International Handbook of
Behavior Modification and Therapy

STUDENT EDITION

International Handbook of
Behavior Modification and Therapy

STUDENT EDITION

Edited by
Alan S. Bellack
Medical College of Pennsylvania at EPPI
Philadelphia, Pennsylvania

Michel Hersen
and
Alan E. Kazdin
Western Psychiatric Institute and Clinic
University of Pittsburgh School of Medicine
Pittsburgh, Pennsylvania

PLENUM PRESS · NEW YORK AND LONDON

Library of Congress Cataloging in Publication Data

Main entry under title:

International handbook of behavior modification and therapy.

   Includes bibliographical references and index.
   1. Behavior therapy—Handbooks, manuals, etc. 2. Behavior modification—Handbooks, manuals, etc. I. Bellack, Alan S. II. Hersen, Michel. III. Kazdin, Alan E.
RC489.B4I54   1985   616.89′142   84-22652
ISBN 0-306-41876-2

This book contains thirteen selected chapters originally published in the
International Handbook of Behavior Modification and Therapy (1982).

© 1985, 1982 Plenum Press, New York
A Division of Plenum Publishing Corporation
233 Spring Street, New York, N.Y. 10013

Printed in the United States of America

Walter and Natalie
Victoria, Gordon, and Helen
Alan, Michael, Daniel, and Steven

Preface to Student Edition

The reaction to the *International Handbook of Behavior Modification and Therapy* has been most enthusiastic. We are gratified by the many positive comments provided by noted behavior therapists with whom we have no affiliation, as well as those from friends and colleagues. Our hypothesis about the need for a comprehensive reference was, apparently, accurate. Moreover, we were fortunate enough to secure a stellar list of contributors who submitted a set of uniformly excellent chapters, many of which have quickly become key references on their respective topics. In addition to the positive feedback, one concern has frequently been brought to our attention. Several colleagues have expressed their regret that the book cannot readily be used as a text in graduate courses, that it is too extensive to be covered in a single graduate seminar. Hence, graduate students may not have ready access to the material.

With that concern in mind, we have constructed the current shortened version. We have selected 13 chapters that comprise a representative curriculum for an introductory graduate seminar on behavior therapy. The chapters comprise three general sections: General Issues, which reflect core principles and practices (history, theory, assessment, and single case research); Treatment of Adult Disorders (anxiety, fear, depression, schizophrenia, medical disorders, and interpersonal problems); and Treatment of Childhood Disorders (behavior problems in the home and classroom, mental retardation, and medical disorders). Each chapter is reprinted in its entirety from the complete *Handbook*. Naturally, this shortened version has excluded several notable topics. However, we felt it wiser to present the complete text of chapters on key topics than to condense many chapters in order to cover more topics. Our view is that graduate students would profit more from in-depth coverage of the various literatures than a more superficial overview of the entire field.

In addition to the individuals mentioned in the Preface to the complete volume, we would like to thank Eliot Werner for his help on this edition, as well as numerous other projects.

ALAN S. BELLACK
MICHEL HERSEN
ALAN E. KAZDIN

Preface to First Edition

The rapid growth of behavior therapy over the past 20 years has been well documented. Yet the geometric expansion of the field has been so great that it deserves to be recounted. We all received our graduate training in the mid to late 1960s. Courses in behavior therapy were then a rarity. Behavioral training was based more on informal tutorials than on systematic programs of study. The behavioral literature was so circumscribed that it could be easily mastered in a few months of study. A mere half-dozen books (by Wolpe, Lazarus, Eysenck, Ullmann, and Krasner) more-or-less comprised the behavioral library in the mid-1960s. Seminal works by Ayllon and Azrin, Bandura, Franks, and Kanfer in 1968 and 1969 made it only slightly more difficult to survey the field. Keeping abreast of new developments was not very difficult, as *Behaviour Research and Therapy* and the *Journal of Applied Behavior Analysis* were the only regular outlets for behavioral articles until the end of the decade, when *Behavior Therapy* and *Behavior Therapy and Experimental Psychiatry* first appeared.

We are too young to be maudlin, but "Oh for the good old days!" One of us did a quick survey of his bookshelves and stopped counting books with *behavior* or *behavioral* in the titles when he reached 100. There were at least half again as many behavioral books without those words in the title. We hesitate to guess how many other behavioral books have been published that he does not own! Another of us subscribes to no less than 10 behavioral journals. A quick count indicated that there are at least 6 others. Moreover, such nonbehavioral publications as *Journal of Consulting and Clinical Psychology, Clinical Psychology Review*, and *Psychological Bulletin* sometimes appear to be more behavioral than anything else.

Needless to say, it is no longer possible to be up-to-date with the entire field. In fact, it is difficult to follow all of the literature in some popular subareas (e.g., behavioral medicine and cognitive behavior therapy). This information overload has a number of undesirable consequences in the research and practice of behavior therapy. It also has a pragmatic implication. Unless one is a prolific book-buyer and journal-subscriber, it is no longer even possible to have a comprehensive behavioral reference library.

Most books currently available fall into one of two classes: elementary surveys (e.g., textbooks) or narrow, highly specialized volumes. Neither type of book meets the need of most professionals for a convenient source of sophisticated reviews. There has been no resource for the person who must get a current but general picture of an area outside of his or her area of specialization. The need for such a resource served as the stimulus for this handbook. Our intention is to provide a basic reference source, in which leaders in the field provide up-to-date reviews of their areas of expertise. Each chapter is intended to give an overview of current knowledge and to identify questions and trends that will be important in the field during the next decade.

In developing the outline for the book, it quickly became apparent that it was impossible to include chapters on every topic studied by behavior therapists. Many readers will find omissions or imbalances in what they regard as vital areas. We have tried to represent major areas of interest and effort. The behavior change chapters, in particular, cover areas that have been subjected to extensive research, rather than areas in which major problems have been solved or exciting new areas with little support as yet. We have also chosen to focus on behavior problems rather than on techniques or models. While many behavior therapists identify with techniques or models (e.g., cognitive behavior therapy), they generally focus on specific problems (e.g., depression and chronic patients). Similarly, the general reader is more likely to be interested in the best treatment for a particular problem than in an overview of a general strategy.

A work of this scope requires the diligent efforts of a great number of people. We would like to thank the contributors for producing a set of uniformly excellent manuscripts. Special appreciation is extended to Mary Newell, Claudia Wolfson, and Lauretta Guerin for their matchless secretarial assistance. Finally, we express our gratitude to our friend and editor, Len Pace, who served a central role in this project from beginning to end.

ALAN S. BELLACK
MICHEL HERSEN
ALAN E. KAZDIN

Contents

PART I

General Issues

In developing this student edition of the *International Handbook of Behavior Modification and Therapy*, we have selected four of the original seven chapters for the first part of the book. Collectively as editors we feel that before the student leaps headlong into the description of the evaluation and treatment of adult and childhood disorders, a very firm grasp of the historical antecedents and the experimental and theoretical foundations is requisite. In addition, two of the areas most representative of the behavioral approach to applied problems (behavioral assessment and single case research) are included in this introductory section. With this as a background, we believe that the subsequent material can then be placed in its proper historical, theoretical, and research perspective.

In looking at this background material, we are struck with the wealth of theory, methodological innovation, and data generated by the behavioral enterprise in what amounts to about three short decades of activity. However, as seen in Chapter 1 by Kazdin, there were some definite historical precursors to contemporary behavior therapy. In his review of the history of behavior therapy, he describes the work on conditioning in Russia, developments in South Africa, England, and the United States, and the formalization of behavior therapy as a clinical entity. The chapter concludes with an overview of the contemporary scene in behavior modification, including the unique characteristics of the movement, the diversity of opinion across behavior modifiers, and the current status of the area.

In Chapter 2, Levis presents a detailed overview of the experimental and theoretical foundations of behavior modification. In addition to evaluating the case for behavioral approaches, he examines some of the basic learning paradigms: classical conditioning, operant conditioning, and avoidance learning. Following the discussion of the formal models of behavioral change, Levis presents the three basic research models that have contributed to the development and refinement of behavioral treatment strategies: (1) infrahuman analogue research; (2) human analogue research); and (3) patient research.

Chapter 3 by Goldfried is most critical in that behavioral assessment, the heart of behavioral approach, is very carefully reviewed. Following discussion of the basic assumptions of behavioral assessment, Goldfried describes the various strategies used, such as observations in the natural environment, role playing, and

1

self-reports. Moreover, the clear relationship between behavioral assessment and treatment is fully documented. Behavioral disorders are classified in terms of difficulties in stimulus control of behavior, deficient behavioral repertoires, aversive behavioral repertoires, difficulties with incentive systems, and aversive self-reinforcing systems. Finally, the future perspectives of behavioral assessment are examined with some emphasis on the comparative validity of traditional and behavioral assessment.

Chapter 4 by Hersen is an overview of the single case method as a tool for evaluation in applied behavior analysis. In this chapter, the raison d'être of single case methodology is explicated vis-à-vis the group comparison design. Indeed, the single case approach has often been described as synonymous with behavior modification. Following a discussion of some general issues, such as intrasubject and intersubject variability, the general procedures followed in single case research are described. Then, Hersen reviews the basic experimental strategies, including the A-B-A designs and their extensions, multiple baseline designs, the changing criterion design, and the simultaneous treatment design. The issue of statistical evaluation in single case research is then discussed, with both the case for and the case against represented. The chapter concludes with considerations of direct replication, clinical replication, and systematic replication.

CHAPTER 1

History of Behavior Modification

Alan E. Kazdin

Introduction

Behavior modification encompasses a variety of conceptual and theoretical positions, methodological approaches, treatment techniques, and historical developments. Because behavior modification is not a monolithic approach, it is important to convey the range of developments that converged over the course of the history of the field. This chapter traces the history of behavior modification as a general movement. Individual conceptual approaches and techniques that comprise behavior modification are obviously important in tracing the history, but they are examined as part of the larger development rather than as ends in their own right. This chapter examines major influences that finally led to the formal development of behavior modification and behavior therapy.[1]

Background

The development of behavior modification can be viewed in part as a reaction to the dominant views within psychiatry and clinical psychology on the nature of abnormal behavior and its treatment. Several sources of dissatisfaction arose that made the field more readily amenable to alternative positions regarding disordered behavior and treatment. Hence, to portray the history of behavior modification, it is important to highlight the traditional approach within psychiatry and clinical psychology.

Alan E. Kazdin • Department of Psychiatry, Western Psychiatric Institute and Clinic, University of Pittsburgh School of Medicine, Pittsburgh, Pennsylvania 15213. Preparation of this chapter was facilitated by a grant from the National Institute of Mental Health (MH31047). The material in the chapter is based on a more extensive examination of the history of behavior modification (Kazdin, 1978b) completed under the auspices of the National Academy of Sciences.

[1] For present purposes, the terms *behavior modification* and *behavior therapy* will be used synonymously. Occasionally, behavior modification and behavior therapy have been distinguished based on such criteria as the theoretical approaches, the treatment techniques, the manner in which the techniques are applied, and the countries in which the techniques have emerged (Franzini & Tilker, 1972; Keehn & Webster, 1969; Krasner, 1971; Yates, 1970). However, consistent distinctions have not been adopted, and the terms usually are used interchangeably in contemporary writing.

Prior to highlighting the context out of which behavior modification grew, it is especially interesting to place many techniques in a different historical perspective. As a movement, behavior modification is new in many ways, but several techniques used in the field emerged much earlier. Selected examples illustrate that what is new, important, and perhaps of greatest historical interest in the field are not the ancestors of current practices but the development of the overall approach that characterizes contemporary behavior modification.

Historical Precursors of Behavioral Techniques

Many treatment techniques developed prior to behavior modification bear a striking similarity to techniques in current use. However, behavior modification is not a conglomeration of various techniques; tracing the history of the field in a way that emphasizes individual techniques might misrepresent the overall thrust of the larger movement. Nevertheless, by way of background, it is interesting to mention that many techniques currently popular in behavior therapy are frequently encountered in the history of treatment—under different names, of course—decades before behavior therapy developed. Consider two among the many types of examples that could be provided: systematic desensitization and reinforcement.

Systematic Desensitization. Desensitization is one of the most well researched and practiced treatment techniques in behavior therapy. Briefly, the technique consists of pairing responses that inhibit anxiety (usually muscle relaxation) with events that provoke anxiety. By pairing relaxation with anxiety-provoking stimuli (actual situations or imaginal representations of them) in a graduated fashion, the anxiety and avoidance reaction can be eliminated. The development of desensitization by Joseph Wolpe (1958) was extremely innovative for a variety of reasons, as discussed later in the chapter. Yet, the underlying rationale and procedure in various forms were evident long before its development in the 1950s.

For example, in France in the 1890s, a procedure that resembled contemporary desensitization was used to relieve tics (Brissaud, 1894). Patients were trained to keep their muscles motionless and to perform exercises to maintain a state of relaxation that would compete with the movements of the tic. Variations of the technique involved performing behaviors incompatible with the response rather than merely remaining motionless (Meige & Feindel, 1907). Indeed, deep breathing exercises and relaxation as a method to overcome tics were relatively popular in France (Pitres, 1888; Tissié, 1899).

More recently, relaxation was used in Germany in the form of "autogenic training," a procedure that was developed in the 1920s (Schultz, 1932; Schultz & Luthe, 1959). The procedure grew out of hypnosis and auto-suggestion and was used to train patients to relax themselves through self-suggestion. Self-induced relaxation successfully treated a range of psychological and physical problems in applications that often closely resembled desensitization.

In the late 1920s, Alexander (1928) suggested that disturbing thoughts could be controlled by "direct switching," that is, thinking of something that was incompatible with the thought that came to mind. Others advocated performing incompatible responses as a way to overcome maladaptive habits or thought patterns (Bagby, 1928). In the 1940s, hierarchical presentation of fear-provoking stimuli was used to overcome combat neuroses. Fear-provoking stimuli associated with combat were presented in a graduated fashion (Schwartz, 1945). In other applications, phobic patients engaged in graded steps of fear-provoking behaviors while performing responses that would compete with anxiety (Terhune, 1949).

Other precursors can be readily identified that apparently influenced the final development of desensitization in various ways. The familiar child case of Peter reported by Mary Cover Jones (1924b) used performance of responses incompatible with anxiety (eating) while the feared stimulus (a rabbit) was presented in progressively closer proximity. Similarly, Edmund Jacobson (1938) successfully applied relaxation to reduce the tension associated with a wide range of disorders, including general anxiety, phobias, hypertension, colitis, insomnia, and tics. Finally, in the early 1940s, Herzberg proposed a treatment of "graduated tasks," in which patients performed a series of tasks *in vivo* to overcome their fears and a variety of other problems (Herzberg, 1945). Even though other precursors of desensitization can be identified, they reflect isolated efforts rather than a continuous historical line culminating in contemporary procedures.

Reinforcement. Reinforcement techniques are used extensively in contemporary behavior modification and have been extended to almost every clinical population from young children to geriatric patients and across a host of problems (Kazdin, 1978a). It is not difficult to find historical precursors of contemporary reinforcement techniques. Unlike precursors to desensitization, the incentive systems that preceded those used in behavior modification occasionally achieved widespread application. Although many examples can be provided, one in particular illustrates the extensive use of rewards to alter behavior and bears extremely close resemblance to current practices.

In England in the early 1800s, Joseph Lancaster devised a reinforcement system for use in the classroom (Lancaster, 1805; Salmon, 1904). The system was developed for classrooms that housed hundreds of students in the same room. The system was developed for largely economic reasons and utilized peer monitors in the class, rather than teachers, to provide rewards. The system relied on what currently is referred to as a *token economy*. Tickets were provided for paying attention and for completing academic tasks. The tickets were backed up by other rewards and prizes to encourage progress in basic academic skills.

A comparison of the specific procedures of this program with those in use in contemporary classroom behavior-modification programs reveals marked similarities (Kazdin & Pulaski, 1977). Interestingly, Lancaster's system became popular throughout the British Empire, Europe, Africa, Russia, Asia, South America, Canada, and the United States (Kaestle, 1973). These applications, primarily in the middle and late 1800s, preceded the development of operant conditioning and the explicit recognition of positive reinforcement and its implications.

General Comments. Historical precursors can be readily identified for many existing behavior-modification techniques, such as flooding, modeling, self-instruction training, variations of operant techniques, aversion therapy, and covert conditioning (Kazdin, 1978b). However interesting such precursors may be, they generally fall outside of the historical purview of contemporary behavior modification. The history of behavior modification reflects a larger movement that synthesizes several influences in psychology more generally. This chapter emphasizes these larger themes, which reveal the movements within psychology, clinical psychology, and psychiatry that led to the formal emergence of behavior modification.

Traditional Approaches in Psychiatry and Clinical Psychology

Behavior modification represents an alternative conceptual approach in research and treatment to the prevailing approach within psychiatry and clinical psychology. The dominant approach has often been referred to as a *disease model* because of its emphasis on extrapolations from medicine. The general approach consists of looking for underlying pathological or disease processes to account for disordered behavior. The underlying processes may reflect organic factors, but reservations about the model have arisen primarily when intrapsychic factors are proposed to account for behavior.

Traditional conceptualizations have emphasized disordered psychological processes within the psyche to account for deviant behavior in cases where organic causal agents cannot be identified. The intrapsychic processes are regarded as being the basis for disordered behavior and as requiring psychological treatment. The intrapsychic approach represents an extension of the disease model to abnormal behavior and has dominated the mental health professions for many years. The development of behavior modification can be viewed in part as a reaction to the intrapsychic conceptualization of abnormal behavior and its treatment.

Perhaps within the disease model, the most significant development from the standpoint of subsequent events in behavior modification is the impact of psychoanalysis on conceptualizations of behavior. In his development of psychoanalysis as a theory of personality and a form of treatment, Sigmund Freud provided a detailed conceptual account of the psychological process, personality mechanisms, and drives that allegedly account for normal and abnormal behavior. The development of psychological symptoms was traced to underlying psychodynamic processes. The general disease model represented by psychoanalysis and the specific propositions of the theory had a tremendous impact on psychiatric diagnosis, assessment, and treatment.

Impact of the Intrapsychic Disease Approach. The general disease model has had important implications for psychiatric diagnosis, assessment, and treatment. With regard to psychiatric diagnosis, the disease model has led to attempts to devise a method of identifying specific and distinct disease entities. A psychiatric diagnostic system developed that delineated various disorders, many of which reflect disease underlying psychological processes ("mental illnesses"). Usually, the concern about these disorders is not with the problematic behaviors themselves but in large part with the underlying psychodynamic factors that have been proposed to account for these disorders. Similarly, in psychological assessment, many efforts have focused on identifying the intrapsychic processes regarded as accounting for the behavior. The underlying intrapsychic processes—as, for example, reflected on projective test performance—received considerable attention, often in place of samples of actual behavior.

Perhaps the greatest impact of the intrapsychic disease model can be seen in the practice of therapy. Psychoanalytically oriented therapy has dominated outpatient treatment in psychiatry and clinical psychology. Treatment consists of focusing on underlying unconscious processes, childhood conflicts, sources of resistance, and other aspects of psychodynamic functioning that are tied to current behaviors through an intricate set of assumptions. Many therapy techniques, such as client-centered therapy (Rogers, 1951), developed as alternatives but often adhered to the overall assumptions about the impact of intrapsychic processes on behavior.

Dissatisfaction with the Disease Model

and Psychoanalysis. Although the disease model has dominated psychiatry and clinical psychology, within the last 30 years dissatisfaction has increased in several areas. Psychoanalysis as the major intrapsychic position generated into its own sources of criticism based on the difficulty in testing various assumptions and the lack of support in many areas where hypotheses have been tested relating psychodynamic processes to behavior (Bailey, 1956; Hovey, 1959; Orlansky, 1949; Sears, 1944). Doubts about the theory focused on specific propositions regarded as stemming from orthodox psychoanalytic theory, such as the notion that underlying psychic processes rather than "symptoms" (overt behavior) invariably needed to be treated. The idea that symptomatic treatment led to the appearance of other maladaptive behaviors or *substitute* symptoms had been questioned seriously (M. C. Jones, 1924b; Mowrer & Mowrer, 1938).

Psychiatric diagnosis has also been the center of criticism. The identification of psychiatric disorders has hardly been a straightforward task, and research on the reliability and validity of the system has led to repeated criticism (e.g., Hersen, 1976; Mischel, 1968; Zubin, 1967). Perhaps more importantly, reservations have been expressed about the utility of diagnosis. Psychiatric diagnosis has had few implications for etiology, prognosis, or treatment. Other objections were made to the diagnosis of psychiatric disorders because most disorders consist of deviant behavior defined by social norms rather than by a demonstrable disease process (Ellis, 1967; Ferster, 1965; Laing, 1967; Scheff, 1966; Szasz, 1960).

A major source of dissatisfaction focused on traditional psychotherapy, particularly psychoanalysis and psychoanalytically oriented therapy. The efficacy of psychotherapy has been seriously questioned by many investigators (Denker, 1946; Landis, 1937; Wilder, 1945; Zubin, 1953). The most influential criticism was that of Hans J. Eysenck (1952), who reviewed the literature and concluded that improvement because of treatment was not better than *spontaneous remission*, that is, the improvements clients experience without formal treatment. Although the conclusions have been challenged (Meltzoff & Kornreich, 1970), Eysenck's critical evaluation stimulated concern about the failure of the traditional psychotherapies and the need for vastly improved research. Even so, subsequent evaluations of psychotherapy research noted that little attention has been devoted to outcome research (Parloff & Rubinstein, 1962).

Criticism of treatment is not restricted to psychotherapy. Institutional care for psychiatric patients has also been under attack because of its largely custodial nature. Major breakthroughs have been made in treatment, primarily chemotherapy. Yet, reservations have been expressed about the need to confine individuals, the depersonalization of institutional life, and the deterioration associated with custodial care (Paul, 1969; Sommer & Osmond, 1961; Wanklin, Fleming, Buck, & Hobbs, 1956). In general, the prospect of discharge for many patients has been poor, and the prospect of readmission for many who have been discharged has been high. Many patients become chronic, and custodial treatment becomes a dominant mode of care.

General Comments. Of course, the impact, benefits, and criticism associated with the disease model in the areas of diagnosis, assessment, and treatment are rich topics in their own right and cannot be elaborated here. From the standpoint of the history of behavior modification, it is important merely to acknowledge the several sources of dissatisfaction with the traditional approach in psychiatry and clinical psychology. The dissatisfaction paved the way for a new approach to enter into the field.

As psychology has grown as a science, experimental findings about behavior and its development have had little impact on the dominant position within psychiatry. Specific psychological constructs, as well as the approach of scientific research, have provided viable alternatives that address many of the criticisms of the disease model. Behavior modification represents a psychological account of behavior relatively free from the medical influences evident in the disease model and psychoanalysis. Behavior modification is not merely a conceptual change; rather, the strengths of behavior modification as an alternative paradigm or approach have been expressly in those areas where the intrapsychic approach has been weak, namely, research and treatment.

Foundations of Behavior Modification

The foundations of behavior modification can be traced by examining developments in philosophy, the physical and biological sciences, and medicine, which are no doubt interrelated and also reflect political and social climates. However, rather direct historical lines can be traced to the foundations of behaviorism in psychology and the antecedents of this movement. In the eighteenth century, developments in the biological and physical sciences exerted a marked impact on psychology. For example, biological research began to progress in identifying the basis of selected organic diseases and their treatment. Theory and research in physics supported a basic scientific approach to understanding physical matter. Also, Darwin's development of the theory of evolution had impact not only on the biological sciences but on the social sciences as well. Darwin emphasized the adaptability of organisms to their environment and the continuity of the species, ideas that directly influenced research in psychology.

The development of behaviorism and its antecedents must be viewed in a larger intellectual climate. Many of the tenets and approaches of behaviorism reflect rather than constitute the overall movement toward a greater appreciation of science and a mechanistic and materialistic approach to topics in the physical, biological, and social sciences. Among the many factors that can be identified, three particularly important antecedents to behavior modification include developments in physiology in Russia, the emergence of behaviorism in America, and developments in the psychology of learning.

Conditioning in Russia

Much of the history of behavior modification can be traced to developments in research on physiology in Russia. In the early 1800s, the influence of scientific research and experimentation increased in Europe. The movement extended to Russia, primarily through the neurophysiological work of Ivan M. Sechenov (1829–1905). Sechenov, who received training in Europe, developed a program of research that helped establish him as the father of Russian physiology.

Sechenov was interested in topics relevant to psychology, which at the time was largely an area of subjective inquiry and speculation about states of consciousness. He believed that the study of reflexes represented a point at which psychology and physiology might merge. Sechenov (1865/1965) suggested that behavior could be accounted for by various "reflexes of the brain." Complex reflexes that accounted for behavior, Sechenov maintained, were developed through learning. Various stimuli in the environment became associated with muscle movements; the repeated association of the stimuli with the movements made the acts habitual. Sechenov's general views about behavior reflected positions that were later embraced by such behaviorists as John B. Watson and B. F. Skinner. Behavior was considered a function of environmental events and learning.

Basically, Sechenov provided two interrelated contributions in the history of behavioral research. First, he advocated the study of reflexes as a way of addressing problems of psychology. The study of reflexes, he believed, provided the basis for understanding behavior. Second, he advocated application of the objective methods of physiology to the problems of psychology. He felt that the research methods of physiology would vastly improve on the subjective and introspective methods of psychology. Sechenov's recognition of the importance of reflexes and his strong advocation of objective research methods were very important. Many of his specific views about the reflexes that caused behavior were speculative, as he recognized. Yet, their impact was marked, in part, no doubt, because of the tremendous respect that Sechenov had earned as a rigorous researcher himself. Sechenov's views influenced two younger contemporaries, Ivan P. Pavlov (1849–1936) and Vladimir M. Bechterev (1857–1927).

Pavlov's work is extremely well known, and hence, I need not elaborate on it here, except to acknowledge his pivotal role in the unfolding history of conditioning. Pavlov's research essentially followed directly from Sechenov's views by using physiological research methods to examine neurological functioning. In his work on digestion, Pavlov investigated reflexes involving primarily glandular secretions. In the process of this research, which earned him a Nobel prize, Pavlov (1902) discovered *psychical secretions*. He found that gastric secretions in the dog would often begin prior to presenting the stimulus (e.g., food); the sight of the food or the approaching experimenter could stimulate secretions. The secretions were referred to as psychical because they were not evoked by physical stimulation. But *psychical* referred to subjective states of the organism and hence was given up and replaced with *conditional reflex* (Pavlov, 1903/1955).[2]

Pavlov's research turned to the investigation of conditioned reflexes. His work spanned several years and involved a large number of investigators in his laboratory who methodically elaborated diverse process associated with the development and the elimination of the conditioned reflexes, such as extinction, generalization, and differentiation. Pavlov's main interest in studying reflexes was to elaborate the activity of the brain. Over the years, his interests in reflexes extended to understanding behavior as well as being reflected in topics of language and psychopathology.

Pavlov's contributions to psychology in general are extensive. His main contribution was in objectively investigating conditioned reflexes from the standpoint of a physiologist. He strongly advocated objectivism in research and was critical of subjective lines of psychological inquiry (e.g., Pavlov, 1906). His programmatic work demonstrated the importance of learning in accounting for animal behavior and eventually provided a research paradigm for investigating human behavior as well.

Bechterev, a contemporary of Pavlov who was also influenced by Sechenov, began a program of research that applied the methods of physiology to the study of the functioning of the brain. Most of Bechterev's work focused on reflexes of the motoric system (i.e., the striated muscles) rather than of the glands and the digestive system studied by Pavlov. Bech-

---

[2] Apparently, *conditional reflex* is closer to the meaning of the Russian term that Pavlov used; it became the more familiar *conditioned reflex* through translation (Hilgard & Bower, 1966).

terev also encountered the conditioned reflexes (which he referred to as "associative
reflexes") and investigated processes associated with their development. Interestingly,
Bechterev's method was more readily applicable to human behavior than was Pavlov's
method because he used shock and muscle
flexion as the unconditioned stimulus and response, respectively. The special surgery and
the assessment of salivation required by Pavlov's early methods were less readily applicable to humans for obvious reasons.

Although Bechterev's work as a neurophy-
siologist is important in its own right, his significant role in the history of behavior modification stems from his interest in problems of
psychiatry and clinical psychology. Bechterev
(1913), more than Pavlov and Sechenov, developed the notion that conditioning could account for a variety of human behaviors and
provided an objective basis for psychology.
Bechterev believed that problems of psychology could be studied by examining reflexes
and developed what he considered a separate
discipline—which he referred to as "reflexology," devoted to that end (Bechterev, 1932).

Reflexology addressed many problems of
psychology including explanations of personality and of normal and deviant behavior. Bechterev attacked psychoanalytic theory from
a scientific standpoint and argued the substantive and methodological superiority of reflexology in its place. Bechterev founded and actively headed a variety of institutes for the
treatment of clinical populations, including
psychiatric patients, alcoholics, epileptics,
and the mentally retarded. Bechterev was
eager to apply information from basic research
on reflexes, which he was conducting at the
time, to clinical populations.

In general, Bechterev's interest in reflexes
and their applicability to behavior was much
broader than that of Pavlov. Bechterev's writings encompassed many of the topics characteristic of more recent developments in behavior modification, including the explanation
of personality and abnormal behavior in terms
of learning. Indeed, it was Bechterev's views
about behavior and its malleability, as a function of conditioning, that Watson initially drew
on when the movement of behaviorism crystallized in America.

The development of conditioning in Russia
represents an extremely significant set of
events in the history of behaviorism. The
emergence of conditioning from physiology
may be an important fact because the objective
methods of physiological research provided an
alternative to the subjective, introspective
methods of psychology. Also, the role of
learning assumed increased importance in
accounting for behavior. Sechenov, Pavlov,
and Bechterev pointed to the importance of
the environment as the source of behavior.

Although the work of Pavlov and Bechterev
was similar, they extended Sechenov's original views in different ways. Pavlov established
lawful relationships on conditioning and provided years of programmatic research that
elaborated many basic processes. Bechterev
also conducted basic work on conditioning,
but he is more readily distinguished by his interests in applying conditioning as a conceptual basis for behavior—all behavior—and for
the treatment of abnormal behavior. To replace psychology Bechterev developed a new
discipline, reflexology, which had considerable impact in Russia. Reflexology itself did not
have much direct impact on American psychology. However, the movement of behaviorism in America drew heavily on reflexology
and provided the radical departure for psychological research that Bechterev had envi-
sioned.

Emergence of Behaviorism

The work on conditioning in Russia was part
of a larger movement toward an increased objectivism and materialism within the sciences.
In the history of behavior modification, expression of this larger movement took the
form of behaviorism in America as espoused
by Watson (1878–1958). Watson's early interest was in animal psychology, which had profited from the objective experimental methods
characteristic of physiology to a much greater
extent than other areas within psychology. As
his research continued, Watson became increasingly convinced that animal psychology
was an objective science that could function
independently of the mentalism characteristic
of other areas of psychology. At the time psychology followed the school of functionalism,

which analyzed consciousness. Introspection had been used to examine the operations of consciousness by having people "observe" their own mental processes. Watson criticized the study of consciousness through introspection as highly mentalistic and subjective.

Essentially, Watson crystallized a movement toward objectivism that was already well in progress. Indeed, in the early years of the nineteenth century, many psychologists were beginning to define psychology as the science of behavior rather than of consciousness or private events (e.g., McDougall, 1908; Meyer, 1911). The movement toward objective research methods was well underway in comparative and animal psychology, which had expanded considerably by the end of the nineteenth century. Prominent among the many available examples is the work by Edward L. Thorndike (1874–1949), who investigated learning among diverse animal species in the late 1890s. Also, Robert Yerkes (1876–1956) began research on diverse species and helped introduce Pavlov's method of conditioning to American psychology (Yerkes & Morgulis, 1909). Research on animal behavior assumed increasing importance after the emergence of Darwin's influential publications outlining his views of evolution (Darwin, 1859, 1871, 1872). Darwin's views on evolution assumed the continuity of the species, so that investigation of infrahuman species was quite relevant to an understanding of human behavior.

Watson's behavioristic position developed in the early 1900s. Although the view can be traced in early lectures, the clearest and most influential statement came from his widely disseminated article "Psychology as the Behaviorist Views It" (Watson, 1913). The article noted that psychology from the behaviorist perspective was purely objective and experimental and excluded introspection as a method of study and consciousness as the appropriate subject matter. Watson wrote several books that addressed various topics of psychology and at the same time conveyed the appropriate domain and methods of the study of behaviorism (Watson, 1914, 1919, 1924).

Watson had many specific views about a variety of topics of psychology. It was important to show that behaviorism could address diverse topics within psychology, such as thoughts, emotions, and instincts. The substantive views that Watson promulgated can be readily distinguished from the methodological tenets of behaviorism. These methodological tenets, which exerted the more lasting impact on behaviorism, were very similar to those advanced by Sechenov, Pavlov, and Bechterev, who had earlier advocated the replacement of speculative and introspective inquiry into subjective states with the objective study of overt behavior. Watson's own work on conditioning had been stimulated directly by translations of Bechterev's work and, later, the work and methods of Pavlov. Indeed, Bechterev had extended conditioning to a wide range of human behaviors and had provided Watson with a detailed view of the implications of conditioning.

In behaviorism, conditioning was initially a method of study meant to replace introspection (Watson, 1913), but eventually, it became a central concept used to explain the development of behavior (Watson, 1924). As Sechenov and Bechterev before him, Watson regarded behavior as a series of reflexes. The assumption had marked heuristic value because it suggested that complex human behavior could be investigated by studying simple reflexes and their combinations.

Watson made conditioning the cornerstone of his approach to behavior. Although arguments can be made that relatively few of the specific methodological tenets were new (Herrnstein, 1969), Watson actively promulgated behaviorism as a movement in order to overthrow existing views in psychology. Aside from his general influence on psychology, Watson's contributions included specific instances of work that had applied implications directly related to behavior modification, which are discussed here later.

Psychology of Learning

The work on conditioning in both Russia and America emphasized the modifiability of behavior, and indeed, this was consistent with the influential views of Darwin on adaptation to the environment. Watson and Bechterev attempted to develop broad theories of behavior based on the conditioned reflex. Conditioning was advocated as the basis of behavior and firmly established learning as a central topic. Complex behaviors were regarded as combinations of simple responses, but explanations restricted to reflex conditioning became increasingly strained.

In America, the psychology of learning began to receive increased attention and was used to explain how behaviors are acquired. The methodological tenets of behaviorism were generally retained, but the specific research paradigms and breadth of theories of learning increased. For behavior modification, early work on the psychology of learning provided important roots. To begin with, the psychology of learning provided the theoretical positions and laboratory paradigms on which behavior modification later freely drew. In addition, proponents of individual theoretical positions occasionally addressed practical problems that touched on learning or maladaptive behavior.

As noted earlier, prior to the development of behaviorism, Thorndike began programmatic animal research that employed objective research methods. Thorndike's research on learning was distinct from that of Pavlov and Bechterev, although at this stage of research, the distinction was not entirely clear (Hilgard & Marquis, 1940). Thorndike did not study how reflexive behavior came to be elicited by other new stimuli. Rather, he was interested in how animals learned new responses that were not in their repertoire to begin with. Among many careful experiments, the most widely known is his work with cats that learned to escape from a puzzle box to earn food. Through "trial and error," the cats became increasingly skilled in escaping from the puzzle box. On the basis of his extensive research showing the influence of consequences on behavior and repeated practice, Thorndike formulated various "laws of learning." The most influential from the standpoint of current work was the law of effect, which noted that "satisfying consequences" increase the bond between a stimulus and a response and "annoying consequences" weaken the bond (Thorndike, 1931). Although the various laws that Thorndike developed evolved over the course of his work (Thorndike, 1932, 1933), the importance of the positive consequences in strengthening behavior remained and has

had a continued impact on contemporary developments in learning and behavior modification.

Several other learning theorists and positions emerged in the years that followed behaviorism. The range of complexity of positions cannot be treated in detail or even adequately highlighted here. Guthrie, Tolman, Hull, Mowrer, and Skinner provided particularly influential views on developments in the psychology of learning and on aspects of behavior modification. For example, Guthrie (1935) viewed learning as a function of the repeated pairing of stimuli and responses. He believed that a response could be established by repeatedly pairing its occurrence with the desired stimulus conditions. Similarly, to eliminate a response, new responses needed to be performed in the presence of stimuli that had previously evoked other (undesirable) responses. Aside from experimental research, Guthrie advanced practical recommendations to break unwanted habits. For example, to overcome fear, Guthrie recommended gradually introducing the fear-provoking stimuli and pairing responses incompatible with fear with these stimuli. This recommendation bears obvious similarity to the contemporary practice of systematic desensitization. Indeed, Guthrie's strong advocacy of the repeated practice of desired responses and of the pairing of responses with appropriate stimulus conditions can be seen in the practice of many contemporary behavioral techniques.

Similarly, Mowrer (1947, 1960) was concerned about the development and elimination of avoidance behavior and proposed the combination of "two factors" to provide an adequate account. Mowrer reasoned that initially, fear is established through Pavlovian conditioning. Fear develops in the organism and is reduced by escaping from the situation through Thorndikean learning. The development of this two-factor theory was important in the history of behavior modification because it provided an account of an important problem in human behavior, namely, avoidance reactions. Hence, there were immediate implications for extending learning conceptualizations to account for maladaptive avoidance behavior and perhaps to develop treatments based on learning.

Perhaps of all the individuals who can be identified with a specific theory or position on learning, B. F. Skinner has had the greatest direct impact on contemporary behavior modification. The impact is readily apparent because the principles of operant conditioning developed in laboratory research have been widely extrapolated to applied settings. In the first few decades of the nineteenth century, the distinction between Pavlovian and Thorndikean learning was not always clear. Fundamental differences between the research paradigms were obscured because of the different types of responses that were studied and the investigation of combined learning paradigms in which both operant and respondent conditioning were intertwined. Attempts were made to clarify the different types of learning by bringing them under a single theoretical framework or by explaining their interrelationship as theorists such as Hull and Mowrer had done.

Skinner (1935, 1937) brought the distinction between respondent and operant learning into sharp focus and delineated special cases where the distinction seemingly was unclear (i.e., cases where operant responses are a function of antecedent stimuli, and learning is under discriminative control). Although the distinction between these types of learning was not new, the importance and implications of the distinction had not been elaborated.

Skinner (1938) began elaborating operant behavior in a series of experimental studies. In addition to advocating a particular type of learning in accounting for the majority of human and animal behavior, Skinner became associated with a particular approach in conceptualizing the subject matter of psychology and in conducting research. The approach, referred to as the *experimental analysis of behavior*, tended to reject theory, to focus on frequency or rate of responding, and to study individual organisms using special experimental designs that departed from the usual research (Skinner, 1938, 1950, 1953b). Aside from experimental work, Skinner pointed to the clinical and social relevance of operant behavior and, to a greater extent than other learning theorists, pointed to possible applications (Skinner, 1953a).

Developments in the psychology of learning cannot be traced in detail here. It is important to note that the psychology of learning occupied a central role in psychological research after the development of behaviorism. The different views that developed and the research they generated provide the underpinnings for the general approaches and specific techniques in contemporary behavior modification. Indeed, many of contemporary debates in behavioral research often have a rather clear precedent in developments in learning theory. For example, the debate over the need for intervening variables, cognitive factors, and the limitations of stimulus–response accounts of behavior reflects major issues in the history of the psychology of learning (Spence, 1950) and remains a source of controversy in contemporary behavior modification (Kazdin, 1979).

Extensions of Conditioning and Learning

Soon after conditioning research was begun, its concepts were extended well beyond the laboratory paradigms from which it was derived. Extensions were quickly made to human behavior, following the early work of Bechterev. For example, in 1907 in Russia and a few years later in the United States, conditioning as a method of study was applied to infants and normal and retarded children (see Krasnogorski, 1925; Mateer, 1918). Also, various forms of psychopathology were interpreted on the basis of conditioning, and the methods were extended to the diagnosis, study, and treatment of selected clinical populations (see Aldrich, 1928; Bechterev, 1923, 1932; Gantt & Muncie, 1942; Reese, Doss, & Gantt, 1953). The relevance of conditioning to psychopathology, personality, and psychotherapy became increasingly apparent over the years. A few events in particular highlight this development, including selected extensions of laboratory paradigms to the study of disordered behavior, applications of conditioning to clinically relevant behavior, and interpretations and extensions of learning to psychotherapy.

Laboratory Paradigms and Analogues

Experimental Neuroses. A particularly significant extension of conditioning was the investigation of experimental neuroses, which consists of experimentally induced states that are regarded as resembling neurotic behavior found in humans. The reactions of laboratory animals to various methods of inducing "neuroses" vary, depending on the species, but they often include avoidance; withdrawal; accelerated pulse, heart, and respiration rates; irritability; and other reactions that bear some resemblance to human anxiety (see Hunt, 1964).

Initial demonstrations of experimental neuroses developed as part of the research in Pavlov's laboratory on differentiation in conditioning dogs. In separate investigations in 1912 and 1913, investigators in Pavlov's laboratory found that when animals were required to make subtle discriminations in the conditioned stimulus, all previously trained conditioned reactions were lost. Moreover, the animals showed distinct disturbances in behavior and became agitated and aggressive. Pavlov (1927) termed the resulting emotional responses "experimentally induced neuroses" and speculated on the neurological bases for the reaction.

Pavlov turned much of his research effort to these unexpected neurotic reactions. Pavlov viewed these reactions, like the conditioned reflex, as a way of investigating higher neurological processes. Yet, he also recognized the potential connection between his results and psychopathology in human behavior. To that end, he familiarized himself with psychiatric disorders by visiting various clinics, and he speculated about the basis of many symptoms of psychopathology, including apathy, negativism, stereotyped movements, fear, and catalepsy (Pavlov, 1928).

The study of experimental neuroses became an area of research in its own right and was continued in America by such researchers as W. Horsely Gantt and Howard S. Liddell. A particularly important extension of research on experimental neuroses, from the standpoint of the development of treatment, was made by Jules H. Masserman, a psychiatrist at the University of Chicago. Masserman (1943) conducted research on experimentally induced neuroses with animals, primarily cats. His work attempted to integrate conditioning concepts with psychopathology and psychoanalytic theory. Moreover, he developed several procedures to overcome the neurotic reactions of the animals. These procedures included animal analogues of contemporary behavior-modification techniques such as modeling (putting a nonfearful animal in the cage with the fearful animal), exposure (physically forcing the animal to have contact with the fear-provoking stimulus), and self-control (self-administration of food by controlling the delivery device). Masserman's main interest in these procedures was in providing an experimental basis for the psychodynamic processes used in psychotherapy. Concepts from psychodynamic therapy (e.g., working through) were used to explain the mechanisms through which the laboratory procedures had ameliorated anxiety in the animals. Hence, this overall thrust is especially interesting because many later developments in behavior modification proceeded in the opposite direction, namely, utilizing laboratory-based procedures and concepts from learning to generate new therapeutic procedures.

Clinically Relevant Applications

Research on conditioning, with few exceptions, was begun with infrahuman subjects. However, the methods were extended to human behavior in a variety of ways. Among the many extensions that can be cited, a few proved to be especially significant in the history of behavior modification.

Conditioning and Deconditioning of Emotions. Certainly one of the most influential applications of conditioning to human behavior was made by Watson, who studied the emotional reactions of human infants. The study of emotional reactions was especially important because Watson was interested in conditioning emotional reactions, in part to show that behavioral concepts and methods could be used to study feelings and private experience.

Watson and Rosalie Rayner reported an influential case in 1920 that attempted to condition fear in an 11-month-old infant named Albert. Albert was not afraid of a variety of stimuli, including a white rat, a rabbit, a dog, and others presented to him as part of an assessment battery prior to the study. The rat was selected as a neutral stimulus because, like the other stimuli, it did not provoke fear. Pairing the presentation of the rat to Albert with a loud noise, produced by striking a hammer on a steel bar, elicited a startle response. Within a matter of only seven pairings of the conditioned stimulus (rat) and the unconditioned stimulus (noise), presentation of the rat alone evoked crying and withdrawal. Moreover, the fear reaction transferred to other objects, including a rabbit, a dog, a fur coat, and cotton wool, which had not elicited fear prior to the conditioning trials.

The case was extremely significant because it was regarded as providing clear evidence that fears can be conditioned. The implications of such an interpretation were great, suggesting at once that learning might account for fears and avoidance behavior and, by implication, that such behaviors might be overcome by alternative learning experiences. The significance of the case is especially noteworthy because the phenomena that were demonstrated proved difficult to replicate (Bregman, 1934; English, 1929); the original study itself is usually inaccurately cited, so that the actual findings are misrepresented (Harris, 1979); and whether the study demonstrated respondent conditioning as usually conceived can readily be challenged by examining the actual procedures that were used (Kazdin, 1978b).

The original report about Albert was only a first step, and the full significance of the demonstration was accentuated three years later by M. C. Jones, a student working under the advice of Watson. Jones (1924b) reported the case of Peter, a 34-month-old boy who was a natural sequel to Albert. Essentially, Peter was afraid of the diverse stimuli that Albert had been conditioned to fear. The task was to develop ways to overcome Peter's fears. Because a rabbit elicited greater fear than other stimuli in the testing situation, it was used as the feared object during treatment. Several procedures were used to overcome fear, primarily the gradual presentation of the rabbit

to Peter under nonthreatening conditions. While Peter ate, the caged rabbit was gradually brought closer to him without eliciting fear. The purpose was to associate pleasant stimuli (food) and responses (eating) with the feared object. Eventually, Peter did not react adversely when the rabbit was free to move outside of the cage, and indeed, he played with it.

In addition to the successful treatment of Peter, Jones (1924a) published a more extensive report that included several different methods of treating institutionalized children who had a variety of fears (e.g., being left alone, being in a dark room, and being near small animals). Two methods appeared to be particularly successful, namely, direct conditioning, in which a feared object was associated with positive reactions (e.g., as had been done with Peter); and social imitation, in which nonfearful children modeled fearless interaction with the stimulus.

The demonstrations by Watson, Rayner, and Jones that fears could be conditioned and deconditioned were of obvious significance by themselves. In addition, the investigators were explicit in pointing out the implications of the findings for existing conceptions of psychopathology. For example, Watson and Rayner (1920) scoffed at the psychoanalytic interpretations that might be applied to Albert's newly acquired fear, despite the fact that the fear had been conditioned in the laboratory. Thus, the demonstrations of the conditioning and deconditioning of fear were placed in the larger arena of psychopathology and its treatment and were posed as a challenge to existing approaches.

Additional Applications

Many extrapolations of conditioning were made to clinically relevant topics similar to those of Watson and his collaborators. For example, the implications of conditioning for educational psychology and child development were suggested by William H. Burnham, who was the adviser of Florence Mateer and encouraged her basic research on respondent conditioning with children. Burnham (1917, 1924) believed that mental hygiene consisted of developing appropriate conditioned reflexes. His major applications of conditioning were to educational settings. Interestingly, his writings anticipated many different behavior modification practices. For example, he encouraged the use of positive consequences in the classroom and gradually providing these consequences for increasingly complex behaviors. These procedures, of course, form an active part of contemporary applications of operant techniques in the classroom.[3] In addition, Burnham suggested that fear could be overcome by employing fear-inhibiting responses, including thoughts and imagery, and by gradually exposing oneself to those situations that provoked fear. These recommendations anticipated contemporary procedures of overcoming anxiety, including variations of systematic desensitization and flooding.

In general, Burnham suggested the utility of conditioning procedures for altering behavior and improving the child's adjustment at school and in the home. In addition to outlining possible applications of conditioning, Burnham was very explicit in noting that learning-based formulations of behavior were more parsimonious than alternative views, such as psychoanalytic theory. Indeed, in anticipation of behavior modification, Burnham (1924) was critical of psychoanalysis, noting that psychoanalytic interpretations of behavior were merely a form of "psychological astrology" (p. 628). The significance of Burnham's position derives from both advocating learning and juxtaposing conditioning formulations as an alternative to psychoanalytic theory.

A significant advance in applying conditioning was the work of Mowrer and Mowrer (1938). In 1935, they began a program to treat enuretic children using the bell-and-pad method. The apparatus was a pad, which was placed in the child's bed and attached to an alarm. The child's urination completed a circuit that triggered an alarm. Eventually, the child learned either to anticipate urination prior to having an accident or, more commonly, to sleep through the night without an accident.

The procedure the Mowrers used to treat enuresis had been available in isolated applications in Europe and Russia. The primary contribution of the Mowrers was their conceptualization of the procedure. The Mowrers viewed the treatment of enuresis from the standpoint of learning and habit training rather than as a function of altering psychodynamic processes. Specifically, they conceptualized enuresis on the basis of respondent conditioning, where various stimuli (e.g., bladder distension) failed to elicit the desired unconditioned response (waking and sphincter control). The bell-and-pad method proved to be very successful in overcoming enuresis (Mowrer & Mowrer, 1938). The marked success of the treatment not only supported the efficacy of the specific procedure but was considered an important advance in using a learning approach to conceptualize and treat problems in general. Indeed, the Mowrers were explicit about the superiority of a learning-based approach compared with a psychoanalytic approach. They viewed psychoanalytic propositions as unparsimonious. Moreover, they challenged the notion that symptom substitution would result from the direct treatment of problematic behavior. The challenge was more than speculative because the Mowrers argued from their favorable follow-up data in treating enuretics.

In general, conditioning concepts were increasingly applied to clinical purposes. The applications extended to treatment and were proposed as a preferable alternative to the psychoanalytic notions that were in vogue at the time. This general pattern is illustrated by the work of Burnham and the Mowrers. However, these cases merely reflect a larger movement.

Personality and Psychotherapy

Integrative Theories of Behavior. The extensions of conditioning were not isolated applications of Pavlov's findings, as the previous section might imply. Conditioning had a marked impact at many different levels. From the 1930s through 1950s, attempts were made to develop general theories to explain normal and abnormal behavior and therapeutic processes based on learning (e.g., French, 1933; Kubie, 1934; Mowrer, 1950).

---

[3] It is worth noting in passing that Burnham's recommendations for mental hygiene primarily involved the application of what are now recognized as techniques derived from operant conditioning. Burnham, however, viewed his work as the application of respondent conditioning, following the breakthroughs of Pavlov, Watson, and others.

An especially noteworthy integrative theory was proposed in 1950 by John Dollard, a sociologist, and Neal E. Miller, an experimental psychologist, who attempted to provide a comprehensive theory of behavior that united learning, psychopathology, and psychotherapy. The work drew heavily on Pavlov, Thorndike, and Hull. The fundamental view was that psychopathology and psychotherapy could be explained by learning concepts and that both symptom development and symptom elimination could be conceived of as learning. Concepts and processes from psychoanalytic theory (e.g., the pleasure principle, transference, neurotic conflict) were reexplained in learning terms (e.g., reinforcement, stimulus generalization, and acquired drives). Concepts that had not been well based and researched were grounded in learning concepts that were the source of active theory and research at the time Dollard and Miller developed their theory.

Other people than Dollard and Miller developed theories of personality and psychotherapy that incorporated learning theory. For example, Julian B. Rotter drew on the work of learning and experimental psychology in general and from specific theorists (Tolman, Thorndike, Hull, and Kurt Lewin) to develop a general theory of behavior (Rotter, 1954). Therapy was also viewed as a learning process, and concepts from the psychology of learning were applied to explain conventional therapy.

In the history of behavior modification, the conceptual work of Dollard and Miller and Rotter is important because it reflects a move toward developing comprehensive theories of behavior that address psychopathology and psychotherapy. Learning theory and research had achieved prominence, if not dominance, in experimental psychology and were viewed as the best candidate for a sound conceptual basis for understanding psychopathology and psychotherapy. The specific theories of Dollard and Miller and Rotter have had little direct impact on contemporary practices in behavior modification. The theories primarily explained existing treatment in terms of learning. Increasingly, learning principles were looked at as a source of new therapy techniques, which ultimately had the greater impact on current

work. However, the conceptualization of existing psychotherapy as a learning process and the serious application of contemporary learning research to personality and psychotherapy were very important first steps.

Verbal Conditioning. Merely reexplaining conventional therapy in learning terms did not greatly stimulate research on psychotherapy. Extrapolations from operant conditioning to the dyadic interaction of therapy, however, generated considerable research that provided an important intermediary step toward applications of learning principles for treatment purposes. Specifically, operant methods were investigated in the context of verbal conditioning. Skinner had extended operant conditioning principles to a variety of behaviors, including verbal behavior, beginning in the 1940s. Skinner proposed that verbal behavior was an operant maintained by the consequences of the listener (Skinner, 1953a, 1957).

Laboratory research began to examine the influence of the experimenter on verbalizations of the subject. The general model of laboratory research in which an animal that responded would receive a reinforcing consequence was adhered to in devising an experimental situation to investigate human verbal behavior. Verbal behavior (e.g., selecting pronouns when constructing sentences) served as the response and was followed by reactions of the experimenter (e.g., statements of "good" or "mmm-hmm"). Several demonstrations showed that specific types of speech and conversation could be influenced by the consequences provided by the listener (Greenspoon, 1962).

Verbal conditioning research initially began in the 1950s and was conducted primarily with college students in an interview type of situation. Within a few years, verbal conditioning was extended to areas of clinical work by applying the methods to various clinical populations and to situations such as diagnostic testing where client behavior could be influenced by the examiner. The major extension of verbal conditioning was to situations resembling psychotherapy. Verbal conditioning research was used in tasks more closely resembling actual client behavior (e.g., speaking freely rather than constructing sentences) while the therapist responded to selected word classes. The word classes increased in clinical focus (e.g., emotional responses, self-acceptance statements, ''hallucinatory'' statements), and the populations included psychiatric patients rather than college students. Increasing parallels were drawn between verbal conditioning and psychotherapy (Krasner, 1955, 1958, 1962), an analogy later bolstered by findings that therapists actually did respond selectively to client behaviors (Truax, 1966).

Generally, verbal conditioning provided an analogue in which isolated processes of dyadic interaction could be investigated. The fact that verbal behavior could be conditioned suggested the role of learning in concrete ways (i.e., how the client talked about things) that were relevant to client change. Moreover, verbal conditioning supported a general approach toward behavior in the therapy session, namely, that behavior might be partially or perhaps even largely a function of external determinants rather than intrapsychic processes. Although many investigators challenged the similarity to psychotherapy of the situations in which verbal conditioning was conducted (Heller & Marlatt, 1969; Luborsky & Strupp, 1962), the fact that parallels were drawn at all increased the salience of learning in relation to psychotherapeutic processes. Also, demonstrations that verbal behavior could be altered by consequences provided by others led to direct extensions in clinical work to the modification of problematic verbal behavior, such as incoherent or irrational speech among psychotic patients (Ayllon & Michael, 1959; Isaacs, Thomas, & Goldiamond, 1960; Rickard, Dignam, & Horner, 1960).

Emergence of Behavior Modification

The extension of learning paradigms to behavior problems was clearly evident in the work of Watson, Rayner, M. C. Jones, and the Mowrers, to mention particularly salient examples. These investigators not only applied learning principles but placed their work in the larger context of psychopathology and therapy in general. Essentially, they viewed their work as representing a new approach to psychopathology. Hence, this initial work il-

lustrates a movement toward treatment that is difficult to distinguish from later conceptualizations and applications that were explicitly labeled as behavior modification. It is difficult to pinpoint a particular date in history at which behavior modification formally emerged. Developments in several places, primarily South Africa, England, and the United States, eventually merged as a formal movement.

Developments in South Africa

Certainly one of the most significant events in the emergence of behavior modification was the work of Wolpe in South Africa. Wolpe's development of systematic desensitization not only provided an innovative technique but in different ways helped crystallize the larger conceptual shift toward behavior therapy. Wolpe was interested in the psychology of learning as a possible source for understanding neurotic reactions and for developing treatment techniques. He was especially interested in the work of Pavlov and Hull and began research on experimental neuroses, using the work of Masserman (1943) as a point of departure.

Wolpe noted that the neurotic reaction established in cats extended to situations other than those in which the reaction was initially induced. Interestingly, the severity of the neurotic reaction appeared to be a function of the similarity of the cats' surroundings to those in the original situation. The more similar the room in which the cats were placed to the room in which fear had been established, the more severe the symptoms. To establish these neurotic reactions originally, Wolpe associated shock with approach toward food; eventually, the neurotic reaction inhibited feeding. This result suggested that feeding might, under different circumstances, inhibit anxiety; that is, the two reactions might be ''reciprocally inhibiting'' (see Wolpe, 1952a, 1954).

To overcome neurotic reactions, Wolpe placed the animals in situations that resembled, in varying degrees, the original situation in which the neurotic reactions had been developed, and he provided opportunities and physical guidance to encourage eating. After eating had been established, Wolpe induced feeding in rooms that more closely resembled the original room, and he continued this procedure until the animal could eat freely in the original room without anxiety. When feeding in the original situation was successfully accomplished, fear was eliminated.

Wolpe (1958) accounted for the "cures" on the basis of inhibition of the anxiety reaction and formulated a general principle of reciprocal inhibition: "If a response antagonistic to anxiety can be made to occur in the presence of anxiety-evoking stimuli so that it is accompanied by a complete or partial suppression of the anxiety responses, the bond between these stimuli and the anxiety responses will be weakened (p. 71)." This principle served as the basis for developing treatments to overcome human fear, an exceedingly important step that greatly extended previous work on experimental neuroses. Wolpe developed the idea that humans could be exposed to anxiety-provoking situations in a way similar to the exposure of the cats to rooms associated with fear. Although Wolpe first exposed clients to actual situations in which anxiety was provoked, he explored the use of imagery in which clients imagined a graded series of situations. Also, following the work of the physiologist Edmund Jacobson (1938), who had used relaxation to treat anxiety and other disorders, Wolpe selected muscle relaxation as a response that could inhibit anxiety in the same way that feeding was used as a response incompatible with fear among the animals.

The procedure that Wolpe developed was systematic desensitization, consisting of relaxation, the development of a graded series of anxiety-provoking situations (hierarchy), and the pairing of the imagination of the hierarchy items with relaxation. This variation is the major technique developed from the reciprocal inhibition principle, but it can be practiced in a variety of ways (e.g., using responses other than relaxation as the incompatible response, *in vivo* presentation of the anxiety-provoking situations).

The significance of the development of psychotherapy based on reciprocal inhibition and many steps and influences along the way cannot be easily highlighted here (see Kazdin, 1978b). Briefly, Wolpe can be credited with several accomplishments. First, he developed

a set of specific therapy techniques. The techniques were provided in the context that suggested their efficacy and superiority to alternative treatment methods (Wolpe, 1952b, 1958). The actual percentage of "cures" with diverse patients was claimed to be high (80%) relative to reports available from other treatment centers using traditional psychotherapeutic treatments. Others who applied learning concepts to psychotherapy had suggested that learning-based treatments were better than traditional treatments. Wolpe, more than others before him, made this issue salient by directly comparing his case data with reports of outcomes from other facilities. The comparison made explicit a challenge to others to develop and test their techniques against desensitization.

Second, the development and theoretical context of reciprocal inhibition therapies were consistent with the *Zeitgeist*. Wolpe drew on the psychology of learning, including the research of Pavlov, Hull, Mowrer, Miller, Masserman, and others, and on physiology in explaining the mechanisms through which behavior change was accomplished. Thus, the technique was placed on a conceptual foundation with a high degree of respectability in terms of its scientific basis.

Third, and related to each of the above, Wolpe developed *new* techniques. Rather than using learning as a basis to explain existing techniques, Wolpe utilized his findings from laboratory work to generate new approaches in clinical treatment. This important leap distinguishes Wolpe's work since many of the findings in experimental neuroses and even the procedures for overcoming neuroses were evident in the work of others (Masserman, 1943). Using experimental work to generate treatment techniques was innovative.

Finally, Wolpe made very specific and testable claims about therapy. He suggested that certain conditions must be included in treatment (e.g., relaxation, hierarchy construction, and the pairing of relaxation with imagination of the hierarchy items). The specificity of Wolpe's treatment encouraged a plethora of research projects in the ensuing years that helped formalize behavior therapy.

Wolpe's influential book, *Psychotherapy by Reciprocal Inhibition,* was written while he was on leave from South Africa in the United

19

States. Aside from publication of the book in 1958, the spread of desensitization and other techniques included in the book was facilitated by Stanley Rachman and Arnold A. Lazarus, who worked with Wolpe in South Africa and helped extend desensitization to England and the United States, respectively. Through their extensive writings, Rachman and Lazarus increased research and clinical practice in behavior therapy and contributed uniquely in their own ways to the final development of the field.

Developments in England

The development of behavior therapy in England began independently of Wolpe's work in South Africa but can be traced during the same period, namely, the early 1950s. The major impetus for formal development of behavior therapy can be traced to Eysenck and work done at the Institute of Psychiatry at the Maudsley Hospital in London.

Eysenck was trained as an experimental psychologist and advocated a rigorous scientific approach to psychiatry and clinical psychology. He incisively criticized traditional psychiatric and psychological practices, including psychiatric diagnosis and psychotherapy. A well-known and highly influential critique was published in 1952, entitled "The Effects of Psychotherapy: An Evaluation." This paper essentially noted that no firm evidence was available that psychotherapy was more effective than improvements likely to occur without formal treatment, that is, spontaneous remission. The paper stirred considerable controversy about the accomplishments of psychotherapy and whether traditional practices were worth the effort (see, for example, Eysenck, 1966).

Concurrently with Eysenck's writings, important developments were taking place at Maudsley. Eysenck, who was head of the research section of the psychology department, and M. B. Shapiro, who was head of the clinical teaching section, were dissatisfied with the role of the psychologist in the psychiatric setting. Eysenck believed that the psychologist should serve as a researcher and rely primarily on findings from general psychology for clinical practice (e.g., Eysenck, 1950, 1952a;

Paynes, 1953). Shapiro (1957) believed that the role of the psychologist should not be the routine administration of psychological tests. Indeed, he felt that traditional assessment devices lacked diagnostic, etiological, and treatment implications. Shapiro maintained that the psychologist should draw on general psychology for leads on how to evaluate and treat the patient.

Eysenck advocated learning-based formulations in conceptual papers about psychopathology and psychotherapy. Shapiro advanced a similar approach in the concrete applications of treatment to alter the behavior of patients at Maudsley. Early applications of interventions based on the work of Pavlov, Hull, and others were reported from Maudsley to alter such problems as enuresis, fear, and tics (e.g., H. G. Jones, 1956; Meyer, 1957; Yates, 1958).

By the late 1950s and early 1960s, extensions of learning to psychopathology and psychotherapy had increased. Eysenck took the lead in using learning theory to explain various disorders such as anxiety and hysteria (Eysenck, 1957). In 1959, he published a paper that explicitly applied learning theory to therapeutic applications and coined this extension as "behavior therapy."[4] This paper helped crystallize the movement toward behavior therapy by distinguishing behavior therapy from Freudian psychotherapy on several criteria.

Many of the distinctions were made sharply, perhaps to polarize the different positions. For example, Freudian psychotherapy was regarded as drawing on uncontrolled observations and as being based on inconsistent theory, whereas behavior therapy was seen as being derived from experimental studies and as being based on consistent and properly formulated theory. Behavior therapy was posed as scientifically superior and clinically more

---

[4] Interestingly, Lindsley and Skinner were the first to use the term *behavior therapy* (Skinner, Solomon, & Lindsley, 1953; Skinner, Solomon, Lindsley, & Richards, 1954). However, the term remained in unpublished reports that did not receive wide circulation. The term became popular primarily through Eysenck's (1959, 1960) early writings on the topic. Lazarus (1958) had used the term earlier than Eysenck, but his use was not adopted or widely publicized.

effective than traditional forms of psychotherapy. Eysenck (1960b, 1966) revised his classic paper, originally published in 1952, and extended the range of his conclusions. He retained the notion that psychotherapy had not been shown to be effective and further suggested that learning-based therapies provided the most promising leads. In short, in different writings, Eysenck made comparisons between behavior therapy and psychotherapy. The individual claims that Eysenck made about the specific differences between the areas might have been challenged, but the comparison clearly placed behavior therapy in the arena as an alternative to traditional Freudian therapy.

The movement toward the formalization of behavior progressed rather quickly in England. By the early 1960s, behavior therapy had emerged explicitly at Maudsley Hospital, representing a convergence of several activities within the setting. Rachman had come from South Africa and had brought with him Wolpe's method of systematic desensitization. From a different origin, Maudsley Hospital had already tried to apply a method of providing patients with graduated tasks to perform in anxiety-provoking situations to overcome their fear. This method was similar to that of Wolpe but derived from Herzberg (1945), who had suggested the procedure to Eysenck. At Maudsley, a psychiatrist, Michael Gelder, and a psychiatrist in training, Isaac Marks, began to apply desensitization in research with phobic patients. Within a very short time, Rachman, Gelder, and Marks began programmatic work applying and evaluating behavior therapy techniques for clinical patients.

Developments in the United States

The development of behavior modification in the United States was much more diffuse than in South Africa and England. Independent lines of work were evident without a central spokesperson, school of thought, or set of proponents. For example, in their work, Watson, the Mowrers, Burnham, and others were relatively isolated from each other, although they reflected a similar thrust. When additional applications in the United States are considered, the diffuseness of the approaches

is even more evident. Selected applications that reflect the movement toward learning-based therapy and eventually behavior modification are illustrated below.

Knight Dunlap and Negative Practice. In the late 1920s and the early 1930s, Knight Dunlap (1875–1949) was interested in the formation and elimination of habits. Dunlap, an experimental psychologist and a colleague of Watson, relied on learning as a basis for changing clinically relevant behavior. He was especially interested in eliminating undesirable habits through repetition, and he developed the procedure referred to as *negative practice* (Dunlap, 1928, 1932). Dunlap believed that habits could be altered by repetition of the undesirable behavior. By repeatedly engaging in the undesired behavior and by expecting improvement, the behavior could be altered. Dunlap reported several case applications where negative practice appeared to be effective in eliminating stuttering, nail biting, daydreaming, tics, thumb sucking, masturbation, and homosexuality.

Dunlap's work is significant in part because he drew on learning to generate treatment. He emphasized the role of repetition, consistent with contiguity views of learning at the time, and believed that clinical treatment in general should draw on the principles of learning (Dunlap, 1932). Later his technique was applied clinically in England and reformulated into Hullian learning theory (Yates, 1958).

Walter L. Voegtlin, Frederick Lemere, and Aversion Therapy for Alcoholics. In the 1930s, aversion therapy began to be applied systematically to the treatment of alcoholism in the United States. Treatment was begun at Shadel Sanatorium in Washington by Walter L. Voegtlin, who was joined by Frederick Lemere a couple of years later. The treatment consisted of pairing nausea with alcohol, consistent with the general paradigm of respondent conditioning. The work can be traced to applications in Russia, primarily that of Kantorovich (1929), who had used electric shock as the unconditioned stimulus and alcohol as the conditioned stimulus to bring about an aversive reaction. Other Russian investigators (e.g., Sluchevski & Friken, 1933) used apomorphine as the unconditioned stimulus with reported success. As a result of these early applications, aversion therapy began to spread throughout Europe and eventually to America.

Voetglin and Lemere began large-scale studies evaluating the effectiveness of aversion therapy (e.g., Lemere & Voegtlin, 1950; Voegtlin, Lemere, & Broz, 1940; Voegtlin, Lemere, Broz, & O'Hollaren, 1942). Follow-up ranged from 1 to 13 years and encompassed over 4,000 patients. The magnitude of the project and its strong commitment to treatment evaluation make the program at Shadel a significant step in the history of behavior modification. Essentially, this work can be considered on a par with many applications of behavior modification that followed in terms of its systematic evaluation, conceptual basis, and therapeutic focus. However, it was reported long before the formal development of behavior modification.

Andrew Salter and Conditioned-Reflex Therapy. A significant development in the history of behavior modification is the work of Andrew Salter, who developed treatments for outpatient psychotherapy. Salter's initial interest was in hypnosis. He was influenced by Hull's (1933) learning-based interpretation of how hypnosis achieves its effects. Hull had suggested that the therapist's speech served as the conditioned stimuli that evoked various reactions on the part of the client.

Salter began to apply hypnosis in private clinical practice and developed techniques of autohypnosis that clients could use effectively as self-control procedures for such problems as stuttering, nail biting, and insomnia (Salter, 1941). However, Salter was interested in expanding his techniques and the conditioning basis of treatment. He drew heavily on the work of Pavlov and Bechterev to provide an explanation for the conditioning that he believed goes on in therapy. Conditioning concepts also were relied on to explain the basis for maladaptive behavior. Salter drew on Pavlov's notions of excitation and inhibition, which had been proposed as neurological processes that accounted for conditioning. Salter suggested that maladjustment comes primarily from excessive inhibition, that is, the inhibition of feelings, thoughts, and behaviors. In 1949, he elaborated his therapeutic procedures based on conditioning notions in his book *Conditioned Reflex Therapy: The Direct Approach to the Reconstruction of Personality*. Conditioned-reflex therapy conveys the conceptual basis of the technique in terms of respondent conditioning. The *direct* approach conveys the therapeutic tasks that Salter required of his patients.

Salter noted that to overcome their inhibitions, clients had to practice expressing themselves in everyday life. Actual practice of the desired behaviors was advocated as the best way to produce therapeutic change. Several adjunctive procedures were used, such as relaxation training for individuals who were anxious and imagery to induce pleasant or relaxing states; but the main recommendation was to facilitate actual performance in everyday situations.

Salter's work is significant for several reasons. To begin with, he developed a theory of maladaptive behavior and therapeutic change based on concepts and contemporary research on conditioning. His conceptual framework drew on several researchers, including Gantt, Masserman, Mowrer, Maier, Hull, and Guthrie, aside from the basic work of Pavlov and Bechterev, as already mentioned. Both psychopathology and psychotherapy were viewed as based on learning.

Second, Salter was concerned with the larger movement toward learning-based therapy as an alternative to traditional psychoanalytically oriented psychotherapy. He referred to work of others such as Watson and Rayner, Voegtlin and Lemere, and Dunlap as successful learning-based approaches. In addition, Salter actively argued that underlying psychodynamic processes were not important in therapeutic change. The main goal of treatment was to change how a person behaves and acts. Salter (1952) criticized psychoanalytic theory and its assumptions about psychotherapy and hence placed behavior therapy in the larger context of representing an alternative to traditional treatment formulations and procedures.

Finally, Salter reported using several treatment techniques that very closely resembled contemporary practices in assertion training, systematic desensitization, self-control, behavioral rehearsal, and imagery-based treatment. Salter applied his conditioned-reflex therapy to a variety of cases and provided the first hint of the range of clinical problems to which learning-based treatments might be applied.

Extensions of Operant Conditioning. In the 1950s and 1960s, operant conditioning was extended to human behavior along several different fronts. The applications illustrate a systematic progression, beginning primarily with conceptual extensions of operant principles, extensions of operant methods to experimentation with humans, and direct clinical applications. Each part of the progression is elaborate and hence can be illustrated only by reference to selected achievements.

To begin with, the breadth of operant conditioning was suggested in conceptual extensions to diverse areas of human behavior (e.g., Keller & Schoenfeld, 1950; Skinner, 1948). For example, Skinner's book *Science and Human Behavior* (1953a) explained the role of operant conditioning principles in government, law, religion, psychotherapy, economics, and education. Of special interest were his extensions to psychotherapy, which suggested that the reinforcement contingencies of the therapist were primarily responsible for any change that was achieved in the client.

Basic laboratory work was initiated to extend operant methods to human behavior. In 1953, Ogden R. Lindsley and Skinner began to apply operant methods to psychotic patients at the Metropolitan State Hospital in Massachusetts. They studied adult and child patients as well as "normal" persons individually in an experimental chamber in order to evaluate the effects of reinforcement. The chamber permitted the performance of a simple response (plunger pulling) followed by reinforcement (e.g., the delivery of candy or cigarettes). Individual patients' behavior was evaluated daily for extended periods (up to several years for some patients) on the basis of the patient's responsiveness to operant contingencies. Although the purpose of the research was merely to extend operant methods to human behavior, the clinical implications were evident. Symptomatic behavior (e.g., hallucinations) occasionally interfered with operant behavior. Developing responses to the apparatus competed with symptomatic behaviors and hence decreased the symptoms. In general, the significance of this initial extension was the appli-

cation of scientific methods to an investigation of the behavior of psychotic patients and their responsiveness to various experimental manipulations (Lindsley, 1956, 1960).

In the early 1950s, Sidney W. Bijou began to apply operant methods to a study of the behavior of children (Bijou, 1957). Bijou developed a laboratory situation to study the responsiveness of children to various contingency manipulations that was similar in many ways to what Lindsley and Skinner had done with psychiatric patients. Bijou conducted several experimental investigations at the University of Washington (e.g., Bijou, 1955, 1957, 1958). By the late 1950s and the early 1960s, Bijou had extended operant conditioning beyond the laboratory to mental retardation and developmental psychology in general (Bijou, 1959, 1963).

Another extension of operant methods to human behavior was made by Charles B. Ferster, who had collaborated closely with Skinner on basic operant research. Ferster came to the Indiana School of Medicine in the late 1950s and began to apply operant methods to a study of the behavior of autistic children. A programmatic series of studies elaborated the nature of the operant behavior of autistic children on a variety of tasks and in a variety of contingency conditions (e.g., Ferster & DeMyer, 1961, 1962). The experiments led Ferster to suggest that the deficits found in autistic children might be overcome by developing more complex response repertoires through operant training. Similarly, in the late 1950s, Arthur Staats began a program of research at Arizona State University, applying operant methods to children with learning disabilities. Children performed individually on a laboratory apparatus where academic responses could earn reinforcers. Through a series of studies, Staats demonstrated the utility of operant methods with normal, retarded, culturally deprived, and disturbed children as they performed tasks that developed reading, writing, and arithmetic skills (e.g., Staats, Finley, Minke, & Wolf, 1964; Staats, Minke, Finley, Wolf, & Brooks, 1964; Staats, Staats, Schulz, & Wolf, 1962).

As laboratory extensions of operant conditioning increased, they began to reflect an increasingly applied relevance. The examples proliferated to such an extent that they would be difficult to document fully. For instance, Barrett and Lindsley (1962) applied operant methods to children in work similar to the work with psychotic patients that Lindsley and Skinner had begun earlier. Individual reports appeared suggesting that operant methods represented more than a method of studying human behavior. Early applications demonstrated that simple responses of the retarded could be altered (Fuller, 1949), tics could be reduced (Barrett, 1962), thumb sucking could be decreased (Baer, 1962), stuttering could be altered (Flanagan, Goldiamond, & Azrin, 1958), and so on.

Of all the applied extensions, two research programs provided particular impetus for extensions of operant techniques. First, the work of Teodoro Ayllon, beginning in 1958, was especially important. Ayllon applied operant techniques to the behaviors of psychiatric patients while at Saskatchewan Hospital. Patients' behaviors on the ward, such as interrupting nurses' work, engaging in violent acts and psychotic talk, or hoarding, were shown to be influenced dramatically by operant consequences (e.g., Ayllon & Michael, 1959; Ayllon, 1963; Ayllon & Haughton, 1964). This series of studies demonstrated very clearly that operant techniques could be applied to the behaviors of patients on the ward that were relevant to their everyday functioning and to their symptomatology. Such work encouraged more extensive and larger-scale applications. For example, Ayllon moved to Anna State Hospital and collaborated with Nathan Azrin on the development of a wardwide token-reinforcement system for a large number of patients (Ayllon & Azrin, 1965, 1968).

Another program that exerted considerable impact began at the University of Washington in the early 1960s. As noted earlier, Bijou began applying operant conditioning methods in laboratory studies. However, this work was extended in child clinical and educational settings. In 1962, Montrose M. Wolf began classroom applications of reinforcement to alter the behavior of retarded students at Rainier School in Washington. Wolf had previously worked with Staats in applying token reinforcement to alter children's reading behavior. When Wolf came to the University of Washington,

he collaborated with others to develop a token reinforcement system at Rainier School that included pioneering studies showing the value of operant procedures in educational settings (Bijou, Birnbrauer, Kidder, & Tague, 1966; Birnbrauer, Bijou, Wolf, & Kidder, 1965). Wolf also was involved with the staff at the laboratory preschool of the University of Washington and developed several programs with children to decrease such behaviors as excessive crawling, crying, and social isolation (e.g., Allen, Hart, Buell, Harris, & Wolf, 1964; Harris, Johnston, Kelley, & Wolf, 1964).

Additional applications emerged from the University of Washington, such as the now-classic report of an autistic boy named Dicky who had many behavioral problems, including tantrums, self-destructive behavior, and refusal to wear glasses, that, if not corrected, might have resulted in partial loss of vision. The successful treatment of Dicky (Wolf, Risley, & Mees, 1964) demonstrated that reinforcement and punishment contingencies could indeed be used to alter important behaviors in clinical cases.

Applications of operant techniques were evident at many different institutions in the early and middle 1960s. The work at the University of Washington was especially important because of the range of applications across settings, the number of projects reported, and their dramatic and carefully demonstrated effects on child behavior. From this research in particular, the influence of applied operant research grew.

General Comments. Spanning the period of the 1940s through the early 1960s, several innovative applications of learning-based treatment could be identified in the United States. However, even up to the very early 1960s, there was relatively little unity that conveyed an overall movement or singular conceptual stance similar to what had developed in England and South Africa. The diffuse movements in the United States included applications and extensions of operant methods and independent development of classical conditioning methods. Even in cases where seemingly similar methods might be unified, they remained somewhat independent. For example, both Voegtlin and Salter had independently drawn on classical conditioning to develop treatment methods; both had even chanced on the same name for their treatments: *conditioned-reflex therapy*. However, they applied very different methods in treatment based on their different clientele and treatment settings (inpatient alcoholics vs. outpatient treatment of diverse problems). The applications reflect a definite move toward learning-based treatments but not a clearly unified movement that could be recognized as such in the United States.

Formalization of Behavior Therapy

Although developments in South Africa, England, and the United States began independently, cross-fertilization and integration of the ideas and techniques followed relatively quickly. Persons active in the initial developments of behavior therapy moved across geographic boundaries to spread the movement further and to integrate separate developments. For example, in the late 1950s and early 1960s, Wolpe left South Africa to visit and eventually to settle in the United States, thereby bringing desensitization to the United States. Wolpe had also visited Eysenck in London. Eysenck had already been interested in reciprocal inhibition. Rachman, who had worked with Wolpe, as mentioned earlier, settled in London and introduced Wolpe's therapy procedures at Maudsley Hospital. Lazarus, who had been in South Africa with Wolpe and Rachman, also settled in the United States. In general, there was some early cross-fertilization of techniques and ideas across the geographical boundaries in which initial developments took place.

Behavior therapy became a visible movement in the early 1960s. Although it is difficult to mark the point at which the movement became identifiable, selected publications seem to have crystallized existing developments. Eysenck (1960a) edited the first book including *behavior therapy* in the title, which brought diverse writings applying learning principles to therapeutic problems. The identity of the field was demarcated further in 1963, when Eysenck started the first behavior therapy journal, *Behaviour Research and Therapy*. Within a matter of a few years, several additional publications emerged that brought together therapeutic applications that were based on learning (Eysenck, 1964; Franks, 1964;

Staats, 1964; Wolpe, Salter, & Reyna, 1964) and behavior therapy or that identified the conditioning therapies as a distinct area of research and approach to treatment. Although books proliferated in the middle 1960s, one completed by Ullmann and Krasner (1965) in the United States was particularly noteworthy for bringing together a variety of case applications of behavioral techniques and for providing a historical overview of the development of behavior modification.

Along with the integration of existing behavioral practices into a single movement, attacks against the disease model conceptualization of abnormal behavior, especially psychoanalytic theory, continued (e.g., Eysenck, 1959; Rachman, 1963; Salter, 1952). Criticism of the existing position helped unify proponents of behavior therapy. Many initial attacks on psychoanalytic theory were polemical and served to delineate behavior therapy as a unique area. Apart from attacking the traditional disease model, behavior therapy became increasingly visible by defending itself from criticism as illustrated in an exchange that was widely circulated (Breger & McGaugh, 1965, 1966; Rachman & Eysenck, 1966).

Aside from publications, the formal development of behavior therapy as a distinct area was aided by the formation of various interest groups and societies. The earliest in the United States was the Association for Advancement of Behavior Therapy, which was formed in 1966 as a multidisciplinary interest group. This organization held annual meetings, published a newsletter, and affiliated with other groups, all of which helped to establish behavior therapy formally. Within a few years, additional organizations emerged, such as the Behavior Therapy and Research Society in 1970, to develop a professional group of behavior therapists rather than simply an interest group. By the late 1960s and the early 1970s, journals, conferences, and organizations devoted to behavior therapy proliferated (see Kazdin, 1978b).

Contemporary Behavior Modification

By the early 1960s, behavior therapy had become a formal movement as ideas spread across different conceptual and geographical boundaries. Behavior therapy consisted of several different developments, including varied theoretical approaches and treatment techniques. However, common denominators of the approach were extracted to provide unity to the field.

Characteristics of Behavior Modification

Behavior modification can be characterized by several assumptions about abnormal behavior as well as by an approach toward treatment and its evaluation. A major characteristic of the field is its reliance on findings or techniques that are derived from general psychology. The psychology of learning has served as the major impetus for and the conceptual basis of many techniques. Learning conceptions are relied on to explain the development and the treatment of abnormal behavior.

A second characteristic of the behavioral approach is the view that normal and abnormal behavior are not qualitatively different. Some behaviors are not "sick" and others "healthy" based on characteristics inherent in the behaviors. There is a continuity of behavior, and psychological principles apply to all behaviors whether or not they are identified as normal. Thus, maladaptive behavior can be unlearned and replaced by adaptive behavior.

A third characteristic of behavior therapy is its direct focus on the maladaptive behavior for which the client seeks treatment. Behavior is not viewed as a sign of disordered intrapsychic processes but is of direct interest in its own right. The direct treatment of behavior does not mean that internal states are necessarily rejected. Indeed, behavior therapy often focuses on thoughts or beliefs when these are conceived of as problems in their own right. However, the focus is on the identified problem rather than on the underlying intrapsychic states considered the basis of the problem.

Another characteristic of behavior modification is its emphasis on the assessment of behavior and the experimental evaluation of treatment. An attempt is made to specify the target problem very carefully so that it can be assessed. This specificity extends to treatment, so that the procedures can be carefully evaluated and systematically replicated. Behavior therapy has a strong commitment to the experimental evaluation of treatment, as evident in several journals heavily committed to outcome research.

Several characteristics of behavior modification reflect a departure from traditional approaches to diagnosis, assessment, and treatment. Diagnosis in behavior modification emphasizes specific problematic behaviors and the conditions under which they are performed. Traditional diagnostic categories generally are eschewed for a careful delineation of the precise behaviors in need of treatment and the influences that may contribute to or that may be used to alter these behaviors (e.g., Cautela & Upper, 1973; Kanfer & Saslow, 1969). Behavioral assessment focuses on the target behavior directly. Behavior is often observed in the actual situations in which it is a problem or under simulated conditions, so that the therapist can see the problem behavior directly (see Ciminero, Calhoun, & Adams, 1977; Hersen & Bellack, 1976). Several response modalities are incorporated into behavioral assessment, in addition to samples of overt behavior, to provide a full picture of the target problem.

Treatment in behavior modification is closely tied to the diagnosis and assessment of behavior. Once the specific maladaptive behaviors are identified and assessed, treatment is directed to the problem behavior itself. The treatment strategies vary considerably according to the problem behavior that is studied. The major treatment approaches that are used include systematic desensitization, flooding, modeling, covert conditioning, aversion therapy, reinforcement and punishment techniques, biofeedback, and cognitive behavior therapy. Each of these refers to general techniques that include a large number of specific variations not easily enumerated here.

Diversity within Behavior Modification

Behavior modification is not a uniform or homogeneous position. At the inception of the field, many independent attempts to provide a scientific and learning-based foundation for psychotherapy were unified under the rubrics *behavior therapy* and *behavior modification*. The justification for unifying different developments was the common reaction against the prevailing view in psychiatry and clinical psychology and the adherence to learning theory, broadly conceived. Differences within the areas of behavior modification were minimized or ignored for the purpose of developing a relatively unified movement to oppose the traditional disease model of abnormal behavior and its treatment.

Actually, behavior modification is extremely diverse. The diversity was evident from the inception of the field but has become increasingly apparent in recent years. After behavior therapy emerged, individual approaches within the field developed over the years, and differences among the approaches could be even more readily identifiable. Consider some of the major dimensions along which diversity exists.

Conceptual Approaches. Different conceptual approaches can be readily identified within behavior therapy, including a stimulus–response (S–R) mediational view, applied behavior analysis, and cognitive behavior modification (Kazdin & Wilson, 1978). The S–R mediational view consists primarily of the application of learning concepts and emphasizes stimulus–response pairing, as derived from the contiguity learning views of Pavlov, Guthrie, Mowrer, and others. Intervening variables and hypothetical constructs are relied on to account for behavior. Illustrative of this general theoretical approach are techniques such as systematic desensitization and flooding, which focus on extinguishing the underlying anxiety that accounts for and sustains avoidant behavior. Characteristic of this approach is an attempt to link mediational constructs to antecedent stimuli and responses that can be readily operationalized.

Applied behavior analysis is quite different as an approach within behavior therapy because it draws primarily on the substantive and methodological heritage of operant conditioning and the experimental analysis of behavior. Emphasis is placed on antecedent and consequent events; mediational states, private events, and cognitions are avoided. Treatment focuses on altering antecedents and consequences in order to alter the target behavior. A unique methodological approach also characterizes applied behavior analysis and includes the experimental evaluation of the performance of individuals using intrasubject-

replication designs, usually in place of between-group designs. Applied behavior analysis includes a variety of techniques based on reinforcement, punishment, extinction, stimulus, control, and other principles derived from laboratory research (Catania & Brigham, 1978).

Cognitive behavior therapy is an approach that stresses thoughts, beliefs, and the assumption that people make their own environment. Maladaptive behavior is viewed as resulting from faulty cognitions, and therapy focuses on eliminating these cognitions and replacing them with thoughts and self-statements that will promote more adaptive behavior. Although behavior is viewed as a result of cognitive symbolic processes (e.g., Bandura, 1977), often behavioral methods are used to alter these cognitive processes, such as practicing and receiving reinforcing consequences for making self-statements that promote the desired behaviors (e.g., Mahoney, 1974; Meichenbaum, 1977).

Additional Dimensions. The diversity of behavior therapy can be illustrated by noting several dimensions in passing. For example, behavior therapy techniques vary in the extent to which they draw on psychological theory and laboratory findings. Many techniques derive from theory in the broad sense, such as S–R learning, operant conditioning, and cognitive theories. Other techniques do not rely on theory. Indeed, drawing on resources in theory or basic research has been discouraged by some authors. For example, Lazarus (1971) has suggested that behavior therapy should include techniques useful in treatment whether or not they derive from theory or laboratory research. Finally, other techniques have emerged from a general learning orientation but have developed from actual practice in applied settings (Azrin, 1977). In short, behavior therapy techniques differ markedly on the extent to which they derive from theory or laboratory research paradigms.

As already hinted at, research methods for evaluating clinical interventions vary considerably in behavior therapy. Different experimental design and data evaluation strategies are evident. Applied behavior analysis relies primarily on single-case experimental designs, evaluated with visual inspection, whereas other areas embrace more traditional between-group research and statistical evaluation.

Current Status

The diversity of views and the different types of techniques and approaches make the term *behavior therapy* almost devoid of meaning (see Lazarus, 1977; Wilson, 1978). The definition of *behavior therapy* has evolved over the course of the field's brief history. Early definitions regarded behavior therapy as a conceptualization of behavior and treatment on the basis of the laws and principles of learning (e.g., Eysenck, 1964; Wolpe & Lazarus, 1966). Although learning theory and findings have been especially useful, the domain has expanded, so that *behavior modification* has been defined more generally as treatment based on experimental findings from the psychology and social sciences (e.g., Krasner & Ullmann, 1973; Yates, 1970).

Because of the expanded definition of the field and the development of alternative and often diametrically opposed conceptual interpretations of behavior and therapeutic change, few characteristics of the field can be set forth that encompass all factions. Currently, the distinguishing characteristics of behavior therapy appear to lie in its approach to treatment and its conceptualization rather than in a specific theoretical basis or set of techniques (Agras, Kazdin, & Wilson, 1979). In general, behavior therapy tends to:

1. Focus on current rather than historical determinants of behavior.
2. Emphasize overt behavior change as the major criterion in evaluating treatment.
3. Rely on basic research from psychology to generate hypotheses about treatment and specific techniques.
4. Specify treatment in objective and operational terms so that the procedures can be replicated.
5. Specify very carefully the target behavior and the techniques for measuring outcome.

In addition to these five characteristics, current behavior therapy still rejects the major tenets of the disease approach in general and the intrapsychic approach in particular. However, the major *positive* characteristics that distinguish behavior therapy reflect more of a general scientific approach toward treatment and clinical practice rather than a particular conceptual stance or set of theoretical propositions.

Summary and Conclusions

When behavior therapy first emerged as a formal movement, it encompassed different conceptual positions and treatment techniques. However, the differences at the inception of the movement were deemphasized to promote the important common characteristics, namely, treatment procedures based on learning and a conceptual alternative to the intrapsychic approaches. Early definitions stressed the ties of behavior therapy to learning theory and conditioning principles as a common ingredient. Within the last 25 years, the field has developed considerably. The heterogeneity of approaches has increased. Consequently, the field cannot be characterized accurately by pointing to a particular set of theories or domain of psychology as the basis of treatment.

A major characteristic of contemporary behavior modification is an empirical approach to treatment and its evaluation. Interestingly, this common feature of the approaches within behavior modification reflects the general methodological tenets of behaviorism to which the overall movement can be traced. Within the general methodological approach, diversity within the field is encouraged at both the conceptual and the technical levels. Approaches are welcome as long as they are amenable to empirical evaluation. On the other hand, behavior modification is not a blind empiricism as applied to psychotherapy, since many techniques and procedures draw quite heavily from scientific psychology and learning theories in particular. Further, advancing research techniques often generate their own theoretical approaches, which are subjected to further validation. The present chapter has traced the major developments that led to the emergence of behavior modification as an overall movement and approach toward therapy.

References

Agras, W. S., Kazdin, A. E., & Wilson, G. T. *Behavior therapy: Toward an applied clinical science.* San Francisco: W. H. Freeman, 1979.

Aldrich, C. A. A new test for learning in the new born: The conditioned reflex. *American Journal of Disease of Children,* 1928, *35,* 36–27.

Alexander, J. *Thought-control in everyday life* (5th ed.). New York: Funk & Wagnalls, 1928.

Allen, K. E., Hart, B. M., Buell, J. S., Harris, F. R., & Wolf, M. M. Effects of social reinforcement on isolate behavior of a nursery school child. *Child Development,* 1964, *35,* 511–518.

Ayllon, T. Intensive treatment of psychotic behavior by stimulus satiation and food reinforcement. *Behaviour Research and Therapy,* 1963, *1,* 53–61.

Ayllon, T., & Azrin, N. H. The measurement and reinforcement of behavior of psychotics. *Journal of the Experimental Analysis of Behavior,* 1965, *8,* 356–383.

Ayllon, T., & Azrin, N. H. *The token economy: A motivational system for therapy and rehabilitation.* New York: Appleton-Century-Crofts, 1968.

Ayllon, T., & Haughton, E. Modification of symptomatic verbal behavior of mental patients. *Behaviour Research and Therapy,* 1964, *2,* 87–97.

Ayllon, T., & Michael, J. The psychiatric nurse as a behavioral engineer. *Journal of the Experimental Analysis of Behavior,* 1959, *2,* 323–334.

Azrin, N. H. A strategy for applied research: Learning based but outcome oriented. *American Psychologist,* 1977, *32,* 140–149.

Baer, D. M. Laboratory control of thumbsucking by withdrawal and re-presentation of reinforcement. *Journal of the Experimental Analysis of Behavior,* 1962, *5,* 525–528.

Bagby, E. *The psychology of personality.* New York: Holt, 1928.

Bailey, P. The great psychiatric revolution. *American Journal of Psychiatry,* 1956, *113,* 387–406.

Bandura, A. *Social learning theory.* Englewood Cliffs, N.J.: Prentice-Hall, 1977.

Barrett, B. H. Reduction in rate of multiple tics by free operant conditioning methods. *Journal of Nervous and Mental Disease,* 1962, *135,* 187–195.

Barrett, B. H., & Lindsley, O. R. Deficits in acquisition of operant discrimination in institutionalized retarded children. *American Journal of Mental Deficiency,* 1962, *67,* 424–436.

Bechterev, V. M. *La psychologie objective.* Paris: Alcan, 1913.

Bechterev, V. M. Die Perversitaten und Inversitaten vom Standpunkt der Reflexologie. *Archiv fuer Psychiatrie und Nervenkrankheiten,* 1923, *68,* 100–213.

Bechterev, V. M. *General principles of human reflexology: An introduction to the objective study of personality.* Trans. E. Murphy & W. Murphy. New York: International Publishers, 1932.

Bijou, S. W. A systematic approach to an experimental analysis of young children. *Child Development,* 1955, *26,* 161–168.

Bijou, S. W. Patterns of reinforcement and resistance to extinction in young children. *Child Development,* 1957, *28,* 47–54.

Bijou, S. W. Operant extinction after fixed-interval schedules with young children. *Journal of Experimental Analysis of Behavior,* 1958, *1,* 25–29.

Bijou, S. W. Learning in children. *Monographs of the Society for Research in Child Development,* 1959, *24,* No. 5 (Whole No. 74).

Bijou, S. W. Theory and research in mental (developmental) retardation. *Psychological Record,* 1963, *13,* 95–110.

Bijou, S. W., Birnbrauer, J. S., Kidder, J. D., & Tague, C. Programmed instruction as an approach to the teaching of reading, writing, and arithmetic to retarded children. *Psychological Record,* 1966, *16,* 505–522.

Birnbrauer, J. S., Bijou, S. W., Wolf, M. M., & Kidder, J. D. Programmed instructions in the classroom. In L. P. Ullmann & L. Krasner (Eds.), *Case studies in behavior modification.* New York: Holt, Rinehart, & Winston, 1965.

Breger, L., & McGaugh, J. L. Critique and reformulation of "learning theory" approaches to psychotherapy and neurosis. *Psychological Bulletin,* 1965, *63,* 338–358.

Breger, L., & McGaugh, J. L. Learning theory and behavior therapy: Reply to Rachman and Eysenck. *Psychological Bulletin,* 1966, *65,* 170–175.

Bregman, E. P. An attempt to modify the emotional attitudes of infants by the conditioned response technique. *Journal of Genetic Psychology,* 1934, *45,* 169–198.

Brissaud, E. Tics et spasmes cloniques de la face. *Journal de Médecine et de Chirurgie Pratiques,* 1894, *65,* 49–64.

Burnham, W. H. Mental hygiene and the conditioned reflex. *Journal of Genetic Psychology,* 1917, *24,* 449–488.

Burnham, W. H. *The normal mind.* New York: Appleton, 1924.

Catania, A. C., & Brigham, T. A. (Eds.), *Handbook of applied behavior analysis: Social and instructional processes.* New York: Irvington, 1978.

Cautela, J. R., & Upper, D. *A behavioral coding system.* Paper presented at meeting of the Association for Advancement of Behavior Therapy, Miami, December, 1973.

Ciminero, A. R., Calhoun, J. S., & Adams, H. E. (Eds.), *Handbook of behavioral assessment.* New York: Wiley, 1977.

Darwin, C. *On the origin of species by means of natural selection.* London: Murray, 1859.

Darwin, D. *The descent of man.* New York: Appleton, 1871.

Darwin, C. *The expression of the emotions in man and animals.* London: Murray, 1872.

Denker, P. G. Results of treatment of psychoneuroses by the general practitioner. *New York State Journal of Medicine,* 1946, *46,* 2164–2166.

Dollard, J., & Miller, N. E. *Personality and psychotherapy.* New York: McGraw-Hill, 1950.

Dunlap, K. A. A revision of the fundamental law of habit formation. *Science,* 1928, *67,* 360–362.

Dunlap, K. *Habits: Their making and unmaking.* New York: Liveright, 1932.

Ellis, A. Should some people be labeled mentally ill? *Journal of Consulting Psychology,* 1967, *31,* 435–446.

English, H. B. Three cases of the conditioned fear response. *Journal of Abnormal and Social Psychology,* 1929, *24,* 221–225.

Eysenck, H. J. Function and training of the clinical psychologist. *Journal of Mental Science,* 1950, *96,* 710–725.

Eysenck, H. J. Discussion on the role of the psychologist in psychiatric practice. *Proceedings of the Royal Society of Medicine,* 1952, *45,* 447–449. (a)

Eysenck, H. J. The effects of psychotherapy: An evaluation. *Journal of Consulting Psychology,* 1952, *16,* 319–324. (b)

Eysenck, H. J. *The dynamics of anxiety and hysteria.* London: Routledge and Kegan Paul, 1957.

Eysenck, H. J. Learning theory and behaviour therapy. *Journal of Mental Science,* 1959, *105,* 61–75.

Eysenck, H. J. (Ed.). *Behavior therapy and the neuroses.* New York: Pergamon, 1960. (a)

Eysenck, H. J. The effects of psychotherapy. In H. J. Eysenck (Ed.), *Handbook of abnormal psychology: An experimental approach.* London: Pittman, 1960. (b)

Eysenck, H. J. (Ed.). *Experiments in behaviour therapy.* New York: Macmillan, 1964.

Eysenck, H. J. *The effects of psychotherapy.* New York: International Science Press, 1966.

Ferster, C. B. Classification of behavioral pathology. In L. Krasner & L. P. Ullmann (Eds.), *Research in behavior modification.* New York: Holt, Rinehart & Winston, 1965.

Ferster, C. B., & DeMyer, M. K. The development of performances in autistic children in an automatically controlled environment. *Journal of Chronic Diseases,* 1961, *13,* 312–345.

Ferster, C. B., & DeMyer, M. K. A method for the experimental analysis of the behavior of autistic children. *American Journal of Orthopsychiatry,* 1962, *1,* 87–110.

Flanagan, B., Goldiamond, I., & Azrin, N. H. Operant stuttering: The control of stuttering behavior through response-contingent consequences. *Journal of the Experimental Analysis of Behavior,* 1958, *1,* 173–177.

Franks, C. M. (Ed.). *Conditioning techniques in clinical practice and research.* New York: Springer, 1964.

Franzini, L. R., & Tilker, H. A. On the terminological confusion between behavior therapy and behavior modification. *Behavior Therapy,* 1972, *3,* 279–282.

French, T. M. Interrelations between psychoanalysis and the experimental work of Pavlov. *American Journal of Psychiatry,* 1933, *89,* 1165–1203.

Fuller, P. R. Operant conditioning of a vegetative human organism. *American Journal of Psychology,* 1949, *62,* 587–590.

Gantt, W. H., & Muncie, W. Analysis of the mental defect in chronic Korsakoff's Psychosis by means of the conditional reflex method. *Bulletin of the Johns Hopkins Hospital,* 1942, *70,* 467–487.

Greenspoon, J. Verbal conditioning and clinical psychology. In A. J. Backrach (Ed.), *Experimental foundations of clinical psychology.* New York: Basic Books, 1962.

Guthrie, E. R. *The psychology of human learning.* New York: Harper, 1935.

Harris, B. Whatever happened to Little Albert? *American Psychologist,* 1979, *34,* 151–160.

Harris, F. R., Johnston, M. K., Kelley, C. S., & Wolf, M. M. Effects of positive social reinforcement on regressed crawling on a nursery school child. *Journal of Educational Psychology,* 1964, *55,* 35–41.

Heller, K., & Marlatt, G. A. Verbal conditioning, behavior therapy, and behavior change: Some problems in extrapolation. In C. M. Franks (Ed.), *Behavior therapy: Appraisal and status.* New York: McGraw-Hill, 1969.

Herrnstein, R. J. Behaviorism. In D. L. Krantz, (Ed.), *Schools of psychology.* New York: Appleton-Century-Crofts, 1969.

Hersen, M. Historical perspectives in behavioral assessment. In M. Hersen & A. S. Bellack (Eds.), *Behavioral assessment: A practical handbook.* Oxford: Pergamon, 1976.

Hersen, M., & Bellack, A. S. (Eds.). *Behavioral assessment: A practical handbook.* Oxford: Pergamon, 1976.

Herzberg, A. *Active psychotherapy.* New York: Grune & Stratton, 1945.

Hilgard, E. R., & Bower, G. H. *Theories of learning.* New York: Appleton-Century-Crofts, 1966.

Hilgard, E. R., & Marquis, P. G. *Conditioning and learning.* New York: Appleton-Century, 1940.

Hovey, H. B. The questionable validity of some assumed antecedents of mental illness. *Journal of Clinical Psychology,* 1959, *15,* 270–272.

Hull, C. L. *Hypnosis and suggestibility.* New York: Appleton, 1933.

Hunt, H. F. Problems in the interpretation of "experimental neurosis." *Psychological Reports,* 1964, *15,* 27–35.

Isaacs, W., Thomas, J., & Goldiamond, I. Application of operant conditioning to reinstate verbal behavior in psychotics. *Journal of Speech and Hearing Disorders,* 1960, *25,* 8–12.

Jacobson, E. *Progressive relaxation.* Chicago: University of Chicago Press, 1938.

Jones, H. G. The application of conditioning and learning techniques to the treatment of a psychiatric patient. *Journal of Abnormal and Social Psychology,* 1956, *52,* 414–419.

Jones, M. C. The elimination of children's fears. *Journal of Experimental Psychology,* 1924, *7,* 382–390. (a)

Jones, M. C. A laboratory study of fear: The case of Peter. *Pedagogical Seminary,* 1924, *31,* 308–315. (b)

Kaestle, C. F. (Ed.), *Joseph Lancaster and the monitorial school movement: A documentary history.* New York: Teachers College Press, 1973.

Kanfer, F. H., & Saslow, G. Behavioral diagnosis. In C. M. Franks (Ed.), *Behavior therapy: Appraisal and status.* New York: McGraw-Hill, 1969.

Kantorovich, N. V. An attempt of curing alcoholism by associated reflexes. *Novoye Refleksologii nervnoy i Fiziologii Sistemy,* 1929, *3,* 436–445.

Kazdin, A. E. The application of operant techniques in treatment, rehabilitation, and education. In S. L. Garfield & A. E. Bergin (Eds.), *Handbook of psychotherapy and behavior change* (2nd ed.). New York: Wiley, 1978. (a)

Kazdin, A. E. *History of behavior modification: Experimental foundations of contemporary research.* Baltimore: University Park Press, 1978. (b)

Kazdin, A. E. Fictions, factions, and functions of behavior therapy. *Behavior Therapy,* 1979, *10,* 629–654.

Kazdin, A. E., & Pulaski, J. L. Joseph Lancaster and

behavior modification in education. *Journal of the History of the Behavioral Sciences,* 1977, *13,* 261–266.

Kazdin, A. E., & Wilson, G. T. *Evaluation of behavior therapy: Issues, evidence, and research strategies.* Cambridge, Mass.: Ballinger, 1978.

Keehn, J. D., & Webster, C. D. Behavior therapy and behavior modification. *Canadian Psychologist,* 1969, *10,* 68–73.

Keller, F. S., & Schoenfeld, W. N. *Principles of psychology.* New York: Appleton-Century-Crofts, 1950.

Krasner, L. The use of generalized reinforcers in psychotherapy research. *Psychological Reports,* 1955, *1,* 19–25.

Krasner, L. Studies of the conditioning of verbal behavior. *Psychological Bulletin,* 1958, *55,* 148–170.

Krasner, L. The therapist as a social reinforcement machine. In H. H. Strupp & L. Luborsky (Eds.), *Research in psychotherapy,* Vol. 2. Washington, D.C.: American Psychological Association, 1962.

Krasner, L. Behavior therapy. In P. H. Mussen (Ed.), *Annual review of psychology,* Vol. 22. Palo Alto, Calif.: Annual Reviews, 1971.

Krasner, L., & Ullmann, L. P. *Behavior influence and personality: The social matrix of human action.* New York: Holt, Rinehart & Winston, 1973.

Krasnogorski, N. I. The conditioned reflexes and children's neuroses. *American Journal of Diseases in Children,* 1925, *30,* 753–768.

Kubie, L. S. Relation of the conditioned reflex to psychoanalytic technic. *Archives of Neurology and Psychiatry,* 1934, *32,* 1137–1142.

Laing, R. D. *The politics of experience.* New York: Pantheon, 1967.

Lancaster, J. *Improvements in education, as it respects the industrious classes of the community* (3rd ed.). London: Darton and Harvey, 1805.

Landis, C. A statistical evaluation of psychotherapeutic methods. In L. E. Hinsie (Ed.), *Concepts and problems of psychotherapy.* New York: Columbia University Press, 1937.

Lazarus, A. A. New methods in psychotherapy: A case study. *South African Medical Journal,* 1958, *32,* 660–664.

Lazarus, A. A. *Behavior therapy and beyond.* New York: McGraw-Hill, 1971.

Lazarus, A. A. Has behavior therapy outlived its usefulness? *American Psychologist,* 1977, *32,* 550–554.

Lemere, F., & Voegtlin, W. L. An evaluation of the aversion treatment of alcoholism. *Quarterly Journal of Studies on Alcohol,* 1950, *11,* 199–204.

Lindsley, O. R. Operant conditioning methods applied to research in chronic schizophrenia. *Psychiatric Research Reports,* 1956, *5,* 118–139.

Lindsley, O. R. Characteristics of the behavior of chronic psychotics as revealed by free-operant conditioning methods. *Diseases of the Nervous System (Monograph Supplement),* 1960, *21,* 66–78.

Luborsky, L., & Strupp, H. H. Research problems in psychotherapy: A three-year follow-up. In H. H. Strupp & L. Luborsky (Eds.), *Research in psychotherapy,* Vol. 2. Washington, D.C.: American Psychological Association, 1962.

Mahoney, M. J. *Cognition and behavior modification.* Cambridge, Mass.: Ballinger, 1974.

Masserman, J. H. *Behavior and neurosis.* Chicago: University of Chicago Press, 1943.

Mateer, F. *Child behavior: A critical and experimental study of young children by the method of conditioned reflexes.* Boston: R. G. Badger, 1918.

McDougall, W. *An introduction to social psychology.* Boston: J. W. Luce, 1908.

Meichenbaum, D. H. *Cognitive behavior modification.* New York: Plenum Press, 1977.

Meige, H., & Feindel, E. *Tics and their treatment.* Trans. S. A. K. Wilson. London: Sidney Appleton, 1907.

Meltzoff, J., & Kornreich, M. *Research in psychotherapy.* New York: Atherton, 1970.

Meyer, M. F. *The fundamental laws of human behavior.* Boston: R. G. Badger, 1911.

Meyer, V. The treatment of two phobic patients on the basis of learning principles. *Journal of Abnormal and Social Psychology,* 1957, *55,* 261–266.

Mischel, W. *Personality and assessment.* New York: Wiley, 1968.

Mowrer, O. H. On the dual nature of learning—a reinterpretation of "conditioning" and "problem solving." *Harvard Educational Review,* 1947, *17,* 102–148.

Mowrer, O. H. *Learning theory and personality dynamics.* New York: Ronald Press, 1950.

Mowrer, O. H. *Learning theory and behavior.* New York: Wiley, 1960.

Mowrer, O. H., & Mowrer, W. M. Enuresis: A method for its study and treatment. *American Journal of Orthopsychiatry,* 1938, *8,* 436–459.

Orlansky, H. Infant care and personality. *Psychological Bulletin,* 1949, *46,* 1–49.

Parloff, M. B., & Rubinstein, E. A. Research problems in psychotherapy. In E. A. Rubinstein & M. B. Parloff (Eds.), *Research in psychotherapy, Volume 1.* Washington, D.C.: American Psychological Association, 1962.

Paul, G. L. Chronic mental patient: Current status—future directions. *Psychological Bulletin,* 1969, *71,* 81–94.

Pavlov, I. P. *The work of the digestive glands.* Trans. W. H. Thompson. London: Charles Griffin, 1902.

Pavlov, I. P. Experimental psychology and psychopathology in animals. Speech presented to the International Medical Congress, Madrid, April 1903. (Also reprinted in I. P. Pavlov, *Selected works.* Moscow: Foreign Languages Publishing House, 1955.)

Pavlov, I. P. The scientific investigation of the psychical faculties or processes in the higher animals. *Science,* 1906, *24,* 613–619.

Pavlov, I. P. *Conditioned reflexes: An investigation of the physiological activities of the cerebral cortex.* London: Oxford University Press, 1927.

Pavlov, I. P. *Lectures on conditioned reflexes.* Trans. W. H. Gantt. New York: International Publishers, 1928.

Paynes, R. W. The role of the clinical psychologist at the Institute of Psychiatry. *Revue de Psychologie Appliquée,* 1953, *3,* 150–160.

Pitres, A. Des spasmes rythmiques hysteriques. *Gazette Medicale de Paris,* 1888, *5,* 145–307.

Rachman, S. (Ed.). *Critical essays on psychoanalysis.* New York: Macmillan, 1963.

Rachman, S., & Eysenck, H. J. Reply to a "critique and reformulation" of behavior therapy. *Psychological Bulletin,* 1966, *65,* 165–169.

Reese, W. G., Doss, R., & Gantt, W. H. Autonomic responses in differential diagnosis of organic and psychogenic psychoses. *Archives of Neurology and Psychiatry,* 1953, *70,* 778–793.

Rickard, H. C., Dignam, P. J., & Horner, R. F. Verbal manipulation in a psychotherapeutic relationship. *Journal of Clinical Psychology,* 1960, *16,* 364–367.

Rogers, C. R. *Client-centered therapy.* Boston: Houghton, Mifflin, 1951.

Rotter, J. B. *Social learning and clinical psychology.* New York: Prentice-Hall, 1954.

Salmon, D. *Joseph Lancaster.* London: British and Foreign School Society, 1904.

Salter, A. Three techniques of autohypnosis. *Journal of General Psychology,* 1941, *24,* 423–438.

Salter, A. *Conditioned reflex therapy.* New York: Straus and Young, 1949.

Salter, A. *The case against psychoanalysis.* New York: Holt, 1952.

Scheff, T. J. *Being mentally ill: A sociological theory.* Chicago: Aldine, 1966.

Schultz, J. H. *Das autogene training.* Leipzig: Georg Thieme, 1932.

Schultz, J. H., & Luthe, W. *Autogenic training.* New York: Grune & Stratton, 1959.

Schwartz, L. A. Group psychotherapy in the war neuroses. *American Journal of Psychiatry,* 1945, *101,* 498–500.

Sears, R. R. Experimental analysis of psychoanalytic phenomenon. In J. M. Hunt (Ed.), *Personality and the behavior disorders.* New York: Roland Press, 1944.

Sechenov, I. M. *Reflexes of the brain: An attempt to establish the physiological basis of psychological processes (1865).* Trans. S. Belsky. Cambridge, Mass.: MIT Press, 1965.

Shapiro, M. B. Experimental method in the psychological description of the individual psychiatric patient. *International Journal of Social Psychiatry,* 1957, *3,* 89–102.

Skinner, B. F. Two types of conditioned reflex and a pseudo type. *Journal of General Psychology,* 1935, *12,* 66–77.

Skinner, B. F. Two types of conditioned reflex: A reply to Konorski and Miller. *Journal of General Psychology,* 1937, *16,* 272–279.

Skinner, B. F. *The behavior of organisms.* New York: Appleton-Century-Crofts, 1938.

Skinner, B. F. *Walden Two.* New York: Macmillan, 1948.

Skinner, B. F. Are theories of learning necessary? *Psychological Review,* 1950, *57,* 193–216.

Skinner, B. F. *Science and human behavior.* New York: Free Press, 1953. (a)

Skinner, B. F. Some contributions of an experimental analysis of behavior to psychology as a whole. *American Psychologist,* 1953, *8,* 69–78. (b)

Skinner, B. F. *Verbal behavior.* New York: Appleton-Century-Crofts, 1957.

Skinner, B. F., Solomon, H. C., & Lindsley, O. R. Studies in behavior therapy. Metropolitan State Hospital, Waltham, Mass., Status Report I, November 1953.

Skinner, B. F., Solomon, H. C., Lindsley, O. R., & Richards, M. E. Studies in behavior therapy. Metropolitan State Hospital, Waltham, Mass., Status Report II, May, 1954.

Sluchevski, I. F., & Friken, A. A. Apomorphine treatment of chronic alcoholism. *Sovetskaya Vrachebnaya Gazeta,* June 1933, 557–561.

Sommer, R., & Osmond, H. Symptoms of institutional care. *Social Problems,* 1961, *8,* 254–263.

Spence, K. W. Cognitive vs. stimulus-response theories of learning. *Psychological Review,* 1950, *57,* 159–172.

Staats, A. W. (Ed.), *Human learning: Studies extending conditioning principles to complex behavior.* New York: Holt, Rinehart & Winston, 1964.

Staats, A. W., Staats, C. K., Schutz, R. E., & Wolf, M. M. The conditioning of textual responses using "extrinsic" reinforcers. *Journal of the Experimental Analysis of Behavior,* 1962, *5,* 33–40.

Staats, A. W., Finley, J. R., Minke, K. A., & Wolf, M. M. Reinforcement variables in the control of unit reading responses. *Journal of the Experimental Analysis of Behavior,* 1964, *7,* 139–149.

Staats, A. W., Minke, K. A., Finley, J. R., Wolf, M., & Brooks, L. O. A reinforcer system and experimental procedure for the laboratory study of reading acquisition. *Child Development,* 1964, *35,* 209–231.

Szasz, T. S. The myth of mental illness. *American Psychologist,* 1960, *15,* 113–118.

Terhune, W. B. Phobic syndrome: Study of 86 patients with phobic reactions. *Archives of Neurology and Psychiatry,* 1949, *62,* 162–172.

Thorndike, E. L. *Human learning.* New York: Century, 1931.

Thorndike, E. L. *The fundamentals of learning.* New York: Teachers College, 1932.

Thorndike, E. L. *An experimental study of rewards.* New York: Teachers College, 1933.

Tissié, P. Tic oculaire et facial droit accompagné de toux spasmodique, traité et guéri par la gymnastique médicale respiratoire. *Journal de Médicine de Bordeaux,* 1899, *29,* 326–330.

Truax, C. B. Reinforcement and non-reinforcement in Rogerian psychotherapy. *Journal of Abnormal Psychology,* 1966, *71,* 1–9.

Ullmann, L. P., & Krasner, L. (Eds.), *Case studies in behavior modification.* New York: Holt, Rinehart & Winston, 1965.

Voegtlin, W. L., Lemere, F., & Broz, W. R. Conditioned reflex therapy of alcoholic addiction. III. An evaluation of the present results in light of previous experiences with this method. *Quarterly Journal of Studies on Alcohol,* 1940, *1,* 501–516.

Voegtlin, W. L., Lemere, F., Broz, W. R., & O'Hollaren, P. Conditioned reflex therapy of chronic alcoholism. IV. A preliminary report on the value of reinforcement. *Quarterly Journal of Studies on Alcohol,* 1942, *2,* 505–511.

Wanklin, J. M., Fleming, D. F., Buck, C., & Hobbs, G. E. Discharge and readmission among mental hospital patients. *Archives of Neurology and Psychiatry,* 1956, *76,* 660–669.

Watson, J. B. Psychology as the behaviorist views it. *Psychological Review,* 1913, *20,* 158–177.

Watson, J. B. *Behavior: An introduction to comparative psychology.* New York: Holt, 1914.

Watson, J. B. *Psychology from the standpoint of a behaviorist.* Philadelphia: Lippincott, 1919.

Watson, J. B. *Behaviorism.* Chicago: University of Chicago Press, 1924.

Watson, J. B., & Rayner, R. Conditioned emotional reactions. *Journal of Experimental Psychology*, 1920, *3*, 1–14.

Wilder, J. Facts and figures on psychotherapy. *Journal of Clinical Psychopathology*, 1945, *7*, 311–347.

Wilson, G. T. On the much discussed nature of behavior therapy. *Behavior Therapy*, 1978, *9*, 89–98.

Wolf, M. M., Risley, T., & Mees, H. Application of operant conditioning procedures to the behavior problems of an autistic child. *Behaviour Research and Therapy*, 1964, *1*, 305–312.

Wolpe, J. Experimental neuroses as learned behavior. *British Journal of Psychology*, 1952, *43*, 243–268. (a)

Wolpe, J. Objective psychotherapy of the neuroses. *South African Medical Journal*, 1952, *26*, 825–829. (b)

Wolpe, J. Reciprocal inhibition as the main basis of psychotherapeutic effects. *Archives of Neurology and Psychiatry*, 1954, *72*, 205–226.

Wolpe, J. *Psychotherapy by reciprocal inhibition*. Stanford, Calif.: Stanford University Press, 1958.

Wolpe, J., & Lazarus, A. A. *Behavior therapy techniques: A guide to the treatment of neurosis*. New York: Pergamon, 1966.

Wolpe, J., Salter, A., & Reyna, L. J. (Eds.). *The conditioning therapies: The challenge in psychotherapy*. New York: Holt, Rinehart & Winston, 1964.

Yates, A. J. The application of learning theory to the treatment of tics. *Journal of Abnormal and Social Psychology*, 1958, *56*, 175–182.

Yates, A. J. *Behavior therapy*. New York: Wiley, 1970.

Yerkes, R., & Morgulis, S. The method of Pavlov in animal psychology. *Psychological Bulletin*, 1909, *6*, 257–273.

Zubin, J. Evaluation of therapeutic outcome in mental disorders. *Journal of Nervous and Mental Disease*, 1953, *117*, 95–111.

Zubin, J. Classification of the behavior disorders. In P. R. Farnsworth, O. McNemar, & Q. McNemar (Eds.), *Annual review of psychology*, Vol. 18. Palo Alto, Calif.: Annual Reviews, 1967.

CHAPTER 2

Experimental and Theoretical Foundations of Behavior Modification

Donald J. Levis

Introduction

The importance of the subject matter of this volume, which deals with issues of the assessment and treatment of human psychological disturbance, cannot be overstressed. A dramatic increase has occurred in the number of individuals requesting solutions to their psychological problems. The cost to society in terms of human suffering, loss of productivity, and dollars is staggering. It was not until World War II that the extent of this problem was recognized. Nearly 5 million men in the United States, almost 1 out of 5, were rejected for military service, and many thousands were discharged following acceptance because of neuropsychiatric problems. The seriousness of the problems was even more clearly demonstrated in the Midtown Manhattan Study conducted by Srole and his co-workers (1962). These investigators reported that fewer than 1 out of 4 persons was judged to be psycho-

logically healthy, and nearly 1 out of 5 persons was considered "incapacitated" by psychological disturbance. Adding to this conclusion is Lemkow and Crocetti's (1958) estimate that between 14 and 20 of every 1,000 children born will be hospitalized in a mental institution within their lifetime. Recent attention has also been focused on the possibility that a large percentage of the presenting physical health problems may be affected by and related to psychological factors.

The mental health field's response to this growing crisis has been slow, inefficient, and ineffectual. Despite an arsenal of over 50 different psychotherapy theories and treatment techniques, many of which are designed to cover a wide variety of psychopathological problems, disenchantment with the status quo exists. Treatment is costly, lengthy, and of dubious effect. Claims of therapeutic efficacy, which not only accompany the introduction of most techniques but are perpetuated in the literature as accepted fact, are almost completely lacking in documentation via controlled research. Furthermore, what research is available for the most part falls short of in-

Donald J. Levis • Department of Psychology, State University of New York at Binghamton, Binghamton, New York 13901.

33

corporating even a minimal degree of methodological sophistication, a conclusion reached by many and tendentiously and at times cogently championed by Eysenck (1960, 1966). Unfortunately, the obvious possibility that traditional psychotherapy may not be an effective therapeutic tool has only scratched the defense system of a field that apparently has generated a fetish for psychotherapy. Nor can the practitioner turn to nonpsychotherapeutic approaches like chemotherapy for a satisfactory solution. At best, psychopharmacology simply provides a "holding" period, and at worst, it delays or prevents an individual from dealing directly with the issues that prevent corrective behavioral change.

The Case for Behavioral Therapeutic Approaches

As a first step in resolving the existing chaos within the mental health field, a solid experimental and theoretical foundation is needed on which treatment techniques can be developed, assessed, and improved. Unfortunately, the vast majority of psychotherapy movements, such as those reflected in the psychoanalytic, Adlerian, existential, and humanistic approaches, have produced theoretical structures that are difficult to test and treatment techniques that lack operational specificity. These movements have also appealed to individuals who manifest little interest in subjecting their efforts to scientific evaluation.

The presentation of this volume reflects yet another new movement, which has been referred to as *behavior modification* or *therapy*. This approach has been labeled the "fourth psychotherapeutic revolution," following moral therapy, psychoanalysis, and community mental health (Levis, 1970a). Although this movement actually encompasses a variety of different theories and techniques, each is based on the learning and conditioning literature.

It is the thesis of this chapter that the behavior modification approach, which utilizes for its development the empirical and theoretical offering of experimental psychology, represents the kind of foundation needed if inroads are to be made on our mental health

problems. The uniqueness of this approach is reflected in its emphasis on behavior and its measurement, in its isolation of relevant environmental variables, in its attempt to develop precise definitions and specifiable operations, and in its stress on experimental control (Greenspoon, 1965).

The fruits of this approach have already materialized with the development of a variety of new techniques that appear quite promising. Although considerable attention has been given to behavior therapy's treatment success, the importance of this movement is independent of any claims of success. Such claims can be found for other techniques prior to 1900 (Tourney, 1967). Considerably more research is needed on a variety of homogeneous patient populations with long-term follow-ups before any concrete conclusions can be reached about any given technique. However, what may prove to be of critical importance is the potential fruitfulness of the philosophy, orientation, and strategy behind this movement, and the possible impact it will have on the rest of the mental health field. Three of these potential assets particularly stand out and are discussed below.

Assets

Emphasis on Learning and Conditioning Principles. Few clinicians would object to the statement that learning plays an important role in the development of psychopathological behavior. In fact, most nonbehavioral explanations of psychopathology acknowledge the role of conditioning and learning in early childhood, the effects of punishment and withdrawal of love by the parents, and the importance of anxiety and fear in motivating human symptomatology. Yet, prior to the advent of the behavior therapy approach, no systematic attempt was made to draw on the established principles of conditioning and learning to develop treatment approaches.

Perhaps the clinical field's inability to show systematic growth is related to the reluctance of other approaches to utilize the tools and procedures of basic researchers in the field of psychology. The development of related applied sciences can be shown to be a direct function of the applied scientists' ability to draw on the established principles developed by basic researchers in the area. Prior to the development of the behavioral approach to treatment, this strategy was largely ignored by the mental health field. The obliviousness of clinicians to the potentially huge volume of human and subhuman data has markedly reduced communication among psychological areas within the field. As Ford and Urban (1967) suggested: "One index of the viability and growth potential of a particular therapeutic approach may well be the extent to which it exposes itself to influences from, and attempts to utilize knowledge from, other domains. If the psychotherapy community does not adopt the responsibility for 'bridge building,' the therapy subject may be the victim" (p. 338).

This lack of integration will be perpetuated as long as the clinician remains deficient in scientific training and unconcerned about the need for a common language to facilitate this communication. The behavior modification approach to clinical problems is an attempt to break down both of the above barriers and clearly represents one of its major contributions to the field.

The Nature of Theory Construction. The strategy common to most nonbehavioral approaches has been to develop complex, all-encompassing theories that are designed to explain the whole and complete human organism. This objective has been achieved by sacrificing clarity, precision, and predictability. Although these theories are occasionally riddled with creative and potentially fruitful ideas, the meshing and interlacing of so many surplus meaning concepts makes experimental analysis difficult, if not impossible. Unfortunately, these theories provide their followers only with a comforting set of terminology and an illusory sense of understanding.

In contrast, the strategy of a behavioral viewpoint is to start from a descriptive, better-defined, and more controllable account of behavior and then systematically and progressively work to build on this foundation. The objective is to produce clarity in communication and operational specificity of variables, which in turn permit the systematic manipulation of critical variables, predictability, and evaluation.

Commitment to Assessment. The last asset to be discussed is perhaps the most important and the most ignored factor in the development of the mental health field. The concern about evaluation in most therapeutic approaches has rarely moved beyond the case history level. Those studies that have attempted experimental analysis have fallen far short of the rigor required of a discipline striving for scientific respectability. The behavioral modification movement has been the only psychotherapeutic approach that has been committed to objective outcome evaluation from its inception. It is well known that therapeutic techniques frequently are reported to be more effective initially (Tourney, 1967), but their effectiveness diminishes eventually. Although the data suggest that one should be cautious in making therapeutic claims, unsupported enthusiastic claims of success still dominate the field.

The behavioral movement is also not free of making premature claims of success, displaying inadequate methodological sophistication, and committing errors of overgeneralization. However, the commitment of the behavioral field to a scientific analysis has resulted in an open system of checks and balances and of self-criticism that in time should result in the establishment of reliable and valid contributions. The existing crisis in the mental health field can be resolved only by an objective evaluation of treatment approaches.

Basic Experimental Learning Paradigms and Principles

The systematic application of learning principles to applied areas has unfortunately been a relatively slow development, gaining impetus only in the last 20 years. The main factors contributing to this delay have been the tendency of psychologists to separate theory and application, a reluctance to use the clinic as a laboratory, and the acceptance of the traditional psychodynamic methods as the model for psychotherapy (Kalish, 1965). The learning psychologist's retreat to the laboratory during the first half of this century was not without its value, because it was during this period that the groundwork for the development of the principles and theories utilized by behavior theorists was laid and well documented. The literature generated on issues of acquisition, response maintenance, extinction, counter-conditioning, generalization and discrimination learning, schedules of reinforcement, punishment, and social imitation and reinforcement proved extremely helpful in the development of applied techniques. Furthermore, the theoretical contributions of Pavlov, Hull, Guthrie, Mowrer, and Tolman shed additional light on the development and treatment of psychopathology. In order to facilitate a better understanding of the rationale underlying the various strategies adopted by contemporary behavior therapists, a review of some of the basic experimental paradigms will be presented here, followed by an outline of some of the theoretical positions that influenced the field's growth.

Classical Conditioning

Changing behavior can be achieved in the laboratory through the use of one of two distinct conditioning procedures, which are commonly referred to as resulting in the development of classical or instrumental learning. Descriptively, the classical conditioning paradigm differs from the instrumental procedure in that the sequence of events presented is *independent* of the subject's behavior. The typical sequence consists of an unconditioned stimulus (UCS), a stimulus known to evoke a regular and measurable response (UCR), and the conditioned stimulus (CS), a stimulus that at the outset of an experiment does not evoke the UCR. The usual order of the sequence used to produce conditioning is to present the CS followed closely in time by the UCS. The regular and measurable response elicited by the UCS is called an *unconditioned response* (UCR). Conditioning is said to have occurred if the CS presentation follows pairings of the CS–UCS results in the elicitation of a conditioned response, which usually resembles the UCR. Pavlov's (1927) work with the conditioning of salivation of dogs illustrates the procedure used in classical conditioning.

The effects of classical conditioning can be demonstrated at almost all levels of animal life. Furthermore, it is just as easily established in primitive animals as in humans, which suggests that conditioning may involve the same mechanism in all species.

Pavlov and his colleagues were responsible for isolating some of the most basic phenomena of classical conditioning learning. These phenomena include:

1. *Conditioning*—the acquisition of a stimulus–response relationship.
2. *Generalization*—the tendency of the organism to transfer as a function stimulus similarity its acquired response to new stimulus situations.
3. *Conditioned discrimination*—the learning to respond only to a specified stimulus or to respond in two different ways to two different stimuli.
4. *Higher-order conditioning*—a conditioning sequence in which a neutral stimulus is conditioned by being paired with a previously conditioned CS.
5. *Extinction*—the training procedure in which the CS is presented in the absence of the UCS, with the resulting effect being a loss in the strength of the CR.
6. *Inhibition*—a hypothetical process that actively prevents the performance of the CR during extinction.
7. *Spontaneous recovery*—the partial reappearance of an extinguished CR following a lapse of time and without any new conditioning.

Operant or Instrumental Learning

Following the work of Thorndike (1911) and Skinner (1938), learned responses have also been developed by procedures labeled *operant* or *instrumental learning*. With the operant procedure, the UCS or reward presentation is made *dependent*—not independent, as in the classical conditioning procedure—on the subject's behavior. An essential aspect of this procedure is that reward (whether negative or positive) follows the subject's response in some systematic manner. For example, every time a rat presses a bar (CR), a food pellet is dispensed (UCS).

Although the condition of operant responses can refer to the selection of isolated responses, the term usually refers to the conditioning of a class of behavior, which in turn is defined by the requirements for reinforcement set by the experimenter or by the environment in a given situation. Thus, unlike the classical conditioning procedures, which is usually confined to the study of isolated responses, operant conditioning widens the range of behaviors that can be studied, including the majority of human behaviors. Thus, as Kazdin (1978) noted, the principles explaining the development, maintenance, and elimination of operants are likely to have wide generality. Some of the basic principles of operant conditioning are outlined below:

1. *Reinforcement.* Reinforcement of a behavior is determined operationally by noting whether an increase in the frequency of a response occurs following certain consequences that are labeled *reinforcers*. If behavior increases following the presentation of an event after a response, the reinforcing state of affairs is referred to as being *positive*. If a behavioral response increases following the removal of an event, the event is labeled a *negative reinforcement*. For example, if a rats' pressing a bar increases following the presentation of food, the food can be labeled a *positive reinforcement*. If such behavior increases following the cessation of shock, shock can be viewed as a *negative reinforcer*.

2. *Punishment.* Punishment refers to an event that is made contingent on a response that results in a decrease in the probability of the response's occurrence. Stimuli that can be classified as punishers can be divided into two classes: those that result in a decrease in responding following the onset of the stimulus event (e.g., electric shock paired with a bar-press response) and those that produce the same result following the withdrawal of an event (e.g., withdrawal of food following a response).

It should be noted that the effects of reward and punishment have important implications for helping us meet the objective of modifying maladaptive human behavior. However, controversy still exists over the effects of punishment on behavior, a source of confusion reflected in Thorndike's early work. His original position was that learning is a reversible process; that reward strengthens behavior and punishment weakens it. Later (1931), he reversed

this position and concluded that although reward does strengthen behavior, punishment does not weaken it. It only results in the suppression of responding. Although recent data provide some support for Thorndike's original position, the issue is far from resolved (Church, 1963; Mowrer, 1960). Such a resolution will have important implications for applied behavior modification.

3. *Extinction.* Extinction, as is the case with classical conditioning procedures, refers simply to a procedural manipulation: the removal of a reinforcer. Although extinction usually results in a decrease or an elimination of responding, it differs from a punishment procedure in that reinforcement is simply discontinued, and its negative effects are not made directly contingent on the occurrence or nonoccurrence of a given response class.

4. *Stimulus control.* Stimulus control is related to the concept of discrimination and to the empirical finding that antecedent events (stimuli) can also control behavior by associating different reinforcement consequences for a particular response class across different stimuli. For example, if Stimulus A is reinforced in one situation and not in another, or if Stimulus A is reinforced in one situation and Stimulus B is not, differential stimulus control over behavior can be established. Thus, *stimulus control* refers to the extent to which antecedent stimuli determine the probability of response occurrence.

5. *Schedules of reinforcement.* It has been established that behavior changes and maintenance can be markedly affected by manipulating the ways in which discriminative or reinforcing stimuli are presented in relation to responses. For example, by varying the frequency and magnitude of reinforcement density, response output can be regulated at high, medium, or low rates of responding. An analysis of certain schedules of reinforcement has resulted in important advances in our understanding of what stimulus reinforcement consequences maintain behavior as well as what changes are needed to alter behavior. The clinical application of such principles has important implications for our quest to alter maladaptive behavior.

6. *Superstitious behaviors.* By the repeated presentation of a reinforcer independent of any

given response class, one can demonstrate that such noncontingent delivery can increase the rate of responding of behavior performed at the time of reinforcement dispensing.

Avoidance Learning: A Combination of Procedures

Bekhterev (1928) provided the reference experiment for the avoidance paradigm by conditioning to a signal the withdrawal response of a hand or foot. In this experiment, which represents the usual form of the avoidance training, the subject could prevent the occurrence of a noxious stimulus such as electric shock by responding to a signal. What makes this paradigm of interest is that it includes both a classical and an operant procedure. The paradigm is designed to present CS–UCS presentations (a classical conditioning procedure) which can be altered if a designated response (operant) is emitted to the CS. If such an operant response is made within the required time period (CS–UCS interval), the UCS is not presented on that trial. Thus, the term *avoidance learning* comes into being.

Most of the laboratory studies of avoidance conditioning use a trial-by-trial procedure in which a discrete warning stimulus is presented. Sidman (1953), however, developed an avoidance procedure within the context of a free-responding situation in which a discrete external signal was not provided. In the Sidman procedure, a noxious stimulus is presented at a fixed interval (e.g., every 20 seconds). If the subject (e.g., rat) makes an appropriate response (e.g., bar press) within the fixed interval, the noxious stimulus is postponed and is therefore avoided for a specified time interval (e.g., 10 seconds). In such a procedure, organisms do learn and develop high rates of responding.

Another procedure closely related to avoidance conditioning and requiring no external warning stimulus is escape training. In this procedure, the subject can turn off (escape) an aversive UCS (e.g., electric shock) by emitting an operant or instrumental response. For example, Mowrer (1940) conditioned a rat to terminate electric shock by pressing a pedal arrangement located at one end of the conditioning chamber.

Implication of Conditioning Principles

The preceding discussion of conditioning procedures and principles represents only a cursory review of the topic. To provide an adequate description of the relevant principles and techniques involved would require a separate volume. A detailed discussion of these topics can be found in Kimble (1961) and Mackintosh (1974).

Until the advent of the behavior therapy movement, the implications of learning principles for the understanding of human maladaptive behavior received only sporadic historical attention. One of the most influential applications of conditioning principles to an understanding of human fear behavior was reported by Watson and Rayner in 1920. These investigators attempted to determine whether they could condition a startle reaction in a child to a previously neutral stimulus. A white rat, which elicited no fear, was paired with a loud, fear-producing noise in the presence of a 11-month-old infant named Albert. After seven such pairings, the presentation of the rat alone elicited avoidance and fearful behavior in the child. This conditioned reaction generalized to other similar stimuli, such as a rabbit, a dog, a fur coat, and cotton. The fear response was not elicited by inanimate objects such as blocks. Extending Watson's work, Mary Cover Jones (1924) attempted to determine whether learning principles could help remove children's fears. Among the techniques employed were principles of extinction, counterconditioning, and social imitation. The impact of the above work is critical in that it suggested the possibility that learning principles may be involved in the development, maintenance, and removal of maladaptive behavior.

Despite the importance of this early work, the systematic application of learning principles has unfortunately developed relatively slowly until recently. However, in recent years, the behavior modification movement has resulted in the use of learning paradigms and principles in the attempt to modify or eliminate maladaptive behavior or to reinforce socially appropriate behavior. Classical conditioning, punishment, escape–avoidance, extinction, and operant paradigms have each been used with apparent success over a wide range of behaviors, including social, sexual, addictive, eating, self-destructive, psychotic, and criminal behaviors. General treatment techniques designed to treat a wide variety of maladaptive behaviors have also emerged based on such learning principles as emotional extinction (implosive and flooding therapy), counterconditioning (systematic desensitization), and higher-order conditioning (covert sensitization procedures).

This initial success in applying laboratory principles to the human situation should strengthen even further the links between experimental and applied psychology. As this relationship becomes stronger, so should there be an increase in the sophistication, applicability, and success of the approach. But for behavioral therapy to remain viable, it must also provide a conceptual framework for understanding, predicting, and eventually preventing maladaptive behaviors. Basic learning theory has already proved helpful in providing an initial conceptual framework from which to start.

Theoretical Foundations

Without question, formal theory construction has played a major and critical role in the development and advancement of the experimental learning field. In the quest to develop a science of behavior, learning theory has kept critical issues at the forefront, has heightened controversy, has resulted in differential predictions, and has stimulated a variety of new research areas. The applied-behavior-therapy movement has also profited from the development of learning theory, since the rationale for a number of its techniques is based directly on classical laboratory theories. However, the direct extrapolation of learning theory to justify applied treatment techniques and to aid us in understanding psychopathology has not proved as successful as the transfer of learning paradigms. Critics (e.g., Breger & McGaugh, 1965) have been correct in their assessment that behavior therapists are working with antiquated models and have yet to establish a direct relationship between theory and treatment techniques.

Part of the above problem stems from the observation that certain clinical phenomena seem to contradict the laboratory findings on which existing learning theory is based. Mowrer (1950) was one of the first theorists to recognize that human "neurotic" behavior appears to represent a paradox in that it is self-punitive, self-defeating, and perhaps self-perpetuated. Patients frequently report being fully aware at a cognitive level that their maladaptive behavior is "irrational" and counterproductive. Such an observation seems contrary to most learning positions, which are essentially hedonistic, stressing what Thorndike (1911) called the "law of effect" and Skinner (1938) the "law of reinforcement." From a learning viewpoint, the symptomatic behavior of the neurotic is functioning in the absence of a UCS. This is in essence why such behavior is labeled irrational, in that failure to exhibit a symptom will not result in any biological harm. Yet, human maladaptive behavior maintains itself over long periods of time in the absence of a biological threat. On the other hand, laboratory data strongly suggest that whether the behavior in question is overt or emotional, unlearning or extinction will follow rather rapidly once the UCS is removed (Mackintosh, 1974).

Classical and modern learning theory has been concerned largely with isolating and explaining general laws of behavior. It has not, as yet, fully addressed the exceptions to these laws reflected in the unusual and puzzling behaviors labeled *psychopathological*. Applied behavior therapists as a group have also not undertaken this task seriously. It is this writer's opinion that this state of affairs exists because behavior therapists have been poorly trained in the areas of theory construction and existing learning theory. It is the further belief of this writer that the existing theories of learning do provide an important starting point from which laws of psychopathology and treatment can be developed and that such a development is critical to the future survival of the behavior therapy movement. Therefore, in this section, the purpose and basic principles of theory construction will be outlined, along with a brief description of those classical and modern learning positions, that may well provide the stepping stones for the development of viable models of psychopathology and treatment.

The Function of Theory

The scientist's task in regard to theory construction has been succinctly stated by Spence (1951):

> Briefly, it may be said that the primary aim of the scientist is to develop an understanding or knowledge of a particular realm of events or data. Such scientific understanding consists in formulating relationships between concepts that have reference to the particular event under observation. Thus, beginning with the sense data or events provided by observation, the scientist abstracts out of them certain ones on which he concentrates. To particular descriptive events and pattern of events he assigns, arbitrarily, language symbols (concepts), and then formulates the relationship observed to hold between these events (or concepts) in the form of laws. These observed regularities or laws provide at least partial explanation of the particular event under consideration, for explanation in science basically consists of nothing more than a statement of relations of a particular event to one or more events. (p. 239)

In other words, the function of theory is to provide a systematic expansion of knowledge mediated by specific empirical propositions, statements, hypotheses, and predictions that are subject to empirical tests. It should be noted that it is only the derivations of propositions derived from the theory that are open to emperical test. The theory itself is assumed; acceptance or rejection of it is determined by its utility, not by its truth or falsity (Hall & Lindzey, 1957, p. 13). The utility of a theory lies essentially in its ability to serve as a guide for empirical studies. Unguided experimentation usually results in an unorganized mass of data.

Although the ordering and interpretation of data are important functions of theory, history supports the claim that a viable theory is one that predicts and explains in advance laws or results that were unknown before. Important theories in science have satisfied this test.

Nonbehavioral theories of psychopathology clearly have not met the above boundary conditions for theory construction. However, the argument is made that human behavior is complex and in need of explanation by postulating a variety of constructs. The language of the laboratory is viewed as inadequate and nondescriptive of human interactions. Unfortunately, the model of human behavior generated by the psychoanalytic, humanistic, and existential movements, although adequate in postdiction, lack prediction. Relationships

among constructs are not adequately explained, and terms and propositions generated by the theories are unclear and full of surplus meaning. For theory to aid in the advancement of knowledge, definitional precision of terms is essential. As Feigl (1953) suggested, "This obvious standard scientific method requires that the concepts used in the formulation of scientific knowledge-claims be as definitely delimited as possible. On the level of the qualitative-classificatory sciences this amounts to the attempt to reduce all border-zone vagueness to a minimum. On the level of quantitative science the exactitude of the concepts is enormously enhanced through the application of the techniques of measurement" (p. 12). Precision of psychological terms requires that they be capable of operational analysis. As Skinner (1945) warned, "we must explicate an operational definition for every term unless we are willing to adopt the vague usage of the vernacular" (p. 270).

Learning theory attempts to meet the tenets of good theory construction, and herein lie its distinct advantage and potential explanatory and predictive power. The issue, of course, is whether it is feasible to apply existing learning or conditioning laws in our quest to understand human psychopathology. Eysenck (1960) perhaps said it best when he reasoned: "If the laws which have been formulated are not necessarily true, but at least partially correct, then it must follow that we can make the deductions from them to cover the type of behavior represented by neurotic patients, construct a model which will duplicate the important and relevant features of the patient and suggest new and possible helpful methods of treatment along lines laid down by learning theory" (p. 5). The issue is, of course, an empirical one, and fortunately, Eysenck's suggestion has already materialized. Learning theory has been responsible for generating a number of new ideas and treatment procedures.

Skinner's Antitheoretical Position

Skinner, who himself has made important contributions to the advancement of learning theory (Skinner, 1938), changed his position and became one of the most eloquent critics of formal theory construction. For Skinner

(1950), a science of behavior must eventually deal with behavior in its relation to certain manipulable variables. He stated that theories in the field generally deal with the intervening steps in these relationships. Therefore, instead of prompting us to search for and explore more relevant variables, these intervening steps frequently serve only to provide verbal answers in place of the factual data we might find through further study. Such a state, from Skinner's viewpoint, can easily create a false sense of security. Skinner further argued that research designed in relation to theory was likely to be wasteful since considerable energy and skill most likely would be devoted to its defense. This energy, he felt, could be directed toward a more "valuable" area of research.

Skinner's position will not be rebutted here, since his viewpoint was mainly taken as a stance against the movement in the 1940s to provide an all-encompassing general theory of behavior. Today, learning theory is much more specific and problem-oriented. Skinner's own attempt to provide an inductive data base for psychology is reflected in the large volume of empirical data published by Ferster and Skinner (1957). This volume, which reports important findings, reads a little like a phone book and falls far short of Skinner's own expectations. The failure of the purely inductive approach has largely been a failure to provide the organizational and integrative structure that theory offers. Today, this point is well recognized by Skinner's followers in the basic research areas. Operant research has clearly moved from an inductive analysis to a functional theoretical structure.

Skinner's antitheoretical stance has influenced and is still influencing many behavior therapists. These individuals, referred to as *operant behavior modifiers*, are mainly interested in the question of what techniques will shape a patient's behavior to the desired outcome, rather than attempting to understand why and how the techniques operate. This strategy has already resulted in the development of some important and interesting techniques, which have greatly enhanced the behavior modification movement. But as the data base of the field increases, the need exists, as was the case in the basic research areas, for better organizational structure, which perhaps

can be best achieved from this orientation by a functional theoretical analysis.

Since formal models of learning also have played a significant role in the development of this new applied field, these implications for the behavior therapy movement are now addressed.

The Impact of Formal Models

The classical theories of learning developed by Pavlov, Hull, Guthrie, and Tolman played a major heuristic role in providing the initial foundations for the development of many of the behavioral modification techniques. It should be understood that these approaches were designed as general theories of behavior and not as models of psychopathology. Today, learning theorists have moved away from such general theories to providing more explicit and detailed models of various empirical findings. However, the influence of the masters can still be felt.

It is the opinion of this reviewer that applied behavioral theorists should also move away from using the classical theories as a foundation for their techniques. Contemporary learning positions may well provide a much stronger base for extrapolating to psychopathology. The need for the applied behavior field to upgrade and sharpen its theoretical foundation is clearly evident. Therefore, only a cursory review of the classical theories is provided here, followed by a description of a couple of contemporary models that may prove of use to the behavior modification field.

Theories of learning can be grouped under a variety of different headings. The subdivisions frequently used are one-factor versus two-factor theories, reinforcement versus nonreinforcement theories, drive versus nondrive theories, and inhibition versus noninhibition theories. It is possible for a given theory to be cross-indexed under more than one heading (e.g., a reinforcement, drive position). For the purposes of this review, the strategy was adopted of grouping theories along the lines of how they conceptualize changing or extinguishing established behaviors. Applied-behavior-therapy techniques are designed to emphasize the principle believed responsible for such changes. Therapeutic techniques have already been developed that emphasize the role of excitation and inhibition, countercon-ditioning, nonreinforced emotional extinction, and changes in cognitive expectancies. It should be noted, however, that these divisions are neither mutually exclusive nor all-inclu-sive.

Excitation and Inhibition Models of Behavior Change

Concepts of excitation and inhibition play both a historical and a contemporary role in theory development. Under this heading, only Pavlov's classic theory is discussed here, but it should be noted that Hull's theory can also be labeled an excitation–inhibition model.

Pavlov's Physiological Theory of the Cerebral Cortex. Pavlov's (1927) theory was one of the first major approaches to have an impact on both the learning and the behavior therapy fields. He viewed conditioning as a function of cortical extinction and cortical inhibition. According to this position, when a "neutral" stimulus (for example, a tone) is presented to a subject, the afferent stimulation elicited by the tone produces an excitatory process at some definite point in the cortex. At the point of cortical stimulation, the excitatory process is believed to spread gradually over the entire sensory area. The intensity of the spreading effect or "irradiation" of excitation is hypoth-esized to decrease as the distance from the point of origin increases. With the onset of the UCS (for example, shock), this process is re-peated, but at a different point in the cortex. Because of the differences in intensity, the ir-radiation is considered greater for the UCS than for the neutral stimulus. Following re-peated presentations of the neutral stimulus and the UCS (CS–UCS pairings), the cortical stimulation elicited by the tone is expected to gravitate toward the stronger cortical stimu-lation of the shock until the locus of the neutral stimulus is of sufficient intensity to elicit a CR.

According to Pavlov, one can reduce the strength of the CS by presenting it in the ab-sence of the UCS (extinction). Under these conditions, the cortical process of excitation is changed to inhibition, which like the pre-vious excitation irradiates to the surrounding region of the cortex. The assumption is further made that when the elicitation of either cor-tical excitation or cortical inhibition occurs, the surrounding areas of the cortex concur-rently produce the opposite process. Borrow-ing a term suggested by E. Hering and C. S. Sherrington, Pavlov called the effect "induc-tion." Excitation in one area of the cortex leads to increased inhibition in another area (negative induction), while inhibition is be-lieved to lead to increased excitation (positive induction).

Implications. Pavlov was the first and one of the few classical theorists to extend his model to explain psychopathology. He rea-soned that when cortical irradiation of the in-hibitory process is extreme, the resultant ef-fect is sleep, while extreme excitation is believed to produce alert, active behavior. A functional breakdown leading to psychopath-ology can occur with the active clashing of the excitatory and inhibitory processes or with the presentation of intense stimulation. According to this model, such excessive cortical excita-tion or inhibition can result in symptoms such as hysteria, neurasthenia, depression, mania, and catatonia.

Pavlov's theory inspired a number of ap-plied behavior therapists, most notably An-drew Salter (1949, 1965), who developed his conditioned-reflex therapy. For Salter, the neurotic individual is suffering basically from an excess of inhibition, thus blocking his or her normal output of excitation. Therapy is therefore designed to encourage the patient to express feelings directly. Wolpe's (1958) "as-sertive" response approach represents a very similar technique and conceptualization.

However, learning theorists long ago aban-doned Pavlov's theoretical thinking, partly because of the lack of direct experimental sup-port and partly because neurophysiologists are committed to the concept of synaptic trans-mission of neural impulses. Nevertheless, the role of the concepts of excitation and inhibi-tion have been incorporated into other more modern theories, such as those proposed by Hull (1943), by Amsel (1958), and more re-cently by Rescorla (1969), Rescorla and Lo Lordo (1965), and Rescorla and Wagner (1972).

Counterconditioning Models of Behavior Change

Counterconditioning theories of extinction have held both historical and contemporary interest. Under this heading the classical models of Hull and Guthrie are described briefly, along with Denny's more recent extension of Hullian theory.

Hull's Monistic Reinforcement Theory. Hull (1943, 1952) attempted to synthesize the data obtained from Pavlov's classical conditioning procedure and Thorndike's trial-and-error learning into a unitary concept of reinforcement (namely, drive reduction). Briefly, the theory states that whenever any receptor activity (a stimulus) and effector activity (a response) occur in close temporal contiguity, and this temporal contiguity is closely associated with the diminution of a need (drive reduction), there will result an increment in the tendency of that afferent impulse to evoke that reaction on later occasions. These increments of successive reinforcements are believed to summate to yield a combined habit strength ($_sH_R$), which is hypothesized to be a simple positive growth function of the number of reinforcements received. Motivational variables like drive are believed to interact in a multiplicative manner with habit strength to produce performance ($D \times {}_sH_R$).

Concurrently with the development of excitatory behavior, Hull, like Pavlov, drew on inhibition theory. In brief, the assumption is made that every response, whether reinforced or not, results in an increment of reactive inhibition (I_R), which according to Hull is a primary negative drive resembling fatigue. The magnitude of I_R is considered an increasing function of the rate of response elicitation and the effortfulness of the response. In short, as I_R builds up, the strength of the response just preceding it becomes weakened, a function of the direct incompatibility of the two responses. It follows that since I_R (fatigue) is a drive, the reduction of this state is reinforcing and therefore is capable of strengthening any response that precedes it closely in time. Since I_R leads to cessation of activity, a resting response is conditioned—or more appropriately, *counterconditioned*—to the CS. Hull

referred to this latter process as conditioned inhibition ($_sI_R$). The total inhibition in the situation results from an additive combination of both I_R and $_sI_R$. Thus, behavior equals $D \times {}_sH_R - (I_R + {}_sI_R)$. With the removal of the UCS (reinforcement), inhibition can exceed the strength of excitation resulting in the extinction or the counterconditioning of the previous learned response.

The implications of the Hullian counterconditioning model of extinction for psychotherapy were first noted by Shoben (1949) and Dollard and Miller (1950), who retranslated existing insight therapy into a learning, reinforcement framework. However, the applied importance of Hullian theory was not fully realized until Joseph Wolpe (1958) extrapolated from the model to develop new behavioral techniques that launched the behavior therapy movement.

Wolpe, borrowing theoretical notions from Hull (1943), Sherrington (1947), and Jacobson (1938), developed the counterconditioning approach of systematic desensitization that is designed to reciprocally inhibit anxiety-eliciting stimulus. He also rekindled interest in assertive training, as well as developing conditioning techniques to reduce sexual inhibition.

Hullian theory, however, may not be the best conceptual framework from which to view Wolpe's reciprocal inhibition therapy. Wolpe interpreted symptoms as avoidance behavior motivated by fear-eliciting stimuli. Although Hull's theory is a general theory of behavior, he never directly applied his theory to the area of avoidance and fear conditioning. Miller (1948) finally made the appropriate extrapolations, but a classical Hullian interpretation of avoidance responding has long since lost the interest of researchers in this area. A recent theoretical extension of Hull's theory that does directly address avoidance behavior has been offered by Denny (1971) and may be found by applied behavior modifiers to be more useful and reflective of the process underlying their techniques.

Denny's Elicitation Theory. Denny (1971, 1976) has offered a counterconditioning model of behavior that stresses concepts like relief and relaxation for the explanation of behavior involving aversive stimuli. In his theory, the removal of a UCS in an established behavior sequence also serves as a UCS or eliciting stimulus for a class of response that is typically antagonistic to the responses that were elicited by the original UCS. For example, in situations that involve aversive stimuli, the removal of these stimuli elicit relief and relaxation, which Denny views as being antagonistic to fear and fear-related behavior. The countercondition effect, then, in turn, mediates approach rather than withdrawal behavior. Relief is a construct that is viewed as essentially autonomic and as occurring almost immediately after the termination of an aversive stimulus. Relaxation is a construct that is viewed as essentially musculoskeletal and as reaching a peak of responding about 2½ minutes after aversive stimulation ends. Relief and relaxation, which make a situation positive and safe, become dominant when the situation is no longer aversive and bring about the extinction of fear-related behavior.

A critical aspect of Denny's elicited-relaxation theory is that relief and relaxation automatically occur when the aversive stimulus is removed or remains harmless. From this model, direct methods for producing relaxation, as used in Wolpe's desensitization procedure, would not be required to produce extinction. Of course, such a procedure should facilitate the extinction procedure. Denny has also suggested that his theory may be useful in explaining the effects of flooding or implosive therapy (Stampfl & Levis, 1967).

Guthrie's Contiguous Conditioning Theory. Guthrie's (1935) theory provides a completely different counterconditioning viewpoint of extinction. According to his contiguity position, all that is necessary for learning to occur is the pairing of a stimulus and a response. Unlike in Hull's theory, reinforcement or reward does not strengthen the learned connection. Rewards are important only in that they change the stimuli or the situation so that no new response can be associated with the previous stimulus. In other words, a reward removes the organism from the stimulus to which the response was conditioned, thus ensuring that unlearning will not take place. The best predictor of learning is the response in the situation that last occurred. According to

Guthrie, learning is permanent unless interfered with by new learning. Therefore, from this model, extinction always occurs as associative inhibition (i.e., through the learning of an incompatible response).

To weaken activities (S–R connections) or remove undesirable behavior, Guthrie suggested three approaches. The first technique involves a gradual stimulus–approximation approach, in which one introduces the stimulus that one wishes to have disregarded, but only in such a faint degree that it will not elicit a response. For example, if a person is afraid of a dog, one could introduce furry objects such as stuffed dogs, then pictures of dogs, then a very small dog, etc.

The second method is to repeat the stimulus until the original response is fatigued and then to continue the sequence until new responses to the signal are learned. For example, if one is afraid of tall buildings, she or he should repeatedly climb the stairs to the top of a tall building until fatigue and exhaustion counteract the fear behavior (a point similar to Hull's prediction).

Finally, Guthrie suggested that behavior can be changed by presenting the stimulus that elicits the undesirable response but then inhibiting the response by presenting a stronger stimulus that elicits an incompatible response. For example, one can let an exhibitor expose himself in the stimulus situation that elicits such behavior and then shock him prior to sexual arousal.

The implications of Guthrie's suggestions for applied behavior change are apparent, but his model in this context has unfortunately been neglected. It clearly deserves more attention.

Behavior Change via Emotional Extinction

It should be noted that *all* major learning positions predict that nonreinforced (UCS absence) presentation of the CS will result in extinction or the unlearning of a previous conditioned response. This is true whether the behavior in question be overt-motor or emotional. As has already been seen, differences exist at a theoretical level about whether the underlying extinction process is facilitated by inhibition, counterconditioning, or simple weakening of the previous response. The major position described in this section was proposed by Mowrer (1947, 1960), who emphasized the principle of CS exposure in the unlearning of emotional responses, which in turn leads to the extinction of overt behavior. As will be seen, Mowrer's model and the existing extensions by Eysenck and Stampfl and Levis are believed to have important theoretical implications for our understanding and treatment of psychopathology.

Mowrer's Two-Factor Theory of Avoidance. Although Mowrer (1947) was influenced by Hull, he broke away from a one-factor or monistic reinforcement position because of the awkwardness Hull's theory in handling problems associated with avoidance learning. For Mowrer, avoidance learning involved two types of learning: one based on the procedure of classical conditioning, which incorporates only a contiguity principle, and one based on operant or instrumental learning, which includes both a contiguity and a drive-reduction notion of reinforcement. In the typical discrete-trial avoidance paradigm, a CS (e.g., a tone) is presented, say, for a five-second period and is followed by a UCS (e.g., shock). With repeated CS–UCS pairing, fear or anxiety is believed to become conditioned to the CS and is mediated by the autonomic nervous system. The conditioning of fear is simply a result of the above classical-conditioning pairing, with drive reduction playing no part in this learning. Fear is conceptualized as having activation or drive properties that result in energizing or increasing the organism's activity. These activation properties are also elicited by UCS onset, resulting in the organism's escaping the shock. The escape response involves motor behavior that is viewed as being mediated by the central nervous system and reinforced by pain reduction. As fear becomes conditioned to the CS, it also activates motor behavior, which results in a response prior to UCS onset. This response is labeled an *avoidance response* and is believed to be learned because it results in the termination of the aversive CS and in a subsequent reduction of fear, which strengthens the avoidance behavior. For the avoidance behavior to become unlearned, one need only estinguish the fear stimuli eliciting the avoidance behavior. To achieve this objective, all one must do is present the CS in the absence of the UCS (Pavlovian extinction). Nonreinforced CS exposure will result in weakening the fear behavior. Once fear is sufficiently weakened, it will cease to activate the avoidance behavior.

In 1960, Mowrer revised the above two-factor theory and extended it to explain appetitive (approach) as well as avoidance theory. In his new model, Mowrer concluded that all learning by implication was a result of the classical conditioning of internal states. The new version remains "two-factor" only in terms of whether the form of reinforcement is incremental (punishment) or decremental (reward).

Mowrer's 1947 version of avoidance behavior, however, still seems to be the preferred interpretation (see Rescorla & Solomon, 1967). The basic tenets of the model have received considerable empirical support (Brown & Jacobs, 1949; Brown, Kalish, & Farber, 1951; Miller, 1948). Although not free of criticism (Herrnstein, 1969), two-factor theory has survived the test of time and is still considered a very viable explanatory model for infrahuman and human avoidance behavior.

For theorists who view human psychological symptoms as avoidance behavior, Mowrer's two-factor theory provides an initial theoretical framework that has already proved profitable to build on. Two such extensions, which clearly illustrate this point, are briefly described below.

Eysenck's Extension. Concerned with the issues involved in the "neurotic paradox," Eysenck (1968, 1976, 1979) has modified Mowrer's theory to explain clinical observations that appear to contrast with the laws of classical learning theory. Three major areas are addressed in this reformation.

First, an attempt is made to explain why certain classes of phobic behavior are much more prevalent than others. To do this, Eysenck challenged the doctrine of equipotentiality, which states that stimuli that are equated for sensory input should be of equal conditionability when paired with a UCS. He argued that a notion such as Seligman's (1971) concept of "CS preparedness" is required. Briefly, Seligman suggested that certain CSs are biologically prepared to be connected more readily with anxiety responses than others.

Eysenck's second modification centers on his observation that basic personality differences are believed to affect conditionability. This conclusion helps to explain differences among nosologies.

And third, and perhaps more importantly, Eysenck reasoned that if we are to explain why symptoms persist for so long in the absence of UCS presentation, the laws of extinction have to be amended and the law of incubation or enhancement of fear needs to be added.

According to Eysenck's (1979) reformulation of the law of Pavlovian extinction, two consequences may follow the presentation of the CS in the absence of the UCS. First, presentation of the CS alone may be followed by a decrement or an extinction of the CR, which is the law of Pavlovian extinction. Second, and contrary to the position of Mowrer and others, CS presentation in the absence of the UCS may lead to an enhancement of the CR. The implication of this latter statement with respect to fear conditioning is that somehow, exposure to the CS alone can enhance or add new fear to the situation despite the fact the UCS has been removed. According to Eysenck, incubation of the CS is more probable when conditioning involves a drive (emotions), a strong UCS, and short CS exposure periods when the UCS is removed. Eysenck's theory clearly has important implications for those behavior theorists interested in developing a viable conditioning model of neurosis. However, his position has not been free of serious criticism (see the commentaries following the Eysenck, 1979, article).

Stampfl and Levis's Extension. Stampfl and Levis (1967, 1969, 1976) not only have extended Mowrer's two-factor theory to the area of psychopathology but also have suggested the use of a new treatment technique developed by Stampfl called *implosive* or *flooding therapy.* In agreement with Eysenck, Stampfl and Levis believe that the critical question from a learning position is why human symptoms (avoidance behaviors) resist extinction for such long periods of time in the absence of any real danger. Laboratory examples of extreme resistance to extinction are rare. However, unlike Eysenck, these authors do not believe that two-factor theory has to be so

drastically modified by adding such concepts as *preparedness* or *incubation* (see Levis, 1979).

Extrapolating from the laboratory model, Stampfl and Levis see most psychopathology as resulting from past specific experiences of punishment and pain, which confer strong emotional reactions to initially nonpunishing stimuli (classical conditioning). The resulting conditioned stimuli provide the motivational source for developing symptom behavior designed to escape or avoid the source of the conditioned aversive stimulation (instrumental conditioning). Furthermore, the past specific conditioning experiences are believed to be encoded in memory and on recall may function as a conditioned emotional stimulus.

According to Stampfl and Levis, the issue of symptom maintenance is best conceptualized by extending the Solomon and Wynne (1954) conservation-of-anxiety hypothesis to encompass complex sets of conditioned cues, ordered sequentially in terms of their accessibility and aversive loadings. Briefly, Solomon and Wynne postulated that exposing an organism to a long CS exposure results in an increase in fear level because of more CS exposure, and that on subsequent trials, such an increase in fear could recondition the avoidance response, resulting in shorter latency responding. Furthermore, the more short-latency avoidance responding that occurs, the less CS exposure experienced and the greater the conservation of fear to the unexposed segments of the CS interval.

If the CS interval comprises a series of complex stimuli that differ on a stimulus dimension from the preceding set, then such conditions should greatly enhance or maximize the conservation-of-anxiety principle. Therefore, from this analysis, the onset of environmental stimulus-eliciting symptoms for human clients is believed to represent only the initial part (S_1) of a chain of stimuli being avoided (S_2, S_3, S_4). As noted earlier, many of these avoided stimuli are assumed to be encoded in memory and capable of functioning on exposure as higher-order, conditioning stimuli. As S_1 is extinguished, S_2 is released from memory, markedly increasing the level of fear and resulting in the reestablishment of avoidance responding to the S_1 segment. As long as the organism is capable of protecting itself or controlling the amount and duration of CS exposure through avoidance behavior, extinction will be retarded considerably (see Levis & Boyd, 1979; Levis & Hare, 1977).

For human symptoms to extinguish, all that one need do is to extinguish the emotional response by presenting the total CS complex in the absence of the UCS. Since the UCS is believed to be long since removed, all that is required is to present an approximation of the CS. Thus, like Pavlov, Hull, and Mowrer, Stampfl and Levis argued that extinction is a direct function of nonreinforced CS exposure, which is the main principle on which the implosive or flooding technique is based.

Extension to Conflict Theory. Fear theorists are drive theorists and thus are cognizant that more than a single drive may be present in a learning situation. If the drive states elicited result in the simultaneous arousal of competitive tendencies, then conflict is said to exist. Miller (1959) has studied this problem extensively, and Dollard and Miller (1950) have provided numerous examples illustrating the important role that conflict plays in the development and maintenance of psychopathology. Since human learning can be motivated by more than a single drive, it is likely that psychopathology involves conflict-learning paradigms that are more complex than that suggested by the simple avoidance model. Levis and Hare (1977) outlined four possible conflict paradigms that may be directly related to the development of psychopathology.

Interaction of Fear and Hunger Drives. The hunger drive and the strong responses it excites may pave the way under certain circumstances for important learning, especially in childhood developmental patterns. As Dollard and Miller (1950, p. 132) pointed out, if a child is repeatedly left to "cry itself out" when hungry, the child may learn that no matter what it tries, it can do nothing that will alleviate the painful experience of hunger. Such training may lay the basis for apathy or helplessness, the behavior of not trying to avoid when in pain (Seligman, 1975). Furthermore, if an intensive hunger develops, the responses involved can attach fearfulness to situational cues like the bedroom, darkness, quietness, being alone, or the absence of the parents. An

approach—avoidance conflict may develop between two primary drives (hunger and externally induced pain) if the child cries when hungry and is subsequently punished for crying or is directly punished for certain eating behaviors that meet with the displeasure of the parents. Thus, by pitting two drives against each other, the desire to eat and the fear of being punished for eating, the resulting conflict can heighten fearfulness and the conditionability of situational cues associated with the stressful situation.

Interaction of Fear and Sex Drives. Probably no other primary drive is so severely inhibited in our society as sex. Research has indicated that the sex drive can produce positive reinforcement effects early in life. For example, Kinsey, Pomeroy, and Martin (1948) concluded that small boys acquire the capacity for orgasm long before they become able to ejaculate. Yet, many parents view such reinforcement as "nasty," "dirty," and "evil." Even in the present "enlightened" age, it is not uncommon for parents to inhibit their childrens' sexual play by directly punishing such behavior or threatening to administer punishment, such as cutting off the penis, if the undesired behavior reoccurs. It is also not uncommon for parents to create an approach—avoidance conflict by directly stimulating their children sexually and then punishing the child's response. It is little wonder that sexual inhibitions play such an important role in the development of many cases of psychopathology. Since sex is a relatively weak primary drive, a frequent learned response is to remove the conflict and guilt associated with the response by the avoidance (repression) of sexual feelings and thoughts. Such conflicts frequently reemerge in adult life, when society partially removes its taboos and places strong pressure on the individual to be active in this area.

Interaction of Fear and Positive Reinforcing Drives Labeled "Affection" or "Love." Stimuli made contingent on positive reinforcement can acquire the capacity to elicit a positive emotional response in the same manner as described for stimuli conditioned to elicit negative affect. To describe an individual as feeling good emotionally, or as having a feeling of well-being and of security, is to say in learning terms that environmental and internal cues previously conditioned to produce positive affect are currently being elicited. A decrease in the positive emotional state experienced is considered a direct function of eliminating or reducing the cues eliciting the positive affect. This is true whether they are labeled *conditioned* or *unconditioned* stimuli. If the loss of positive affect is of sufficient magnitude, the experience generates a negative emotional state resulting in the aversive conditioning of those situational cues correlated with the reduction in stimulation of the positive affective cues. Depending on the individual's previous conditioning history, such a sequence of events can elicit additional cues (thoughts, images, memories) representing similar conditioning sequences. The resulting compounding of negative affective stimuli can generate the strong negative emotional states frequently described by clinicians as representing feelings of guilt, worthlessness, and depression (Stampfl & Levis, 1969).

Thus, goal-directed behavior designed to elicit a positive emotional state may become inhibited because of the presence of previously conditioned stimuli that were associated with a reduction in the positive emotional state (e.g., rejection). The presence of such aversive stimuli may result in the anticipation that such negative consequences may occur again if the positive goal-directed behavior is carried out. This, in turn, should result in an inhibition of such behavior in an attempt to avoid the possible ngative outcome. Whether such behavior is engaged in depends on the conditioning and the motivational strength of the two sets of approach–avoidance stimuli (Miller, 1951). For a fairly typical conditioning sequence depicting the above process and believed to reflect a common childhood occurrence, the reader is referred to an article by Stampfl and Levis (1969).

Interaction of Fear, Anger, and Frustration Drives. As previous models have suggested, the excessive or severe use of punishment as a behavioral controller leads to the conditioning of fear to previously nonfearful stimuli. Punishment can also have the effect of inhibiting ongoing, goal-directed behavior. The blocking of such responses frequently creates a state of frustration, which has been shown experimentally to lead to an increase in drive

(anger) and to behavior labeled as aggression (Amsel, 1958). The affects of the interaction of these two emotions (fear and anger) on the development of psychopathology are well documented in the clinical literature. It is not surprising that Dollard and Miller (1950) concluded, "Lift the veil of repression covering the childhood mental life of a neurotic person and you come upon the smoking responses of anger" (p. 148).

The conflict resulting from the interaction of fear and anger frequently leads, in theory, to behavior best described in the context of a multiprocess approach–avoidance paradigm (see Stampfl & Levis, 1969). The first stage consists of conditioned anxiety's being associated with cues correlated with a desired approach response. This is achieved by pairing the goal-directed response with punishment (pain). Because the goal-directed behavior is thwarted, frustration is elicited, in addition to pain, and may lead to aggressive behavior. Especially in the case of children, such aggressive tendencies are usually followed by more punishment, inhibiting the aggressive responses. With sufficient repetition of the above sequence, aggressive responses will, in turn, become inhibited by conditioned anxiety.

By channeling the aggressive behavior into internal cues involving thoughts, images, or ruminations concerning the punishing agent, a partial discharge of the anger response can occur. However, if the punishing agent is a source of considerable positive primary and secondary reinforcement, such as in the case of a mother who plays a protective, nurturant role, the stage is set for an additional conflict. By the child's harboring aggressive impulses toward such a figure, the strength and positive reinforcement obtained from viewing the mother as a supportive, loving figure is decreased.

The above conflict can be resolved by avoiding (suppressing) the aggressive fantasies and responses associated with the aggressive behavior. Such behavior is engaged in so as to avoid diminishing the positive reinforcement associated with the child's conceptualization of the punishing agent and to reduce additional secondary anxiety (guilt) over expressing the internal aggressive cues. If the avoidance pattern is not completely successful in removing the conflict, defense mechanisms such as displacement, reaction formation, and projection may develop. A depressive reaction is also believed to be a frequent outgrowth of such conditioning sequences.

Depression can play added functional roles in that the self-punitive effects of the reaction may help reduce the secondary anxiety of guilt as well as setting the stage for the attainment of positive responses from the punisher or other individuals (secondary gain). Furthermore, such conditioning experience usually leads to a decrease in assertive behavior in an effort to avoid increasing the probability of additional conditioning trials.

The above four conditioning models are only suggestive of some possible interactions that can occur to produce symptoms. Clearly, the models are speculative in nature and in need of scientific evaluation at the human level of analysis. Yet, such speculation may prove to be useful in determining directions in which therapy might proceed.

Cognitive Models of Behavior Change

Historically, cognitive models of learning have not been popular with those who hold an S–R, behavioristic viewpoint. Issues of contention have largely focused on the lack of theoretical precision and parsimony and on the difficulty of establishing an empirical framework. Nevertheless, cognitive interpretations have become more popular in the recent learning literature and have had a similar impact on the behavior therapy movement. In the following section, Tolman's classic theory is discussed along with some recent contributions.

Tolman's Sign Learning. Tolman (1932) departed from the traditional stimulus–response orientation of conditioning in an attempt to develop a theoretical system that would be applicable to all of psychology. Tolman attempted to integrate into one theory the facts of classical conditioning, trial-and-error learning, and "inventive" or higher learning processes.

According to Tolman, all learning is sign-gestalt learning, or the acquiring of bits of "knowledge" or "cognitions." Sign-gestalts can be conceptualized as consisting of three parts: a sign, a significate, and a behavior route leading from sign to significate. In Tolman's language a sign-gestalt is equivalent to an expectation by the organism that the sign, if behaved to in such and such a way (the behavior route), will lead to this or that significate.

When signs (certain sets of stimuli) become integrated within the nervous system with certain sign-gestalt expectations, learning occurs. Hypotheses are created and rejected. When one is confirmed, it (the expectation) is learned. Unlearning, or extinction, requires the disconfirmation of a previously learned hypothesis. In Tolman's viewpoint, reinforcement, in the sense of an S–R position, is not essential for learning to occur.

Breger and McGaugh's Informational Analysis. Tolman's theory had little impact on the development of the behavior modification movement, largely because of its cognitive emphasis. Behavior therapy's identity initially resided in its emphasis on changing overt behavior and freeing itself of mentalistic concepts. However, a few earlier attempts were made to introduce cognitive notions into the behavioral movement. Breger and McGaugh (1965), for example, suggested that the problem of neurosis may be better understood by incorporating concepts like information storage and retrieval. From this viewpoint, neurosis is seen as a learned set of central strategies that guide the person's adaptation to his or her environment. Therefore, neurosis is not viewed as symptoms, and therapy is conceived of as involving the learning of a new set of strategies via a new language, that is, a new syntax as well as a new vocabulary.

Rotter's Expectancy-Reinforcement Theory. A cognitive influence can also be found in Rotter's (1954, 1970) "expectancy-reinforcement" theory, which was also designed to provide a different learning framework within which the clinician could operate. Although Rotter was influenced by Hull and others, Tolman's impact is clearly seen in Rotter's position. Behavior for Rotter is goal-directed, and the directional aspect of behavior is inferred from the effect of the reinforcing conditions. An individual's behaviors, needs, and goals are viewed as belonging to a functionally related system. The behavior potential is considered a function of both the individual's expectancy of the goal and the reinforcement value of the external reinforcement. Emphasis is placed on a person's social interactions as opposed to his or her internal feelings as an explanation or criterion for pathology. It is not so much the underlying motivation that needs to be altered or removed according to Rotter as it is the manner in which the patient has learned to gratify needs. The question asked is "What is the patient trying to obtain by a given behavior," rather than "What is being avoided?" Once the answer to this question has been ascertained, the assumption is made that the present mode of responding is viewed by the patient as the best way to obtain the desired goal. In addition, more efficient behaviors for achieving the same goal are either not available in the patient's repertoire or are believed to lead to punishment or the frustration of another need. The task of the therapist then becomes one of manipulating expectancies and reinforcement values in such a way as to bring about new behaviors.

The cognitive viewpoints of Rotter and Breger and McGaugh have provided mainly a framework from which to operate rather than providing alternative behavioral techniques. This point, plus the fact the behavior modification movement initially was in large part a reaction against cognitive, insight-oriented therapies, minimized the influence of any learning-based cognitive positions. However, recently there has been a renewed interest in a cognitive-based behavioral viewpoint that has become a substantial influence within the behavioral therapy movement (Mahoney, 1977). The position that changing cognitions are central to changing overt behavior has led to the development of a variety of new techniques focusing on changing thought processes (e.g., cognitive restructuring, thought stopping, and covert assertion).

S–R-oriented behavior therapists (Levis, 1980; Wolpe, 1978) have been quick to criticize this new development, suggesting that an emphasis on changing cognitions will not only remove the identity of the behavioral movement but result in a return to the less objective, insight-oriented treatment approaches.

Whatever the final outcome of this new debate, cognitive-behavioral modification is here to stay, at least in the immediate future. However, even supporters of this movement should recognize that the theoretical foundations on which cognitive-behavioral modification is based are deplorably weak. What clearly is needed is to update the cognitive-behavioral approach by incorporating the theoretical thinking of modern-day cognitive psychology. An excellent start in this direction has been offered by Bowrer (1978).

Seligman and Johnston's Expectancy Theory. Two other models developed from infrahuman experimentation are worthy of note. Seligman and Johnston (1973) have proposed a cognitive-expectancy model of avoidance conditioning. Avoidance behavior is initially learned via a process of fear conditioning similar to that in the models previously outlined. However, unlike traditional S–R theorists, Seligman and Johnston have argued that once the UCS is removed, fear extinction will be rapid. Yet, they noted that in some cases, avoidance responding is quite resistant to extinction. At the clinical level, this clearly appears to be the normal state of affairs. From their viewpoint, fear has long since extinguished, and what is motivating responding is a cognitive expectancy that if responding is stopped, pain will follow. From this model, extinction results only if the expectancy is changed to one in which absence of responding will not be followed by an aversive consequence. If one extrapolates this model to a therapeutic situation, then the task of therapy is not to extinguish fear-producing cues but to change the expectancies of response-contingent outcomes.

Seligman's Learned-Helplessness Theory. In a related theoretical development, Maier and Seligman (1976) attempted to explain why infrahuman subjects under certain experimental manipulations failed to learn to avoid or escape aversive consequences. This position is referred to as *learned-helplessness theory* and has been extended by Seligman (1975) to explain human depression. Three stages are postulated in the development of learned helplessness. The first stage consists of the organism's receiving information that the probability of the outcome is independent of performing a given response class. The distinction between controllable and uncontrollable reinforcement is central to the theory.

The concepts of controllability are operationally defined within a response-reinforced contingency space. If the conditional probability of that outcome (i.e., reinforcement), given a specific response, does not differ from the conditional probability of that outcome in the absence of that response, then the outcome is independent of responding and, by definition, uncontrollable. On the other hand, if the conditional probability of the outcome, given a specific response, is not equal to the conditional probability of the outcome in the absence of that response, then the outcome is controllable. A person or infrahuman is "helpless" with respect to some outcome when the outcome occurs independently of all voluntary responses.

The critical stage of the theory involves the organism's registering and processing cognitively the information obtained from the contingency exposure in which responding was independent of outcome. This event can be subdivided into two processes for the organism subject to helplessness: (1) learning that a contingency exists concering the independence of responding and outcome, and (2) developing the expectation that responding and outcome will remain independent on future trials. Coinciding with the second stage is a reduction in the motivation (activity) to control the outcome and thus the designation of nonmotivational theory once depression or helplessness is learned. The final stage includes the generalization and transference of the expectation that responding and outcome are independent of new learning situations. The behavioral outcome of this generalization is referred to as the *learned-helplessness effect* or *depression*.

Abramson, Seligman, and Teasdale (1978) have extended Seligman's earlier position to include attribution theory. They have added to the model the response class of self-esteem, which is considered orthogonal to controllability, presumably being dependent on attributional considerations. For these writers, the expectation of response–outcome performance is regarded only as a sufficient condition for depression. Other factors like physiological and hormonal states, postpartum conditions, chemical depletions, and loss of interest in reinforcers may also produce depression in

the absence of expectations of uncontrollability.

From the above discussion of theory and its applied implications, it should be recognized that formal theory aids in the scientist's quest to heighten diversified viewpoints, strategies, and predictions. It should also be noted that many important theoretical models have not been presented here that may at some point also contribute in a significant way to the applied-behavior-therapy movement (see Hilgard & Bower, 1966; Mackintosh, 1974). For example, experimental work on modeling and imitation learning at the infrahuman level stimulated Bandura (1962) to develop and research important principles that have resulted in behavior techniques usable at the human level. As was noted in relation to the value of extrapolating learning principles and paradigms, theory also plays an important role in making a workable and profitable marriage between behavioral science and the application of this knowledge.

Methodological Foundations

The behavior modification movement's reliance on the principles and theories of experimental psychology has also resulted in this field's adoption or acceptance of the validity of certain research strategies. For example, many of the established principles that form the foundation of various behavioral techniques are based on infrahuman or human laboratory research. Furthermore, its identification with experimental psychology has also required that the behavioral movement adopt the methodological principles of the behavioral scientist. Although at times a source of controversy, the acceptance of each of the points of heritage has strengthened and clarified the rationale and commitment of this new applied science. The following section attempts to highlight some of the positive fallout of such a strategy.

Infrahuman Analogue Research

Most of the behavior principles and theories just reviewed were initially and sometimes solely developed from research data that utilized laboratory animals, especially the rat, as subject material. Skepticism naturally arises concerning the applicability of these laws to human behavior, since marked differences are apparent between rat behavior and human's social and verbal development. Nevertheless, many of the principles developed at the infrahuman level have been shown to operate at the human level. It may also turn out that data collected from infrahuman species will prove more useful for generalizing than the vast amount of research now being conducted with humans. If, say, maladaptive behavior is tied to the conditioning of emotional or autonomic responses, and if mediated internal cues such as words, thoughts, images, and memories in the human turn out to follow essentially the same conditioning laws as extroceptive stimuli, the argument for the implications of infrahuman research becomes much stronger. Not only does the rat provide a less complex organism, which may be more advantageous for deciphering basic laws, it is also equipped with an autonomic nervous system not unlike that of the human. Further, animals are expendable and can be used in expermentation that for ethical reasons cannot be carried out on humans. They also have the advantage of being less complex than the human, which increases the probability of isolating basic principles of behavior. In fact, if infrahuman experimentation provides a vehicle for illustration and confirmation of suspected hypotheses about the human, the effort is more than worthwhile.

Despite the various arguments pro and con and the obvious need for confirmation at the human level, the value of infrahuman research in developing other sciences like biology, behavioral genetics, and medicine is beyond debate. And as far as behavior therapy is concerned, animal research has been directly responsible for influencing the development of the applied behavioral movement. Both Wolpe and Stampfl's research with animals was instrumental in developing their respective theories, and Skinner's work with animals has had a profound influence on the operant conditioning approach. Justified or not, these infrahuman findings have given impetus to the development of treatment techniques that previously were undeveloped or unhighlighted. This is certainly no small accomplishment (Levis, 1970a).

Human Analogue Research

Human laboratory or analogue research has also become an ingrained part of the methodological arsenal of the applied behavioral movement. These studies, usually carried out in a laboratory setting with college students, mainly involve studying the fears and avoidance behaviors of nonpatient populations. Cooper, Furst, and Bridger (1969) were one of the first teams to criticize this strategy by suggesting that the treatment of nonclinical fears may be irrelevant to an understanding of treating clinical neuroses. Cooper et al. were quite correct then, and unfortunately, the criticism still applies today: too much of the analogue research was and is used by behavior therapists to validate their techniques, a major error of overgeneralization. The naiveté of some behavior therapists in attempting to justify the validity of their techniques without documenting them with clinical populations is disconcerting. Even today, reviews frequently fail to discriminate between research performed with analogue and clinical populations.

Human analogue research, however, has been proved of value as a vehicle for obtaining information about various treatment manipulations, for isolating critical principles of behavior change associated with a given technique, for developing and testing ideas or hypotheses in a controlled setting, for clarifying theoretical issues, and for establishing the validity and reliability of previous findings. The laboratory setting using nonpatient populations is useful because it permits the selection of an adequate sample of homogeneous target behaviors, the equation of avoidance tendencies, the operational definition of independent and dependent measures, and the selection of appropriate control conditions. Such experimental precision is exceedingly difficult, if not impossible, when one is using patient populations (Levis, 1970b).

The value of the analogue population is based on essentially the same strategy that led investigators to study the rat so intensively. Studying less complex sets of behaviors under more controlled conditions may well be more advantageous for deciphering basic laws. This strategy has clearly helped the behavioral therapy movement in isolating and developing important principles in the areas of assessment, treatment, and theory (see Bandura, 1978, an excellent article on this subject).

Patient Research

Perhaps the most important aspect of the behavior modification movement is its continual commitment to objective assessment and scientific analysis. Not only have behavior therapists embraced the methodological techniques developed by behaviorism and experimental psychology, but they have also built on these, adding to the arsenal available to applied scientists. However, more advances in this area are badly needed. Experimental precision is exceedingly difficult to achieve when using a clinical population to assess therapeutic techniques. Anyone who has conducted therapy-outcome research is aware of the numerous problems that continually confront the researcher. Difficulty with administrative interference, cooperation of staff, control over patient selection and drug administration, issues of ethics, and sample size are only a few of the frustrations facing the investigators.

The complexity of the therapeutic interaction also necessitates the use of numerous control groups to deal with such issues as the therapist's skill, experience, commitments, and potential extratherapeutic factors, such as the patient's expectations or uncontrolled demand effects. It is precisely because of this lack of experimental control that outcome research has not even begun to consider the questions raised at the analogue level of analysis. In fact, it is because of the control problem that patient research has not had much of an impact on the scientific community. Appropriate design and statistical techniques for evaluation are readily available, but the issue is one of implementation.

In an attempt to resolve the problem of the large sample sizes required by the traditional between-group analysis, a number of behavior therapists have adopted the philosophy developed by Skinner and other operant researchers of using within-group analysis of small samples. In such a design, each subject serves as his or her own control. Such a strategy has already been proved of value in establishing useful behavioral principles at the infrahuman level of analysis, and it appears to be the only methodological solution with those populations for whom adequate sample size or homogeneous behavioral patterns cannot be obtained.

However, the use of these designs with humans creates new methodological problems that are not a factor when conducting animal research. For one thing, the within-group analysis of a small sample (ABA design) is based on the assumption that large numbers of subjects are not required if environmental variance can be eliminated or controlled. This kind of control may be readily achieved by using the rat or pigeon Skinner box, but it is almost impossible or too costly to maintain within the clinical setting. For another thing, the experimental manipulation (e.g., reinforcement administration) is free of bias at the infrahuman level because it is usually programmed by an apparatus. At the human level, such manipulations are usually made with the aid of other humans or in the presence of an experimenter. Drug research has overwhelmingly documented the methodological point that such manipulations, unless done on a completely blind basis, can result in subtle communications (suggestive and demand effects) to patients, resulting in the alteration of behavior in the absence of any experimental effect (the so-called placebo effect). Such dangers must be considered when evaluating research of this type.

It should be clear from the above comments that new designs are needed at the applied level that reinforce the feasibility of conducting patient research. Ideally, these designs should permit research on small samples while addressing the issue of control. One possibility that may have merit involves the combination of a between-group design with a within-group analysis. One major difficulty in evaluating any therapeutic technique is the lack of control over how effectively the technique is administered. The therapist's skill and expertise, personality interaction, and suggestive effects are currently allowed to vary, greatly increasing error variance. Control groups can be added to the design, but they are costly and imprecise.

One of the key advantages of the behavioral approaches is that the procedural technique used and the principles outlined for creating behavioral change can be operationalized. However, this is rarely done on a subject-by-subject basis or for that matter even on a group basis. For example, systematic desensitization maintains that for therapy to work, the relaxation response must be dominant over the anxiety response. Implosive therapy argues that therapy will be effective if the cues introduced elicit a high level of anxiety and if extinction of this response results from continual repetition. Error variance would be markedly reduced if the boundary condition of the technique used were established on a subject-by-subject basis. That is to say, the technique administration needs to be monitored by an objective dependent measure.

For systematic desensitization, a measure for relaxation (e.g., EMG) and for anxiety (e.g., GSR) would be needed. For implosive therapy, a measure of anxiety is required. Thus, with appropriate monitoring, it can be empirically established whether the boundary conditions for a given technique were met by the subject. When it has been established that they have been met, a direct correspondence should be achieved with symptom reduction. If symptom reduction does not occur, the principle suggested by the therapy is not effective with the population tested. If the boundary conditions are not met and behavior changes occur, such changes must be attributed to a principle other than that suggested by the therapy.

Because of space limitations, all of the implications of the above design cannot be addressed. But it is the writer's conclusion that only two groups would be required: an experimental group and a nontreated, control-baseline group. With adequate replications, such a design would provide a quantitative index for establishing whether a relationship exists between meeting the boundary conditions of the technique and symptom reduction and for determining whether extratherapeutic factors are effectively operating. Whether or not the above ideas are workable requires testing. But the objective of an economical design is correct, and the future of the clinical areas is dependent on reaching an adequate solution. The behavioral therapy movement is committed to achieving this objective and enhancing scientific rigor.

Epilogue

In a relatively short time, the behavior therapy movement has made many important inroads, which have been achieved largely through the strategy of extrapolating from extensive laboratory research and theory dealing with conditioning and learning principles. As Stampfl (1970) observed:

Research of this nature has yielded relatively precise statements of the relationship existing between critical variables (for example, immediacy of reinforcement and schedules of reinforcements) and behavioral variables. The relatively precise statements of the relationship between critical independent variables and behavioral change makes the task of the applied practitioner a vastly simpler one. When confronted with the problem of what might be tried to modify behavior, the applied operant practitioner has a ready set of behavioral principles that furnish guidelines for the initiation of procedures in relation to the behavioral problem considered. One can hardly overemphasize the advantages that result from the knowledge and confidence provided by the basic behavioral principles established through laboratory research. (p. 103)

Additional attractive features of the behavior modification movement are also apparent. For one thing, behavior therapy is based on principles that are readily observed in everyday experience. Behavior certainly appears to be directed and modified in social cultures by rewards and punishments. As Stampfl (1970) noted, such observations give a strong presumptive face validity to the procedures used. Furthermore, the strength of the approach is reflected in the attitude of those involved in the movement. Behavior therapists are willing to tackle almost any behavioral problem on an empirical basis and to relinquish any preconceptions as to which behaviors are susceptible to change. This refusal to accept *a priori* conclusions on clinical dogma is critical for the field's advancement. Without this attitude, important contributions to the treatment of the difficult behavior problems of chronic schizophrenics, autistic children, juvenile delinquents, and other diagnostic populations might never have been attempted or achieved.

Despite the applied behavioral movement's numerous achievements, many of which are reviewed in this volume, the future holds the promise of even more exciting contributions. These dividends will materialize if the foundations on which the movement rests are not ignored and are continually developed.

References

Abramson, L. Y., Seligman, M. E. P., & Teasdale, J. P. Learned helplessness in humans: Critique and reformulation. *Journal of Abnormal Psychology*, 1978, *87*, 49–74.

Amsel, A. The role of frustrative nonreward in noncontinuous reward situations. *Psychological Bulletin*, 1958, *55*, 102–119.

Bandura, A. Social learning through imitation. In M. R. Jones (Ed.), *Nebraska symposium on motivation*. Lincoln: University of Nebraska Press, 1962.

Bandura, A. On paradigms and recycled ideologies. *Cognitive Therapy and Research*, 1978, *2*, 79–103.

Bekhterev, V. M. *General principles of human reflexology*. Trans. E. & W. Murphy. New York: International, 1928.

Breger, L., & McGaugh, J. L. Critique and reformulation of "learning-theory" approaches to psychotherapy and neurosis. *Psychological Bulletin*, 1965, *63*, 338–358.

Brown, J. S., & Jacobs, A. The role of fear in the motivation and acquisition of responses. *Journal of Experimental Psychology*, 1949, *39*, 747–759.

Brown, J. S., Kalish, H. I., & Farber, I. E. Conditioned fear as revealed by magnitude of startle response to an auditory stimulus. *Journal of Experimental Psychology*, 1951, *41*, 317–328.

Church, R. M. The varied effects of punishment on behavior. *Psychological Review*, 1963, *70*, 369–402.

Cooper, A., Furst, J. B., & Bridger, W. H. A brief commentary on the usefulness of studying fears of snakes. *Journal of Abnormal Psychology*, 1969, *74*, 413–414.

Denny, M. R. Relaxation theory and experiments. In F. R. Brush (Ed.), *Aversive conditioning and learning*. New York: Academic Press, 1971.

Denny, M. R. Post-aversive relief and relaxation and their implications for behavior therapy. *Journal of Behavior Therapy and Experimental Psychiatry*, 1976, *7*, 315–322.

Dollard, J., & Miller, N. E. *Personality and psychotherapy*. New York: McGraw-Hill, 1950.

Eysenck, H. J. (Ed.). *Behaviour therapy and the neuroses*. New York: Pergamon, 1960.

Eysenck, H. J. *The effects of psychotherapy*. New York: International Science Press, 1966.

Eysenck, H. J. A theory of the incubation of anxiety fear responses. *Behaviour Research and Therapy*, 1968, *6*, 309–322.

Eysenck, H. J. The learning theory model of neurosis—a new approach. *Behaviour Research and Therapy*, 1976, *14*, 251–267.

Eysenck, H. J. The conditioning model of neurosis. *The Behavioral and Brain Sciences*, 1979, *2*, 155–166.

Feigl, H. The scientific outlook: Naturalism and humanism. In H. Feigl & M. Brodbeck (Eds.), *Readings in the philosophy of science*. New York: Appleton-Century-Crofts, 1953.

Ferster, C. B., & Skinner, B. F. *Schedules of reinforcement*. New York: Appleton-Century-Crofts, 1957.

Ford, D. H., & Urban, H. B. Psychotherapy. *Annual Review of Psychology*, 1967, *17*, 333–372.

Greenspoon, J. Learning theory contributions to psychotherapy. *Psychotherapy: Theory, Research and Practice*, 1965, *2*, 145–146.

Guthrie, E. R. *The psychology of learning*. New York: Harper, 1935.

Hall, C., & Lindzey, G. *Theories of personality*. New York: Wiley & Sons, 1957.

Herrnstein, R. Method and theory in the study of avoidance. *Psychological Review*, 1969, *76*, 49–69.

Hilgard, E. R., & Bower, G. H. *Theories of learning*. New York: Appleton-Century-Crofts, 1966.

Hull, C. L. *Principles of behavior*. New York: Appleton-Century-Crofts, 1943.

Hull, C. L. *A behavior system: An introduction to behavior therapy concerning the individual organism*. New Haven, Conn.: Yale University Press, 1952.

Jacobson, E. *Progressive relaxation*. Chicago: University of Chicago Press, 1938.

Jones, M. C. The elimination of children's fears. *Journal of Experimental Psychology*, 1924, *7*, 383–390.

Kalish, H. I. Behavior therapy. In B. Wolman (Ed.), *Handbook of clinical psychology*. New York: McGraw-Hill, 1965.

Kazdin, A. E. *History of behavior modification: Experimental foundations of contemporary research*. Baltimore: University Park Press, 1978.

Kimble, G. A. *Hilgard and Marquis' conditioning and learning*. New York: Appleton-Century-Crofts, 1961.

Kinsey, A., Pomeroy, W., & Martin, C. *Sexual behavior in the human male*. Philadelphia: W. B. Saunders, 1948.

Levis, D. J. & Boyd, T. L. Symptom maintenance: An infrahuman analysis and extension of the conservation of anxiety principle. *Journal of Abnormal Psychology*, 1979, *88*, 107–120.

Levis, D. J., & Hare, N. A review of the theoretical rationale and empirical support for the extinction approach of implosive (flooding) therapy. In M. Hersen, R. M. Eisler, & P. M. Miller (Eds.), *Progress in behavior modification, Vol. 4*. New York: Academic Press, 1977.

Lemkow, P. V., & Crocetti, G. M. Vital statistics of schizophrenia. In L. Bellak (Ed.), *Schizophrenia: A review of the syndrome*. New York: Grune & Stratton, 1958.

Levis, D. J. Behavioral therapy: The fourth therapeutic revolution? In D. J. Levis (Ed.), *Learning approaches to therapeutic behavior change*. Chicago: Aldine Publishing Company, 1970. (a)

Levis, D. J. The case for performing research on nonpatient populations with fears of small animals: A reply to Cooper, Furst, and Bridger. *Journal of Abnormal Psychology*, 1970, *76*, 36–38. (b)

Levis, D. J. A reconsideration of Eysenck's conditioning model of neurosis. *The Behavioral and Brain Sciences*, 1979, *2*, 172–174.

Levis, D. J. Do cognitive constructs enhance or threaten the survival of clinical behaviorism? In W. W. Tryon, C. B. Ferester, C. M. Franks, A. E. Kazdin, D. J. Levis, & G. S. Tryon, On the role of behaviorism in clinical psychology. *Pavlovian Journal of Biological Science*, 1980, *15*, 15–17.

Mackintosh, N. J. *The psychology of animal learning.* New York: Academic Press, 1974.

Mahoney, J. J. Cognitive therapy and research: A question of questions. *Cognitive Therapy and Research,* 1977, *1,* 5–16.

Maier, S. F., & Seligman, M. E. P. Learned helplessness: Theory and evidence. *Journal of Experimental Psychology: General,* 1976, *105,* 3–46.

Miller, N. E. Studies of fear as an aquirable drive. I: Fear as motivation and fear-reduction as reinforcement in the learning of a new response. *Journal of Experimental Psychology,* 1948, *38,* 89–101.

Miller, N. E. Learnable drives and rewards. In S. S. Stevens (Ed.), *Handbook of experimental psychology.* New York: Wiley, 1951.

Miller, N. E. Liberalization of basic S-R concepts: Extensions to conflict behavior, motivation and social learning. In S. Koch (Ed.), *Psychology: A study of a science,* Vol. 2. New York: McGraw-Hill, 1959.

Mowrer, O. H. Anxiety-reduction and learning. *Journal of Experimental Psychology,* 1940, *27,* 497–516.

Mowrer, O. H. On the dual nature of learning—A reinterpretation of "conditioning" and "problem-solving." *Harvard Educational Review,* 1947, *17,* 102–148.

Mowrer, O. H. Pain, punishment, guilt, and anxiety. *Anxiety.* New York: Grune & Stratton, 1950.

Mowrer, O. H. *Learning theory and behavior.* New York: Wiley, 1960.

Pavlov, I. P. *Conditioned reflexes.* London: Oxford University Press, 1927.

Rescorla, R. A. Pavlovian conditioned inhibition. *Psychological Bulletin,* 1969, *72,* 77–94.

Rescorla, R. A., & Lo Lordo, V. M. Inhibition of avoidance behavior. *Journal of Comparative and Physiological Psychology,* 1965, *59,* 406–412.

Rescorla, R. A., & Solomon, R. L. Two-process learning theory: Relationships between Pavlovian conditioning and instrumental learning. *Psychological Review,* 1967, *74,* 151–182.

Rescorla, R. A., & Wagner, R. R. A theory of Pavlovian conditioning variations in the effectiveness of reinforcement and nonreinforcement. In A. H. Black & W. F. Prokasy (Eds.), *Classical conditioning. Vol. 2: Current research and theory.* New York: Appleton-Century-Crofts, 1972.

Rotter, J. B. *Social learning and clinical psychology.* Englewood Cliffs, N.J.: Prentice-Hall, 1954.

Rotter, J. B. Some implications of a social learning theory for the practice of psychotherapy. In D. J. Levis (Eds.), *Learning approaches to therapeutic behavior change.* Chicago: Aldine, 1970.

Salter, A. *Conditioned reflex therapy.* New York: Farrar, Straus, 1949.

Salter, A. The theory and practice of conditioned reflex therapy. In J. Wolpe, A. Salter, L. J. Reyna's (Eds.), *The conditioning therapies.* New York: Holt, Rinehart & Winston, 1965.

Seligman, M. E. P. Phobias and preparedness. *Behavior Therapy,* 1971, *2,* 307–320.

Seligman, M. E. P. *Helplessness: On depression, development and death.* San Francisco: W. H. Freeman, 1975.

Seligman, M. E. P., & Johnston, J. C. A cognitive theory of avoidance learning. In F. J. McGuigan & D. B. Lumsden (Eds.), *Contemporary prospectives in learning and conditioning.* Washington: Scripta Press, 1973.

Sherrington, C. S. *The integrative action of the central nervous system.* Cambridge: Cambridge University Press, 1947.

Shoben, E. J. Psychotherapy as a problem in learning theory. *Psychological Bulletin,* 1949, *46,* 366–392.

Sidman, M. Two temporal parameters of the maintenance of avoidance behavior in the rat. *Journal of Comparative and Physiological Psychology,* 1953, *46,* 253–261.

Skinner, B. F. *The behavior of organisms: An experimental analysis.* New York: Appleton-Century, 1938.

Skinner, B. F. The operational analysis of psychological terms. *Psychological Review,* 1945, *52,* 270–278.

Skinner, B. F. Are theories of learning necessary? *Psychological Review,* 1950, *57,* 193–216.

Solomon, R. L., & Wynne, L. C. Traumatic avoidance learning: The principle of anxiety conservation and partial irreversibility. *Psychological Review,* 1954, *61,* 353–385.

Spence, K. W. Theoretical interpretations of learning. In C. P. Stone (Ed.), *Comparative psychology.* New York: Prentice-Hall, 1951.

Srole, L., Langner, T. S., Michael, S. T., Opler, M. K., & Rennie, T. A. C. *Mental health in the metropolis: Midtown Manhattan Study,* Vol. 1. New York: McGraw-Hill, 1962.

Stampfl, T. G. Comment. In D. J. Levis (Ed.), *Learning approaches to therapeutic behavior change.* Chicago: Aldine, 1970.

Stampfl, T. G., & Levis, D. J. The essentials of implosive therapy: A learning-theory-based psychodynamic behavioral therapy. *Journal of Abnormal Psychology,* 1967, *72,* 496–503.

Stampfl, T. G., & Levis, D. J. Learning theory: An aid to dynamic therapeutic practice. In L. D. Eron & R. Callahan (Eds.), *Relationship of theory to practice in psychotherapy.* Chicago: Aldine, 1969.

Stampfl, T. G., & Levis, D. J. Implosive therapy: A behavioral therapy. In J. T. Spence, R. C. Carson, & J. W. Thibaut (Eds.), *Behavioral approaches to therapy.* Morristown, N.J.: General Learning Press, 1976.

Thorndike, E. S. *Animal intelligence.* New York: Macmillan, 1911.

Throndike, E. L. *Human learning.* New York: Macmillan, 1931.

Tolman, E. C. *Purposive behavior in animals and man.* New York: Macmillan, 1932.

Tourney, G. A history of therapeutic fashions in psychiatry, 1800–1966. *American Journal of Psychiatry,* 1967, *124*(6), 784–796.

Watson, J. B., & Rayner, R. Conditioned emotional reaction. *Journal of Experimental Psychology,* 1920, *3,* 1–4.

Wolpe, J. *Psychotherapy by reciprocal inhibition.* Stanford, Calif.: Stanford University Press, 1958.

Wolpe, J. Cognition and causation in human behavior and its therapy. *American Psychologist,* 1978, *33,* 437–446.

CHAPTER 3

Behavioral Assessment

AN OVERVIEW

Marvin R. Goldfried

Introduction

Within the past decade, the field of behavioral assessment has grown dramatically. This growth is reflected by the numerous books on this topic (Barlow, 1980; Ciminero, Adams, & Calhoun, 1977; Cone & Hawkins, 1977; Haynes, 1978; Haynes & Wilson, 1979; Nay, 1980; Hersen & Bellack, 1976, 1981; Keefe, Kopel, & Gordon, 1978; Kendall & Hollon, 1981; Mash & Terdal, 1976, 1980; Merluzzi, Glass, & Genest, 1981; Wiggins, 1973), as well as by two journals devoted to behavioral assessment (*Behavioral Assessment* and *Journal of Behavioral Assessment*). Such increased interest is due to the recognition that effective clinical behavior therapy is only as good as its initial behavioral analysis, and that clinical outcome research on behavior therapy cannot be undertaken without adequate measures of change.

Despite such interest in behavioral assessment—perhaps even because of it—we face the potential danger of developing measures that are poorly conceived and developed. This was clearly the case in the 1940s, when there was an indiscriminate proliferation of projective techniques (see Rabin, 1968). Although the conceptual underpinnings of behavioral assessment do not parallel those associated with projective techniques, it should not be assumed that we are immune from many of the pitfalls that the field of assessment has experienced in the past. This unfortunate tendency for history to repeat itself may occur with behavioral assessment, as the need for measures outstrips the procedures currently available.

This chapter provides an overview of the field of behavioral assessment; it deals with the underlying theoretical and methodological assumptions associated with such procedures, outlines some of the currently available assessment methods, discusses the relationship between behavior therapy and behavioral assessment, and ends with a note on future perspectives.

Portions of this chapter were adapted from Goldfried and Davison (1976), Goldfried (1976), and Goldfried and Linehan (1977).

Marvin R. Goldfried • Department of Psychology, State University of New York at Stony Brook, Stony Brook, New York 11794. Preparation of this chapter was facilitated by grant MH 24327 from the National Institute of Mental Health.

Basic Assumptions

The distinction between traditional and behavioral approaches to assessment has been discussed at length by Goldfried (1976), Goldfried and Kent (1972), Mischel (1968), and Wiggins (1973). Each of these writers has noted that behavioral assessment is characterized by relatively fewer inferential assumptions, remaining instead closer to observables. This holds true for the behavioral conceptualization of human functioning, as well as the interpretation of the person's response to situations within the assessment setting.

One of the earliest arguments for using operational terms in assessing and changing human behavior can be found in Johnson's *People in Quandaries* (1946):

> To say that Henry is mean implies that he has some sort of inherent trait, but it tells us nothing about what Henry has done. Consequently, it fails to suggest any specific means of improving Henry. If, on the other hand, it is said that Henry snatched Billy's cap and threw it in the bonfire, the situation is rendered somewhat more clear and actually more helpful. You might never eliminate "meanness," but there are fairly definite steps to be taken in order to remove Henry's incentives or opportunities for throwing caps in bonfires. . . .
>
> What the psychiatrist has to do . . . is to get the person to tell him not what he is or what he *has*, but what he *does*, and the conditions under which he does it. When he stops talking about what *type* of person he is, what his outstanding *traits* are, and what type of disorder he *has*—when he stops making these subject–predicate statements, and begins to use actional terms to describe his behavior and its circumstances—both he and the psychiatrist begin to see what specifically may be done in order to change both the behavior and the circumstances. (p. 220)

Within the scope of contemporary behavioral assessment, *personality* is typically construed as an intervening variable that provides a summary of the individual's reactions to a wide variety of life situations. Stated in this way, however, the concept *personality* has little practical utility for behavioral assessment, in that it would be a near-impossible task to obtain systematic samples of all day-to-day situations. In actual practice, behavioral assessment has instead focused on behavior patterns associated with a given class of performance capabilities, such as social skills or fearfulness.

The concept of *behavioral capability* refers to whether or not an individual has given response available in his or her repertoire. The specific focus of assessment is on the determination of which capabilities a person has in any given class of situations. It should be clear that the specification of "capabilities" relates to maladaptive behavioral repertoires as well as to behavioral competencies. Thus, it may be inferred that a person who is observed to berate others is capable of taking on an aggressive role or has aggressive capabilities.

A capabilities conceptualization of personality functioning, when viewed within the broad context of psychometric methodology, relates most directly to *content validity*, where careful item-sampling becomes a most important issue. As described in the *Standards for Educational and Psychological Tests* (American Psychological Association, American Educational Research Association, and National Council on Measurement in Education, 1974), "Evidence of content validity is required when the test user wishes to estimate how an individual performs in the universe of situations the test is intended to represent" (p. 28). Although content validity has long been described as an important aspect of test construction, it has typically been related to achievement tests, not personality assessment.

In their discussion of the behavioral-analytic approach to assessing competence, Goldfried and D'Zurilla (1969) have outlined a procedure for establishing the content validity of behavioral measures. The initial step consists of a *situational analysis*, involving a sampling of typical situations in which a given behavior of interest is likely to occur (e.g., aggressive behavior, heterosexual interaction). The next phase consists of a *response enumeration*, which entails a sampling of typical responses to each of the situations generated during the situational analysis. Both this phase and the previous one may be carried out by means of direct observations, that is, reports from individuals who have occasion to observe the behaviors within a naturalistic setting, as well as self-observations by those for whom the assessment is specifically designed. The final phase of the criterion analysis uses a *response evaluation* to judge each response with regard to capability level. In the measurement of competence, these judgments are carried out by significant others in the environment who typically label behavior patterns as being effective or maladaptive. In other instances, such as the assessment of empathic or fearful behavior, these judgments are made in light of how well they fit the definition of the behavioral capability of interest to the investigator. Each situation may have associated with it an array of different responses, which can be grouped functionally according to their judged capability level. One may then use this three-stage criterion analysis to select the items in one's measuring instrument and also to find the empirically derived criteria for scoring the measure.

The basic assumption underlying this approach to establishing scoring criteria is that there exist common standards or behavioral norms for effectiveness within the particular life setting in question, and that these standards are relatively stable over the period of time during which the assessment is to take place. In light of the rapidly changing value system associated with many aspects of our society, this assumption may at times prove to be faulty. It should be emphasized, however, that failure to confirm empirically the existence of a stable set of behavioral norms would have implications not only for the establishment of scoring criteria, but also for the selection of criterion behaviors against which any validation could take place. However, this problem would be present in any attempt to predict human behavior, whether it be behavioral or traditional.

Although the behavioral-analytic model was originally developed for the study of the effectiveness of college freshmen (Goldfried & D'Zurilla, 1969), it has been applied to a wide variety of different content areas. Thus, the behavioral-analytic model has been used to develop measures of social competence (Levenson & Gottman, 1978; Mullinix & Galassi, 1981), heterosocial skills (Bellack, Hersen, & Lamparski, 1979; Kulich & Conger, 1978; Perri & Richards, 1979), interpersonal skills among retarded adults (Bates, 1980), children's social skills (Edleson & Rose, 1978), skill deficits in delinquent boys (Freedman, Rosenthal, Donahoe, Schlundt, & McFall, 1978), depression (Funabiki & Calhoun, 1979),

assertiveness (MacDonald, 1974), guilt over assertion (Klass, 1980), methods of coping with chronic illness (Turk, 1979), occupational skills (Mathews, Whang, & Fawcett, 1980), and managerial effectiveness (Bernstein, 1978).

It should also be emphasized that the behavioral-analytic model for test construction focuses only on sampling and not on methodological issues. Once a criterion analysis is conducted, the assessor must consider the format for measuring the obtained situation–response interactions. Should one observe the individual in a naturalistic setting? Should one somehow contrive situations within the laboratory setting and then observe the person's response? Should the individual sit back and imagine the situation and then verbalize how he or she might react to it if it were actually occurring? Should the measuring procedure take the form of a structured interview? Should it involve a paper-and-pencil test? In deciding on which procedure to employ, various issues of method variance become relevant, such as the reactivity of the measuring procedure and the reliability of the observers or scorers, as well as the comparative validities of the several assessment procedures.

Behavioral Assessment Methods

There are a variety of different approaches that one may employ in sampling an individual's response to certain life situations. Behavioral assessment has made use of (1) direct observation in naturalistic settings; (2) the observation of responses to situations that have been contrived by the assessor; (3) responses that manifest themselves in role-playing situations; and (4) the individual's own self-report of behavior. Each of these different approaches to assessment is discussed below.

Observations in Naturalistic Settings

In attempting to implement the criterion-sampling orientation to behavioral assessment described in the previous section, it follows logically that behavioral assessors would have turned to the use of direct observation in naturalistic settings. Not only can such observation allow one to measure the various dimensions of the behavior of interest (e.g., frequency, strength, pervasiveness), but it can also provide a good opportunity for understanding those variables that may be currently maintaining the behavior.

Naturalistic observation is hardly an invention of behavior therapists. Psychologists, anthropologists, and sociologists have made use of such procedures long before the current behavioral orientation came into being. For example, Barker and Wright emphasized the importance of observing the "stream of behavior" in its appropriate ecological setting. They illustrated this approach to observation dramatically in their book *One Boy's Day* (1951) in which they provided a detailed account of the activities of a 7-year-old boy whom observers literally followed around for an entire day. Any such attempt to observe the natural stream of behavior represents an admirable if not staggering undertaking, as is attested to by the fact that Barker and Wright's observational data for a single day encompass an entire book.

Largely as a function of practical considerations, behaviorally oriented assessors have typically been more goal-oriented in making their observations than were Barker and Wright. Thus, depending on the particular purpose of the assessment, behavioral codes are customarily devised that outline the categories of behavior to be attended to during the observation procedure. Different codes have been devised by investigators for observing behavior as it occurs in various settings, such as schools, homes, and hospitals. These observations are typically carried out at specified periods of time and are tailored to the particular subject population being assessed.

An early attempt to employ behavioral observations within the school setting is described by O'Leary and Becker (1967). The main goal of their observation was to evaluate the effect of a token reinforcement program with a class consisting of disruptive children. Teams of trained observers recorded the incidence of various behavioral categories for specific time periods, typically lasting 1½ hours each. The observers sat toward the rear of the classroom and attempted to be as unobtrusive as possible. Included among the categories within the behavioral code were such

behaviors as making disruptive noises, speaking without raising one's hand, and pushing. Based on extensive research and continual revisions, the code has been refined and updated (O'Leary & O'Leary, 1972) for future applications.

An observation code has also been developed for the assessment of positively reinforcing behaviors (Bersoff & Moyer, 1973). Included among the 10 behavioral categories in this code are positive reactions (e.g., the administration of concrete rewards, verbal or nonverbal praise, attention, and physical contact), behaviors that presumably are neutral with respect to their reinforcement qualities (e.g., asking questions), and responses of an aversive nature (e.g., admonishment and nonverbal disapproval).

The use of behavioral observation codes involving frequency counts of various categories of behavior has provided researchers and clinicians with an invaluable approach for evaluating the effectiveness of various therapeutic intervention programs. Despite the obvious utility of such behavioral codes, one may nonetheless raise questions as to the relevance of data that they may ignore. Of particular importance is the likelihood that an individual behaving in a given way is probably reacting to some antecedent event in her or his environment, and that the behavior being observed may also have certain environmental consequences.

Toward the goal of evaluating the antecedent and/or consequent occurrences that may maintain any particular behavior, Patterson, Ray, Shaw, and Cobb (1969) developed an observational code to evaluate the interaction between an individual and significant others in the environment. The observations specifically focus on predelinquent boys, particularly as they interact with members of their families within the home setting. The code essentially attempts to take the complex stream of behavior and break it down into categories focused on various aspects of the child's behavior (e.g., yelling, talking, teasing, hitting, and crying) and the way in which other members of the family react to him (e.g., positive physical contact, ignoring, and disapproval). The behavioral code is utilized by trained observers who go directly to the home and record the family interactions on a time-sampling basis.

A code for assessing the interaction among adults has been developed by Lewinsohn and Shaffer (1971), who have focused specifically on the observation of depressed individuals. Here, too, observers go directly into the home and time-sample the interaction among family members at mealtime. Although the distinction may be difficult to make at times, Lewinsohn and Shaffer's code attempts to classify an individual's behavior as being either an "action" or a "reaction" to another family member's behavior. Among the class of "actions" are such categories as criticism, information request, statement of personal problem, and complaint. The "reactions," which are presumed to have the potential of maintaining a given behavior, may be either "positive" or "negative." Among the positive categories are approval, laughter, and interest; the negative reactions comprise such responses as disagreement, criticism, punishment, and ignoring.

Within the context of observations in hospital settings, Paul and his associates (Mariotto & Paul, 1974; Paul & Lentz, 1977; Paul, Tobias, & Holly, 1972) developed a time-sample behavioral checklist for use with chronic psychiatric patients. Among the behaviors recorded by trained observers are such categories as verbalized delusions or hallucinations, repetitive and stereotypic movements, grimacing or frowning without apparent stimulus, physical assault, blank staring, and various other forms of inappropriate behavior. Interobserver reliability is high for this checklist, with coefficients typically in the .90s.

Although it might appear at first blush that direct naturalistic observation is the procedure par excellence for carrying out a behavioral assessment, nonetheless, certain methodological problems are associated with this approach. Although there has been a considerable amount of research focusing on method assumptions in naturalistic observations, relatively little attention has been paid to the question of the representativeness of the behaviors sampled. In the case of the time-sample behavioral checklist developed by Paul for use with psychiatric patients, this is not much of an issue, as the observations are carried out

for 2-second intervals during each of the patient's waking hours. Where the issue of sampling assumptions does come into play, however, is with codes in which the observations are made only during certain times and at certain places. The question becomes the legitimacy of generalizing from what is observed to some larger class of behaviors or interactions. As yet, virtually no research efforts have been directed toward this most important issue.

One of the method assumptions associated with naturalistic observations is the extent to which the observers actually interfere with or influence the phenomena they are attempting to assess. This has been labeled the *reactivity* problem within behavioral observation methods. In studying this problem, Purcell and Brady (1966) attempted to determine the extent to which being monitored by a miniature wireless radio transmitter would alter the verbal behavior of a group of adolescents. The subjects were monitored 1 hour per day for a total of 10 successive days, and they seemed to behave more naturally after the first few days. However, the indications that their behavior became more natural were based on somewhat weak criteria, such as the decrease in the number of references made to the transmitter, the amount of talking done, and impressionistic reports of the subjects themselves.

The reactivity issue was followed up by Moos (1968), who studied the effect of wearing a radio transmitter on a group of psychiatric patients observed both when they were wearing the transmitter and when the transmitter was absent. Moos's findings indicated that the effect of being monitored by the radio transmitter was small, and that when it did occur, it occurred in the more disturbed patients. He also found an interaction between individual differences and the setting in which the observation was taking place. One limitation to keep in mind in interpreting these data, however, is that what was really determined was not simply the effect of being observed but the patients' reactions to wearing a transmitter when they knew they were otherwise being observed. In other words, there was no "pure" measure of the patients' behavioral tendencies. The same interpretative limitation applies to the more recent study by Johnson and Bolstad (1975), who found that tape-recorded family interactions were no different when observers were present or absent.

The problem of reactivity is obviously a complex issue, and one that is not easy to study. The nature of the reactivity that may exist probably depends on the subject's knowledge of what aspect of his or her behavior is being observed. There is ample research evidence to indicate that when people are made self-conscious about certain aspects of their behavior by means of self-monitoring, there is a clear effect on the frequency of this behavior (Kazdin, 1974b). However, if individuals are told that they are being observed by someone but are not informed as to what aspects of their behavior are being noted, then the effects are likely to be a more general self-consciousness, and perhaps an attempt to second-guess what the observer is looking for.

With the exception of the ethically questionable procedure of observing individuals without their knowledge, the possibility of reactivity remains a methodological issue to which a behavioral assessor must attend. Thus, observers are usually instructed to remain as unobtrusive as possible (e.g., to "become part of the furniture"). One should also allow for a period of acclimation, to let subjects become accustomed to the presence of observers, and this initial period of observation should not be used as part of the actual baseline against which any behavior change is compared.

Another potential difficulty in satisfying method assumptions has to do with the observers themselves and the extent to which any source of bias may be associated with the observation process. In this regard, unreliability among independent observers may be a function of differential expectancies about what is supposed to be occurring and/or idiosyncratic interpretations of the behavior code.

Researchers in the area of behavioral observation have been concerned about the findings of Rosenthal (1966) and others that an experimenter or observer effect may exist under certain circumstances. The question here is whether any initial hypotheses or expectations regarding what is "supposed to be seen" can influence the observation process itself. Some data by Kent, O'Leary, Diament, and Dietz (1974) suggest that, to the extent to which one uses a behaviorally anchored observational code, biases resulting from differential expectancy can be kept to a minimum. This study used the code described in O'Leary and O'Leary (1972), and the authors experimentally manipulated observers' expectations regarding the type of change likely to occur. In one condition, the observers were told that the therapeutic treatment procedures being used on the children they were observing were expected to produce a decrease in disruptive behavior. In the second condition, the observers were told that no behavior change was anticipated. In reality, both groups of observers viewed the same videotapes, which in fact showed no change in the frequency of disruptive behavior from baseline to treatment phase. The study did not show any differences in the *use of the behavioral code* as a function of differential expectations; in contrast, the overall, more *impressionistic judgments* of change in the two conditions were significantly influenced by initial expectations. The influence on global impression is particularly striking, especially since these observers had just carried out concrete and detailed observations providing information contrary to their overall impressions.

A follow-up study by O'Leary, Kent, and Kanowitz (1975) showed that it *was* possible to influence the observer so that a biased observation would emerge even with the use of a concrete behavioral code. The observers were informed that the children they would be rating on the videotapes were participating in a token reinforcement program in which two specific disruptive classes of behavior were being modified while two others were not being treated. As was the case in the previous study, the tapes revealed no actual behavior change whatsoever. Each time the observers coded the behavior and turned in their data, the experimenter provided them with differential feedback. If the data submitted were consistent with what was initially stated as an anticipated predicted change, the experimenter offered positive feedback (e.g., "These tokens are really reducing the level of vocalization"). If no change from baseline was manifested in the observation, but one was actually "predicted," the experimenter would say such things as "We really ought to be picking up some decreases in the rate of playing by now." The results of this study revealed that when the observers received this differential feedback, they eventually presented the "expected" results.

In dealing with the expectancy issue, then, every attempt should be made to define the behavioral categories as concretely and operationally as possible. Observers should not be informed of the changes expected, and, if possible, they should be kept "blind" as to the experimental or therapeutic manipulations applied to the individuals being observed. Further, the observational data should not be inspected in any detail while the study is under way, so that any inadvertent reinforcement for what the observer has recorded may be avoided.

A related methodological problem is the extent to which independent observers can reliably utilize a given behavioral code. Although it seems evident that potential sources of unreliability are reduced when one utilizes a coding system focusing on specific behaviors, it should also be pointed out that most behavioral codes nonetheless require a certain amount of interpretation. For example, if one is attempting to observe the incidence with which children in a classroom are engaging in "off-task" behavior (i.e., not doing their work), some problems of interpretation may arise. Such a category represents a large behavior class, under which a wide variety of specific behaviors may fall, and the observer needs to be familiar with the potential specific behaviors that can be scored in this category, and to be able to differentiate them from "on-task" behaviors. There are times, however, when a judgment about a specific behavior may be most difficult to make. What of a child who is supposed to be doing his or her arithmetic assignment in class but spends periods of time toying with his or her pencil? Should this be considered an instance of off-task behavior? Or is this recurrent behavior something the child engages in when he or she pauses to concentrate on a problem? For each particular observational code, the specificity of guidelines for resolving such ambiguities can have substantial bearing on observer reliability.

A typical finding reported for each of the behavioral observational codes described above has been that interobserver reliability is in fact quite good. But what has emerged in looking at this issue more closely is that a kind of reactivity exists when observers realize that *their* behavior is being observed. This effect was dramatically demonstrated in a study by Reid (1970), who trained and examined the performance of observers in the use of a behavioral code and then had them apply the code in observations of behavior they viewed on videotape recordings. Before viewing the videotapes, the observers were led to believe that no reliability check would be made and that they would be the only ones doing the rating. The results indicated that in comparison with a reliability coefficient of .76 when the observers thought their reliability was being evaluated, there was a sharp drop to a coefficient of .51 once the raters felt that they were completely on their own.

Elaborating this phenomena are some findings by Romanczyk, Kent, Diament, and O'Leary (1973), who not only confirmed Reid's finding that interobserver reliability was higher when the observers felt that their accuracy was being evaluated but additionally found that interobserver agreement could be increased further by providing the raters with information as to exactly who was going to be checking their reliability. In other words, it was possible for the observers to modify their interpretation of the code so as to be more consistent with the criteria employed by the specific person doing the reliability check.

Another potential source of unreliability that sometimes goes unnoticed is the "drift" problem (O'Leary & Kent, 1973). A typical procedure in the application of behavioral codes involves the use of terms of observers. Following the observation periods, the teams often have the opportunity to compare their observations more closely and to discuss among themselves any potential sources of unreliability. As a result of working together, various ambiguities in the use of a code are clarified. Although this at first does not seem to be an undesirable practice, a problem arises when each team begins to develop its own idiosyncratic interpretation of the code. This problem is not readily apparent, as the reliability checks made between pairs of observers lead one to conclude that interobserver agreement is good. However, even though teams of observers are in fact reliably applying the behavioral code, they may drift away from each other with regard to what they are actually observing. To the extent that such drift occurs, the different teams of observers are unwittingly utilizing different behavioral codes.

As in the case of the expectancy problem, unreliability among observers may be kept to a minimum by clarifying any ambiguities inherent in the behavioral code. Further, a more extensive training period can be utilized, the reliability of observers can be constantly monitored, and teams of observers can be continually rotated so as to prevent any potential drift.

One final point might be made in this discussion of observations in naturalistic settings. From a practical point of view, it may not always be feasible to have trained observers readily available. In fact, much of what has been described thus far is much more likely to be carried out within the context of a research program than in routine clinical work. The reason should be obvious: the systematic implementation of many of these observation procedures can be very costly. As a practical compromise, behavioral observations have been carried out by individuals typically present in the subject's naturalistic environment, such as friends, spouses, parents, teachers, nurses, and other significant individuals. Although their observations are not likely to be detailed or precise as those of more highly trained observers, there is a definite advantage in obtaining information from individuals who have occasion to view the subject over relatively long periods of time, in a wide variety of situations, and with minimal likelihood of reactivity. Among the various behavior checklists that have been employed are those that utilize the observations of psychiatric nurses (Honigfeld, Gillis, & Klett, 1966), classmates (Wiggins & Winder, 1961), and teachers (Ross, Lacey, & Parton, 1965).

Situation Tests

A basic limitation associated with observations in naturalistic settings is that one typically has little control over the situation to which the subject or client must respond. Although every attempt is made to standardize the setting in which the observation is to take place—such as carrying out home observations during dinnertime—little can be done to control exactly what goes on at this time and place. Thus, depending on what may be said or done to the person being observed, his or her behavior can vary greatly. As a way of circumventing these shortcomings, behavioral assessors have made use of various situation tests.

Although situation tests have been used for assessment purposes in the past (e.g., Office of Strategic Services Assessment Staff, 1948), their use by behavioral assessors has focused specifically on confronting the subject with situations likely to elicit the type of behavior toward which the assessment is specifically directed. Not only is the individual's behavior objectively observed in such situations but, whenever relevant, subjective and physiological measures of anxiety are employed as well.

One frequently employed situation test was devised by Paul (1966) in conjunction with an outcome study on the effectiveness of systematic desensitization in treating speech anxiety. The situation test, which was used as a measure of improvement, required subjects to present a 4-minute speech before a live audience. Immediately before giving the talk, they were administered self-report and physiological measures of anxiety. During the speech itself, trained observers in the audience recorded various overt signs of anxiety, coding such behaviors as extraneous hand movements, hand tremors, pacing, and absence of eye contact. This type of situation test has proved useful in a variety of other clinical outcome studies (e.g., Goldfried & Trier, 1974; Meichenbaum, Gilmore, & Fedoravicious, 1971).

Situation tests have also been employed for the assessment of interpersonal anxiety (e.g., Borkovec, Fleischmann, & Caputo, 1973; Borkovec, Stone, O'Brien, & Kaloupek, 1974; Kanter & Goldfried, 1979). In these assessments, the subject is required to maintain a brief conversation with one or two trained confederates of the experimenter, the interaction is videotaped, and the subject's performance is evaluated in terms of behavioral, subjective report and physiological indexes of anxiety.

Research on this procedure has demonstrated that the interaction situation is capable of eliciting emotional arousal in individuals for whom interpersonal anxiety is a problem.

The interpersonal skills of chronic psychiatric patients have been assessed by means of the Minimal Social Behavior Scale, a procedure originally developed by Farina, Arenberg, and Guskin (1957). The scale is applied within a standardized interview requiring the interviewer to do various things (e.g., drop a pencil on the floor) or to ask various questions (e.g., "How are you today?"). The scale comprises 32 different items, each of which is scored as eliciting either an appropriate or an inappropriate response. The scoring criteria are clearly spelled out, and the interrater reliability is high. Although one may legitimately raise the question whether the behavior observed within the context of the particular interview setting is a representative sample of the patient's behavior in all situations, the scale has nonetheless been shown to be sensitive to behavior change following drug treatment and to discriminate among patients at varying levels of functioning (Farina *et al.*, 1957; Ulmer & Timmons, 1966).

Numerous attempts have been made to assess assertive behavior by means of controlled situation tests (e.g., Kazdin, 1974a; McFall & Lillesand, 1971; McFall & Marston, 1970; McFall & Twentyman, 1973). Subjects were called on the telephone, and some unreasonable request was made of them. This request, which varied from study to study, entailed either purchasing a subscription to several magazines or lending one's lecture notes immediately prior to a final examination. The subject's response was unobtrusively recorded and later evaluated by judges for its assertiveness. In most of these studies, however, the assessment procedure failed to discriminate between individuals who were otherwise found to have changed as a function of assertion training. Although it is certainly possible that the inability to obtain positive results could have resulted from a failure to sample adequately from situations in which the subject actually achieved behavior change, positive results found in one instance by McFall and Twentyman (1973) suggest that the methodology may have been at fault. Instead of

making a single unreasonable request during the telephone conversation, they presented the subject with a series of seven increasingly unreasonable requests. The telephone calls were made less than a week before a scheduled final examination and began by simply asking the subject to spend a few minutes discussing the lecture material. The subject was then confronted with a series of more and more outlandish requests, which culminated in a request to lend out his or her lecture notes for two full days prior to the examination. By extending the nature of the interaction in this manner, the assessment procedure was found to be more sensitive in detecting changes resulting from assertion training.

Situation tests have also been employed in observations of the way in which parents interact with their children. This procedure is frequently done behind a one-way mirror, with the situation constructed in such a way as to sample the type of instances in which the child's problematic behaviors typically occur. For example, if the child's primary problem consists of having difficulty in working independently, one might set up a section of the room where he or she is asked to carry out various homework problems while his or her mother is involved in some other task in another section of the room. The behavior of both parent and child can then be observed, providing data useful in a functional analysis of the child's difficulties.

One additional example of a situation test should be discussed, not only because it represents one of the more frequently used behavioral assessment procedures but also because it may serve to illustrate some of the potential methodological problems inherent in situation tests. The assessment procedure is the Behavioral Avoidance Test (BAT), which is used as a means of evaluating the strength of fears and phobias. Although the exact procedures have varied somewhat from study to study (see Bernstein & Nietzel, 1973), the test basically requires that the individual enter a room in which the feared object is present (e.g., a snake in a cage), walk closer to the object, look at it, touch it, and, if possible, hold it. In addition to evaluating how closely the subject is willing to approach the object, subjective, physiological, and overt behavioral indexes of anxiety may be assessed as well. In addition to various small-animal phobias (e.g., snakes, rats, spiders, dogs), more clinically relevant fears have also been assessed by means of the BAT, such as the fear of enclosed places and heights.

For several years, behavioral assessors utilizing the BAT in their research have assumed that the measure provided them with a completely accurate assessment of an individual's phobia. More recent tests of the method assumptions underlying this procedure, however, have revealed that this may not always be the case. When an individual enters an assessment session, whether for research or clinical purposes, there are certain socially defined characteristics of the situation that can influence his or her response. An illustration of such so-called demand characteristics of situations was first demonstrated by Orne (1962), who showed that the mere participation in an experiment was reactive, causing subjects to behave in ways that were perhaps atypical of them. In one experiment, for example, Orne had a group of subjects enter a room and gave them the tedious task of adding up columns of figures on a sheet of paper, after which they were instructed to tear the paper into small pieces, throw them in the air, and begin with a new list of figures. The subjects persisted at this task for long periods of time, simply because it was the thing to do in this situation.

In the case of the BAT, research evidence is accumulating to the effect that here, too, subjects' perception of the demand characteristics of the assessment can greatly influence the extent to which they will approach the feared object or stay in the phobic situation. A study by Miller and Bernstein (1972), for example, divided a group of claustrophobic subjects into two experimental conditions, after which they were individually put in a small, dark chamber. Under a low-demand condition, subjects were told that they could leave the room at any point by simply signaling, whereas under a high-demand condition, they were encouraged to stay in the room regardless of how anxious they might be. Following this experimental procedure, the conditions were reversed, so that the subjects who were initially in the low-demand group were

now in the high-demand group, and vice versa. The findings clearly demonstrated the very powerful effect that the demand-characteristic instructions had on the subjects' behavior, in that the subjects under low-demand instructions behaved more phobically than those under the high-demand condition. This was true when a comparison was made between groups of subjects and also when the instructions were changed for each subject individually. A second finding of some interest was that the experimental instructions, although they had a clear effect on the subjects' behavior, had no impact on their anxiety reactions as measured by either subjective report or physiological measures.

Further investigation of the effect of demand characteristics when the BAT was used to assess small-animal phobias has similarly revealed that changing the subjects' perception of the task requirements can significantly influence their willingness to approach caged rats (Smith, Diener, & Beaman, 1974) and snakes (Bernstein & Neitzel, 1973). The Smith et al. study additionally confirmed the finding noted by Miller and Bernstein (1972) that although the demand characteristics of the situation can significantly alter approach behavior, they have relatively little impact on the subjective and physiological indexes of anxiety.

In evaluating the BAT in light of the research findings on demand characteristics, as well as with the hindsight that the early users of this assessment procedure obviously did not have, it is not at all surprising that subjects' approach behavior is influenced by factors unrelated to their actual phobia. All of us are aware of instances in which otherwise fearful individuals have been able to do things "on a dare," or in which people have displayed unusual acts of courage despite the high level of anxiety they might have been experiencing at the time.

The nature of the demand characteristics one chooses to convey in administering the BAT should probably vary as a function of the experimenter's or clinician's purpose for the assessment. If one wishes to screen out all but the most phobic of individuals, then the demand characteristics for approaching the feared objects should be set as high as possible. If, however, one wishes to predict how the individual is likely to respond in a more naturalistic context—such as when one is out in the woods and notices a snake climbing down a tree—then the BAT should be contrived so as to parallel the real-life situation more accurately. The exact way in which this parallel may be implemented and validated constitutes a challenge to the ingenuity of behavioral assessors.

One of the problems associated with the assessment of phobic behavior is that it is comprised of an operant as well as a respondent, the implication of which is that it can at times be influenced by external contingencies. The fact that demand characteristics are not necessarily an issue in all situation tests, however, is clearly illustrated in a study by Borkovec, Stone, O'Brien, and Kaloupek (1974). Borkovec *et al.* found that instructions to behave "in a relaxed, nonanxious manner" had no influence on subjects' performance in a situation test of heterosexual anxiety. In comparison with the assessment of phobic behavior, this situation test focused solely on anxiety, as measured by self-report, behavior signs, and physiological indexes. In all likelihood, the potential influence of demand characteristics on situation tests depends on the extent to which the behavior being measured is under the subject's voluntary control.

In concluding this discussion of situation tests, there is a possible methodological issue inherent in all of them that has yet to be investigated, namely, the *difficulty level* of the task presented to the subject. Take, for example, the use of a situation test for assessing public-speaking anxiety. Although practical limitations obviously limit what can actually be implemented, one can easily think of a wide variety of situations in which to place the speech-anxious individual: audiences may vary in their size and composition, the length of the speech can be short or long, the preparation period can be extensive or minimal, the topic can be familiar or strange, and numerous other variations may be introduced to vary the aversiveness of the situation.

What most users of situation tests have not addressed themselves to is just how difficult the task should be for the subject. To take the extremes, it is obvious that speaking to two individuals for a brief period of time about a topic with which one is familiar is likely to elicit less anxiety than speaking at length to a group of several hundred about an unfamiliar topic. In a situation test used to assess change in clinical outcome studies, there is probably some interaction between the effectiveness of one's treatment procedure and the difficulty level reflected in the test situation. More powerful and extensive therapeutic interventions are likely to have more of an impact on higher levels of anxiety, whereas briefer and less effective therapies will probably reflect changes at lower levels only. Thus, depending on how one constructs the situation test in such research, the experimental findings are likely to vary. What may be called for in the use of the situation tests in the future, then, is to present a series of increasingly difficult tasks to the subject, thereby providing a potentially more sensitive measure of behavior change.

Role Playing

Although there are similarities between certain situation tests as described above and a role-playing approach to assessment, the primary distinction between the two is that the situation test focuses on placing subjects in the real-life situation, whereas role playing requires subjects to react "as if" the event were occurring to them in real life. Although the line between the two may be a fine one at times, it is probably wise to maintain this distinction until it has been demonstrated empirically that the differences between the two procedures are nonfunctional.

The use of role playing for assessment purposes was described several years ago in a report by Rotter and Wickens (1948), whose stated rationale for the procedure is quite consistent with a behavioral orientation to assessment. They suggested that sampling behavioral interactions has considerable potential for providing the assessor with useful information, primarily because of the extent to which it parallels criterion behavior. Rotter and Wickens were interested mainly in demonstrating the feasibility of conducting such an assessment, and consequently, they report no validity data for their procedure. The subjects in their study were required to respond to various simulated situations, and their behavior in these instances was rated by judges according to the degree to which "social aggressiveness" was reflected. This report is important in that it offers an early statement of the potential utility of this procedure.

Another early use of role playing as an assessment device is reported in a study by Stanton and Litwak (1955), who provided validity data of a most encouraging sort. Using foster parents and college students as their subject populations, they attempted to assess "interpersonal competence." The subjects were presented with three situations—meeting a troubled friend, handling an interfering parent, and criticizing an employee—and their responses were rated for competence with the aid of a behavior checklist. Highly significant correlations were found between observers' ratings of the subjects' behavior during role-playing situations and evaluations obtained from individuals who knew the subjects well. For the foster parents, a correlation of .82 was found with social workers' ratings; in the case of students, friends' ratings correlated .93 with the scores obtained from the role-playing assessment. Not unexpected, but nonetheless providing discriminant validity, was the finding that criterion ratings provided by individuals who did not know the subjects well did not correlate nearly as well with the role-playing assessment. Moreover, when the role playing was compared with an assessment based on 12 hours of intensive interviews, the role playing was found to fare considerably better in matching the ratings of well-acquainted individuals.

In more recent years, role playing has gained in popularity among behavioral assessors as a means of evaluating the effectiveness of various therapeutic procedures. One of the initial uses of role playing in this context is described by Rehm and Marston (1968), who developed a procedure for assessing heterosexual anxiety in males. In an attempt to standardize the procedure and to make it otherwise more practically feasible, a series of 10 social situations was presented on audiotape. Each situation begins with a description of the context, after which there is a comment by a female requiring some response on the part of the subject.

For example, one situation starts with the narrator describing a scene in the college cafeteria in which the subject is walking out, when he suddenly is approached by a female. At this point in the tape, a female voice states, "I think you left this book." For each of these situations, the subject is asked to imagine that it is actually occurring to him at the moment and to respond as he would in real life. The response is recorded on a separate tape recorder and evaluated later for such characteristics as anxiety, adequacy of response, length of response, and delay before responding. In comparisons with the scores of subjects not volunteering for a therapy program focusing on heterosexual anxiety, the role-playing scores for those participating in the clinical research were found by Rehm and Marston to be significantly different. Performance on the role-playing assessment was furthermore found to change as a function of the therapeutic intervention.

A role-playing assessment procedure similar to that used by Rehm and Marston was investigated by Arkowitz, Lichtenstein, McGovern, and Hines (1975), who compared the performance of high versus low socially competent males as determined independently on the basis of their frequency of dating and their subjective comfort, social skills, and general satisfaction in their heterosexual behaviors. Two role-playing situations were studied, one conducted *in vivo* with a female confederate and the other involving a role-played telephone conversation. In the face-to-face situation, subjects were asked to imagine that they had just met this female and were attempting to get to know her better. In the telephone conversation, the subject was instructed to ask the female confederate for a date. The primary finding was that the low socially competent individuals displayed a lower rate of verbal activity than the high socially competent subjects in each of these role-played situations.

In a comprehensive program designed to assess and facilitate interpersonal skills among psychiatric inpatients, Goldsmith and McFall (1975) employed the behavioral-analytic model (Goldfried & D'Zurilla, 1969) in developing a role-playing assessment procedure. Twenty-five separate situations were sampled from various aspects of the patients' typical day-today interactions, each of which was then presented to them on audiotape with instructions to respond as they would in a real-life situation. The subjects' responses to each situation were rated on the basis of certain predetermined and reliably applied criteria for interpersonal effectiveness. Goldsmith and McFall found that as a result of a behavior training program designed to facilitate interpersonal skills, the scores of these patients on the role-playing assessment procedures showed significant improvement. No change was found for control subjects who had been assigned to attention-placebo or no-contact conditions.

Another related problem area that has been assessed by means of role-playing procedures is assertive behavior. The initial work in this area was reported by McFall and Marston (1970), who sampled several situations representative of instances in which college students might be required to assert themselves. These included being interrupted by a friend while attempting to study, having one's laundry lost by the cleaners, and being asked to work by an employer at a time that would be inconvenient. Following the methodology originally devised by Rehm and Marston (1968), the situations were presented to subjects on audiotapes, and their responses were recorded on a second tape recorder. In this particular study, the subjects' responses were not scored; instead, independent judges carried out a paired comparison between the subjects' behavior before and after assertion training. These judges' ratings, which were completely blind as to which interaction was obtained before and which after therapy, revealed significant improvement in role-played assertive behavior.

A later report by McFall and Lillesand (1971) indicated that when assertiveness was rated on the basis of a 5-point scale, interrater reliability was in the .90s. McFall and Lillesand also reported some experimentation with a modification of the role-played assessment procedure. Rather than presenting the situation and asking the subject to give his or her typical response, the interaction was extended so as to parallel more closely what might occur in a real-life situation. Specifically, if the subject was successful in refusing the unreasonable request, the taped confederate would

press him or her further, for a total of five "pushes." This variation in the assessment procedure also revealed changes reflecting the effects of assertion training.

A series of studies on the role-playing assessment of assertive behavior within a population of psychiatric patients has also been carried out by Eisler and his associates (Eisler, Hersen, & Agras, 1973a,b; Eisler, Hersen & Miller, 1973; Eisler, Miller, & Hersen, 1973; Hersen, Eisler, Miller, Johnson, & Pinkston, 1973). The role-playing assessment procedure consisted of 14 situations in which a male psychiatric patient was required to interact with a female confederate in such standard impositions as having someone cut ahead in line, having one's reserved seat taken at a ball game, having a steak delivered overcooked at a restaurant, and having a service station carry out extensive repairs on one's car without previous approval. Unlike most role-playing measures of assertive training, the Eisler interaction is carried out *in vivo*, and the ratings of assertiveness are based on videotape recordings of the interaction. The reliability of ratings is generally high for both an overall rating of assertiveness and ratings of several behavioral components. Among those components that have been found to improve as a result of assertion training are duration of reply, affective quality of response, loudness of response, and content of assertive reply (Eisler, Hersen, & Miller, 1973).

Although much of the work on the use of role playing as an assessment procedure is promising, relatively little attention has been paid to any potential methodological problems that may serve to attenuate its effectiveness, such as the failure to satisfy both method and sampling assumptions (see Goldfried & Kent, 1972). Among the method assumptions that need to be satisfied is the extent to which the behavior of the confederate can be appropriately standardized. Standardization can be achieved by providing the confederate with detailed guidelines and adequate training, or more simply by presenting a tape-recorded stimulus situation.

Although most users of role-playing assessment report good interrater reliability, virtually no attempt has been made to control for the possible occurrence of a "halo effect."

That a halo effect may be an issue is reflected in the study by Rotter and Wickens (1948). They found that when a given subject's role-played responses to two separate situations were rated by the same judges, the average interrater reliability of the subject's behavior in these two situations was .78. However, when different judges were used to rate the subjects' behavior in the two separate situations, the average correlations were only .55. The erroneously imposed cross-situational consistency may very well have accounted for the spuriously higher correlation obtained originally. As discussed in conjunction with behavioral observation in naturalistic settings, there are numerous potential sources of bias when one sets out to observe and code human behavior. Thus, the issues of observer expectancies, continual monitoring of reliability, and the possibility of drift among pairs of observers need to be attended to in the coding of role-playing interactions as well.

The question of demand characteristics has yet to be a topic of empirical investigation in the use of role-playing assessment. Are subjects truly "in role" during the assessment procedure, or are they somehow responding to some unique aspects of the demand characteristics within the assessment setting? Is it easier or more difficult for subjects to behave as they typically would when the stimulus situation is presented on audiotape as compared with an *in vivo* interaction? Are there any individual differences associated with subjects' abilities to immerse themselves naturally in the role-playing interaction? These are only some of the questions related to method assumptions that need to be answered.

With regard to the question of sampling assumptions, most developers of role-playing assessment procedures have used only a few situations, selected more or less on an *a priori* basis. Among the exceptions have been the procedures outlined by Bates (1980), Bellack, Hersen, and Lamparski (1979), DeLange, Lanham, and Barton (1981), Edleson and Rose (1978), Freedman *et al.* (1978), Goldsmith and McFall (1975), Mathews *et al.* (1980), and Perri and Richards (1979), who conducted an empirically based situational analysis. Unless one assumes cross-situational consistency with whatever variable one is assessing (e.g., social skills or assertiveness), some form of empirical sampling is essential if one wishes to generalize the finding of the assessment.

Self-Report

In using self-report procedures, behavioral assessors have focused on the report of specific behavioral interactions, on subjective reports of emotional response, and on perceptions of environmental settings. Each of these areas of assessment is described below.

Self-Report of Overt Behavior. The behavioral characteristic that has been the focus of most self-report measures of overt behavior is assertiveness. For example, Wolpe and Lazarus (1966) described a series of 30 questions that they recommend be asked of clients in assessing the extent to which they may be inhibited in expressing their opinion in interpersonal situations. More recent questionnaires, based in part on the questions described by Wolpe and Lazarus, have been devised by Rathus (1973), Galassi, DeLo, Galassi, and Bastien (1974), Gambrill and Richey (1975), and Gay, Hollandsworth, and Galassi (1975). Although the formats of these more recent questionnaires are slightly different, the assessment inventories are more similar than they are different. In fact, some of the items are virtually identical. The questionnaires are similarly limited in the sense that they fail to satisfy the sampling assumptions essential in the development of behavioral assessment procedures. For the most part, the items in these inventories were taken from previous questionnaires or were determined on an *a priori* basis. In using these inventories, the general trait of assertiveness is assumed, and no subscales reflecting different aspects of one's interactions (e.g., with friends, strangers, or authority figures) are available.

A more sophisticated approach to the development of a measure of assertiveness may be seen in the work of McFall and Lillesand (1971), whose focus was specifically on the ability of college students to refuse unreasonable requests. Their Conflict Resolution Inventory consists of 35 items, each of which is specific to a particular situation in which some unreasonable request might be made of the subject. For example, one such item is "You are in the thick of studying for exams when a person whom you know only slightly comes into your room and says, 'I'm tired of studying. Mind if I come in and take a break for awhile?'" For each item, subjects are to indicate the likelihood that they would refuse each of the requests and how comfortable they would feel about either refusing or giving in. Unlike the developers of the other assertiveness questionnaires described above, McFall and Lillesand derived their items empirically on the basis of extensive pilot work, in which the sample of college students used in generating the initial item pool was similar to the subject population to whom the assessment measure was later to be applied. The Conflict Resolution Inventory has been found to be useful as a dependent variable in clinical outcome studies (McFall & Lillesand, 1971; McFall & Twentyman, 1973), in which change was found to occur as a function of assertion training.

Self-Report of Emotion. Although the assessment of overt behavior—whether via self-reports of behavior, naturalistic observation, situation tests, or role playing—holds considerable promise, there is more to human functioning than a person's overt behavior can reveal. As noted earlier, several reports indicate that even when demand characteristics influence an individual's performance on a behavioral avoidance test, subjective reports of anxiety remain unaffected (Miller & Bernstein, 1972; Smith, Diener, & Beaman, 1974). Furthermore, there are instances, as in an outcome study on acrophobia reported by Jacks (1972), in which subjective reports of anxiety may be more sensitive to differential change than is approach behavior.

A measure frequently used by behavioral assessors in the self-report of anxiety is the Fear Survey Schedule (Geer, 1965). The schedule consists of a series of 51 potentially anxiety-arousing situations and objects (e.g., snakes, being alone, looking foolish), which subjects are asked to rate for the degree of fear typically elicited in them. The schedule is at best a gross screening device and should probably be viewed as nothing more than that. Although some researchers have attempted to carry out extensive factor analyses of the

schedule to determine the potential dimensions of fear, such research activities are of dubious value, especially as no attempt was originally made to sample representatively the full range of fears and phobias typically present in most individual's lives.

Although several attempts have been made to use the Fear Survey Schedule to predict subjects' reactions to a behavioral avoidance task, the data on its predictive efficiency have been mixed. In viewing these conflicting findings, it is important to keep in mind that these two measures of fear are of a very different form, in the sense that one is primarily verbal and the other more behaviorally observable. Moreover, these two measures appear to focus on different aspects of anxiety. In the case of the Fear Survey Schedule, subjects are asked to state how afraid they would feel when in the presence of certain situations or objects. When subjects are placed in the behavioral avoidance task, the primary measure consists of the extent to which they will approach the feared object. As noted earlier, there are often situations in which the demand characteristics or the task requirements are such that individuals, despite their feelings of fear and trepidation, will approach a feared object or remain in anxiety-producing circumstances.

In the context of research on the way in which demand characteristics affect performance on the behavioral avoidance test, Bernstein (1973) demonstrated that the Fear Survey Schedule could differentially predict approach behavior, depending on the situational context in which the behavioral avoidance test was carried out. When the test was carried out in a clinic context, subjects' initial reports on the Fear Survey Schedule were predictive of their actions. However, the verbal reports of subjects who participated in the avoidance test conducted in a laboratory setting had no relationship to their likelihood of approaching a feared object.

Whatever assets the Fear Survey Schedule may have as a relatively quick and easily administered screening device, there are nonetheless certain limitations that severely restrict its utility. Perhaps the most telling of these is the fact that subjects are required to indicate their degree of fear about situations or objects that are described in only general and very vague terms (e.g., "being criticized"). The nature of the situation (e.g., who is doing the criticizing and what the criticism is about) is left unspecified. Furthermore, the nature of the person's anxiety response (e.g., sweaty palms, increased heart rate, or desire to run away) is not assessed by the questionnaire.

A commonly used self-report measure of anxiety that takes into account the nature of the situation, as well as each of the possible components of the anxiety response, is described by Endler, Hunt, and Rosenstein (1962). Their assessment prodecure, called the S–R Inventory of Anxiousness, consists of a series of potentially anxiety-arousing situations that are briefly described in writing, after which there are several rating scales reflecting varying ways in which a person might become anxious. For example, one such situation is "You are about to take an important final examination," for which subjects are asked to indicate the extent to which their "heart beats faster," they "get an uneasy feeling," their "emotions disrupt action," and several other reactions indicative of anxiety.

The S–R inventory is important for its utility as a dependent measure and also as a vehicle for studying the question of cross-situational behavioral consistency. In keeping with the behavioral orientation to assessment, which emphasizes the importance of the situation to which an individual reacts, research with the S–R inventory is useful in learning more about the extent to which individual differences and consistencies may manifest themselves in various types of situations.

Both the Fear Survey Schedule and the S–R Inventory of Anxiousness ask subjects to indicate their typical reaction. In a sense, these self-reports are hypothetical, since they are based on the subjects' *recollections* of how they reacted in the past to certain types of situations. Consistent with the overall philosophy that behavioral assessment should focus directly on criterion behavior, it seems only reasonable that behavioral assessors have also made attempts to elicit self-reports of emotional reactivity during the time the individual is actually *in* certain situations, rather than recollecting them. Among the several available subjective measures of situational state anxiety are Spielberger, Gorsuch, and Lushene's (1970) State–Trait Anxiety Inventory and Zuckerman and Lubin's (1965) Multiple Affect Adjective Checklist. The former measures involve a series of descriptive statements, such as "I am tense," "I am jittery," and "I feel calm," which the subject is asked to rate on a 4-point scale for their accuracy as a self-descriptive statements. In the case of the Multiple Affect Adjective Checklist, feelings of depression and hostility, as well as those of anxiety, are assessed. For both of these measures, appropriate changes are frequently found in response to various kinds of experimental manipulations, such as those intended to elicit or reduce stress.

In addition to focusing on various negative emotional states, behavioral assessors have also developed self-report measures to assess positive feelings. For example, Cautela and Kastenbaum (1967) developed a Reinforcement Survey Schedule, which in part parallels the Fear Survey Schedule. Various objects and situations are presented in questionnaire form, and subjects are asked to indicate the extent to which they prefer each of them. This measure suffers from numerous problems, not the least of which is the fact that the items themselves were not empirically derived from a pool of potentially reinforcing events or objects.

In contrast, the Pleasant Events Schedule constructed by MacPhillamy and Lewinsohn (1972) includes items generated from an actual situational analysis. College students were asked to specify "events, experiences, or activities which you find pleasant, rewarding, or fun," and the net result of this sampling was a series of 320 items of both a social and a nonsocial type. In responding to the Pleasant Events Schedule, subjects are asked to indicate not only how often each of these various events might have occurred within the past month but also how pleasant and enjoyable they were. If for some reason subjects have not experienced any particular event, they are simply asked to estimate how enjoyable it might have been if it had occurred. This more sophisticated approach to the assessment of potential reinforcers has been found to be useful in research in the area of depression (Lewinsohn & Graf, 1973; Lewinsohn & Libet, 1972).

Self-Report of Environment. Consistent with the behavioral assessor's interest in the nature of the social environment with which individuals must interact, there is a growing interest in what has been referred to as *social ecology* (Insel & Moos, 1974; Moos, 1973). Moos and his colleagues have been actively involved in developing questionnaires for assessing the social-psychological impact made by various environments, including psychiatric wards, community-oriented psychiatric treatment programs, correctional institutions, military basic-training companies, university student residences, junior and senior high-school classrooms, work environments, and social, therapeutic, and decision-making groups. The questionnaires focus on the individual's perception of various aspects of her or his social environment and include such items as "On this ward everyone knows who's in charge," "Members are expected to take leadership here," and "Members here follow a regular schedule every day."

In assessments of the impact made by varying environmental settings, three dimensions appear to be common across several diverse environmental contexts: the nature and intensity of interpersonal relationships (e.g., peer cohesion and spontaneity); personal development opportunities (e.g., competition and intellectuality); and the stability and responsivity of the social system to change (e.g., order and organization, innovation). In much the same way as the assessment of behavioral characteristics within an individual is relevant to behavioral change, so the various environmental assessment questionnaires have implications for the modification of social environments (Moos, 1974).

Behavioral Assessment and Behavior Therapy

If one interprets behavior therapy in its broadest sense as involving the application of what we know about psychology in general to problems that may manifest themselves within the clinical setting, it follows that the number and variety of behavior therapy procedures available to the clinician are large and forever changing (Goldfried & Davison, 1976). This is clearly a double-edged sword, which provides one with several potentially effective treatment methods, and also with the dilemma of which to use in any given case. With this dilemma in mind, Goldfried and Pomeranz (1968) have argued that "assessment procedures represent a *most crucial and significant* step in the effective application of behavior therapy" (p. 76).

In considering behavioral assessment in the clinical setting, it is useful to make a conceptual distinction between (1) those variables associated with a behavioral analysis of the maladaptive behavior and (2) those that have implications for the selection and implementation of the most relevant therapeutic procedures. In essence, the first set of variables sheds light on *what* has to be manipulated in order to bring about behavior change, while the second set provides information about *how* best to bring about this change.

Variables Associated with Maladaptive Behavior

Viewing the client's maladaptive behavior as a dependent variable, the therapist is required to decide which of many potential independent variables one can best "manipulate" to bring about behavior change. There has been some confusion in the literature about whether behavior therapists actually are manipulating "underlying causes" when attempting to modify problem behaviors. If by *underlying causes* one necessarily means early social learning experiences, then the answer is no. This answer does not imply, however, that the treatment always focuses on the presenting problem. Take, for example, the man whose marriage is foundering because of the frequent arguments he has with his wife. In carrying out a behavioral analysis, it may be revealed that the arguments typically occur when he has been drinking. When does he drink? Whenever he's had a hard day at work. What contributes to the pressure at work? The excessively high standards he imposes on his own performance. Here the therapist would probably focus more on the husband's unrealistic standards of self-evaluation and not on the fighting behavior itself. In other words, the behavioral analysis may "uncover" other relevant variables—not early social learning experiences, but additional concurrent variables within the chain of potential determinants of behavior.

In deciding which variables should be manipulated, the behavior therapist can select from one or more of the following: (1) the antecedent stimulus variables, which may elicit or set the stage for the maladaptive behavior; (2) organismic variables, whether psychological or physiological; (3) the overt maladaptive behavior itself; and (4) the consequent changes in the environmental situation, including the reactions of others to the maladaptive behavior. While the distinction among these four types of variables may at times be arbitrary, it is useful to discuss each separately.

Stimulus Antecedents. Although once highly centralistic, clinicians and personality theorists have begun to recognize the significant role of the environment as an important determinant of behavior. In considering the role of antecedent stimulus events, one may draw a distinction between those that elicit emotional or autonomic responses and those that function as discriminative cues for occurrence of maladaptive instrumental responses.

In dealing with such maladaptive emotional responses as anxiety or depression, the behavior therapist operates under the assumption that some external situation is eliciting the behavior. We must admit, however, that at times it may be no easy task to specify exactly which events in the client's life are determining his or her emotional response. Some individuals report being anxious all of the time or being in very chronic and pervasive states of depression. In such a case, the client's emotional reaction apparently becomes so salient that he or she is unable to pinpoint its functional antecedents. Other clients may be able to indicate general classes of situations to which they are reacting (e.g., heights, enclosed spaces, or social-evaluative situations). Although this general indication clearly simplifies the task of assessment, the need nonetheless exists for greater specification of those situations that have been eliciting the emotional upset.

In the assessment of the discriminative stimuli that set the stage for maladaptive instrumental behaviors that will be reinforced, the therapist must obtain detailed information on the precise nature of the situation, such as time, place, and frequency. Mischel (1968) has argued convincingly that an individual's response, whether it be deviant or nondeviant, is greatly influenced by the specific nature of the situation in which the behavior occurs. We have all had the experience of being surprised when a friend or colleague acts "out of character" in certain situations. Clinically, it is not uncommon to observe a child who presents a behavior problem at home but creates no difficulties in the school. As in the specification of stimuli that elicit maladaptive emotional responses, relevant discriminative stimuli must be described in detail (e.g., What is it about the school setting that differs from the home environment?).

The way individuals interpret events is often important in determining the stimulus antecedents of their behavior. The issue of defining the effective stimulus has prompted those involved in research on perception to focus on the significant role played by the physiological and cognitive states of the individual. We refer to these factors as *organismic variables*.

Organismic Variables. While the increasing recognition of environmental variables as determinants of behavior is a welcome trend, the exclusion of all inferential concepts and the refusal to consider mediating factors can seriously limit the therapist's ability to understand and modify behavior. The completely environmentalistic, noninferential orientation to the study of human functioning, which Murray (1938) has called the *peripheralistic approach*, can limit one's understanding of human behavior as much as an entirely centralistic orientation can. Although an individual's attitudes, beliefs, and expectations may often be modified by changes in overt behavior, there are times when such organismic variables should themselves be the target for direct modification.

One type of mediator consists of the client's

expectations, or set, about certain situations. As suggested by Dollard and Miller (1950), Beck (1967), and Ellis (1962), the way in which people label or categorize events can greatly color their emotional reaction in such situations. In addition to interpreting situations in ways that can create problems, people may also create difficulties by the way they label their own behavior. To the extent that individuals construe their maladaptive behavior as indicative of "going crazy," being out of control, or manifesting a serious physical illness, their problems will be compounded. Another important mediating variable consists of the standards one sets for self-reinforcement. Although clients may be functioning at an appropriate level of proficiency according to societal standards, their primary problem may result from the fact that they construe their behavior as being substandard; in such instances, it would appear that the standard is unrealistic and in need of modification.

In the assessment of organismic variables, one should attend also to any physiological factors that may contribute to the maladaptive behavior. Included here would be the direct and side effects of any psychoactive drugs, the client's general energy level, states of fatigue, and other similar physiological and constitutional factors that might influence his or her behavior. It is not uncommon, for example, for depression to coincide with some women's menstrual periods. It is clear that presenting problems such as headaches, forgetfulness, sexual inadequacy, and other potentially biologically mediated problems require a thorough physical examination.

Response Variables. The primary focus here should be consistent with the general guidelines suggested by Mischel (1968): "In behavioral analysis the emphasis is on what a person *does* in situations rather than on inferences about what attributes he *has* more globally" (p. 10). In other words, the assessment of response variables should focus on situation-specific samples of the maladaptive behavior, including information on duration, frequency, pervasiveness, and intensity.

Although the distinction is at times difficult to make, it is important to differentiate responses that are primarily *respondents* from those that are *operants*. Respondents, where consequences play a relatively minimal role in maintaining the response, typically include such emotional reactions as anxiety, depression, anger, and sexual arousal. Operant or instrumental behavior, on the other hand, includes those responses for which the consequent reinforcement plays a significant role. Examples of maladaptive instrumental behaviors are typically seen in children, particularly where the primary difficulty consists of "behavioral problems." The extensive work done with token economies in schools and institutional settings has similarly focused on instrumental behaviors. Still further examples of operant behavior seen in clinical settings are social skill deficits, such as lack of assertiveness and inappropriate heterosexual behaviors.

There are times when one cannot distinguish between operants and respondents. For example, children who consistently delay going to bed at night because they are "afraid to be alone" may pose assessment problems. The same is true of a multitude of other problems of a primarily avoidant nature, which may be maintained both by an emotional reaction to antecedent stimuli and by consequent changes in the environment following the avoidance response.

Consequent Variables. To a great extent, many of our day-to-day responses, both adaptive and maladaptive, are maintained by their consequences. In determining whether something "pays off," the timing of the consequences can play a significant role. For example, the so-called neurotic paradox (Mowrer, 1950) refers to behaviors having immediate positive consequences, but long-term negative ones, as in the case of alcohol or drug addiction. A frequently existing positive reinforcement may consist of the reactions of significant others. Such reinforcements can include approval and praise, but in some cases, they may simply be attention, as when a parent or teacher becomes angry over a child's refusal to obey a given command. In addition to the delay and content of reinforcement, one should note also the frequency of reinforcement, as in the case of depressed individuals who have few reinforcing events in their life situation.

Variables Associated with the Selection and Implementation of Techniques

In addition to using assessment procedures to determine which variables—whether antecedent, organismic, response, or consequent—need to be modified, the clinician must also make an assessment to find the most appropriate therapeautic technique. Unlike many other clinicians, behavior therapists choose from a wide range of possible procedures. In part, the selection of therapeutic technique is determined by the target in need of modification. For example, if a detailed behavioral analysis done with a test-anxious client reveals that the difficulties arise because this individual does not study, one would obviously not utilize a technique such as desensitization. Or, for a client whose anxiety in social situations is due to an actual behavioral deficit, some sort of skill-training procedure would be more appropriate than desensitization.

At present, we have relatively little empirical data on specific variables associated with the effective implementation of the various behavior therapy procedures. Some findings are just beginning to become available, such as Kanter and Goldfried's (1979) report that cognitive restructuring may be more appropriate than desensitization in cases of social anxiety. However, most of our clinical decisions are based on the intrinsic nature of the procedure itself (e.g., you cannot use systematic desensitization with a client who is unable to conjure up an aversive image) as well as on clinical experience in the use of the various procedures.

There are certain client characteristics that are relevant to the selection and implementation of therapeutic procedures. The client's ability to report specific concrete examples is frequently crucial in the implementation of a number of therapeutic techniques. One clinical observation is that those clients who have the greatest initial difficulty in reporting actual behavioral sample tend to be brighter and more "psychologically sophisticated." Clients who have this difficulty must be trained to be more specific (e.g., via repeated instructions, selective reinforcement, and homework assignments) before anything can be done therapeutically.

A number of the techniques used by behavior therapists include ongoing homework assignments, in which clients must keep a record of various behavioral events between sessions or practice certain skills *in vivo*. If clients tend to be disorganized or to procrastinate, which may or may not be part of the primary target behaviors toward which the therapy is being directed, they will probably be less likely to carry through on the between-session assignments. In such instances, the therapist must decide to rely less on homework or must attempt to persuade or otherwise aid the client to follow through on these tasks.

The therapist should also be attuned to clients' standards for self-reinforcement. Clients with perfectionistic standards may expect too much too fast and consequently may become discouraged with the gradualness of behavior change. It is important to take great care to discuss this potential difficulty with such clients prior to the actual implementation of whatever technique is to be used. One can also dispel potential dissatisfaction by focusing continually on the client's appropriate evaluation of behavior change as it begins to occur. A fuller discussion of this issue can be found in Goldfried and Robins (in press).

In addition to client variables, certain environmental variables may be important in the selection and implementation of therapeautic procedures. Included here are such considerations as the availability of appropriate role models in a client's life or the extent to which certain reinforcers are likely to be available for certain behaviors. In the treatment of sexual problems, for example, the availability of a partner can have obvious implications for the specific therapeutic procedures utilized. Other examples are the various phobias, where the feasibility of *in vivo* desensitization depends on the availability of fear-related situations or objects.

At present, one typically uses clinical intuition and experience as an aid in determining what seems to be the most appropriate behavior-therapy technique for a particular client. Clinical practice involves selecting a few seemingly relevant techniques and then trying each in turn until one proves to be effective. A better strategy would seem to involve the use of a thorough "criterion analysis" of each behavior-therapy procedure, with the goal being the determination of those variables necessary for the selection of the most effective treatment for any given client. In the most comprehensive sense, the relevant research question is "*What* treatment, by *whom,* is most effective for *this* individual with *that* specific problem, and under *which* set of circumstances?" (Paul, 1967, p. 111).

Classification of Behavior Disorders

The Kraepelinian system of classifying deviant behavior has been criticized on a number of counts, not the least of which is its scant relevance to a behavioral approach to the understanding and modification of behavior (Adams, Doster, & Calhoun, 1977; Kanfer & Saslow, 1969). Alternate classification systems that are more behavioral in nature have been described by Adams *et al.* (1977) and Staats (1963). What follows is based on Staats's suggestions, which have been elaborated on by Bandura (1968) and Goldfried and Sprafkin (1974). In outlining various categories of deviant behaviors, this interim approximation attempts to take into account stimulus as well as client variables. Further, it categorizes deviant behaviors according to the variables that are probably maintaining them.

Difficulties in Stimulus Control of Behavior

Within this general category, the distinction is drawn between the failure of environmental stimuli to control maladaptive *instrumental* behavior and the tendency of some stimuli to elicit maladaptive *emotional* reactions.

Defective Stimulus Control. In instances of defective stimulus control, the individual presumably possesses an adequate behavioral repertoire but is unable to respond to socially appropriate discriminative stimuli. An extreme example of defective stimulus control would be an individual who tells jokes at a funeral. Although the jokes may be objectively funny (i.e., the behavioral repertoire is adequate), they are clearly out of place in that particular situation. An example with more clinical relevance is those children so eager to show the teacher they know the correct an-

swer that they continually speak out of turn in class. Assuming the child is capable of maintaining silence at times, he or she must learn to respond to those situational cues that indicate when it is appropriate to speak up. There are numerous clinical examples that show how parents inadvertently train their children to respond to incorrect discriminative stimuli. For example, parents often complain that their children will not obey them when they speak quietly, but only when they shout. The child has probably learned that neither aversive nor positive consequences follow ordinary requests, but that failure to heed an angry parent's request can result in a variety of aversive consequences. Such children are clearly capable of obeying but do not do so when the parents want them to.

Inappropriate Stimulus Control. In this category, one would include intense aversive emotional reactions elicited by objectively innocuous cues. These emotional reactions have presumably been conditioned to these specific stimuli, either by direct or by vicarious social learning experiences. Anxiety, gastrointestinal disturbances, insomnia, and other direct or indirect manifestations of intense emotional reactions would be included in this category. Such problems are frequently complicated by attempts to avoid these emotional states (as in the case of phobias) and also by the symbolic presentation of aversive stimuli, that is, ruminating about fears.

Deficient Behavioral Repertoires

This category includes behavior problems in which individuals lack the skills needed to cope effectively with situational demands. For example, they may never have learned what to say or do in social, academic, or vocational situations. Although the problem may be construed as a skill deficit, the clinical picture is often complicated by such individuals' failure to achieve adequate social reinforcement. They may even experience punishing consequences, such a loss of status, ridicule, and rejection. As a result, clients manifesting behavioral deficits frequently report negative subjective attitudes, including anxiety, depression, lack of self-confidence, and sometimes generalized anger toward others.

Aversive Behavioral Repertoires

The defining characteristic of this category is a maladaptive behavior pattern that is aversive to other individuals surrounding the client. Included here, then, would be persons who manifest antisocial behavior, who are overly aggressive, or who in some other ways are inconsiderate of others. Some writers have characterized these individuals as manifesting a "behavioral excess." In contrast to clients with behavioral deficiencies, individuals with aversive behavioral repertoires know what to say and do in various situations, but they ultimately make life difficult for themselves by being obnoxious or otherwise bothersome to others.

Difficulties with Incentive Systems (Reinforcers)

Included here are deviant behaviors that are functionally tied to reinforcing consequences, either because the incentive system of the individual is deficient or inappropriate, or because the environmental contingencies are creating problems.

Defective Incentive System in the Individual. In these instances, social stimuli that are reinforcing for most people are not capable of controlling the individual's behavior. Thus, attention, approval, and praise may not be positively reinforcing, nor may criticism or disapproval be negatively reinforcing. Two clinical examples are autistic children, whose behavior cannot be readily controlled by conventional social reinforcers (Rimland, 1964), and delinquents, for whom social reinforcers in the larger society have little relevance, as their behavior conforms to the standards of a subculture.

Inappropriate Incentive System in the Individual. This category includes those persons for whom the incentive system itself is maladaptive, that is, those things reinforcing to the individual are harmful and/or culturally disapproved. Excessive involvement with alcohol, drugs, and sexual practices such as pedophilia are some clinical examples.

Absence of Incentives in the Environment. Problems in this category include situations in which reinforcement is lacking in an individual's particular environment. The most clearly delineated example is a state of prolonged depression resulting from the loss of a spouse. More subtle examples are apathy and boredom.

Conflicting Incentives in the Environment. Much maladaptive behavior stems from conflicting environmental consequences. The clearest clinical examples are children whose maladaptive behavior appears to pay off, where there is a contradiction between what has been labeled by the environment as maladaptive and what, in fact, the environment is inadvertently reinforcing. Sometimes certain individuals in the environment positively reinforce a deviant behavior, as with the class clown who attracts the attention of his or her peers, despite the fact that the teacher disapproves of his or her actions. More subtly, parents or teachers may reinforce children for lack of persistence by helping them as soon as they experience some difficulty in handling a situation. Problems associated with conflicting incentives in the environment are not limited to children. As pointed out by Goffman (1961), Rosenhan (1973), and others, institutional settings, including psychiatric hospitals, may inadvertently foster behavior that is then labeled as deviant. On the more interpersonal level, individuals may verbally encourage their spouses to behave in one way but may act otherwise to discourage or even outrightly punish such attempts.

Aversive Self-Reinforcing Systems

Assuming that cognitive processes are capable of maintaining various forms of behavior, it is important to recognize that individuals are capable of reinforcing themselves for adequate behavior. If individuals' standards for "adequacy" are unrealistically high, they are likely to find themselves in few situations where their performance merits self-reinforcement, regardless of how adequate they may be according to external criteria. The consistent lack of self-reinforcement may lead to chronic states of depression and subjective feelings of inadequacy.

Although the system outlined above can be useful in carrying out a behavioral analysis of deviate behavior, it should be viewed as only a first attempt to categorize maladaptive behavior within a social learning context. Obviously, the categories are not mutually exclusive. Any one person may manifest a number of behavioral problems, which can be classified according to several of the headings. Further, certain behavior problems may be so complex as to warrant a multiple classification. Still, the system can serve its purpose by isolating those environmental or client variables that can be manipulated for maximum therapeutic benefit.

Future Perspectives

In concluding this overview of behavioral assessment, I would like to raise some additional considerations yet to be answered by behaviorally oriented researchers and clinicians. These issues are practically and conceptually complex and clearly present a challenge to the ingenuity of behavioral assessors.

Comparative Validity of Behavioral and Traditional Assessment

In light of the growing interest in behavioral assessment procedures, it is somewhat surprising to find that virtually no research has been carried out to compare their validity and predictive efficiency with more traditionally oriented methods. When one recognizes that problems with the validity and reliability of many traditional assessment procedures were, to a large extent, responsible for the rejection of traditional models of human functioning, this lack of comparative research is even more surprising. Although a few isolated studies have tended to support a more behaviorally oriented approach to assessment (Goldfried & Kent, 1972), there are insufficient findings at present to draw any firm conclusions regarding the comparative validity of both orientations. Just as one can view behavior therapy as a broad orientation for approaching the full gamut of clinical problems, so can one construe behavioral assessment as providing clinical psychology with a new paradigm for measuring human functioning. As has been demonstrated with various behavior therapy procedures, the acceptance of a behaviorally

oriented approach to assessment by clinical psychology in general is not likely to occur until it can be shown that it does a better job than what is currently available.

Standardization of Procedures

A direction in which we need to move is toward the eventual standardization of the assessment measures used in our outcome research and clinical work. By varying the assessment methodologically from study to study—in ways that are not always very apparent—we make it extremely difficult to compare and synthesize our findings. For example, when role playing has been used as an outcome measure, the procedures have varied by virtue of whether the subject offers a single response or several responses in an extended interaction, whether the procedure entails a live interaction or the situation is presented on audiotape, what is the content of the items used, and what particular scoring criteria are employed.

What we need to do is to work toward achieving an interim consensus on the best few measures currently available for assessing each class of behaviors of interest, and then to encourage comparative research so as to narrow down the pool to only those procedures that have been demonstrated to be most valid. Once we have decided on the best methods for assessing a given variable, the next step may be to use these measures until it can be demonstrated empirically that others may surpass them in validity and discriminability. Until that time occurs, I would even go so far as to suggest that journal editors not consider for publication any studies using measures that have been shown to have inferior validity. This is not to say that we should leave no room for improvement or refinement, but that we avoid the proliferation of procedures that serve only to add confusion, not growth, to the field.

Need for a Theoretical Framework

One of the major problems with behavioral assessment—and with behavior therapy in general—is that we have no "theory" to guide our work. Although we clearly have developed an important technology for assessing and modifying various "behaviors of interest," we need to have clearer direction as to exactly what we should be interested in, as well as the parameters and determinants of such behaviors. In talking about *theory*, I am referring not to any highly conceptual scheme but to a compilation of close-to-observable functional relationships between various behaviors and their determinants. Those of us involved in the clinical application of behavior therapy can offer a rich source of hypotheses about those variables that we need to investigate empirically in order to build up a pool of such functional relationships.

Summary

This chapter has discussed some of the underlying theoretical and methodological assumptions associated with behavioral assessment procedures, contrasting them with more traditional approaches to personality assessment. Consistent with an abilities conceptualization of personality, the relevance of behavioral assessment to proficiency tests and the assessment of competence has been noted. Some of the more frequently used methods of behavioral assessment were discussed, including direct observations in naturalistic settings and the sampling of responses to situations that have been contrived by the assessor, responses that manifest themselves in role-playing situations, and the person's own self-reports of overt behavior, emotions, and perceived environmental settings. Some of the methodological problems associated with each of these procedures were also considered. The relationship between behavioral assessment and behavior therapy was outlined, and those variables associated with clinical behavioral assessment were described. In addition, a system for classifying clinical problems within a behavioral framework was outlined.

The chapter ends by raising some unanswered questions that we need to deal with in order to advance the field, including those surrounding the comparative validity of behavioral and traditional assessment, the need to standardize our procedures, and the need for a low-level theoretical framework within which behavioral assessment can take place.

References

Adams, H. E., Doster, J. A., & Calhoun, K. S. A psychologically based system of response classification. In A. R. Ciminero, K. S. Calhoun, & H. E. Adams (Eds.) *Handbook of Behavioral Assessment*. New York: Wiley-Interscience, 1977.

American Psychological Association, American Educational Research Association, and National Council on Measurement in Education. *Standards for educational and psychological tests*. Washington, D.C.: American Psychological Association, 1974.

Arkowitz, H., Lichtenstein, E., McGovern, K., & Hines, P. The behavioral assessment of social competence in males. *Behavior Therapy*, 1975, *6*, 3–13.

Bandura, A. A social learning interpretation of psychological dysfunctions. In P. London & D. Rosenhan (Eds.), *Foundations of abnormal psychology*. New York: Holt, Rinehart & Winston, 1968, pp. 293–344.

Barker, R. G., & Wright, H. F. *One boy's day*. New York: Harper & Row, 1951.

Barlow, D. H. (Ed.), *Behavioral assessment of adult dysfunctions*. New York: Guilford Press, 1980.

Bates, P. The effectiveness of interpersonal skills training on the social skill acquisition of moderately and mildly retarded adults. *Journal of Applied Behavioral Analysis*, 1980, *13*, 237–248.

Beck, A. T. *Depression: Clinical, experimental, and theoretical aspects*. New York: Harper & Row, 1967.

Bellack, A. S., Hersen, M., & Lamparski, D. Role-play tests for assessing social skills: Are they valid? Are they useful? *Journal of Consulting and Clinical Psychology*, 1979, *47*, 335–342.

Bernstein, D. A., & Nietzel, M. T. Procedural variation in behavioral avoidance tests. *Journal of Consulting and Clinical Psychology*, 1973, *41*, 165–174.

Bernstein, G. S. *Behavior manager effectiveness inventory*. Unpublished manuscript, 1978.

Bersoff, D. N., & Moyer, D. Positive reinforcement observation schedule (PROS): Development and use. Paper presented at the annual meeting of the American Psychological Association, Montreal, August 1973.

Borkovec, T. D., Fleischmann, D. J., & Caputo, J. A. The measurement of anxiety in an analogue social situation. *Journal of Consulting and Clinical Psychology*, 1973, *41*, 157–161.

Borkovec, T. D., Stone, N. M., O'Brien, G. T., & Kaloupek, D. G. Evaluation of a clinically relevant target behavior for analog outcome research. *Behavior Therapy*, 1974, *5*, 503–513.

Cautela, J. R., & Kastenbaum, R. A. A reinforcement survey schedule for use in therapy, training, and research. *Psychological Reports*, 1967, *20*, 1115–1130.

Ciminero, A. R., Adams, H. E., & Calhoun, K. S. *Handbook of Behavioral Assessment*. New York: Wiley-Interscience, 1977.

Cone, J. D., & Hawkins, R. P. (Eds.). *Behavioral assessment: New directions in clinical psychology*. New York: Brunner-Mazel, 1977.

Delange, J. M., Lanham, S. L., & Barton, J. A. Social skills training for juvenile delinquents: Behavioral skill training and cognitive techniques. In D. Upper & S. Ross (Eds.), *Behavioral group therapy*. Champaign, Ill.: Research Press, 1981.

Dollard, J., & Miller, N. E. *Personality and psychotherapy*. New York: McGraw-Hill, 1950.

Edleson, J. L., & Rose, S. D. A behavioral roleplay test for assessing children's social skills. Paper presented at the Twelfth Annual Convention of the Association for the Advancement of Behavior Therapy, Chicago, 1978.

Eisler, R. M., Hersen, M., & Agras, W. S. Effects of videotape and instructional feedback on non-verbal marital interactions: An analogue study. *Behavior Therapy*, 1973, *4*, 551–558. (a)

Eisler, R. M., Hersen, M., & Agras, W. S. Videotape: A method for the controlled observation of non-verbal interpersonal behavior. *Behavior Therapy*, 1973, *4*, 420–425. (b)

Eisler, R. M., Hersen, M., & Miller, P. M. Effects of modeling on components of assertive behavior. *Journal of Behavior Therapy and Experimental Psychiatry*. 1973, *4*, 1–6.

Eisler, R. M., Miller, P. M., & Hersen, M., Components of assertive behavior. *Journal of Clinical Psychology*, 1973, *24*, 295–299.

Ellis, A. *Reason and emotion in psychotherapy*. New York: Lyle Stuart, 1962.

Endler, N. S., Hunt, J. McV., & Rosenstein, A. J. An S-R inventory of anxiousness, *Psychological Monographs*, 1962, *76*, (17, Whole No. 536).

Farina, A., Arenberg, D., & Guskin, S. A scale for measuring minimal social behavior. *Journal of Consulting Psychology*, 1957, *21*, 265–268.

Freedman, B. J., Rosenthal, L., Donahoe, C. P., Jr., Schlundt, D. J., & McFall, R. M. A social-behavioral analysis of skill deficits in delinquent and nondelinquent adolescent boys. *Journal of Consulting and Clinical Psychology*, 1978, *46*, 1448–1462.

Funabiki, D., & Calhoun, J. F. Use of a behavioral-analytic procedure in evaluating two models of depression. *Journal of Consulting and Clinical Psychology*, 1979, *47*, 183–185.

Galassi, J. P., DeLo, J. S., Galassi, M. D., & Bastien, S. The college self-expression scale: A measure of assertiveness. *Behavior Therapy*, 1974, *5*, 165–172.

Gambrill, E. D., & Richey, C. A. An assertion inventory for use in assessment and research. *Behavior Therapy*, 1975, *6*, 550–561.

Gay, M. L., Hollandsworth, J. G., & Galassi, J. P. An assertiveness inventory for adults. *Journal of Counseling Psychology*, 1975, *4*, 340–344.

Geer, J. H. The development of a scale to measure fear. *Behaviour Research and Therapy*, 1965, *13*, 45–53.

Goffman, E. *Asylums*. Garden City, N.Y.: Doubleday, 1961.

Goldfried, M. R. Behavioral assessment. In I. B. Weiner (Ed.), *Clinical methods in psychology*. New York: Wiley-Interscience, 1976.

Goldfried, M. R., & Davison, G. C. *Clinical behavior therapy*. New York: Holt, Rinehart & Winston, 1976.

Goldfried, M. R., & D'Zurilla, T. J. A behavioral-analytic model for assessing competence. In C. D. Spielberger (Ed.), *Current topics in clincal and community psychology*. New York: Academic Press, 1969.

Goldfried, M. R., & Kent, R. N. Traditional versus behavioral personality assessment: A comparison of methodological and theoretical assumptions. *Psychological Bulletin*, 1972, *77*, 409–420.

Goldfried, M. R., & Linehan, M. Basic issues in behavioral assessment. In A. R. Ciminero, H. E. Adams, & K. S. Calhoun, *Handbook of behavioral assessment*. New York: Wiley Interscience, 1977.

Goldfried, M. R., & Pomeranz, D. M. Role of assessment in behavior modification. *Psychological Reports*, 1968, *23*, 75–87.

Goldfried, M. R., & Robins, C. On the facilitation of self-efficacy. *Cognitive Therapy and Research*, in press.

Goldfried, M. R., & Sprafkin, J. N. *Behavioral personality assessment*. Morristown, N.J.: General Learning Press, 1974.

Goldfried, M. R., & Trier, C. S. Effectiveness of relaxation as an active coping skill. *Journal of Abnormal Psychology*, 1974, *83*, 348–355.

Goldsmith, J. B., & McFall, R. M. Development and evaluation of an interpersonal skill-training program for psychiatric inpatients. *Journal of Abnormal Psychology*, 1975, *84*, 51–58.

Haynes, S. N. *Principles of behavioral assessment*. New York: Gardner, 1978.

Haynes, S. N., & Wilson, C. C. *Behavioral assessment*. San Francisco: Jossey-Bass, 1979.

Hersen, M., & Bellack, A. (Eds.). *Behavioral assessment: A practical handbook. New York: Pergamon, 1976.

Hersen, M., & Bellack, A. (Eds.). *Behavioral assessment: A practical handbook. New York: Pergamon, 1976.

Hersen, M., & Bellack, A. (Eds.), *Behavioral assessment: A practical handbook. (2nd Ed.). Elmsford, N.Y.: Pergamon, 1981.

Hersen, M., Eisler, R. M., Miller, P. M., Johnson, M. B., & Pinkston, S. G. Effects of practice instructions and modeling on components of assertive behavior. *Behaviour Research and Therapy*, 1973, *11*, 443–451.

Honigfeld, G., Gillis, R. D., & Klett, C. J. Nosie-30: A treatment-sensitive ward behavior scale. *Psychological Reports*, 1966, *19*, 180–182.

Insel, P. M., & Moos, R. H. Psychological environments: Expanding the scope of human ecology. *American Psychologist*, 1974, *29*, 179–188.

Jacks, R. N. Systematic desensitization versus a self-control technique for the reduction of acrophobia. Unpublished doctoral dissertation. Stanford University, 1972.

Johnson, S. M., & Bolstad, O. D. Reactivity to home observation: A comparison of audio recorded behavior with observers present or absent. *Journal of Applied Behavioral Analysis*, 1975, *8*, 181–185.

Johnson, W. *People in quandaries*. New York: Harper & Row, 1946.

Kanfer, F. H., & Saslow, G. Behavioral diagnosis. In C. M. Franks (Ed.), *Behavior Therapy: Appraisal and status*. New York: McGraw-Hill, 1969.

Kanter, N. J., & Goldfried, M. R. Relative effectiveness of rational restructuring and self-control desensitization in the reduction of interpersonal anxiety. *Behavior Therapy*, 1979, *10*, 472–490.

Kazdin, A. E. Effects of covert modeling and model reinforcement on assertive behavior. *Journal of Abnormal Psychology*, 1974, *83*, 240–252. (a)

Kazdin, A. E. Self-monitoring and behavior change. In M. J. Mahoney & C. E. Thoresen (Eds.). *Self-control:*

Power to the person. Monterey, Calif.: Brooks/Cole, 1974. (b)

Keefe, F. J., Kopel, S. A., & Gordon, S. B. *A practical guide to behavioral assessment.* New York: Springer, 1978.

Kendall, P. C., & Hollon, S. D. (Eds.), *Assessment strategies for cognitive-behavioral interventions.* New York: Academic Press, 1981.

Kent, R. N., O'Leary, K. D., Diament, C., & Dietz, A. Expectation biases in observational evaluation of therapy change. *Journal of Consulting and Clinical Psychology,* 1974, *42,* 774–780.

Klass, E. T. A cognitive-behavioral approach to research on guilt. Paper presented at 25th Anniversary Conference on Rational-Emotive Therapy, June 1980, New York City.

Kulich, R. J., & Conger, J. A step towards a behavior analytic assessment of heterosocial skills. Paper presented at Association for Advancement of Behavior Therapy, Chicago, 1978.

Levenson, R. W., & Gottman, J. M. Toward the assessment of social competence. *Journal of Consulting and Clinical Psychology,* 1978, *46,* 453–462.

Lewinsohn, P. M., & Graf, M. Pleasant activities and depression. *Journal of Consulting and Clinical Psychology,* 1973, *41,* 261–268.

Lewinsohn, P. M., & Libet, J. Pleasant events, activity schedules, and depressions. *Journal of Abnormal Psychology,* 1972, *79,* 291–295.

Lewinsohn, P. M., & Shaffer, M. Use of home observations as an integral part of the treatment of depression: Preliminary report and case studies. *Journal of Consulting and Clinical Psychology,* 1971, *37,* 87–94.

Macdonald, M. *A behavioral assessment methodology applied to the measurement of assertiveness.* Doctoral dissertation, University of Illinois, 1974.

MacPhillamy, D. J., & Lewinsohn, P. M. Measuring reinforcing events. *Proceedings of the 80th Annual Convention, American Psychological Association* 1972.

Mariotto, M. J., & Paul, G. L. A multimethod validation of the inpatient multidimensional psychiatric scale with chronically institutionalized patients. *Journal of Consulting and Clinical Psychology,* 1974, *42,* 497–508.

Mash, E. J., & Terdal, L. G. (Eds.) *Behavioral therapy assessment.* New York: Springer, 1976.

Mash, E., & Terdal, L. (Eds.), *Behavioral assessment of childhood disorders.* New York: Guilford Press, 1980.

Mathews, R. M., Whang, P. L., & Fawcett, S. B. Development and validation of an occupational skills assessment instrument. *Behavioral Assessment,* 1980, *2,* 71–85.

McFall, R. M., & Lillesand, D. B. Behavior rehearsal with modeling and coaching in assertion training. *Journal of Abnormal Psychology,* 1971, *77,* 313–323.

McFall, R. M., & Marston, A. An experimental investigation of behavior rehearsal in assertive training. *Journal of Abnormal Psychology,* 1970, *6,* 295–303.

McFall, R. M., & Twentyman, C. T. Four experiments in the relative contributions of rehearsal, modeling, and coaching to assertive training. *Journal of Abnormal Psychology,* 1973, *81,* 199–218.

Meichenbaum, D. H., Gilmore, J. B., & Fedoravicious, A. Group insight versus group desensitization in treating

speech anxiety. *Journal of Consulting and Clinical Psychology,* 1971, *36,* 410–421.

Merluzzi, T. V., Glass, C. R., & Genest, M. *Cognitive assessment.* New York: Guilford Press, 1981.

Miller, B., & Bernstein, D. Instructional demand in a behavioral avoidance test for claustrophobic fears. *Journal of Abnormal Psychology,* 1972, *80,* 206–210.

Mischel, W. *Personality and assessment.* New York: Wiley, 1968.

Moos, R. H. Behavioral effects of being observed: Reactions to a wireless radio transmitter. *Journal of Consulting and Clinical Psychology,* 1968, *32,* 383–388.

Moos, R. H. Conceptualizations of human environments. *American Psychologist,* 1973, *28,* 652–665.

Moos, R. H. *Evaluating treatment environments: A social ecological approach.* New York: Wiley, 1974.

Mowrer, O. H. *Learning theory and personality dynamics.* New York: Ronald, 1950.

Mullinix, S. D., & Gallasi, J. P. Deriving the content of social skills training with a verbal response components approach. *Behavioral Assessment,* 1981, *3,* 55–66.

Murray, H. A. *Explorations in personality.* New York: Oxford University Press, 1938.

Nay, W. R. *Multimethod clinical assessment.* New York: Gardner, 1979.

Office of Strategic Services Assessment Staff. *Assessment of men.* New York: Rinehart, 1948.

O'Leary, K. D., & Becker, W. C. Behavior modification of an adjustment class: A token reinforcement program. *Exceptional Children,* 1967, *33,* 637–642.

O'Leary, K. D., & Kent, R. Behavior modification for social action: Research tactics and problems. In L. A. Hamerlynck, L. C. Handy, & E. J. Mash (Eds.), *Critical issues in research and practice.* Champaign, Ill.: Research Press, 1973.

O'Leary, K. D., & O'Leary, S. G. (Eds.). *Classroom management.* Elmsford, N.Y.: Pergamon Press, 1972.

O'Leary, K. D., Kent, R. N., & Kanowitz, J. Shaping data collection congruent with experimental hypothesis. *Journal of Applied Behavior Analysis,* 1975, *8,* 43–51.

Orne, M. T. On the social psychology of the psychological experiment: With particular reference to demand characteristics and their implication. *American Psychologist,* 1962, *17,* 776–783.

Patterson, G. R., Ray, R. S., Shaw, D. A., & Cobb, J. Manual for coding of family interactions, 1969. Available from ASIS/NAPS, c/o Microfiche Publications, 305 E. 46th Street, New York, N.Y. 10017. Document #01234.

Paul, G. L. *Insight vs. desensitization in psychotherapy.* Stanford, Calif.: Stanford University Press, 1966.

Paul, G. L. Insight versus desensitization in psychotherapy two years after termination. *Journal of Consulting Psychology,* 1967, *31,* 333–348.

Paul, G. L., & Lentz, R. J. *Psychosocial treatment of chronic mental patients.* Cambridge, Mass.: Harvard University Press, 1977.

Paul, G. L., Tobias, L. L., & Holly, B. L. Maintenance psychotropic drugs in the presence of active treatment programs: A "triple-blind" withdrawal study with long-term mental patients. *Archives of General Psychiatry,* 1972, *27,* 106–115.

Perri, M. G., & Richards, C. S. Assessment of heterosocial skills in male college students: Empirical development of a behavioral role-playing test. *Behavior Modification,* 1979, *3,* 337–354.

Purcell, K., & Brady, K. Adaptation to the invasion of privacy: Monitoring behavior with a miniature radio transmitter. *Merrill-Palmer Quarterly of Behavior and Development,* 1966, *12,* 242–254.

Rabin, A. I. Projective methods: An historical introduction. In A. I. Rabin (Ed.), *Projective techniques in personality assessment.* New York: Springer, 1968.

Rathus, S. A. A 30-item schedule for assessing assertive behavior. *Behavior Therapy,* 1973, *4,* 398–406.

Rehm, L. P., & Marston, A. R. Reduction of social anxiety through modification of self-reinforcement: An instigation therapy technique. *Journal of Consulting and Clinical Psychology,* 1968, *32,* 565–574.

Reid, J. B. Reliability assessment of observation data: A possible methodological problem. *Child development,* 1970, *41,* 1143–1150.

Rimland, B., *Infantile autism.* New York: Appleton-Century Crofts, 1964.

Romanczyk, R. G., Kent, R. N., Diament, C., & O'Leary, K. D. Measuring the reliability of observational data: A reactive process. *Journal of Applied Behavior Analysis,* 1973, *6,* 175–184.

Rosenhan, D. L., On being sane in insane places. *Science,* 1973, *179,* 250–258.

Rosenthal, R. *Experimenter effects in behavioral research.* New York: Appleton-Century-Crofts, 1966.

Ross, A. O., Lacey, H. M., & Parton, D. A. The development of a behavior checklist for boys, *Child Development,* 1965, *36,* 1013–1027.

Rotter, J. B., & Wickens, D. D. The consistency and generality of ratings of "social aggressiveness" made from observations of role playing situations. *Journal of Consulting Psychology,* 1948, *12,* 234–239.

Smith, R. E., Diener, E., & Beaman, A. L. Demand characteristics and the behavioral avoidance measure of fear in behavior therapy analogue research. *Behavior Therapy,* 1974, *5,* 172–182.

Spielberger, C. D., Gorsuch, R. L., & Lushene, R. E. *The state-trait anxiety inventory (STAI) test manual for form X.* Palo Alto, Calif.: Consulting Psychologists Press, 1970.

Staats, A. W. (with contributions by C. K. Staats). *Complex human behavior.* New York: Holt, Rinehart & Winston, 1963.

Stanton, H. R., & Litwak, E. Toward the development of a short form test of interpersonal competence. *American Sociological Review,* 1955, *20,* 668–674.

Turk, D. C. Factors influencing the adaptive process with chronic illness: Implications for intervention. In I. Sarason & C. Spielberger (Eds.), *Stress and anxiety,* Vol. 6. Washington, D.C.: Hemisphere, 1979.

Ulmer, R. A., & Timmons, E. O. An application and modification of the minimal social behavior scale (MSBS): A short objective, empirical, reliable measure of personality functioning. *Journal of Consulting Psychology,* 1966, *30,* 1–7.

Wiggins, J. S. *Personality and prediction: Principles of personality assessment.* Reading, Mass.: Addison-Wesley, 1973.

Wiggins, J. S., & Winder, C. L. The peer nomination inventory: An empirical derived sociometric measure of adjustment in preadolescent boys. *Psychological Reports,* 1961, *9,* 643–677.

Wolpe, J., & Lazarus, A. A. *Behavior therapy techniques.* New York: Pergamon, 1966.

Zuckerman, M., & Lubin, B. *Manual for the multiple affect adjective checklist.* San Diego, Calif.: Educational and Industrial Testing Service, 1965.

CHAPTER 4

Single-Case Experimental Designs

Michel Hersen

Introduction

Behavior modification and therapy perhaps are best distinguished from other therapeutic and educational approaches by their dependence on the experimental-empirical methods for solving human problems. Thus, in evaluating the efficacy of emerging therapeutic and educational techniques, a large variety of experimental strategies has been carried out by behavioral researchers. Included, of course, are both group-comparison designs (cf. Kazdin, 1980) and single-case experimental designs (cf. Hersen & Barlow, 1976).

Although group comparison and single-case design strategies are both well within the armamentarium of behavioral researchers, the single-case design approach to evaluating technical efficacy is almost uniquely tied in with the behavioral movement of the last two decades. That is, the single-case research approach has been followed not only in clinical psychology (Leitenberg, 1973), psychiatry

Michel Hersen • Department of Psychiatry, Western Psychiatric Institute and Clinic, University of Pittsburgh School of Medicine, Pittsburgh, Pennsylvania 15261. Preparation of this chapter was facilitated by Grant MH 28279-01A1 from the National Institute of Mental Health.

(Barlow & Hersen, 1973), and education (Risley & Wolf, 1972; Thoresen, 1972), but also in the practice of social work (Thomas 1978), physical rehabilitation (Martin & Epstein, 1976) and behavioral medicine (Barlow, Blanchard, Hayes, & Epstein, 1977). Thus, the widespread application attests to both its popularity and its utility.

The importance of the single-case experimental study to behavior therapy was best illustrated by Yates (1970). Indeed, he felt compelled to define behavior therapy specifically in relation to single-case methodology. He argued that "Behavior therapy is the attempt to utilize systematically that body of empirical and theoretical knowledge which has resulted from the application of the experimental method in psychology and its closely related disciplines (physiology and neurophysiology) in order to explain the genesis and maintenance of abnormal patterns of behavior; and to apply that knowledge to the treatment or prevention of those abnormalities by means of controlled experimental studies of single cases, both descriptive and remedial" (p. 18). This strong link between behavior therapy and research is reflected in the single-case publications in psychological (e.g., *Journal of Consulting and Clinical Psychology*), psychiatric (*American*

Journal of Psychiatry, Archives of General Psychiatry), and, of course, the behavioral journals (e.g., *Behavior Modification, Behaviour Research and Therapy, Behavior Therapy, Journal of Applied Behavior Analysis, Journal of Behavior Therapy and Experimental Psychiatry*).

In this chapter, we first briefly trace the history of the single-case approach, particularly as it relates to the problems and limitations of the group comparison method. This is to be followed by a discussion of more general issues involved in research, such as variability, intrasubject averaging, and the generality of findings. Next, we outline the basic procedures followed in single-case evaluations: repeated measurement, choice of a baseline, changing of one variable at a time, length of phases, distinction between reversal and withdrawal, and evaluation of irreversible procedures. Then we discuss and illustrate A-B-A designs and their extensions (e.g., interaction designs, drug evaluations). This is followed by our examination of additional design strategies (e.g., the three types of multiple-baseline designs, the multiple-schedule and simultaneous-treatment designs and the changing criterion design). Next, we tackle the thorny issue of the role of statistical analyses in evaluating treatment efficacy in single case studies. Highlighted are the arguments in support of and against the use of such statistical techniques. Finally, we discuss the importance of replication in single-case research. Three types of replication methods are to be considered: direct, clinical, and systematic.

History

A historical perusal clearly shows that the single-case approach, as currently applied, owes its heritage to many disciplines (cf. Hersen & Barlow, 1976, Chapter 1; Kazdin, 1978). There can be no doubt that the single case study has been important in the development of physiology, medicine, early experimental psychology, and psychoanalysis. In all of these disciplines, many critical findings have emerged from the careful study of individual organisms and subjects.

The tradition of single-case research dates back to the 1830s, as exemplified by the work of Johannes Müller and Claude Bernard in physiology. More important from a historical perspective, however, is the contribution of Paul Broca in 1861. At that time, Broca was treating a patient who had suffered a severe speech loss. However, the patient died while still under his care. Broca subsequently performed an autopsy and discovered a lesion in the man's cerebral cortex (i.e., in the third frontal convolution). He correctly assumed that this part of the brain controlled speech functions. As pointed out by Hersen and Barlow (1976), Broca's clinical method was an extension of prior work done in laboratories in which parts of the brains of experimental animals were systematically excised (i.e., the extirpation of parts). The relationship of such surgical excisions and subsequent behavioral changes in single organisms was meticulously studied, thus providing "an anatomical map of brain functions." The critical point to be underscored here is that findings of wide generality were gleaned on the basis of experimental work with very few research subjects.

It is generally agreed that Fechner's publication in 1860 of *Elemente der Psychophysik* heralded the beginning of experimental psychology. In this treatise, Fechner described studies he had conducted, using individual subjects, to determine sensory thresholds and just-noticeable differences in a variety of sense modalities. Although he did apply some statistical methods in evaluating his work, such statistics were employed to ascertain variability within a given subject. Following Fechner's studies in psychophysics, Wundt and his colleagues evaluated sensation and perception, while Ebbinghaus assessed the processes of learning, developing a new tool for conducting such research: the nonsense syllable. Both of these giants in the history of psychology accomplished their goals by studying individual subjects. Later, in the early part of the twentieth century, Pavlov's classical experiments in physiology, learning, and conditioning were all conducted with single organisms.

With the emergence of the group comparison methods, bolstered by the statistical genius of R. A. Fisher in the 1930s (i.e., inferential statistics), interest in the single-case approach during the middle part of this century waned considerably. Of course, the psychoanalysts did (and continue to) publish their descriptions of protracted treatments of individual patients. Probably the first was Breuer and Freud's case history published in 1895 (1957), describing the systematic treatment of Anna O's hysterical symptoms. (Parenthetically, we might note that Hersen and Barlow [1976, Chapter 1] have likened Breuer and Freud's approach to the multiple-baseline design across behaviors.) Nonetheless, these reports, albeit of tremendous therapeutic import, generally had subjective interpretations of results in that usually, no hard data were presented. However, the psychoanalytic case study certainly may be considered one of the antecedents to the single-case experimental tactic.

In the 1920s and 1930s, there were some sporadic descriptions of the behavioral treatment of individual cases of unusual interest (cf. Max, 1935; Watson & Rayner, 1920). But these single-case descriptions appear to have had little impact on therapeutic attitudes of the day and on subsequent strategies developed to assess therapeutic efficacy.

There are several other historical antecedents that warrant our attention. Most outstanding, of course, is the operant work of B. F. Skinner and his students in the 1940s and 1950s. Skinner (1966) has stated his philosophy of research in very succinct form: "instead of studying a thousand rats for one hour each, or a hundred rats for ten hours each, the investigator is likely to study one rat for a thousand hours" (p. 21). The specific experimental strategies used in the experimental analysis of behavior (with special emphasis on research with animals) were compiled and elucidated in Sidman's (1960) now-classic tome entitled *Tactics of Scientific Research*. However, this book was written prior to the plethora of behavior therapy studies that appeared in the 1960s, the 1970s, and now in the 1980s. (For a more comprehensive description of the use of single-case strategies as applied to humans in therapeutic endeavors, the reader is referred to Hersen and Barlow, 1976.)

In the more clinical realm, the contribution of Shapiro (1966) and Chassan (1967) must not be overlooked. Both were committed to the intensive study of the single case in a methodologically rigorous manner. Although neither of the two used the current nomenclature (e.g., A-B-A) for describing their single-case strategies, a number of the reported cases (e.g., Shapiro & Ravenette, 1959) bear a striking similarity to the prototypical A-B-A design. However, for the most part, the work of Shapiro and Chassan may be described as correlational. That is, the experimental control of therapeutic variables over dependent measures is not as clearly specified as in the reports of today's behavior analysts (cf. Hersen & Barlow, 1976; Kazdin, 1975; Leitenberg, 1973).

Group Comparison Designs

It was in the late 1940s and 1950s that the effects of psychotherapy began to be evaluated in large-scale group-comparison designs (see Rubenstein & Parloff, 1959, for a review of the issues). However, very quickly some of the major shortcomings were pointed out in both the therapeutic techniques themselves (cf. Eysenck, 1952) and the design strategies carried out by clinical researchers (cf. Bergin, 1966). Eysenck (1952) compared the improvement rates of treated patients and "spontaneous remission" rates (evaluated from insurance company records) and concluded that the effects of psychotherapy (as then practiced) were negligible at best. This finding, of course, sparked a tremendous controversy in the psychological world, which still rages at times. Bergin (1966) reevaluated the disappointing results of psychotherapy when contrasted with control group procedures and discovered that some patients improved as a function of treatment, whereas others actually worsened. Indeed, the statistical averaging of results (employing the group comparison method) led to a canceling of treatment effects for a fairly substantial number of patients.

Bergin's (1966) work in particular clearly indicated some of the limitations of the group comparison approach to studying the efficacy of psychotherapy. As noted by Hersen and Barlow (1976), "These difficulties or objections, which tend to limit the usefulness of a group comparison approach in applied research, can be classified under five headings: (1) ethical objectives, (2) practical problems in collecting large numbers of patients, (3) averaging of results over the group, (4) generality of findings, and (5) inter-subject variability'' (p. 14).

We briefly comment here on each of these limitations in turn. *First*, with regard to ethical concerns, the primary one is that in the group comparison strategy, the control group subjects do not receive treatment and, of consequence, are denied potential benefits. This objection, naturally, is predicated on the notion (albeit erroneous at times) that the treatment being evaluated is efficacious in the first place (cf. Eysenck, 1952). *Second*, the practical problems in identifying and matching subjects in large-scale group-comparison studies, in addition to selecting and remunerating suitable therapists, are overwhelming. Moreover, this approach to research is time-consuming and usually requires large federal allocations. It is not at all uncommon for a three- to four-year outcome study in psychotherapy to cost the National Institute of Mental Health upwards of $500,000. *Third*, already discussed, are the pitfalls involved in the statistical averaging of patients who improve or worsen as a function of treatment. Such problems led Paul (1967) to conclude that psychotherapy researchers should identify the patient who would profit from a specific therapy under very specific circumstances. *Fourth* is the issue of generality of findings. Inasmuch as group averaging may ''wash out'' the individual effects of particular treatments, the practicing clinician in the community cannot ascertain which specific patient characteristics may be correlated with improvement. Nonetheless, if a study of this kind is planned prospectively (usually a factorial design), such information may be teased out statistically. *Fifth* is the concern with intersubject variability. Although ideally in the group comparison study a frequent objective is to contrast homogeneous groups of patients, in practice this often is neither feasible nor practicable. (It is obviously impossible to control for the individual learning histories of patients, irrespective of whether the presenting symptoms are identical.) Thus, again, the unique response of the individual patient to treatment is lost. Also, in most group comparison studies, the effects of treatment are indicated on a pre–post basis. As a result, the vicissitudes

of therapeutic response throughout the full course of treatment are not clarified. This certainly is one area of marked import to every practicing clinician, who knows through experience about the ''ups and downs'' of responsivity to treatment, regardless of the theoretical approach cherished.

Experimental Analysis of Behavior

In addition to the problems inherent in evaluating the effects of psychotherapy in group comparison designs, some other factors contributed to the growing importance of the single-case approach in the late 1960s and through the 1980s. First was the then-prevalent scientist–practitioner split. That is, many clinical psychologists pursued esoteric research interests that had little or no bearing on the work they conducted with their patients. Indeed, often the research carried out by such clinicians was only of academic import. As late as 1972, Matarazzo pointed out that ''Even after 15 years, few of my research findings affect my practice. Psychological science *per se* doesn't guide me one bit. I still read avidly but this is of little direct practical help. My clinical experience is the only thing that has helped me in my practice to date'' (Bergin & Strupp, 1972, p. 340). As argued by Hersen and Barlow (1976), ''Since this view prevailed among prominent clinicians who were well acquainted with research methodology, it follows that clinicians without research training or expertise were largely unaffected by the promise or substance of scientific evaluation of behavior change procedures'' (p. 22).

With the advent of behavior therapy and the emergence of a new journal devoted to the experimental study of the individual in depth (*Journal of Applied Behavior Analysis*), much of the scientist–practitioner split was bridged. Although initially the great majority of the work was operant in nature, more recently other types of therapeutic strategies (e.g., systematic desensitization) have also been assessed by means of single-case methodology (see Van Hasselt, Hersen, Bellack, Rosenblum, & Lamparski, 1979). Generally, single-case research as now practiced is referred to as the *experimental analysis of behavior*.

General Issues

Intrasubject Variability

To determine the sources of variability in the subject is probably the most important task of the single-case researcher. The assessment of variability, of course, is facilitated by observing the individual over time under highly standardized conditions (i.e., repeated measurement). In the quest to determine the causes of variability, the greater the control over the subject's environment (external and internal), the greater the likelihood of accurately identifying such variability. As noted by Hersen and Barlow (1976), the task is made easier by studying lower organisms (e.g., the white rat):

In response to this, many scientists choose to work with lower life forms in the hope that laws of behavior will emerge more rapidly and be generalizable to the infinitely more complex area of human behavior. Applied researchers do not have this luxury. The task of the investigator in the area of human behavior disorders is to discover functional relations among treatments and specific behavior disorders over and above the welter of environmental and biological variables impinging on the patient at any given time. Given these complexities, it is small wonder that most treatments, when tested, produce small effects. (p. 35)

In identifying sources of variability at the human level, the researcher needs to consider biological, cognitive, and environmental variables. Although these three systems are obviously interconnected, each has some unique contributions to the problem. Biological or cyclical variability in humans (and animals, for that matter) is best represented by the female's estrus cycle. As is well known clinically and is equally well documented empirically (see Hersen & Barlow, 1976, Chapter 4), the dramatic hormonal changes that occur in women throughout the entire cycle (be it 24, 28, or 30 days) often yield equally dramatic changes in mood, affect, and behavior. Applied behavioral researchers evaluating effects of therapeutic interventions, particularly in female subjects whose menstrual changes in behavior are extreme, need to consider this factor when deriving conclusions from their data. Thus, it is quite conceivable that a behavioral intervention may coincide with a given part of the cycle, yielding changes in behavior (either improvement or worsening) and thus confounding the possible controlling effects of the specific behavioral technique. Indeed, what behavioral change does take place simply may be due to biological (internal) mechanisms. Certainly in the case of the woman whose postmenses mood typically improves, improved mood after the introduction of a behavioral treatment for depression may have nothing to do with the behavioral intervention. To the contrary, improved mood most likely is the progression of natural biological events rather than therapeutic efficacy.

Although of somewhat more recent interest to applied behavioral researchers (cf. Bellack & Schwartz, 1976; Hersen, 1979; Meichenbaum, 1976), the importance of the subject's cognitions can be neither ignored nor discounted. The strict operant interpretation of behavior, albeit more parsimonious, probably fails to reflect completely what truly distinguishes humans from the lower species. Thus, when repeated measurements are conducted, the subject's emotional-cognitive state requires attention, both as to how he or she feels and thinks over time (a dependent measure) and also as to how such thinking and feeling themselves can be causative agents for altering overt behavior.

Finally, but hardly least of all, we must consider the contribution of the external environment (i.e., the contingencies of reinforcement) on specific behavioral manifestations. To date, most of the work in single-case methodology has been devoted to elucidating the environmental variables that control directly observable motor responses (cf. Kazdin, 1975). For example, in a case of conversion reaction where the patient presented himself as unable to walk, Kallman, Hersen, and O'Toole (1975) clearly documented how the family's reactions to the symptoms resulted directly in the patient's continued symptomatology. That is, the family tended to reinforce the patient's verbalizations about symptoms (as well as serving him meals in bed and absolving him from all household responsibilities) while concurrently ignoring any of the few positive verbal and motoric initiatives he did take. It was only when the family was instructed and taught to reverse the contingencies (i.e., to ignore symptomatic presentation and to reinforce positive verbal and motor behaviors) that there was a marked change in the patient's behavior that maintained itself through a lengthy post-treatment follow-up period.

Intersubject Variability

To this point, we have focused our discussion on the attempt to ascertain the sources of variability within the individual subject. However, another type of variability that concerns the single-case researcher involves the differences between and among subjects in reaction to a therapeutic or educational procedure. Small and large differences in responding between and among subjects is termed *intersubject variability*. We have already touched on this issue when discussing the limitations and problems of the group comparison approach to research. There we pointed out how some patients may improve as a function of treatment, while others may worsen. But when the entire treatment group's data are averaged and contrasted with the control condition, no statistically significant differences emerge. From the aforementioned, it is clear that intersubject variability poses an enormous problem for the group comparison researcher, even if homogeneous groups are to be contrasted. For the single-case researcher who is conducting replications of treatments in a series of patients (presumably homogeneous with regard to a particular disorder), intersubject variability is also a problem but may result in subsequent refinements of procedures. In addition, with extensive intersubject variability, the power of a particular procedure may be determined in addition to an evaluation of its possible limitations.

More specifically, a behavioral treatment for depression may prove efficacious for both males and females who have had no prior episodes of the disorder. On the other hand, for those patients who have suffered several prior depressive episodes, the same technique may be only partially effective. Under these circumstances, the single-case researcher may alter some aspect of the treatment strategy in the hope of getting improved results. As stated by Hersen and Barlow (1976), "The task confronting the applied researcher at this point is

to devise experimental designs to isolate the cause of change, or lack of change. One advantage of single case experimental designs is that the investigator can begin an immediate search for the cause of an experimental behavior trend by altering his experimental designs on the spot. This feature, when properly employed, can provide immediate information on hypothesized sources of variability" (p. 40).

On the other hand, the same behavioral treatment applied to depressives who have had prior episodes may yield absolutely no change if the patients in addition are severely obsessive. At this point, the upper limits of the behavioral strategy may have been discovered, and it behooves the single-case researcher to consider either a different behavioral strategy or the combined (synergistic) effects of the behavioral-pharmacological approach (cf. Hersen, 1979).

Magnitude of Change

In the section on statistical analysis, we consider in some detail the advantages and disadvantages of the statistical versus the visual evaluation of data trends. However, here it is important to consider the magnitude of change brought about by a particular intervention. Because of the frequently exploratory nature of single-case work, it is especially important to document the power of the technique under consideration. For example, in the treatment of a depressed individual, one may be able to document a statistically significant change if the Beck Depression Inventory (BDI) score decreases, say, from 20 at baseline to about 15 following treatment. However, the question to be raised at this juncture is: How meaningful (clinically and socially) is this 5-point diminution? Certainly, a score of 15 on the BDI still represents a considerable residue of depression. Thus, although potentially of statistical significance, the therapeutic technique would have to yield a much greater change if it is to be considered of value to the practicing clinician. In his incisive review of this issue, Kazdin (1977) has argued about the importance of providing social validation. That is, to be given clinical credence, a therapeutic technique should be able to bring about sufficient change so that the treated individual approaches the *social norm*. Thus, in the case of our depressive, the change brought about should lead to a posttreatment score of 0–5 on the BDI. Otherwise, the norm for the non-pathological population will not have been closely enough approached.

Generality of Findings

As will be apparent in the following sections of this chapter, the main objective of the experimental analysis-of-behavior model (i.e., the single-case design) is to demonstrate the functions of the therapeutic or educational strategy that control the target behavior of interest. However, single-case researchers are intent on demonstrating this functional relationship not only in the individual case but also for other individuals who bear similar characteristics. This, then, is referred to as *subject generality*. That is, the same therapeutic strategy should prove effective over a number of patients with homogeneous features. Such features may relate to sex of the patients, their age, their diagnosis, their premorbid personality structure, or the family history of the disorder under investigation.

A second kind of generality concerns the *behavior change agent* (i.e., the therapist or educator). Given the same type of patient and the identical therapeutic strategy, do the unique characteristics of the therapist affect the outcome? More specifically, is the male therapist who carries out assertion training with an unassertive female client as effective as the female therapist doing the same treatment who is also highly committed to the goals of the woman's movement? This naturally is an empirical question whose answer can be determined only via careful replication across different therapists (see the sections on direct, clinical, and systematic replication).

A third type of generality deals with the *setting* in which the therapeutic or educational technique is being applied. That is, will a given intervention work as well in one type of setting as in another? For example, if the flooding treatment of an agoraphobic in a rural setting appears to work, will the same therapy for an agoraphobic living in an urban center prove as efficacious?

The three types of generality discussed above are problems for the single-case researcher. Indeed, critics of the single-case approach most often point to generality of findings as one of the weaker features of this research strategy:

The most obvious limitation of studying a single case is that one does not know if the results from this case would be relevant to other cases. Even if one isolates the active therapeutic variable in a given client through a rigorous single case experimental design, critics . . . note that there is little basis for inferring that this therapeutic procedure would be equally effective when applied to clients with similar behavior disorders (client generality) or that different therapists using this technique would achieve the same results (therapist generality). Finally, one does not know if the technique would work in a different setting (setting generality). This issue, more than any other, has retarded the development of single case methodology in applied research and has caused many authorities on research to deny the utility of studying a single case for any other purpose than the generation of hypotheses. . . . Conversely, in the search for generality of applied research findings, the group comparison approach appeared to be the logical answer. (Hersen & Barlow, 1976, p. 53)

However, as the old adage goes, "Appearances can be misleading." A careful scrutiny of the group comparison strategy reveals that there are limitations here, too, on establishing generality of findings. These have been discussed in considerable detail in Hersen and Barlow (1976, Chapter 2), and the interested reader is referred to that source. However, for purposes of exposition at this point, there are two problems that warrant our attention. The *first* is that one cannot automatically infer that the results from a homogeneous group of subjects are necessarily representative of the population of such subjects. *Second,* and probably of paramount importance, it is difficult to take the average response of a group of subjects and generalize to the individual case. In the section on replication (direct, clinical, and systematic), we examine how single-case researchers have attempted to document the general applicability of their findings.

Variability as Related to Generality

On the surface, one would think that variability and generality are unrelated. However, on closer inspection it is clear that by identifying as many sources of variability as possible, single-case researchers are able to improve and refine their techniques so that overall treatments have greater applicability to a wider range of subjects. Sidman (1960) contended that

Tracking down sources of variability is then a primary technique for establishing generality. Generality and variability are basically antithetical concepts. If there are major undiscovered sources of variability in a given set of data, any attempt to achieve subject or principle generality is likely to fail. Every time we discover control of a factor that contributes to variability, we increase the likelihood that our data will be reproducible with new subjects and in different situations. Experience has taught us that precision of control leads to more extensive generalization of data. (pp. 50–51)

Of course, Sidman was referring primarily to work with infrahuman species. Although the same principles hold in clinical and educational investigation with human subjects, the methods for achieving control and ferreting out sources of variability are both more difficult and more time-consuming. It is highly unlikely that the kind of environmental control that one is capable of obtaining in the animal laboratory will ever be possible in the clinical situation, because of the multiplicity of variables impinging on humans as well as because of the more obvious ethical considerations.

General Procedures

Repeated Measurement

The hallmark of the single-case experimental design is that dependent measures are repeatedly taken during baseline and treatment phases. Such measures may involve the observation of motoric behavior (e.g., the number of social interactions per half hour of free play in a socially isolated child), the assessment of physiological functioning (e.g., the heart rate of a phobic patient on presentation of the feared stimulus), or the evaluation of the cognitive-attitudinal state of the subject (e.g., the score on a self-report anxiety or depression scale).

Irrespective of the measurement system under consideration, "the operations involved in obtaining such measurements . . . must be clearly specified, observable, public, and replicable in all respects. . . . Secondly, measurements taken repeatedly, especially over ex-

tended periods of time must be done under exacting and totally standardized conditions with respect to measurement devices used, personnel involved, time or times of day; . . . instructions to the subject, and the specific environmental conditions (e.g., location) where the measurement session occurs" (Hersen & Barlow, 1976, p. 71).

Each of the measurement systems poses some unique challenges to the single-case researcher. When motoric measures are taken and human observers are used, independent reliability checks are required. These reliability checks can be expressed either as a percentage of agreement for interval data (with 80% considered minimally acceptable) or as a correlation for continuous data (with $r = .80$ considered minimally acceptable). (For a more comprehensive survey of behavioral assessment strategies, see Chapter 4.)

When physiological measures are repeatedly taken, this too must be done under totally standardized conditions. Here, investigators must be concerned not only with the functioning of the electronic devices but with the subject's adaptation to the equipment. In addition, concern for fatigability is of some importance, particularly if intertrial time periods are not sufficiently long. In cases where sexual responding in males is being repeatedly evaluated, assessment sessions should be programmed to guarantee maximum possible responding. Thus, the fatigue factor, if not properly attended to in this instance, might lead to a confounding of conclusions. This could occur if decreased deviant sexual responding to stimuli is erroneously attributed to treatment but is, in fact, simply a function of fatigue.

A major problem in using repeated self-reports of subjects in single-case evaluations of treatments involves the external validity of such data. As noted by Hersen and Barlow (1976), "When using this type of assessment technique, the possibility always exists, even in clinical subjects, that the subject's natural responsivity will not be tapped, but that data in conformity to experimental demand are being recorded" (p. 73). That is, the subject verbally responds to what he or she perceives as the therapist's expectation at that point in the treatment. Of course, the use of alternate forms of the scale and the establishment of external validity by correlating self-report with motoric and physiological indexes are two methods for avoiding some of the pitfalls of attitudinal measures. However, there is ample evidence in the behavioral literature that desynchrony exists among the three response systems (i.e., motoric, physiological, and cognitive) (Hersen, 1973, 1978). Indeed, there is the suggestion that clinical subjects' self-reports of how they feel should be given credence, irrespective of how motoric and physiological data change during the course of treatment (cf. Hersen, 1978). It is assumed that if sufficient improvements do not take place in motoric and physiological areas, but the cognitive-attitudinal system remains unmodified, treatment should be considered only partially successful.

A specific issue faced by the single-case researcher who works in the psychiatric setting (Hersen & Bellack, 1978) that obviously can affect the standardization of data is the different composition of the staff at various times. Not only may variable levels of staff cooperation yield a differing quality in the data collected within a stated time period (e.g., the morning), but the marked staff differences in number and attitude during day, evening, and weekend shifts are variables that may lead to confounded data. Thus, when conducting single-case research in the psychiatric setting, standardization of data collection times and data collectors (e.g., nursing personnel) assumes even greater importance.

Choosing a Baseline

With the exception of the B-A-B design, where treatment precedes baseline assessment, in most single-case experimental designs the initial period of observation involves the natural frequency of occurrence of the behavior of interest. This initial phase is referred to as *baseline* and is labeled *A*. Baseline serves as the standard by which subsequent treatment phases are contrasted.

In the ideal case, the assessment of baseline functioning yields a stable pattern of data, thus facilitating the interpretation of treatment effects in the B phase. However, more often than not, such stability of data is not to be

found. This is less of a problem for the basic animal researcher, who is in a position to program the subject's responding through the application of a variety of interval- and ratio-scheduling methodologies. It is understandable, then, why Sidman's (1960) definition of stability is a 5% range of variability. If variability exceeds that range, it is recommended that the experimenter evaluate sources of variability systematically.

In evaluating human subjects, the experimenter's flexibility in creating and choosing a baseline is much more constricted. Generally, the applied researcher does not have the luxury of "creating" ideal baseline conditions and is compelled to accept the baseline pattern as a given. Furthermore, the applied researcher is usually under time constraints; hence there is less opportunity to search for the manifold causes of variability. However, sometimes adjustment in the measurement scale being used may reduce extensive variability. That is, at times, the measurement interval may not be appropriate for the behavior under study and therefore leads to extraneous variability.

In the following discussion, we illustrate some of the baseline patterns typically encountered when conducting applied research with human subjects. Problems inherent in each of the patterns and methods for dealing with them are outlined.

Hersen and Barlow (1976) have identified and illustrated eight specific baseline patterns (see Table 1). These, of course, are the most representative, but many other possibilities, combinations, and permutations exist. Each of the baseline patterns illustrated contains six data points. In single-case research, an oft-raised question is: "How many points do I

Table 1. Baseline Patterns

1. Stable baseline
2. Increasing baseline (target behavior worsening)
3. Decreasing baseline (target behavior improving)
4. Variable baseline
5. Variable–stable baseline
6. Increasing–decreasing baseline
7. Decreasing–increasing baseline
8. Unstable baseline

need for an appropriate baseline assessment?'' Although this is a straightforward question, the answer to it is a bit complex. The first issue, of course, is how many data points are required in order to ascertain some trend in the data. Barlow and Hersen (1973) argued that, ''A minimum of three separate observation points, plotted on the graph, during this baseline phase are required to establish a trend in the data'' (p. 320). Sometimes more data points are needed if the baseline is initially variable or unstable. But, of course, the exigencies of a treatment situation may, at time, demand that the investigator forego experimental purity and institute treatment as rapidly as possible.

An upward trend in the data is represented by three successively increasing points. Conversely, a decreasing trend in the data is represented by three successively decreasing points. However, the power of the trend is dictated by the slope of the curve, with steeper slopes indicating greater power. The statistical methods for assessing slopes and trends in single-case research have been reviewed by Kazdin (1976). However, to date, despite considerable controversy in the field (cf. Baer, 1977; Michael, 1974a; Jones *et al.*, 1977; Thoresen & Elashoff, 1974), most applied behavioral researchers rely on a visual analysis of the data.

The stable baseline is depicted in Figure 1. As is quite apparent, there is some minor variability in tic frequency, but this variability is

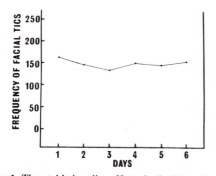

Figure 1. The stable baseline. Hypothetical data for mean numbers of facial tics averaged over three daily 15-minute videotaped sessions. (From Fig. 3-1 in *Single Case Experimental Designs* by Michel Hersen and David H. Barlow. Copyright 1976 by Pergamon Press, New York. Reprinted by permission.)

minimal, with the data essentially representing a straight line (i.e., no upward or downward trend). The application of treatment following such a baseline would permit an unambiguous interpretation of its effect (no change, improvement, or worsening).

As indicated in Table 1, the second pattern is the increasing baseline, where the target behavior is worsening. This, of course, is an acceptable pattern that could lead to a meaningful interpretation if subsequent treatment were to reverse the trend. However, if treatment were ineffective, then no difference in the slope of the curve might be noted. On the other hand, if treatment were detrimental to the patient, it would be difficult to determine whether the data in the intervention phase simply represent a continuation of the trend begun in baseline or whether they indicate further deterioration due to the treatment itself. However, a marked change in the slope of the curve could be interpreted as a deterioration effect due to treatment.

The third pattern is one where the baseline is decreasing and the target behavior is improving. This pattern is problematic inasmuch as subsequent treatment application might just result in a continuation of the trend begun in baseline. If there were a marked change in the slope of the curve, the improvement might be attributed to treatment, but this would be difficult to evaluate via visual inspection. Generally, in this instance, treatment would have to be withdrawn and reinstituted if its controlling effects are to be established. If treatment were to lead to a worsening of the patient's condition, then a reversed trend in the data would be apparent.

The fourth pattern, portrayed in Figure 2, is the variable baseline. We should note that this is a pattern frequently encountered in applied clinical research. The figure shows a tic frequency ranging from 24 to 255; no clear trend is apparent in the data. Nonetheless, there is a clear pattern of alternating low and high data points. Some investigators who obtain this pattern block the data by averaging tic frequency over a two-day period. This would lead to an apparently stable pattern, at least visually. However, this is an artificial manner of dealing with variability that is ''cosmetic'' but does not alter the basic pattern. In

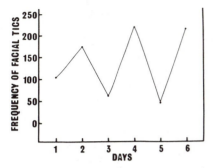

Figure 2. The variable baseline. Hypothetical data for mean number of facial tics averaged over three 15-minute videotaped sessions. (From Fig. 3-4 in *Single Case Experimental Designs* by Michel Hersen and David H. Barlow. Copyright 1976 by Pergamon Press, New York. Reprinted by permission.)

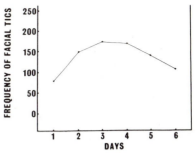

Figure 3. The increasing–decreasing baseline. Hypothetical data for mean number of facial tics averaged over three daily 15-minute videotaped sessions. (From Fig. 3-6 in *Single Case Experimental Designs* by Michel Hersen and David H. Barlow. Copyright 1976 by Pergamon Press, New York. Reprinted by permission.)

light of the extreme variability seen in this pattern, subsequent interpretations of a treatment effect could be quite difficult unless the treatment itself were successful in reducing both variability and tic frequency. As recommended by Sidman (1960), if time permits, the researcher should attempt to identify the source(s) of variability. But in the clinical situation, this usually is not the case.

As can be seen in Table 1, the fifth pattern is the variable–stable baseline. Here, despite initial variability, the investigator extends the baseline observation until the data are less variable. Indeed, this is one of the methods for dealing with the fourth pattern: the variable baseline. After stability is achieved, the institution of a given treatment should once again lead to an unambiguous interpretation of the resulting data. The only problem here is that extensive baseline observation may not be possible or ethical in certain clinical situations (e.g., severe head-banging or severe depression where suicidal ideation is present).

The sixth pattern (increasing–decreasing baseline), presented in Figure 3, is one where after an initial period of deterioration, improvement is quite apparent in the subject's condition. But as in the case of the decreasing baseline, the subsequent treatment application might only result in the continuation of the trend in the second part of baseline (i.e., continued improvement). Therefore, here, as in the case of the decreasing baseline, withdrawal and reinstatement of treatment are

needed to document the effects controlling the intervention strategy.

The seventh pattern (decreasing–increasing baseline) is the converse of the sixth: improvement followed by deterioration. In this instance, application of treatment that results in a reversal of data trends permits a clear interpretation of the effect. However, in the event that treatment is detrimental to the patient, visual inspection should prove extremely difficult unless there is a marked change in the slope of the curve.

The final pattern, the unstable baseline, is graphically portrayed in Figure 4. In this example, we have an extended baseline assessment that fails to reveal any particular pattern in the data. Thus, even the cosmetics of block-

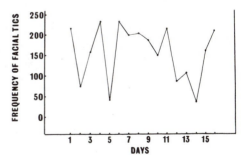

Figure 4. The unstable baseline. Hypothetical data for mean number of facial tics averaged over three daily 15-minute videotaped sessions. (From Fig. 3-8 in *Single Case Experimental Designs* by Michel Hersen and David H. Barlow. Copyright 1976 by Pergamon Press, New York. Reprinted by permission.)

ing would fail to yield visual improvement as to stability. As noted by Hersen and Barlow (1976), "To date, no completely satisfactory strategy for dealing with this type of baseline has appeared; at best, the kinds of strategies for dealing with variable baseline are also recommended here" (p. 82).

Changing One Variable at a Time

One of the basic tenets of the single-case approach is that only one variable is altered at a time when proceeding from one phase to the next (Barlow & Hersen, 1973; Hersen & Barlow, 1976). It should be noted that if two variables are manipulated simultaneously from one phase to another, then it is impossible to determine which of the two was responsible for or contributed most to behavioral change. This one-variable structure holds irrespective of whether the beginning, the middle, or the end phase is being evaluated.

Let us examine this basic tenet in greater detail. In the A-B-A-B design, for example, only one variable is changed from one adjacent phase to the next. Baseline is followed by treatment, which is succeeded by baseline and then treatment again. If treatment consists of a single therapeutic strategy—say, social reinforcement—then only one variable is altered from A to B. However, many treatments (e.g., social skills training) consist of a mélange of techniques (i.e., instructions, feedback, modeling, and social reinforcement). Thus, in an A-B-A-B design involving the application of such treatment, B represents the full combination of techniques. In this analysis, it is not possible to evaluate the separate contribution of each technique. However, in an A-B-A-B-BC-B design, where A is baseline, B is feedback, and C is social reinforcement, the separate contributions of feedback and social reinforcement to the overall treatment effect can be determined.

Although the one-variable rule is generally adhered to by behavioral researchers, examples in the literature may be found where incorrect applications have been carried out and published. Two prime examples are the A-B-A-C design, where the investigator erroneously assumes that the differential effects

of A and C can be determined, and the A-B-A-BC design, where the investigator assumes that the combined effects of BC may be contrasted with the original B phase. Not only is this idea erroneous in terms of the one-variable tenet, but the investigator has failed to consider the additional factor of the sequencing of possible treatment effects and the time lapses between treatment applications. With respect to these two examples, it should be pointed out that the experimental error is most frequently committed toward the latter part of the experimental analysis.

We might also note that in drug evaluations, the one-variable rule also holds but has some additional implications. Instead of progressing from a baseline phase (where no treatment is being administered) to a treatment phase (active drug), an additional step (i.e., placebo) is needed to control for the mere fact that the subject is ingesting a substance. Thus, a typical drug evaluation accomplished in the experimental single-case design might involve the following sequence: (1) no drug; (2) placebo; (3) active drug; (4) placebo; and (5) active drug. This design, labeled A-A'-B-A'-B, allows for evaluation of the contribution of the placebo over baseline and the drug over and above placebo alone.

Length of Phases

A number of factors need to be considered when determining length of baseline and treatment phases in single-case research. Included are time limitations, staff reactions, the relative length of adjacent phases, and ethical considerations. Johnston (1972) argued that "It is necessary that each phase be sufficiently long to demonstrate stability (lack of trend and constant range of variability) and to dispel any doubts of the reader that the data shown are sensitive to and representative of what was happening under the described conditions" (p. 1036).

In the ideal case, of course, the investigator attempts to secure a relatively equal number of data points per phase. This is especially important in the A-B-A-B design; otherwise, if, for example, a treatment phase were substantially longer than the preceding baseline, effects could be attributed to the extended time factor rather than to the treatment *per se* (see Hersen & Barlow, 1976, p. 101).

An excellent example of an A-B-A-B design with equal phases (with the exception of the last B phase) was presented by Miller (1973). In this study, the effects of retention control training were evaluated in a secondary enuretic child, with two targets (number of enuretic episodes and frequency of daily urination) selected as dependent measures (see Figure 5). The reader will note the relative stability in the baseline, the initial effects of the treatment, the return to baseline stability, and the renewed effects of the treatment during the second B phase. However, the second B phase was extended to 7 data points (instead of 3) to ensure the permanence of the treatment effects. This is a procedure commonly carried out in the last phase of the A-B-A-B design, and it has clinical implications, but the importance of the equality of the data points in the A-B-A phase of the study is clear.

Sometimes, when the targeted behavior is potentially injurious to the subject under study (e.g., head banging) and/or the staff in the institution are eager to get the behavior under

control very quickly because it is annoying, the initial baselines and the subsequent withdrawals of treatment (second and third A phases) may be very brief as contrasted with the intervention phases. Here, it is quite clear that ethical considerations have precedence over experimental rigor.

Still another factor related to length of phase is the carry-over effects of treatment to baseline. In the A-B-A-B design evaluating a behavioral strategy, this occurs in the second A phase, where the experimenter is unable to recover the initial baseline level that appeared in the first A phase. This is one of the primary reasons that Bijou, Peterson, Harris, Allen, and Johnston (1969) stated that "In studies involving stimuli with reinforcing properties, relatively short experimental periods are advocated, since long ones might allow enough time for the establishment of new conditioned reinforcers" (p. 202).

A special problem concerning carry-over effects involves evaluations of pharmacological treatments in single-case designs. Whereas with a behavioral intervention it is possible to terminate treatment (hopefully with minimal carry-over effects from treatment to baseline), in pharmacological applications the biological effects of the drug may actually persist into the placebo and baseline phases. Thus, it generally is not feasible to evaluate the long-term effects of drugs in single-case studies without the use of additional phases ("washout" phases, where there is no intervention) interposed between treatment and placebo. However, for the short-term evaluation of drugs, where they are rapidly introduced and removed, the single-case strategy is quite satisfactory (see Liberman & Davis, 1975).

Reversal and Withdrawal

In the behavioral literature (e.g., Baer, Wolf, & Risley, 1968; Barlow & Hersen, 1973; Kazdin, 1973), the A-B-A-B design is considered prototypical of the reversal strategy: "When speaking of a reversal, one typically refers to the removal (withdrawal) of the treatment variable that is applied after baseline measurement has been concluded. In practice, the reversal involves a withdrawal of the B

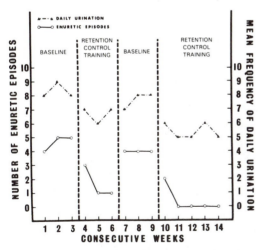

Figure 5. Number of enuretic episodes per week and mean number of daily urinations per week for Subject 1. (From "An Experimental Analysis of Retention Control Training in the Treatment of Nocturnal Enuresis in Two Institutionalized Adolescents" by Peter M. Miller, *Behavior Therapy*, 1973, *4*, 288–294, Fig. 1. Copyright 1973 by *Behavior Therapy*. Reprinted by permission.)

phase (in the A-B-A design) after behavioral change has been successfully demonstrated. If the treatment (B phase) indeed exerts control over the targeted behavior under study, a decreased or increased trend (depending on which direction indicates deterioration) in the data should follow its removal" (Hersen & Barlow, 1976, p. 92).

However, although the word *reversal* is used to describe the A-B-A-B design and the removal of treatment in the second A phase, Leitenberg (1973) and, more recently, Hersen and Barlow (1976) argued that the term *withdrawal* better describes the technical operation carried out by the applied behavioral researcher. Also, Leitenberg (1973) and Hersen and Barlow (1976) contended that there is a specific experimental strategy that is to be labeled the *reversal design*. An illustration of this design appears in Figure 6. Allen, Hart, Buell, Harris, and Wolf (1964) evaluated the effects of social reinforcement in a 4½-year-old withdrawn girl attending a preschool nursery. The target behaviors selected for study were the percentage of interaction with adults and the percentage of interaction with children. As can be seen in Figure 6, during baseline, a greater percentage of social interaction took place with adults than with children. In the second phase, the teacher was instructed to reinforce the child socially when she was interacting with other children and to ignore her when she was interacting with adults. In the next phase, the teacher was instructed to *reverse* the contingencies (i.e., to reinforce interaction with adults and to ignore interactions with children). Again, interaction with adults increased while interaction with children decreased. According to Leitenberg (1973), this is a *true* reversal (of differential attention) and is vastly different from simple withdrawal of treatment in the second A phase of the A-B-A-B design. In the fourth phase of the Allen *et al.* (1964) study, the contingencies were once more reversed, this reversal leading to increased interaction with children and decreased interaction with adults.

We should note parenthetically, however, that despite this distinction drawn between withdrawal and reversal, most applied behavioral researchers persist in referring to the A-B-A-B design as a reversal strategy. In short, the distinction made has not been reinforced by journal editors.

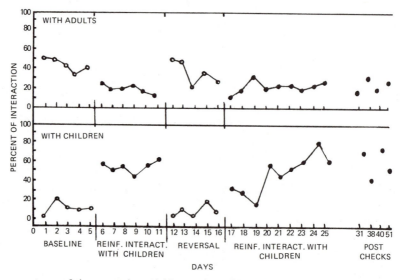

Figure 6. Daily percentages of time spent in social interaction with adults and with children during approximately 2 hours of each morning session. (From "Effects of Social Reinforcement on Isolate Behavior of a Nursery School Child" by K. E. Allen *et al.*, *Child Development*, 1964, *35*, 511–518, Fig. 2. Copyright 1964 by The Society for Research in Child Development, Inc. Reprinted by permission.)

Evaluating Irreversible Procedures

In single-case research, variables such as feedback, social reinforcement, and a variety of punishment techniques can be readily introduced and withdrawn in a number of designs (withdrawal and reversal). However, one variable, instructions, cannot be withdrawn in the technical sense. That is, once an instructional set has been given to the subject a number of times, simply ceasing to remind him or her of the instructions cannot be equated with cessation of feedback or reinforcement. Indeed, there is an analogy here to the physical discontinuation of a drug whose biological effect in the body may persist through the placebo and baseline phases of experimentation. Nonetheless, it is possible to study the very short-term effects of an instructional set that is periodically introduced and removed (Eisler, Hersen, & Agras, 1973) and the effects of changing the instructional set from a positive to a negative expectation (Barlow, Agras, Leitenberg, Callahan, & Moore, 1972). But usually, instructions tend to be maintained as a constant across the various phases of treatment, so that only one therapeutic variable is changed at a time (cf. Kallman *et al.,* 1975). When this is not possible, alternative experimental strategies, such as the multiple-baseline design, may be used to evaluate specific instructional effects on targeted behaviors (e.g., Hersen & Bellack, 1976).

Basic A-B-A Designs

A-B Design

The A-B design is the simplest of the single-case strategies, with the exception of the so-called B design, where measures are repeatedly taken throughout the course of treatment (i.e., in an uncontrolled case study with repeated measures). On the other hand, in the A-B design, the natural frequency of the behavior under study is first assessed in baseline (A). Then, in the B phase, treatment is instituted.

Of the single-case strategies, the A-B design is one of the weakest in terms of inferring causality. Indeed, the design is often referred to as correlational in that the effects of treatment that control the dependent measures are not completely documented unless treatment is withdrawn subsequent to B (i.e., the A-B-A design). Thus, in the A-B design, it is possible that changes in B are not the direct result of treatment *per se* but perhaps of some other factor, such as passage of time, that is correlated with the treatment.

Nonetheless, the A-B design does have its use and certainly represents a vast improvement over the uncontrolled case study. Also, for therapeutic or educational problems that have long proved recalcitrant, if intervention in B yields behavioral improvement, then with *some* degree of confidence one may attribute the effects to the specific intervention. However, only by demonstrating such change in a withdrawal or reversal design will dispel the remaining doubts of the more ''hard-headed'' operant researcher.

An example of an A-B design that also includes follow-up was presented by Epstein and Hersen (1974). The subject was a 26-year-old psychiatric inpatient who had suffered from gagging episodes for about two years in spite of numerous medical interventions. However, the problem appeared to have no direct medical etiology; hence the patient was admitted to the psychiatric service of a Veterans Administration hospital. During baseline (A), the patient was asked to record on an index card the specific time and frequency of each gagging episode. During treatment (B), the patient was given $2 in canteen books (exchangeable at the hospital commissary) for an $n - 1$ decrease in his gagging rate from the previous day. In treatment, the emphasis was on the patient's managing his disorder himself, with canteen booklets serving as the incentive. During the 12-week follow-up, the patient continued recording his gagging rate at home, with self-reports corroborated by his wife.

Figure 7 baseline data reveal a gagging frequency of 8–17 instances per day. The institution of treatment led to a marked decrease, to 0 on Day 14. However, renewed symptomatology was evidenced on Day 15, and treatment was continued, with the criterion for Day 15 reset to that originally used for Day 13. Improvements were noted between Days 15 and 18, and treatment was continued an additional six days.

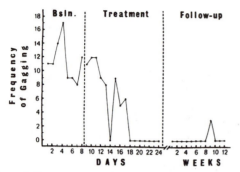

Figure 7. Frequency of gagging during baseline treatment and follow-up. (From "Behavioral Control of Hysterical Gagging" by L. H. Epstein and M. Hersen, *Journal of Clinical Psychology*, 1974, *30*, 102–104, Fig. 1. Copyright 1974 by the American Psychological Association. Reprinted by permission.)

From a design perspective, the reader should note the initial variability in baseline, which then stabilized to some degree. Further, the length of the treatment phase was double that of the baseline; it was extended for obvious clinical considerations (i.e., renewed symptomatology on Day 15).

Although the treatment appeared to be efficacious, it is possible that some unidentified variable, correlated with reinforcement procedures, led to behavioral change. But as previously noted, the A-B design does not allow for a completely unambiguous interpretation of causality. However, given the longevity of this patient's disorder and the repeated failure of medical interventions, there is a good likelihood that the treatment *per se* caused the improvement.

A-B-A Design

The A-B-A design corrects for one of the major shortcomings of the A-B design: lack of experimental control. Removal of treatment in the second A phase is used to confirm experimental control over the dependent measure initially suggested when improvement occurs in B. However, the A-B-A design is not completely adequate either, as it terminates in a no-treatment phase. For very obvious clinical and ethical reasons, this is problematic; at times, the experimenter may have intended to follow the more complete A-B-A-B strategy, but for any number of reasons, the subject

terminates the treatment prematurely. Even under these circumstances, data from A-B-A designs are of value.

Let us consider an example of an A-B-A design published by Hersen *et al.* (1973) some years ago. In this study, the investigators evaluated the effects of a token economy on neurotic depression in a married, white, 52-year-old farmer who had become depressed following the sale of his farm. The two dependent measures selected for study were the number of points earned and the behavioral ratings of depression (talking, smiling, and motor activity), with higher ratings indicating less depression. During baseline (A), the patient was able to earn points, but they had no exchange value. In B (token economy), the patient had to purchase privileges on the ward with points earned. Then, in the third phase (A), baseline procedures were reinstated.

The results of this experimental analysis are presented graphically in Figure 8. Inspection of baseline shows that the number of points earned was increasing, whereas decreased behavioral ratings of depression indicated a slight worsening of the patient's condition. It is quite clear that with the introduction of

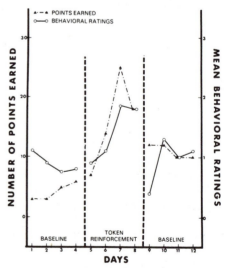

Figure 8. Number of points earned and mean behavioral ratings for Subject 1. (From "Effects of Token Economy on Neurotic Depression: An Experimental Analysis" by Michel Hersen *et al.*, *Behavior Therapy*, 1973, *4*, 392–397, Fig. 1. Copyright 1973 by *Behavior Therapy*. Reprinted by permission.)

token reinforcement in the B phase, there was a sharp increase both in the number of points earned and in the behavioral ratings, suggesting the efficacy of the intervention. Removal of treatment in the second A phase led to a marked diminution of points earned; decreased behavioral ratings also confirmed the controlling effects of the treatment.

From a design perspective, the fact that the number of points earned in baseline was on the increase makes it a bit more difficult to interpret the greater number of points earned during token reinforcement. However, the marked change in the slope of the curve during the token economy phase is highly suggestive. Moreover, data in the second A phase (showing a marked decrease in the number of points earned) confirmed the initial impression of the token economy's controlling effects. The data for behavioral ratings, because of the specific trends obtained, are definitely less ambiguous to interpret and clearly indicate the controlling effects of the token economy.

A-B-A-B Design

The A-B-A-B design, as previously noted, controls for deficiencies inherent in the A-B-A strategy, and elsewhere it has been termed the "equivalent time-samples design" (Campbell & Stanley, 1966). Not only does this design end on a treatment phase (B), but it provides two opportunities for showing the controlling effects of treatment over the dependent measure (B to A and A to B).

Let us now examine a recent example of the successful use of an A-B-A-B single-case design. Lombardo and Turner (1979) evaluated the effects of thought stopping in a 26-year-old male psychiatric inpatient who was severely obsessive. Obsessions focused on "imaginal relationships" he had had with other patients on the ward during previous hospitalizations. Although the patient attempted to control obsessive ruminations through distraction, this approach failed to reduce the disorder's full intensity.

In all phases of the experimental analysis, the patient was instructed to note the beginning and ending times of each obsessive episode, thus allowing a determination of both the rate of ruminations and the total time per day. Baseline (A) consisted of six days of observation. Treatment (thought stopping) began on Day 7 and consisted of the patient raising his right index finger whenever he had obtained a vivid obsessive image. At that point, the therapist shouted, "Stop," and the patient lowered his finger: "Fading of 'STOP' intensity and transfer of control from therapist to patient in all training was accomplished as follows. Initially, the therapist provided the 'STOP,' first shouting, then saying it loudly, then using a normal speaking voice, then saying it softly, and finally whispering 'STOP.' The patient then verbalized 'STOP' in the same manner with an additional final step of saying 'STOP' covertly. Depending upon how rapidly the patient gained control, four to six repetitions of stopping were used at each voice intensity" (Lombardo & Turner, 1979, p. 269). Treatment was discontinued on Day 18 and recommenced on Day 28. In addition, a six-week follow-up was carried out.

The results of this study appear in Figure 9. Following a period of baseline stability (the modal response was 40 minutes), thought stopping led to a marked decrease of obsessions to a 0 level. When treatment was then withdrawn in the second A phase (baseline), obsessions increased considerably, well over baseline levels, albeit in a very unstable fashion. However, reintroduction of the treatment led to renewed improvement to a 0 level, maintained through Days 33–40. Furthermore, improvement continued throughout the six-week follow-up period.

Although the functional effects of treatment appeared to be documented, "this conclusion must be tempered by the fact that controls were not provided for the possible therapeutic effects of instructions and therapist as well as patient expectancies" (Lombardo & Turner, 1979, p. 270). This kind of problem is definitely more prevalent when self-report data are used as opposed to motoric and physiological measures. As earlier noted, motoric and physiological measures are less susceptible to such confounding.

B-A-B Design

The B-A-B design, although not as complete an experimental analysis as the A-B-A-B de-

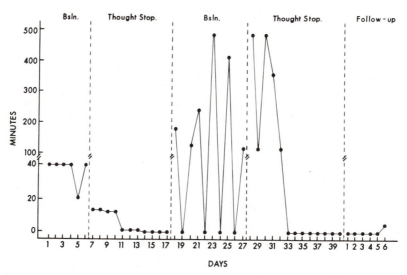

Figure 9. Duration of obsessive ruminations during baseline, treatment, and six-week follow-up. (From "Thought-Stopping in the Control of Obsessive Ruminations" by T. W. Lombardo and S. M. Turner, *Behavior Modification*, 1979, *3*, 267–272, Fig. 1. Copyright by Sage Publications. Reprinted by permission.)

sign, is superior to the A-B-A strategy, as it ends in a treatment phase. Since the experimental analysis begins in a treatment phase in the B-A-B design, the natural frequency (i.e., rate) of the behavior under investigation is not initially obtained. On the other hand, the B-A-B design may be useful for experimentation in institutional settings, particularly if the staff are eager to get some disruptive or unpleasant behavior under quick control. In such instances, the staff will undoubtedly require persuasion with regard to withdrawal of the treatment in the second phase (i.e., in A).

Let us consider an example of a B-A-B design in which the effects of token economic procedures on work performance were evaluated for 44 chronic schizophrenic patients (Ayllon & Azrin, 1965). In the first phase (B), the patients were awarded tokens contingently for engaging in a variety of hospital-ward work activities. Tokens, of course, were exchangeable for a large menu of "backup" reinforcers. In the second phase (A), the patients were given tokens noncontingently, based on the individual rates obtained in B. In the third phase (B), treatment was reinstated.

The results of this study are depicted in Figure 10. During the first B phase, the group of patients averaged a total of 45 work hours per day. When the contingency was removed in

A, the work level dropped to 1 hour by Day 36. The reinstatement of the treatment in the second B phase led to a marked increase of work output similar to that in the first phase. The data in the second B phase clearly document the controlling effects of the token economy on the work performance of these chronic schizophrenic patients.

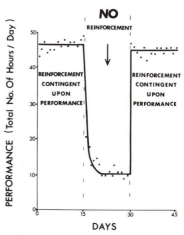

Figure 10. The total number of hours of the on-ward performance by a group of 44 patients. (From "The Measurement and Reinforcement of Behavior of Psychotics" by T. Ayllon and N. H. Azrin, *Behaviour Research and Therapy*, 1965, *8*, 357–383, Fig. 4. Copyright 1965 by Pergamon Press, Ltd. Reprinted by permission.)

Inasmuch as group data were averaged in this experimental analysis, Ayllon and Azrin (1965) also presented individual data, indicating that 36 of the 44 patients were affected by the contingency in force; 8 of the patients did not respond to token economic procedures. As argued by Hersen and Barlow (1976), when group data are presented graphically, the investigator should also display data for selected subjects: "Individual data presented for selected subjects can be quite useful, particularly if data trends differ. Otherwise, difficulties inherent in the traditional group comparison approach (e.g., averaging out of effects, effects due to a small minority while the majority remains unaffected by treatment) will be carried over to the experimental analysis procedure" (Hersen & Barlow, 1976, p. 190).

Extensions of the A-B-A Design

Extensions of the basic A-B-A design have appeared in numerous behavioral publications. In this section, we will consider three categories of such extensions.

The first involves a more extended replication of the basic A-B pattern (e.g., A-B-A-B-A-B: Mann, 1972) or the A-B-A-C-A design, where the controlling effects of B and C on A are examined in one study (e.g., Wincze *et al.*, 1972). However, in the A-B-A-C-A design, it is not possible to make a comparison of the relative effects of B and C, since these two interventions are confounded by a third factor: time.

The second category we will look at involves the additive or interactive effects of two therapeutic variables (e.g., A-B-A-B-BC-B design). Here, given the appropriate data trends, it is possible to evaluate the contribution of C above and beyond that of B.

Finally, the third category is concerned with the assessment of pharmacological treatments. As already noted, there are some unique problems in evaluating the effects of drugs in single-case designs (e.g., the need for placebo phases and the carry-over effects). Also, it should be noted that at this juncture the use of single-case analyses for pharmacological interventions is not widespread. Thus,

in our discussion, we will highlight possibilities for the future.

A-B-A-B-A-B and A-B-A-C-A-C' Designs

Mann (1972) repeatedly evaluated the effects of contingency contracting (A-B-A-B-A-B design) in his efforts to treat an overweight subject. At the beginning of the study, the subject surrendered a number of prize possessions (i.e., variables) to the investigator, which could be regained (one at a time), contingent on a 2-pound weight loss over a previous low within a designated time period. By contrast, a 2-pound weight gain led to the subject's permanent loss of the valuable, to be disposed of by the investigator in equitable fashion. That is, he did not profit in any way from the subject's loss.

As can be seen in Figure 11, the institution of the treatment (contingency contracting) led to marked decreases in weight, with interposed baseline data evincing a plateauing effect or an upward trend. In short, the controlling effects of the contingency contract on weight loss were firmly demonstrated several times in this experimental analysis.

Wincze *et al.* (1972) evaluated the effects of feedback and token reinforcement on the verbal behavior of a delusional psychiatric inpatient using an A-B-A-C-A-C'-A design. During each of the phases of study, the patient was asked daily to respond to 15 questions selected at random from a pool of 105. The proportion of the responses containing delusional material was recorded for the individual sessions, as was the percentage of delusional talk on the ward monitored by nurses 20 times a day.

During A (baseline), no contingencies were in effect, and the patient received "free" tokens. Feedback (B) involved the patient's being corrected whenever he responded delusionally. Tokens were still given to him noncontingently in this phase. In A, baseline procedures were reinstituted. In the fourth phase (C), tokens were earned *contingently* for nondelusional talk. This was followed by a return to baseline conditions. In C', tokens were awarded contingently for nondelusional talk that exceeded a given criterion (nondelusional talk more than 90%). Finally, in the last phase

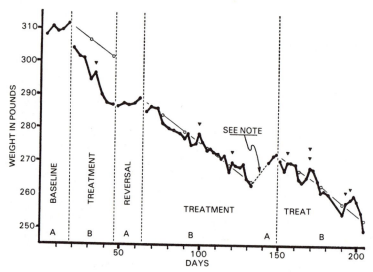

Figure 11. A record of the weight of Subject 1 during all conditions. Each open circle (connected by the thin solid line) represents a 2-week minimum-weight-loss requirement. Each of the solid dots (connected by the thick solid line) represents the subject's weight on each of the days he was measured. Each triangle indicates the point at which the subject was penalized by a loss of valuables, either for gaining weight or for not meeting the 2-week minimum-weight-loss requirement. *Note*: The subject was ordered by his physician to consume at least 2,500 calories per day for 10 days, in preparation for medical tests. (From "The Behavior Therapeutic Use of Contingency Contracting to Control on Adult Behavior Problem: Weight Control" by R. A. Mann, *Journal of Applied Behavior Analysis*, 1972, *5*, 99–109, Fig. 1. Copyright 1972 by the Society for the Experimental Analysis of Behavior, Inc. Reprinted by permission.)

(A), baseline procedures were reinstated for the fourth time.

The results of this study appear in Figure 12. These data indicate that none of the treatment variables applied effected any change in delusional talk on the ward. Similarly, feedback (B) yielded no effects on delusional talk in individual sessions. But token sessions (Phase 4) and token bonus (Phase 6) procedures led to decreased delusional talk in individual sessions, thus demonstrating the controlling power of these treatments over the dependent measure. However, as has already been underscored, this design does not permit

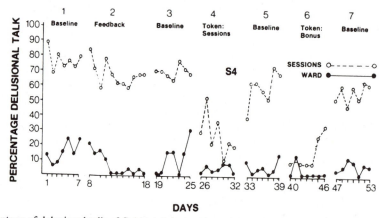

Figure 12. Percentage of delusional talk of Subject 4 during therapist sessions and on the ward for each experimental day. (From "The Effects of Token Reinforcement and Feedback on the Delusional Verbal Behavior of Chronic Paranoid Schizophrenics" by J. P. Wincze *et al.*, *Journal of Applied Behavior Analysis*, 1972, *5*, 247–262, Fig. 4. Copyright 1972 by the Society for the Experimental Analysis of Behavior, Inc. Reprinted by permission.)

an analysis of the relative effects of token sessions and the token bonus treatment.

Interaction Designs

As previously pointed out in Hersen and Barlow (1976), "Most treatments contain a number of therapeutic components. One task of the clinical researcher is to experimentally analyze these components to determine which are effective and which can be discarded, resulting in a more efficient treatment. Analyzing the separate effects of single therapeutic variables is a necessary way to begin to build therapeutic programs, but it is obvious that these variables may have different effects when interacting with other treatment variables. In advanced states of the construction of complex treatments it becomes necessary to determine the nature of these interactions" (p. 213).

As clearly noted in an earlier section, the importance of the one-variable rule (i.e., changing one variable across phases) holds in particular in interaction designs. In some instances, the introduction of one therapeutic variable will lead to some behavioral change, but the addition of a second variable will lead to still further increases, as marked by a significant change in the slope of the curve (see Hersen & Barlow, 1976, p. 217). In other instances, the first variable may lead to a min-

imal effect, while the second suggests considerable additional effects. Let us consider one such example.

Kallman *et al.* (1975) evaluated the effects of reinforcing standing and walking on the mean distance in yards walked per instruction in a white, 42-year-old married, patient suffering from a conversion reaction (i.e., an inability to walk). Figure 13 shows that in the first phase, when standing was reinforced with verbal praise, only minimal efforts were made to walk. In the second phase, when walking and standing were both reinforced, a marked linear increase in walking was noted. In the third phase, standing alone was reinforced; the result was a plateauing effect. However, when reinforcement for standing and walking was reinstituted in the fourth phase, further improvements in walking appeared. In the next two phases, reinforcement for standing and walking were maintained, but with the addition of a walker in the fifth phase and its removal in the sixth. The nomenclature for the first six phases of this study is as follows: (1) B; (2) BC; (3) B; (4) BC; (5) BCD; and (6) BC. An evaluation of the analysis clearly indicates the controlling effects of C (reinforcing walking) over B (reinforcing standing), but it does not reveal the controlling effects of the walker (BCD) over no walker (BC), inasmuch as improvements in walking continued after the walker was removed.

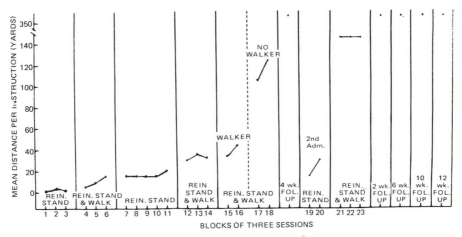

Figure 13. Mean distances walked during all phases of treatment and follow-up. (From "The Use of Social Reinforcement in a Case of Conversion Reaction" by W. M. Kallman *et al.*, *Behavior Therapy*, 1975, 6, 411–413, Fig. 1. Copyright 1975 by *Behavior Therapy*. Reprinted by permission.)

Let us consider still another example of the interaction design, an evaluation of the effects of feedback and reinforcement on the eating behavior of an anorexia nervosa patient (Agras *et al.*, 1974). This study was done in an A-B-BC-B-BC design, with A as baseline, B as reinforcement, and C as feedback. Throughout the study, the patient was provided four meals daily, each consisting of 1,500 calories. Reinforcement consisted of granting the patient privileges, contingent on weight gain. Feedback, on the other hand, involved giving the patient specific information as to weight, caloric intake, and actual mouthfuls consumed.

The data presented in Figure 14 show a slight increase in weight during baseline but decreased caloric intake. The introduction of reinforcement led to decreased weight and a continued decrease in caloric intake. When feedback was added to reinforcement in the third phase, a marked increase in weight and

caloric intake was noted. This leveled off when feedback was removed in Phase 4 but increased when feedback once again was added to reinforcement in the final phase. In summary, this study failed to document the controlling effects of reinforcement on weight gain and caloric intake, but it definitely reflects the controlling effects of feedback on these two dependent measures.

Drug Evaluations

So far in this chapter, we have touched on some of the issues related to the evaluation of pharmacological agents in single-case designs (namely, the placebo phase and the carry-over effects from adjacent phases). A third important issue in drug research, of course, is the use of double-blind assessments; that is, neither the patient nor the assessor is aware of whether a placebo or an active drug is being

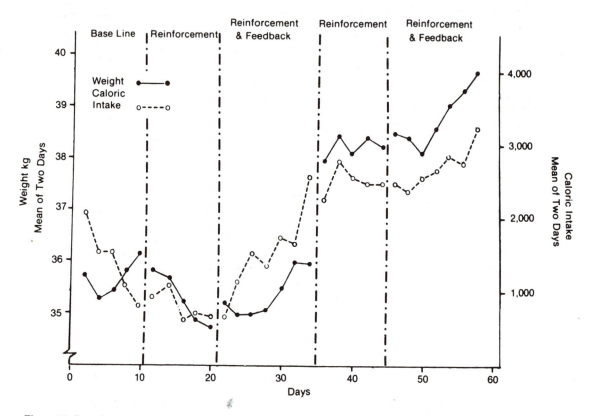

Figure 14. Data from an experiment examining the effect of feedback on the eating behavior of a patient with anorexia nervosa. (From "Behavior Modification of Anorexia Nervosa" by W. S. Agras *et al.*, *Archives of General Psychiatry*, 1974, *30*, 279–286, Fig. 4. Copyright 1974, American Medical Association. Reprinted by permission.)

administered. In the single-blind assessment, only the patient typically is unaware of whether he or she is receiving a drug or a placebo.

Hersen and Barlow (1976) have pointed out the difficulties inherent in conducting the double-blind assessment in single-case analysis:

A major difficulty in obtaining a "true" double-blind trial in single case research is related to the experimental monitoring of data (i.e., making decisions as to when baseline observation is to be concluded and when various phases are to be introduced and withdrawn) throughout the course of investigation. It is possible to program phase lengths on an *a priori* basis, but then one of the major advantages of the single case strategy (i.e., its flexibility) is lost. However, even though the experimenter is fully aware of treatment changes, the spirit of the double-blind trial can be maintained by keeping the observer . . . unaware of drug and placebo changes. . . . We might note here additionally that despite the use of the double-blind procedure, the side effects of drugs in some cases . . . and the marked changes in behavior resulting from removal of active drug therapy in other cases often betray to nursing personnel whether a placebo or drug condition is currently in operation. (p. 206)

In spite of the aforementioned difficulties, which equally plague the group comparison researcher, there are some good examples of single-case work using drugs. In some, the drug is a constant across phases while behavioral strategies are evaluated (cf. Wells, Turner, Bellack, & Hersen, 1978); in others, the addition of a drug to a behavioral intervention

is assessed (Turner, Hersen, & Alford, 1974; Turner, Hersen, Bellack, & Wells, 1979); in still others (Liberman *et al.*, 1973; Williamson, Calpin, DiLorenzo, Garris, & Petti, 1981), the primary effects of the drug are evaluated.

Listed in Table 2 are some of the possible design strategies for assessing drugs. Designs 4–15 are all experimental in that the controlling effects of the drug on targeted behaviors may be ascertained. Also indicated is whether a single- or double-blind procedure is possible. Let us consider a published example of one of the designs (Number 13).

Liberman *et al.* (1973) assessed the effects of placebo and Stelazine on the social interaction of a 21-year-old chronic schizophrenic patient who was quite withdrawn. Social interaction was evaluated by noting the patient's willingness to engage in 18 daily half-minute chats with nursing personnel on the ward. Refusals to engage in such chats were labeled asocial responses. In the first phase (A), the patient was withdrawn from all medication. In the next phase (A'), he was administered a placebo, followed by 60 mg per day of Stelazine (Phase B). Next, he was withdrawn from Stelazine (Phase A'), and then Stelazine was reinstated (Phase B).

As can be seen in Figure 15, removal of the drugs in the first phase led to increased asocial behavior. With the introduction of placebo,

Table 2. Single-Case Experimental Drug Strategies[a]

No.	Design[b]	Type	Blind possible
1.	A-A$_1$	Quasi-experimental	None
2.	A-B	Quasi-experimental	None
3.	A$_1$-B	Quasi-experimental	Single or double
4.	A-A$_1$-A	Experimental	None
5.	A-B-A	Experimental	None
6.	A$_1$-B-A$_1$	Experimental	Single or double
7.	A$_1$-A-A$_1$	Experimental	Single or double
8.	B-A-B	Experimental	None
9.	B-A$_1$-B	Experimental	Single or double
10.	A-A$_1$-A-A$_1$	Experimental	Single or double
11.	A-B-A-B	Experimental	None
12.	A$_1$-B-A$_1$-B	Experimental	Single or double
13.	A-A$_1$-B-A$_1$-B	Experimental	Single or double
14.	A-A$_1$-A-A$_1$-BA$_1$-B	Experimental	Single or double
15.	A$_1$-B-A$_1$-C-A$_1$-C	Experimental	Single or double

[a] *From* Hersen and Barlow (1976), Table 6.1.
[b] A = no drug; A$_1$ = placebo; B = drug 1; C = drug 2.

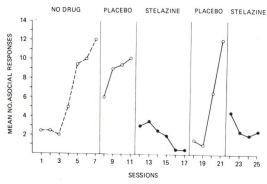

Figure 15. Average number of refusals to engage in a brief conversation. (From "Research Design for Analyzing Drug-Environment-Behavior Interactions" by R. P. Liberman *et al.*, *Journal of Nervous and Mental Disease*, 1973, *156*, 432–439, Fig. 2. Copyright © 1973 The Williams & Wilkins Co. Reprinted by permission.)

there was initial improvement and then a return of asocial behavior. The introduction of Stelazine in the third phase led to a marked improvement, followed by deterioration when Stelazine was removed in the fourth phase. The reinstitution of Stelazine in the fifth phase clearly documents the controlling effects of the drug on improved social responding.

Additional Designs

Although the basic A-B-A design and its numerous extensions have been used extensively and successfully by applied behavioral researchers to evaluate many therapeutic and educational problems, at times some of these designs simply are not appropriate. Inappropriateness may be due to practical, ethical, or design considerations. For example, if a given therapeutic procedure cannot be reversed or withdrawn (e.g., therapeutic instructions), then a different design (such as the multiple-baseline design across behaviors) could be employed to document the controlling effects of instructions on independent target behaviors. On the other hand, if an investigator is intent on showing the effects of some kind of shaping procedure where behavior is to be accelerated or decelerated, then the changing-criterion design would be more suitable. Finally, if the relative efficacy of two treatment strategies is to be contrasted in a single subject, then

the simultaneous treatment design (sometimes referred to as the *multielement* or *alternating-treatment design*) is the design strategy of choice.

Let us now consider each of these designs in turn, beginning with the three varieties of the multiple-baseline strategy.

Multiple Baseline

Baer *et al.* (1968) first described the multiple-baseline design as follows: "In the multiple-baseline technique, a number of responses are identified and measured over time to provide baselines against which changes can be evaluated. With these baselines established, the experimenter then applies an experimental variable to one of the behaviors, produces a change in it, and perhaps notes little or no change in the other baselines" (p. 94). The investigator then applies treatment to succeeding behaviors until some criterion point has been achieved. Generally, the treatment is then withheld until baseline stability has been achieved.

The strategy described above is referred to as the *multiple-baseline design across behaviors*. An assumption, of course, is that the targeted behaviors are independent of one another. Otherwise, treatment for one may lead to covariation in a second, thus obfuscating the controlling effects of the treatment. In essence, the multiple-baseline design across behaviors is a series of A-B designs, with every succeeding A phase applied to one targeted behavior until treatment has finally been applied to each. Treatment effects are inferred from the untreated baselines. That is, the controlling effects of treatment on dependent measures are documented if, and only if, change occurs when treatment is directly applied. In this respect, the design certainly is weaker than that in the A-B-A-B design, where the effects of controlling variables are directly shown.

Let us consider an example of the multiple-baseline design across behaviors. Bornstein *et al.* (1977) assessed the effects of social skills training on the role-played performance of an unassertive 8-year-old female third-grader (Jane). During baseline, specific behaviors were assessed (ratio of eye contact to speech duration, loudness of speech, number of requests, and overall assertiveness) in role-played scenarios requiring assertive responding. As can be seen in Figure 16, the baseline levels of responding for target behaviors were low. Treatment applied to each baseline under time-lagged and cumulative conditions led to marked increases in responding. The reader should note that only when social skills treatment was directly applied to each of the first three targeted behaviors did changes take place. There was no evidence that the targeted behaviors were correlated, nor did concurrent change take place in untreated target measures. In short, the controlling effects of social skills treatment were demonstrated. It also should be noted that although overall assertiveness was not directly treated, independent ratings of overall assertiveness reflected improvement throughout the course of treat-

ment, with all treatment gains generally maintained in follow-up.

Unless there is a specific theoretical rationale or the investigator has had prior experience working with a given set of target behaviors, there is no accurate way to predict whether the three or more targeted behaviors selected for treatment truly are independent of one another. Following the initial logic of the multiple-baseline design across behaviors, if change in target behaviors 1 and 2 occur as a result of treatment application to only the first, then the controlling effects of the treatment will not have been demonstrated. The baselines are correlated, but that does not necessarily imply that the treatment in general is ineffective. Kazdin and Kopel (1975) have offered a solution to this dilemma sometimes encountered in applied clinical research. They argue that

> In case of ambiguity with the effects of a multiple-baseline design, it often is possible to include a partial reversal in the design for one of the behaviors. The reversal phase, or return to baseline, need not be employed for all of the behaviors (i.e., baselines) for which data are collected. Indeed, one of the reasons for using a multiple-baseline design is to avoid the ABAB design and its temporary removal of treatment. However, when the specific effect of the intervention is not evident in a multiple-baseline design, one may have to resort to a temporary withdrawal of the intervention for one of the baselines to determine the effect of the intervention. (p. 607)

A problem with the Kazdin and Kopel solution is that in the case of instructions, a *true* reversal or withdrawal is not possible. Thus, their recommendations apply best to the assessment of such techniques as feedback, reinforcement, and modeling.

A second type of multiple-baseline strategy is the one across settings. That is, a given treatment is applied to one subject (or group of subjects) across several different settings (e.g., different classroom periods). The logic of the design, however, remains the same. Baselines for separate settings increase in length, with treatment applied under time-lagged and cumulative conditions. Generally, only one behavior is targeted for time-lagged treatment. But there is no reason that concurrent changes in other behaviors should not be monitored.

An example of a multiple-baseline design across settings was presented by Allen (1973).

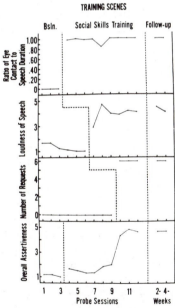

Figure 16. Probe sessions during baseline, social skills treatment, and follow-up for training scenes for Jane. A multiple-baseline analysis of ratio to speech duration of eye contact while speaking, loudness of speech, number of requests, and overall assertiveness. (From "Social-Skills Training for Unassertive Children: A Multiple-Baseline Analysis" by M. R. Bornstein *et al.*, 1977, *10*, 183–195, Fig. 1. Copyright 1977 by the Society for the Experimental Analysis of Behavior, Inc. Reprinted by permission.)

In his study, the subject was an 8-year-old boy with minimal brain damage who was attending a special summer camp. The target selected for modification was the child's high rate of bizarre verbalizations in four separate camp settings: walking on a trail, in the dining hall, in the cabin, and during education sessions. Treatment simply involved instructing the camp counselors to systematically ignore such bizarre verbalizations. (Previously, these verbalizations had attracted considerable social reinforcement from the counselors.)

The results of this experimental analysis appear in Figure 17. Following seven days of baseline, treatment was implemented for walking on the trail, with a resultant decrease in bizarre talk. However, no concurrent changes

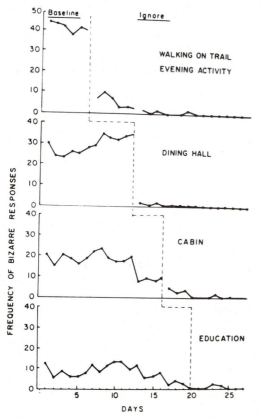

Figure 17. Daily number of bizarre verbalizations in specific camp settings. (From "Case Study: Implimentation of Behavior Modification Techniques in Summer Camp Setting" by G. J. Allen, *Behavior Therapy*, 1973, *4*, 570–575, Fig. 1. Copyright 1973 by *Behavior Therapy*. Reprinted by permission.)

were noted in the dining hall. Only when treatment was specifically applied to the dining hall did bizarre talk decrease. Note, however, that when treatment was applied in the dining hall, there were some concurrent decreases in bizarre talk in the cabin. Similarly, when treatment was applied in the cabin, there were some concurrent decreases noted during education sessions. Thus, the last two baselines were not totally independent. Indeed, this was an instance in which Kazdin and Kopel's (1975) recommendation of a partial reversal (withdrawal) for Baselines 3 and 4 would have added confirmatory evidence to the treatment's effectiveness.

A third type of multiple-baseline design strategy is the one across subjects. Although not strictly a *single case* study, the general principles of the multiple-baseline strategy apply. As described by Hersen and Barlow (1976), "a particular treatment is applied in sequence across *matched* subjects presumably exposed to 'identical' environmental conditions. Thus, as the same treatment variable is applied to succeeding subjects, the baseline for each subject increases in length. In contrast to the multiple baseline design across behaviors (the within-subject multiple baseline design), in the multiple baseline across subjects a single targeted behavior serves as the primary focus of inquiry. However, there is no experimental contraindication to monitoring concurrent . . . behaviors as well" (p. 228).

A recent example of the multiple-baseline design across subjects appeared in a paper by Ortega (1978). In this study, Ortega evaluated the effects of relaxation training on the spasticity level of four cerebral palsied adults. The dependent measures involved two timed trials of the Placing Test and the Turning Test from the Minnesota Rate of Manipulation Tests, which test the speed and dexterity of finger, hand, and arm movements.

Figure 18 shows that all four subjects' performance on the two tests was slow, but that slight improvements generally occurred throughout baseline as a function of repeated trials. However, only when progressive relaxation exercises were practiced by each subject did marked changes in speed take place. Moreover, follow-up data indicate that performance improvement was maintained for at least three

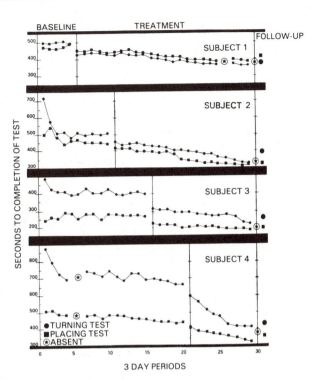

Figure 18. The time required to complete two trials of both the Placing Test and the Turning Text, from the Minnesota Rate of Manipulation Tests, during baseline, treatment, and follow-up phases of research. Testing sessions, which measured the amount of time required to complete various manual manipulations involving pegs and pegboard, were conducted every third working day throughout the experiment. During the treatment condition, relaxation exercises were performed every working day. Subject 1 was absent throughout Test Period 26 because of illness. Subject 4 was vacationing during Periods 5 and 6. Severe cold weather and heavy snows forced the closure of both sheltered workshop-facilities for eight working days, so Test Period 30 was canceled. (From "Relaxation Exercise with Cerebral Palsied Adults Showing Spasticity" by D. F. Ortega, *Journal of Applied Behavior Analysis*, 1978, *11*, 447–451, Fig. 1. Copyright 1978 by the Society for the Experimental Analysis of Behavior, Inc. Reprinted by permission.)

weeks. Performance improvement from baseline to treatment (averaged over the four subjects) was 28% on the Turning Test and 21% on the Placing Test.

Changing-Criterion Design

The changing-criterion design (cf. Hartmann & Hall, 1976) appears to be ideal for assessing shaping programs to accelerate or decelerate behaviors (e.g., increasing activity in overweight individuals; decreasing alcohol consumption in heavy drinkers). As a strategy, it bears characteristics similar to those of the A-B design and has some features of the multiple-baseline strategy. Following initial baseline observation, treatment is applied until a given criterion is achieved and stability at that level appears. Then, a more rigorous criterion is selected, and treatment is applied until the performance level is met. Changes in criterion level as a result of the second treatment are contrasted with the lower criterion in Treatment 1. Treatment is thereby continued in this stepwise fashion until the final criterion is met. "Thus, each phase of the design provides a

baseline for the following phase. When the rate of the target behavior changes with each stepwise change in the criterion, therapeutic change is replicated and experimental control is demonstrated" (Hartmann & Hall, 1976, p. 527).

An excellent example of the changing-criterion design was provided by Hartmann and Hall (1976) in their evaluation of a smoking-deceleration program. The baseline smoking level is graphically depicted in Panel A of Figure 19. In B (treatment), the criterion rate was established as 95% of baseline (i.e., 45 cigarettes per day). An escalating-response cost of $1 was set for smoking Cigarette 47, $2 for Cigarette 48, etc. If the subject smoked fewer than the criterion number of cigarettes, an escalating bonus of 10 cents per cigarette was established. Subsequent treatment in C through G involved the same contingencies, with the criterion for each succeeding phase set at 94% of the previous one.

The experimental analysis clearly shows the efficacy of the contingencies established in reducing cigarette smoking by 6% or more from the preceding phase. In addition, within the individual analysis, there were six clear

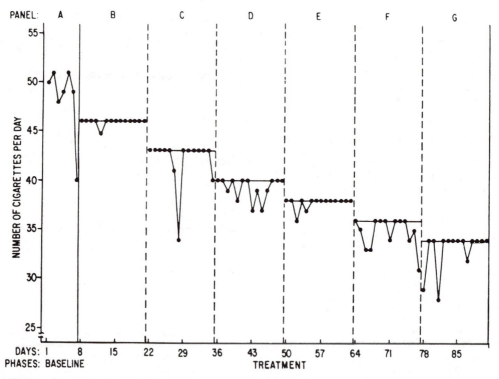

Figure 19. Data from a smoking-reduction program used to illustrate the stepwise criterion-change design. The solid horizontal lines indicate the criterion for each treatment phase. (From "The Changing Criterion Design" by D. P. Hartmann and R. V. Hall, *Journal of Applied Behavior Analysis*, 1976, *9*, 527–532, Fig. 2. Copyright 1976 by the Society for the Experimental Analysis of Behavior, Inc. Reprinted by permission.)

replications of the treatment's effect. In short, we agree with Hartmann and Hall (1976) that "the changing criterion design is capable of providing convincing demonstrations of experimental control, seems applicable to a wide range of problematic behaviors, and should be a useful addition to applied individual subject methodology" (p. 532).

Simultaneous Treatment Design

In the simultaneous treatment design (cf. Kazdin & Geesey, 1977; Kazdin & Hartmann, 1978), there is the opportunity to compare two or more treatments within a single subject. This, of course, is in marked contrast to the other strategies we have discussed to this point, wherein design limitations *do not* allow for such comparisons.

As with all single-case designs, there are particular circumstances under which the simultaneous treatment design may be imple-

mented. Thus, there must be the opportunity to evaluate at least two stimulus dimensions (e.g., different times of day, locations, or treatment agents). In a classroom study, different time periods may be the stimulus dimension (morning versus afternoon). During the baseline phase, the targeted behavior is evaluated in each of the stimulus dimensions. Then two (or possibly more) interventions (e.g., individual versus group contingencies) are applied concurrently in each of the stimulus dimensions. In order to avoid a possible treatment–stimulus dimension confound, each of the two interventions is counterbalanced across dimensions. For example, on the first day, Treatment A is administered in the morning; Treatment B is administered in the afternoon. On the second day, Treatment B is administered in the morning; Treatment A is administered in the afternoon, etc. The results of the two treatments are plotted and visually examined. (It is possible to evaluate the effects of counterbalanced treatment with statistical analyses similar to those employed in the analysis of a Latin square design; see Benjamin, 1965.) In the third phase of the study, the most efficacious treatment is applied across each of the stimulus conditions.

Let us look at an example of this design in a study carried out by Kazdin and Geesey (1977). In this investigation of classroom behavior, the effects of token reinforcement for the subject alone versus token reinforcement for the subject and the rest of his class were evaluated, with percentage of attentive behavior as the dependent measure. This study was done in counterbalanced fashion for two separate classroom periods. Figure 20 (bottom part) reveals that the percentage of attentive behavior during baseline ranged from 40% to 60%. Implementation of the token program for the subject alone (i.e., self) led to an average percentage of attentive behavior of 72.5%. By contrast, the token program for the subject and the rest of the class (i.e., class: backup reinforcers were earned for himself and the entire class) led to 91% attentive behavior. Thus, in the third phase, the superior procedure was continued across both class periods, with a mean percentage of attentive behavior of 91.2% attained.

In further considering the simultaneous treatment design, Kazdin and Hartmann (1978) pointed out that the behaviors selected for

study must be those that can rapidly shift and that *do not* evince carry-over effects after termination. By necessity, this would preclude the evaluation of certain drugs in this kind of design. Also, because of the counterbalancing requirement, relatively few behaviors can be evaluated (probably not more than three). Finally, "The client must make at least two sorts of discriminations. First, the client must discriminate that the treatment agents and time periods are not associated with a particular intervention because the interventions vary across each of the dimensions. Second, the client must be able to distinguish the separate interventions. One would expect that the greater the discrimination made by the client the more likely there will be clear effects or discrepancies between (among) treatments" (Kazdin & Hartmann, 1978, p. 919).

Statistical Analysis

There has probably been no aspect of single-case research in recent times more fraught with controversy than that involving statistical analysis (cf. Baer, 1977; Hartmann, 1974; Jones *et al.*, 1977; Kazdin, 1976; Keselman & Leventhal, 1974; Kratchowill, Alden, Demuth, Dawson, Panicucci, Arntson, McMurray, Hempstead, & Levin, 1974; Michael 1974a,b; Thoresen & Elashoff, 1974). The crit-

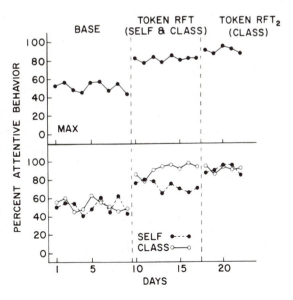

Figure 20. Attentive behavior of Max across experimental conditions. Baseline (base): no experimental intervention. Token reinforcement (token rft): implementation of the token program, in which tokens earned could purchase events for himself (self) or the entire class (class). Second phase of token reinforcement (token rft$_2$): implementation of the class exchange intervention across both time periods. The upper panel presents the overall data collapsed across time periods and interventions. The lower panel presents the data according to the time periods across which the interventions were balanced, although the interventions were presented only in the last two phases. (From "Simultaneous-Treatment Design Comparisons of the Effects of Earning Reinforcers for One's Peers versus for Oneself" by A. E. Kazdin and S. Geesey, *Behavior Therapy*, 1977, *8*, 682–693, Fig. 2. Copyright 1977 by *Behavior Therapy*. Reprinted by permission.)

ics and the advocates of the use of statistics are equally intense about attempting to persuade colleagues and students to their respective positions. In this section, it is not our purpose to attempt to resolve the controversy. Rather, it is our explicit intention to look at the arguments and to ferret out the data in relation to these arguments. In so doing, we will briefly examine the opposing positions while considering some of the recommended statistical procedures.

The Case Against

The basic argument against the use of statistics in single-case research involves the distinction between *clinical* and *statistical* significance. Indeed, one of the specific arguments against the group comparison method is that statistics do not give the experimenter a "true" picture of the individual pattern of results. That is, positive and negative treatment effects cancel out; in addition, statistics may possibly yield significance from very weak overall treatment strategies. Thus, if the effect of treatment is not sufficiently substantial to be detected by visual inspection (i.e., considerable overlap of data between baseline and treatment phases), then the treatment applied is not clinically potent and its controlling effects have not been clearly documented. On the other hand, if treatment is of sufficient potency to yield considerable clinical change, then there is the expectation that such change may approach the social norm (i.e., social rather than statistical validation) (see Kazdin, 1977). This being the case, statistical analysis should prove superfluous.

Kazdin (1976) has summarized the case against statistical analysis in single-subject research as follows: "Individuals who advocate non-statistical criteria for evaluation caution against 'teasing out' subtle effects because these effects are least likely to be replicable. Moreover, involving statistical significance as the only criterion for evaluation does not encourage the investigator to obtain clear unequivocal experimental control over behavior. Finally, many investigators believe that in clinical work statistical evaluation is simply not relevant for assessing therapeutic change" (p. 272).

The Case For

The advocates of statistical analyses for single-case research recommend them for several reasons. The most persuasive argument has been presented by Jones *et al.* (1977). In contrasting the statistical approach with visual analysis for a number of studies published in the *Journal of Applied Behavior Analysis,* it was found that in some instances, time-series analyses (cf. Glass, Willson, & Gottman, 1975) confirmed the experimenters' conclusions based on visual inspection. In other instances, time-series analyses did not confirm the experimenters' conclusions. In still other cases, time-series analyses indicated the presence of statistically significant findings not identified by the experimenters. Consequently, Jones *et al.* (1977) concluded that "All three kinds of supplementary information provided by time-series analysis are useful. It is rewarding to have one's visual impressions supported by statistical analysis. It is humbling and/or educational to have other impressions not supported. And it is clearly beneficial to have unseen changes in the data detected by a supplementary method of analysis. It is difficult to see how operant researchers can lose in the application of time-series analysis to their data" (p. 166).

Statistical analysis may prove helpful when baseline stability is difficult to establish and considerably overlap exists between the baseline and the treatment phases. As pointed out by Kazdin (1976), "Whereas visual inspection of the data often entails noting distinct changes in trends across phases, statistical analysis can scrutinize continuous shifts across phases where there is no change in trend" (p. 270).

A third use advocated for statistical analysis is for investigations in so-called new areas of research. Presumably, in these newer areas, therapeutic techniques are unlikely to be fully refined and developed; hence, there is a lesser likelihood that marked clinical differences will appear on visual inspection. Thus, in the early stages of research, it is argued that statistics may reveal small but important differences with clinical implications.

A fourth reason offered for the use of statistical analyses (cf. Kazdin, 1976) is the increased intrasubject variability in uncontrolled research settings (e.g., in the natural environment). Again, the argument put forth is that the statistical approach may detect changes that could eventually have some clinical impact when the specific therapeutic or educational strategy is later refined.

T Test and ANOVA

A number of *t*-test and analysis-of-variance (ANOVA) techniques have been adapted for use in single-case research across the different phases of a given study (cf. Gentile, Roden, & Klein, 1972; Shine & Bower, 1971). If we compare the ANOVA in single-case research and group comparison designs, the treatment factor in the single-case study is analogous to the between-group factor. Similarly, the number of observations within a phase is comparable to the within-group factor. In developing their ANOVA technique, Gentile *et al.* (1972) assumed that the performance of a response within a phase is independent of each other response. However, it should be noted that they were aware of "the high autocorrelation of adjacent observations" (Kazdin, 1976, p. 276). To control for this factor, Gentile *et al.* suggested combining nonadjacent phases in the A-B-A-B design (i.e., $A_1 + A_2$; $B_1 + B_2$) in computing the statistical analysis.

Despite the correction factor suggested by Gentile *et al.*, there are two basic problems in using the ANOVA model. First and foremost is the issue of dependency. As argued by Kazdin (1976), "combining phases does not at all affect the problem of non-independent data points and the decreased variability among observations *within* phases, two factors that can positively bias *F* tests" (p. 277). The second is that the ANOVA essentially contrasts the means of each phase. Thus, the statistical model proposed fails to take into account data trends as represented by the slope of the curve. In short, it would appear that the criticisms of applications of traditional group statistics to the single-case study are warranted (see Hartmann, 1974; Keselman & Leventhal, 1974).

Time-Series Analysis

Time-series analysis controls for the problems alluded to above in that the statistical strategy takes into account change in the level, change in the slope of the curve, and the presence or absence of drift or slope in the curve (see Jones *et al.,* 1977). Indeed, Figure 21 depicts six illustrative treatment effects that may be ascertained through the use of time-series analyses. As noted by Jones *et al.,* in some instances the mere visual analysis of such data might yield erroneous conclusions.

Despite the obvious utility of the time-series approach, it is not without its limitations. First, to meet the requirements of the analysis, a fairly large number of observations may be required (i.e., 50–100). Although feasible in some investigations, this number would preclude the use of statistics in many others where short-term treatment effects are being evaluated. Second, and equally important at this time, time series analysis requires computerized programs and the ready availability of the requisite facilities. Although in time we would expect them to proliferate, these facilities are now relatively scarce.

Additional Comments

There can be no doubt that statistical analysis for single-case research has its merits and should proliferate in the future. Also, the reader should keep in mind that many other statistical strategies (not discussed in this chapter) have appeared and undoubtedly will continue to appear in the press. (For a more comprehensive coverage of the area, the reader is referred to Kazdin, 1976; Kratchowill, 1978.)

Replication

In the previous section, we looked at some of the statistical techniques that might serve to confirm (or even to supplant) the experimenter's visual analysis of his or her data. The objective in using a statistical technique is to guarantee that the visual inspection of trends indicating controlling effects of treatment variables on dependent measures is indeed valid. Assuming a high concordance between a visual and a statistical analysis of the data (thus confirming the treatment's efficacy for the one subject), the question, of course, remains

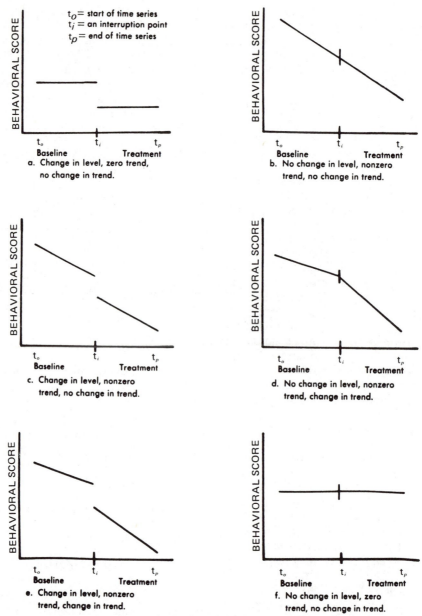

Figure 21. Six illustrative treatment effects: combinations of level and trend changes detectable by time-series analysis. (From "Time-Series Analysis in Operant Research" by R. R. Jones *et al.*, *Journal of Applied Behavior Analysis*, 1973, 6, 517–531, Fig. 1. Copyright 1973 by the Society for the Experimental Analysis of Behavior, Inc. Reprinted by permission.)

whether the same effect can be repeated in a different subject. Thus, replication is concerned with the reliability and the generality of findings.

Elsewhere, Hersen and Barlow (1976) noted that "Replication is at the heart of any science. In all science, replication serves at least two purposes: First, to establish the reliability of previous findings and, second, to determine the generality of these findings under differing conditions. These goals, of course, are intrinsically interrelated. Each time that certain results are replicated under different conditions, this not only establishes generality of findings, but also increases confidence in the reliability of these findings" (p. 317).

The importance of replication in single-case research should be quite obvious from a strictly scientific standpoint. Also, however, critics of the single-case research approach have chastised applied behavioral researchers for reporting chance findings in single cases, despite the apparent demonstration of experimental control in each. Thus, as in the use of statistics in the experimental analysis of behavior, replication (or its absence) is a controversial point.

In this section, we are concerned with the description of three types of replication strategies referred to in Hersen and Barlow (1976): (1) direct; (2) clinical; and (3) systematic. For each type of replication series, the specific issues and guidelines are considered.

Direct Replication

Sidman (1960) has defined direct replication as "repetition of a given experiment by the same investigator" (p. 72). This could involve replication of a procedure within the same subject or across several similar subjects. As argued by Hersen and Barlow (1976), "While repetition on the same subject increases confidence in the reliability of findings and is used occasionally in applied research, generality of findings across clients can be ascertained only by replication on different subjects" (p. 310). Generally, the same investigator (or research team) repeats the study in the same setting (e.g., school, hospital, or clinic) with a set of clients who present with a similar educational or psychological disorder (e.g., unipolar nonpsychotic depression). Although such clients may differ to some extent on demographic variables such as age, education, and sex, it is better for a direct replication series if these are closely matched. This is of special importance for instances where failure to replicate occurs. In such cases, failure, then, should not be attributed to differences in demographic variables. Of paramount concern is that the identical procedure be applied across the different subjects. Otherwise, possible failures or unusual successes may occur, with attribution to subject characteristics erroneously assumed.

Hersen and Barlow (1976) have described several series where direct replications have been undertaken. In one, the initial experiment was successful followed by two replications in the treatment of agoraphobia (Agras, Leitenberg, & Barlow, 1968). (The same held true for a study reported by Hersen et al., 1973 on token economy and neurotic depression.) In a second example (Mills, Agras, Barlow, & Mills, 1973), there were four successful replications with design modifications during replications. In still another series (Wincze, Leitenberg, & Agras, 1972), there were mixed results in nine replications.

When mixed results occur, the investigator should search for the causes of failure and refine the treatment procedures. According to Hersen and Barlow (1976), if one successful experiment is followed by three successful replications, then it is useful to begin a systematic replication series, in which different behaviors in the same setting or similar behavior in different settings are treated by different therapists. If, on the other hand, one successful treatment is followed by two failures to replicate, the investigator should carefully study the variables that account for the failure. This can be as important as a successful attempt at direct replication, inasmuch as new hypotheses may be generated, leading to vastly improved treatments.

Clinical Replication

Hersen and Barlow (1976) have defined "*clinical replication* as the "administration of a treatment package containing two or more distinct treatment procedures by the same investigator or group of investigators. These procedures would be administered in a specific setting to a series of clients presenting similar combinations of multiple behavioral and emotional problems, which cluster together" (p. 336). Examples might be schizophrenia or childhood autism (e.g., Lovaas, Koegel, Simmons, & Long, 1973).

"The usefulness of this effort also depends to some extent on the consistency or reliability of the diagnostic category. If the clustering of the target behaviors is inconsistent, then the patients within the series would be so heterogeneous that the same treatment package could not be applied to successive patients. For this reason, and because of the advanced nature of the research effort, clinical replications are presently not common in the literature'' (Hersen & Barlow, 1976, p. 336).

Guidelines for clinical replication are essentially the same as for direct replication. However, interclient characteristics are, by definition, likely to be more heterogeneous, thus necessitating a longer replication series than in the case of direct replication. Also, successful clinical replication should lead to a systematic replication series.

Systematic Replication

Systematic replication is defined ''as any attempt to replicate findings from a direct replication series, varying settings, behavior change agents, behavior disorders, or any combination thereof. It would appear that any successful systematic replication series in which one or more of the above-mentioned factors is varied also provides further information on generality of findings across clients since new clients are usually included in these efforts'' (Hersen & Barlow, 1976, p. 339).

As for specific guidelines, systematic replication ideally begins after one successful initial experiment and three direct replications have been carried out. However, although the word *systematic* is included, usually such a series is carried out by researchers, either concurrently or in succession, in a number of settings. Some researchers may be in direct communication with one another, but more frequently, it turns out that they are simply working on similar problems, hence the possibility (albeit not really systematic) of replications with variation. Probably the largest such series in the behavioral literature is the one involving dozens of single-case studies showing the efficacy of differential procedures for adults and children (cf. Hersen & Barlow, 1976, pp. 344–352).

In examining a systematic replication series, it is important to note differences in therapists, treatment settings, and clients. In that sense,

the objective of a systematic replication series is to determine exceptions to the rule (i.e., those instances in which a given treatment strategy will not work for a given client or for a particular therapist). This certainly was the case when Wahler (1969) found that differential attention *was not* an effective treatment for dealing with oppositional children. Thus, the limits of applicability of differential attention were ascertained.

Since a systematic replication series involves decentralized research (i.e., in several research settings) and since the search for exceptions to the rule is inevitable in any scientific endeavor, there really can be no finite ending to a systematic replication series. As more data are adduced, however, clinicians applying a given technique should have a greater sense of its likelihood of being effective and successful. This, then, should decrease the trial-and-error approach followed by many practitioners of therapeutic and educational strategies.

Summary and Conclusions

Of the research strategies employed by behavioral researchers, the single-case approach has been the one uniquely tied in with the behavioral tradition. As a research strategy, the single-case approach has had a long and interesting history. In this chapter, we first examined the historical roots of the current experimental analysis-of-behavior model. Then, we considered general issues, such as intrasubject variability, intersubject variability, generality of findings, and variability as related to generality. We next looked at some of the general procedures that characterize most single-case research (repeated measurement, choice of a baseline, the changing of one variable at a time, length of phases, reversal and withdrawal, and evaluation of irreversible procedures). This was followed by a discussion of basic A-B-A designs, their extensions, and the additional designs required when conditions for the A-B-A strategies cannot be met. We briefly looked at the thorny issue of statistical analysis in single-case research and ended with a discussion of direct, clinical, and systematic replication.

In conclusion, we should point out that the field is not static and that newer design and statistical techniques will undoubtedly emerge over the course of the next few years. This, of course, is a healthy phenomenon that we can only applaud. Moreover, we should acknowledge that there are some inherent limitations in all design strategies, including single-case analysis, that all researchers need to recognize. Thus, we see nothing inherently wrong in, at times, using the single-case approach to generate treatment hypotheses that subsequently may be refined and then pitted against one another in larger-scaled group-comparison studies.

References

Agras, W. S., Leitenberg, H., & Barlow, D. H. Social reinforcement in the modification of agoraphobia. *Archives of General Psychiatry*, 1968, *19*, 423–427.

Agras, W. S., Barlow, D. H., Chapin, H. N., Abel, G. G., & Leitenberg, H., Behavior modification of anorexia nervosa. *Archives of General Psychiatry*, 1974, *30*, 279–286.

Allen, G. J. Case study: Implimentation of behavior modification techniques in summer camp setting. *Behavior Therapy*, 1973, *4*, 570–575.

Allen, K. E., Hart, B. M., Buell, J. S., Harris, F. R., & Wolf, M. M. Effects of social reinforcement on isolate behavior of a nursery school child. *Child Development*, 1964, *35*, 511–518.

Ayllon, T., & Azrin, N. H. The measurement and reinforcement of behavior of psychotics. *Behaviour Research and Therapy*, 1965, *8*, 357–383.

Baer, D. M. Perhaps it would be better not to know everything. *Journal of Applied Behavior Analysis*, 1977, *10*, 167–172.

Baer, D. M., Wolf, M. M., & Risley, T. R. Some current dimensions of applied behavior analysis. *Journal of Applied Behavior Analysis*, 1968, *1*, 91–97.

Barlow, D. H., & Hersen, M. Single-case experimental designs: Uses in applied clinical research. *Archives of General Psychiatry*, 1973, *29*, 319–325.

Barlow, D. H., Agras, W. S., Leitenberg, H., Callahan, E. J., & Moore, R. C. The contribution of therapeutic instruction to covert sensitization. *Behaviour Research and Therapy*, 1972, *10*, 411–415.

Barlow, D. H., Blanchard, D. B., Hayes, S. C., & Epstein, L. H. Single case designs and clinical biofeedback experimentation. *Biofeedback and Self-Regulation*, 1977, *2*, 221–236.

Bellack, A. S., & Schwartz, J. S. Assessment for self-control programs. In M. Hersen & A. S. Bellack (Eds.), *Behavioral assessment: A practical handbook*. New York: Pergamon Press, 1976.

Benjamin, L. S. A special latin squre for the use of each subject "as his own control." *Psychometrika*, 1965, *30*, 499–513.

Bergin, A. E. Some implications of psychotherapy research for therapeutic practice. *Journal of Abnornal Psychology*, 1966, *71*, 235–246.

Bergin, A. E., & Strupp, H. H. *Changing frontiers in the science of psychotherapy*. New York: Aldine-Atherton, 1972.

Bijou, S. W., Peterson, R. F., Harris, F. R., Allen, K. E., & Johnston, M. S. Methodology for experimental studies of young children in natural settings. *Psychological Record*, 1969, *19*, 177–210.

Bornstein, M. R., Bellack, A. S., & Hersen, M. Social-skills training for unassertive children: A multiple-baseline analysis. *Journal of Applied Behavior Analysis*, 1977, *10*, 183–195.

Breuer, J., & Freud, S. *Studies on hysteria*. New York: Basic Books, 1957.

Campbell, D. T., & Stanley, J. C. Experimental and quasi-experimental designs for research and teaching. Chicago: Rand-McNally, 1966.

Chassan, J. B. *Research design in clinical psychology and psychiatry*. New York: Appleton-Century-Crofts, 1967.

Eisler, R. M., Hersen, M., & Agras, W. S. Effects of videotape and instructional feedback on nonverbal marital interaction: An analog study. *Behavior Therapy*, 1973, *4*, 551–558.

Epstein, L. H., & Hersen, M. Behavioral control of hysterical gagging. *Journal of Clinical Psychology*, 1974, *30*, 102–104.

Eysenck, H. J. The effects of psychotherapy: An evaluation. *Journal of Consulting Psychology*, 1952, *16*, 319–324.

Fisher, R. A. On the mathematical foundations of the theory of statistics. In *Theory of statistical estimation* (Proceeding of the Cambridge Philosophical Society), 1925.

Gentile, J. R., Roden, A. H., & Klein, R. D. An analysis of variance model for the intrasubject replication design. *Journal of Applied Behavior Analysis*, 1972, *5*, 193–198.

Glass, G. V., Willson, V. L., & Gottman, J. M. *Design and analysis of time-series experiments*. Boulder: Colorado Associated University Press, 1974.

Hartmann, D. P. Forcing square pegs into roundholes: Some comments on "an analysis-of-variance model for the intrasubject replication design." *Journal of Applied Behavior Analysis*, 1974, *7*, 635–638.

Hartmann, D. P., & Hall, R. V. The changing criterion design. *Journal of Applied Behavior Analysis*, 1976, *9*, 527–532.

Hersen, M. Self-assessment of fear. *Behavior Therapy*, 1973, *4*, 241–257.

Hersen, M. Do behavior therapists use self-reports as the major criteria? *Behavioural Analysis and Modification*, 1978, *2*, 328–334.

Hersen, M. Limitations and problems in the clinical application of behavioral techniques in psychiatric settings. *Behavior Therapy*, 1979, *10*, 65–80.

Hersen, M., & Barlow, D. H. *Single case experimental designs: Strategies for studying behavior change*. New York: Pergamon Press, 1976.

Hersen, M., & Bellack, A. S. (Eds.). *Behavioral assessment: A practical handbook*. New York: Pergamon Press, 1976.

Hersen, M., & Bellack, A. S. (Eds.). *Behavior therapy*

in the psychiatric setting. Baltimore: Williams & Wilkins, 1978.

Hersen, M., Eisler, R. M., Alford, G. S., & Agras, W. S. Effects of token economy on neurotic depression: An experimental analysis. *Behavior Therapy,* 1973, *4,* 392–397.

Johnston, J. M. Punishment of human behavior. *American Psychologist,* 1972, *27,* 1033–1054.

Jones, R. R., Vaught, R. S., & Weinrott, M. Time-series analysis in operant research. *Journal of Applied Behavior Analysis,* 1977, *10,* 151–166.

Kallman, W. M., Hersen, M., & O'Toole, D. H. The use of social reinforcement in a case of conversion reaction. *Behavior Therapy,* 1975, *6,* 411–413.

Kazdin, A. E. Methodological and assessment considerations in evaluating reinforcement programs in applied settings. *Journal of Applied Behavior Analysis,* 1973, *6,* 517–531.

Kazdin, A. E. *Behavior modification in applied settings.* Homewood, Ill.: Dorsey Press, 1975.

Kazdin, A. E. Statistical analysis for single-case experimental designs. In M. Hersen & D. H. Barlow (Eds.), *Single case experimental designs: Strategies for studying behavior change.* New York: Pergamon Press, 1976.

Kazdin, A. E. Assessing the clinical or applied importance of behavior change through social validation. *Behavior Modification,* 1977, *1,* 427–451.

Kazdin, A. E. *History of behavior modification.* Baltimore: University Park Press, 1978.

Kazdin, A. E. *Research design in clinical psychology.* New York: Harper & Row, 1980.

Kazdin, A. E., & Geesey, S. Simultaneous-treatment design comparisons of the effects of earning reinforcers for one's peers versus for oneself. *Behavior Therapy,* 1977, *8,* 682–693.

Kazdin, A. E., & Hartmann, D. P. The simultaneous-treatment design. *Behavior Therapy,* 1978, *9,* 912–922.

Kazdin, A. E., & Kopel, S. A. On resolving ambiguities of the multiple-baseline design: Problems and recommendations. *Behavior Therapy,* 1975, *6,* 601–608.

Keselman, H. J., & Leventhal, L. Concerning the statistical procedures enumerated by Gentile *et al.:* Another perspective. *Journal of Applied Behavior Analysis,* 1974, *7,* 643–645.

Kratochwill, T. R. (Ed.). *Single subject research: Strategies for evaluating change.* New York: Academic Press, 1978.

Kratochwill, T., Alden, K., Demuth, D., Dawson, D., Panicucci, C., Arntson, P., McMurray, N., Hempstead, J., & Levin, J. A further consideration in the application of an analysis-of-variance model for the intrasubject replication design. *Journal of Applied Behavior Analysis,* 1974, *7,* 629–633.

Leitenberg, H. The use of single-case methodology in psychotherapy research. *Journal of Abnormal Psychology,* 1973, *82,* 87–101.

Liberman, R. P., & Davis, J. Drugs and behavior analysis. In M. Hersen, R. M. Eisler, & P. M. Miller (Eds.), *Progress in behavior modification,* Vol. 1. New York: Academic Press, 1975.

Liberman, R. P., Davis, J., Moon, W., & Moore, J. Research design for analyzing drug-environment-behavior interactions. *Journal of Nervous and Mental Disease,* 1973, *156,* 432–439.

Lombardo, T. W., & Turner, S. M. Thought-stopping in the control of obsessive ruminations. *Behavior Modification,* 1979, *3,* 267–272.

Lovaas, O. I., Koegel, R., Simmons, J. Q., & Long, J. D. Some generalization and follow-up measures on autistic children in behavior therapy. *Journal of Applied Behavior Analysis,* 1973, *5,* 131–166.

Mann, R. A. The behavior-therapeutic use of contingency contracting to control an adult behavior problem: Weight control. *Journal of Applied Behavior Analysis,* 1972, *5,* 99–109.

Martin, J. E., & Epstein, L. H. Evaluating treatment effectiveness in cerebral palsy: Single subject designs. *Physical Therapy,* 1976, *56,* 285–294.

Max, L. W. Breaking up a homosexual fixation by the conditioned reaction technique: A case study. *Psychological Bulletin,* 1935, *32,* 734 (abstract).

Meichenbaum, D. A cognitive-behavior modification approach to assessment. In M. Hersen & A. S. Bellack (Eds.), *Behavioral assessment: A practical handbook.* New York: Pergamon Press, 1976.

Michael, J. Statistical inference for individual organism research: Mixed blessing or curse? *Journal of Applied Behavior Analysis,* 1974, *7,* 647–653. (a)

Michael, J. Statistical inference for individual organism research: Some reactions to a suggestion by Gentile, Roden, & Klein. *Journal of Applied Behavior Analysis,* 1974, *7,* 627–628. (b)

Miller, P. M. An experimental analysis of retention control training in the treatment of nocturnal enuresis in two institutionalized adolescents. *Behavior Therapy,* 1973, *4,* 288–294.

Mills, H. L., Agras, W. S., Barlow, D. H., & Mills, J. R. Compulsive rituals treated by response prevention: An experimental analysis. *Archives of General Psychiatry,* 1973, *28,* 524–529.

Ortega, D. F. Relaxation exercise with cerebral palsied adults showing spasticity. *Journal of Applied Behavior Analysis,* 1978, *11,* 447–451.

Paul, G. L. Strategy of outcome research in psychotherapy. *Journal of Consulting Psychology,* 1967, *31,* 104–118.

Risley, T. R., & Wolf, M. M. Strategies for analysing behavioral change over time. In J. Nesselroade & H. Reese (Eds.), *Life-span developmental psychology: Methodological issues.* New York: Academic Press, 1972.

Rubenstein, E. A., & Parloff, M. B. Research problems in psychotherapy. In E. A. Rubenstein & M. B. Parloff (Eds.), *Research in psychotherapy,* Vol. 1. Washington, D.C.: American Psychological Association, 1959.

Shapiro, M. B. The single case in clinical-psychological research. *Journal of General Psychology,* 1966, *74,* 3–23.

Shapiro, M. B., & Ravenette, A. T. A preliminary experiment of paranoid delusions. *Journal of Mental Science,* 1959, *105,* 295–312.

Shine, L. C., & Bower, S. M. A one-way analysis of variance for single subject designs. *Educational and Psychological Measurement,* 1971, *31,* 105–113.

Sidman, M. *Tactics of scientific research: Evaluating experimental data in psychology.* New York: Basic Books, 1960.

Skinner, B. F. Operant behavior. In W. K. Konig (Ed.),

Operant behavior: Areas of research and application. New York: Appleton-Century-Crofts, 1966.

Thomas, E. J. Research and service in single-case experimentation: Conflicts and choices. *Social Work Research and Abstracts,* 1978, *14,* 20–31.

Thoresen, C. E. The intensive design: An intimate approach to counseling research. Paper read at American Educational Research Association, Chicago, April 1972.

Thoresen, C. E., & Elashoff, J. D. "An analysis-of-variance model for intrasubject replication design": Some additional comments. *Journal of Applied Behavior Analysis,* 1974, *7,* 639–641.

Turner, S. M., Hersen, M., & Alford, H. Case histories and shorter communications. *Behaviour Research and Therapy,* 1974, *12,* 259–260.

Turner, S. M., Hersen, M., Bellack, A. S., & Wells, K. C. Behavioral treatment of obsessive-compulsive neurosis. *Behaviour Research and Therapy,* 1979, *17,* 95–106.

Van Hasselt, V. B., Hersen, M., Bellack, A. S., Rosenblum, N., & Lamparski, D. Tripartite assessment of the effects of systematic desensitization in a multiphobic child: An experimental analysis. *Journal of Behavior Therapy and Experimental Psychiatry,* 1979, *10,* 51–56.

Wahler, R. G. Oppositional children: A guest for parental reinforcement control. *Journal of Applied Behavior Analysis,* 1969, *2,* 159–170.

Watson, J. B., & Rayner, R. Conditioned emotional reactions. *Journal of Experimental Psychology,* 1920, *3,* 1–14.

Wells, K. C., Turner, S. M., Bellack, A. S., & Hersen, M. Effects of cue-controlled relaxation on psychomotor seizures: An experimental analysis. *Behaviour Research and Therapy,* 1978, *16,* 51–53.

Williamson, D. A., Calpin, J. P., DiLorenzo, T. M., Garris, R. P., & Petti, T. A. Combining dexedrine (dextro-amphetamine) and activity feedback for the treatment of hyperactivity. *Behavior Modification,* 1981, *5,* 399–416.

Wincze, J. P., Leitenberg, H., & Agras, W. S. The effects of token reinforcement and feedback on the delusional verbal behavior of chronic paranoid schizophrenics. *Journal of Applied Behavior Analysis,* 1972, *5,* 247–262.

Yates, A. J. *Behavior Therapy.* New York: Wiley, 1970.

PART II

Adult Disorders

Behavior therapy is often characterized by nonbehavior therapists as a set of discrete procedures. This results partially from the fact that we do not have a single, all-encompassing theory to explain all behavior and treatment procedures. Of course, behavior therapists pay allegiance to "learning theory." But, the "principles" of learning provide more of a general backdrop and frame of reference for our work, rather than a specific, tightly knit theory. The misperceptions of nonbehavior therapists are also based on the behavior theory of the 1960s, which was limited to a few highly publicized techniques: notably, systematic desensitization and token economies.

Our discipline has changed and expanded dramatically in the past 20 years, and that early characterization is no longer appropriate. Treatments have been developed for a host of additional disorders. Moreover, there are now a variety of alternative treatments for many individual disorders. In some cases, these alternatives result from competing models for the nature of the disorder (e.g., depression as a result of a cognitive distortion or a social skills deficits). Frequently, the empirical literature does not definitively support any one model, and the choice of treatment depends on the preferences of the therapist and patient. In the case of other disorders, the treatment variations seem to be more appropriate for different subcategories of patients, based on the specific nature of their disorder. For example, systematic desensitization appears to be the treatment of choice for simple phobias, cognitive therapies appear to be especially appropriate for social phobias, and exposure treatments appear to be most effective for agoraphobia. Although the data are not as clear, cognitive therapy seems to be more appropriate for those depressed patients who have cognitive distortions, whereas social skills training seems to be appropriate for depressed patients who have skill deficits and a restricted social network. Each chapter in this section examines alternative models and treatments for the respective disorders. They also discuss the current state of knowledge about patient–treatment matching and they reflect the differing states of our knowledge about the different disorders. In so doing, they highlight the breadth and diversity of behavior therapy strategies.

In preparing a text on behavior therapy, one is always faced with the difficult choice of organizing the book around techniques or disorders. Given our belief that future research will enable us to more carefully match techniques to specific patient characteristics, we have chosen to organize around disorders. Orienting around techniques offers the advantage of providing a conceptually integrated perspective (i.e., a specific model is described, followed by discussion of the various treatment procedures which flow from it, as with cognitive behavior therapy). Conversely, a technique oriented perspective can have a negative impact on clinical practice. If the clinician conceptualizes problems primarily by the available treatment techniques rather then specific problems presented by the client, there is a danger that the client will be shoehorned into a superficially relevant treatment rather than receiving a carefully tailored intervention.

Based on that viewpoint, we have elected to organize this and the subsequent section of the book around disorders. In Chapter 5, Emmelkamp provides an excellent overview of the various behavioral treatments for fear and anxiety, with an emphasis on clinical studies and issues. Lewinsohn and Hoberman discuss the major behavioral theories and treatments for depression in Chapter 6. Chapter 7, by Curran, Monti, and Corriveau, covers various strategies for work with schizophrenics, with an emphasis on token economies and social skills training. Reflecting the current emphasis on behavioral medicine, Taylor examines procedures for treating a variety of medical disorders in Chapter 8. Finally, Bellack and Morrison discuss the nature of interpersonal dysfunction and social skills training strategies in Chapter 9.

In addition to the five chapters preented here, the complete handbook contains chapters on alcohol and drug problems, obesity, cigarette dependence, crime and delinquency, sexual dysfunctions and sexual deviation, obsessive compulsive disorders, and marital distress. In determining which chapters to reprint here, we considered the clinical significance of the disorders in the general community, the frequency of referral to behavior therapists, and the empirical support for the various interventions. We believe that the five chapters in this section describe effective interventions for the most serious and most frequently appearing problems.

CHAPTER 5

Anxiety and Fear

Paul M. G. Emmelkamp

Introduction

Most behavioral research in the area of anxiety and fear has been of the analogue type. Researchers have typically employed volunteers, usually students, with small animal phobias (e.g., snake phobia) or social anxiety (e.g., speech anxiety, dating anxiety) as subjects. While some researchers have selected only highly fearful subjects, others have used mildly fearful subjects or those with low fear. For instance, in a study by De Moor (1970), about one-third of the sample of "snake phobics" could touch the snake at the pretest; Melnick (1973) employed subjects with "dating anxiety" who dated less than twice a week. Analogue researchers have usually excluded subjects from participation who have real psychological problems. To give just a few examples, subjects who were undergoing or had undergone any form of psychiatric treatment (e.g., Mathews & Rezin, 1977; Mealiea & Nawas, 1971) or who manifested emotional disorder or psychological difficulties (e.g., Barrett, 1969; Beiman, Israel, & Johnson, 1978; De Moor, 1970) have been excluded. However, it should be noted that subjects with

psychological difficulties may be more similar to phobic patients than subjects without such problems.

Analogue studies are often not internally valid. Several studies have demonstrated that demand characteristics can influence behavioral assessment in such studies. For instance, in a study of Emmelkamp and Boeke-Slinkers (1977a) using snake phobics as subjects, the level of demand for approach behavior in a behavioral avoidance test was varied. Both high-demand and low-demand subjects were regarded as phobic if they could not touch the snake with a gloved hand. On the basis of the results of the low-demand test, 16.9% of the subjects would have been classified as phobic and would have qualified for treatment, whereas on the basis of the high-demand test, the percentage would have been only 6.8%. Thus, behavioral avoidance tests used in analogue studies are easily influenced by demand characteristics. Other studies clearly indicate the influence of situational and instructional effects on behavioral assessment procedures (e.g., Barrios, 1978; Bernstein, 1974; Bernstein & Nietzel, 1973, 1974; Smith, Diener, & Beaman, 1974).

There are several important differences between clinical and analogue populations. Phobic patients differ from controls and phobic students on various measures of psychopath-

Paul M. G. Emmelkamp • Department of Clinical Psychology, Academic Hospital, Oostersingel 59, Groningen, The Netherlands.

ology (Emmelkamp, 1979a). In addition, subjects in analogue and clinical studies may differ markedly with respect to approach contingencies (Hayes, 1976). Even though both types of subjects may show substantial avoidance behavior, phobic patients may experience much stronger approach contingencies than subjects in laboratory studies. Furthermore, the kind of phobias treated in clinical and analogue studies differ widely. While analogue researchers have typically employed students with small-animal phobias or social anxiety as subjects, agoraphobia forms the greatest category of phobias seen in clinical settings. Because of the differences between clinical and analogue populations, the clinical value of such studies has been questioned (e.g., Cooper, Furst, & Bridger, 1969; Emmelkamp, 1980a).

The difficulty in generalizing results from analogue studies to clinical patients is illustrated by the differential effectiveness of treatment with analogue populations, on the one hand, and with clinical populations, on the other. For many years, the behavioral treatment of phobias was dominated by systematic desensitization. In contrast with analogue studies, where this procedure has consistently been found to be effective in improving minor fears, a recent review (Emmelkamp, 1979a) suggests that this procedure has only small effects on socially anxious and agoraphobic patients. Branham and Katahn (1974) compared desensitization and no treatment, with both volunteer students and patients as subjects. Volunteers improved significantly more than patients. In their volunteer sample, desensitization was significantly superior to the control condition, whereas in their patient sample, desensitization was no more effective than no treatment. With cognitive modification procedures, the same picture arises. Cognitive modification procedures have been found to be quite effective with analogue populations. However, recent studies at out department show that these procedures have clinically insignificant effects with agoraphobic (Emmeikamp, Kuipers, & Eggeraat, 1978) and obsessive-compulsive patients (Emmelkamp, Van de Helm, Van Zanten, & Plochg, 1980). Other studies have found differential effectiveness with biofeedback (Shepherd & Watts,

1974) and relaxation (Borkovec & Sides, 1979) for patients and for volunteers.

It is not my purpose to dismiss the findings of analogue studies entirely. Whether analogue research is relevant or not depends on the question that one wants to investigate. Since several recent papers (Bandura, 1978; Borkovec & Rachman, 1979; Kazdin, 1978) deal with this issue, I will not discuss it further. However, while analogue studies may be of some value for certain research questions, the clinical effectiveness of treatments can be studied only with clinical patients as subjects.

In this chapter, I first briefly discuss the current status of behavioral theories concerning the functioning of phobic behavior; then, the effectiveness of nonbehavioral treatments (i.e., psychopharmaca and psychotherapy) is discussed. The bulk of the chapter is devoted to a critical analysis of behavioral treatments. In a separate section, the *clinical* effectiveness of behavioral procedures with socially anxious and agoraphobic patients is reviewed. In the last section, some future trends are discussed.

Historical Perspective

Current Status of the Process Learning Theory of Fear Acquisition

In the early days of behavior therapy, therapists held that phobic reactions could be adequately explained in terms of conditioning. Until several years ago, Mowrer's (1950) theory of fear acquisition was widely accepted by behavior therapists as a model for the development of clinical phobias. In Mowrer's view, classically conditioned fear motivates avoidance behavior, which leads to a reduction of fear and a strengthening of the avoidance behavior (negative reinforcement). According to this theory, anxiety and avoidance are causally linked, and avoidance behavior should be reduced as soon as anxiety is eliminated.

The two-stage theory of learning is disputed by several lines of evidence (Emmelkamp, 1979a; Eysenck, 1976; Rachman, 1976, 1977). First, a traumatic experience relating to the genesis of phobias often cannot be found. For instance, both phobic volunteers (Fazio, 1972;

Murray & Foote, 1979; Rimm, Janda, Lancaster, Nahl & Dittmar, 1977) and phobic patients (Buglass, Clarke, Henderson, Kreitman, & Presley, 1977; Goldstein & Chambless, 1978; Goorney & O'Connor, 1971; Lazarus, 1971; Liddell & Lyons, 1978; Solyom, Beck, Solyom, & Hugel, 1974) are often unable to recall any traumatic experience in the setting in which they were subsequently phobic. Second, repeated failures to condition phobias are an even greater problem for the conditioning theory. Several studies have failed to replicate the famous "Little Albert" experiment of Watson and Rayner (1920), who conditioned a phobia in a 1-year-old child. And finally, the conditioning paradigm is inadequate (1) in explaining the gradual development of phobias as sometimes seen in phobic patients and (2) in explaining the preponderance of phobias such as agoraphobia or snake phobia as compared with the infrequency of phobias for hammers and electrical appliances.

Several modifications and alternative theories have been proposed, but to date, evidence based on research with clinical patients is lacking (Emmelkamp, 1979a). For instance, some have argued that clinical phobias can develop through *vicarious learning* (e.g., Bandura, 1977) or that fear can be acquired through the *transmission of information and instruction* (e.g., Rachman, 1977). Although there is some evidence that children often share their parents' fears, which may be explained in terms of observational and instructional learning, other explanations are equally plausible (e.g., genetic influences or similar traumatic experiences). As far as retrospective reports of phobic subjects are concerned, the data are inconclusive. Few of the subjects in the Fazio (1972) and Rimm *et al.* (1977) studies reported vicarious learning experiences, while Murray and Foote (1979) found that fear was often acquired through observational and instructional experiences that communicate negative information.

According to Seligman (1971), phobias are instances of highly *prepared* learning; in his view, the human species has been preprogrammed through evolution to acquire phobias easily for potentially dangerous situations. Öhman and his colleagues have conducted a series of ingenious experiments to test the preparedness theory experimentally (for review, see Öhman, 1979). The results of their experiments, conducted with normal volunteer subjects, indicate that conditioned electrodermal responses to fear-relevant stimuli (e.g., pictures of spiders or snakes) showed much higher resistance to extinction than responses conditioned to neutral stimuli (e.g., pictures of flowers or mushrooms). However, the effect of the stimulus content variable was less clear-cut during the acquisition phase. Thus, the experiments partially supported the preparedness theory.

Despite the bulk of evidence in favor of preparedness provided by this series of experiments, the results of these studies need to be qualified in several ways. In passing, it should be noted that all experiments have been conducted by only one research group. Cross-validation of this theory in a different center would be valuable. Moreover, the laboratory model of fear acquisition seems to be of questionable relevance to clinical phobias (Emmelkamp, 1979a). Finally, the preparedness theory does not seem to have any implication for the treatment of phobias.

Another influential theory concerning phobic behavior has been proposed by cognitive-behavior therapists. In their view, anxiety reactions are mediated by faulty *cognitions* or anxiety-inducing self-instructions. Several studies have been conducted to test this theory. Two types of faulty thinking have been investigated: (1) negative self-statements and (2) irrational beliefs.

Studies investigating the influence of self-instructions on anxiety indicated that negative self-statements may enhance arousal (May & Johnson, 1973; Rimm & Litvak, 1969; Rogers & Craighead, 1977; Russell & Brandsma, 1974). However, in a study with phobic subjects, Rimm *et al.* (1977) found that only half of the subjects reported *in vivo* thoughts preceding fear in the phobic situation. According to the cognitive theory, the thoughts always should precede the fear.

Irrational thinking is identified with Ellis's (1962) theory, suggesting that phobics have a tendency to think irrationally and that these irrational beliefs produce their anxiety reactions. Several studies indicate that irrational beliefs are related to phobic anxiety (Goldfried & Sobocinsky, 1975; Rimm *et al.*, 1977). While the results of these studies might indicate that such irrational beliefs are causally linked to anxiety evocation, it is equally plausible that increased emotional arousal in certain situations may sensitize individuals to certain irrational expectancies (Goldfried & Sobocinski, 1975). The studies reviewed so far are of questionable relevance to clinical phobias, because of none of these studies investigated the thoughts of phobic patients.

Recently, Sutton-Simon and Goldfried (1979) reported a study involving patients, although not necessarily phobic, who requested psychotherapy at a community clinic. In this study, the relationship between two types of faulty thinking (irrational beliefs vs. negative self-statements) on the one hand and type of phobia (social anxiety vs. acrophobia) on the other was investigated. The results showed that social anxiety was correlated only with irrational thinking, while acrophobia was correlated with both types of faulty thinking.

In my opinion (Emmelkamp, 1980a), behavioral interpretations of phobic behavior have been rather naive and simple and can offer at best only a partial explanation. In addition to conditioning and cognitive factors, we have to search for other factors as well. One suggestion is that a more comprehensive theory of phobia development should take into account the role of *interpersonal conflicts*. Although the evidence on this point is less than satisfactory (Emmelkamp, 1979a), comprising mainly anecdotes, clinical observations do suggest the importance of clients' interpersonal relationships in the development of clinical phobias, especially in the case of agoraphobia. Moreover, a really comprehensive theory of fear acquisition should also take into account the role that the client's system plays in the functioning of the phobic behavior. It is not sufficient merely to point out that family members "reinforce" the phobic behavior of the identified patient; their motives to do so and the reason that the patient lets them do so deserve special attention. Conceptualizing interpersonal conflicts solely in terms of conditioning may seriously hinder progress in this area.

Another point that deserves more attention is the role of individual differences in phobia acquisition. Although far from conclusive, there is some evidence (Emmelkamp, 1979a) that level of emotional arousal, hormonal processes, and premorbid dependency may significantly contribute to the development of phobias.

Obviously, several factors interact in determining phobic behavior. In my opinion, laboratory studies using either animals or volunteer students as subjects are not useful in developing and evaluating a more comprehensive theory of phobia development.

Nonbehavioral Treatments

Until Wolpe's (1958) introduction of systematic desensitization for the treatment of phobias, treatment for this condition consisted of psychopharmacological or insight-oriented psychotherapy. In this section, research with respect to the effectiveness of psychopharmacology and psychotherapy is reviewed.

Psychopharmaca. Both monoamine oxidase inhibitors (MAOIs) and tricyclic antidepressants have been reported to be beneficial in the treatment of anxiety neurosis and phobic states. However, most of these studies have severe methodological flaws (e.g., no adequate controls, retrospective assessment of results, lack of independent assessments, and no homogeneous population).

Monoamine Oxidase Inhibitors. More recently, several controlled researches into the effectiveness of MAOIs have been conducted. Tyrer, Candy and Kelly (1973) found phenelzine more effective as compared with placebo after eight weeks, but the clinical improvement was not very impressive. Solyom, Heseltine, McClure, Solyom, Ledwidge, and Steinberg (1973) compared phenelzine with various behavioral treatments (systematic desensitization, aversion relief, and flooding, all in imagination). Although the effect of phenelzine was the most rapid, two weeks after the termination of treatment all 6 (out of 10) patients who had stopped taking the drug had relapsed, as compared with only 10% of the patients who had been treated by behavior therapy.

Lipsedge, Hajioff, Huggins, Napier, Pearce,

Pike, and Rich (1973) compared iproniazid with systematic desensitization (in imagination) and placebo. While both treatments proved to be more effective than placebo, no significant differences between systematic desensitization and iproniazid were found. Finally, Solyom, Solyom, La Pierre, Pecknold, and Morton (1981) compared phenelzine and placebo and could not find any difference between them.

Thus, there is some evidence that MAOIs may have beneficial effects on phobic cases, but the effects found were rather small. This conclusion needs to be qualified in several ways. First, most studies instructed patients to expose themselves *in vivo* between treatment sessions. Thus, the effects of MAOIs have not been assessed independently of the effects of exposure *in vivo*. In the only study that attempted to separate these effects (Solyom *et al.*, 1981), phenelzine proved to be no more effective than placebo. Second, discontinuation of medication generally leads to relapse (Lipsedge *et al.*, 1973; Solyom *et al.*, 1973; Tyrer *et al.*, 1973). Third, side effects have often been reported with the use of this class of drugs, including difficulty with micturition, inhibition of ejaculation and anorgasmia, fatigue, dry mouth, blurred vision, edema, and insomnia (e.g., Kelly, Guirguis, Frommer, Mitchell-Heggs, & Sargant, 1970; Mountjoy, Roth, Garside, & Leitch, 1977; Solyom *et al.*, 1973; Tyrer *et al.*, 1973). Fourth, severe interaction with some foods containing a high concentration of amines (Blackwell, 1963) and other drugs (Sjöqvist, 1963) and hepatotoxicity (Pare, 1964) have been reported. Finally, as far as comparisons with behavioral treatments are concerned, only "weak" forms of behavioral treatment have been involved. No study has directly compared MAOIs with prolonged exposure *in vivo*, which is far more effective than systematic desensitization, especially with agoraphobics. Briefly, MAOIs have little to recommend them in the treatment of phobias and anxiety states.

Imipramine. Zitrin, Klein, and Woerners (1978) compared the relative effectiveness of imipramine and behavior therapy. Behavior therapy consisted of systematic desensitization in imagination and assertive training. In order to have treatment time equivalent to behavior therapy, patients who received imipramine were also given supportive psychotherapy. Three conditions were compared: (1) behavior therapy plus imipramine; (2) behavior therapy plus placebo; and (3) supportive psychotherapy plus imipramine. The treatment consisted of 26 weekly sessions. The preliminary results indicate that imipramine had beneficial effects for patients who experienced spontaneous panic attacks (including agoraphobics). Imipramine had no therapeutic effects on simple phobics. Rather, it led to a high dropout rate due to medication side effects.

Psychotherapy. Reports of psychoanalysts concerning the treatment of phobias have involved theoretical essays on the dynamics of the patients; the effectiveness of treatment is rarely discussed (Emmelkamp, 1979a). However, Friedman (1950) reported that "after the dynamics of the case were worked through, many patients failed to recover" (p. 274). Other psychoanalysts have also reported unsatisfactory results. Both Freud and Fenichel used exposure *in vivo* in the treatment of phobic cases, which seems to have been forgotton by their followers. Freud wrote (1959), "One can hardly ever master a phobia if one waits till the patient lets the analysis influence him to give it up. . . . one succeeds only when one can induce them through the influence of the analysis . . . to go about alone and struggle with the anxiety while they make the attempt" (Freud, 1959, p. 399). Fenichel (1963) stated the same point, perhaps even more clearly: "The analyst must actively intervene in order to induce the patient to make his first effort to overcome the phobia; he must induce the patient to expose himself to the feared experiences" (p. 215). One can only wonder why the suggestion of these authorities have not been taken seriously by their followers.

Several authors have reported on the treatment of anxiety neurosis and phobias with psychotherapy (Errera & Coleman, 1963; Miles, Barrabee, & Finesinger, 1951; Robert, 1964; Terhune, 1949). These studies have serious methodological flaws, such as no control groups, retrospective assessment of results, no independent assessment of results, and no homogeneous population. In addition, more often than not the results are confounded by additional medication, electroconvulsive therapy (ECT), or unsystematic exposure *in vivo*, which preclude the drawing of any conclusion with respect to the effectiveness of psychotherapy.

Several studies have compared the effectiveness of psychotherapy and behavioral treatments. Only prospective studies involving real clinical phobic patients are discussed here. Gelder and Marks (1966) were the first to conduct such a study. In their study, systematic desensitization and psychotherapy were compared with severe agoraphobic inpatients. After 60–70 sessions, no significant differences were found between the treatments. Overall improvement was small. In a subsequent study involving mixed phobic patients as subjects (Gelder, Marks, & Wolff, 1967), systematic desensitization proved to be more effective than individual or group psychotherapy at the posttest, despite the fact that the desensitization patients had received less treatment than the psychotherapy patients. In a following study in this series (Gelder & Marks, 1968), seven patients who were unimproved after group psychotherapy were treated with desensitization. The patients improved three times as much after four months of desensitization as after two years of group psychotherapy. Finally, Dormaar and Dijkstra (1975) and Gillan and Rachman (1974) also found systematic desensitization to be superior to psychotherapy, although in the Dormaar and Dijkstra study, the between-group difference was not statistically significant.

In summary, systematic desensitization has been found to be more effective than psychotherapy where mixed phobic patients or socially anxious patients (Dormaar & Dijkstra, 1975) were concerned. With agoraphobics, systematic desensitization was no more effective than psychotherapy.

Current Empirical Status

In this section, the current empirical status of behavioral procedures is reviewed. This section is divided in two parts. The first part evaluates the theoretical underpinnings of various treatments and presents an integrated treatment model. The second part is devoted

to an evaluation of the clinical effectiveness of treatments, especially with socially anxious and agoraphobic patients.

Behavioral Procedures

Systematic Desensitization. In desensitization, clients are first trained in muscular relaxation; then, they move gradually up a hierarchy of anxiety-arousing situations, while remaining relaxed. Systematic desensitization may be applied either in imagination or *in vivo*, but most studies involved the imaginal variant.

Although numerous studies have demonstrated the effectiveness of systematic desensitization in reducing circumscribed phobias in analogue populations, the theoretical underpinnings of this procedure are still vague. Several theoretical explanations have been put forward, including reciprocal inhibition (Wolpe, 1958), counterconditioning (Davison, 1968), cognitive processes (Emmelkamp, 1975a), and psychoanalytic interpretations (Silverman, Frank, & Dachinger, 1974). Since a detailed review of the research in this area could fill a whole volume, only the major research findings are presented in this section.

Reciprocal Inhibition and Counterconditioning. Both the reciprocal inhibition and the counterconditioning interpretations hold that a graded hierarchy and an incompatible response (relaxation) are essential for the successful desensitization of fear. However, desensitization with relaxation has been found to be as effective as desensitization without relaxation (graded exposure). Marks (1975) reviewed research in this area and found no evidence that relaxation enhanced the effectiveness of imaginal exposure to the phobic stimuli. More recent studies have also demonstrated that desensitization with relaxation is no more effective than graded exposure to the hierarchy items (e.g., Goldfried & Goldfried, 1977; Ladouceur, 1978). Even more importantly, studies with clinical phobics have also found negative results with respect to relaxation in a systematic desensitization context (Agras, Leitenberg, Barlow, Curtis, Edwards, & Wright, 1971; Benjamin, Marks, & Huson, 1972; Gillan & Rachman, 1974). Briefly, there is no evidence that the effects of systematic desensitization should be interpreted in terms of counterconditioning or reciprocal inhibition.

Cognitive Factors. There has been a continuous debate over the influence of cognitive factors, particularly the expectancy of therapeutic gain on systematic desensitization (Davison & Wilson, 1973; Emmelkamp, 1975a,b; Wilson & Davison, 1975; Wilkins, 1979). One strategy of evaluating the influence of cognitive (i.e., expectancy) factors on systematic desensitization is to compare desensitization with placebo conditions. However, most studies that have followed this strategy do not permit the drawing of any conclusions with respect to expectancy factors, because the credibility of the placebo controls has not been adequately assessed. Several studies (e.g., Borkovec & Nau, 1972; McGlynn & McDonell, 1974; Nau, Caputo, & Borkovec, 1974) have demonstrated that the "expectancy of improvement" produced by a placebo therapy must be assessed rather than assumed. In many cases, placebo rationales have not been as credible as the rationale of systematic desensitization. Nevertheless, it is noteworthy that several studies could not find any difference in effectiveness between systematic desensitization and placebo conditions (e.g., Holroyd, 1976; Kirsch & Henry, 1977; Lick, 1975; Marcia, Rubin, & Efran, 1969; McGlynn, 1971; McGlynn, Gaynor, & Puhr, 1972; McGlynn, Reynolds, & Linder, 1971; McReynolds, Barnes, Brooks, & Rehagen, 1973; Tori & Worell, 1973).

A different approach to the study of the influence of expectancy on treatment outcome is to vary instructional sets. Two strategies can be distinguished (Emmelkamp, 1975a). First, subjects who are given a therapeutically oriented instructional set are compared with subjects who are led to believe that they are participating in experimental procedures concerned with physiological reactions. Studies that have followed this strategy have generally found a clear expectancy effect. Second, all subjects are informed that they are to receive therapy, but the instructions concerning the anticipated outcome are varied (positive, neutral, or negative). Studies following this paradigm have produced conflicting results. However, as noted earlier (Emmelkamp, 1975a), "it is inappropriate to conclude that expectancy does not play an important part in the systematic desensitization procedure, because all subjects had received a therapeutic instruction" (p. 5). These therapeutic instructions may lead to expectations of improvement regardless of what the subject is subsequently told. In addition, regardless of instructions given by the experimenter, systematic desensitization may be experienced at face value as a treatment.

Several alternative explanations have been proposed to explain the expectancy effects, particularly experimenter bias (Wilkins, 1973) and demand characteristics (Borkovec, 1973). In his review of expectancy studies, Wilkins (1973) concluded that the studies reporting an expectancy effect involved therapists who were not blind to the experimental manipulations, whereas in studies failing to demonstrate an expectancy effect, the therapists were blind. However, several studies have found expectancy effects with experimenters who were unaware of the expectancy manipulations applied to the subjects (Emmelkamp & Straatman, 1976; Emmelkamp & Walta, 1978; Rosen, 1974; Sullivan & Denney, 1977). Thus, experimenter bias does not adequately explain the differences found in expectancy studies.

Borkovec (1973) proposed that the subjects' characteristics could explain the contradictory results among expectancy studies. In a retrospective analysis of expectancy studies, he suggested that the studies failing to find an expectancy effect employed fearful subjects, whereas studies demonstrating expectancy effects employed low-fear subjects. The post hoc classification of fearful–low-fear subjects, as used by Borkovec (1973) has been criticized by Emmelkamp (1975b); his reanalysis of the studies reviewed by Borkovec indicates that several studies that did find expectancy effects involved highly fearful subjects. More recently, several studies found expectancy effects regardless of the phobic level of the subjects (Emmelkamp & Boeke-Slinkers, 1977b; Sullivan & Denney, 1977). Thus, contrary to Borkovec's (1973) hypothesis, highly fearful subjects were no less susceptible to expectancy effects than were low-fear subjects.

Finally, assessment in most expectancy studies has been limited to self-report and behavioral tests. Thus, it could be argued that expectancy might influence the subjective and behavioral components of fear, but not the physiological component. Indeed, Borkovec (1972) and Rappaport (1972) failed to obtain expectancy effects on physiological indexes of anxiety. However, Beiman (1976) and Kirsch and Henry (1977) demonstrated expectancy effects on physiological measures. Thus, expectancy influences have been demonstrated on subjective, behavioral, and psychophysiological indexes of anxiety.

In summary, expectancy factors appear to play an important role in systematic desensitization. It is still questionable whether systematic desensitization is not merely a highly effective placebo procedure. In order to investigate to what extent desensitization produces an effect independent of expectancy factors, the procedure should be compared with pseudotherapies with the same credibility and face validity (Emmelkamp, 1975a).

Psychoanalytic Interpretation. Silverman, Frank, and Dachinger (1974) hypothesized that part of the effectiveness of systematic desensitization resides in the fact that it activates an unconscious fantasy of merging with the therapist as mother substitute, an activation that is made particularly likely by the use of the muscle relaxation procedure. To test this hypothesis, these authors compared two variants of systematic desensitization with insect-phobic subjects. Instead of using relaxation as an incompatible response, the subjects were given subliminal exposures of either a symbiosis gratification stimulus (*Mommy and I are one*) or a neutral stimulus (*People walking*). The group that received subliminal exposure to the symbiotic gratification stimulus manifested more improvement than the group with the neutral stimulus, thus supporting the authors' hypothesis that the effectiveness of systematic desensitization resides in its activation of unconscious merging fantasies.

Emmelkamp and Straatman (1976) replicated the study by Silverman *et al.* (1974) with special reference to demand characteristics, using snake-phobic volunteers as subjects. In this experiment, *Mommy and I are one* was used as the symbiotic gratification stimulus and *Snake and I are one* as the neutral stimulus; it was assumed that to subjects with a snake phobia, this stimulus would be more rel-

evant than the stimulus *People walking*. The results indicated that sytematic desensitization with a symbiotic gratification stimulus was not more effective than desensitization with a neutral stimulus. Rather, it was shown that subjects receiving the neutral stimulus improved more on the behavioral avoidance test. The difference in outcome from the Silverman *et al.* (1974) study may be explained by the fact that the neutral stimulus *Snake and I are one* was experienced as more relevant than the simulus *Mommy and I are one*. Thus, there seems to be no support for a psychoanalytic reinterpretation of the effectiveness of systematic desensitization.

Systematic Desensitization as Self-Control. Instead of a passive conditioning conceptualization, Goldfried (1971) argued that systematic desensitzation should be viewed as a self-control procedure, in which clients are taught to exert voluntary control over their feelings of anxiety. Several modifications of the standard systematic-desensitization procedure were recommended by Goldfried: first, relaxation is conceptualized as a coping skill; second, different fears are placed within a single multidimensional hierarchy; third, the clients are instructed to stay in the imaginal situation, when anxiety occurs, and to cope with anxiety by relaxing it away; and finally, the clients have to apply relaxation skills in real-life anxiety-provoking situations.

Since self-control desensitization focuses on applying relaxation coping skills whenever proprioceptive cues of anxiety or tension are perceived, the effects of this procedure should transfer across anxiety-arousing situations. As far as targeted anxieties are concerned, self-control desensitization has been found to be as effective as traditional desensitization (Deffenbacher & Parks, 1979; Spiegler, Cooley, Marshall, Prince, Puckett, & Skenazy, 1976; Zemore, 1975) or more effective (Denney & Rupert, 1977). The studies that have compared traditional and self-control desensitization on generalization measures have provided conflicting results. Several studies (Deffenbacher & Parks, 1979; Zemore, 1975) did find a transfer of treatment effects across anxiety-arousing situations, whereas others did not (Denney & Rupert, 1977; Spiegler *et al.*, 1976). More importantly, however, in neither study was self-control desensitization found to be superior to standard desensitization with respect to nontargeted anxiety reduction.

Goldfried and Goldfried (1977) compared two self-control desensitization procedures with speech-anxious subjects: one with a hierarchy relevant to speech anxiety and the second involving a hierarchy totally unrelated to public-speaking situations. No differential effectiveness was found between the two self-control desensitization conditions, an outcome that suggests that the learning of an active coping skill is an important factor in self-control desensitization.

Several other self-management procedures have been developed in which clients are trained in relaxation as a coping skill: clients are trained to recognize the physiological cues of tension and to apply relaxation whenever tension is perceived (e.g., applied relaxation, Deffenbacher, 1976, and anxiety management, Suinn & Richardson, 1971; Suinn, 1976). In contrast to self-control desensitization, no hierarchy of anxiety-arousing situations is used. In anxiety management training, the client imagines a single highly anxiety-arousing situation and actively attempts to relax away anxiety feelings. In applied relaxation, clients have to apply relaxation to stressful and anxiety-provoking situations in real life.

Several studies indicate that relaxation presented as a coping skill is more effective than standard relaxation exercises (Chang-Liang & Denney, 1976; Goldfried & Trier, 1974). Other studies have found relaxation to be as effective as desensitization, provided that both are presented as self-management procedures (Deffenbacher, Mathis, & Michaels, 1979; Deffenbacher & Payne, 1977; Snyder & Deffenbacher, 1977). Finally, Deffenbacher and Shelton (1978) found anxiety management to be more effective than standard systematic desensitization, at least at follow-up. However, the positive results of self-management relaxation procedures may be attributed to expectancy factors. McGlynn, Kinjo, and Doherty (1978) compared cue-controlled relaxation with an equally credible placebo treatment and could not find any difference in effectiveness.

Imaginal versus in vivo Exposure. Wolpe's (1963) statement that "there is almost invari-

ably a one to one relationship between what the patient can imagine without anxiety and what he can experience in reality without anxiety" (p. 1063) receives little support. A transfer gap between what a client can imagine without feeling anxiety and what the client can deal with *in vivo* without feeling tension has been reported a number of times (e.g., Agras, 1967; Barlow, Leitenberg, Agras, & Wincze, 1969; Hain, Butcher, & Stevenson, 1966; Meyer & Crisp, 1966; Sherman, 1972). Clients who had been successfully desensitized in imagination nevertheless proved to react with anxiety when they were confronted with the phobic stimuli *in vivo.*

Several studies have directly compared systematic desensitization in imagination and *in vivo.* The results indicated that *in vivo* exposure is far more effective (Dyckman & Cowan, 1978; Barlow *et al.,* 1969; Litvak, 1969; Sherman, 1972). It is noteworthy that much effort has gone into studying imaginal desensitization; few studies have been conducted with respect to systematic desensitization in real life. Presumably, the consensual notion that imaginal desensitization is equivalent to *in vivo* desensitization originated in the conceptualization of desensitization in conditioning terms and has been reinforced for years by the lack of tests with real clinical patients.

Flooding. Flooding therapies are derived from the work of Stampfl (Stampfl & Levis, 1967, 1968) on implosive therapy. The implosive procedure used by Stampfl and his associates has been claimed to be based on the principle of extinction. During treatment, the therapist presents a *complex* of conditioned stimuli to the patient without primary reinforcement and without allowing an avoidance response. The therapist tries to maximize anxiety throughout the treatment, which eventually leads to "extinction." Sessions are continued until a significant reduction in anxiety is achieved. It is essential to the implosive approach not only that the "symptom-contingent" cues are presented, but also that the patient is exposed to the aversive stimuli assumed to be underlying the patient's problems ("hypothesized-sequential cues"). Hypothesized cues are defined as "those which are not directly correlated with symptom onset but which represent 'guesses' as to the remaining components of the avoided CS complex" (Levis & Hare, 1977, p. 321). These hypothesized cues may concern such dynamic themes as aggression, guilt, punishment, rejection, loss of control, and oral, anal or sexual material. For a detailed excursion into implosive theory, the reader is referred to Levis and Hare (1977).

Apart from the psychodynamic cues, the implosive therapy for phobias has got wide attention from behavior therapists. So far, only one study has compared implosive therapy with psychodynamic cues and implosive therapy without such cues (Prochaska, 1971). Both procedures were found to be about equally effective. Almost all controlled studies (both with analogue and with clinical populations) have conducted implosive therapy without such psychodynamic cues. Since the therapeutic procedures used differ considerably from the implosive therapy as originally developed by Stampfl, the term *flooding* will be used throughout this chapter.

Duration of Exposure. One of the most important variables in determining the effectiveness of flooding seems to be the duration of exposure to the stimulus variable within each session. Too early termination of flooding sessions may lead to an exacerbation instead of a reduction of fear. In fact, the patient is then allowed to escape the fearful situation (either in imagination or *in vivo*), and the escape may lead to an immediate anxiety reduction (negative reinforcement). It is noteworthy that in most studies with clinical patients, much longer exposure duration has been used than has typically been carried out in analogue research. In the analogue studies, flooding sessions last from 20 to 60 min. In contrast, however, in clinical studies where flooding has been found to be effective, it lasts up to several hours.

The process of anxiety reduction during *flooding-in-imagination* sessions has been examined in several studies. Only a few clinical studies have assessed physiological changes continuously during flooding sessions. In an uncontrolled study (Watson, Gaind, & Marks, 1972) (10 patients with specific phobias), heart rate tended to return to resting levels in time. However, considerable variation was observed between patients. Most patients showed their greatest anxiety early in the sessions, others showed the greatest anxiety only to particular themes, and a few patients showed no significant change in heart rate during flooding in imagination. In the Stern and Marks (1973) study, there was little tachycardia or skin conductance activity throughout flooding in imagination. It should be noted that in both the Watson *et al.* (1972) and the Stern and Marks (1973) study, patients listened to tape-recorded flooding themes. Clinical studies are lacking that have assessed arousal during flooding in imagination conducted by a live therapist.

Foa and Chambless (1978) assessed *subjective* anxiety throughout flooding in imagination with agoraphobic and obsessive-compulsive patients. Patients were instructed to imagine the scenes described by the therapist as vividly as possible. Flooding sessions lasted 90 min. Patients had to indicate their anxiety every 10 min on a scale of 0–100. Figure 1 shows the mean SUDS of the agoraphobics during second and last (eight) treatment sessions. The results of this study showed that habituation of subjective anxiety occurs within sessions. Most often, it follows a curvilinear pattern. In addition, evidence was provided for habituation across sessions. It is interesting to see that in the Foa and Chambless study, subjective anxiety started to decline only after 50 min, whereas in most analogue studies, the duration of exposure during flooding is often much shorter.

One clinical study (Stern & Marks, 1973) compared short (20-min) and long (80-min) fantasy sessions. No significant differences were found. However, as already noted, the treatment was given with a tape recorder and did not lead to significant changes in arousal.

Let us now turn our attention to analogue studies. In a study with spider phobics, Mathews and Shaw (1973) found habituation within sessions on both heart rate and skin conductance measures but not on subjective anxiety. However, the subjects had to listen to tape-recorded material, and the exposure duration was only 48 min. Moreover, the experimenters may have provided the possibility of escape to their subjects, since their subjects had to open their eyes and then rate their anx-

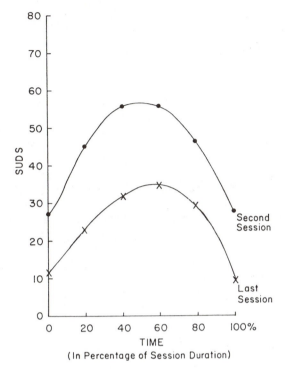

Figure 1. Mean SUDS during second and last treatment sessions with agoraphobics ($N = 6$). (From "Habituation of Subjective Anxiety during Flooding in Imagery" by E. B. Foa and D. L. Chambless, *Behavior Research and Therapy*, 1978, *16*, 391–399, Fig. 3. Copyright 1978 by Pergamon Press. Reprinted by permission.)

iety every 8 min. The results of the Mc-Cutcheon and Adams (1975) study shed further light on the habituation of physiological arousal during flooding in imagination: A 20-min tape-recorded flooding session (imagery of witnessing a surgical operation) did not lead to habituation. In fact, there appeared to be an increase in arousal as measured by the nonspecific fluctuation of the galvanic skin response (GSR). In a second study, flooding lasted 60 min. After an intial increase in arousal, as in their first experiment, arousal finally decreased, thus showing a curvilinear habituation curve. A similar pattern of habituation during flooding was found by Orenstein and Carr (1975), as measured by heart rate.

Let us turn now to habituation during *flooding in vivo*. In the study by Watson *et al.* (1972), heart rate was monitored during pro-

longed exposure *in vivo*. In general, the heart rate tended to return to resting levels. Similar results were found by Nunes and Marks (1975).

In the Watson *et al.* (1972) study, flooding in fantasy evoked less tachycardia than exposure *in vivo*. Even after habituation to imaginal stimuli had occurred, the patients responded with much tachycardia when exposed to the phobic stimuli *in vivo*. During the *in vivo* sessions, both habituation within and across sessions was found.

In the study by Stern and Marks (1973), heart rate was monitored during exposure *in vivo* with agoraphobics. They compared short (four half-hour) sessions with long (two-hour) sessions. Prolonged *in vivo* sessions were clearly superior to shorter ones. There was little decrement in heart rate and subjective anxiety during the first hour. During the second hour, improvement was significantly greater. Findings with agoraphobics contradict those of specific phobics. In the latter category, heart rate was found to decrease much earlier (Watson *et al.*, 1972). Finally, in a study by Rabavilas, Boulougouris, and Stefanis (1976) with 12 obsessive-compulsive patients, prolonged exposure *in vivo* (80 min) was found to be superior to short exposure *in vivo* (10 min). In fact, short exposure had a deteriorating effect on the patients' affective state.

To summarize the results of clinical and analogue studies, there is evidence that habituation of physiological arousal and subjective anxiety occurs when the duration of exposure lasts long enough. The duration of exposure and the anxiety reduction as its result are the boundary conditions for treatment to be called *flooding*. Obviously, it is important to continue flooding until anxiety has declined. However, which criterion should be used for the termination of sessions is as yet far from clear: Should anxiety be reduced on psychophysiological, subjective, or behavioral measures, or should anxiety reduction occur across all these systems?

Only one analogue study (Gauthier & Marshall, 1977) has been reported that addresses itself to this question. The investigators compared variants of termination of flooding sessions with snake-phobic volunteers. The treatment consisted of three sessions of imaginal exposure. The criterion for session termination in the "subjective" group was the subject's report of not feeling any anxiety. In the "autonomic group," the criterion was the reduction of the heart rate to the resting rate. In the "behavioral" condition, session termination was determined by agreement between two observers that anxiety had declined. Finally, in the last group, all criteria (i.e., autonomic, subjective, and behavioral) had to be met before the session was terminated. The results of this study revealed that session termination determined by the observers led to the greatest reduction in anxiety as measured behaviorally and by self-reports. The "autonomic" group, in which session termination was determined by heart-rate reduction, did not do much better than the control groups. There was almost no difference between the "subjective" and the "behavioral" groups. The group in which all criteria were used to determine session termination did no better than the controls. The results of this study indicate that behavioral and subjective anxiety reduction may be more important criteria for session termination than heart-rate reduction. Research into this question with clinical patients is lacking.

Horrific Cues. Another continuing debate in the flooding literature concerns the stimulus content during flooding. Some therapists have used actual depictions of the feared situations, whereas others have employed depictions of horrifying scenes, often including adverse consequences to the patient. For example, during flooding, one can have a car-phobic patient imagine that he is driving a car on a busy motorway or have him imagine that he is involved in a terrible car accident. Although Bandura (1969) has suggested the use of the term *flooding* for realistic scenes and the term *implosion* for horrifying scenes with adverse consequences, this distinction is confusing, since the use of horrifying themes is only one detailed aspect of implosion therapy as originally developed by Stampfl. For present purposes, I shall distinguish flooding without adverse consequences and flooding with adverse consequences, even though such a distinction is rather artificial. Even if adverse consequences to the subject are excluded, the content of

flooding scenes may differ considerably. For instance, flooding scenes can contain either coping statements or helplessness statements (Mathews & Rezin, 1977). In some studies (e.g., De Moor, 1970), even reassuring statements have been used with snake-phobic subjects: "You really never looked at a snake. Now, look at it. A long body getting thinner at the ends. One end is the tail, it's a pointed one. The other end is the head, a very little head with two piercing eyes, a little mouth and a very little forked tongue flicking in and out. Look at it. *That's what a snake is all about*" (p. 49). Unfortunately, in most studies, the details of the flooding procedures used are not reported. Therefore, cross-study comparisons are virtually impossible.

Several studies have compared flooding with and without horrifying scenes. The results of a study by Foa, Blau, Prout, and Latimer (1977) with rat-phobic students are equivocal. After four 40-min sessions, flooding with and flooding without horrifying cues were about equally effective with regard to the subject's willingness to approach a live rat, in addition to subjective ratings of anxiety. However, the independent evaluator found that the subjects who had been treated by flooding with horrifying cues improved significantly more with respect to interference of their fear in everyday life as compared with pleasant flooding and no-treatment control subjects.

Marshall, Gauthier, Christie, Currie, and Gordon (1977) also compared flooding without horrific images with flooding with a horrifying content, using spider-phobic volunteers as subjects. The treatment consisted of three 45-min sessions of taped stimulus material. The pleasant flooding condition was found to be more effective.

Finally, the work by Mathews and his colleagues is relevant with respect to this issue. Mathews and Shaw (1973) compared flooding with pleasant scenes and flooding with horrifying scenes using spider-phobic volunteers as subjects. Treatment consisted of one session only. Flooding with pleasant scenes was found to be the most effective.

Stimulus content with flooding in the studies so far reviewed may have been confounded by the degree of helplessness depicted in the scenes. In the studies by Foa *et al.* (1977),

Marshall *et al.* (1977), and Mathews and Shaw (1973), during flooding with horrifying themes subjects were depicted as helpless. For instance, in the scenes used by Mathews and Shaw (1973), the subjects are described as being covered by spider webs and powerless to escape. Mathews and Rezin (1977) compared horrifying with pleasant and coping with no-coping rehearsal in a 2×2 factorial design. The subjects were dental-phobic volunteers, who referred themselves for treatment following announcements in a local paper. The treatment in each condition consisted of four sessions of 50-min duration. The scenes were presented by tape. Coping rehearsal had no effect on anxiety. However, pleasant themes led to more anxiety reduction than horrifying themes. Moreover, an interaction effect was found with respect to dental attendance. Coping rehearsal had most effect when combined with horrifying themes; pleasant themes did not reduce avoidance.

To summarize the analogue studies reviewed so far, it may be concluded that the inclusion of horrifying stimuli during flooding in imagination does not enhance effectiveness. Rather, it seems that flooding with pleasant scenes is more effective. In addition, coping statements may increase the effectiveness of flooding, at least when horrifying stimuli are used. However, these conclusions must be qualified in several ways. In the first place, all studies were of the analogue type. Thus, generalization of the results to the population of clinical patients seems unwarranted. Second, Mathews and Rezin (1977), Mathews and Shaw (1973), and Marshall *et al.* (1977) used taped stimulus material. It is quite possible that during taped flooding scenes, cognitive avoidance on the part of the subject is more likely when horrifying cues are presented than when pleasant scenes are offered. If cognitive escape and avoidance occur during flooding, habituation of the anxiety may be prevented; and theoretically, this state may even lead to an exacerbation of the fear. Unfortunately, the studies did not investigate this particular issue.

It seems to me that flooding should always use realistic themes: Patients should be able to imagine themselves in the depicted situations. The point at issue here is that for some patients horrifying cues may be quite realistic, whereas for others these cues may be quite unrealistic and therefore can be easily avoided by internal statements like "That isn't real; that will not happen to me." If we agree that flooding themes should be realistic in order to prevent cognitive avoidance, it follows that flooding treatment should be tailor-made. Let me illustrate my point with a clinical example. In our flooding treatment with agoraphobic patients, we have included such "horrifying scenes" as feeling dizzy, getting a panic attack, and fainting; people looking at the patient and making comments about him/her while he/she is lying down; and being taken to a mental hospital. However, only those horrifying cues were used of which the patient was really afraid. For example, patients who feared going insane were flooded on this theme, whereas flooding for patients who feared being observed in public consisted of such scenes. Thus, even within a relatively homogeneous population of phobic patients, the situations the patients are really afraid of might differ from patient to patient. Therefore, flooding scenes should be adapted to the individual fears.

Now, let us turn back to the analogue studies. The horrifying themes used seem to have been quite unrealistic for most of the spider-phobic or rat-phobic subjects. For instance, as already mentioned, the spider phobics in the Mathews and Shaw (1973) study had to imagine that they were covered by webs and had no possibility of escape. I wonder how many spider phobics are really afraid of having this happen. In fact, Mathews and Shaw (1973) found no difference between horrifying cues and realistic cues in terms of self-reported anxiety *during* flooding, a finding that seems to emphasize my point.

Before meaningful conclusions can be drawn with respect to the contribution of horrific cues to flooding in imagination, studies are needed in which *realistic* flooding themes with and without horrific cues are compared with each other: The content of these scenes must be based on the patients' fears. In addition, treatment has to be given by a life therapist to prevent any possible cognitive avoidance-behavior on the parts of the subject.

Several studies have investigated the effects of anxiety evocation during exposure *in vivo*.

In the early days of exposure *in vivo*, guidelines for conducting treatments were derived from implosion and flooding theory; it was thought to be essential to maximize anxiety during exposure *in vivo* before extinction or habituation could occur. In the first controlled study that included flooding *in vivo* with phobic patients (Marks *et al.*, 1971), therapists tried to evoke anxiety deliberately during exposure *in vivo*. Hafner and Marks (1976) allocated 12 agoraphobics randomly across high-anxiety and low-anxiety conditions. In the high-anxiety condition, the patients were encouraged to confront their symptoms during exposure *in vivo*; the therapists' reassurance was minimized. Instead, throughout the exposure *in vivo* procedure, the therapist tried to induce anxiety by statements such as "Imagine yourself feeling worse and worse, giddy, sweaty, nauseated, as if you are about to vomit any moment. . . . you fall to the floor half conscious, people gather round you, someone calls for an ambulance" (p. 77). In the low-anxiety condition, the patients were allowed to distract themselves, and they were even encouraged to do relaxation exercises. No anxiety-inducing statements were made by the therapists. The patients in the high-anxiety condition experienced more anxiety and panic attacks than the patients in the low-anxiety condition. However, *no* differences in improvement were found between both conditions; thus, deliberately inducing anxiety during exposure *in vivo* did not enhance improvement.

In an analogue study by Kirsch, Wolpin, and Knutson (1975), speech-anxious college students were treated with several variants of exposure *in vivo*. The results of this study revealed that delivering a speech without anxiety provocation was more effective than when anxiety was deliberately provoked by a "booing" audience. However, the treatment consisted of five sessions of 4 min only; this rather short exposure time precludes drawing any conclusions.

Imaginal Exposure versus In Vivo Exposure. Several clinical studies have been conducted comparing flooding in imagination with flooding *in vivo* (Emmelkamp & Wessels, 1975; Mathews, Johnston, Lancashire, Munby,

Shaw, & Gelder, 1976; Stern & Marks, 1973; Watson, Mullett, & Pillay, 1973). All of these studies involved the treatment of agoraphobics.

Watson *et al.* (1973) compared both treatments in a crossover design. The treatment was conducted in groups. Flooding *in vivo* was found to be more effective than imaginal flooding. However, flooding was applied by means of a tape recorder. Another methodological flaw concerns the differences in treatment time. Patients received six *in vivo* sessions as compared with three fantasy sessions.

In the study by Stern and Marks (1973), flooding *in vivo* was also found to be superior. However, delay or carry-over effects may partly explain the superior results of flooding *in vivo*, since flooding in imagination always preceded flooding *in vivo*. In addition, imaginal treatment was tape-recorded.

Two studies in which (1) imaginal flooding, (2) flooding *in vivo*, and (3) a combined procedure were compared in a between-group design produced conflicting results. In the study by Emmelkamp and Wessels (1975), four sessions of exposure *in vivo* were found to be superior to imaginal exposure; the effects of the combined procedure were between those of the imaginal and *in vivo* conditions. However, after 16 sessions, Mathews *et al.* (1976) found no differences among these three procedures. The following differences between both studies might explain the conflicting results (Emmelkamp, 1977). First of all, the procedures actually used may have been quite different. The procedures of Emmelkamp and Wessels resembled flooding, whereas for the Mathews *et al.* procedures, the term *gradual exposure* seems more appropriate. More important is the mixing of exposure *in vivo* and in imagination in the imaginal condition in the study by Mathews *et al.* Their patients were instructed to practice at home between treatment sessions. Since they treated their patients once a week, there was ample opportunity for the practice at home. In fact, a check of the diaries completed by the patients revealed that on the average, they went out once a day throughout the treatment. In the Emmelkamp and Wessels study, the patients were not instructed to practice between treatment sessions, and since the treatment was conducted three times weekly, there was little room for self-practice between treatment sessions.

Johnston, Lancashire, Mathews, Munby, Shaw, and Gelder (1976) reported the results of measures taken during the treatment in the Mathews et al. study. On measures of the immediate effects of treatment, exposure in vivo had consistent positive effects, whereas imaginal flooding had little or no effect. These results suggest that the long-term effects after imaginal flooding were indeed due to the exposure in vivo between treatment sessions.

In conclusion, flooding in vivo has been found to be far more effective than flooding in imagination, when agoraphobics are the subjects. Finally, one study (Rabavilas et al., 1976) compared flooding in imagination and flooding in vivo with obsessive-compulsive patients. Here, flooding in vivo was also found to be superior to imaginal flooding.

Flooding versus Desensitization. Numerous studies have been carried out comparing systematic desensitization with flooding. However, these studies have yielded equivocal results. Several studies (Boudewyns & Wilson, 1972; Marks et al., 1971; Hussain, 1971; Marshall et al., 1977) found flooding to be more effective; others found systematic desensitization superior to flooding (Hekmat, 1973; Mealiea & Nawas, 1971; Smith & Nye, 1973; Suarez, Adams, & McCutcheon, 1976; Willis & Edwards, 1969). Still others found them to be about equally effective (Barrett, 1969; Borkovec, 1972; Calef & MacLean, 1970; Cornish & Dilley, 1973; Crowe, Marks, Agras, & Leitenberg, 1972; De Moor, 1970; Gelder et al., 1973; Horne & Matson, 1977; Mylar & Clement, 1972; Shaw, 1976; Solyom et al., 1973). Research in this area is encumbered by the vague theoretical notions and terminological confusion concerning flooding. Therefore, straightforward comparisons across studies are rather difficult.

Table 1 summarizes the main features of the studies that compared systematic desensitization and flooding. It should be noted that apart from the studies by Boudewyns and Wilson (1972), Boulougouris et al. (1971), Crowe et al. (1972), Gelder et al. (1973), Hus-

sain (1971), Shaw (1976), and Solyom et al. (1973), all other comparisons have involved analogue populations (most often small-animal phobias).

1. *Clinical studies.* The study by Boudewyns and Wilson (1972) involved a heterogeneous sample of psychiatric patients. The outcome was assessed by means of the Minnesota Multiphasic Personality Inventory (MMPI) and the Mooney Problem Checklist. Although flooding was found to be somewhat more effective than a modified desensitization procedure, the results are difficult to evaluate because of the heterogeneous sample and the unsatisfactory measures.

Two studies of clinical phobics found flooding to be superior to desensitization. Hussain (1971) compared both treatments (in imagination) in a crossover design. Half of the patients received thiopental as the first treatment, and the other half received saline. The thiopental–flooding condition proved to be more effective than the other treatments. However, because of several methodological flaws (all patients treated by the same therapist, inadequate statistical analysis, and no "blind" observer), the conclusions are not definitive. Another study in which flooding was found to be more effective than systematic desensitization on clinical as well as physiological measures of fear was reported by Marks et al. (1971). In this study, both treatments involved six sessions of imaginal exposure followed by two sessions of exposure in vivo. The superiority of flooding was most pronounced in the agoraphobics.

In the study by Gelder et al. (1973), both treatments also were carried out in imagination and in vivo. Their treatments involved three information sessions and eight imaginal sessions followed by four in vivo sessions. In contrast with the Marks et al. (1971) study, no differences were found between flooding and desensitization. As the imaginal part of the treatment used in both studies was similar, differences in outcome are probably due to the differences in exposure in vivo that the patients received. First, Gelder et al. (1973) made no attempt to differentiate both treatments in the exposure in vivo phase, whereas in the Marks et al. (1971) study, exposure in

Table 1. Flooding versus Systematic Desensitization

Study	Population	Treatment	Sessions (minutes)	Mode of treatment presentation	Results
A. Phobic patients					
Crowe, Marks, Agras, & Leitenberg (1972)	Mixed (n = 14)	Flooding / SD^a / Reinforced practice (block design)	4 × 50	L^d	3 > 2^b (behavioral measure)
Gelder, Bancroft, Gath, Johnston, Mathews, & Shaw (1973)	18 Agoraphobics / 18 Other phobics	Flooding / SD / Nonspecific control	15 × 45 – 60	L	1 = 2^c / 1 & 2 > 3 (agoraphobics)
Hussain (1971)	Agoraphobics or social phobics (n = 40)	Flooding-thiopental / Flooding saline / SD-thiopental / SD-saline (crossover)	6 × 45	L	1 > 2, 3, & 4
Marks, Boulougouris, & Marset (1971)	9 Agoraphobics / 7 Specific	Flooding / SD (crossover)	8 × 50 – 70	L	1 > 2
Shaw (1976)	Social phobics (n = 30)	Flooding / SD / Social skills	10 × 60 / 10 × 60 / 10 × 75	L	1 = 2 = 3
Solyom, Heseltine, McClure, Solyom, Ledwidge, & Steinberg (1973)	39 Agoraphobics and social phobics / 11 Other phobics	Flooding / SD / Aversion relief / Phenelzine / Placebo	12 × 60 / 12 × 60 / 24 × 30 / 6 × 60 / 6 × 60	L	1 > 2 (FSS only) / 3 > 1, 2, 4, & 5 (psychiatric rating) / 4 > 5 (psychiatric rating)
B. Analogue studies					
Barrett (1969)	Snake phobia	Flooding / SD / No treatment	± 2 / ± 12	L	1 = 2 / 1 & 2 > 3 / 1 more efficient
Borkovec (1972)	Snake phobia	Flooding / SD / Placebo / No treatment	4 × 50	L	1 = 2

Study	Fear	Treatments	Sessions		Results
Calef & MacLean (1970)	Speech anxiety	Flooding SD No treatment	5 × 60	L	1 = 2 1 & 2 > 3
Cornish & Dilley (1973)	Test anxiety	Flooding SD Counseling No treatment	4 × 40	T[e]	1 = 2 1 & 2 > 4
De Moor (1970)	Snake phobia	Flooding SD No treatment	5 × 20	L	1 = 2 1 & 2 > 3
Hekmat (1973)	Rat phobia	Flooding SD Semantic desensitization Pseudodesensitization	2 × 40 5 × 40	L	2 & 3 > 1 4 > 1 (behavioral measure) 2 & 3 > 4
Horne & Matson (1977)	Test anxiety	Flooding SD Modeling Study skills No treatment	10 × 60	L	1, 2 & 3 > 4 & 5 (test anxiety) 3 > 2 > 1 (test anxiety) 2, 3 & 4 > 1 & 5 (grade point average)
Marshall, Gauthier, Christie, Currie, & Gordon (1977)	Snake phobia	Flooding SD Placebo No treatment	3 × 40	L	1 > 2 1 & 2 > 3 & 4 3 = 4
Mealiea & Nawas (1971)	Snake phobia	Flooding Implosive desensitization SD Placebo No treatment	5 × 30	T	3 > all others (behavioral measure) 1 = 5 (behavioral measure) 2 & 4 > 5 (behavioral measure) 1 = 2 = 3 = 4 = 5 (self-report)
Mylar & Clement (1972)	Speech anxiety	Flooding SD No treatment	5 × 60	T	1 = 2 1 & 2 > 3
Smith & Nye (1973)	Test anxiety	Flooding SD No treatment	7 × 45	L	1 = 2 (test anxiety) 2 > 1 (other measures)

(Continued)

Table 1. Flooding versus Systematic Desensitization (*Continued*)

Study	Population	Treatment	Sessions (minutes)	Mode of treatment presentation	Results
Suarez, Adams, & McCutcheon (1976)	Surgical operation	Flooding SD No treatment	3 × 30	?	1 = 2 (behavioral measure) 2 > 1 (self-report)
Willis & Edwards (1969)	Mouse phobia	Flooding SD Placebo	± 4 × ?	L	2 > 1 & 3 1 = 3

[a] SD = systematic desensitization.
[b] a > b = Treatment a superior to treatment b.
[c] a = b = Treatment a about as effective as Treatment b.
[d] L = treatment presented by live therapist.
[e] T = treatment presented by tape.

vivo was relaxed during desensitization and forceful during flooding (Marks, 1975). Second, the different results might be explained by different amounts of self-exposure *in vivo* between treatment sessions. Since Marks *et al.* treated patients three times a week rather than once a week (as in the Gelder *et al.* study), there was in the former study less time between sessions for an effect to develop from self-exposure *in vivo*. That self-exposure *in vivo* may have beneficial effects on its own was recently demonstrated by McDonald, Sartory, Grey, Cobb, Stern, and Marks (1979).

In the studies by Crowe *et al.* (1972), Shaw (1976), and Solyom *et al.* (1973), systematic desensitization and flooding were carried out in imagination. Both procedures were found to be about equally effective.

To summarize the studies of phobic patients, it can be concluded that desensitization in imagination and flooding in imagination are about equally effective. Moreover, the way in which exposure *in vivo* is carried out might be crucial.

2. Analogue studies. In most studies that found systematic desensitization (SD) to be superior to flooding, the flooding was not correctly carried out. First, in the studies by Horne and Matson (1977), Hekmat (1973), Mealiea and Nawas, (1971), and Willis and Edwards (1969), a hierarchy was used. If we assume that one essential characteristic of flooding is anxiety evocation, the use of a hierarchy seems not to be the optimal procedure to achieve this. Second, often insufficient time was provided for anxiety to dissipate. For instance, flooding in the study by Hekmat (1973) consisted of one session only in which five different scenes had to be visualized in 40 min. In the study by Mealiea and Nawas (1971), each flooding session lasted only 30 min, which is much too short a time for anxiety reduction to occur in most subjects. In fact, anxiety reduction within sessions was prevented in several subjects in the study by Willis and Edwards (1969), since they stated, "treatment may have been terminated somewhat prematurely because it was felt that the S. had reached the upper level of her tolerance" (p. 393). Finally, Mealiea and Nawas (1971) used taped flooding material.

Since procedural descriptions in the Suarez

et al. (1976) study are lacking, the results are difficult to evaluate. To date, only one study, in which flooding was carried out within the boundary conditions, shows SD on some measures to be more effective than flooding (Smith & Nye, 1973). Smith and Nye compared SD, flooding, and a no-treatment control with test-anxious subjects. The treatment consisted of seven 45-min sessions. During flooding, the subjects were exposed (five-sessions) to anxiety-inducing stimuli until they exhibited behavioral evidence of reduced anxiety. Both treatments led to significant improvements on the Test Anxiety Scale. However, on the A-state questionnaire and increase in grade-point averages, SD was found to be superior. It should be noted that the flooding group had a higher pretreatment mean grade-point average than the SD subjects. A ceiling effect might be responsible for their lack of change, as Smith and Nye (1973) have pointed out.

The studies that found both procedures to be about equally effective are also marred by several procedural and methodological flaws. Cornish and Dilley (1973) and Mylar and Clement (1972) used taped stimulus material, which might have led to cognitive avoidance on the part of the subjects. In addition, Borkovec (1972), Calef and MacLean (1970), and Mylar and Clement (1972) used a graded approach (hierarchy) during flooding. In the Borkovec (1972) study, each scene was presented only twice, and in the Calef and MacLean (1970) study, the treatment was conducted in groups. Thus, the progress with new material during flooding was not determined by anxiety reduction but predetermined by the experimenter. Finally, in the study by De Moor (1970), flooding sessions lasted only 20 min. Since the boundary conditions of flooding were not met, definitive conclusions from these studies seem unwarranted.

In the study by Barrett (1969), flooding was carried out according to the rules: scenes were presented until they ceased to elicit anxiety. Although flooding was found to be about as effective as SD, the treatment time with SD subjects was much longer. Therefore, Barrett concluded that flooding was more efficient. However, both treatments were conducted by the same therapist, a condition that might have confounded results.

Finally, one analogue study (Marshall *et al.,* 1977) found flooding to be more effective than SD with snake-phobic subjects. Both treatments were carried out with tapes. The subjects had to imagine the most intense scene of the fear hierarchy (picking up the snake); these instructions were accompanied by slides showing snakes. Immediately after each session, the subjects had to participate in a behavioral avoidance test, which required them to approach the snake. Thus, the treatment consisted of a combination of imaginal rehearsal and *in vivo* exposure. Flooding produced greater behavioral changes than desensitization.

In summary, any conclusions are premature. There is no evidence that SD is superior to flooding or vice versa. The methodological and procedural flaws are so grave and the procedures used are so far removed from clinical practice that most of the efforts that have gone into this enterprise seem to have been a waste of time.

Successive Approximation and Self-Controlled Exposure. While in systematic desensitization it is assumed that anxiety must first be inhibited before avoidance behavior can be reduced, in successive approximation the avoidance behavior is changed directly, a process that may eventually lead to a decrease in anxiety (Leitenberg, Agras, Butz, & Wincze, 1971). Working within an operant-conditioning paradigm, Leitenberg and his colleagues demonstrated that graded exposure *in vivo* in an anxiety-arousing situation, plus contingent reinforcement by means of verbal praise for approach behavior, was successful in the treatment of a variety of clinical phobic cases (Agras, Leitenberg, & Barlow, 1968; Agras, Leitenberg, Barlow, & Thomson, 1969; Agras, Leitenberg, Wincze, Butz, & Callahan, 1970) and in the treatment of such common fears as fear of heights, fear of snakes, fear of painful electric shock, and (in young children) fear of darkness (Leitenberg & Callahan, 1973). This treatment procedure has been called *successive approximation, reinforced practice,* or *shaping.*

Several studies have compared successive approximation with other behavioral treatments. Successive approximation proved to be more effective than systematic desensitization

in imagination with phobic volunteers (Barlow, Agras, Leitenberg, & Wincze, 1970; McReynolds & Grizzard, 1971) and with phobic patients (Crowe *et al.,* 1972). Successive approximation and flooding were found to be about equally effective with phobic patients, including agoraphobics (Crowe *et al.,* 1972; Everaerd, Rijken, & Emmelkamp, 1973).

Reinforcement versus Feedback. In successive approximation, reinforcement and feedback have been confounded, since patients are given both social reinforcement and contingent feedback for time spent in the phobic situation. In order to investigate the relative contribution of feedback and reinforcement, Emmelkamp and Ultee (1974) compared successive approximation and self-observation using agoraphobics as subjects. With both procedures, the patient had to walk a course leading in a straight line from the patient's home, with instructions to turn back on experiencing undue anxiety. With successive approximation, the patient was informed by the therapist about the time he/she had stayed away after each trial; in addition, the patient was reinforced whenever there was an increase in the time spent outside. The differences between successive approximation and self-observation are that during the latter procedure, the patient observes his/her progress by recording the time he/she is able to spend outside (feedback) and that he/she is never reinforced by the therapist. The patient had to record the duration of each trial in a notebook. No difference in effect was found between successive approximation and self-observation: Thus, verbal praise contingent on achievement did not enhance the effects of graduated exposure plus feedback. The effectiveness of graduated exposure plus feedback has further been demonstrated in analogue (Becker & Costello, 1975) and clinical studies (Emmelkamp, 1974, 1980; Emmelkamp & Emmelkamp-Benner, 1975; Emmelkamp & Wessels, 1975; Leitenberg, Agras, Allen, Butz, & Edwards, 1975).

Whether feedback enhanced the effectiveness of graduated exposure was studied by Rutner (1973) in an analogue study involving rat-fearful female volunteers as subjects. The treatment consisted of self-controlled exposure to a live rat. Each subject was instructed to look into a box containing a rat and to keep viewing the rat for as long as she could before releasing a handle that terminated the trial. *In toto*, 35 experimental trials were conducted. Four experimental conditions were created: (1) exposure only; (2) exposure plus self-monitored feedback; (3) exposure plus therapeutically oriented instruction; and (4) exposure plus therapeutically oriented instruction with feedback. The results indicated that feedback enhanced the effectiveness of self-controlled exposure, while no significant effects were found for either the therapeutically oriented instruction or the interaction factor. Thus, the results of this study showed the importance of precise trial-by-trial feedback in self-controlled exposure *in vivo*.

Self-Control of Exposure Time. With both successive approximation and self-observation procedures, the exposure time is controlled by the patient. Whether such self-control enhances the effects of graduated exposure *in vivo* was studied by Hepner and Cauthen (1975), using snake-phobic volunteers as subjects. Graduated exposure under subject control with feedback was compared with graduated exposure under therapist control with feedback. Self-control of exposure time proved to be superior to therapist control in reducing avoidance behavior. Presumably, the cognitive process of enhancement of the self-attribution of personal competence is associated with self-controlled exposure *in vivo*.

In summary, self-controlled exposure *in vivo* has been found to be quite effective in clinical trials. There is little evidence that reinforcement enhances the effectiveness of this procedure. The results of analogue studies indicate that both feedback and self-control of exposure time are important factors that both enhance the effectiveness of graduated exposure *in vivo*.

Covert Reinforcement. The procedure of covert positive reinforcement, originally developed by Cautela (1970), has been applied to phobic cases. The procedure involves a positive stimulus presented in imagination after the subject imagines approach behavior in a phobic situation. The procedure is conceptualized in operant terms. Apart from a few clinical case studies, all controlled studies concern analogue populations.

Several studies found covert positive rein-

forcement more effective than no treatment control groups (Bajtelsmit & Gershman, 1976; Finger & Galassi, 1977; Guidry & Randolph, 1974; Hurley, 1976; Kostka & Galassi, 1974; Ladouceur, 1974, 1977, 1978; Marshall, Boutilier, & Minnes, 1974) and attention–placebo groups (Flannery, 1972; Guidry & Randolph, 1974; Ladouceur, 1977, 1978; Marshall *et al.*, 1974). However, in the Bajtelsmit and Gershman (1976) study, covert positive reinforcement was found to be no more effective than placebo. Comparative evaluations of covert positive reinforcement and systematic desensitization have found both procedures to be about equally effective (Kostka & Galassi, 1974; Ladouceur, 1978; Marshall *et al.*, 1974).

The theoretical rationale of the procedure has been seriously questioned. The results of several studies indicate that covert reinforcement is not a crucial element of this procedure, since omitting the reinforcer or noncontiguous presentation of the reinforcer led to similar outcome (Bajtelsmit & Gershman, 1976; Hurley, 1976; Ladouceur, 1974, 1977, 1978; Marshall *et al.*, 1974). The results of these studies cast doubt on the operant model underlying this procedure. The rationale of covert positive reinforcement was most seriously challenged by the findings of Bajtelsmit and Gershman (1976): Covert reinforcement following anxious behavior was as effective as when it followed the desired behavior. According to the operant model, reinforcement of anxiety should have led to an increase instead of a reduction of anxiety.

The most parsimonious explanation for the effects of covert positive reinforcement appears to be exposure to the phobic stimuli. Only one study (Flannery, 1972) tested the relative effectiveness of covert reinforcement presented either after imaginal or after *in vivo* exposure; *in vivo* exposure was found to be the most effective. Controlled clinical studies using this technique are lacking.

Cognitive Therapy. Behavior therapy is "going cognitive," as demonstrated by the vast increase of articles dealing with cognitive behavior modification in the behavioral journals (Ledwidge, 1978). Most of the cognitive-behavior-modification studies have involved phobic or anxiety-related problems. Now, at least 30 controlled studies in this area have been reported, but we are still far from a definitive evaluation of the usefulness of the cognitive approach for anxiety-related problems. First, almost all the controlled studies involved analogue populations, most often students, who were treated for relatively mild problems. Second, the category of cognitive behavior modification contains such diverse treatment procedures as rational emotive therapy, systematic rational restructuring, self-instructional training, stress inoculation, attentional training, and stimulus reappraisal. The evaluation of these various procedures and cross-study comparisons is often complicated by inadequate reports of the treatment procedures actually used. Third, almost two-thirds of these studies deal with social evaluative anxiety or unassertiveness. It is interesting to note that only two studies deal with snake phobias (Meichenbaum, 1971; Odom, Nelson, & Wein, 1978). The interested reader may take a look at Table 1, which summarizes the studies comparing systematic desensitization and flooding, and may be surprised by the fact that seven studies involve small-animal phobias, while only two studies involve social anxiety. The preponderance of social evaluative anxiety as a target behavior in the cognitive modification studies might indicate that cognitive procedures are more useful with this type of anxiety than with small-animal phobias.

The cognitive-behavior-modification procedures can be divided roughly into two categories: (1) procedures that focus on insight into irrational beliefs and on challenging these beliefs, for example, rational emotive therapy (Ellis, 1962) and systematic rational restructuring (Goldfried, Decenteceo, & Weinberg, 1974); and (2) procedures that focus on the modification of the client's internal dialogue, for example, self-instructional training (Meichenbaum, 1975). In the latter procedure, productive or coping self-statements are rehearsed. It should be noted, however, that in self-instructional training, "insight" into negative or unproductive self-statements is often an integral part of the treatment procedure. Research on social evaluative anxiety, test anxiety, and specific phobias as target behaviors are discussed here separately.

Social Evaluative Anxiety. In this section, studies are discussed that deal with speech anxiety, communication apprehension, interpersonal anxiety, dating anxiety, and unassertiveness. Even though there are some technical differences in both procedures, for present purposes no differentiation will be made between rational emotive therapy and systematic rational restructuring, since both procedures appear to be very similar.

Several studies have compared rational emotive therapy with *systematic desensitization* and have provided conflicting results. In the study by Di Loreto (1971), systematic desensitization was found to be more effective than rational emotive therapy. In contrast with the results of this study, rational emotive therapy proved to be more effective than self-control desensitization in the study by Kanter and Goldfried (1979). Further, it was found that a combined treatment approach (rational emotive therapy plus self-control desensitization) was more effective than self-control desensitization, but *less* effective than rational restructuring alone.

Both Meichenbaum (1971) and Thorpe (1975) found self-instructional training to be superior to systematic desensitization with unassertive subjects. Weissberg (1977) compared (1) desensitization; (2) desensitization with coping imagery; and (3) self-instructional training plus desensitization. No consistent differences among the three treatments were found.

Cognitive therapy has been compared with other treatment approaches, too. Although Di Loreto (1971) found no significant differences between rational therapy and client-centered therapy, an interesting interaction effect was found: Rational emotive therapy was more effective with introvert clients, while client-centered therapy was more effective with extravert clients.

Karst and Trexler (1970) compared (1) rational emotive therapy, (2) *fixed-role therapy* (Kelly, 1955), and (3) a no-treatment control. Both therapies were superior to no treatment; fixed-role therapy proved to be more effective than rational therapy on some measures.

Several studies have investigated the issue of whether unassertiveness should be considered the result of social skills deficits or the result of unproductive self-statements or ir-rational beliefs. Some studies involving a comparison of social skills training and cognitive modification found no significant differences between the two procedures (Alden, Safran, & Weideman, 1978; Fremouw & Zitter 1978; Thorpe, 1975). One study (Linehan, Goldfried, & Powers-Goldfried, 1979) found social skills training to be more effective than a cognitive modification procedure. Finally, Glass, Gottman, and Shmurak (1976) found cognitive restructuring more effective than skills training with respect to transfer of training to nontraining situations. However, the results indicated that skills training was the most effective treatment for the training situations and the total situations on a role-play test.

Several studies found a combined cognitive–social skills treatment to be no more effective than either social skills treatment alone (Carmody, 1978; Glass *et al.*, 1976) or cognitive therapy alone (Glass *et al.*, 1976). In contrast to these studies, the results of other studies indicate that a combined cognitive–social skills approach might be superior. For instance, using as subjects unassertive women in an outpatient clinical setting, Wolfe and Fodor (1977) compared (1) social skills training; (2) social skills training plus rational therapy; (3) a consciousness-raising group; and (4) a waiting-list control group. Both skills training and the combined procedure were superior to the consciousness-raising group and the waiting-list control group on the behavioral measure. Only the patients who had received rational therapy showed anxiety reduction. Derry and Stone (1979) also found a combined procedure to be more effective than social skills training alone. However, the treatment in both the Wolfe and Fodor (1977) and Derry and Stone (1979) study involved two sessions only, so that only limited conclusions can be drawn.

In a well-executed study, Linehan *et al.* (1979) compared (1) social skills training; (2) rational therapy; (3) a combined approach, and (4) pseudotherapy and a waiting list. The results of this study indicated that the combined cognitive–social skills treatment was superior to all other conditions.

In summary, studies comparing the effect of cognitive restructuring and skills training have produced conflicting results. However, several studies indicate that cognitive modification might enhance the effectiveness of social skills training.

Test Anxiety. The effectiveness of various cognitive-restructuring procedures has been investigated with test-anxious subjects. Cognitive restructuring has been found to be superior to systematic desensitization (Holroyd, 1976; Meichenbaum, 1972) and to prolonged exposure in imagination (Goldfried, Linehan, & Smith, 1978). In Holroyd's (1976) study, the effects of a combined procedure (cognitive restructuring plus desensitization) were not found to be consistently different from desensitization and a pseudotherapy.

According to Liebert and Morris (1967), a distinction should be made between the cognitive ("worry") and the emotional (affective and physiological responses) components of test anxiety. Little and Jackson (1974) investigated whether a treatment approach aimed at both the cognitive and the emotional component of test anxiety was more effective than treatments that focused on one component only. Therefore, they compared the following conditions: (1) attention training (cognitive component); (2) relaxation training (emotional component); (3) attention training plus relaxation; (4) placebo; and (5) no treatment as a control. The results indicated that the combined procedure was more effective than relaxation and attentional training by themselves.

More recently, Finger and Galassi (1977) also compared (1) attentional training; (2) relaxation; (3) attentional training plus relaxation; and (4) no treatment. While all the treatments resulted in beneficial effects, the treatments did not differentially affect the cognitive component and the emotional component of test anxiety. The findings obtained with the two major self-report measures, "emotionality" and "worry," indicated that improvement resulted from each treatment, regardless of whether the treatment focused on the cognitive or the emotional component.

There is some evidence that focusing on the emotional component only, as is typically done in systematic desensitization and relaxation training, is not appropriate in the case of test anxiety. The results of laboratory studies (Hollandsworth, Glazeski, Kirkland, Jones, & Van Norman, 1979; Holroyd, Westbrook, Wolf, & Bradhorn, 1978) indicate that low and high test-anxious subjects exhibit almost similar arousal levels during testing. Although the level of arousal during test taking does not adequately discriminate effective and ineffective test-takers, the use of negative self-verbalizations may do so. Hollandsworth *et al.* (1979) found that low-anxious subjects labeled their arousal as facilitative, while high-anxious subjects viewed their arousal as debilitative. Hollandsworth *et al.* (1979) suggested that it may be more productive to train test-anxious subjects to relabel arousal as facilitative, rather than attempting to reduce it by means of relaxation.

Specific Phobias. Two studies have been conducted using snake-phobic volunteers as subjects. Meichenbaum (1971) compared variants of videotaped modeling: (1) mastery model; (2) mastery model plus self-statements; (3) coping model; and (4) coping model plus self-statements. A coping model was found to be more effective than a mastery model. Self-statements did not enhance the effectiveness of the mastery model. With the coping models, the addition of self-statements yielded more positive results on the difficult tasks of the behavioral avoidance test only.

Odom *et al.* (1978) compared (1) exposure *in vivo* (guided participation); (2) systematic desensitization; (3) cognitive restructuring; (4) verbal extinction; (5) placebo; and (6) no treatment. On the behavioral measure and fear thermometer, exposure *in vivo* was found to be superior to all other conditions. Cognitive restructuring was found to be more effective on the psychophysiological modality (heart rate) only.

Cognitive restructuring was found to be as effective as prolonged exposure in imagination in a study by D'Zurilla, Wilson, and Nelson (1973) involving volunteers who were afraid of dead rats. The results of this study further indicated that systematic desensitization was no more effective than no treatment as a control.

Finally, a study by Girodo and Roehl (1978) should be mentioned. Using volunteers with a fear of flying, they compared (1) information giving; (2) self-instructional training; and (3) a combined procedure. The anxiety ratings that were obtained during a normal flight indicated that self-instructional training was no more effective than prior information-giving.

Rational Therapy versus Self-Instructional Training. As already noted, cognitive restructuring procedures differ in their emphasis on insight into irrational beliefs and the training of incompatible positive self-statements. Several studies have been conducted to investigate which component of cognitive restructuring is the most productive. In a study of speech-anxious teenagers, Thorpe, Amatu, Blakey, and Burns (1976) compared (1) general insight (discussion of Ellis's irrational beliefs; (2) specific insight (discussion of irrational ideas relevant to public speaking); (3) self-instructional training; and (4) a combination of specific insight and self-instructional training. The results indicated that insight (general and specific) contributes more to cognitive restructuring than self-instructional training or a combination of insight and self-instructional training. However, the reverse was found by Glogower, Fremouw, and McKroskey (1978). Here, self-instructional training was found to be superior to specific insight into negative self-statements. In addition, it was found that a procedure that combined specific insight and self-instructional training was consistently more effective than any single procedure, although this difference did not reach significance. Finally, Carmody (1978) compared the effectiveness of two variants of assertion training. The results of this study indicated that assertiveness training plus rational therapy along the lines of Ellis was as effective as assertiveness training plus self-instructional training.

In summary, studies comparing various components (i.e., insight vs. self-instructional training) have produced conflicting results. A related issue is whether during self-instructional training coping statements of a specific nature are more productive than more generalized coping statements. The relative contribution of specific coping statements and generalized coping statements was investigated by Hussian and Lawrence (1978), who used test-anxious volunteers as subjects. Generalized coping statements included statements such as

"When fear comes, just pause." Specific coping statements referred to test taking and preparation, such as "I know I'm well prepared for this test, so just relax"; or "The test is a challenge, nothing to get worked up over." The results of this study indicated that the test-specific statements were more productive than the generalized coping statements.

Sutton-Simon and Goldfried (1979) investigated the differential involvement of two forms of faulty thinking (irrational thinking and negative self-statements) in two types of anxiety (social anxiety and fear of heights). In contrast to social anxiety, which was significantly correlated with only irrational thinking, acrophobia was correlated with both irrational thinking and negative self-statements. The results of this study suggest that it might be more productive to match cognitive treatment procedures with types of faulty thinking rather than treating all anxiety-related problems with an identical cognitive treatment package.

Concluding Remarks. Almost all studies in the cognitive area have involved analogue populations. It is remarkable that the journal *Cognitive Therapy and Research,* which is devoted entirely to the cognitive approach, has not yet published one study involving real clinical phobic patients. So far, only a few studies have involved real clinical patients, and the picture that arises on the basis of these studies is far less optimistic with respect to the cognitive approach. Only one study (Wolfe & Fodor, 1977) in the area of social evaluative anxiety involved real patients, but the external validity of this study is presumably small. Patients were selected who had a score not more than one-and-one-half standard deviations above or below the mean of the Rathus Assertiveness Schedule. The use of this criterion might have excluded patients with social anxiety and unassertiveness as the major problem. Other studies with clinical patients, involving agoraphobics (Emmelkamp, Kuipers, & Eggeraat, 1978; Emmelkamp & Mersch, 1982) and obsessive-compulsives (Emmelkamp *et al.,* 1980), have produced inconclusive results.

Although cognitive modification procedures have yielded beneficial effects, it is far from clear whether the effects can be attributed to a modification of cognitive processes. Only a few studies found a change in irrational beliefs after cognitive restructuring. In addition, it is questionable if these changes in cognitions are specific for the cognitive procedures. For instance, Alden *et al.* (1978) found an even greater reduction of irrational beliefs after assertion training than after cognitive restructuring.

Biofeedback. Biofeedback procedures are often applied in the treatment of anxiety or phobic states. In this section, an overview is given of the research that has been conducted in this area. Most of the research has concerned electromyographic feedback and heart-rate feedback.

Electromyographic Feedback. A number of researchers have investigated whether electromyographic (EMG) biofeedback results in a reduction of anxiety symptoms. Studies involving normal volunteers as subjects have produced equivocal results. Several studies (Coursey, 1975; Haynes, Moseley, & McGowan, 1975; Reinking & Kohl, 1975) found EMG feedback superior to relaxation instructions as far as changes in EMG level were concerned; no differences were found on other measures. However, other studies found EMG feedback no more effective (Schandler & Grings, 1976) or even less effective than relaxation procedures (Beiman *et al.,* 1978).

Several controlled studies have been conducted with anxious patients as subjects. Both Canter, Kondo, and Knott (1975) and Townsend, House, and Addario (1975) found EMG feedback superior to control conditions, when EMG was taken as the primary dependent variable. As far as anxiety symptoms were concerned, *no* significant differences were reported between EMG and relaxation (Canter *et al.,* 1975) and between EMG and group psychotherapy (Townsend *et al.,* 1975). Finally, it is noteworthy that Jessup and Neufeld (1977) could not demonstrate a significant change on the EMG measure in a study involving psychiatric patients. Perhaps even more significantly, noncontingent tone presentation (control condition) led to significant changes in heart rate and anxiety measures, while EMG feedback (contingent tone) did not.

Counts, Hollandsworth, and Alcorn (1978) sought to determine whether biofeedback could enhance the effectiveness of cue-controlled relaxation in the treatment of test anxiety. The results of this study indicated that biofeedback did not contribute to the effectiveness of cue-controlled relaxation.

In summary, there is no evidence that EMG feedback has something to offer that other treatments (e.g., relaxation) do not. The few differences that have been found in favor of EMG feedback all concerned EMG level as the dependent variable. Although it has generally been assumed that high levels of frontal EMG are related to anxiety, a study by Burish and Horn (1979) indicates that this is not the case. While several arousal-producing situations were successful in increasing arousal as measured by self-report and physiological measures, these situations had *no* effect on EMG levels.

Heart-Rate Feedback. Gatchel and his colleagues have investigated whether heart-rate biofeedback can be used in the treatment of speech anxiety. In the first study of this series (Gatchel & Proctor, 1976), heart-rate control was found to be more effective than a condition of no heart-rate control on physiological indexes, self-report, and observers' rating. There was also a near-significant expectancy effect, indicating that improvement was at least partially due to expectancy factors. In a subsequent study (Gatchel, Hatch, Watson, Smith, & Gaas, 1977), the relative effectiveness of heart-rate feedback and muscle relaxation was assessed. Therefore, the effects of (1) heart-rate feedback, (2) relaxation, (3) relaxation plus heart-rate feedback, and (4) false heart-rate feedback (placebo) were compared in a between-group design. The results indicated that all treatments (including placebo) improved on self-report measures, with no differences among the groups. Only on physiological indexes during the posttest speech situation did the placebo group differ from the active treatment groups. Moreover, the combined procedure was found to be the most effective on this measure. Finally, the last study of this series (Gatchel, Hatch, Maynard, Turns, & Taunton-Blackwood, 1979) replicated the placebo effect found in the Gatchel *et al.* (1977) study. The results of this study demonstrated that false heart-rate feedback was as effective as true heart-rate feedback and systematic desensitization on self-report indexes and overt motor components of anxiety. Only on heart-rate level, was heart-rate feedback found to be more effective relative to desensitization and placebo. No significant group differences were found for skin conductance and EMG indexes. Moreover, the results indicated that the placebo effect was not short-lived, since identical results were obtained at one-month follow-up.

Nunes and Marks (1975, 1976) investigated whether true heart-rate feedback enhanced the effectiveness of exposure *in vivo*. In contrast to the studies by Gatchel and his colleagues, this study involved real patients with specific phobias. Although it was found that heart-rate feedback substantially reduced heart rate, this effect did not generalize to skin conductance or to subjective anxiety. In addition to the studies by Nunes and Marks, some case reports have been published demonstrating the effectiveness of heart-rate feedback with phobic patients (e.g., Blanchard & Abel, 1976; Wickramasekera, 1974; Gatchel, 1977). However, these studies have typically confounded exposure and biofeedback and thus prevent the drawing of any conclusion.

Finally, the results of several studies indicate that heart-rate feedback is more effective with low-anxious subjects than with high-anxious subjects (Blankstein, 1975; Shepherd & Watts, 1974). The results of the Shepherd and Watts study are the most interesting, since they compared student volunteers with agoraphobic patients. It was found that agoraphobic patients did significantly worse than phobic students in decreasing their heart rate.

In summary, while heart-rate feedback may lead to some control over heart rate, this control does not lead to a greater reduction of subjective anxiety relative to control conditions. Thus, feedback of heart rate seems to have little to offer in the treatment of anxiety. Furthermore, it should be noted that heart rate feedback during exposure to a phobic stimulus may even inhibit approach behavior, as was found in two analogue studies with snake-phobic volunteers (Carver & Blaney, 1977a,b).

In 1974, Engel had already questioned the usefulness of heart-rate feedback in the treatment of anxiety: "it may not be feasible to treat anxiety by teaching subjects to slow their heart rates since heart rate is merely one peripheral manifestation of anxiety and not the illness itself. If one taught an anxious patient to slow his heart, the end results could be an anxious patient whose heart beats slower'' (p. 303). The present review suggests that this is indeed the case.

Concluding Remark. Despite claims made by the proponents of biofeedback, there is no substantial evidence that biofeedback is of any value in the treatment of anxiety-related disorders. The application of biofeedback in this area seems to have been more beneficial to the industry than to anxious and phobic patients.

Modeling. Modeling procedures have been successfully applied in the treatment of phobias. However, it should be noted that almost all studies in this area have dealt with analogue populations (most often animal phobics). Thus, the utility of modeling procedures with clinical phobic cases remains to be demonstrated.

Modeling procedures vary in several aspects: The model may be presented live (*overt modeling*), displayed on film (*symbolic modeling*), or imagined covertly (*covert modeling*). In addition, guided participation *in vivo* after observing the therapist's approach behavior is referred to as *participant modeling*.

No meaningful modeling procedure can be applied devoid of exposure to the phobic stimulus. Thus, it is questionable whether the effects of modeling should be ascribed to vicarious learning processes. Rather, an explanation in terms of exposure is equally plausible. Several studies have sought to test whether modeling was more effective than mere exposure to the phobic stimuli. These studies have provided conflicting results. Rankin (1976) found modeling more effective than mere exposure after anxiety was reduced through prior exposure to the phobic stimulus; modeling was no more effective than exposure when both were presented as the first treatment.

The results of other studies comparing modeling and exposure procedures (including systematic desensitization) are difficult to evaluate since modeling is often mixed with relaxation and narratives. Denney and Sullivan (1976) attempted to separate the effects of modeling and relaxation: Several variants of exposure and modeling were compared. Modeling alone was more effective than mere exposure to the phobic object. However, when

both exposure and modeling were combined with relaxation and narratives, modeling was no more effective than exposure. In my opinion, the results of this study might be interpreted in terms of treatment-generated "expectancies." It is quite possible that the modeling subjects believed they were receiving a valid treatment, whereas the exposure-only subjects did not. On the other hand, when exposure was made equally credible as a treatment procedure by adding relaxation and narratives, the effects of modeling did not surpass the effects of exposure. Unfortunately, expectancy ratings are lacking. The above hypothesis suggests that the effects of modeling may be ascribed to placebo factors rather than to vicarious learning. Current research efforts do not yet provide sufficient evidence to rule out an interpretation of modeling effects in terms of a cognitive expectancy model.

During *covert modeling,* clients imagine rather than watch models approach and handle fearful stimuli. The covert modeling studies have been reviewed by Kazdin and Smith (1979) and are not repeated here. Briefly, while several studies found covert modeling effective in comparison with control conditions, in other studies control conditions were found to be equally effective.

Participant modeling involves two stages: The therapist initially models approach behavior to the phobic stimulus, followed by the therapist's guiding the subject's participation through progressively more demanding tasks. Participant modeling has been found to be far more effective than modeling alone (Bandura, Adams, & Beyer, 1977; Blanchard, 1970; Lewis, 1974; Ritter, 1969) and than covert modeling (Thase & Moss, 1976). The participant-modeling approach consists of two components: (1) modeling and (2) gradual exposure *in vivo*. To date, there is no evidence that the modeling component is an esssential feature of this approach; modeling does not enhance the effectiveness of gradual exposure *in vivo* with obsessive-compulsive patients (Emmelkamp, in press).

Several recent studies have contributed to further clarification of the role of exposure *in vivo* in participant modeling. The results of these studies (Bandura, Jeffery, & Gajdos, 1975; Smith & Coleman, 1977) indicate that self-directed practice enhances the effectiveness of participant modeling. In the Smith and Coleman (1977) study, rat-phobic volunteers were assigned to one of three groups. After treatment by means of participant modeling, the subjects received either self-directed practice (subject without therapist) with the treatment rat or self-directed treatment with varied rats, or they continued with participant modeling. Both self-directed practice conditions led to greater fear reduction to generalization stimuli than did the participant-modeling condition. The results of this study indicate that successful performance in real-life situations might be more important than modeling.

In summary, whether modeling potentiates the effects of exposure procedures is still a question for further studies. Moreover, the relative contribution of modeling may depend on the target behavior under study. While modeling is presumably of limited value with agoraphobics, it might be more important in the treatment of socially anxious patients who lack adequate social skills. Further, the need for additional work with clinical patients is underscored. Modeling therapies applied to clinical phobic patients are currently based on extrapolations from laboratory data and require further examination in clinical cases.

A Cognitive Expectancy Model. It is clear that all procedures reviewed so far have beneficial effects in the treatment of fear and anxiety, at least in analogue populations. The mechanisms by which these procedures achieve their results are, however, far from being understood. While it is obvious that almost all procedures contain elements of exposure to phobic stimuli, this fact does not elucidate the therapeutic processes involved. Exposure is merely a description of what is going on during treatment and not an explanation of its process.

In my opinion, the conditioning explanation presumed to underlie the various treatment techniques seems no longer tenable. Rather, cognitive processes appear to be more important. Elsewhere (Emmelkamp, 1975a), I have presented a cognitive expectancy model to explain the effects of various behavioral treatments on anxiety and fear. This model emphasizes *self-observation of improvement* and *expectancy of therapeutic gain*. All imaginally

based treatments consist of exposure to the phobic stimuli. However, it is not exposure *per se* but self-observation of improvement that seems to be the crucial factor. Through continuous exposure to the phobic stimuli, habituation may occur. Eventually, the patient observes that the imagining of fearful situations no longer arouses anxiety. However, this discovery does not mean that the real-life phobic situation no longer arouses anxiety (e.g., Agras, 1967; Barlow *et al.,* 1969). There is a transfer gap between what patients can imagine without feeling anxiety and what they can perform in real life without anxiety. In my opinion, the self-observation that imagined phobic stimuli no longer arouse anxiety—combined with the therapeutic suggestion of improvement—prompts reality testing *in vivo.* Through successful performance in the real-life situations, habituation *in vivo* is eventually effected. Briefly, while exposure plays a role in the "first" and "second" stages of the treatment process, other important variables seem to be the patient's self-observation of improvement and the expectancy of therapeutic gain. Thus, the effect of exposure depends on the attitude and the set of the patient.

Such other procedures as "self-control relaxation" and cognitive restructuring may work through a similar mechanism. Having learned a coping skill, patients are instructed to venture into the phobic situations *in vivo.* The self-observation of successful performance *in vivo* may lead to further cognitive changes and may motivate further coping efforts.

There is now sufficient evidence that imaginal treatments are often redundant. Treatment may start directly with exposure *in vivo.* The routine use of imaginal procedures with phobic patients seems unwarranted. However, I do not mean to say that all imaginal treatments should be abandoned. Imaginal procedures are still the treatment of choice when real-life exposure is difficult to arrange (e.g., thunderstorm phobias) or when habituation in imagination is the primary aim of treatment (e.g., obsessional ruminations, Emmelkamp & Kwee, 1977).

Self-directed treatments may have several advantages as compared with therapist-directed treatments. In the latter treatments, patients may attribute their improvement to their therapist rather than to their own efforts. Therefore, it seems therapeutically wise to fade out the role of the therapist as soon as possible. The few comparative clinical studies (with agoraphobics and obsessive-compulsives) indicate that self-directed treatment *in vivo* is at least as effective as therapist-directed treatment (Emmelkamp, 1974; Emmelkamp & Kraanen, 1977; Emmelkamp & Wessels, 1975). Moreover, there is some evidence that therapist-directed treatment followed by self-directed practice is more effective than either approach alone (Emmelkamp, 1974).

Finally, the results of analogue studies comparing therapist-directed treatment (participant modeling) and self-directed treatment indicate the superiority of the self-directed approach (Bandura *et al.*, 1975; Smith & Coleman, 1977). Compared with subjects who received therapist-directed treatment, subjects who had the benefit of independent-mastery experiences displayed greater fear reduction.

Clinical Outcome Studies

In this section, research with clinical patients is reviewed. This review is limited to the behavioral treatment of social anxiety and agoraphobia, because of the preponderance of these conditions in clinical settings. A more detailed review of the clinical effectiveness of behavioral treatments is provided elsewhere (Emmelkamp, 1979a).

Social Anxiety. In contrast with the numerous analogue studies that deal with social anxiety, speech anxiety, dating anxiety, unassertiveness, etc. (reviewed by Arkowitz, 1977; Curran, 1977), relatively few studies in the area of social anxiety have used real patients. Studies using patients who are socially inadequates or unassertive are included in the present review, since most patients with social interaction difficulties experience anxiety in social situations (Hall & Goldberg, 1977).

Generally, three behavioral theories concerning the functioning of social anxiety can be distinguished: (1) skills-deficit theory; (2) conditioned-anxiety theory; and (3) cognitive theory. These theories are associated with different therapeutic strategies. If anxiety experienced in social situations is the result of an inadequate handling of these situations due to a lack of interpersonal skills, anxiety may be overcome through social skills training. On the other hand, if patients do have adequate skills but are inhibited in social situations by conditioned anxiety, then treatments that deal directly with this anxiety may be effective. Finally, if anxiety is mediated by faulty thinking, cognitive restructuring may be the treatment of choice.

Systematic Desensitization. Several studies have investigated the effectiveness of systematic desensitization with socially anxious patients (Hall & Goldberg, 1977; Marzillier, Lambert & Kellett, 1976; Shaw, 1976; Trower, Yardley, Bryant, & Shaw, 1978; Van Son, 1978). In general, limited clinical improvements were achieved. In only three studies was systematic desensitization compared with no-treatment conditions, and in neither study did desensitization subjects improve significantly more than controls. In addition, Dormaar and Dijkstra (1975) found no significant between-group differences between psychotherapy and desensitization. Finally, Kanter and Goldfried (1979), using socially anxious community residents as subjects, found systematic desensitization as self-control more effective than a waiting-list control; however, overall improvement was small.

Briefly, systematic desensitization is of limited value with socially anxious patients. The results of studies dealing with real patients contrast with those of studies using analogue populations. In the latter studies, desensitization has consistently been found to be effective in the treatment of social anxiety.

Social Skills Training. Social skills training seems to be of more value in the treatment of social anxiety. However, the evidence in favor of this approach is far from conclusive. Although several studies could not find consistent differences between systematic desensitization and social skills training (Hall & Goldberg, 1977; Shaw, 1976; Trower *et al.*, 1978, social phobics; Van Son, 1978) social inadequates, the results of other studies indicate that social skills training may be superior (Marzillier *et al.*, 1976; Trower *et al.*, 1978, social inadequates; Van Son, 1978, erythophobics).

The skills-deficit model assumes that social

anxiety is caused by a lack of adequate social skills. Thus, the effectiveness of skills training may be interpreted as support for this hypothesis. Alternatively, the effects of this treatment may be due not to skills training *per se* but to exposure *in vivo* to anxiety-arousing situations. During the treatment sessions, the patients are exposed to anxiety-arousing situations and have to give up their avoidance behavior, which may lead eventually to anxiety reduction. Furthermore, the homework patients usually have to carry out between treatment sessions results in a further exposure to real-life situations.

Cognitive Approach. Relatively few studies have examined the effectiveness of cognitive therapy with clinically relevant populations. In the Kanter and Goldfried (1979) study referred to earlier, the following treatment conditions were compared: (1) cognitive restructuring; (2) self-control desensitization; (3) cognitive restructuring plus self-control desensitization; and (4) waiting-list control. Cognitive restructuring proved to be superior to the desensitization and control groups. It is noteworthy that the combined treatment (cognitive restructuring plus desensitization) was *less* effective than cognitive restructuring alone.

Further evidence for the effectiveness of cognitive restructuring was provided by Wolfe and Fodor (1977). The results of their study indicated that both skills training and cognitive restructuring yielded improvements on the behavioral measure; cognitive restructuring, however, was the only condition that led to anxiety reduction.

Concluding Remarks. Both skills training and cognitive restructuring seem to be promising treatments for socially anxious patients, although further studies are certainly needed before more definitive conclusions can be drawn. The effectiveness of systematic and prolonged exposure *in vivo* has not been studied, presumably because such an exposure is difficult to arrange in real life situations. It is well to remember that both cognitive restructuring and social skills training contain elements of exposure *in vivo*. For instance, *in vivo* homework assignments are an integral part of Ellis's rational emotive therapy: "For unless phobic individuals act against their irrational beliefs that they must not approach

fearsome objects or situations and that it is horrible if they do, can they ever really be said to have overcome such beliefs?" (Ellis, 1979, p. 162).

Most research in this area has been plagued by the uniformity myth that all socially anxious patients are similar. Generally, researchers do not distinguish among various categories of socially anxious patients: A functional analysis is not made, but patients are randomly assigned to treatment conditions. It is too easy, however, to conceptualize social anxiety in terms of a single theory. Cognitive restructuring, social skills training, and exposure procedures surely can be critical elements in treatment, but no method is so powerful that it can be applied universally across socially anxious patients. For patients who lack adequate social skills, the training of such skills seems essential. On the other hand, for those patients who do have the necessary social skills but whose anxiety is mediated by faulty thinking, cognitive therapy combined with exposure *in vivo* to test the newly acquired cognitions may be the treatment of choice.

Agoraphobia. Systematic desensitization seems to have little to offer in the treatment of agoraphobia (Cooper, Gelder, & Marks, 1965; Evans & Kellam, 1973; Gelder & Marks, 1966; Gelder *et al.*, 1967; Marks *et al.*, 1971; Marks & Gelder, 1965; Yorkston, Sergeant, & Rachman, 1968). Studies that involved both agoraphobics and specific phobics generally found that systematic desensitization was more effective for specific phobics than with agoraphobics. In contrast to the above-cited researchers, Gelder *et al.* (1973) found no differential effectiveness of desensitization for agoraphobics and for other phobics. However, most of the improvements found may be attributed to exposure *in vivo*: Most changes seemed to have occurred *after* systematic desensitization during four sessions of exposure *in vivo*.

Aversion relief is also of little value in the treatment of agoraphobia. Solyom, McClure, Heseltine, Ledwidge, and Solyom (1972) investigated the effects of this treatment on agoraphobics. Overall improvement was rather small: Patients rated their main phobia as unimproved.

As already discussed, flooding in imagination is less effective than flooding or prolonged exposure *in vivo*. There is no evidence that flooding in imagination is more effective than systematic desensitization in imagination. Most studies that found favorable results for flooding in imagination have confounded imagination and *in vivo* exposure (e.g., Mathews *et al.*, 1976). Briefly, the rather small effects of systematic desensitization, aversion relief, and flooding in imagination do not warrant widespread clinical application. In the last few years, research on agoraphobics has been concentrated on the development of exposure *in vivo* programs, which will be discussed in some detail.

Prolonged Exposure In Vivo. Although prolonged exposure *in vivo* may be applied in individual cases (e.g., Emmelkamp & Wessels, 1975), group exposure *in vivo* seems to offer several advantages. Besides the aspect of saving the therapist time, groups may provide the patient with coping models and may lead to fewer dropouts. It should be noted, however, that both Emmelkamp and Emmelkamp-Benner (1975) and Hand, Lamontagne, and Marks (1974) reported cases of negative modeling during group exposure *in vivo*. For instance, one group treated by Emmelkamp and Emmelkamp-Benner (1975) was dominated by a patient who repeatedly simulated heart attacks. Studies comparing individual and group exposure *in vivo* found no clear differences in effectiveness (Emmelkamp & Emmelkamp-Benner, 1975; Hafner & Marks, 1976).

To illustrate this treatment approach, the prolonged exposure treatment conducted by Emmelkamp *et al.* (1978) is described in some detail. During the first half hour of the first session, the patients exchanged information about the onset and the development of their phobias, and the therapists gave the treatment rationale. The role played by avoidance behavior in maintaining phobias was emphasized, and the patients were instructed to remain in the phobic situations until they had experienced anxiety reduction. Then, the patients and the therapists took a short walk to the center of the town, the place where the patients would have to walk more on their own in the future. After 90 min of prolonged exposure *in vivo*, the patient's experiences were assessed in a brief group discussion at the hospital. During prolonged exposure *in vivo*, the patients were exposed to anxiety-provoking situations, at first in groups of two or three patients but, as the treatment progressed, more and more on their own. Difficult situations were, for example, walking in busy streets, shopping in department stores and supermarkets, and riding in buses. The therapists consciously faded from the groups and, after a few sessions, were present only at the discussions preceding and following the exposure periods.

Various investigators in three different centers have found prolonged exposure *in vivo* conducted in groups to be a very effective treatment for agoraphobics (Emmelkamp *et al.*, 1978; Emmelkamp & Mersch, 1982; Emmelkamp, 1979b; Hafner & Marks, 1976; Hand *et al.*, 1974; Teasdale, Walsh, Lancashire, & Mathews, 1977). Often, dramatic improvements with respect to anxiety and avoidance are achieved even in a few days, but generally, a lack of continuing improvement has been found when treatment ends (e.g., Emmelkamp & Mersch, 1982; Emmelkamp, 1979b; Hafner & Marks, 1976; Teasdale *et al.*, 1977).

Self-Management Programs. In Andrews's (1966) view, the phobic patient is characterized by dependency relationships with others and by an avoidance of activity that involves the independent handling of difficult and fear-arousing situations. This lack of independency constitutes a fairly broad pattern of responses and not just a response to the phobic stimulus itself. In agoraphobics, Emmelkamp and Cohen-Kettenis (1975) found a significant correlation between external locus of control and phobic anxiety. This finding suggests that an agoraphobic can be characterized as someone who avoids anxiety-arousing situations because of a lack of internal control. In light of this consideration, acquiring self-control may be an important therapeutic goal for agoraphobics. If this reasoning is correct, then treatment for agoraphobics should focus on teaching generalizable coping skills.

Problems with respect to a lack of continuing improvement when formal treatment ends may be prevented by self-management programs in the patient's natural environment. An additional advantage of this approach is that the most severe agoraphobics, who are unable to visit a therapist, can be treated. To date, two treatment programs, have been developed that can be managed by patients in their own environment.

The first self-management program was developed by Emmelkamp (1974). The treatment consisted of self-controlled exposure plus feedback (self-observation). After an instructional phase in the presence of the therapist, the patient had to carry on alone. The procedure involved a graduated approach by the patient to the actual feared situation. Right from the first session, the client had to enter the phobic situation. The client had to walk alone a route through the city with instructions to turn back on experiencing undue anxiety. The client had to record the duration of each trial and to write it down in a notebook. Then she/he had to enter the phobic situation in the same way. This procedure was repeated until the 90-min. session was over. At the end of each session, the patient had to send the results to the therapist.

In a study by Emmelkamp (1974), the effects of the following treatments were compared: (1) self-observation; (2) flooding; (3) flooding followed by self-observation; and (4) no-treatment control. Each flooding session consisted of 45 min of flooding in imagination, immediately followed by 45 min of flooding *in vivo*. During self-observation, the therapist was present only at the first few sessions. At the following sessions, the patients had to practice alone. All treatments proved to be superior to no treatment. No significant differences were found between flooding and self-observation, despite the fact that the therapist's involvement was at least twice as much during flooding. In addition, flooding plus self-observation proved to be the most effective. The effectiveness of self-observation as a self-management procedure was further demonstrated in the studies by Emmelkamp (1980b), Emmelkamp and Emmelkamp-Benner (1975), Emmelkamp and Wessels (1975), and Emmelkamp and Kuipers (1979). In conrast to the results found with prolonged exposure *in vivo*, with this self-management program most patients went on to make further gains during follow-up. (Emmelkamp, 1974, 1980b; Emmelkamp & Kuipers, 1979).

More recently, Mathews, Teasdale, Munby, Johnston, and Shaw (1977) developed another self-management program for agoraphobics. Their program differs from our program in that their patients' spouses were actively involved in planning and encouraging practice attempts. Furthermore, their patients had to remain in the phobic situation long enough for anxiety to decline, rather than to return on experiencing undue anxiety, as in self-observation. Mathews, Jannoun and Gelder (1979) reported the results of two controlled studies, demonstrating the effectiveness of this program. As in our self-observation program, there was a trend toward continuing improvement between posttest and follow-up.

The role of the partner in the Mathews *et al.* program is questionable. By using the partner as a cotherapist, the therapist may inadvertently reinforce the dependent relationship between patient and partner. One study (Mathews *et al.*, 1979) compared home practice with the partner with home practice alone. While the partner condition was more effective at the posttest, it is interesting to see that only the condition of home practice alone showed continuing improvement between posttest and follow-up. Moreover, it should be remembered that the self-management program developed by Emmelkamp produced at least equivalent change without the help of the patient's partner.

Spaced versus Massed. Until recently, there was little evidence of whether massed practice of exposure *in vivo* was superior to spaced practice or vice versa. Foa and Turner (1979) compared 10 sessions of massed practice with 10 sessions of spaced practice in a crossover design. In the massed-practice condition, the treatment was conducted on consecutive days, whereas in the spaced condition, the sessions were held only once a week. The results indicated that massed practice was more effective than spaced practice. Foa and Turner (1979) suggested that the massed condition may be superior because massed practice provides less opportunity for accidental exposure between treatment sessions and for the reinforcement of avoidance or escape behavior.

Follow-Up. Follow-up in the various studies into exposure *in vivo* ranges from a few weeks to one year. Thus, there is little evidence of termination persistence effects. Recently, we conducted a follow-up study (Emmelkamp & Kuipers, 1979) with 70 agoraphobics who were treated at an average of four years ago in the trials of Emmelkamp (1974), Emmelkamp and Ultee (1974), Emmelkamp and Wessels (1975), and Emmelkamp and Emmelkamp-Benner (1975). Although the treatment procedures varied from study to study (including self-controlled exposure *in vivo*, flooding or prolonged exposure *in vivo*, and flooding in imagination), all patients had been treated by exposure *in vivo*. After the clinical trial, a number of patients were further treated individually. The number of treatment sessions averaged around 18 (clinical trial plus further treatment).

The results on the anxiety and avoidance scales at pretest, postest, and follow-up are shown in Figure 2. The improvements that were achieved during the treatment were maintained and partly continued during follow-up. Hafner (1976) found the emergence of fresh symptoms one year after exposure *in vivo* treatment with a number of his agoraphobics. However, in the present study, the patient did not report the emergence of other problems than agoraphobia. Moreover, it should be noted that results at follow-up revealed even further continuing improvement in depression.

As can be seen in Figure 2, the treatment led to clinically significant improvements at

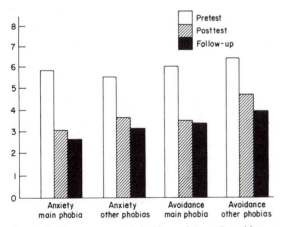

Figure 2. Mean scores on phobic anxiety and avoidance scales. (From "Agoraphobia: A Follow-Up Study Four Years after Treatment" by P. M. G. Emmelkamp and A. Kuipers, *British Journal of Psychiatry,* 1979, *134,* 352–355, Fig. 1. Copyright 1979 by the British Journal of Psychiatry. Reprinted by permission.)

four-year follow-up. However, there was a great variance in the results of the treatment. Some patients were symptom-free, some were moderately improved, and a few patients did not benefit at all. Obviously, while exposure *in vivo* procedures may be quite effective for a number of agoraphobics, it is not the panacea for the treatment of agoraphobia.

There are several factors that may complicate treatment by exposure procedures. For present purposes, I will limit the discussion to (1) anxiety-inducing cognitions and (2) interpersonal problems. Of course, I do not mean to say that these are the only factors that may complicate treatment by exposure *in vivo*.

Cognitive Approach. Agoraphobics often complain of anxiety-inducing thoughts. With a number of patients these "negative" cognitions change "spontaneously" as a result of treatment by exposure *in vivo*. For example, during exposure *in vivo*, patients may notice that the awful things that they fear, such as fainting, getting a heart-attack or "going crazy," do not take place. However, while we have found these cognitive changes in a number of patients, clearly not *all* patients do change their cognitions during treatment, and in some patients, these cognitive changes are only short-lived.

Another point also deserves attention. Although the patients are exposed to the phobic situation *in vivo*, real exposure may still be avoided by the patients through thoughts, as, for example, "there is a hospital; if something goes wrong, there will be help." Similarly, *after* treatment sessions, some patients "reassure" themselves with such statements as "Well, this time nothing did go wrong because I had a good day, but tomorrow I can get a real attack." Thus, the patients may use private speech that interferes with real exposure to the anxiety-inducing situations. Although as yet no research has been conducted into the effects of such negative private speech, it is tempting to assume that such cognitive avoidance militates against the effects of *in vivo* exposure.

In the last few years, we have directed some research into cognitive change methods for agoraphobics and obsessive-compulsives. In our first study (Emmelkamp *et al.,* 1978), cognitive restructuring was compared with prolonged exposure *in vivo* in a crossover design. Both prolonged exposure *in vivo* and cognitive restructuring were conducted in groups. Each procedure consisted of five sessions. Exposure *in vivo* was found to be far more effective than cognitive restructuring on the behavioral measure, on phobic anxiety, and on avoidance scales. However, treatment was conducted in a relatively short time period (one week), which might be too short to result in significant cognitive changes. Moreover, the use of the crossover design precluded conclusions about the long-term effectiveness of our cognitive package.

In a following study (Emmelkamp & Mersch, 1982), three treatments were compared in a between-group design: (1) cognitive restructuring; (2) prolonged exposure *in vivo*; and (3) a combination of cognitive restructuring and prolonged exposure *in vivo*. Each session lasted 2 hr, and each treatment consisted of eight sessions. During cognitive restructuring, more emphasis was placed on insight into unproductive thinking than in the cognitive procedure used by Emmelkamp *et al.* (1978). In each session, the patient had to analyze their own feelings in terms of Ellis's ABC theory. In the combined procedure, half of the time was spent on self-instructional training, the other half on prolonged exposure *in vivo*. During the latter phase of the combined treatment,

the patients were instructed to use their positive self-statements during their *in vivo* exercises. The results of the patients' ratings on the phobic anxiety and avoidance scales (Watson & Marks, 1971) are presented in Figure 3. At the posttest, prolonged exposure *in vivo* and the combined procedure were clearly superior to cognitive restructuring. At the one-month follow-up, however, the differences between the treatments partly disappeared because of a continuing improvement in the cognitive modification group and a slight relapse in the exposure *in vivo* condition. Thus, although the short-term effects were similar to the results of the Emmelkamp *et al.* (1978) study, in the long run, cognitive modification was about equally effective. Unfortunately, self-instructional training did not enhance the effects of exposure *in vivo*. At follow-up, the results of the combined procedure were comparable with the results of the exposure and cognitive procedures.

Similar results were found in a study with obsessive-compulsive patients (Emmelkamp *et al.*, 1980), in which 10 sessions of exposure *in vivo* were compared with 10 sessions of a combined procedure, which consisted of self-instructional training and exposure *in vivo*. Each session lasted 2 hr. The results on the anxiety and avoidance scales are presented in Figure 4. Self-instructional training did not

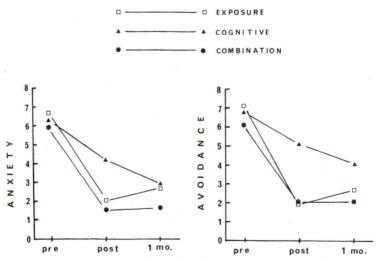

Figure 3. Mean scores on phobic anxiety and avoidance scales. (From "Cognition and Exposure *in Vivo* in the Treatment of Agoraphobia: Short Term and Delayed Effects" by P. M. G. Emmelkamp and P. Mersch, *Cognitive Therapy and Research*, 1982, 6, 77–88. Fig. 1. Copyright 1982 by Plenum Press. Reprinted by permission.)

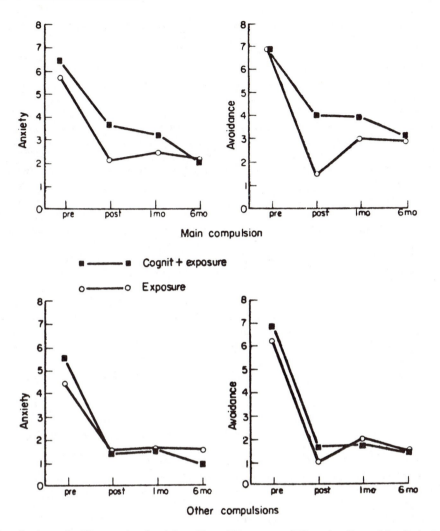

Figure 4. Contributions of self-instructional training. (From "Treatment of Obsessive-Compulsive Patients: The Contribution of Self-Instructional Training to the Effectiveness of Exposure," by P. M. G. Emmelkamp *et al., Behaviour Research and Therapy,* 1980, *18,* 61–66, Fig. 2. Copyright 1980 by Pergamon Press. Reprinted by permission.)

enhance treatment effectiveness, either at the posttest or at the one- or six-month followups.

The results of our studies with clinical populations using cognitive procedures have not yet given an answer for the usefulness of the cognitive approach for clinical patients. However, these results have stressed the necessity of conducting outcome research with real patients instead of with students in need of some credit points for their course requirements.

Although as yet no definitive conclusions can be drawn with respect to the usefulness of the cognitive approach for clinical phobics, a comparison of our studies leads to a few suggestions about effective parameters: (1) Cognitive therapy conducted over a longer time interval might prove to be more effective than when conducted over a short period; and (2) Insight into unproductive thinking might prove to be more relevant than self-instructional training.

Interpersonal Problems. The interpersonal problems of phobic patients might also complicate treatment by exposure *in vivo.* Both psychotherapists (e.g., Fry, 1962; Goodstein

& Swift, 1977) and behavior therapists (Goldstein-Fodor, 1974; Goldstein, 1973; Goldstein & Chambless, 1978; Wolpe, 1973) have stressed the importance of the client's interpersonal relationships in the development of agoraphobia. According to Goldstein and Wolpe, female agoraphobics wish to flee the marriage but cannot because of their fears of being alone. Goldstein-Fodor holds that agoraphobia in women develops because the patients in infancy were reinforced for stereotypical female behavior like helplessness and dependency. In her view, interpersonal trappedness, particularly the feeling of being dominated with no outlet for assertion, might enhance the tendency to develop agoraphobia. However, experimental studies to test these notions are sparse and are not discussed here (see review by Emmelkamp, 1979a).

More important to our present discussion is whether such interpersonal factors interfere with treatment by exposure *in vivo*. Therefore, in a recent study by Emmelkamp (1980b), two types of interpersonal problems were distinguished: (1) problems with the significant partner and (2) unassertiveness. Agoraphobics were divided for low and high marital satisfaction and for low and high assertiveness on the basis of their scores on questionnaires. After four treatment sessions with self-controlled exposure *in vivo*, it appeared that low-assertive patients improved as much as high-assertive patients. Moreover, patients with low marital satisfaction improved as much as patients with high marital satisfaction. The effects of the treatment were not influenced by the interpersonal problems of agoraphobics either at the posttest or at the one-month follow-up. However, one should interpret these results cautiously. First, only short-term effects were assessed, since the treatment involved four sessions only. Second, the assignment to conditions was based on self-report questionnaires. Thus, patients may have faked their responses on the questionnaires, although we have no evidence that this was the case. Finally, this study should not be seen as proof or disproof of the system-theoretic hypothesis. A true test of the system-theoretic hypothesis concerning agoraphobia would require a demonstration that improvement in the agoraphobic patient was uninfluenced by family factors.

If lack of assertion is at the root of agoraphobia, as some have suggested, then agoraphobics may profit from assertiveness training. Emmelkamp (1979b) reported a study in which assertiveness training was compared with prolonged exposure *in vivo*. Only low-assertive agoraphobics were accepted in this experiment. The preliminary data of this study indicate that assertiveness training is less effective than exposure *in vivo*. Nevertheless, assertion training did lead to clinically significant improvements in some agoraphobics. In addition, it should be noted that assertion training may teach patients a more adequate handling of interpersonal stress situations, which might prevent relapse in the future.

Although a number of agoraphobics have problems with their partners, they often want treatment for their phobias instead of for these problems. In our experience, few agoraphobics accept help for marital difficulties. Recently, Cobb, McDonald, Marks and Stern (1979) compared marital treatment with exposure *in vivo*; the subjects were both agoraphobics and obsessive-compulsives who also manifested marital discord. The results indicated that exposure *in vivo* led to improvements with respect to both the compulsive and phobic problems and the marital relationship, while marital therapy improved only the marital interaction. Further studies in this area are surely needed.

Future Perspectives

This section delineates some issues for further investigation, though these suggestions are by no means exhaustive.

Behavioral Analysis

One of the major issues for further research relates to a differential diagnosis and treatment tailored to the individual needs of patients. Most studies have used a between-groups design: Subjects are randomly assigned to different treatments. It would be advisable for researchers to put a larger emphasis on making a functional analysis of the problem behavior, rather than neglecting individual differences by assigning patients randomly to groups.

So far, research on phobic patients has focused narrowly on the removal of phobias. It should be noted that clinical phobias are often complicated by other problems. Obviously, complex problems deserve complex treatments. Studies of agoraphobics (Emmelkamp, 1979b) and of obsessional patients (Emmelkamp & Van der Heyden, 1980) indicate that for some patients, assertiveness training might be at least as effective as treatments that focus on the phobias and obsessions directly.

For clinical purposes, the effects of proper combinations of various treatments need to be evaluated. To give just one example, for some agoraphobics exposure *in vivo* may suffice as treatment, whereas for others this approach needs to be supplemented by assertiveness training, cognitive restructuring, or marital therapy. Such clinical decisions are often based on intuition and need to be supplemented by hard data.

Prevention

Another issue for future research concerns the prevention of anxiety and fear. Several studies have evaluated the effectiveness of immunization programs (including systematic desensitization, modeling, and cognitive rehearsal) in preventing snake phobias (Jaremko & Wenrich, 1973); fears of dental treatment (Melamed, 1979); and speech anxiety (Cradock, Cotler, & Jason, 1978; Jaremko & Wenrich, 1973). Generally, the results of these studies demonstrate the utility of immunization programs in preventing anxiety. However, Cradock *et al.* (1978) could not find any difference in the behavioral manifestations of anxiety for systematic desensitization and cognitive rehearsal relative to their control group.

The studies cited above can be criticized along several lines. First, only short-term effects were assessed. Thus, whether immunization programs are effective in preventing phobias in later life is still questionable. Further, some of these studies (e.g., Jaremko & Wenrich, 1973) may have included subjects who were already phobic prior to the intervention program. In that case, the term *treatment* is more appropriate than the term *prevention*.

In my opinion, meaningful prevention programs can be applied only when we have a better understanding of the etiology of phobic disorders. It is well to remember that attempts to explain the acquisition of fears have created the widest conceptual disagreements among behavior therapists. The various speculations put forth by behavior therapists clearly suggest the many variables that require examination as critical determinants of the development of phobic behavior. This view implies that a great deal of research has yet to be done before meaningful prevention programs can be developed.

Drug-Assisted Exposure

Several recent studies have investigated whether drugs enhance the effectiveness of exposure *in vivo*. Neither beta blockers (Butollo, Burkhardt, Himmler, & Müller, 1978; Hafner & Milton, 1977; Ullrich, Ullrich, Cromback, & Peikert, 1972) nor MAOIs (Solyom *et al.*, 1981) seem to enhance the effects of exposure *in vivo*. Only diazepam has been found to have some effects, particularly with specific phobics (Hafner & Marks, 1976; Johnston & Gath, 1973; Marks, Viswanathan, Lipsedge, & Gardner, 1972). In addition, there is some evidence suggesting that diazepam might influence anxiety experienced *during* exposure sessions. For those few patients for whom exposure *in vivo* is too terrifying, diazepam-assisted exposure might offer a solution.

Whether imipramine might potentiate the effects of exposure *in vivo* has not been studied. However, data from the study by Zitrin *et al.* (1978) indicate that imipramine has beneficial effects in patients who experience spontaneous panic attacks. Studies investigating whether imipramine facilitates exposure *in vivo* are surely needed.

Therapeutic Relationship

Nonbehavioral psychotherapists presume the therapeutic relationship to be of paramount importance in the process of therapy. The relationship between therapist and patient has been neglected in the behavioral literature (De Voge & Beck, 1978).

As far as behavior therapy for phobias is concerned, the role of the therapist is largely ignored. There are, however, a few studies that shed some light on this issue. For example, analogue studies by Morris and Suckerman (1974a,b) demonstrated that a warm therapeutic voice produced significantly better results than a cold voice. Thus, even with desensitization in an analogue context, therapist variables appear to be of importance.

Let us now turn our attention to clinical studies. In several studies, a significant therapist interaction was found (e.g., Mathews *et al.* 1976, 1979). The "therapist effect" found in these studies indicates that the improvements achieved cannot be ascribed solely to technical procedures.

A study by Rabavilas and Boulougouris (1979) contributes to an understanding of the role of the therapist during behavioral treatment. Phobic and obsessive-compulsive patients who had been treated with exposure *in vivo* had to rate their therapists' qualities at follow-up. The results indicated that therapists' respect, understanding, and interest was positively related to outcome. However, gratification of patients' dependency needs was negatively related to outcome.

Subsequent studies pertaining to relationship factors should use direct observational measures of therapist–patient interactions in addition to ratings of therapists' qualities. Another research strategy that might prove to be fruitful is to vary therapeutic styles experimentally. The therapeutic relationship, then, is an important target for further research.

Summary

Phobics are typically considered a homogeneous group. This uniformity myth has plagued behavioral research: Generally, outcome research has been technique- rather than problem-oriented. As we have seen, a good deal of effort has been directed toward evaluating various techniques. But it is essential to note that there are important differences among

various categories of phobic behavior. Therefore, conclusions cannot be generalized from one population (e.g., social anxiety) to another population (e.g., agoraphobia).

In the early days, behavioral treatments for anxiety and fear were defined as the application of "established laws of learning" or were viewed as being based on "modern learning theories." The claim that these procedures are exclusively based on learning paradigms seems no longer tenable nowadays. The present review suggests that additional factors, such as the therapeutic relationship, the expectancy of therapeutic gain, and the self-observation of improvements, play an important role. The preceding review indicates that *in vivo* procedures are more powerful than imaginal ones. Taken together, these data lead to the clinical emphasis on *in vivo* treatments and self-attributed success experiences to enhance therapeutic changes.

The clinical utility of most behavioral procedures is questionable. To give just one example, although systematic desensitization has been found to be effective in improving specific phobias, the benefits of this treatment for social phobics and agoraphobics are doubtful. Generalizing results from analogue populations to clinical populations, as has typically been done in the past, ignores crucial differences between these populations. The time may be ripe for taking a fresh look at the value of analogue studies. In my opinion, the hard job, but the only one that will lead to meaningful conclusions, is to develop and evaluate treatments using real clinical patients as subjects.

References

Agras, W. S. Transfer during systematic desensitization therapy. *Behaviour Research and Therapy*, 1967, 5, 193–199.

Agras, W. S., Leitenberg, H., & Barlow, D. H. Social reinforcement in the modification of agoraphobia. *Archives of General Psychiatry*, 1968, 19, 423–427.

Agras, W. S., Leitenberg, H., Barlow, D. H., & Thomson, L. E. Instructions and reinforcements in the modification of neurotic behavior. *American Journal of Psychiatry*, 1969, 125, 1435–1439.

Agras, W. S., Leitenberg, H., Wincze, J. P., Butz, R. A., & Callahan, E. J. Comparison of the effects of instructions and reinforcement in the treatment of a neurotic avoidance response: A single case experiment. *Journal of Behavior Therapy and Experimental Psychiatry*, 1970, *1*, 53–58.

Agras, W. S., Leitenberg, H., Barlow, D. H., Curtis, N. A., Edwards, J., & Wright, D. Relaxation in systematic desensitization. *Archives of General Psychiatry*, 1971, *25*, 511–514.

Alden, L., Safran, J., & Weideman, R. A comparison of cognitive and skills training strategies in the treatment of unassertive clients. *Behavior Therapy*, 1978, *8*, 843–846.

Andrews, J. D. W. Psychotherapy of phobias. *Psychological Bulletin*, 1966, *66*, 455–480.

Arkowitz, H. Measurement and modification of minimal dating behavior. In M. Hersen, R. M. Eisler, & P. M. Miller (Eds.), *Progress in behavior modification*, Vol. 5. New York: Academic Press, 1977.

Bajtelsmit, J. W., & Gershman, L. Covert positive reinforcement: Efficacy and conceptualization. *Journal of Behavior Therapy and Experimental Psychiatry*, 1976, *7*, 207–212.

Bandura, A. *Principles of behavior modification*. New York: Holt, Rinehart & Winston, 1969.

Bandura, A. *Social learning theory*. Englewood Cliffs, N.J.: Prentice-Hall, 1977.

Bandura, A. On paradigms and recycled ideologies. *Cognitive Therapy and Research*, 1978, *2*, 79–103.

Bandura, A., Jeffery, R. W., & Gajdos, E. Generalizing change through participant modeling with self-directed mastery. *Behaviour Research and Therapy*, 1975, *13*, 141–152.

Bandura, A., Adams, N. E., & Beyer, J. Cognitive processes mediating behavioral change. *Journal of Personality and Social Psychology*, 1977, *35*, 125–139.

Barlow, D. H., Leitenberg, H., Agras, W. S., & Wincze, J. P. The transfer gap in systematic desensitization: An analogue study. *Behaviour Research and Therapy*, 1969, *7*, 191–196.

Barlow, D. H., Agras, W. S., Leitenberg, H., & Wincze, J. P. An experimental analysis of the effectiveness of "shaping" in reducing maladaptive avoidance behavior: an analogue study. *Behaviour Research and Therapy*, 1970, *8*, 165–173.

Barrett, C. L. Systematic desensitization versus implosive therapy. *Journal of Abnormal Psychology*, 1969, *74*, 587–592.

Barrios, B. A. Note on demand characteristics in analogue research on small animal phobias. *Psychological Reports*, 1978, *42*, 1264–1266.

Becker, H. G., & Costello, C. G. Effects of graduated exposure with feedback of exposure times of snake phobias. *Journal of Consulting and Clinical Psychology*, 1975, *43*, 478–484.

Beiman, I. The effects of instructional set on physiological response to stressful imagery. *Behaviour Research and Therapy*, 1976, *14*, 175–180.

Beiman, I., Israel, E., & Johnson, S. During training and posttraining effects of live and taped extended progressive relaxation, self-relaxation, and electromyogram feedback. *Journal of Consulting and Clinical Psychology*, 1978, *46*, 314–321.

Benjamin, S., Marks, I. M., & Huson, J. Active muscular relaxation in desensitization of phobic patients. *Psychological Medicine*, 1972, *2*, 381–390.

Bernstein, D. A. Manipulation of avoidance behavior as a function of increased or decreased demand on repeated behavioral tests. *Journal of Consulting and Clinical Psychology*, 1974, *42*, 896–900.

Bernstein, D. A., & Nietzel, M. T. Procedural variations in behavioral avoidance tests. *Journal of Consulting and Clinical Psychology*, 1973, *41*, 165–174.

Bernstein, D. A., & Nietzel, M. T. Behavioral avoidance tests: The effects of demand characteristics and repeated measures on two types of subjects. *Behavior Therapy*, 1974, *5*, 183–192.

Blackwell, B. Hypertensive crisis due to mono-amine oxidase inhibitors. *Lancet*, 1963, *2*, 849–851.

Blanchard, E. B. The relative contributions of modeling, informational influences, and physical contact in the extinction of phobic behavior. *Journal of Abnormal Psychology*, 1970, *76*, 55–61.

Blanchard, E. B., & Abel, G. G. An experimental case study of the biofeedback treatment of a rape-induced psychophysiological cardiovascular disorder. *Behavior Therapy*, 1976, *7*, 113–119.

Blankstein, K. R. Heart rate control, general anxiety, and subjective tenseness. *Behavior Therapy*, 1975, *6*, 699–700.

Borkovec, T. D. Effects of expectancy on the outcome of systematic desensitization and implosive treatments for analogue anxiety. *Behavior Therapy*, 1972, *3*, 29–40.

Borkovec, T. D. The role of expectancy and physiological feedback in fear research: A review with special reference to subject characteristics. *Behavior Therapy*, 1973, *4*, 491–505.

Borkovec, T. D., & Nau, S. D. Credibility of analogue therapy rationales. *Journal of Behavior Therapy and Experimental Psychiatry*, 1972, *3*, 257–260.

Borkovec, T. D., & Rachman, S. The utility of analogue research. *Behaviour Research and Therapy*, 1979, *17*, 253–261.

Borkovec, T. D., & Sides, J. K. Critical procedural variables related to the physiological effects of progressive relaxation: A review. *Behaviour Research and Therapy*, 1979, *17*, 119–125.

Boudewyns, P. A., & Wilson, A. E. Implosive therapy and desensitization therapy using free association in treatment of inpatients. *Journal of Abnormal Psychology*, 1972, *79*, 252–268.

Boulougouris, J. C., Marks, I. M., & Marset, P. Superiority of flooding (implosion) to desensitization for reducing pathological fear. *Behaviour Research and Therapy*, 1971, *9*, 7–16.

Branham, L., & Katahn, M. Effectiveness of automated desensitization with normal volunteers and phobic patients. *Canadian Journal of Behavioral Sciences*, 1974, *6*, 234–245.

Buglass, D., Clarke, J., Henderson, N., Kreitman, N., & Presley, A. S. A study of agoraphobic housewives. *Psychological Medicine*, 1977, *7*, 73–86.

Burish, T. G., & Horn, P. W. An evaluation of frontal EMG as an index of general arousal. *Behavior Therapy*, 1979, *10*, 137–147.

Butollo, W., Burkhardt, P., Himmler, C., & Müller, M.

Mehrdimensionale Verhaltenstherapie und Beta-Blocker bei functionellen Dysrytmien und chronischen körperbezogenen Angstreaktionen. Paper read at the meeting of the German Society of Psychosomatic Medicine, Cologne, 1978.

Calef, R. A., & MacLean, G. D. A comparison of reciprocal inhibition and reactive inhibition therapies in the treatment of speech anxiety. *Behavior Therapy*, 1970, *1*, 51–58.

Canter, A., Kondo, C. Y., & Knott, J. R. A comparison of EMG feedback and progressive muscle relaxation training in anxiety neurosis. *British Journal of Psychiatry*, 1975, *127*, 470–477.

Carmody, T. P. Rational-emotive, self-instructional, and behavioral assertion: Facilitating maintenance. *Cognitive Therapy and Research*, 1978, *2*, 241–253.

Carver, C. S., & Blaney, P. H. Avoidance behavior and perceived arousal. *Motivation and Emotion*, 1977, *1*, 61–73. (a)

Carver, C. S., & Blaney, P. H. Perceived arousal, focus of attention, and avoidance behavior. *Journal of Abnormal Psychology*, 1977, *86*, 154–162. (b)

Cautela, J. R. Covert reinforcement. *Behavior Therapy*, 1970, *2*, 192–200.

Chang-Liang, R., & Denney, D. R. Applied relaxation as training in self-control. *Journal of Counseling Psychology*, 1976, *23*, 183–189.

Cobb, J. P., McDonald, R., Marks, I. M., & Stern, R. S. *Marital versus exposure treatment for marital plus phobic-obsessive problems.* Unpublished manuscript, 1979.

Cooper, A., Furst, J. B., & Bridger, W. H. A brief commentary on the usefulness of studying fear of snakes. *Journal of Abnormal Psychology*, 1969, *74*, 413–414.

Cooper, J. E., Gelder, M. G., & Marks, I. M. Results of behaviour therapy in 77 psychiatric patients. *British Medical Journal*, 1965, *1*, 1222–1225.

Cornish, R. D., & Dilley, J. S. Comparison of three methods of reducing test anxiety: Systematic desensitization, implosive therapy, and study counseling. *Journal of Counseling Psychology*, 1973, *20*, 499–503.

Counts, D. K., Hollandsworth, J. G., & Alcorn, J. D. Use of electromyographic biofeedback and cue-controlled relaxation in the treatment of test anxiety. *Journal of Consulting and Clinical Psychology*, 1978, *46*, 990–996.

Coursey, R. D. Electromyograph feedback as a relaxation technique. *Journal of Consulting and Clinical Psychology*, 1975, *43*, 825–834.

Cradock, C., Cotler, S., & Jason, L. A. Primary prevention: Immunization of children for speech anxiety. *Cognitive Therapy and Research*, 1978, *2*, 389–396.

Crowe, M. J., Marks, I. M., Agras, W. S., & Leitenberg, H. Time-limited desensitization implosion and shaping for phobic patients: A cross-over study. *Behaviour Research and Therapy*, 1972, *10*, 319–328.

Curran, J. P. Skills training as an approach to the treatment of heterosexual-social anxiety: A review. *Psychological Bulletin*, 1977, *84*, 140–157.

Davison, G. C. Systematic desensitization as a counterconditioning process. *Journal of Abnormal Psychology*, 1968, *73*, 91–99.

Davison, G. C., & Wilson, G. T. Processes of fear-reduction in systematic desensitization: Cognitive and social reinforcement factors in humans. *Behavior Therapy*, 1973, *4*, 1–21.

Deffenbacher, J. L. Relaxation in vivo in the treatment of test anxiety. *Journal of Behavior Therapy and Experimental Psychiatry*, 1976, *7*, 289–292.

Deffenbacher, J. L., & Parks, D. H. A comparison of traditional and self-control desensitization. *Journal of Counseling Psychology*, 1979, *26*, 93–97.

Deffenbacher, J. L., & Payne, D. M. J. Two procedures for relaxation as self-control in the treatment of communication apprehension. *Journal of Counseling Psychology*, 1977, *24*, 255–258.

Deffenbacher, J. L., & Shelton, J. L. Comparison of anxiety management training and desensitization in reducing test and other anxieties. *Journal of Counseling Psychology*, 1978, *25*, 277–282.

Deffenbacher, J. L., Mathis, H., & Michaels, A. C. Two self-control procedures in the reduction of targeted and nontargeted anxieties. *Journal of Counseling Psychology*, 1979, *26*, 120–127.

De Moor, W. Systematic desensitization versus prolonged high intensity stimulation (flooding). *Journal of Behavior Therapy and Experimental Psychiatry*, 1970, *1*, 45–52.

Denney, D. R., & Rupert, P. A. Desensitization and self-control in the treatment of test anxiety. *Journal of Counseling Psychology*, 1977, *24*, 272–280.

Denney, D. R., & Sullivan, B. J. Desensitization and modeling treatments of spider fear using two types of scenes. *Journal of Consulting and Clinical Psychology*, 1976, *44*, 573–579.

Derry, P. A., & Stone, G. L. Effects of cognitive-adjunct treatments on assertiveness. *Cognitive Therapy and Research*, 1979, *3*, 213–223.

De Voge, J. T., & Beck, S. The therapist-client relationship in behavior therapy. In M. Hersen, R. M. Eisler, & P. M. Miller (Eds.), *Progress in Behavior Modification*, Vol. 6. New York: Academic Press, 1978.

Di Loreto, A. O. *Comparative psychotherapy: An experimental analysis.* Chicago: Aldine, 1971.

Dormaar, M., & Dijkstra, W. Systematic desensitization in social anxiety. Paper read at the Conference of the European Association of Behaviour Therapy, 1975.

Dyckman, J. M., & Cowan, P. A. Imagining vividness and the outcome of in vivo and imagined scene desensitization. *Journal of Consulting and Clinical Psychology*, 1978, *48*, 1155–1156.

D'Zurilla, T. J., Wilson, G. T., & Nelson, R. A preliminary study of the effectiveness of graduated prolonged exposure in the treatment of irrational fear. *Behavior Therapy*, 1973, *4*, 672–685.

Ellis, A. *Reason and emotion in psychotherapy.* New York: Lyle-Stuart, 1962.

Ellis, A. A note on the treatment of agoraphobics with cognitive modification with prolonged exposure *in vivo*. *Behaviour Research and Therapy*, 1979, *17*, 162–164.

Emmelkamp, P. M. G. Self-observation versus flooding in the treatment of agoraphobia. *Behaviour Research and Therapy*. 1974, *12*, 229–237.

Emmelkamp, P. M. G. Effects of expectancy on systematic desensitization and flooding. *European Journal of Behavioral Analysis and Modification*, 1975, *1*, 1–11. (a)

Emmelkamp, P. M. G. Face-validity and behaviour therapy. *European Journal of Behavioral Analysis and Modification*, 1975, *1*, 15–19. (b)

Emmelkamp, P. M. G. Phobias: Theoretical and behavioural treatment considerations. In J. C. Boulougouris & A. D. Rabavilas (Eds.), *The treatment of phobic and obsessive compulsive disorders*. New York: Pergamon, 1977.

Emmelkamp, P. M. G. The behavioral study of clinical phobias. In M. Hersen, R. M. Eisler, & P. M. Miller (Eds.), *Progress in Behavior Modification*, Vol. 8. New York: Academic Press, 1979. (a)

Emmelkamp, P. M. G. Recent advances in the treatment of clinical phobias. Paper presented at the Ninth Conference of the European Association of Behaviour Therapy, Paris, September 1979. (b)

Emmelkamp, P. M. G. Relationship between theory and practice in behavior therapy. In W. De Moor, & H. Wijngaarden (Eds.), *Psychotherapy*. Amsterdam: Elsevier, 1980. (a)

Emmelkamp, P. M. G. Agoraphobics' interpersonal problems: Their role in the effects of exposure *in vivo* therapy. *Archives of General Psychiatry*, 1980, *37*, 1303–1306. (b)

Emmelkamp, P. M. G. Obsessive-compulsive disorders: A clinical-research approach. In I. Hand (Ed.), *Obsessions and compulsions—Recent advances in behavioral analysis and modification*. New York: Springer, in press.

Emmelkamp, P. M. G., & Boeke-Slinkers, I. Demand characteristics in behavioral assessment. *Psychological Reports*, 1977, *41*, 1030. (a)

Emmelkamp, P. M. G., & Boeke-Slinkers, I. *The contribution of therapeutic instruction to systematic desensitization with low-fearful and high-fearful subjects*. Unpublished manuscript. University of Groningen, 1977. (b)

Emmelkamp, P. M. G., & Cohen-Kettenis, P. Relationship of locus of control to phobic anxiety and depression. *Psychological Reports*, 1975, *36*, 390.

Emmelkamp, P. M. G., & Emmelkamp-Benner, A. Effects of historically portrayed modeling and group treatment on self-observation: A comparison with agoraphobics. *Behaviour Research and Therapy*, 1975, *13*, 135–139.

Emmelkamp, P. M. G., & Kraanen, J. Therapist controlled exposure *in vivo* versus self-controlled exposure *in vivo*: A comparison with obsessive-compulsive patients. *Behaviour Research and Therapy*, 1977, *15*, 491–495.

Emmelkamp, P. M. G., & Kuipers, A. Agoraphobia: A follow-up study four years after treatment. *British Journal of Psychiatry*, 1979, *134*, 352–355.

Emmelkamp, P. M. G., & Kwee, K. G. Obsessional ruminations: A comparison between thought-stopping and prolonged exposure in imagination. *Behaviour Research and Therapy*, 1977, *15*, 441–444.

Emmelkamp, P. M. G., & Mersch, P. Cognition and exposure in vivo in the treatment of agoraphobia: Short term and delayed effects. *Cognitive Therapy and Research*, 1982, *6*, 77–88.

Emmelkamp, P. M. G., & Straatman, H. A psychoanalytic reinterpretation of the effectiveness of systematic desensitization: Fact or fiction? *Behaviour Research and Therapy*, 1976, *14*, 245–249.

Emmelkamp, P. M. G., & Ultee, K. A. A comparison of successive approximation and self-observation in the treatment of agoraphobia. *Behavior Therapy*, 1974, *5*, 605–613.

Emmelkamp, P. M. G., & Van der Heyden, H. The treatment of harming obsessions. *Behavioural Analysis and Modification*, 1980, *4*, 28–35.

Emmelkamp, P. M. G., & Walta, C. The effects of therapy-set on electrical aversion therapy and covert sensitization. *Behavior Therapy*, 1978, *9*, 185–188.

Emmelkamp, P. M. G., & Wessels, H. Flooding in imagination vs flooding *in vivo*: A comparison with agoraphobics. *Behaviour Research and Therapy*, 1975, *13*, 7–16.

Emmelkamp, P. M. G., Kuipers, A., & Eggeraat, J. Cognitive modification versus prolonged exposure *in vivo*: A comparison with agoraphobics. *Behaviour Research and Therapy*, 1978, *16*, 33–41.

Emmelkamp, P. M. G., Van der Helm, M., Van Zanten, B., & Plochg, I. Treatment of obsessive-compulsive patients: The contribution of self-instructional training to the effectiveness of exposure. *Behaviour Research and Therapy*, 1980, *18*, 61–66.

Engel, B. T. Operant conditioning of cardiac function: Some implications for psychosomatic medicine. *Behavior Therapy*, 1974, *5*, 302–303.

Errera, P., & Coleman, J. V. A long-term follow-up study of neurotic phobic patients in a psychiatric clinic. *Journal of Nervous and Mental Disease*, 1963, *136*, 267–271.

Evans, P. D., & Kellam, A. M. P. Semi-automated desensitization: A controlled clinical trial. *Behaviour Research and Therapy*, 1973, *11*, 641–646.

Everaerd, W. T. A. M., Rijken, H. M., & Emmelkamp, P. M. G. A comparison of "flooding" and "successive approximation" in the treatment of agoraphobia. *Behaviour Research and Therapy*, 1973, *11*, 105–117.

Eysenck, H. J. The learning model of neurosis. *Behaviour Research and Therapy*, 1976, *14*, 251–267.

Fazio, A. F. Implosive therapy with semiclinical phobias. *Journal of Abnormal Psychology*, 1972, *80*, 183–188.

Fenichel, O. *Psychoanalytic theory of neurosis*. New York: Norton, 1963.

Finger, R., & Galassi, J. P. Effects of modifying cognitive versus emotiality responses in the treatment of test anxiety. *Journal of Consulting and Clinical Psychology*, 1977, *45*, 280–287.

Flannery, R. B. A laboratory analogue of two covert reinforcement procedures. *Journal of Behavior Therapy and Experimental Psychiatry*, 1972, *3*, 171–177.

Foa, E. B., & Chambless, D. L. Habituation of subjective anxiety during flooding in imagery. *Behaviour Research and Therapy*, 1978, *16*, 391–399.

Foa, E. B., & Turner, R. M. Massed vs. spaced exposure sessions in the treatment of agoraphobia. Paper presented at the 9th European Conference of Behavior Modification, Paris, Sept. 1979.

Foa, E. B., Blau, J. S., Prout, M., & Latimer, P. Is horror a necessary component of flooding (implosion)? *Behaviour Research and Therapy*, 1977, *15*, 397–402.

Fremouw, W. J., & Zitter, R. E. A comparison of skills training and cognitive restructuring—Relaxation for the treatment of speech anxiety. *Behavior Therapy*, 1978, 9, 248–259.

Freud, S. Turnings in the world of psycho-analytic therapy. In *Collected papers*, Vol. 2. New York: Basic Books, 1959, pp. 392–402.

Friedman, J. H. Short-term psychotherapy of "phobia of travel." *American Journal of Psychotherapy*, 1950, 4, 259–278.

Fry, W. F. The marital context of an anxiety syndrome. *Family Process*, 1962, 1, 245–252.

Gatchel, R. J. Therapeutic effectiveness of voluntary heart rate control in reducing anxiety. *Journal of Consulting and Clinical Psychology*, 1977, 45, 689–691.

Gatchel, R. J., & Proctor, J. D. Effectiveness of voluntary heart rate control in reducing speech anxiety. *Journal of Consulting and Clinical Psychology*, 1976, 44, 381–389.

Gatchel, R. J., Hatch, J. P., Watson, P. J., Smith, D., & Gaas, E. Comparative effectiveness of voluntary heart rate control and muscular relaxation as active coping skills for reducing speech anxiety. *Journal of Consulting and Clinical Psychology*, 1977, 45, 1093–1100.

Gatchel, R. J., Hatch, J. P., Maynard, A., Turns, R., & Taunton-Blackwood, A. Comparison of heart rate biofeedback, and systematic desensitization in reducing speech anxiety: Short- and Long-term effectiveness. *Journal of Consulting and Clinical Psychology*, 1979, 47, 620–622.

Gauthier, J., & Marshall, W. L. The determination of optimal exposure to phobic stimuli in flooding therapy. *Behaviour Research and Therapy*, 1977, 15, 403–410.

Gelder, M. G., & Marks, I. M. Severe agoraphobia: A controlled prospective trial of behaviour therapy. *British Journal of Psychiatry*, 1966, 112, 309–319.

Gelder, M. G., & Marks, I. M. Desensitization and phobias: A crossover study. *British Journal of Psychiatry*, 1968, 114, 323–328.

Gelder, M. G., and Marks, I. M., & Wolff, H. H. Desensitization and psychotherapy in the treatment of phobic states: A controlled enquiry. *British Journal of Psychiatry*, 1967, 113, 53–73.

Gelder, M. G., Bancroft, J. H. J., Gath, D. H., Johnston, D. W., Mathews, A. M., & Shaw, P. M. Specific and non-specific factors in behaviour therapy. *British Journal of Psychiatry*, 1973, 123, 445–462.

Gillan, P., & Rachman, S. An experimental investigation of desensitization in phobic patients. *British Journal of Psychiatry*, 1974, 124, 392–401.

Girodo, M., & Roehl, J. Cognitive preparation and coping self-talk: Anxiety management during the stress of flying. *Journal of Consulting and Clinical Psychology*, 1978, 46, 978–989.

Glass, C. R., Gottman, J. M., & Shmurak, S. H. Response acquisition and cognitive self-statement modification approaches to dating-skills training. *Journal of Counseling Psychology*, 1976, 23, 520–526.

Glogower, F. D., Fremouw, W. J., & McCroskey, J. C. A component analysis of cognitive restructuring. *Cognitive Therapy and Research*, 1978, 2, 209–223.

Goldfried, M. R. Systematic desensitization as training in self-control. *Journal of Consulting and Clinical Psychology*, 1971, 37, 228–234.

Goldfried, M. R., & Goldfried, A. P. Importance of hi-erarchy content in the self-control of anxiety. *Journal of Consulting and Clinical Psychology*, 1977, 45, 124–134.

Goldfried, M. R., & Sobocinski, D. The effect of irrational beliefs on emotional arousal. *Journal of Consulting and Clinical Psychology*, 1975, 43, 504–510.

Goldfried, M. R., & Trier, C. S. Effectiveness of relaxation as an active coping skill. *Journal of Abnormal Psychology*, 1974, 83, 348–355.

Goldfried, M. R., Decenteceo, E. T., & Weinberg, L. Systematic rational restructuring as a self-control technique. *Behavior Therapy*, 1974, 5, 247–254.

Goldfried, M. R., Linehan, M. M., & Smith, J. L. The reduction of test anxiety through rational restructuring. *Journal of Consulting and Clinical Psychology*, 1978, 37, 228–234.

Goldstein, A. J. Learning theory insufficiency in understanding agoraphobia: A plea for empiricism. *Proceedings of the European Association for Behaviour Therapy*. Münich: Urban & Schwarzenberg, 1973.

Goldstein, A. J., & Chambless, D. L. A reanalysis of agoraphobia. *Behavior Therapy*, 1978, 9, 47–59.

Goldstein-Fodor, I. G. The phobic syndrome in women. In V. Franks & V. Burtle (Eds.), *Women in therapy*. New York: Brunner/Mazel, 1974.

Goodstein, R. K., & Swift, K. Psychotherapy with phobic patients: The marriage relationship as the source of symptoms and focus of treatment. *American Journal of Psychotherapy*, 1977, 31, 284–293.

Goorney, A. B., & O'Connor, P. J. Anxiety associated with flying. *British Journal of Psychiatry*, 1971, 119, 159–166.

Guidry, L. S., & Randolph, D. L. Covert reinforcement in the treatment of test anxiety. *Journal of Counseling Psychology*, 1974, 21, 260–264.

Hafner, R. J. Fresh symptom emergence after intensive behaviour therapy. *British Journal of Psychiatry*, 1976, 129, 378–383.

Hafner, R. J., & Marks, I. M. Exposure *in vivo* of agoraphobics: Contributions of diazepam, group exposure, and anxiety evocation. *Psychological Medicine*, 1976, 6, 71–88.

Hafner, R. J., & Milton, F. The influence of propranolol on the exposure *in vivo* of agoraphobics. *Psychological Medicine*, 1977, 7, 419–425.

Hain, J. D., Butcher, H. C., & Stevenson, I. Systematic desensitization therapy: An analysis of results in twenty-seven patients. *British Journal of Psychiatry*, 1966, 112, 295–307.

Hall, R., & Goldberg, D. The role of social anxiety in social interaction difficulties. *British Journal of Psychiatry*, 1977, 131, 610–615.

Hand, I., Lamontagne, Y., & Marks, I. M. Group exposure (flooding) *in vivo* for agoraphobics. *British Journal of Psychiatry*, 1974, 124, 588–602.

Hayes, S. C. The role of approach contingencies in phobic behavior. *Behavior Therapy*, 1976, 7, 28–36.

Haynes, S. N., Moseley, D., & McGowan, W. T. Relaxation training and biofeedback in the reduction of frontalis muscle tension. *Psychophysiology*, 1975, 12, 547–552.

Hekmat, H. Systematic versus semantic desensitization and implosive therapy: A comparative study. *Journal of Consulting and Clinical Psychology*, 1973, 40, 202–209.

Hepner, A., & Cauthen, N. R. Effect of subject control and graduated exposure on snake phobias. *Journal of Consulting and Clinical Psychology,* 1975, *43,* 297–304.

Hollandsworth, J. G., Glazeski, R. C., Kirkland, K., Jones, G. E., & Van Norman, L. R. An analysis of the nature and effects of test anxiety: Cognitive, behavioral, and physiological components. *Cognitive Therapy and Research,* 1979, *3,* 165–180.

Holroyd, K. A. Cognition and desensitization in the group treatment of test anxiety. *Journal of Consulting and Clinical Psychology,* 1976, *44,* 991–1001.

Holroyd, K. A., Westbrook, T., Wolf, M., & Bradhorn, E. Performance, cognition, and physiological responding in test anxiety. *Journal of Abnormal Psychology,* 1978, *87,* 442–451.

Horne, A. M., & Matson, J. L. A comparison of modeling, desensitization, flooding, study skills, and control groups for reducing test anxiety. *Behavior Therapy,* 1977, *8,* 1–8.

Hurley, A. D. Covert reinforcement: The contribution of the reinforcing stimulus to treatment outcome. *Behavior Therapy,* 1976, *7,* 374–378.

Hussain, M. Z. Desensitization and flooding (implosion) in treatment of phobias. *American Journal of Psychiatry,* 1971, *127,* 1509–1514.

Hussian, R. A., & Lawrence, P. S. The reduction of test, state, and trait anxiety by test-specific and generalized stress inoculation training. *Cognitive Therapy and Research,* 1978, *2,* 25–37.

Jaremko, M., & Wenrich, W. A prophylactic usage of systematic desensitization. *Journal of Behavior Therapy and Experimental Psychiatry,* 1973, *4,* 103–108.

Jessup, B. A., & Neufeld, R. W. J. Effects of biofeedback and "autogenic relaxation" techniques on physiological and subjective responses in psychiatric patients: A preliminary analysis. *Behavior Therapy,* 1977, *8,* 160–167.

Johnston, D. W., & Gath, D. Arousal levels and attribution effects in diazepam-assisted flooding. *British Journal of Psychiatry,* 1973, *123,* 463–466.

Johnston, D. W., Lancashire, M., Mathews, A. M., Munby, M., Shaw, P. M., & Gelder, M. G. Imaginal flooding and exposure to real phobic situations: Changes during treatment. *British Journal of Psychiatry,* 1976, *129,* 372–377.

Kanter, N. J., & Goldfried, M. R. Relative effectiveness of rational restructuring and self-control desensitization in the reduction of interpersonal anxiety. *Behavior Therapy,* 1979, *10,* 472–490.

Karst, T. O., & Trexler, L. D. Initial study using fixed-role and rational-emotive therapy in treating public speaking anxiety. *Journal of Consulting and Clinical Psychology,* 1970, *34,* 360–366.

Kazdin, A. E. Evaluating the generality of findings in analogue research. *Journal of Consulting and Clinical Psychology,* 1978, *46,* 673–686.

Kazdin, A. E., & Smith, G. A. Covert conditioning: A review and evaluation. *Advances in Behaviour Research and Therapy,* 1979, *2,* 57–98.

Kelly, D., Guirguis, W., Frommer, E., Mitchell-Heggs, N., & Sargant, W. Treatment of phobic states with antidepressants, a retrospective study of 246 patients. *British Journal of Psychiatry,* 1970, *116,* 387–398.

Kelly, G. A. *The psychology of personal constructs.* New York: Norton, 1955.

Kirsch, I., & Henry, D. Extinction versus credibility in the desensitization of speech anxiety. *Journal of Consulting and Clinical Psychology,* 1977, *45,* 1052–1059.

Kirsch, I., & Henry, D. *Self-desensitization and meditation in the reduction of public speaking anxiety.* Unpublished manuscript, 1979.

Kirsch, I., Wolpin, M., & Knutson, J. L. A comparison of in vivo methods for rapid reduction of "stage fright" in the college classroom: A field experiment. *Behavior Therapy,* 1975, *6,* 165–171.

Kostka, M. P., & Galassi, J. P. Group systematic desensitization versus covert positive reinforcement in the reduction of test anxiety. *Journal of Counseling Psychology,* 1974, *21,* 464–468.

Ladouceur, R. An experimental test of the learning paradigm of covert positive reinforcement in deconditioning anxiety. *Journal of Behavior Therapy and Experimental Psychiatry,* 1974, *5,* 3–6.

Ladouceur, R. Rationale of covert positive reinforcement: Additional evidence. *Psychological Reports,* 1977, *41,* 547–550.

Ladouceur, R. Rationale of systematic desensitization and covert positive reinforcement. *Behaviour Research and Therapy,* 1978, *16,* 411–420.

Lazarus, A. A. *Behavior therapy and beyond.* New York: McGraw-Hill, 1971.

Ledwidge, B. Cognitive behavior modification: A step in the wrong direction? *Psychological Bulletin,* 1978, *85,* 353–375.

Leitenberg, H., & Callahan, E. J. Reinforced practice and reduction of different kinds of fear in adults and children. *Behaviour Research and Therapy,* 1973, *11,* 19–30.

Leitenberg, H., Agras, S., Butz, R., & Wincze, J. Relationship between heart rate and behavioral change during the treatment of phobias. *Journal of Abnormal Psychology,* 1971, *78,* 59–68.

Leitenberg, H., Agras, W. S., Allen, R., Butz, R., & Edwards, J. Feedback and therapist praise during treatment of phobia. *Journal of Consulting and Clinical Psychology,* 1975, *43,* 396–404.

Levis, D. J., & Hare, A. A review of the theoretical rationale and empirical support for the extinction approach of implosive (flooding) therapy. In M. Hersen, R. M. Eisler, & P. M. Miller (Eds.), *Progress in behavior modification,* Vol. 4. New York: Academic Press, 1977.

Lewis, S. A. A comparison of behavior therapy techniques in the reduction of fearful avoidance behavior. *Behavior Therapy,* 1974, *5,* 648–655.

Lick, J. Expectancy, false galvanic skin response feedback, and systematic desensitization in the modification of phobic behavior. *Journal of Consulting and Clinical Psychology,* 1975, *43,* 557–567.

Liddell, A., & Lyons, M. Thunderstorm phobias. *Behaviour Research and Therapy,* 1978, *16,* 306–308.

Liebert, R. M., & Morris, L. W. Cognitive and emotional components of test anxiety: A distinction and some initial data. *Psychological Reports,* 1967, *20,* 975–978.

Linehan, M. M., Goldfried, M. R., & Powers-Goldfried,

A. Assertion therapy: Skills training or cognitive restructuring. *Behavior Therapy*, 1979, *10*, 372–388.

Lipsedge, M. S., Hajioff, J., Huggins, P., Napier, L., Pearce, J., Pike, D. J., & Rich, M. The management of severe agoraphobia: A comparison of iproniazid and systematic desensitization. *Psychopharmacologia*, 1973, *32*, 67–88.

Little, S., & Jackson, B. The treatment of test anxiety through attentional and relaxation training. *Psychotherapy: Theory, Research and Practice*, 1974, *11*, 175–178.

Litvak, S. B. A comparison of two brief group behavior therapy techniques on the reduction of avoidance behavior. *Psychological Record*, 1969, *19*, 329–334.

Marcia, J. E., Rubin, B. M., & Efran, J. S. Systematic desensitization: Expectancy change or counter-conditioning? *Journal of Abnormal Psychology*, 1969, *74*, 382–387.

Marks, I. M. Behavioural treatments of phobic and obsessive-compulsive disorders: A critical appraisal. In M. Hersen, R. M. Eisler, & P. M. Miller (Eds.), *Progress in behavior modification*, Vol. 1. New York: Academic Press, 1975.

Marks, I. M., Boulougouris, J., & Marset, P. Flooding versus desensitization in the treatment of phobic patients: A cross-over study. *British Journal of Psychiatry*, 1971, *119*, 353–375.

Marks, I. M., Viswanathan, R., Lipsedge, M. S., & Gardner, R. Enhanced relief of phobias by flooding during waning diazepam effect. *British Journal of Psychiatry*, 1972, *121*, 493–506.

Marshall, W. L., Boutilier, J., & Minnes, P. The modification of phobic behavior by covert reinforcement. *Behavior Therapy*, 1974, *5*, 469–480.

Marshall, W. L., Gauthier, J., Christie, M. M., Currie, D. W., & Gordon, A. Flooding therapy: Effectiveness, stimulus characteristics, and the value of brief in vivo exposure. *Behaviour Research and Therapy*, 1977, *15*, 79–87.

Marzillier, J. S., Lambert, C., & Kellett, J. A controlled evaluation of systematic desensitization and social skills training for social inadequate psychiatric patients. *Behaviour Research and Therapy*, 1976, *14*, 225–228.

Mathews, A. M., & Rezin, V. Treatment of dental fears by imaginal flooding and rehearsal of coping behaviour. *Behaviour Research and Therapy*, 1977, *15*, 321–328.

Mathews, A. M., & Shaw, P. M. Emotional arousal and persuasion effects in flooding. *Behaviour Research and Therapy*, 1973, *11*, 587–598.

Mathews, A. M., Johnston, D. W., Lancashire, M., Munby, M., Shaw, P. M., & Gelder, M. G. Imaginal flooding and exposure to real phobic situations: Treatment outcome with agoraphobic patients. *British Journal of Psychiatry*, 1976, *129*, 362–371.

Mathews, A. M., Teasdale, J. D., Munby, M., Johnston, D. W., & Shaw, P. M. A home-base treatment program for agoraphobia. *Behavior Therapy*, 1977, *8*, 915–924.

Mathews, A., Jannoun, L., & Gelder, M. Self-help methods in agoraphobia. Paper presented at the Conference of the European Association of Behavior Therapy, Paris, Sept. 1979.

May, J. R., & Johnson, J. Physiological activity to internally elicited arousal and inhibitory thoughts. *Journal of Abnormal Psychology*, 1973, *82*, 239–245.

McCutcheon, B. A., & Adams, H. E. The physiological basis of implosive therapy. *Behaviour Research and Therapy*, 1975, *13*, 93–100.

McDonald, R., Sartory, G., Grey, S. J., Cobb, J., Stern, R., & Marks, I. M. The effects of self-exposure instruction on agoraphobic outpatients. *Behaviour Research and Therapy*, 1979, *17*, 83–86.

McGlynn, F. D., & McDonell, R. M. Subjective ratings of credibility following brief exposures to desensitization and pseudotherapy. *Behaviour Research and Therapy*, 1974, *12*, 141–146.

McGlynn, F. D., Reynolds, E. J., & Linder, L. H. Experimental desensitization following therapeutically oriented and physiologically oriented instructions. *Journal of Behavior Therapy and Experimental Psychiatry*, 1971, *2*, 13–18.

McGlynn, F. D., Gaynor, R., & Puhr, J. Experimental desensitization of snake-avoidance after an instructional manipulation. *Journal of Clinical Psychology*, 1972, *28*, 224–227.

McGlynn, F. D., Kinjo, K., Doherty, G. Effects of cue-controlled relaxation, a placebo treatment, and no-treatment on changes in self-reported test anxiety among college students. *Journal of Clinical Psychology*, 1978, *34*, 707–714.

McReynolds, W. T., & Grizzard, R. H. A comparison of three fear reduction procedures. *Psychotherapy: Theory, Research and Practice*, 1971, *8*, 264–268.

McReynolds, W. T., Barnes, A. R., Brooks, S., & Rehagen, N. J. The role of attention-placebo influences in the efficacy of systematic desensitization. *Journal Consulting and Clinical Psychology*, 1973, *41*, 86–92.

Mealiea, W. L., & Nawas, M. M. The comparative effectiveness of systematic desensitization and implosive therapy in the treatment of snake phobia. *Journal of Behavior Therapy and Experimental Psychiatry*, 1971, *2*, 185–194.

Meichenbaum, D. H. Examination of model characteristics in reducing avoidance behavior. *Journal of Personality and Social Psychology*, 1971, *17*, 298–307.

Meichenbaum, D. H. Cognitive modification of test anxious college students. *Journal of Consulting and Clinical Psychology*, 1972, *39*, 370–380.

Meichenbaum, D. H. Self instructional methods. In F. H. Kanfer & A. P. Goldstein (Eds.), *Helping people change*. New York: Pergamon, 1975.

Melamed, B. G. Behavioral approaches to fear in dental settings. In M. Hersen, R. M. Eisler, & P. M. Miller (Eds.), *Progress in behavior modification*, Vol. 7. New York: Academic Press, 1979.

Melnick, J. A. A comparison of replication techniques in the modification of minimal dating behavior. *Journal of Abnormal Psychology*, 1973, *81*, 51–59.

Meyer, V., & Crisp, A. H. Some problems in behavior therapy. *British Journal of Psychiatry*, 1966, *112*, 367–381.

Miles, H., Barrabee, E., & Finesinger, J. Evaluation of psychotherapy: With a follow-up study of 62 cases of anxiety neurosis. *Psychosomatic Medicine*, 1951, *13*, 83–106.

Morris, R. J., & Suckerman, K. R. The importance of the

therapeutic relationship in systematic desensitization. *Journal of Consulting and Clinical Psychology*, 1974, *42*, 147. (a)

Morris, R. J., & Suckerman, K. R. Therapist warmth as a factor in automated systematic systematic desensitization. *Journal of Consulting and Clinical Psychology*, 1974, *42*, 244–250. (b)

Mountjoy, C. Q., Roth, M., Garside, R. F. & Leitch, I. M. A clinical trial of phenelzine in anxiety depressive and phobic neuroses. *British Journal of Psychiatry*, 1977, *131*, 486–492.

Mowrer, O. H. *Learning theory and personality dynamics*. New York: Arnold Press, 1950.

Murray, E. J., & Foote, F. The origins of fear of snakes. *Behaviour Research and Therapy*, 1979, *17*, 489–493.

Mylar, J. L., & Clement, P. W. Prediction and comparison of outcome in systematic desensitization and implosion. *Behaviour Research and Therapy*, 1972, *10*, 235–246.

Nau, S. D., Caputo, J. A., & Borkovec, T. D. The relationship between therapy credibility and simulated therapy response. *Journal of Behavior Therapy and Experimental Psychiatry*, 1974, *5*, 129–134.

Nunes, J. S., & Marks, I. M. Feedback of true heart rate during exposure *in vivo*. *Archives of General Psychiatry*, 1975, *32*, 933–936.

Nunes, J. S., & Marks, I. M. Feedback of true heart rate during exposure *in vivo*: Partial replication with methodological improvement. *Archives of General Psychiatry*, 1976, *33*, 1346–1350.

Odom, J. V., Nelson, R. O., & Wein, K. S. The differential effectiveness of five treatment procedures on three response systems in a snake phobia analog study. *Behavior Therapy*, 1978, *9*, 936–942.

Ohman, A. Fear relevance, autonomic conditioning, and phobias: A laboratory model. In S. Bates, W. S. Dockens, K. Götestam, L. Melin, & P. O. Sjöden (Eds.), *Trends in behavior therapy*. New York: Academic Press, 1979.

Orenstein, H., & Carr, J. Implosion therapy by tape-recording. *Behaviour Research and Therapy*, 1975, *13*, 177–182.

Pare, C. M. B. Side-effects and toxic effects of antidepressants. *Preceedings of Royal Society of Medicine*, 1964, *57*, 757–758.

Prochaska, J. O. Symptom and dynamic cues in the implosive treatment of test anxiety. *Journal of Abnormal Psychology*, 1971, *77*, 133–142.

Rabavilas, A. D., & Boulougouris, J. C. Therapeutic relationship and long term outcome with flooding treatment. Paper presented at the Ninth Conference of the European Association of Behaviour Therapy, Paris, Sept. 1979.

Rabavilas, A. D., Boulougouris, J. C., & Stefanis, C. Duration of flooding sessions in the treatment of obsessive-compulsive patients. *Behaviour Research and Therapy*, 1976, *14*, 349–355.

Rachman, S. The passing of the two-stage theory of fear and avoidance: Fresh possibilities. *Behaviour Research and Therapy*, 1976, *14*, 125–134.

Rachman, S. The conditioning theory of fear-acquisition: A critical examination. *Behaviour Research and Therapy*, 1977, *15*, 375–387.

Rankin, H. Are models necessary? *Behaviour Research and Therapy*, 1976, *14*, 181–183.

Rappaport, H. Modification of avoidance behavior: Expectancy, autonomic reactivity, and verbal report. *Journal of Consulting and Clinical Psychology*, 1972, *39*, 404–414.

Reinking, R. H., & Kohl, M. L. Effects of various forms of relaxation training on physiological and self-report measures of relaxation. *Journal of Consulting and Clinical Psychology*, 1975, *43*, 595–600.

Rimm, D., & Litvak, S. Self-verbalization and emotion arousal. *Journal of Abnormal Psychology*, 1969, *74*, 181–187.

Rimm, D. C., Janda, L. H., Lancaster, D. W., Nahl, M., & Dittmar, K. An exploratory investigation of the origin and maintenance of phobias. *Behaviour Research and Therapy*, 1977, *15*, 231–238.

Ritter, B. The use of contact desensitization, demonstration-plus-participation and demonstration alone in the treatment of acrophobia. *Behaviour Research and Therapy*, 1969, *7*, 157–164.

Robert, A. H. House-bound housewives: A follow-up study of a phobic anxiety state. *British Journal of Psychiatry*, 1964, *110*, 191–197.

Rogers, T., & Craighead, W. E. Physiological responses to self-statements: The effects of statement valence and discrepancy. *Cognitive Therapy and Research*, 1977, *1*, 99–119.

Rosen, G. M. Therapy set: Its effect on subjects' involvement in systematic desensitization and treatment outcome. *Journal of Abnormal Psychology*, 1974, *83*, 291–300.

Russell, P. L., & Brandsma, J. M. A theoretical and empirical integration of the rational emotive and classical conditioning theories. *Journal of Consulting and Clinical Psychology*, 1974, *42*, 389–397.

Rutner, I. T. The effects of feedback and instructions on phobic behavior. *Behavior Therapy*, 1973, *4*, 338–348.

Schandler, S. L., & Grings, W. W. An examination of methods for producing relaxation during short-term laboratory sessions. *Behaviour Research and Therapy*, 1976, *14*, 419–426.

Seligman, M. E. P. Phobias and preparedness. *Behavior Therapy*, 1971, *2*, 307–320.

Shaw, P. M. *A comparison of three behaviour therapies in the treatment of social phobia*. Paper read at the British Association for Behavioral Psychotherapy, Exeter, 1976.

Shepherd, G. W., & Watts, F. N. Heart rate control in psychiatric patients. *Behavior Therapy*, 1974, *5*, 153–154.

Sherman, A. R. Real-life exposure as a primary therapeutic factor in the desensitization treatment of fear. *Journal of Abnormal Psychology*, 1972, *79*, 19–28.

Silverman, L. H., Frank, S. G., & Dachinger, P. A. A psychoanalytic reinterpretation of the effectiveness of systematic desensitization: Experimental data bearing on the role of merging fantasies. *Journal of Abnormal Psychology*, 1974, *83*, 313–318.

Sjöqvist, F. Interaction between mono-amine oxidase inhibitors and other substances. *Proceedings of the Royal Society of Medicine*, 1963, *58*, 967–978.

Smith, G. P., & Coleman, R. E. Processes underlying

generalization through participant modeling with self-directed practice. *Behaviour Research and Therapy*, 1977, *15*, 204–206.

Smith, R. E., & Nye, S. L. A comparison of implosive therapy and systematic desensitization in the treatment of test anxiety. *Journal of Consulting and Clinical Psychology*, 1973, *44*, 37–42.

Smith, R. E., Diener, E., & Beaman, A Demand characteristics and the behavioral avoidance measures of fear in behavior therapy analogue research. *Behavior Therapy*, 1974, *5*, 172–182.

Snyder, A. L., & Deffenbacher, J. L. Comparison of relaxation as self-control and systematic desensitization in the treatment of test anxiety. *Journal of Consulting and Clinical Psychology*, 1977, *45*, 1202–1203.

Solyom, L., McClure, D. J., Heseltine, G. F. D., Ledwidge, B., & Solyom, C. Variables in the aversion relief therapy of phobics. *Behavior Therapy*, 1972, *3*, 21–28.

Solyom, L., Heseltine, G. F. D., McClure, D. J., Solyom, C., Ledwidge, B., & Steinberg, L. Behaviour therapy versus drug therapy in the treatment of phobic neurosis. *Canadian Psychiatric Association Journal*, 1973, *18*, 25–31.

Solyom, L., Beck, P., Solyom, C., & Hugel, R. Some etiological factors in phobic neurosis. *Canadian Psychiatric Association Journal*, 1974, *19*, 69–78.

Solyom, C., Solyom, L., La Pierre, Y., Pecknold, J. C., & Morton, L. Phenelzine and exposure in the treatment of phobias. *Journal of Biological Psychiatry*, 1981, *16*, 239–248.

Spiegler, M. D., Cooley, E. J., Marshall, G. J., Prince, H. T., Puckett, S. P., & Skenazy, J. A. A self-control versus a counterconditioning paradigm for systematic desensitization: An experimental comparison. *Journal of Counseling Psychology*, 1976, *23*, 83–86.

Stampfl, T. G., & Levis, D. J. Essentials of implosive therapy: A learning-theory-based psychodynamic behavioral therapy. *Journal of Abnormal Psychology*, 1967, *72*, 496–503.

Stampfl, T. G., & Levis, D. J. Implosive therapy: A behavioral therapy? *Behaviour Research and Therapy*, 1968, *6*, 31–36.

Stern, R., & Marks, I. M. Brief and prolonged flooding: A comparison in agoraphobic patients. *Archives of General Psychiatry*, 1973, *28*, 270–276.

Suarez, Y., Adams, H. E., & McCutcheon, B. A. Flooding and systematic desensitization: Efficacy in subclinical phobics as a function of arousal. *Journal of Consulting and Clinical Psychology*, 1976, *44*, 872.

Suinn, R. M. Anxiety management training to control general anxiety. In J. D. Krumboltz & C. E. Thoresen (Eds.), *Counseling Methods*. New York: Holt, Rinehart, & Winston, 1976.

Suinn, R. M., & Richardson, F. Anxiety management training: A non-specific behavior therapy program for anxiety control. *Behavior Therapy*, 1971, *2*, 498–511.

Sullivan, B. J., & Denney, D. R. Expectancy and phobic level: Effects on desensitization. *Journal of Consulting and Clinical Psychology*, 1977, *45*, 763–771.

Sutton-Simon, K., & Goldfried, M. R. Faulty thinking patterns in two types of anxiety. *Cognitive Therapy and Research*, 1979, *3*, 193–203.

Teasdale, J. D., Walsh, P. A., Lancashire, M., & Mathews, A. M. Group exposure for agoraphobics: A replication study. *British Journal of Psychiatry*, 1977, *130*, 186–193.

Terhune, W. The phobic syndrome. *Archives of Neurology and Psychiatry*, 1949, *62*, 162–172.

Thase, M. E., & Moss, M. K. The relative efficacy of covert modeling procedures and guided participant modeling in the reduction of avoidance behavior. *Journal of Behavior Therapy and Experimental Psychiatry*, 1976, *7*, 7–12.

Thorpe, G. L. Desensitization, behavior rehearsal, self-instructional training and placebo effects on assertive-refusal behavior. *European Journal of Behavioural Analysis and Modification*, 1975, *1*, 30–44.

Thorpe, G. L., Amatu, H. I., Blakey, R. S., & Burns, L. E. Contributions of overt instructional rehearsal and "specific insight" to the effectiveness of self-instructional training: A preliminary study. *Behavior Therapy*, 1976, *7*, 504–511.

Tori, C., & Worell, L. Reduction of human avoidant behavior: A comparison of counterconditioning, expectancy and cognitive information approaches. *Journal of Consulting and Clinical Psychology*, 1973, *41*, 269–278.

Townsend, R. E., House, J. F., & Addario, D. A comparison of biofeedback mediated relaxation and group therapy in the treatment of chronic anxiety. *American Journal of Psychiatry*, 1975, *32*, 598–601.

Trower, P., Yardley, K., Bryant, B. M., & Shaw, P. The treatment of social failure: A comparison of anxiety-reduction and skills-acquisition procedures on two social problems. *Behavior Modification*, 1978, *2*, 41–60.

Tyrer, P., Candy, J., & Kelly, D. A study of the clinical effects of phenelzine and placebo in the treatment of phobic anxiety. *Psychopharmacologica*, 1973, *32*, 237–254.

Ullrich, R., Ullrich, R., Crombach, G., & Peikert, V. *Three flooding procedures in the treatment of agoraphobics*. Paper read at the European Conference on Behaviour Modification, Wexford, Ireland, 1972.

Van Son, M. J. M. *Sociale vaardigheidstherapie*. Amsterdam: Swets and Zeitlinger, 1978.

Watson, J. P., & Marks, I. M. Relevant and irrelevant fear in flooding—A crossover study of phobic patients. *Behavior Therapy*, 1971, *2*, 275–293.

Watson, J., & Rayner, R. Conditioned emotional reactions. *Journal of Experimental Psychology*, 1920, *3*, 1–22.

Watson, J. P., Gaind, R., & Marks, I. M. Physiological habituation to continuous phobic stimulation. *Behaviour Research and Therapy*, 1972, *10*, 269–278.

Watson, J. P., Mullett, G. E., & Pillay, H. The effects of prolonged exposure to phobic situations upon agoraphobic patients treated in groups. *Behaviour Research and Therapy*, 1973, *11*, 531–546.

Weissberg, M. A comparison of direct and vicarious treatments of speech anxiety: Desensitization, desensitization with coping imagery, and cognitive modification. *Behavior Therapy*, 1977, *8*, 606–620.

Wickramasekera, I. Heart rate feedback and the management of cardiac neurosis. *Journal of Abnormal Psychology*, 1974, *83*, 578–580.

Wilkins, W. Expectancy of therapeutic gain: An empirical and conceptual critique. *Journal of Consulting and Clinical Psychology*, 1973, *40*, 69–77.

Wilkins, W. Expectancies and therapy effectiveness: Emmelkamp versus Davison and Wilson. *Behavioural Analysis and Modification*, 1979, *3*, 109–116.

Willis, R. W., & Edwards, J. A. A study of the comparative effectiveness of systematic desensitization and implosive therapy. *Behaviour Research and Therapy*, 1969, *7*, 387–395.

Wilson, G. T., & Davison, G. C. "Effects of expectancy on systematic desensitization and flooding." A critical analysis. *European Journal of Behavioural Analysis and Modification*, 1975, *1*, 12–14.

Wolfe, J. L., & Fodor, I. G. Modifying assertive behavior in women: A comparison of three approaches. *Behavior Therapy*, 1977, *8*, 567–574.

Wolpe, J. *Psychotherapy and reciprocal inhibition*. Stanford, Calif.: Standford University Press, 1958.

Wolpe, J. Quantitative relationships in the systematic desensitization of phobias. *American Journal of Psychiatry*, 1963, *119*, 1062–1068.

Wolpe, J. *The practice of behavior therapy*. New York: Pergamon, 1973.

Yorkston, N. J., Sergeant, H. G. S., & Rachman, S. Methohexitone relaxation for desensitizing agoraphobic patients. *Lancet*, 1968, *2*, 651–653.

Zemore, R. Systematic desensitization as a method of teaching a general anxiety-reducing skill. *Journal of Consulting and Clinical Psychology*, 1975, *43*, 157–161.

Zitrin, C. M., Klein, D. F., & Woerner, M. G. Behavior therapy, supportive psychotherapy, imipramine and phobias. *Archives of General Psychiatry*, 1978, *35*, 307–316.

CHAPTER 6

Depression

Peter M. Lewinsohn and Harry M. Hoberman

Introduction

The behavioral study of depression has reached
its adolescence. As recently as 5 years ago,
Becker (1974) observed that the behaviorists
had relatively little to say about depression.
The first behaviorally oriented single-case
studies began to appear in the literature only
some 10 years ago (e.g., Burgess, 1969; Johansson, Lewinsohn, & Flippo, 1969; Lazarus, 1968). It was not until 1973 that the first
group-design studies appeared in the literature (McLean, Ogston, & Grauer, 1973; Shipley & Fazio, 1973). Thus, the systematic investigation of depression within a behavioral
framework is a very recent phenomenon.
Since 1973, at least 42 outcome studies of behavioral treatments of depression have been
reported, and several major reviews have appeared (e.g., Blaney, 1979; Craighead, 1979;
Hollon, 1979; Parloff, Wolfe, Hadley, & Waskow, 1978; Rehm & Kornblith, 1979; Rush
& Beck, 1978). In a short period of time, both
the scope and the number of behavioral studies
of depression have increased dramatically.
Stimulated by the increasing evidence that a
variety of structured behavioral and cognitive

therapies are effective in ameliorating depression, this prolific activity has resulted in an
increased acceptance of such approaches among
clinicians.

Overview

The purpose of this chapter is to review the
steadily accumulating literature on behavioral
and cognitive theories of and interventions for
depression in adults. The intention of the authors is to be "illuminatory"; we seek to clarify the assumptions and implications of the
major behavioral theories and therapies for a
subset of affective disorders, what is referred
to as *unipolar depression*. Bipolar and psychotic depression are not discussed. To the
end of clarification, the chapter begins with a
review of the historical development of behavioral approaches to depression. Epidemiological considerations relevant to depression are then noted. Next, the major theories
or models of depression are discussed, including experimental findings on the mechanisms
hypothesized to be significant in the onset and
maintenance of depressive behavior. Following this discussion, the assessment of depression level and of behaviors functionally related
to depression is considered. Subsequently,
theory-based treatment strategies, as well as

Peter M. Lewinsohn and Harry M. Hoberman • Psychology Department, University of Oregon, Eugene,
Oregon 97403.

more eclectic intervention procedures, are examined; relevant outcome studies of cognitive and/or behavioral therapies are evaluated. Finally, in light of the preceding review of significant research findings, new directions in the behavioral study and treatment of depressive behavior are discussed.

Historical Perspective

Psychoanalytic formulations (e.g., Abraham, 1960; Bibring, 1953; Freud, 1917/1957; Jacobson, 1971) dominated the psychological study of depression for many years. The psychoanalytic position compares depression with grief reactions, suggesting that depression may occur following the loss of a real or a fantasied love object in conjunction with certain intrapsychic processes, such as a loss of self-esteem and internalized hostility. However, this conceptualization has not been productive in generating empirical research or in developing treatment procedures specific to depression.

Despite this void, behavioral researchers, as was indicated, have only recently begun to study the phenomena of depression. Several reasons have been suggested to explain why behavior modification was late in attacking the problem of depressive disorders (Craighead, 1979; Lewinsohn, Weinstein, & Shaw, 1969):

1. The early proponents of behavior modification focused on circumscribed problems that were amenable to study in the experimental-clinical laboratory.
2. A major symptom of depression refers to a subjective state; depression had traditionally not been defined in terms of *specific* somatic-motor behaviors, which until the 1970s were the focus of behavioral assessment and intervention.
3. It was difficult to fit depression within the "learning theory" formulation espoused during the early years of behavior modification. As the theoretical underpinnings of behavior modification were broadened (e.g., Bandura, 1977; Mahoney, 1974) and the diagnostic description of depression improved, the behavioral treatment of depression began moving into the mainstream of behavior modification.

Two significant developments or trends can be seen as contributing to the advance of behavioral research on depression. The first trend concerns the empirical delineation of depressive behaviors. As a result of many historical influences, depression emerged as a ubiquitous and elusive phenomenon. A number of weakly defined diagnostic entities (neurotic, psychotic, involutional melancholic, etc.) were said to represent different kinds of affective disorders. In conducting the first descriptive study of clinically depressed individuals, Grinker, Miller, Sabshin, Nunn, and Nunnally (1961) utilized behavior and symptom checklists to investigate the components of the depression syndrome. Through factor analysis, they identified several patterns of feelings and of behavior that delineated the phenomena of depression (dysphoria, self-depreciation, guilt, material burden, social isolation, somatic complaints, and a reduced rate of behavior). In so doing, Grinker *et al.* (1961) made it possible to define depression operationally in terms of several distinct symptom clusters.

The second trend developed as several behavioral theorists attempted to link depression to principles of learning and, in particular, to the concept of reinforcement. The first attempt at a behavioral analysis of depression is contained in Skinner's *Science and Human Behavior* (1953), in which depression is described as a weakening of behavior due to the interruption of established sequences of behavior that have been positively reinforced by the social environment. This conceptualization of depression as an extinction phenomenon, and as a reduced frequency of emission of positively reinforced behavior, has been central to all behavioral positions. Ferster (1965, 1966) provided more detail by suggesting that such diverse factors as sudden environmental changes, punishment and aversive control, and shifts in reinforcement contingencies can give rise to depression (e.g., to a reduced rate of behavior).

Lazarus (1968) also hypothesized depression to be due to insufficient or inadequate

reinforcement. In his view, the antecedent for depression is a reaction to an actual or anticipated reduction of great magnitude in positive reinforcers. Depressive behavior is maintained by lack of ability, opportunity, or capacity to recognize or utilize available reinforcers. Wolpe (1971) hypothesized depression to be a protective, inhibitory type of behavior in response to prolonged, intense anxiety. Costello (1972) argued that depression results not from the loss of reinforcers *per se* but instead from the loss of reinforcer effectiveness.

Lewinsohn and his associates (Lewinsohn & Shaw, 1969, 1975b, 1976) have also maintained that a low rate of response-contingent positive reinforcement constitutes a sufficient explanation for parts of the depressive syndrome, such as the low rate of behavior. The Lewinsohn group amplified the "behavioral" position through several additional hypotheses:

1. A causal relationship between the low rate of response-contingent positive reinforcement and the feeling of dysphoria.
2. An emphasis on the maintenance of depressive behaviors by the social environment through the provision of contingencies in the form of sympathy, interest, and concern.
3. An emphasis on deficiencies in social skill as an important antecedent to the low rate of positive reinforcement.

The therapeutic implications of these conceptualizations were relatively straightforward. Since the onset of depression was assumed to be preceded by a reduction in response-contingent positive reinforcement, improvement should follow from an increase in positive reinforcement. Hence, the principal goal of treatment should be to restore an adequate schedule of positive reinforcement for the patient by altering the level, the quality, and the range of his/her activities and interpersonal interactions.

Working within a cognitive framework, Beck (1963, 1964, 1967, 1970, 1976; and Beck, Rush, Shaw, & Emery, 1978, 1979) developed both a theory and a therapy for depression that has paralleled and, in a number of important ways, interacted with the development of behavioral approaches to depression. Beck assigned the primary causal role in depression to negative cognitions. Such distorted or unrealistic cognitions were postulated as producing misinterpretations of experiences that lead to the affective reactions and the other behaviors associated with depression.

Currently, the most influential theoretical formulations and clinical approaches may be roughly divided into those that emphasize "reinforcement" and those that emphasize "cognitions" in the etiology of depression. While these two conceptualizations differ fundamentally in where they place the locus of causation, it is important to recognize their similarities: both assume that the depressed patient has *acquired* maladaptive reaction patterns that can be *unlearned,* and the treatments in both are aimed at the modification of relatively specific behaviors and cognitions rather than at a general reorganization of the patient's personality.

Major Theories of Depression

Despite a variety of problems (Eastman, 1976; Blaney, 1977), a number of behavioral formulations have been proposed to explain the phenomena of depression. As noted, contemporary theories of depression fall into two general categories: reinforcement and cognitive (which includes self-control) theories. All of these concern themselves with tracing the course of depression, including its genesis and maintenance, and they have direct implications for treatment. Each formulation assumes one central mechanism to be causal in depression and only secondarily takes account of other symptoms and problem behaviors. Some empirical support has been provided for each of the theories. Two kinds of data are typically presented to justify theoretical formulations: treatment outcome studies and correlational studies using depressed individuals. In the first approach, theorists test their models by way of treatment comparisons. If a theory-based treatment is successful in reducing depression level, the model is said to have been supported. Studies of the second kind present evidence demonstrating covariation between depression level and other variables. As is well known, correlation does not prove causation, and from the available literature, it is impossible to know whether the distinguishing characteristics of depressives that have been identified in correlational studies are of etiological significance or result from the disorder.

Reinforcement Theories[1]

The behavioral or social learning theory of depression, initially proposed by Lewinsohn, Weinstein, and Shaw (1969), has been responsible for generating a substantial amount of empirical research on the phenomena of depression. On the basis of the results of a number of correlational studies on aspects of depressed persons' behavior, as well as from treatment outcome studies (Brown & Lewinsohn, 1982; Lewinsohn, Youngren, & Grosscup, 1980; Sanchez, Lewinsohn, & Larson, 1980; Zeiss, Lewinsohn, & Muñoz, 1979), a model of depression centered on the construct of reinforcement has been progressively refined (Lewinsohn & Amenson, 1978; Lewinsohn & Graf, 1973; Lewinsohn & Talkington, 1979; Lewinsohn, Youngren, & Grosscup, 1980; MacPhillamy & Lewinsohn, 1974).

In contrast to more strictly cognitive theories, Lewinsohn has suggested that the feeling of dysphoria is the central phenomenon of depression. Cognitive symptoms (e.g., low self-esteem, pessimism, feelings of guilt) are viewed as depressives' efforts to explain to themselves, and to others, why they feel bad. The large number of available labeling alternatives (e.g., "I'm sick"; "I'm inadequate") may account for the variety of the specific cognitive symptoms shown by different individuals. Lewinsohn's theory suggests that dysphoria is a direct result of a reduction in the rate of response-contingent reinforcement.

[1] Considerable variation exists in the definition of depression employed in the different research studies. Consequently, in order to allow meaningful comparisons across studies, a distinction is made here between depression as defined by rigorous criteria (e.g., diagnostic criteria) and depression as defined by weak criteria (e.g., a high Beck Depression Inventory [BDI] score). Individuals in the former classification are referred to as *patients*, while those in the latter classification are termed *subjects*.

Thus, the relative presence or absence of reinforcing events is postulated as playing the major role in the development and maintenance of depression.

As defined by Glazer (1971), a reinforcer is "any event, stimulus, or state of affairs that changes subsequent behavior when it temporally follows an instance of that behavior" (p. 1). Throughout the various theoretical interpretations of reinforcement mechanisms, this description of reinforcing situations has remained relatively constant. Some consequences increase the probability of the behavior they follow (positive reinforcers); others reduce the probability of the behavior they follow (aversive events). Whether an event has positive or negative reinforcing properties is inferred from its empirical effect on the behavior. As used by Lewinsohn, Youngren, & Grosscup (1980), *reinforcement* is defined by the rate and the quality of a person's interactions with his/her environment. Research has shown that the rate of occurrence of positively reinforcing and of aversive events are independent of one another (e.g., Lewinsohn & Amenson, 1978). Dysphoria is assumed to result when there is either too little positive reinforcement or too much punishment. A low rate of response-contingent positive reinforcement might occur in three ways. First, events contingent on behavior may not be reinforcing, perhaps, as Costello (1972) has suggested, because of a loss of reinforcer effectiveness. Second, events that are reinforcing may become unavailable. For example, an incapacitating injury may prevent an individual from engaging in sports or social activities that have previously been significant in maintaining his/her behavior. Third, reinforcers may be available, but because the individual lacks the necessary repertoire (e.g., social skill), the individual is unable to elicit them. These possibilities are, of course, not mutually exclusive.

Conversely, aversive events or punishment is assumed to play a role in depression when aversive events occur at a high rate; when the individual has a heightened sensitivity to aversive events; and lastly, if the individual lacks the necessary coping skills to terminate aversive events. Finally, Lewinsohn *et al.* (1969) have suggested a feedback loop for the maintenance of depressive behaviors as operants.

Initially, depressive behaviors (dysphoria and associated symptoms and the low rate of behavior) are elicited or caused by the low rate of reinforcement. Very often, however, the social environment provides social reinforcements in the form of sympathy, interest, and concern, which strengthen and maintain depressive behaviors. These reinforcements are typically provided by a small segment of the depressed person's social environment (e.g., the immediate family). However, since most people in the depressed person's environment (and eventually even his/her family) find these depressive behaviors aversive (Coyne, 1976), they will avoid him/her as much as possible, thus further decreasing the person's rate of receiving positive reinforcement and further accentuating the depression.

As the relationship between reinforcement and depression is central to Lewinsohn's conceptualization, a great deal of the research generated by this group has focused on (1) developing methods of identifying reinforcing and punishing events; (2) comparing the rates of positive reinforcement and of the occurrence of aversive events in depressed and nondepressed groups; and (3) trying to identify specific reinforcement events of special importance in depression.

Lewinsohn and his associates have developed several psychometric instruments: the Pleasant Events Schedule (PES) (MacPhillamy & Lewinsohn, 1971); the Unpleasant Events Schedule (UES) (Lewinsohn, 1975b); and the Interpersonal Events Schedule (IES) (Youngren, Zeiss, & Lewinsohn, 1975). Each of these instruments attempts to measure events assumed to have reinforcing properties. Frequency ratings are obtained for the rate of occurrence of particular behaviors (events) during the preceding month. Additionally, subjective impact scores are obtained; these are assumed to reflect the potential reinforcing value of the events in question. Finally, a multiplicative function of frequency and impact ratings is derived for each event. The sum of these cross-product scores is assumed to be an approximate measure of response-contingent reinforcement obtained over a specific period of time.

Studies using these instruments have consistently shown the depressed to have lower rates of positive reinforcement and higher rates of negative reinforcement and have also shown that predicted changes occur as a function of clinical improvement. Lewinsohn and Graf (1973) found that depressed persons had significantly lower mean numbers of pleasant activities averaged over 30 days. MacPhillamy and Lewinsohn (1974) administered the PES to 120 paid volunteer subjects; the results indicated that the depressed group evidenced significantly lower positive reinforcement because of lower levels of engagement in pleasant activities, decreased enjoyability of the events, and a restricted range of activities. Finally, Lewinsohn, Youngren, and Grosscup (1980) demonstrated that after treatment, depressives who evinced a decrease in depression level showed a corresponding increase in PES cross-product scores and consistent improvement in enjoyability ratings.

An early experiment by Lewinsohn, Lobitz, and Wilson (1973) presented data consistent with the hypothesis that depressives are more sensitive to aversive stimuli (e.g., mild electric shock) when compared with psychiatric and normal control groups. More recently, Lewinsohn, and Amenson (1978) and Lewinsohn and Talkington (1979) found that compared with controls, depressed persons did not report significant differences in the frequency of moderately unpleasant events. While the total amount of experienced aversiveness was substantially higher for depressives than for controls, this difference was the result of depressed persons generally rating events as more aversive.

Youngren and Lewinsohn (1980) attempted to distinguish interpersonal behaviors and events that especially raise difficulties for depressed persons. The results showed that depressed persons reported significantly lower rates of engagement and higher rates of experienced discomfort in social activity and in giving and receiving positive responses. Consequently, it appears that they derive less positive social reinforcement from these interpersonal behaviors and events. Assertion was also found to be a problem for depressives. Additionally, it was found that depressed individuals uniquely reported more discomfort as a result of negative cognitions concerning personal interactions. After treatment, depressed individuals demonstrated significant increases in the frequency and amount of reinforcement obtained from social activity and giving and receiving positive interpersonal responses. Significant decreases in the degree of discomfort associated with negative cognitions regarding interpersonal interactions were also found for the depressed as compared with the controls.

A related, but somewhat different, strategy for identifying events with potential reinforcing or punishing properties has been to ask people to monitor the occurrence of specified events and to complete mood ratings on a daily basis for periods of 30 days or more. By studying the correlations between the occurrence of events and mood level, it has been possible to show a statistically significant ($p < .01$) covariation between feeling good and the occurrence of pleasant events and between feeling bad and the occurrence of aversive events. Specific event–mood correlations for an individual are assumed to identify particular events that have reinforcing or punishing impact for that person. Events that are correlated with mood for a substantial (10% or more) proportion of the population (mood-related events) are assumed to represent events that have reinforcing or punishing properties in the population at large. Hence, mood-related events are assumed to bear a critical relationship to the occurrence of depression; and they are assumed to be the major types of events that act as reinforcement for people. Data consistent with these hypotheses are discussed by Lewinsohn and Amenson (1978).

A significant association between mood and number and kind of pleasant activities engaged in was demonstrated by Lewinsohn and Libet (1972) and Lewinsohn and Graf (1973). Similarly, Lewinsohn, Youngren, and Grosscup (1980) reported significant covariations between feeling good and the frequency of pleasant events. A study by Graf (1977) indicated that depressed persons who increased mood-related pleasant events improved more than depressed persons who increased non-mood-related pleasant events.

Significant covariations have also been found between feeling bad and the occurrence of aversive events (Lewinsohn, Youngren, & Grosscup, 1980). The rate of occurrence of mood-related unpleasant events was shown to be uniquely elevated in depressives by Lewinsohn and Amenson (1978). This study found the mood-related items, for both the UES and the PES, to be especially discriminating between the depressed and the nondepressed.

Lewinsohn and his associates have also been interested in the social behavior of depressed individuals because the lack of social skill could be one of the antecedent conditions producing a low rate of positive reinforcement and a high rate of punishment. Social skill is defined as the ability to emit behaviors that are positively reinforced by others and that terminate negative reactions from others. An individual may be considered skillful to the extent that he/she elicits positive and avoids negative consequences from the social environment. On the basis of an extensive analysis of social interactional data obtained by observing depressed and nondepressed individuals in group therapy interactions and in their home environment (e.g., Lewinsohn, Weinstein, & Alper, 1970; Lewinsohn and Shaffer, 1971; Libet & Lewinsohn, 1973), the depressed as a group were found to be less socially skilled than the nondepressed control groups. Coyne (1976) also found that in phone conversations with normal individuals, depressed persons (as compared with nondepressed persons) induced more negative affects and elicited greater feelings of rejection from others, suggesting that depressed individuals relate to others in a fashion that reduces the likelihood that they will be reinforced.

In another study, Youngren and Lewinsohn (1980) contrasted the verbal and nonverbal behavior and interpersonal style of depressed patients with that of nondepressed controls in group and dyadic laboratory interactions. Differences on the verbal and nonverbal measures, while generally in the predicted direction, were often small and not uniquely related to depression. In the group situation, but not in dyadic interactions, the depressed were rated by others as less socially skilled. On ratings of interpersonal style scales (e.g., friendly, speaks fluently), the depressed rated themselves more negatively and received more negative ratings from others compared with controls. After treatment, the depressed improved on all ratings of interpersonal style.

Prkachin, Craig, Papageorgis, and Reith (1977) studied the receptive and expressive skills of depressed, psychiatric control, and normal control subjects within a nonverbal communication paradigm. The results indicated that the facial expressions of depressed subjects were the most difficult to judge correctly, while no differences were apparent between the other two groups. Prkachin *et al.* interpreted their findings as suggesting that depressed individuals exhibit a deficit in nonverbal communicative behavior (e.g., their expressive behavior is both ambiguous and nonresponsive) and as supporting Lewinsohn's hypothesis that a lack of social skill represents a major antecedent condition for the occurrence of depression.

While many studies can thus be cited that, in general, are consistent with the hypothesis that depressed individuals are less socially skillful and that they obtain less reinforcement in social interaction, the specific nature of the behavioral (overt) deficits associated with depression have, as yet, not been clearly delineated. Further research is needed that is aimed at the identification of discriminating behaviors through empirical analysis (Jacobson, 1979). The results may be situation-specific, or they may be influenced by the duration of the interaction and its demands for intimacy. Also, the sex of the individual acts as a moderator variable (Hammen & Peters, 1977).

Cognitive Theories

Cognitive theorists such as Beck (1967), Ellis and Harper (1961), Rehm (1977), and Seligman (1974, 1975) have advanced hypotheses that attribute a causal role to cognitions in the etiology of depression. But they differ in regard to the specific nature of the cognitions that are assumed to lead to depression.

Beck. Beck and his associates (1967, 1976; and Beck, Rush, Shaw, & Emery, 1978, 1979) conceive of depression as a disorder of thinking. The signs and symptoms of the depressive syndrome are a *consequence* of the activation of negative cognitive patterns. Affect, according to Beck, is intimately linked with cognition. Between an event and an individual's emotional reaction to that event, a cognition or an automatic thought intervenes that determines the resulting affect. When the cognitions represent an inaccurate or distorted appraisal of the event, the subsequent affect will be inappropriate or extreme. Beck (1976) believes that the dysphoria or sadness associated with depression derives from an individual's tendency to interpret her/his experiences in terms of being deprived, deficient, or defeated.

Several specific cognitive structures are postulated as being central in the development of depression: the cognitive triad, schemata and cognitive errors (Beck, Rush, Shaw, & Emery, 1979). The cognitive triad consists of three cognitive patterns asserted to dominate depressive ideation: a negative view of oneself (depressed individuals perceive themselves as inadequate, defective, and lacking the attributes necessary to obtain happiness); a negative view of the world (depressed individuals believe that the world presents unreasonable demands and/or obstacles to reaching important life goals); and a negative view of the future (depressed individuals believe that their current difficulties will continue indefinitely).

Beck has also postulated the existence of superordinate schemata that lead to the systematic filtering or distortion of the stimuli that confront the individual. These schemata represent stable cognitive patterns of the individual that mold raw data (sensory inputs) in the direction of making them accord with these prepotent schemata (Beck *et al.*, 1979). The existence of such schemata, asserts Beck, explains why depressed persons cling to painful attitudes ("I am unlovable") despite objective evidence to the contrary. As a result of the increased domination of dysfunctional schemata, systematic errors in the logic of depressives' thinking are said to occur. Such errors are automatic and involuntary and include arbitrary inference (drawing conclusions without evidence or despite contrary evidence); selective abstraction (ignoring the context of an event by fixating on a detailed aspect of a situation while ignoring more salient features); overgeneralization (drawing a general conclusion on the basis of limited detail or limited occurrences of an event); magnification and minimization (undue exaggerating or limiting of the significance of the information); personalization (attaching subjective significance to external events when no basis exists for making such a connection); and absolutistic thinking (placing all experiences in one or two opposite categories) (Beck *et al.,* 1979).

Several different kinds of studies were initially conducted by Beck and his associates (summarized in Beck, 1967) to test these hypotheses. Early studies focused on the content of various types of ideational productions, involving dreams, early memories, storytelling, and responses to picture cards. The productions of depressed patients were found to show a greater frequency of themes of failure and fewer successes and to focus on personal defects and rejection, and their responses to verbal tests involving self-concept tended to be more negative.

In recent years, a considerable amount of experimental literature has accumulated relating to the variety of predictions implied by Beck's theory. This research, conducted by Beck and his co-workers, as well as a number of other investigators, has focused on the effects of success and failure, perceptual distortion, memory distortion, negative expectancies, and other cognitive deficits in depressed individuals.

Effects of Success and Failure. A number of studies focused on the differential effects of success and failure experiences on self-esteem, mood, and expectation of future success on the task-and-performance evaluation in depressed and in nondepressed groups. Critical to Beck's theory is the prediction that following a failure experience, the depressed, compared with the nondepressed, will become *more negative* (in their self-esteem, mood, expectancies, and performance evaluation) and *less* positive following a success experience. On the basis of the cognitive mechanisms postulated by Beck, it would be expected that the depressed should be particularly responsive to negative information about themselves and unresponsive to positive information.

The experimental procedure for testing the effects of success and failure has typically been similar to one developed by Diggory and Loeb (1962), in which "success" and "failure" were experimentally produced either by manipulating the time allowed for completing the task or by manipulating the length of the task. This and similar tests have consistently been shown to produce systematic change in self-esteem (e.g., Flippo & Lewinsohn, 1971).

One of the earliest studies was done by Rosenzweig (1960), who hypothesized that following a failure or success experience, the self-concept of depressed persons changes on the evaluative dimension more than does the self-concept of nonpsychiatric control subjects. Rosenzweig found depressed patients to be less consistent, but not more negative, in their self-concept ratings following either a success or a failure experience. Loeb, Feshback, Beck, and Wolf (1964) compared depressed and nondepressed male psychiatric patients prior to and immediately following experimentally induced "superior" and "inferior" performance conditions. Prior to and immediately following the experimental task, the subjects rated their mood; after the task, they were also assessed for self-confidence and expectation of future performance. Trends were found for depressed patients to show more negative mood and lower expectancies after inferior performances. However, a number of findings were obtained contrary to what Beck's theory would predict: depressives were more optimistic and had higher expectancies following superior performances.

In another experiment, Loeb, Beck, Diggory, and Tuthill (1967) manipulated success and failure on a card-sorting task. Inspection of the means suggests a comparable change in probability-of-future-success estimates following success and following failure in individuals with high and low depression. Using anagrams as the experimental task and self-esteem ratings as the dependent variable, Flippo and Lewinsohn (1971) found that the magnitude of change from before to after three different failure–success conditions did not differ between depressed and nondepressed subjects. Alloy and Abramson (1979) found greater *positive* change in depressed than in nondepressed subjects on mood ratings following "win" or "lose" tasks.

Klein and Seligman (1976) and Miller and Seligman (1973, 1975, 1976)—and learned helplessness studies in general—have found depressed students to exhibit *smaller* expectancy changes following success and failure on a skill task than nondepressed students. In addition, Abramson, Garber, Edwards, and Seligman (1978) reported that relative to hospitalized control subjects and schizophrenics, unipolar depressives showed small expectancy changes in a skill task.

The results of laboratory studies relevant to the prediction of differential effects of success and failure from Beck's theory have thus provided little support for the theory.

Perceptual Distortion. Studies have also been directed at Beck's hypothesis that the depressed person screens out or fails to integrate "successful experiences that contradict his negative view of himself" (Beck, 1976, p. 119). From this hypothesis, it may be predicted that depressed individuals will distort their perception of environmental feedback in a negative direction. DeMonbreun and Craighead (1977) and Craighead, Hickey, and DeMonbreun (1979) failed to find differences between depressed and nondepressed subjects in immediate perception of positive, negative, and ambiguous feedback information, which was provided after each response on the experimental task.

Alloy and Abramson (1979) studied the ability of depressed and nondepressed subjects to detect the degree of contingency between responding and outcomes in a series of problems that varied in the actual degree of objective contingency between the performance responses and outcomes obtained. No differences between more and less depressed subjects were found in their ability to detect the degree of contingency between their responses and environmental outcomes on three contingency problems. In problem situations lacking contingency, the nondepressed subjects showed an illusion of control in the high-density but not in the low-density problem, while the depressed were relatively accurate in both problems. In a third experiment, the nondepressed judged that they had more control (erroneously) in a "win" situation than in a "lose" situation, while the depressed subjects accurately reported that responding and not responding were equally effective regardless of whether they were winning or losing money.

Judgments of contingency of the depressed individuals were remarkably accurate. The nondepressed subjects, by contrast, tended to overestimate the degree of contingency for frequent and/or desired outcomes and to underestimate the degree of contingency between their responses and their outcomes when the contingent outcomes were undesired.

Another experiment (Lewinsohn, Mischel, Chaplin, & Barton, 1980a) also found *less* perceptual distortion in depressed than in nondepressed individuals. The findings indicated that nondepressed persons perceived themselves more positively than others saw them, while the depressed saw themselves as they were seen. If social reality is defined by the extent of agreement with objective observers, the depressed were the most realistic in their self-perceptions, while the controls were engaged in self-enhancing distortions.

Thus, laboratory studies have not provided support for the perceptual distortion hypothesis. If anything, nondepressed persons distort their perceptions, while the depressed are quite accurate in theirs.

Memory Distortion. Studies have also been conducted to investigate the presence of selective memory effects in depressed individuals. From Beck's theory, more forgetting of hedonically positive (pleasant) and less selective forgetting of hedonically negative (unpleasant) information would be expected. The results have generally supported these predictions. Wener and Rehm (1975) found that at the end of a series of trials, depressed subjects reported that they were correct less often than nondepressed subjects. Buchwald (1977) asked subjects to estimate the percentage of "right" responses and found a significant negative correlation between a measure of depression and estimates of "right" for female but not for male subjects. Nelson and Craighead (1977) reported that compared with the control group, depressed subjects underestimated the number of "bad" responses. DeMonbreun and Craighead (1977), also introducing their memory probe at the end of the experiment, found that the depressed "recalled" having received less positive feedback than did the controls. It is possible that the obtained differences reflect differences in incidental learning rather than in memory formation, retention, and retrieval (i.e., of hedonically toned information through intentional learning). It is also impossible to determine whether the hedonic selectivity of depressed individuals, which is suggested by the studies, constitutes an enduring characteristic of depressed individuals that predisposes them to become depressed (as required by Beck's hypothesis) or whether the hedonic selectivity is secondary to being in a depressed state.

Relevant to this last question are a series of studies that very strongly suggest that the state of depression increases the accessibility of memories of unpleasant events relative to the accessibility of memories of pleasant events. Lloyd and Lishman (1975) asked depressed patients, in response to a standard set of stimulus words, to retrieve from memory pleasant or unpleasant experiences from their past life. With increasing depression, subjects retrieved unpleasant experiences faster than pleasant experiences, a reversal of the pattern shown by nondepressed subjects. Lloyd and Lishman (1975) suggested that depression exerts its effects mainly by speeding up the recall of unpleasant memories. In a well-designed study, Teasdale and Fogarty (1979) extended these findings by showing that a mood induction procedure, in which student subjects were made happy on one occasion and depressed on another, exerted a significant effect on the time taken to retrieve pleasant memories relative to the time taken to retrieve unpleasant memories. In contrast to the findings of Lloyd and Lishman (1975), Teasdale and Fogarty's (1979) results indicate that depression exerts its effect by increasing the latency of pleasant memories.

Negative Expectancies. Beck's construct of negative expectancies has also been the subject of several investigations. Weintraub, Segal, and Beck (1974) devised a test consisting of incomplete stories involving a principal character with whom the subject was asked to identify. The expected relationship between negative expectancies and depression level was found. Another study (Beck, Weissman, Lester, & Trexler, 1974) made use of the Hopelessness Scale which consists of 20 true–false items. This scale was found to correlate well with clinical ratings of hopelessness

and was sensitive to change in patients' state of depression over time.

A related study was conducted specifically to test Beck's cognitive triad (Lewinsohn, Larson, & Muñoz, 1978; Muñoz, 1977). To incorporate the distinctions between self and the world, and present and future, a test (the Subjective Probability Questionnaire: Muñoz & Lewinsohn, 1976c) was constructed along three dichotomous and crossed dimensions: self versus world, present versus future, and positive versus negative. Depressives had higher expectancies about negative, and lower expectancies for positive, events pertaining to the self (in the present and in the future) but not about the "world."

Other Cognitive Deficits. Studies have also been aimed at other cognitive distortions hypothesized by Beck to be characteristic of depressed individuals. Using the Dysfunctional Attitude Scale (Weissman & Beck, 1978) to probe respondents' degree of agreement with beliefs hypothesized by Beck to characterize depressed patients, Weissman and Beck (1978) found a substantial, and statistically significant, correlation between the Dysfunctional Attitude Scale and the Beck Depression Inventory (Beck, 1976) and the Depression Scale of the Profile of Mood States (McNair, Lorr, & Droppleman, 1971). Substantial correlation was also found between the Dysfunctional Attitude Scale and a measure of cognitive distortion developed by Hammen and Krantz (1976). In this study depressed individuals were found to select a greater number of depression-distorted responses.

Ellis. Ellis (e.g., Ellis & Harper, 1961) attaches primary importance to irrational beliefs in the development of depression. Depression in this view occurs when a particular situation triggers an "irrational belief." It is this belief that is hypothesized to cause the person to overreact emotionally to the situation. For example, the person may become depressed after being rejected because he/she believes that "if one is not loved by everyone, one is unlovable."

The prediction that depressives subscribe more to irrational beliefs in general was tested and supported by Muñoz (1977) and by Nelson (1977). In these studies, the subjects were asked to indicate their degree of agreement or disagreement with absolute statements of various kinds (e.g., ''The main goal and purpose of life is achievement and success''). Attempting to delineate the specific nature of the irrational beliefs associated with depression, Lewinsohn, Larson, and Muñoz (1978) identified beliefs that in their, and in Nelson's, study had been found to be discriminating (at a high level of statistical significance) between depressed and nondepressed persons. Factors obtained from a factor analysis of the most discriminating items were then contrasted with factors derived from a factor analysis of a set of nondiscriminating beliefs. A particular set of ''irrational'' beliefs was identified to which depressed individuals subscribed more than nondepressed individuals.

Rehm. Rehm (1977) has developed a self-control theory of depression in which negative self-evaluations, as well as low rates of self-reinforcement and high rates of self-punishment, are seen as leading to the low rate of behavior that characterizes depressed individuals. Rehm's theory builds on Kanfer's (1971) notion of behavioral self-control. Three processes are postulated to be important: self-monitoring, self-evaluation, and self-reinforcement. Self-monitoring is the observation of one's own behavior. Rehm suggested that depressed persons self-monitor in two characteristic ways: they attend selectively to negative events and they attend selectively to the immediate versus the delayed outcomes of their behavior. Self-evaluation involves assessing one's performance against an internal standard. Two forms of maladaptive self-evaluation are said to characterize depressives: they often fail to make accurate internal attributions of causality (for success experiences), and they tend to set stringent criteria for self-evaluation (i.e., they have high thresholds for positive self-evaluation and low thresholds for negative self-evaluation). Self-reinforcement is the self-administration of overt or covert contingent reward or punishment. In controlling behavior, self-reinforcement is theorized to supplement external reinforcement; it functions to maintain behavior, especially where long-term goals are involved, when external reinforcement is delayed.

The self-control model thus accounts for the diverse symptoms of depression by a variety of cognitive deficits. Self-monitoring of negative events is assumed to result in a negative view of the self, the world, and the future. Strict evaluatory criteria are asserted to produce lowered self-esteem and feelings of helplessness. Finally, a lack of self-reward is postulated to be associated with retarded activity levels and lack of initiative, while excessive self-punishment is said to be reflected in negative self-statements and other forms of self-directed hostility.

Several studies have been conducted to test Rehm's hypotheses about the role of self-reinforcement and self-punishment in depression. The rates that subjects self-reinforce or self-punish in these experiments is assumed to be an analogue measure of the person's tendency to self-reinforce and to self-punish in other settings, but no evidence for the validity of this assumption has been provided.

An early self-reinforcement study was conducted by Rozensky, Rehm, Pry, and Roth (1977), using hospitalized medical patients who had been divided into high- and low-depression groups. The high-depression group were found to give themselves fewer self-rewards and more self-punishment than the low-depression group. This was true despite the lack of differences in the number of correct responses.

Other studies have yielded less consistent results. Roth, Rehm, and Rozensky (1975) found that the depressed gave themselves significantly more self-punishments but did not differ from the control group on the number of self-rewards administered. Nelson and Craighead (1977) found no differences between depressed and nondepressed subjects in regard to self-punishment. The nondepressed reinforced more than the depressed (and then justified this by their objective accuracy scores) after low-density but not high-density reinforcement.

Ciminero and Steingarten (1978) found no differences in performance, self-evaluation, and self-reinforcement between depressed and nondepressed groups on a task involving the Digit Symbol subtest of the Wechsler Adult Intelligence Scale (Wechsler, 1955). When subjects were assigned to low- or high-standard conditions and repeated the task, the results suggested that differential rates of self-reinforcement exist only when standards are available regarding performance. Using a similar procedure, Garber, Hollon, and Silverman (1979) found that female depressed subjects gave themselves fewer rewards following substandard performance than nondepressed females. Depressed male subjects, however, did not show such a pattern.

Lobitz and Post (1979) used a word association task, the Digit Symbol Test, and a Ward Assistance Task to test hypotheses about self-reinforcement. Two groups of hospitalized psychiatric patients (clinically depressed and clinically nondepressed) were used. The dependent measures included a scale of level of self-expectation (obtained prior to each task) and a self-reward measure (tokens), which was obtained following self-evaluation. The depressed group was significantly lower on all three measures. However, the intercorrelations among the three dependent measures were substantial. When level of self-expectation was used as the covariate, no significant differences between groups in level of self-reward were obtained. In other words, the differences between the depressed and the nondepressed on a self-reward measure were completely predictable from the level-of-expectation scores, which, of course, were obtained prior to the subject's engagement in the experimental task. Lobitz and Post suggested that the deficits in self-reinforcement found in their study and in previous studies (e.g., Nelson & Craighead, 1977) may be accounted for by the cognitive set (low self-expectations) that the subjects brought to the tasks and that a more global factor, such as low self-esteem, could be underlying all variables.

A very different approach to testing aspects of Rehm's hypothesis is represented in another study (Lewinsohn, Larson, & Muñoz, 1978; Muñoz, 1977). Starting with the assumption that the hedonic content of thoughts (positive vs. negative) constitutes a measure of covert reinforcement, a psychometric instrument, the Cognitive Events Schedule (Muñoz & Lewinsohn, 1976a), was constructed. On the basis of Rehm's hypotheses, depressed patients were expected, and found, to be characterized by a greater number of negative and a fewer number of positive thoughts about the self. In addition, the interaction between diagnostic

groups and hedonic quality (positive vs. negative) was highly significant because in the depressed group, the excess of negative thoughts was much greater than the deficit of positive thoughts. Rehm and Plakosh (1975) found that depressed compared with nondepressed subjects expressed a greater preference for immediate as opposed to delayed rewards.

In short, then, mixed experimental support exists for the self-control theory of depression. Some findings provide evidence for certain predictions of the theory, while others do not. The results of Lobitz and Post suggest an important qualification to the research in this area.

Seligman. Working from an experimental paradigm developed initially with dogs and other animals, Seligman (1974, 1975) has proposed a theory of human depression, the central tenet of which concerns the effect of the independence of behavior and outcomes (noncontingency). The critical issue is uncontrollability; consequently, the distinction between controllable and uncontrollable events is critical to Seligman's position. With repeated instances of uncontrollability, the organism learns that responding is independent of reinforcement. This fact is *transformed* into a cognitive representation, called an *expectation,* that responding and outcomes are independent. This expectation is the causal condition for the motivational (reduced responding), cognitive (interference with later instrumental learning), and emotional (first fear, and then depression) debilitation that accompanies helplessness.

The term *learned helplessness* was first used to describe interference with avoidance responding in dogs produced by inescapable shock. Indeed, the debilitating consequences of exposure to situations in which responses and outcomes are unrelated have been observed across a wide variety of experimental situations and within a large number of species (Seligman, 1975). The main psychological phenomena of learned helplessness are (1) passivity; (2) retarded learning; (3) lack of aggressiveness and competitiveness; and (4) weight loss and undereating. The critical antecedent for learned helplessness is not trauma *per se,* but not having control over trauma. A key assumption of Seligman's theory of depression is that "if the symptoms of learned helplessness and depression are equivalent then what we have learned experimentally about the cause, cure, and prevention of learned helplessness can be applied to depression" (1973, p. 43). Depressed individuals are presumed to have been, or to be, in situations in which responding and reinforcement are independent. As a result, the depressed person believes that he/she is helpless. Recovery of belief that responding produces reinforcement is the critical attitudinal change for the cure of depression.

The learned-helplessness theory has stimulated much research, and one issue of the *Journal of Abnormal Psychology* (February 1978) was devoted to a review of methodological and conceptual issues and empirical findings on the relationship between learned helplessness and depression.

A number of different experimental paradigms have been used to study predictions from the learned-helplessness theory. Using a triadic design analogous to that employed in animal helplessness studies, Seligman and his associates (e.g., Hiroto, 1974) have compared subjects exposed to three prior conditions: contingent, noncontingent, or no trauma (aversive noise). All groups were subsequently tested in a human shuttle box for escape–avoidance responses to noise. The results were similar to those obtained in other species; students who had received prior exposure to noncontingent noise showed impaired performance on the requisite escape–avoidance response in the shuttle box test, compared with students receiving prior exposure to contingent noise or no noise.

In their studies on the locus-of-control construct, Rotter and his associates (e.g., James, 1957; James & Rotter, 1958) demonstrated that the outcomes of previous trials have a greater effect on expectancies of future success on skill tasks when the person believes that outcomes are dependent on responses (internal) than when the person believes that outcomes are independent of responses (external). Using this logic, Miller and Seligman (1976) and Klein and Seligman (1976) examined verbalized expectancies of success on skill and chance tasks for subjects who were, again, given prior exposure to contingent, noncon-

tingent, or no trauma (an aversive tone). The subjects exposed to prior uncontrollable noises showed less expectancy change in the skill task than the students exposed to prior controllable noises or no noises, although the groups did not differ in a chance task. Furthermore, depth of depression was significantly correlated with small expectancy change in skill tasks but did not correlate with expectancy changes in chance tasks. Similarly to nondepressed subjects who received experience with uncontrollable events, naive depressed students exhibited *smaller* expectancy changes following success (Klein & Seligman, 1976; Miller & Seligman, 1973, 1975) and failure (Klein & Seligman, 1976; Miller & Seligman, 1975, 1976) in a skill task. In addition, Abramson, Garber, Edwards, and Seligman (1978) reported that unipolar depressives also showed small expectancy changes in a skill task relative to hospitalized control subjects and schizophrenics. On the assumption that expectancy changes in chance and skill tasks represent valid indexes of people's beliefs about response–outcome contingencies, these studies have been used to infer that depressives believe less in the relationship between outcomes and responding. This assumption has been questioned by a number of theorists (Buchwald, Coyne & Cole, 1978; Costello, 1978; Huesmann, 1978), who have suggested that the above-mentioned studies do not provide convincing evidence for the specific cognitive deficit postulated by learned-helplessness theory.

A more direct method for the assessment of depressed and nondepressed persons' perception of response–outcome contingencies is provided in a recent experiment by Alloy and Abramson (1979). In a series of experiments, depressed and nondepressed students were confronted with problems that varied in the actual degree of objective contingency between the performance responses and the outcomes obtained. Surprisingly, the judgments of contingency of the depressed students were remarkably accurate; if anything, the results suggest that nondepressives have difficulty in assessing response–outcome relationships.

The emotional component of learned helplessness has also come under investigation. The helplessness theory requires that exposure to uncontrollable events result in depressive affect. In some studies (Gatchel, Paulus, & Maples, 1975), nondepressed college students exposed to uncontrollable noise became depressed in comparison with either a group that received controllable noises or a group that received no noise. But in other studies (Miller & Seligman, 1975), the different treatments with noise did not produce significantly different effects on depressive mood. When the helplessness manipulation does affect depression ratings, it also typically affects anxiety as well as ratings of hostility (Alloy & Abramson, 1979; Gatchel *et al.*, 1975). The fact that research indicates that the helplessness induction results in anxiety and hostility as well as depression raises the question of whether such helplessness bears a unique relation to depression or whether there is a sequence of emotional reactions to the experience of noncontrol (Klinger, 1975; Wortman & Brehm, 1975) and the discrepancies between studies result because various subjects had arrived at various points in the sequence when the dependent measures were collected.

An interesting "paradox" has been discussed by Abramson and Sackheim (1977), who noted that despite viewing events (as in the learned-helplessness theory) as uncontrollable and themselves as helpless, depressives blame themselves for those events; that is, depressive individuals assume the responsibility for events that they believe they neither cause nor control. A recent study by Peterson (1979) provides empirical support for this so-called paradox in depression.

In response to these and other criticisms, Seligman (Abramson, Seligman, & Teasdale, 1978) has recently proposed a reformulation of the learned-helplessness theory by incorporating extensions from attribution theory (Weiner, Frieze, Kukla, Reed, Rest, & Rosenbaum, 1971; Weiner, Nierenberg, & Goldstein, 1976). The reformulated theory suggests that the attributions the individual makes for the perceived noncontingency between his/her acts and outcomes (personal helplessness) are the source of subsequent expectations of future noncontingency (expected uncontrollability). The dimensions of attributions said to be particularly relevant to learned helplessness and depression include internality–ex-

ternality, globality–specificity, and stability–instability. The depressive attributional style is hypothesized to (1) consist in a tendency to make internal attributions for failure but external attributions for success; (2) make stable attributions for failure but unstable attributions for success; and (3) make global attributions for failure but specific attributions for success. The person is more likely to be depressed, it is hypothesized, if his/her attributions for failure and lack of control are internal ("It is my fault"), global ("I am incompetent"), and stable ("I will always be like that"), while his/her attributions for successes are external ("I was lucky"), specific ("in this particular situation"), and unstable ("just this time").

The low self-esteem associated with depression is hypothesized to result from internal attributions for personal helplessness, while the affect (depression) results from the expectation that bad outcomes will result in the future. The severity of the motivational and cognitive deficits of depression is postulated as depending jointly on the strength (or the certainty) of the expectation of aversive outcomes *and* the strength of the uncontrollability. The severity of the affective and self-esteem deficits is said to be governed by the importance of uncontrollable outcomes.

Recently, Seligman, Abramson, Semmel, and Von Baeyer (1979) have presented evidence for the reformulated theory. Using a new Attributional Style Scale (Semmel, Abramson, Seligman, & Van Baeyer, 1978) with a sample of college students, they computed correlations between the Beck Depression Inventory and the Attributional Style Scale scores. For bad outcomes, the depression measure correlated with internality, stability, and globality; for good outcomes, the depression measure correlated with externality and instability, but not significantly with specificity. In a prospective pilot study, the same students who had completed the Attributional Style Scale, and who were faced with an exam, rated what grade they would consider a failure before they took the exam. It was found that students who actually attained what they considered a grade low enough to be a failure were more likely to *become* depressed (i.e., it was found that students, who, eight weeks before, had made stable and global attributions for failure on the Attributional Style Scale, were more likely to be depressed after attaining a low grade on the exam).

In conclusion, limited experimental evidence exists in support of the original learned-helplessness theory of depression. A reformulation of that model based on attributional theory has been proposed; a preliminary study suggests that the association between degree of depression and attributional style is in the direction predicted by the revised theory of learned helplessness.

Epidemiological Considerations in Depression

A number of research findings of an epidemiological nature are relevant to an understanding of depression. The prevalence (number of cases of diagnosable episodes of depression at any point in time) has typically been estimated at between 3% and 4% (Lehman, 1971). The National Institute of Mental Health (1970) estimated that in any given year, 15% of all adults experience a clinically significant depressive episode. The commonness of depression is further illustrated by the finding (Amenson & Lewinsohn, 1979) that more than half (62% of the women and 49% of the men) of the subjects in two general community samples were diagnosed, by the Research Diagnostic Criteria (RDC) (Spitzer, Endicott, & Robins, 1978) criteria, as having experienced a diagnosable episode of depression at some time during their lives. The oft-quoted metaphor that depression is the common cold of mental health (e.g., Seligman, 1975) seems most appropriate.

Perhaps the most consistent epidemiological finding concerning depression is the substantial sex difference in prevalence: a female preponderance (often 2:1) is almost always reported (Weissman & Klerman, 1977). In their extensive study on the sex difference in prevalence of unipolar depression, Amenson and Lewinsohn (1979) found that the incidences of depression (i.e., the number of persons without a history of previous depression who became depressed during the course of the study) in men and women were quite comparable

(6.9% vs. 7.1%). Women did not have longer-lasting episodes; nor were there any differences in age at first onset. The major difference between the sexes was observed in persons with a history of previous depression. Women with a history of previous depression were much more likely to become depressed again (21.8%) than men with a history of previous depression (12.9%). Thus, it is clear that persons with a previous history of depression, and especially females, are at very high risk, and treatment and *prevention* programs should be aimed at them.

The relationship between age and depression is less clear. On the basis of the studies reviewed by Gurland (1976), it appears that when psychiatric diagnosis is used as the criterion, high rates of depressive disorders occur between the ages of 25 and 65 years, with a decline in younger and older groups. However, these data are probably distorted by the demonstrated underutilization of mental health services on the part of elderly people and by the tendency on the part of clinicians to underdiagnose depression among elderly people (Ernst, Badash, Beran, Kosovsky, & Kleinhauz, 1977). There is confusion among practitioners and researchers alike about how to distinguish between complaints due to "normal aging" and those that are due to real depressive disorder (Gurland, 1976; Raskin & Jarvik, 1979).

Another important epidemiological fact about depression is its time-limited and episodic nature (e.g., Beck, 1967; Weissman & Paykel, 1974). The mean length of episodes is reported as seven months by Robins and Guze (1969), and the median as 22 weeks by Amenson and Lewinsohn (1979). With and without treatment, most depressed patients improve. However, there is a small minority of patients (approximately 15%) who remain chronic, or in partial remission, and this subgroup needs to be studied more carefully (Weissman & Klerman, 1977).

Although exact suicide rates among depressed persons are difficult to pinpoint, the probability of self-injurious and suicidal behavior is significantly elevated in depressed populations. The suicide rate of depressed individuals exceeds that of people with any other psychological disorder (Becker, 1974). Lehman (1971) estimated that 1 out of 200 depressed persons commit suicide. The death rate, from all causes, for depressed females is twice, and for males triple, the normal rate. Any clinician involved in the diagnosis and treatment of depressed individuals needs to be able to assess the risk of suicide and to take appropriate preventive steps. Several studies (e.g., Burglass & Horton, 1974) indicate that on the basis of relatively simple information, it is possible to make quantitative predictions about the probability of serious suicidal behavior on the part of the patient.

Assessment of Depression

A major difficulty with the term *depression* is that it is commonly used both as a construct and as a designation of specific behavioral events. In the former usage, the term *depression* is used in a diverse set of circumstances, and the nature of these circumstances is frequently neither well defined nor consistent from one clinician to another. Used as a construct, *depression* implies the existence of a distinct and consistent set of internal events and behaviors that is characteristic of all "depressed" individuals.

Inadequacies in the use of the construct of *depression* have led some behavior therapists to reject such a diagnostic label because of its lack of precise behavioral referents. This position denies the existence of a unique syndrome (or symptom cluster) for which a specific term (*depression*) is needed. Rather, they concern themselves with the occurrence of specific behaviors in individual depressed patients, such as the low rate of social behavior, sadness, and verbal expressions of guilt and personal inadequacy.

While there can be no question of the legitimacy of this position, which focuses attention on the details of the individual patient's behaviors, certain evidence suggests that this may not be the most adequate conceptualization of depression. Analyses of the behaviors that are commonly exhibited by persons who have been diagnosed as depressed (e.g., "bootstrap" approaches, such as that of Grinker et al., 1961) indicate substantial agreement as to the constituents of the depression syndrome that extends across studies.

That is, good agreement exists as to the behaviors and symptoms that characterize "depressed" individuals.

The fact that considerable agreement can be found on the behavioral components of the depression syndrome has been used to postulate the existence of a syndrome that may be labeled as *depression,* even though some specific behavioral manifestations of depression differ from one individual to the next. While not denying the importance of schedules of reinforcement or of the operant characteristics of depressive behaviors, this position views depression as a *psychopathological condition* or syndrome whose existence can be defined in terms of the occurrence (frequency and intensity) of certain kinds of behaviors and symptoms. This syndrome includes verbal statements of dysphoria, self-depreciation, guilt, material burden, social isolation, somatic symptoms, and a reduced rate of behavior.

Given this conceptualization, the assessment of depressed patients has several related goals:

1. *Differential diagnosis.* Assessment must first determine whether or not depression is *the,* or at least *a,* problem for the individual.
2. *Functional diagnosis and identification of targets for intervention.* Assessment should also identify events and behavior patterns that are functionally related to the person's depression.
3. *Evaluation.* Evaluation involves periodic assessment not only of changes in depression level but also of concomitant changes in the events presumed to be related to the patient's depression. This two-pronged approach to assessment allows the therapist (researcher) to evaluate the effectiveness of treatment in changing the targeted behavior patterns and also to determine whether these are accompanied by changes in depression level.

Differential Diagnosis

The diagnosis of depression is rendered difficult because the term *depression* does not have a single, generally accepted set of referents. Consequently, individuals who are labeled depressed are quite heterogeneous. Given this heterogeneity it is especially important that one explicitly define the criteria that are used to diagnose patients as depressed.

The differential diagnosis of depression can be accomplished by four different, but complementary, methods: (1) psychiatric diagnosis; (2) symptom ratings; (3) self-report depression scales; and (4) observations of overt behavior.

Psychiatric Diagnosis. Even though behaviorally oriented clinicians, and many others, have questioned the adequacy of psychiatric diagnosis, it is by far the most commonly used diagnostic procedure. Furthermore, there is evidence that with the use of recently developed interview schedules, such as the Schedule for Affective Disorders and Schizophrenia (Endicott & Spitzer, 1978), and diagnostic systems, such as the Research Diagnostic Criteria (RDC) (Spitzer *et al.*, 1978), very good interrater reliability, can be achieved.

The RDC provides operational definitions for many of the subtypes of depression that have at one time or another been thought to be important; these subtypes are treated as not being mutually exclusive. Thus, the RDC is the most elaborate and probably the best currently available diagnostic system for the affective disorders. Its use in research studies is recommended, so that patient samples can be compared across studies. The other major diagnostic systems are the Diagnostic and Statistical Manual of mental disorders, second edition (DSM II; 1968), now replaced by the DSM III (1980).

The DSM II allowed for four "psychotic" depressions (schizoaffective, involutional melancholia, manic-depressive, and psychotic depressive reaction) and for one "neurotic" depression (depressive neurosis). Involutional melancholia has been eliminated from the newer schemata because there is little rational basis for using a separate diagnostic category simply on the basis of the age of onset of the disorder (Beck, 1967; Rosenthal, 1968). The neurotic versus psychotic depression *dichotomy*, which implied that these were qualitatively different types of disorders, has also been eliminated.

Patients with manic, and those with a history of both manic and depressive, episodes have always been recognized as a separate diagnostic group. In the DSM III, a manic episode is defined by the presence of at least one distinct period of elevated, expansive, or irritable mood, associated with a specified number of manic symptoms. Whether or not the patient is also psychotic (defined by the presence of delusions or hallucinations) is indicated by a "level-of-severity" rating. A diagnosis of bipolar affective disorder is given to a patient who is currently depressed and who also has a history of one or more manic episodes, or vice versa. The general distinction between unipolar and bipolar depressions is becoming increasingly recognized as important to therapy outcome. There is evidence that these two subgroups differ in response to pharmacological intervention (Morris & Beck, 1974) and that they may have different genetic and/or biochemical bases (Becker, 1977; Cadoret & Tanna, 1977).

The DSM III uses one major category ("Affective Disorders") within which three subgroups are distinguished. The first group is termed "Episodic Affective Disorders." The term *episodic* is used to indicate that there is a period of disorder that is clearly distinguishable from previous functioning. The second group is referred to as "Chronic Affective Disorders." The term *chronic* is used to indicate a long-standing (lasting at least two years) disorder that usually does not have a clear onset. The disturbance in mood and related symptoms may be sustained throughout the period or may be intermittent. The third group, "Atypical Affective Disorders," is a residual category for individuals with a mood disturbance that cannot be classified as either episodic or chronic. Within each of the three groups, distinctions are made between manic (hypomanic), major depressive (unipolar), and bipolar (cyclothymic) disorders, based on whether both manic and depressive episodes are involved or only one of them is involved.

Symptom Ratings. Another way of measuring the presence and severity of the manifestations of depression is through ratings on items presumed to represent the symptoms of depression. Such items, and their broader dimensions, have been identified in descriptive studies of depressed individuals (e.g., Grinker *et al.*, 1961). On the basis of such studies, there is considerable agreement as to the constituents of the depression syndrome. The symptoms of depression may be grouped into six general categories: dysphoria, reduced rate of behavior, social-interactional problems, guilt, material burden, and somatic symptoms. Depressed patients manifest different combinations of these.

The task of assessing the presence and severity of the phenomena of depression is facilitated by the use of one of several available interviewer rating-scales. Among the better-known scales are the Feelings and Concerns Checklist (Grinker *et al.*, 1961), the Hamilton Rating Scale for Depression (Hamilton, 1960, 1967), and the more global ratings of the Raskin Depression Scales (Raskin, Schulterbrandt, Reatig, Crook, & Odle, 1974). Other similar rating scales are the Psychiatric Judgment of Depression Scale (Overall, 1962) and the Depression Rating Scale (Wechsler, Grosser, & Busfield, 1963). When used by well-trained raters, these scales possess high interrater reliability. They differentiate significantly between depressed and nondepressed patients, and between depressed patients differing with respect to intensity of depression.

Levitt and Lubin (1975) list 23 self-administered depression scales. Only the more popular ones are mentioned here. All of them have been shown to correlate significantly with each other (e.g., Lubin, 1967; Zung, Richards, & Short, 1965) and to correlate substantially with interview ratings. They differ from each other in terms of the number of items, the types of symptoms represented by the items, and the time frame for which ratings are made. Since elderly individuals tend to acknowledge more somatic symptoms (Gaitz, 1977) and to check fewer socially undesirable items (Harnatz & Shader, 1975), there is a significant question about whether the self-report depression scales are in fact measuring the same phenomena in the elderly as they do in younger persons (Gallagher, McGarvey, Zelinksi, & Thompson, 1978). With the exception of the Minnesota Multiphasic Personality Inventory (MMPI)—D Scale (Dahlstrom, Welsh, & Dahlstrom, 1972) and the Depression Adjective Checklist (Lubin, 1967), available measuring instruments have not been standardized on elderly samples.

The best known of the self-report measures for depression is the D Scale of the MMPI. It

has been used widely for the measurement of depression for clinical and research purposes. For example, Lewinsohn and his colleagues (e.g., Lewinsohn & Libet, 1972) have used multiple MMPI criteria to define depressed populations for research.

By far the most popular brief self-report depression inventory is the Beck Depression Inventory (BDI; Beck, Ward, Mendelson, Mock, & Erbaugh, 1961) consisting of 21 items. Beck and Beck (1972) developed a shorter version of the BDI that has only 13 items, which correlated .96 with the original BDI. Another useful test is the Self-Rating Depression Scale (SDS; Zung *et al.*, 1965; Zung, 1973), which consists of 20 statements.

The Center for Epidemiologic Studies—Depression Scale (CES-D; Radloff, 1977) is a 20-item self-report scale selected from previously validated scales (e.g., the MMPI-D Scale, the Zung SDS, and the BDI). The wording of the items is simple. The time frame for rating is clearly specified in the directions and refers to the *past week*.

The Depression Adjective Check List (DACL) was developed by Lubin (1965, 1967, 1977) and consists of seven parallel lists of adjectives designed to provide a measure of what has been called *state depression* (i.e., the individual's mood at a particular moment in time). The subject is asked to "Check the words which describe *How you feel now—today*." The availability of alternate forms and their brevity make the DACL especially useful for repeated measurement research. The DACL differs from the previously described self-report depression scales in sampling a much more limited range of depression behavior (i.e., depressed affect), in contrast to the BDI and the SDS, which include items involving overt-motor, physiological, and other cognitive manifestations. The DACL is somewhat less valuable for pre- and posttreatment assessment because of the large day-to-day intrasubject variability of DACL scores.

An even simpler method of assessing depressed affect is to have patients rate their mood on a line that is defined as representing a continuum from "best mood" to "worst mood."

Assessment of Overt Behavior. The construct of depression includes a variety of relatively specific overt behaviors, and a number of methods have been developed to measure them. A Ward Behavior Checklist for use with hospitalized patients has been described by Williams, Barlow, and Agras (1972). The presence or absence of simple, observable behavior is rated by aides using a time-sampling procedure (e.g., once per hour). Excellent interrater reliability (96%) was reported for this scale.

There have been other attempts to count specific behaviors in depressed patients. Reisinger (1972) used a time-sampling method to count the frequency of crying and smiling behavior. Interrater reliability exceeded 90% for observation periods of up to two hours. Johansson, Lewinsohn, and Flippo (1969) and Robinson and Lewinsohn (1973) used a coding system developed by Lewinsohn (1974) to partition verbal behavior into discrete response categories. McLean, Ogston, and Grauer (1973) described a simplified method of measuring verbal behavior based on Lewinsohn's coding system. Patients were required to make half-hour tape recordings of a problem discussion with their spouse at home. These recordings were separated into 30-sec intervals and coded for positive and negative initiations and reactions. Interrater agreement was high.

Fuchs and Rehm (1977) videotaped 10-min segments of interaction among groups of depressed subjects. The number of statements spoken in 10 min was counted. Interrater agreement ranged from 83% to 100% with a mean of 87%.

Kupfer, Weiss, Detre, Foster, Delgado, and McPartland (1974) described an apparatus that records activity in inpatient settings. A miniature transmitter, with a range of 100 feet, is worn on a leather wristband. Receivers transform data into pulses, which are read out digitally as the number of counts per minute. This measure of psychomotor activity was shown to possess high reliability (e.g., between wrist and ankle transmitters). It has also been shown to be correlated with various sleep parameters, such as EEG movement, minutes awake, time asleep, REM (rapid-eye-movement) time, and REM activity.

Functional Diagnosis and Identification of Targets for Intervention

Functional diagnosis involves pinpointing specific person–environment interactions and events related to depression. This part of the diagnostic process is needed to guide the formulation of a treatment plan designed to change the events contributing to depression. Behavior patterns may be postulated as being functionally related to depression on the basis of three criteria: (1) if the pattern occurs with increased, or decreased frequency in depressed vis-à-vis appropriate control groups; (2) if the behavior–environment interaction is present when the person is depressed but is absent, or attenuated, when the person is not depressed; and (3) if the occurrence of the person–environment interaction covaries with fluctuations in daily mood.

The following areas may be listed as functionally related to depression: social-interactional problems, depressive cognitions, a low rate of engagement in pleasant activities, and a high rate of occurrence of unpleasant events.

Social Behavior: Significance and Assessment. There now appears to be a general consensus that depressed persons, as a group, manifest social-interactional problems (e.g., Lewinsohn, Biglan, & Zeiss, 1976; Weissman & Paykel, 1974; Youngren & Lewinsohn, 1980). Complaints about various inadequacies in social relationships are frequently among the problems that are identified by the patient.

An instrument designed to assess aspects of social behavior by self-report is the Interpersonal Events Schedule (IES; Youngren, Zeiss, & Lewinsohn, 1975). The IES consists of a list of 160 items, all of which involve interpersonal activities or cognitions concerning such interactions. The item pool was drawn largely from a variety of preexisting instruments. Subjects complete ratings of the frequency and the subjective comfort and discomfort of events. A cross-product score of these ratings is assumed to provide an approximate measure of the response-contingent positive social reinforcement obtained, or of the interpersonal aversiveness experienced.

At the level of self-report, the following have been found to be associated with depression: (1) infrequent engagement, discomfort, and low levels of obtained pleasure in social activity (Youngren & Lewinsohn, 1980; (2) discomfort in being assertive (Langone, 1979; Sanchez, 1977; Youngren & Lewinsohn, 1980); and (3) discomfort experienced in conjunction with negative cognitions concerning personal interactions (Youngren & Lewinsohn, 1980). Depressed persons tend to feel that they are boring, worry about appearing foolish, feel themselves to be inferior and socially incompetent, and have conflicted interactions with their spouse or partner (Lewinsohn & Talkington, 1979; Weissman & Paykel, 1974).

It is essential to be specific in describing and delineating particular social skill problems if manifested by a given depressed individual and to focus interventions on the modification of the behaviors relevant to these problems. Several reviews of the literature relevant to the assessment of social behavior have appeared in the last few years (e.g., Arkowitz, Lichtenstein, McGovern, & Hines, 1975; Curran, 1977; Lewinsohn & Lee, 1981; Sundberg, Snowden, & Reynolds, 1978), and hence no systematic review is attempted here.

Cognitions: Significance and Assessment. There is no doubt that the phenomena of depression include cognitive manifestations, and a number of relevant assessment devices have been developed.

Negative Expectancies. The relevance of negative expectations to depression has been stressed by Beck (1967), and a number of different tests have been developed to measure expectancies. Weintraub *et al.* (1974) devised a test consisting of incomplete stories involving a principal character with whom the subject was asked to identify; the subject was asked to select alternative story completions. The expected relationship between negative expectancies and depression level was found. Another instrument designed to assess a respondent's negative expectancies is the Hopelessness Scale (Beck *et al.* 1974), which consists of 20 true–false items. The scale was found to have a high degree of internal consistency, showed good correlation with clinical ratings of hopelessness, and was sensitive to changes in the patient's state of depression over time.

The Subjective Probability Questionnaire (SPQ) is yet another attempt to operationalize Beck's cognitive triad (Muñoz & Lewinsohn, 1976c). The SPQ consists of 80 statements constructed along three dichotomous and crossed dimensions: self versus world, present versus future, and positive versus negative. Respondents indicate on an 11-point scale (0

= 0% probability; 10 = 100% probability) "What you think the chances are that the statement is true or that it will become true." The SPQ has been shown to possess a good test–retest reliability and to discriminate well between depressed and nondepressed samples (Muñoz, 1977).

Cognitive Distortion. A number of different conceptual distortions have been hypothesized by Beck (1963) as being uniquely associated with depression. A measure of cognitive distortion in depression has been developed by Hammen and Krantz (1976; Krantz & Hammen 1978). The Hammen and Krantz procedure assesses an individual's interpretations of events depicted in brief stories, and it measures the presence of a tendency to select the most depressed and distorted response options. Depressed individuals have consistently been found to select a greater number of depressed and distorted responses.

Irrational Beliefs and Dysfunctional Attitudes. A number of scales have been developed to measure the degree to which respondents hold various irrational beliefs (Murphy & Ellis, 1976). Nelson (1977) found a significant correlation between scores on the Irrational Beliefs Test (Jones, 1968) and the Beck Depression Inventory. The Personal Belief Inventory (PBI; Muñoz & Lewinsohn, 1976b) consists of 30 statements representing irrational beliefs hypothesized to be important in the occurrence of depression. The PBI was found to discriminate well between depressed and nondepressed control groups. A methodologically similar instrument is represented by the Dysfunctional Attitudes Scale (Weissman & Beck, 1978), which consists of 40 Likert-type items and has two alternate forms. The Dysfunctional Attitude Scale also probes the respondent's degree of agreement with beliefs hypothesized by Beck as characterizing depressed patients.

Negative Thoughts. The Cognitive Events Schedule (CES; Muñoz & Lewinsohn, 1976a) was intended to probe for the content of thoughts by asking the respondent to report the frequency of occurrence, and the emotional impact, of each of 160 thoughts during the past 30 days. The frequency of occurrence of each specific thought is rated on a 3-point scale, and its impact is rated on a 5-point scale.

193

Paralleling the SPQ, CES items were constructed along three dichotomous and crossed dimensions: self versus world, present versus future, and positive versus negative. Depressed individuals have been shown to report a much larger number of negative and a smaller number of positive thoughts than nondepressed controls (Lewinsohn, Larson, & Munoz, 1978).

Attributions of Causality. The causation of outcomes is central to learned-helplessness theory. Locus of control is assumed to be a cognitive set within this framework, and it has been typically measured with the Locus of Control Scale (Rotter, 1966, 1975). Dimensions of behavioral attributions can be assessed with the Multidimensional Multiattributional Causality Scale (Lefcourt, 1978). Seligman *et al.* (1979) reported on the use of their Attributional Style Scale; the results were in accord with the reformulated learned-helplessness theory.

Engagement in Pleasant Activities: Significance and Assessment. It is well established that depressed individuals as a group engage in relatively few activities, and in even fewer activities that they consider pleasant or rewarding.

The patient's rate of engagement in pleasant activities can be assessed in several ways:

1. The patient may fill out the Pleasant Events Schedule (PES; MacPhillamy & Lewinsohn, 1971). The PES contains 320 events generated by exhaustively sampling events that were reported to be sources of pleasure by highly diverse samples of people. The person is asked to rate both the frequency and the subjective enjoyability of each event; a multiplicative cross-product of these ratings is assumed to provide an approximate measure of response-contingent positive reinforcement. Extensive normative data and results consistent with the construct validity of the scale have been presented elsewhere (Lewinsohn & Amenson, 1978; MacPhillamy & Lewinsohn, 1975).
2. The subject may monitor his/her daily rate of engagement in pleasant activities over a period of time through the use of "activity schedules" (Lewinsohn, 1976).

An activity schedule consists of the items judged by the patient to be most pleasant, and patients are asked to indicate at the end of each day which of the activities he/she performed. Fuchs and Rehm (1977) employed an activity schedule procedure in a self-control–oriented therapy program.

3. Harmon, Nelson, and Hayes (1978) described the use of a portable timer that is carried by the patient and that is used to cue self-monitoring on a variable-interval schedule of one hour. The person is provided with a list of the variable intervals used to set the timer and is asked to set the timer for the first interval on awakening in the morning and to reset it for the next interval immediately after being cued. When cued, the person is instructed to record a description of her/his activity, in addition to a numerical rating of pleasantness from 1 to 5. In contrast to the procedure used by the Lewinsohn group, which is not reactive (Lewinsohn, 1976), the Harmon *et al.* procedure apparently was quite reactive, resulting in substantial increases in engagement in pleasant activities.

Aversive Events: Significance and Assessment. Aversive events have been shown to be related to depression in the following ways:

1. Aversive events have been found to precede the occurrence of clinical depression (e.g., Brown, Bhrolchain, & Harris, 1975; Paykel, Myers, Dienelt, Klerman, Lindenthal, & Pepper, 1969).
2. Depressed persons have been found to be particularly sensitive to aversive events (e.g., Lewinsohn, Lobitz, & Wilson, 1973; Lewinsohn & Talkington, 1979).
3. The rate of occurrence of aversive events covaries with dysphoria (Lewinsohn & Talkington, 1979; Rehm, 1978).

The most frequently used assessment device for the occurrence of life events has been the Social Readjustment Rating Scale (SRRS; Holmes & Rahe, 1967). It consists of 43 items intended to represent fairly common events arising from family, personal, occupational, and financial situations that require, or signify, changes in ongoing adjustment. The occurrence of the events during the preceding six months is established during an interview. Weights are assigned to each item based on ratings made by a sample of judges (Holmes & Rahe, 1967). However, there are many serious methodological and conceptual problems that limit the potential usefulness and the theoretical interpretation of results obtained with the SRRS (Rabkin & Struening, 1976). Instruments that incorporate refinements suggested by criticisms of the SRRS are the PERI (Psychiatric Epidemiology Research Interview) developed by Dohrenwend, Krasnoff, Askenasy, and Dohrenwend (1978), the LES (Life Experiences Survey) developed by Sarason, Johnson, and Siegel (1977), and the UES (Unpleasant Events Schedule) developed by Lewinsohn and Talkington (1979).

Events for the PERI were selected from a population of events generated by asking respondents, "What was the last major event in your life that, for better or worse, interrupted or changed your usual activities?" The 102 events obtained were then rated on the dimension of "change" by a probability-randomized sample from New York City (Dohrenwend, 1978).

The LES is a 57-item self-report measure that asks respondents to indicate the events that they have experienced during the past year. The respondents are then asked to indicate (1) whether they viewed the event as positive or negative at the time and (2) to rate the impact of the particular event on their lives. The LES thus approaches the individualized approach to the measurement of life events advocated by Brown (e.g., Brown, 1974).

The UES consists of 320 events generated on the basis of an extensive search of events considered unpleasant, distressing, and aversive by many people. As with the PES, individuals are asked to rate both the frequency and the subjective aversiveness of an event; a multiplicative cross-product is derived from these ratings. Data on the psychometric properties of the UES—including test–retest reliability, aspects of validity and internal consistency, and relationships with depression—are provided in Lewinsohn and Talkington (1979) and Lewinsohn, Tursky, and Arconad (1979).

Therapeutic Programs for Depression

While the number of fundamental empirical studies of the etiology and the behavior of depression has grown "arithmetically" in recent years, the number of behavioral treatment-outcome studies of depression has grown "exponentially." Treatment strategies and methods reflect the diversity of models of depression. While different therapies posit specific strategies for alleviating depression, commonalities among the various approaches have been noted (Blaney, 1979; Rehm & Kornblith, 1979). There seems little doubt that a variety of structured behavioral and cognitive therapies are, in fact, efficacious in ameliorating depression (Rehm & Kornblith, 1979). In particular, two studies—Rush, Beck, Kovacs, and Hollon (1977) and McLean and Hakstian (1979)—have demonstrated the superiority of cognitive and/or behavioral treatments over chemotherapy.

Decreasing Unpleasant Events and Increasing Pleasant Activities

A treatment approach has evolved out of Lewinsohn's research and theory emphasizing the role of reinforcement in the etiology and maintenance of depression (Lewinsohn, Biglan, & Zeiss, 1976; Lewinsohn, Youngren, & Grosscup 1980). Being depressed is regarded as resulting from few person–environment interactions with positive outcomes and/or an excess of such interactions with aversive or punishing outcomes. Consequently, this approach aims to change the quality and the quantity of the depressed patient's interactions in the direction of increasing positive and decreasing negative events. The treatment is time-limited (12 sessions) and highly structured, and a therapist's manual is available (Lewinsohn & Grosscup, 1978). During the diagnostic phase, which precedes treatment, extensive use is made of the Pleasant Events Schedule (MacPhillamy & Lewinsohn, 1971) and of the Unpleasant Events Schedule (Lewinsohn, 1975b) to begin to pinpoint specific person–environment interactions related to the patient's depression. An Activity Schedule (Lewinsohn, 1976), consisting of 80 items rated by the patient as most pleasant and frequent and 80 items rated by the patient as most unpleasant and frequent, is constructed. Then, patients begin daily monitoring of the occurrence of pleasant and unpleasant activities and of their mood. The covariation of certain pleasant and unpleasant events with changes in mood is used to pinpoint specific person–environment interactions influencing the patient's dysphoria. Subsequently, the treatment provides assistance to the patient in decreasing the frequency and the subjective aversiveness of unpleasant events in his/her life and then concentrates on increasing pleasant ones.

The general goal of the treatment is to *teach* depressed persons skills that they can use to change problem patterns of interaction with the environment, as well as the skills needed to maintain these changes after the termination of therapy. To accomplish the goals of treatment, the therapist makes use of a wide range of cognitive-behavioral interventions, such as assertion, relaxation training, daily-planning and time-management training, and cognitive procedures intended to allow the person to deal more adaptively with aversive situations. A more detailed description and case illustrations are presented in Lewinsohn, Sullivan, and Grosscup (1980).

Lewinsohn, Youngren, and Grosscup (1980) examined the relationship between reinforcement and depression across four samples of depressives as a result of treatment. They found that the rate of positive reinforcement increased as a function of improvement in clinical depression level. Similarly, the rate of experienced aversiveness diminished as clinical depression decreased. In Lewinsohn, Sullivan, and Grosscup (1980), a program of increasing pleasant events was tested across two samples of depressed individuals, while another sample of patients received therapy emphasizing both decreasing unpleasant events and increasing pleasant events. All three samples demonstrated highly significant amounts of clinical improvement.

Interpersonal Therapy

The interpersonal disturbance model of depression postulated by McLean (McLean, Ogston, & Grauer, 1973; McLean, 1976) regards the depressed person's interaction with

his/her social environment as the basis of the development and the reversal of depression. As McLean views it, depression results when individuals lose the ability to control their interpersonal environment. When ineffective coping techniques are utilized to remedy situational life problems, the consequence may be depression.

From this interpersonal conception of the etiology and the maintenance of depression, McLean (McLean, 1976; McLean & Hakstian, 1979) has developed a treatment program that incorporates techniques of both a behavioral and a cognitive nature, and that has several distinctive features. The unique aspects of McLean's therapy include an emphasis on decision making regarding appropriate intervention components and the incorporation of procedures for involving relevant social-network members (e.g., the spouse) in treatment.

Like most behaviorally oriented treatments, interpersonal therapy is highly structured and is time-limited to approximately 12 weeks. Six specific therapeutic components are suggested by McLean: communication training, behavioral productivity, social interactions, assertiveness, decision making and problem solving, and cognitive self-control.

Communication training attempts to correct two problems: (1) aversive marital interactions producing spouse avoidance-behavior and (2) a constricted quantity and range of interaction sources. Therapy involves a structured type of communication training. It aims to provide an opportunity for positive feedback and enhanced self-esteem and to facilitate other forms of social interaction.

The primary treatment block, especially important in the early stages of therapy, is called *behavioral productivity*. As McLean has noted, successful performance or mastery experiences are the most powerful antidepressant. Tasks are explicitly graduated, with attention focused on the task and what has been accomplished. Reinforcement, preferably of a social nature from significant others, is made contingent on the successful performance of behavioral tasks.

Social interaction, by acting as a reinforcer and by providing an incompatible response to withdrawal, is used to moderate the experience of depression. Graduated performance assignments are employed to promote social engagement and are prompted by rehearsal and by resource-person accompaniment.

Assertiveness training, decision-making, and problem-solving skills, and *cognitive self-control techniques* are implemented as required by the particular individual's condition.

McLean *et al.* (1973) conducted a study to compare the therapeutic efficacy of an earlier version of McLean's therapeutic program to a varied comparison group. Twenty patients, referred by physicians, were randomly assigned to one of two treatment conditions. The experimental group received training in social learning principles, communication skills, and behavioral contracts. Treatment for the comparison group varied as a function of the treatment agency that they were initially referred from but usually involved either medication, group therapy, individual psychotherapy, or some combination of these. The results showed that the experimental condition produced a significant decrease in problem behaviors, as well as improvements in verbal communication style. The experimental group was also less depressed than the control group at the end of treatment. At a three-month follow-up, the treatment effects were maintained.

More recently, McLean and Hakstian (1979) conducted a large-scale treatment outcome study. One hundred and seventy-eight moderately clinically depressed patients were selected on interview screening and psychometric criteria. The subjects were randomly assigned to one of four treatment conditions: behavior therapy as described in McLean (1976), short-term psychotherapy, relaxation training, and drug treatment (amitriptyline). The therapists were selected on the basis of their preferred treatment modality. The patients encouraged their spouses or significant others to participate in the treatment sessions; the treatment took place over 10 weeks of weekly sessions.

The results demonstrated the unequivocal superiority of the behavioral intervention. Behavior therapy was best on 9 of 10 outcome measures immediately after treatment and marginally superior at follow-up (best on 7 of 10 outcome measures). Additionally, behavior therapy showed a significantly lower attrition rate (5%) than the other conditions, which had dropout rates of 26–36%. The psychotherapy treatment proved to be least effective in the

post-treatment and follow-up evaluation periods. Generally it fared worse than the control condition (relaxation training).

Cognitive Therapy

Beck's model of depression assigns the primary causal significance in depression to automatic negative cognitions. Such distorted or unrealistic cognitions are thought to produce misinterpretations of experiences, which lead to affective reactions and other behaviors associated with depression. As one would expect, cognitive therapy aims to assist the client in identifying certain assumptions and themes that are supporting recurrent patterns of stereotypical negative thinking and in pointing out the specific stylistic errors in thinking. Detailed treatment protocols are presented in Rush and Beck (1978) and in Beck, Rush, Shaw, and Emery (1978, 1979).

Cognitive therapy is conceived of as a short-term, time-limited intervention. While both behavioral and cognitive techniques are seen as important in alleviating depression in cognitive therapy, Beck has argued that the former should precede the latter in treatment. In his view, often depressives are initially unable to engage directly in cognitive tasks. At the same time, he considers it a priority to restore a patient's behavioral functioning quickly to counteract withdrawal and to induce involvement in constructive activities. Consequently, behavioral assignments are given to increase environmental input. Additionally, these series of "experiments" enable the patient to test the validity of his/her ideas about him/herself.

To these ends, a number of behavioral techniques are utilized. Graduated task assignments in conjunction with cognitive rehearsal are employed so that patients can test their beliefs about their competence. Activity schedules (e.g., hourly assignments) are also assigned, and patients may be asked to place mastery and pleasure ratings on their scheduled activities. Finally, assertiveness training and role playing may be implemented.

As a patient begins to change his/her negative estimations of his/her capabilities as a result of behavioral exercises, the therapist focuses more directly on the assumed core of depression, namely, cognitions. The therapist teaches the close relationship between feelings, behavior, and thoughts by presenting evidence that the negative way of thinking contributes to depression. The patient learns that there are many ways of interpreting any situation and that a particular interpretation is related to specific feelings. Thus, the therapist assists the patient in searching for alternative interpretations and solutions to problem events. Among the cognitive techniques utilized to ameliorate depression, the triple-column exercise is of particular importance. Patients are asked to identify upsetting events, the nature of the feelings those events elicit, and the automatic negative cognitions associated with dysphoria, and to examine and test the validity of such cognitions on the basis of concrete evidence.

Considerable evidence exists that cognitive therapy is an effective treatment for depression. Rush, Khatami, and Beck (1975) reported that the cognitive and behavioral techniques used in their study produced effective and lasting results with three severely depressed persons with a history of recurrent relapses who had responded poorly to antidepressant medication. Using an A-B-A design, Schmickley (1976) employed cognitive therapy to treat 11 outpatients selected on the basis of MMPI and BDI scores and clinical interview data. While the self-report and observation measures showed improvement during treatment, during the withdrawal phase the improvement lessened. The treatment was not reinstituted and no follow-up was reported.

Gioe (1975) selected 40 college students on the basis of BDI scores. Comparisons were made among a cognitive modification condition, cognitive modification in combination with a "positive group experience," a treatment condition consisting of the "positive group experience" alone, and a waiting-list control. All treatments were given in a group modality, and the results, measured by the BDI, showed that the combined treatment was significantly better than the other conditions. No follow-up was reported.

Taylor and Marshall (1977) compared cognitive therapy with a behavioral approach based on treatment strategies suggested by Ferster (1965), Lazarus (1968), and Lewinsohn (1975a). The subjects were 28 college students selected on the basis of their BDI scores, who were randomly assigned to one of four treatment conditions: cognitive therapy, behavior therapy, a combined cognitive-behavioral treatment, and a waiting-list control. The treatment consisted of six individual sessions. While both the cognitive and the behavioral treatments were more effective than being in the control group according to self-report measures, the combined treatment was more effective than either treatment alone. At a one-month follow-up, however, no significant differences between the cognitive and the behavioral groups could be identified, though the depression scores were generally lower for the cognitive treatment group.

Kovacs and Rush (1976) compared "cognitive-behavioral psychotherapy" with tricyclic antidepressant medication in treating 33 outpatients selected on the basis of scores on the BDI, the Hamilton Scale, and therapists' ratings of symptoms. All subjects were seen individually. Both treatment conditions were found to produce similar decreases in symptoms, although more chemotherapy subjects dropped out of treatment. At six-month follow-up, gains were maintained for both conditions.

Finally, Rush *et al.* (1977) replicated Kovacs and Rush's study with a sample of 41 outpatients carefully selected by means of BDI, Hamilton Scale, and MMPI scores, as well as clinical criteria. The subjects were randomly assigned to treatments and received a mean of 11 weeks of active treatment. Again, the results showed that a higher percentage of chemotherapy patients dropped out of treatment. In contrast to the earlier study, cognitive therapy led to significantly greater improvement on the dependent measures. At three- and six-month follow-ups, this trend continued but was statistically significant only at the three-month period. An important finding was that while only 16% of those treated with cognitive therapy reentered therapy during the follow-up period, *68%* in the chemotherapy sample did so.

Self-Control Therapy

As already noted, Rehm (1977) has proposed a model of depression that emphasizes cognitive distortion processes and the importance of self-administered contingent reward and punishment. Three processes—self-monitoring, self-evaluation, and self-reinforcement—are hypothesized to interact in a feedback loop. Depression, according to Rehm, can be accounted for by a number of deficits in self-control behavior.

A self-control behavior therapy for depression has been described by Fuchs and Rehm (1977). This six-week cumulative, sequential program consists of three phases, during which emphasis is placed on training self-monitoring, self-evaluating, and then self-reinforcing skills. Each phase consists of two therapy sessions. Primarily didactic, the first session of each phase involves a presentation and discussion of self-control principles relevant to the assumed deficits of depression, plus a behavioral homework assignment. In the second of these sessions, the patients review their preceding week's assignment. The principles of self-control are reiterated by the therapist, and appropriate use of these concepts by patients is reinforced.

The self-monitoring phase of treatment involves the use of logs to record positive activities; daily average mood is also noted. In the self-evaluation phase, patients are instructed in setting subgoals for desirable positive activities associated with good mood and to rate their accomplished behaviors toward those goals. Finally, during the self-reinforcement phase, the patients are presented with the general principles of reinforcement and taught to self-reinforce, overtly and covertly.

Fuchs and Rehm (1977) compared a group behavior-therapy program based on self-control principles to a non-specific group-therapy condition and to a waiting-list control-group conditions. The subjects were volunteers who were selected on the basis of MMPI scores and interview criteria. After a six-week treatment period, those in the self-control condition showed clear improvement, which was superior to the control conditions. At a six-week follow-up, the treatment effects were maintained, although differences between conditions had dissipated somewhat.

Rehm, Fuchs, Roth, Kornblith, and Romano (1979) compared 24 volunteer subjects with moderate depression on two treatment conditions: self-control therapy and a social skills treatment (essentially, assertion train-

ing). The results indicated that the social skills subjects improved more in social skills, while the self-control subjects improved more on self-control dependent measures. At six-week follow-up, the treatment effects were maintained.

A Psychoeducational Approach

The most recent experimental development in the behavioral and cognitive treatment of depression has been the use of an explicit educational experience (i.e., a course entitled "Coping with Depression") as the vehicle for treatment (Lewinsohn & Brown, 1979). The course consists of 12 two-hour class sessions spaced out over eight weeks. The typical number of participants has been eight. The course utilizes a textbook *Control Your Depression* (Lewinsohn, Muñoz, Youngren, & Zeiss, 1978) and represents a multicomponent approach emphasizing general self-help skills (two sessions), self-control techniques relevant to thoughts (two sessions), pleasant activities (two sessions), relaxation (two sessions), interpersonal interaction (two sessions), and maintenance (two sessions). The efficacy of the course was evaluated in an initial study (Brown & Lewinsohn, in press; Lewinsohn & Brown, 1979), which was designed to compare three different modes of teaching the course (class, individual tutoring, and minimal phone contact) with a waiting-list control condition. Large and statistically significant clinical improvement was shown in all of the active conditions, which together were significantly superior to the waiting control condition. Improvement shown at the termination of the course was maintained at the one-month and at the six-month follow-up.

An important feature of the "Coping With Depression" courses is that the participants are able to meet in groups to assist each other in overcoming their depression. With relatively few exceptions (e.g., Barerra, 1979; Fuchs & Rehm, 1977), previous cognitive-behavioral treatments have been offered within an individual therapy mode. This is not surprising, since most authorities in the area of group therapy (e.g., Yalom, 1975) advise against homogeneous groups of depressed patients. Our results indicate that within the structure presented by the course, depressives work together very effectively. Another feature of the course is that it represents a community-oriented outreach approach to impact on the great majority of depressives who never avail themselves of the services of clinics and mental health professionals. The educational focus reduces the stigma involved in seeking "psychiatric" or "psychological" treatment, which is especially important to the elderly depressed.

"Eclectic" Tactics in Treating Depression

Several investigators have explored therapy programs whose elements are not commonly associated with the treatment of depression. Perhaps the most distinctive of these are the comparisons between running or jogging and individual psychotherapy in two studies conducted and reported by Greist, Klein, Eischens, Faris, Gurman, and Morgan (1979). In their pilot study, 28 patients were randomly assigned to running or either time-limited or time-unlimited psychotherapy. The subjects were selected on the basis of scores on the Depression Symptom Checklist-90 (Derogatis, Lipman, & Covi, 1973). Also, they had to meet RDC criteria for minor depression. The results of two studies indicated that the running treatment was as effective in alleviating depressive symptomatology and target complaints as either of the psychotherapy treatments.

Assertion training has also been used with depressed individuals. It was first reported in case studies by Wolpe and Lazarus (1966). Lazarus (1968) trained a depressed outpatient to make assertive statements and requests of significant others with whom she was experiencing frequent conflict. As a result of these skills, her depressive symptoms were reportedly alleviated, although no data were presented. Following the application of assertiveness training in the treatment of one of his patients, Seitz (1971) reported a significant decrease in the level of depression.

Sanchez, Lewinsohn, and Larson (1980) reported the results of a treatment outcome study in which subassertive depressed outpatients were randomly assigned either to an assertion-training group or to a "traditional" (i.e., insight-oriented) therapy group. The re-

sults indicated that assertion training was effective in increasing self-reported assertiveness and in alleviating depression. Additionally, it was more effective than the traditional psychotherapy that lasted for a comparable period of time.

Because marital relationships are often a problem for depressed individuals (Coleman & Miller, 1975; Weiss & Aved, 1978; Weissman & Paykel, 1974), treatment approaches focusing on the marital relationship have also been described (e.g., Lewinsohn & Shaw, 1969; McLean, Ogston, & Grauer, 1973; Stuart, 1967).

Final Comments

It is clear that cognitive-behavioral approaches and conceptualizations are characterized by great diversity but that empirical support for the therapeutic efficacy of each has been provided. Since all are theoretically derived (i.e., they are specifically designed to modify *the* specific cognitions and/or behaviors assumed by the theory to be a critical antecedent of depression), a question needs to be raised: How could they all be effective? Our own thinking has been greatly influenced by the results of a particular treatment outcome (Zeiss *et al.*, 1979). In this study, three treatments (cognitive, pleasant activities, and social skill training) were compared. The results indicated that while all three treatments were equally effective in reducing depression level, the changes on the intervening dependent measures were not specific to the treatment (i.e., the thinking of the social skill treatment patients changed as much as the thinking of those in the cognitive treatment and vice versa). The major finding of this study (i.e., that the treatments did not selectively impact the relevant target behaviors) was completely unexpected, and we feel that it has theoretical and clinical implications.

On the basis of these results, we have tried to hypothesize what the "critical components" might be for successful short-term cognitive-behavioral therapy for depression (Zeiss, Lewinsohn, & Muñoz, 1979), to wit:

1. Therapy should begin with an elaborated, well-planned rationale.

2. Therapy should provide training in skills that the patient can utilize to feel more effective in handling his/her daily life.
3. Therapy should emphasize the independent use of these skills by the patient outside the therapy context and must provide enough structure so that the attainment of independent skill is possible for the patient.
4. Therapy should encourage the patient to believe that improvement in mood is caused by the patient's increased skillfulness, not by the therapist's skillfulness.

Similarly, McLean and Hakstian (1979) noted that high structure, a social learning rationale, a goal attainment focus, and increasing social interaction were significant elements in the behavioral treatment of depression.

Conclusions and Recommendations

It is clear that the past 10 years have been a period of very busy and exciting progress in the psychological treatment of depression and in depression theory. Great strides have been made in the differential diagnosis of depressive disorders. Existing assessment procedures have the capacity to generate reliable and replicable data on patients' depression in terms of specific symptoms, manifestations, severity level, and perhaps even subtypes. Investigators should be expected to define their populations in much more rigorous terms than has been the case in the past. It is no longer defensible for researchers (or clinicians) to base their diagnosis of depression entirely on arbitrary cutoff scores on self-report inventories like the Beck Depression Inventory (Beck, 1967). Self-report depression measures like the Center for Epidemiologic Studies–Depression Scale (Radloff, 1977) are very useful as screening devices but need to be followed by a clinical interview.

An area of weakness is the differential diagnosis and treatment of depression among the elderly. Differential diagnosis in the elderly is complicated both by the increase in the incidence of physical illness and of somatic symp-

toms with age and by the difficulty in distinguishing the symptoms of depression from those of senile dementia (Epstein, 1976). More work needs to be done to develop instruments appropriate to elderly populations and to standardize existing instruments across the total age range. Existing treatment programs will need to be modified and then tested with elderly persons (e.g., Gallagher, in press).

Depression in childhood and early adolescence is becoming an area of increasing importance and interest. Promising new developments are being reported, particularly in the area of assessment. A self-report rating of childhood depression, the Children's Depression Inventory (CDI), has been developed by Kovacs and Beck (1977). A Peer Nomination Inventory of Depression (PNID) has been found to possess good psychometric properties and has been used to identify depression in normal populations of children (Lefkowitz & Tesiny, 1980).

At the level of depression theory, there has been a shift from global (and obviously too simple) single-sentence theoretical statements ("Depression is due to . . .") to more sophisticated conceptualizations that begin to recognize the complexity and the diversity of the phenomena of depression. The general outline of the end point of depression theorizing may have been anticipated by Akiskal and McKinney (1973) and by Becker (1974) in their attempts to provide "unified" hypotheses to integrate the many relevant clinical, experimental, genetic, biochemical, and neurophysiological findings.

At the level of empirical research, it is important that studies include a carefully defined and matched nondepressed "psychiatric control" group (i.e., persons who show psychological deviations *other* than depression). The inclusion of a psychiatric control group permits the attribution of observed group differences to depression rather than to psychological deviation. Research is also needed to assess the *etiological* significance of the various variables that have been shown to be uniquely associated with depression. On the basis of existing research findings, it is impossible to determine whether the factors that have been shown to be correlated with depression constitute antecedent conditions for the occurrence of depression, or whether they are secondary to depression. Support for the etiological significance of the problem behaviors that have been found to be associated with depression can come only from longitudinal studies of the sequence of events leading to depression.

At a recent conference convened by the National Institute of Mental Health (Rehm, 1979), it was concluded that there is promising evidence of the efficacy of behavior therapies in the treatment of depression. At the same time, a number of serious limitations to this conclusion were noted. Among other things, the treatments that have been developed differ in certain specific components, although they also overlap to a considerable degree. Yet, the *effective* ingredients of behavior therapy programs for depression are essentially unknown. The *relative* contribution of specific components, and of so-called nonspecific effects, clearly needs to be investigated, and the results of such studies will be important theoretically.

Not all therapeutic elements are appropriate for every depressed individual. Hence, research efforts need to be concerned with matching patients to treatments. Additionally, attention needs to be focused on developing and testing maintenance programs for depressives treated by behavioral and cognitive treatments. More needs to be known, as well, about the distinguishing characteristics of patients who do not respond to behavioral and cognitive treatments. Finally, as research produces evidence of antecedent conditions and/or predispositional variables in the etiology of depression, prevention programs directed at high-risk populations should be tested and employed.

References

Abraham, K. Notes on the psychoanalytic investigation and treatment of manic-depressive insanity and allied conditions. *Selected Papers on Psychoanalysis*. New York: Basic Books, 1960.

Abramson, L. Y., & Sackheim, H. A. A paradox in depression: Uncontrollability and self-blame. *Psychological Bulletin*, 1977, *84*, 838–851.

Abramson, L. Y., Garber, J., Edwards, N. B., & Seligman, M. E. P. Expectancy changes in depression and schizophrenia. *Journal of Abnormal Psychology*, 1978, *87*, 102–109.

Abramson, L. Y., Seligman, M. E. P., & Teasdale, J. D. Learned helplessness in humans: Critique and reformulation. *Journal of Abnormal Psychology*, 1978, *87*, 49–74.

Akiskal, H. S., & McKinney, W. T., Jr. Depressive disorders: Toward a unified hypothesis. *Science*, 1973, *182*, 20–29.

Alloy, L. B., & Abramson, L. Y. Judgment of contingency in depressed students: Sadder but wiser? *Journal of Experimental Psychology: General*, 1979, *108*, 441–485.

Amenson, C. S., & Lewinsohn, P. M. An investigation into the observed sex differences in prevalence of unipolar depression. *Journal of Abnormal Psychology*, 1981, *90*, 1–13.

Arkowitz, H., Lichtenstein, E., McGovern, K., & Hines, P. The behavioral assessment of social competence in males. *Behavior Therapy*, 1975, *6*, 3–13.

Bandura, A. *Social learning theory*. Englewood Cliffs, N.J.: Prentice-Hall, 1977.

Barrera, M. An evaluation of a brief group therapy for depression. *Journal of Consulting and Clinical Psychology*, 1979, *47*, 413–415.

Beck, A. T. Thinking and depression: Idiosyncratic content and cognitive distortions. *Archives of General Psychiatry*, 1963, *9*, 324–333.

Beck, A. T. Thinking and depression. II: Theory and therapy. *Archives of General Psychiatry*, 1964, *10*, 561–571.

Beck, A. T. *Depression: Clinical, experimental and theoretical aspects*. New York: Harper & Row, 1967.

Beck, A. T. Cognitive therapy: Nature and relation to behavior therapy. *Behavior Therapy*, 1970, *1*, 184–200.

Beck, A. T. *Cognitive therapy and the emotional disorders*. New York: International Universities Press, 1976.

Beck, A. T., & Beck, R. W. Screening depressed patients in family practice—A rapid technique. *Postgraduate Medicine*, 1972, *52*, 81–85.

Beck, A. T., Ward, C. H., Mendelson, M., Mock, J., & Erbaugh, J. An inventory for measuring depression. *Archives of General Psychiatry*, 1961, *4*, 561–571.

Beck, A. T., Weissman, A., Lester, D., & Traxler, L. The measurement of pessimism: The hopelessness scale. *Journal of Consulting and Clinical Psychology*, 1974, *42*, 861–865.

Beck, A. T., Rush, A. J., Shaw, B. F., & Emery, G. *Cognitive therapy of depression: A treatment manual*. Unpublished manuscript, University of Pennsylvania, 1978.

Beck, A. T., Rush, A. J., Shaw, B. F., & Emery, G. *Cognitive therapy of depression*. New York: Guilford Press, 1979.

Becker, J. *Depression: Theory and research*. New York: V. H. Winston & Sons, 1974.

Becker, J. *Affective disorders*. Morristown, N.J.: General Learning Press, 1977.

Bibring, E. The mechanism of depression. In P. Greenacre (Ed.), *Affective disorders*. New York: International Universities Press, 1953.

Blaney, P. H. Contemporary theories of depression: Critique and comparison. *Journal of Abnormal Psychology*, 1977, *86*, 203–223.

Blaney, P. H. The effectiveness of cognitive and behavior therapies. In L. P. Rehm (Ed.), *Behavior therapy for depression: Present status and future directions*. New York: Academic Press, 1981.

Brown, G. W. Meaning, measurement and stress of life-events. In B. S. Dohrenwend & B. P. Dohrenwend (Eds.), *Stressful life events: Their nature and effects*. New York: Wiley, 1974.

Brown, G. W., Bhrolchain, M. N., & Harris, T. Social class and psychiatric disturbance among women in an urban population. *Sociology*, 1975, *9*, 225–254.

Brown, R. A., & Lewinsohn, P. M. *A psychoeducational approach to the treatment of depression: Comparison of group, individual and minimal contact procedures*, in preparation.

Buchwald, A. M. Depressive mood and estimates of reinforcement frequency. *Journal of Abnormal Psychology*, 1977, *86*, 443–446.

Buchwald, A. M., Coyne, J. C., & Cole, C. S. A critical evaluation of the learned helplessness model of depression. *Journal of Abnormal Psychology*, 1978, *87*, 180–193.

Burgess, E. The modification of depressive behaviors. In R. Rubin & C. M. Franks (Eds.), *Advances in behavior therapy, 1968*. New York: Academic Press, 1969.

Burglass, D., & Horton, J. A scale for predicting subsequent suicidal behavior. *British Journal of Psychiatry*, 1974, *124*, 573–578.

Cadoret, R. J., & Tanna, V. L. Genetics of affective disorders. In G. Usdin (Ed.), *Depression: Clinical, biological and psychological perspectives*. New York: Brunner/Mazel, 1977.

Ciminero, A. R., & Steingarten, K. A. The effects of performance standards on self-evaluation and self-reinforcement on depressed and nondepressed individuals. *Cognitive Therapy and Research*, 1978, *2*, 179–182.

Coleman, R. E., & Miller, A. G. The relationship between depression and marital adjustment in a clinic population: A multitrait-multimethod study. *Journal of Consulting and Clinical Psychology*, 1975, *43*, 647–651.

Costello, C. G. Depression: Loss of reinforcers or loss of reinforcer effectiveness. *Behavior Therapy*, 1972, *3*, 240–247.

Costello, C. G. A critical review of Seligman's laboratory experiments of learned helplessness and depression in humans. *Journal of Abnormal Psychology*, 1978, *87*, 21–31.

Coyne, J. C. Depression and the response of others. *Journal of Abnormal Psychology*, 1976, *85*, 186–193.

Craighead, W. E. Issues resulting from treatment studies. In L. P. Rehm (Ed.), *Behavior therapy for depression: Present status and future directions*. New York: Academic Press, 1981.

Craighead, W. E., Hickey, K. S., & DeMonbreun, B. G. Distortion of perception and recall of neutral feedback in depression. *Cognitive Therapy and Research*, 1979, *3*, 291–298.

Curran, J. P. Skills training as an approach to the treatment of heterosexual-social anxiety: A review. *Psychological Bulletin*, 1977, *84*, 140–157.

Dahlstrom, W. G., Welsh, G. S., & Dahlstrom, L. E. *An MMPI handbook*. Minneapolis: University of Minnesota Press, 1972.

DeMonbreun, W., & Craighead, W. E. Distortion of perception and recall of positive and neutral feedback in depression. *Cognitive Therapy and Research*, 1977, *1*, 311–329.

Derogatis, L. R., Lipman, R. S., & Covi, L. SCL-90: An outpatient psychiatric rating scale—Preliminary report. *Psychopharmacology Bulletin*, 1973, *9*, 13–27.

Diagnostic and statistical manual of mental disorders, Second edition. Washington, D.C.: American Psychiatric Association, 1968.

Diagnostic and statistical manual of mental disorders, Third edition. Washington, D.C.: American Psychiatric Association, 1980.

Diggory, J. C., & Loeb, A. Motivation of chronic schizophrenics by information about their abilities in a group situation. *Journal of Abnormal and Social Psychology*, 1962, *65*, 48–52.

Dohrenwend, B. S., Krasnoff, L., Askenasy, A. R., & Dohrenwend, B. P. Exemplification of a method for scaling life events: The Peri life events scale. *Journal of Health and Social Behavior*, 1978, *19*, 205–229.

Eastman, C. Behavioral formulations of depression. *Psychological Review*, 1976, *83*, 277–291.

Ellis, A., & Harper, R. A. *A guide to rational living*. Hollywood, Calif.: Wilshire, 1961.

Endicott, J., & Spitzer, R. L. A diagnostic interview, the schedule for affective disorders and schizophrenia. *Archives of General Psychiatry*, 1978, *35*, 837–844.

Epstein, S. Anxiety, arousal, and the self-concept. In I. G. Sarason & C. D. Spielberger (Eds.), *Stress and anxiety*, Vol. 3. Washington, D.C.: Hemisphere, 1976.

Ernst, P., Badash, D., Beran, B., Kosovsky, R., & Kleinhauz, M. Incidence of mental illness in the aged: Unmasking the effect of a diagnosis of chronic brain syndrome. *Journal of the American Geriatrics Society*, 1977, *25*, 371–375.

Ferster, C. B. Classification of behavior pathology. In L. Krasner & L. P. Ullmann (Eds.), *Research in behavior modification*. New York: Holt, Rinehart & Winston, 1965.

Ferster, C. B. Animal behavior and mental illness. *Psychological Record*, 1966, *16*, 345–356.

Flippo, J. R., & Lewinsohn, P. M. Effects of failure on the self-esteem of depressed and nondepressed subjects. *Journal of Consulting and Clinical Psychology*, 1971, *36*, 151.

Freud, S. Mourning and melancholia. In *The complete works of Sigmund Freud, Vol. XIV*. London, Hogarth Press, 1957. (Originally published, 1917.)

Fuchs, C. Z., & Rehm, L. P. A self-control behavior therapy program for depression. *Journal of Consulting and Clinical Psychology*, 1977, *45*, 206–215.

Gaitz, C. M. Depression in the elderly. In W. Fann, I. Karacan, A. Pokorny, & R. Williams (Eds.), *Phenomenology and treatment of depression*. New York: Spectrum, 1977.

Gallagher, D. Behavioral group therapy with elderly depressions: An experimental study. In D. Upper & S. Ross (Eds.), *Behavioral group therapy*. Champaign, Ill.: Research Press, 1981.

Gallagher, D., McGarvey, W., Zelinski, E., & Thompson, C. W. Age and factor structure of the Zung depression scale. Unpublished mimeo, 1978.

Garber, J., Hollon, S. D., & Silverman, V. *Evaluation and reward of self vs. others in depression.* Paper presented at the Annual Meeting of Association for Advancement of Behavior Therapy, San Francisco, 1979.

Gatchel, R. J., Paulus, P. B., & Maples, C. W. Learned helplessness and self-reported affect. *Journal of Abnormal Psychology*, 1975, *84*, 589–620.

Gioe, V. J. *Cognitive modification and positive group experience as a treatment for depression.* Paper presented at the Association for Advancement of Behavior Therapy, San Francisco, 1975.

Glazer, R. (Ed.). *The nature of reinforcement.* New York: Academic Press, 1971.

Graf, M. G. *A mood-related activities schedule for the treatment of depression.* Unpublished doctoral dissertation, Arizona State University, 1977.

Greist, J. H., Klein, M. H., Eischens, R. R., Faris, J., Gurman, A. J., & Morgan, W. P. Running as treatment for depression. *Comprehensive Psychiatry*, 1979, *20*, 41–54.

Grinker, R. R., Miller, J., Sabshin, M., Nunn, R., & Nunnally, J. C. *The phenomena of depressions.* New York: Paul B. Hoeber, 1961.

Gurland, B. J. The comparative frequency of depression in various adult age groups. *Journal of Gerontology*, 1976, *31*, 283–292.

Hamilton, D. A rating scale for depression. *Journal of Neurology, Neurosurgery, and Psychiatry*, 1960, *23*, 56–61.

Hamilton, D. Development of a rating scale for primary depressive illness. *Journal of Clinical and Social Psychology*, 1967, *6*, 278–296.

Hammen, C. L., & Krantz, S. *The story completion test.* Unpublished mimeo, University of California at Los Angeles, 1976.

Hammen, C. L., & Peters, S. D. Differential responses to male and female depressive reactions. *Journal of Consulting and Clinical Psychology*, 1977, *45*, 994–1001.

Harnatz, J., & Shader, R. Psychopharmacologic investigations in healthy elderly volunteers: MMPI depression scale. *Journal of American Geriatrics Society*, 1975, *23*, 350–354.

Harmon, T. H., Nelson, R. O., & Hayes, S. C. *Self-monitoring of mood vs. activity by depressed clients.* Paper presented at the Association for Advancement of Behavior Therapy, Chicago, 1978.

Hiroto, D. S. Locus of control and learned helplessness. *Journal of Experimental Psychology*, 1974, *102*, 187–193.

Hollon, S. D. Comparisons and combinations with alternative approaches. In L. P. Rehm (Ed.), *Behavior therapy for depression: Present status and future directions.* New York: Academic Press, 1981.

Holmes, T. H., & Rahe, R. H. The social readjustment rating scale. *Journal of Psychosomatic Research*, 1967, *11*, 213–218.

Huesmann, L. R. Cognitive processes and models of depression. *Journal of Abnormal Psychology*, 1978, *87*, 194–198.

Jacobson, E. *Depression—Comparative studies of normal, neurotic, and psychotic conditions.* New York: International Universities Press, 1971.

Jacobson, N. S. The assessment of overt behavior. In L. P. Rehm (Ed.), *Behavior therapy for depression: Present status and future directions.* New York: Academic Press, 1981.

James, W. H. *Internal versus external control of reinforcement as a basic variable in learning theory.* Unpublished doctoral dissertation, Ohio State University, 1957.

James, W. H., & Rotter, J. B. Partial and one hundred percent reinforcement under chance and skill conditions. *Journal of Experimental Psychology*, 1958, *55*, 397–403.

Johansson, S. L., Lewinsohn, P. M., & Flippo, J. F. *An application of the Premack principle to the verbal behavior of depressed subjects.* Paper presented at the meeting of the Association for Advancement of Behavior Therapy, Washington, D.C., 1969.

Jones, R. G. *A factored measure of Ellis' irrational beliefs system.* Wichita, Kansas: Wichita Test Systems, Inc., 1968.

Kanfer, F. H. The maintenance of behavior by self-generated stimuli and reinforcement. In A. Jacobs & L. B. Sachs (Eds.), *The psychology of private events: Perspectives on covert response systems.* New York: Academic Press, 1971.

Klein, D. C., & Seligman, M. E. P. Reversal of performance deficits in learned helplessness and depression. *Journal of Abnormal Psychology*, 1976, *85*, 11–26.

Klinger, E. Consequences of commitment to and disengagement from incentives. *Psychological Review*, 1975, *82*, 1–25.

Kovacs, M., & Beck, A. T. An empirical-clinical approach toward a definition of childhood depression. In J. G. Schulterbrandt & A. Raskin (Eds.), *Depression in childhood: Diagnosis, treatment, and conceptual models.* New York: Raven Press, 1977.

Kovacs, M., & Rush, A. J. *Cognitive psychotherapy versus anti-depressant medication in the treatment of depression.* Paper presented at Eastern Psychological Association, New York, April 1976.

Krantz, S., & Hammen, C. *The assessment of cognitive bias in depression.* Unpublished mimeo, University of California at Los Angeles, 1978.

Kupfer, D. J., Weiss, G. F., Detre, T. P., Foster, F. G., Delgado, J., & MacPartland, R. Psychomotor activity in affective states. *Archives of General Psychiatry*, 1974, *30*, 765–768.

Langone, M. Assertiveness and Lewinsohn's theory of depression: An empirical test. *The Behavior Therapist*, 1979, *2*, 21.

Lazarus, A. A. Learning theory and the treatment of depression. *Behaviour Research and Therapy*, 1968, *6*, 83–89.

Lefcourt, H. M. Locus of control for specific goals. In L. C. Perlmuter & R. A. Monty (Eds.), *Choice and perceived control.* Hillside, N.J.: Lawrence Erlbaum, 1978.

Lefkowitz, M. M., & Tesiny, E. P. Assessment of childhood depression. *Journal of Consulting and Clinical Psychology*, 1980, *48*, 43–50.

Lehman, H. E. Epidemiology of depressive disorders. In

R. R. Fieve (Ed.), *Depression in the 70's: Modern theory and research.* Princeton, N.J.: Excerpta Medica, 1971.

Levitt, E. E., & Lubin, B. *Depression.* New York: Springer, 1975.

Lewinsohn, P. M. Manual of instructions for the behavior ratings used for the observations of interpersonal behavior. In E. J. Mash & L. G. Terdal (Eds.), *Behavior therapy assessment: Diagnosis design, and evaluation.* New York: Springer, 1974.

Lewinsohn, P. M. The behavioral study and treatment of depression. In M. Hersen, R. M. Eisler, & P. M. Miller (Eds.), *Progress in behavior modification,* Vol. 1. New York: Academic Press, 1975. (a)

Lewinsohn, P. M. The unpleasant events schedule: A scale for the measurement of aversive events. Unpublished mimeo, University of Oregon, 1975. (b)

Lewinsohn, P. M. Activity schedules in the treatment of depression. In C. E. Thoresen & J. D. Krumboltz (Eds.), *Counseling methods.* New York: Holt, Rinehart & Winston, 1976.

Lewinsohn, P. M., & Amenson, C. S. Some relations between pleasant and unpleasant mood-related events and depression. *Journal of Abnormal Psychology,* 1978, *87,* 655–654.

Lewinsohn, P. M., & Brown, R. A. *Learning how to control one's depression: An educational approach.* Paper presented at the meeting of the American Psychological Association, New York, 1979.

Lewinsohn, P. M., & Graf, M. Pleasant Activities and depression. *Journal of Consulting and Clinical Psychology,* 1973, *41,* 261–268.

Lewinsohn, P. M., & Grosscup, S. J. *Decreasing unpleasant events and increasing pleasant events: A treatment manual for depression.* Unpublished manuscript, University of Oregon, 1978.

Lewinsohn, P. M., & Lee, W. M. L. Assessment of affective disorders. In D. H. Barlow (Ed.), *Behavioral assessment of adult disorders.* New York: Guilford Press, 1981.

Lewinsohn, P. M., & Libet, J. Pleasant events, activity schedules, and depressions. *Journal of Abnormal Psychology,* 1972, *79,* 291–295.

Lewinsohn, P. M., & Shaffer, M. Use of home observations as an integral part of the treatment of depression: Preliminary report and case studies. *Journal of Consulting and Clinical Psychology,* 1971, *37,* 87–94.

Lewinsohn, P. M., & Shaw, D. Feedback about interpersonal behavior as an agent of behavior change: A case study in the treatment of depression. *Psychotherapy and Psychosomatics,* 1969, *17,* 82–88.

Lewinsohn, P. M., & Talkington, J. Studies on the measurement of unpleasant events and relations with depression. *Applied Psychological Measurement,* 1979, *3,* 83–101.

Lewinsohn, P. M., Weinstein, M., & Shaw, D. Depression: A clinical-research approach. In R. D. Rubin & C. M. Frank (Eds.), *Advances in behavior therapy,* 1968. New York: Academic Press, 1969.

Lewinsohn, P. M., Weinstein, M., & Alper, T. A behavioral approach to the group treatment of depressed persons: A methodological contribution. *Journal of Clinical Psychology,* 1970, *26,* 525–532.

Lewinsohn, P. M., Lobitz, W. C., & Wilson, S. "Sensitivity" of depressed individuals to aversive stimuli. *Journal of Abnormal Psychology,* 1973, *81,* 259–263.

Lewinsohn, P. M., Biglan, A., & Zeiss, A. M. Behavioral treatment of depression. In P. O. Davidson (Ed.), *The behavioral management of anxiety, depression and pain.* New York: Brunner/Mazel, 1976.

Lewinsohn, P. M., Larson, D. W., & Muñoz, R. F. *The measurement of expectancies and other cognitions in depressed individuals.* Paper presented at the Association for Advancement of Behavior Therapy, Chicago, 1978.

Lewinsohn, P. M., Muñoz, R. F., Youngren, M. A., & Zeiss, A. M. *Control your depression.* Englewood Cliffs, N.J.: Prentice-Hall, 1978.

Lewinsohn, P. M., Tursky, S. P., & Arconad, M. *The relationship between age and the frequency of occurrence, and the subjective impact, of aversive events.* Unpublished mimeo, University of Oregon, 1979.

Lewinsohn, P. M., Mischel, W., Chaplin, W., & Barton, R. Social competence and depression: The role of illusory self-perception? *Journal of Abnormal Psychology,* 1980, *89,* 203–212.

Lewinsohn, P. M., Sullivan, M. J., & Grosscup, S. J. Changing reinforcing events: An approach to the treatment of depression. In *Psychotherapy: Theory, Research and Practice,* 1980, *17,* 322–334.

Lewinsohn, P. M., Youngren, M. A., & Grosscup, S. L. Reinforcement and depression. In R. A. Depue (Ed.), *The psychobiology of the depressive disorders: Implications for the effects of stress.* New York: Academic Press, 1980.

Libet, J., & Lewinsohn, P. M. The concept of social skill with special reference to the behavior of depression persons. *Journal of Consulting and Clinical Psychology,* 1973, *40,* 304–312.

Lloyd, G. G., & Lishman, W. A. Effect of depression on the speed of recall of pleasant and unpleasant experiences. *Psychological Medicine,* 1975, *5,* 173–180.

Lobitz, W. C., & Post, R. D. Parameters of self-reinforcement and depression. *Journal of Abnormal Psychology,* 1979, *88,* 33–41.

Loeb, A., Feshbach, S., Beck, A. T., & Wolfe, A. Some effects of reward upon the social perception and motivation of psychiatric patients varying in depression. *Journal of Abnormal and Social Psychology,* 1964, *68,* 609–611.

Loeb, A., Beck, A. T., Diggory, J. C., & Tuthill, R. Expectancy, level of aspiration, performance, and self-evaluation in depression. *Proceedings of the 75th Annual Convention of the American Psychological Association, 1967,* pp. 193–194.

Lubin, B. Adjective check lists for measurement of depression. *Archives of General Psychiatry,* 1965, *12,* 57–62.

Lubin, B. *Manual for the depression adjective check lists.* San Diego: Educational and Industrial Testing Service, 1967.

Lubin, B. *Bibliography for the depression adjective check lists: 1966–1977.* San Diego, Calif.: Educational and Industrial Testing Service, 1977.

MacPhillamy, D. J., & Lewinsohn, P. M. *A scale for the*

measurement of positive reinforcement. Unpublished mimeo, University of Oregon, 1971.

MacPhillamy, D. J., & Lewinsohn, P. M. Depression as a function of levels of desired and obtained pleasure. *Journal of Abnormal Psychology,* 1974, *83,* 651–657.

MacPhillamy, D., & Lewinsohn, P. M. *Manual for the Pleasant Events Schedule.* Unpublished mimeograph, University of Oregon, 1975.

Mahoney, M. J. *Cognition and behavior modification.* Cambridge, Mass.: Ballinger, 1974.

McLean, P. Therapeutic decision making in the behavioral treatment of depression. In P. O. Davidson (Ed.), *The behavioral management of anxiety, depression, and pain.* New York: Brunner/Mazel, 1976.

McLean, P. D., & Hakstian, A. R. Clinical depression: Comparative efficacy of outpatient treatments. *Journal of Consulting and Clinical Psychology,* 1979, *47,* 818–836.

McLean, P. D., Ogston, K., & Grauer, L. A behavioral approach to the treatment of depression. *Journal of Behavior Therapy and Experimental Psychiatry,* 1973, *4,* 323–330.

McNair, D., Lorr, M., & Droppleman, L. *EITS manual for the profile of mood states.* San Diego, Calif.: Educational and Industrial Testing Service, 1971.

Miller, W. R., & Seligman, M. E. P. Depression and the perception of reinforcement. *Journal of Abnormal Psychology,* 1973, *82,* 62–73.

Miller, W. R., & Seligman, M. E. P. Depression and learned helplessness in man. *Journal of Abnormal Psychology,* 1975, *84,* 228–238.

Miller, W. R., & Seligman, M. E. P. Learned helplessness, depression, and the perception of reinforcement. *Behaviour Research and Therapy,* 1976, *14,* 7–17.

Morris, J. B., & Beck, A. T. The efficacy of anti-depressant drugs: A review of research, 1958–1972. *Archives of General Psychiatry,* 1974, *30,* 667–674.

Muñoz, R. F. A cognitive approach to the assessment and treatment of depression. *Dissertation Abstracts International, 1977, 38,* 2873B (University Microfilms No. 77-26, 505, 154.)

Muñoz, R. F., & Lewinsohn, P. M. *The Cognitive Events Schedule.* Unpublished mimeo, University of Oregon, 1976. (a)

Muñoz, R. B., & Lewinsohn, P. M. *The Personal Belief Inventory,* Unpublished mimeo, University of Oregon, 1976. (b)

Muñoz, R. F., & Lewinsohn, P. M. *The Subjective Probability Questionnaire.* Unpublished mimeo, University of Oregon, 1976. (c)

Murphy, R., & Ellis, A. *Rationality scales: A bibliography.* New York: Institute for Rational Living, 1976.

National Institute of Mental Health. *Special report: The depressive illnesses.* 1970.

Nelson, R. E. Irrational beliefs in depression. *Journal of Consulting and Clinical Psychology,* 1977, *45,* 1190–1191.

Nelson, R. E., & Craighead, W. E. Selective recall of positive and negative feedback, self-control behaviors, and depression. *Journal of Abnormal Psychology,* 1977, *86,* 379–388.

Overall, J. E. Dimensions of manifest depression. *Journal of Psychiatric Research,* 1962, *1,* 239–245.

Parloff, M. B., Wolfe, B., Hadley, S., & Waskow, I. *Assessment of psychosocial treatment of mental disorders:*

Current status and prospects. Unpublished mimeo, 1978.

Paykel, E. S., Myers, J. K., Dienelt, M. N., Klerman, G. L., Lindenthal, J. J., & Pepper, M. P. Life events and depression: A controlled study. *Archives of General Psychiatry,* 1969, *21,* 753–760.

Peterson, C. Uncontrollability and self-blame in depression: Investigation of the paradox in a college population. *Journal of Abnormal Psychology,* 1979, *88,* 620–624.

Prkachin, K., Craig, K., Papageorgis, D., & Reith, G. Nonverbal communication deficits in response to performance feedback in depression. *Journal of Abnormal Psychology,* 1977, *86,* 224–234.

Rabkin, J. G., & Struening, E. L. Life events, stress, and illness. *Science,* 1976, *194,* 1013–1020.

Radloff, L. The CES-D Scale: A self-report depression scale for research in the general population. *Applied Psychosocial Measurement,* 1977, *1,* 385–401.

Raskin, A., & Jarvik, L. F. (Eds.), *Psychiatric symptoms and cognitive loss in the elderly.* Washington, D.C.: Hemisphere Publications, 1979.

Raskin, A., Schulterbrandt, J. G., Reatig, N., Crook, T. H., & Odle, D. Depression subtypes and response to phenelzine, diazepam, and a placebo. *Archives of General Psychiatry,* 1974, *30,* 66–75.

Rehm, L. P. A self-control model of depression. *Behavior Therapy,* 1977, *8,* 787–804.

Rehm, L. P. Mood, pleasant events, and unpleasant events: Two pilot studies. *Journal of Consulting and Clinical Psychology,* 1978, *46,* 854–859.

Rehm, L. P. (Ed.). *Behavior therapy for depression: Present status and future directions.* New York: Academic Press, 1981.

Rehm, L. P., & Kornblith, S. J. Behavior therapy for depression: A review of recent developments. In M. Hersen, R. M. Eisler, & P. M. Miller (Eds.), *Progress in behavior modification,* Vol. 7. New York: Academic Press, 1979.

Rehm, L. P., & Plakosh, P. Preference for immediate reinforcement in depression. *Journal of Behavior Therapy and Experimental Psychiatry,* 1975, *6,* 101–103.

Rehm, L. P., Fuchs, C. Z., Roth, D. M., Kornblith, S. J., & Romano, J. M. A comparison of self-control and social skills treatments of depression. *Behavior Therapy,* 1979, *10,* 429–442.

Reisinger, J. J. The treatment of "anxiety depression" via positive reinforcement and response cost. *Journal of Applied Behavior Analysis,* 1972, *5,* 125–130.

Robins, E., & Guze, S. B. Classification of affective disorders: The primary-secondary, the endogenous-reactive, and the neurotic-psychotic concepts. In T. A. Williams *et al.* (Eds.), *Recent advances in the psychobiology of the depressive illnesses.* Chevy Chase, Md.: U.S. Department of Health, Education, and Welfare, 1969, pp. 283–295.

Robinson, J. C., & Lewinsohn, P. M. An experimental analysis of a technique based on the Premack principle for changing the verbal behavior of depressed individuals. *Psychological Reports,* 1973, *32,* 199–210.

Rosenthal, S. H. The involutional depressive syndrome. *American Journal of Psychiatry,* 1968, *124,* May Supplement.

Rosenzweig, S. The effects of failure and success on evaluation of self and others: A study of depressed patients and normals. *Dissertation Abstracts*, 1960, *21*, 675.

Roth, D., Rehm, L. P., Rosensky, R. A. *Self-reward, self-punishment, and depression.* Unpublished mimeo, University of Pittsburgh, 1975.

Rotter, J. B. Generalized expectancies of internal vs. external control of reinforcement. *Psychological Monographs*, 1966, *80* (Whole No. 609), 1.

Rotter, J. B. Some problems and misconceptions related to the construct of internal vs. external locus of control. *Journal of Consulting and Clinical Psychology*, 1975, *43*, 56–67.

Rozensky, R. H., Rehm, L. P., Pry, G., & Roth, D. Depression and self-reinforcement behavior in hospitalized patients. *Journal of Behavior Therapy and Experimental Psychiatry*, 1977, *8*, 35–38.

Rush, A. J., & Beck, A. T. Behavior therapy in adults with affective disorders. In M. Hersen & A. S. Bellack (Eds.), *Behavior therapy in the psychiatric setting.* Baltimore: Williams & Wilkins, 1978.

Rush, A. J., Khatami, M., & Beck, A. T. Cognitive and behavioral therapy in chronic depression. *Behavior Therapy*, 1975, *6*, 398–404.

Rush, A. J., Beck, A. T., Kovacs, M., and Hollon, S. Comparative efficacy of cognitive therapy and imipramine in the treatment of depressed outpatients. *Cognitive Therapy and Research*, 1977, *1*, 17–37.

Sanchez, V. *A comparison of depressed, psychiatric control, and normal subjects on two measures of assertiveness.* Unpublished master's thesis, University of Oregon, 1977.

Sanchez, V., & Lewinsohn, P. M. Assertive behavior and depression. *Journal of Consulting and Clinical Psychology*, 1980, *48*, 119–120.

Sanchez, V. C., Lewinsohn, P. M., & Larson, D. W. *Assertion training: Effectiveness in the treatment of depression.* Unpublished manuscript, University of Oregon, 1979.

Sarason, I. G., Johnson, J. H., & Siegel, J. M. *Assessing the impact of life change: Development of the life experience survey.* Unpublished mimeo, University of Washington, 1977.

Schmickley, V. G. The effects of cognitive behavior modification upon depressed outpatients. Dissertation Abstracts International, 1976, 37, 987B–988B. (University Microfilms No. 76-18, 675.)

Seitz, F. A behavior modification approach to depression: A case study. *Psychology*, 1971, *8*, 58–63.

Seligman, M. E. P. Fall into helplessness. *Psychology Today*, 1973, *7*, 43–48.

Seligman, M. E. P. Depression and learned helplessness. In R. J. Friedman, & M. M. Katz (Eds.), *The Psychology of depression: Contemporary theory and research.* New York: Wiley, 1974.

Seligman, M. E. P. *Helplessness: On depression, development, and death.* San Francisco: Freedman, 1975.

Seligman, M. E. P., Abramson, L. Y., Semmel, A., & Von Baeyer, C. Depressive attributional style. *Journal of Abnormal Psychology*, 1979, *88*, 242–247.

Semmel, A., Abramson, L. Y., Seligman, M. E. P., & Von Baeyer, C. A. *Scale for measuring attributional style.* Manuscript in preparation, University of Pennsylvania, 1978.

Shipley, C. R., & Fazio, A. F., Pilot study of a treatment for psychological depression. *Journal of Abnormal Psychology*, 1973, *82*, 372–376.

Skinner, B. F. *Science and human behavior.* New York: Free Press, 1953.

Spitzer, R. L., Endicott, J., & Robins, E. Research diagnostic criteria. *Archives of General Psychiatry*, 1978, *35*, 773–782.

Stuart, R. B. Operant-interpersonal treatment of marital discord. *Journal of Consulting and Clinical Psychology*, 1967, *33*, 675–682.

Sundberg, N. D., Snowden, L. R., & Reynolds, W. M. Toward assessment of personal competence and incompetence in life situations. *Annual Review of Psychology*, 1978, *29*, 179–221.

Taylor, F. G., & Marshall, W. L. Experimental analysis of a cognitive-behavioral therapy for depression. *Cognitive Therapy and Research*, 1977, *1*, 59–72.

Teasdale, J. D., & Fogarty, S. J. Differential effects of induced mood on retrieval of pleasant and unpleasant events from episodic memory. *Journal of Abnormal Psychology*, 1979, *88*, 248–257.

Wechsler, D. *Wechsler adult intelligence scale.* New York: The Psychological Corporation, 1955.

Wechsler, H., Grosser, F., & Busfield, B. The depression rating scale: A quantitative approach to the assessment of depressive symptomatology. *Archives of General Psychiatry*, 1963, *9*, 334–343.

Weiner, B., Frieze, I., Kukla, A., Reed, L., Rest, S., & Rosenbaum, R. M. *Perceiving the causes of successes and failure.* Morristown, N.J.: General Learning Press, 1971.

Weiner, B., Nierenberg, R. & Goldstein, M. Social learning (locus of control) versus attributional (causal stability) interpretations of expectancy of success. *Journal of Personality*, 1976, *44*, 52–68.

Weintraub, M., Segal, R. M., & Beck, A. T. An investigation of cognition and affect in the depressive experience of normal men. *Journal of Consulting and Clinical Psychology*, 1974, *42*, 911.

Weiss, R. L., & Aved, B. M. Marital satisfaction and depression as predictors of physical health status. *Journal of Consulting and Clinical Psychology*, 1978, *56*, 1379–1384.

Weissman, A., & Beck, A. T. *A preliminary investigation of the relationship between dysfunctional attitudes and depression.* Unpublished manuscript, University of Pennsylvania, 1978.

Weissman, M., & Klerman, G. L. Sex differences and the epidemiology of depression. *Archives of General Psychiatry*, 1977, *34*, 98–111.

Weissman, M., & Paykel, E. G. *The depressed woman: A study of social relationships.* Chicago: University of Chicago Press, 1974.

Wener, A. E., & Rehm, L. P. Depressive affect: A test of behavioral hypotheses. *Journal of Abnormal Psychology*, 1975, *84*, 221–227.

Williams, J. G., Barlow, D. H., & Agras, W. S. Behavioral measurement of severe depression. *Archives of General Psychiatry*, 1972, *27*, 330–337.

Wolpe, J. Neurotic depression: An experimental analog, clinical syndromes, and treatment. *American Journal of Psychotherapy*, 1971, *25*, 362–368.

Wolpe, J., & Lazarus, A. A. *Behavior therapy techniques.* New York: Pergamon Press, 1966.

Wortman, C. B., & Brehm, J. W. Responses to uncontrollable outcomes: An integration of reactance theory and the learned helplessness model. In L. Berkowitz (Ed.), *Advances in experimental social psychology.* Academic Press, 1975.

Yalom, I. D. *The theory and practice of group psychotherapy* (2nd ed.). New York: Basic Books, 1975.

Youngren, M. A., & Lewinsohn, P. M. The functional relationship between depression and problematic interpersonal behavior. *Journal of Abnormal Psychology,* 1980, *89,* 333–341.

Youngren, M. A., Zeiss, A., & Lewinsohn, P. M. *Interpersonal events schedule.* Unpublished mimeo, University of Oregon, 1975.

Zeiss, A. M., Lewinsohn, P. M., & Muñoz, R. F. Nonspecific improvement effects in depression using interpersonal skills training, pleasant activity schedules, or cognitive training. *Journal of Consulting and Clinical Psychology,* 1979, *47,* 427–439.

Zung, W. W. K. From art to science: The diagnosis and treatment of depression. *Archives of General Psychiatry,* 1973, *29,* 328–337.

Zung, W. W. K., Richards, C. B., & Short, M. J. Self-rating depression scale in an outpatient clinic. *Archives of General Psychiatry,* 1965, *13,* 508–516.

CHAPTER 7

Treatment of Schizophrenia

James P. Curran, Peter M. Monti, and Donald P. Corriveau

Introduction

Although some theorists, such as Szasz (1961, 1976), charge that schizophrenia is a myth and does not exist, the vast majority of mental health workers would quite adamantly maintain that schizophrenia is an extremely pervasive disorder. Definitional problems notwithstanding, the behavioral disturbances that generally characterize this construct appear throughout the world irrespective of culture, race, language, or time. Furthermore, there is no solid evidence that the incidence has changed in the last 150 years. Out of the U.S. population, 2–3% are estimated to be included in this classification (Keith, Gunderson, Reifman, Buchsbaum & Mosher, 1976). According to the National Institute of Mental Health, about 25% of all patients admitted to state mental hospitals are diagnosed as schizophrenic, and 50% of the inpatient populations in state mental hospitals bear the same diagnosis. Schizophrenics clearly comprise the vast majority of psychiatric patients residing in long-term custodial facilities. The chronicity of this disorder is reflected in a 50% readmission rate within only 2 years after discharge (Mosher, Govera, & Menn, 1972). The expected length of stay within an institution increases with subsequent readmission (Kraft, Binner, & Dickey, 1967). Once a schizophrenic patient has spent two years in a mental hospital, the probability of release is only 6% (Ullmann, 1967). The prognosis for rehabilitation is alarmingly poor. A staggering 65–85% of discharged patients with the schizophrenic diagnosis are unable to function more than minimally in the community. Gunderson and Mosher (1975) also estimate that beyond the $2–$4 billion directly spent on treatment costs, the loss of productivity attributable to this disorder is beyond $10 billion.

Despite years of research devoted to both studying the etiology of schizophrenia and developing viable remedial interventions, the overall progress in this area of research is, at best, only modest. Several authors have cited the failures of traditional treatment methods, especially individual psychotherapy, with schizophrenics (May, 1968; Stahl & Leitenberg, 1976). While chemotherapy has shown some success in alleviating some of the symptoms associated with this disorder, the prognosis of rehabilitation into the community remains notoriously poor, and recidivism rates

James P. Curran, Peter M. Monti, and Donald P. Corriveau • Department of Psychology, Brown University Medical School and Veterans Administration Medical Center, Providence, Rhode Island 02912.

remain uncomfortably high (Coleman, 1976; Hersen, 1979). While relatively new to this research area, behavioral principles of treatment have been systematically applied to schizophrenic populations for approximately 30 years. The major thrust of this chapter is to examine critically behavior therapy's contribution to this major health problem.

In this chapter, we separately review published studies in three broad areas of behaviorally oriented treatment procedures. We begin by examining those studies that appear to share as a common denominator a central focus on specific, well-delineated behavioral objectives. Although the major impetus for these treatments comes mainly from operant paradigms, this behavioral technology has been gradually influenced by social learning theory and other branches of psychology. The second area of treatment that we review includes treatments that fit under the general label of *token economies*. The major influence behind the development of this behavioral area appears to be pragmatic concerns with ward management, which has led to the application of contingency management procedures to target variables much wider in scope and more practical in implication. The third and last major area to be reviewed is the general area currently referred to as *social skills training*. As a whole, this relatively new research area has addressed the frequently reported interpersonal deficits in schizophrenic populations. Treatment efforts have specifically focused on training interpersonal competencies. Since the target behaviors examined and trained by social skill investigators appear crucial in posttreatment adjustment to the community, the social skills research area has, at the very least, great potential in establishing viable treatment procedures for schizophrenic patients.

Before examining the behavioral literature, a few important issues need to be addressed. Definitional problems are perhaps the most salient issues beleaguering the general area of schizophrenia research. To adequately understand the controversies and theoretical nuances within this general area, it is first important to note that as with other disorders subsumed under current nosological systems, the concept of schizophrenia was developed primarily within what is now called the *medical model* or the *disease model*. In its simplest form, the medical model is an orientation in which an analysis of symptomatology leads to a diagnosis of the underlying disease. Even today, the issue of whether schizophrenia should be considered a unitary or a multimodal disease entity continues to be debated in the literature (cf. Rieder, 1974; Tuma, 1968). An interesting observation is that about two decades before Kraepelin laid down psychiatry's first comprehensive system of classification, much debate revolved around the value of "disease entities." In his own formulations, Kraepelin adopted a disease model and has always been credited for grouping a variety of abnormal behaviors under one heading, *dementia praecox*. Unfortunately, Kraepelin's descriptions of this disorder contain concurrent conceptualizations of both behavioral observations and theoretical inferences. His descriptions of symptoms include hallucinations, delusions, thought disorders, attentional problems, and a dissociation between thought and affect. Beyond these descriptions, however, Kraepelin strongly emphasized that the deterioration of psychological processes (dementia) usually began early in life (hence, the word *praecox*) and was always in part irreversible. Aligning himself with other medical contemporaries, Kraepelin assumed that he had discovered a "disease entity," but recent theorists charge that he had simply invented a concept (Kendell, 1978; Szasz, 1978). Therefore, his formulations have received much criticism and revision.

Eugen Bleuler, who coined the word *schizophrenia*, rejected deterioration as an essential criterion of schizophrenia, yet accepted Kraepelin's inference of an underlying cerebral defect. Bleuler placed particular emphasis on four categories of fundamental symptoms: altered affectivity, altered associations, ambivalence, and autism (often called *Bleuler's four As*). Bleuler emphasized these symptoms above all others, including delusions and hallucinations.

Historically, attempts to define, let alone understand, the concept of schizophrenia have always generated a cloud of confusion, producing nearly as many definitions as diagnosticians. In the 1920s, each large teaching center employed its own system of classification, developed to meet its own esoteric needs. Zubin (1967) detailed how the original nosological system construed by the American Psychiatric Association was compiled by majority voting because of the vast disagreement among its members. Despite these valiant efforts to operationalize definitional criteria, reliability across diagnosticians has often been alarmingly poor (Zubin, 1967). In a series of classic articles, Zigler and Phillips (1961a,b) implied that the then-current nosological system focused much of its efforts on etiology and therefore fostered an inferential instead of an empirical approach. Despite the truism that diagnoses were based on symptoms, these researchers found that few symptoms could be predicted based on diagnosis.

The last decade, however, has witnessed numerous concerted efforts to operationalize major psychiatric syndromes. The first major comprehensive set appears to be the St. Louis Criteria (Feighner, Robins, Guze, Woodruff, Winokur, & Muñoz, 1972). Since then, several rival operational definitions have appeared in the field, including the New Haven Criteria (Astrachan, Harrow, Adler *et al.*, 1972); Carpenter's Flexible Criteria (Carpenter, Strauss, & Bartko, 1973); the Research Diagnostic Criteria of Spitzer, Endicott, and Robins (1975); and Schneider's first-rank symptoms (see Kendell, Brockington, & Leff, 1979). Two international studies have helped clarify the way *schizophrenic* is used in different parts of the world. Both the US–UK Diagnostic project (Cooper, Kendell, Gurland, Sharpe, Copeland, & Simon, 1972) and the International Pilot Study of Schizophrenia (WHO, 1973) relied extensively on the Present State Examination (PSE), a standard interviewing procedure that appears highly reliable. A computer program called CATEGO has been developed to profile these symptoms (Wing, Cooper, & Sartorius, 1974). Most recently, the American Psychiatric Association has published a major revision of its Diagnostic and Statistical Manual of Mental Disorders (American Psychiatric Association, 1980). Although it would be premature to evaluate its strengths and limitations, the task force, headed by Robert L. Spitzer, that developed this revision should be commended for its increased reliance on empirical development and verification. The classificatory system contained in this manual is supported by an abundance of operational definitions and has clear potential for significantly improved diagnostic reliability.

Behavior therapists, in their haste to reject the basic tenets of the medical model, have often shunned the use of diagnostic labels. Instead of persevering with symptomatology and its theoretical relation to diagnosis, etiology, and disease process and treatment, behavior therapists have traditionally narrowed their interests to specific problem behaviors. Concepts such as diagnosis and treatment have been reformulated into the generation of hypotheses and verification of functional relationships between environment and behaviors. By separating itself from conventional nosological systems, behavior therapists' selection of target variables is mostly arbitrary and these variables are selected, at times, solely for the convenience of the experimenter. Regrettably, this approach has fostered several unfortunate consequences.

First, behavior therapists' selective choice of target behaviors has done little to assure congruence between the criteria used for diagnosis or admission and the variables targeted for treatment. Behavior therapists may, in fact, become overly specific in their identification of target behaviors.

Second, although behavior therapists' emphasis on target behaviors to some extent circumvents issues of diagnosis in individual case studies, greater attention must be given to identifying a subject population for group designs. Unless these criteria are delineated more precisely, comparisons across group studies become meaningless. A review of the literature on behavioral interventions with schizophrenics shows that the diagnostic criteria are not even specified in the vast majority of these studies. Case studies, which sometimes report successes and sometimes report treatment failures, become quite difficult to evaluate when diagnostic criteria are not specified.

Third, the relative contribution of any group study may be jeopardized by the potential heterogeneity within its subject population. For example, several treatment studies simultaneously select subjects from vastly different major classificatory groupings (personality disorders, neurotics, and psychotics), who are then treated identically. Before we can systematically examine which behavioral treatments are more efficacious for particular groups of patients, we must be able to identify these patient groups reliably. While current nosological systems are not without problems, it would behoove behavioral researchers to include some of the more objective diagnostic schemes discussed above (cf. Endicott, Foreman, & Spitzer, 1979).

Definitional issues notwithstanding, our present intention is to examine the general applicability of behavioral interventions to a schizophrenic population. Although a complete and thorough review of the behavioral literature is beyond the scope of this chapter, our initial goal is to reflect on behavior therapists' successes and failures with a wide variety of target behaviors, most notably those commonly employed as diagnostic criteria for the classification of schizophrenia. At the risk of appearing unduly critical, we place particular emphasis on delineating the major weaknesses of our current technology. By bringing attention to these weaknesses, we hope to generate future renewed interest in the development and research of improved treatment strategies.

Operant Paradigms

The systematic application of behavioral principles to a schizophrenic population is best traced to the work of Lindsley and Skinner, beginning in 1954. Essentially, these investigators extended their operant technology developed from research with animals lower on the phylogenetic scale to a series of experiments with schizophrenics. Following the same initiative for experimental control, they used a small experimental room with very little furniture or other distracting stimuli. A review of this early experimental work is particularly interesting (see Inglis, 1966; Lindsley, 1956, 1960). Lindsley experimented with a variety of reinforcers and measured a variety of responses. Furthermore, since he recorded the patients' behavior regularly over long periods of time (in some cases, years), Lindsley had

several opportunities to observe the cyclical nature of such phenomena as psychotic episodes. In essence, Lindsley's work helped to provide the framework for an operant orientation often referred to as *behavior modification*. This orientation provided two major contributions to the treatment of schizophrenics. The first represents the development of behavioral principles whose main target variables were specific symptomatologies. The second contribution is in the area of ward management or, more specifically, "token economies." In a later section of this chapter, we devote considerable attention to both the potential benefits and the limitations of token economies. First, let us examine the application of operant principles to the target behaviors that characterize schizophrenic symptomatology.

In the treatment literature, several operant-oriented treatments have been applied to the modification of delusional speech. The majority of these studies share a general emphasis on increasing appropriate speech with positive reinforcement. In one of the first studies to modify delusional verbal behavior, Rickard and his colleagues (Rickard, Digman, & Horner, 1960; Rickard & Dinoff, 1962) used a verbal reinforcement procedure and reported a dramatic decrease in the delusional talk of a 60-year-old male who had been hospitalized for 20 years. These investigators simply expressed interest and approval whenever this patient's verbalizations were found to be appropriate. Whenever the speech became delusional, the therapist simply turned away from the patient. Although the results were very suggestive, the investigators unfortunately used an A-B design, which precluded strong conclusions.

In another study, Ayllon and Haughton (1964) also used a single-case design and reported more impressive results in light of their reversal design. In this study, nurses recorded a series of verbal interactions with each of three patients. Verbal interactions were limited to a maximum of three minutes, and these were recorded for 15–20 days before any experimental manipulation. Each interaction was classified as either psychotic or neutral. Contingent reinforcement, which was successively applied to each class of verbal behavior, consisted of listening and showing interest to the patient and intermittently providing candy or cigarettes. The extinction procedures entailed withholding both social attention and tangible reinforcers. The results showed that when contingent reinforcement was applied to neutral verbalizations, that response class increased in frequency. Conversely, when that procedure was applied to psychotic verbalization, the frequency of that response class increased. When the extinction procedure was applied to either response class, the frequency of that response class decreased below that of baseline levels. In addition to the small number of subjects, however, one limitation of this study was the absence of reliability checks on the nurses' recordings.

Wincze, Leitenberg, and Agras (1972) incorporated a more sophisticated design and compared the effects of both feedback and reinforcement procedures in reducing the delusional talk of 10 paranoid schizophrenics. Recordings of delusional talk were made both within therapeutic sessions and on the ward. Reliability checks of these recordings were always high (usually above 90% agreement). Additionally, a psychiatric resident naive to the design of the study supplied general "improvement" ratings at the beginning and end of each experimental phase. The results of this study indicate that the feedback procedure showed some success in reducing the percentage of delusional speech for about half the subjects, but it also produced adverse reactions in at least three subjects. The reinforcement procedure appeared to be more consistent, reducing delusional talk in seven of the nine subjects who completed this phase of the program. The results of the psychiatric interviews showed either no change at all in some of the patients or gradual improvement over the course of the experiment regardless of the experimental contingencies (e.g., feedback, baseline, or reinforcement).

These results are important in two ways. First, they indicate the potential limitations of feedback procedures with a psychotic population, an issue less salient with normal or neurotic populations (e.g., Leitenberg, Agras, Thompson, & Wright, 1968). Second, the data are important in highlighting the crucial problem of generalization. The effects of both treatment procedures were clearly specific to the therapeutic environment. The reductions of delusional speech during therapeutic sessions were far greater than those observed on the ward.

Major difficulties in obtaining generalization of treatment effects are also illustrated in a study by Liberman, Teigen, Patterson, and Baker (1973), who attempted to reduce the delusional speech of four chronic patients by providing "evening chats" with the therapists of their choice. The length of this interaction covaried directly with the amount of rational speech observed in an interview occurring earlier in the day, and the "chat" was terminated whenever the patient emitted irrational speech. These authors found an appreciable reduction of delusional speech in both the daily interview and the evening chat, but no generalization to ward surroundings was found. In fact, one of the four patients actually increased his delusional talk on the ward. In a subsequent study, Patterson and Teigen (1973) gave specific ward training to one of these four original patients, who subsequently showed improvement on the ward and was later discharged.

Difficulty in obtaining generalization effects is a problem shared by the majority of individual behavioral programs involving schizophrenics. Another potential limitation of this research area is the lack of strong empirical evidence documenting the maintenance of treatment effects. Although early behavioral studies should be commended for their groundbreaking attempts at developing their behavioral interventions, relatively few early studies reported adequate follow-up data. Although some studies suggest that decreases in delusional speech *per se* may continue after discharge, these effects appear to be maximized when family members are programmed to reinforce rational speech and to ignore irrational speech (cf. Nydegger, 1972). While addressing the maintenance issue, Liberman, Wallace, Teigen, and Davis (1974) have specifically called for the use of simultaneous procedures to decrease delusional speech and reinforce rational conversation. The suggestion that punishment procedures be used to reduce delusional speech, however, is not without risk, since treatment effects are often temporary and erratic. Davis, Wallace, Liberman, and Finch (1976) used a time-out procedure to reduce delusional statements and found only temporary and specific effects. Delusional references were reduced only in the observational samples where contingencies were applied. Moreover, the authors observed that when the time-out procedure was applied, the patient often placed a hand over the mouth and mumbled what were presumably delusional statements.

Problems in obtaining adequate generalization of treatment effects are well known to investigators who have attempted to reinstate speech in mute schizophrenic patients. Isaacs, Thomas, and Goldiamond (1960) attempted to reinstate speech in two patients who had been mute for 14 and 19 years. In a clever shaping procedure, one patient was initially reinforced with a stick of gum for simply looking at the gum. Once this response was established, the patient was additionally required to make a vocalization. Finally, the patient was required to say, "Gum, please." Eventually, the patient answered direct questions presented in group sessions. The specificity of these treatment effects, however, soon became apparent. Although the patient spoke to the experimenter on the ward, his verbal behavior failed to generalize to other ward personnel. To increase the generalization of reinstated verbal behavior to people other than the experimenters, the investigators were required to bring a nurse into the therapeutic room and to reinstate the shaping procedure. Thus, although the generalization was extremely poor, the results did demonstrate the conditionability of verbal behavior.

An even more convincing demonstration of the effect of positive reinforcement on verbal behavior is found in a study by Sherman (1965). He employed both imitation and fading procedures with three schizophrenic patients who had been hospitalized for 20–45 years and had a history of mutism ranging from 16 to 43 years. After speech had been reinstated with these procedures, Sherman used a reversal procedure to rule out alternative explanations. In this experimental phase of the study, the subjects were reinforced for not replying to the experimenter for 30 seconds. Under these reverse contingencies, the subjects did not speak.

An additional problem in this research area has been noted by investigators who have experimented with various modes of reinforcement. While the use of tangible reinforcers such as cigarettes or candy with mute or near-mute schizophrenics has consistently been shown to be effective (Thomson, Fraser, & McDougall, 1974; Wilson & Walters, 1966), procedures that rely on vicarious learning have questionable effectiveness with this patient population. Wilson and Walters (1966), for example, found that modeling without reinforcement was much less effective than modeling with reinforcement.

Other Behavioral Procedures

One area of clinical research that has incorporated a wider range of behavioral treatments is represented by those studies aimed at reducing hallucinatory behavior. Rutner and Bugle (1969) applied a self-monitoring procedure to a long-term female patient who experienced hallucinations of a controlling nature. For the first 3 days of their program, the patient privately recorded the following frequencies of hallucinations: 181, 80, and 11. Following these private recordings, the patient's chart was placed on public display, and she received praise and social reinforcement from both staff and other patients whenever a reduction in hallucinatory behavior was evident. During the course of this case study, the patient reported that hallucinations decreased to 0 within 13 days and remained completely suppressed at a six-month follow-up.

Bucher and Fabricatore (1970) treated a schizophrenic patient who complained of disturbing hallucinations by providing him with a portable shock device and instructing him to deliver a shock to himself whenever he experienced a hallucination. After several days, the patient reported that he was no longer hallucinating and was subsequently discharged. Unfortunately, the general applicability of this procedure appears to be greatly restricted. The authors warned that very few chronic patients could be persuaded to follow this procedure. These restrictions were also reported by Anderson and Alpert (1974), who, after a two-week unsuccessful attempt with the shock device and procedure used by Bucher and Fabricatore, were prompted to develop an alternative procedure. Their particular patient apparently exhibited ritualistic hand and face movements, which reportedly accompanied hallucinations. Since these ritualistic behaviors were very disruptive of his normally routine activities, such as eating meals, he was positively reinforced for reducing the time it took to eat meals. One experimentally blind observer independently recorded the frequencies of these behaviors. The results of this new procedure showed a dramatic reduction in these behaviors when the contingencies were applied, and a reversal procedure witnessed a rapid return to baseline.

The effectiveness of self-administered shock procedures in reducing hallucinations was examined in a group-design study by Weingaertner (1971) with 45 schizophrenic inpatients. Weingaertner compared a self-shock condition to a self-administered "placebo" condition (subjects wore the same shock apparatus on their belts, which ostensibly delivered subliminal shock) and to an untreated control condition. His results showed that all three groups reported fewer hallucinations and improved as well on other symptomatology ratings following the two-week treatment. However, no significant differences were found between the groups. Weingaertner concluded that the major change agent was patient expectations. In viewing these results, the issue of self-administration itself must be considered. In a case report, Alford and Turner (1976) found positive results in reducing hallucinations when shock was administered by the experimenter. Again, further research is needed to examine this issue.

Following a somewhat different paradigm, Haynes and Geddy (1973) used a "time-out" procedure with a female patient hospitalized for over 20 years. Since the subject had difficulty describing her subjective experiences, let alone monitoring them, these investigators operationally defined a hallucination as observations that the patient was mumbling to herself or yelling loudly without any visible provocation. Their time-out procedure consisted of removing the patient from the ward and isolating her in an unfurnished time-out room for 10 minutes. Although time-out procedures, like other punishment procedures, appear generally more effective when applied continuously, every time the behavior is emitted, these authors applied the procedure in only some instances, about four times a day. Nonetheless, the procedure proved effective in reducing the frequency of baseline observations from 80% to 30% after 35 days. No further reduction beyond this rate was achieved.

Another separate group of investigations, following Davison's (1969) general suggestion to examine antecedent conditions, speculated that the hallucinatory behavior of schizophrenics may be related to anxiety. Although phobic or anxiety-motivated behavior is not typically included in any conceptualization of the primary-rank symptoms of schizophrenics, some patients diagnosed as schizophrenic nonetheless emit behavior that would fit the research criteria for phobic behavior. Not surprisingly, systematic desensitization has been tried in both single-case and group research with this population. Unfortunately, the general efficacy of this procedure with a psychiatric population appears equivocal. A review of single-case reports reveals a proportionate rate of success and failure. Slade (1972), for example, attempted a functional analysis of the hallucinations and situational antecedents of a 19-year-old schizophrenic. It appeared that the patient experienced tension before hallucinating episodes, which subsided thereafter. Slade also reported that mood states deteriorated during episodes of hallucinations. In his systematic desensitization procedure, Slade included an *in vitro* hierarchy of tension-provoking stimuli and reported that hallucinations significantly reduced in frequency, especially at follow-up. Unfortunately, the patient was later rehospitalized with depression, albeit free of hallucinations. In a later controlled study, however, Slade (1973) was unable to replicate his earlier success. In another study, Lambley (1973) attempted to desensitize distressing thoughts, but his patient was again reporting hallucinations and uncomfortable thoughts at a 6-month follow-up. In another study, Alumbaugh (1971) reported success in reducing anxiety associated with cigarette smoking. Unfortunately, his results are seriously confounded because of the introduction of a concurrent procedure that reduced cigarette-smoking behavior itself.

Two case studies that do report success include as a common denominator the incorporation of an *in vivo* hierarchy. Cowden and Ford (1962) reported the success of a systematic desensitization procedure with a patient diagnosed as paranoid schizophrenic who was extremely panicky and frightened when he talked with other people. Other forms of treatment with this patient were all unsuccessful. Following the desensitization procedure, the patient was reported as more talkative, more relaxed, and more productive in his work, and he was then able to leave the hospital grounds at the conclusion of treatment. Similarly, Weidner (1970) successfully applied an *in vivo* hierarchy to a paranoid patient who would not leave the hospital grounds for fear of assassination by the CIA. Following treatment, this patient was reportedly able to leave the hospital grounds on a pass.

Although these case reports suggest that systematic desensitization may indeed be effective with some patients, the results of published group studies are extremely difficult to evaluate. One well-controlled study examining the effects of systematic desensitization in reducing anxiety in a schizophrenic population is that of Zeisset (1968). This study specifically examined "interview anxiety" recorded by experimentally blind observers. Although Zeisset found moderate success with systematic desensitization, the results are tempered by the fact that the subjects included both neurotic and psychotic patients selected principally because they could converse *without* overt delusional or hallucinatory behavior. Two other group studies, which at first glance appear to demonstrate the ineffectiveness of this procedure with schizophrenic patients, may not provide a fair examination. In the first of these (Serber & Nelson, 1971), a nonstandard procedure was employed. In the second study, Weinman, Gelbart, Wallace, and Post (1972) compared desensitization with socioenvironmental therapy or relaxation alone in increasing assertive behavior. Unfortunately, this study failed to provide any convincing evidence that the target behavior (interpersonal assertion) was related in any way to anxiety. In fact, the authors noted that if their

patients could not describe an anxiety-related situation, one was provided for them from six "standardized" situations.

At best, the demonstrated efficacy of desensitization with schizophrenics is equivocal. It is interesting to note that Wolpe (1958, 1961), who first introduced this technique, cautioned against the application of this procedure to psychotic patients. For different theoretical reasons, Wilkins (1971) has suggested that systematic desensitization is effective in large part because of increased expectancy of therapeutic outcome or increased cognitive or attentional control. Given the cognitive and communicative deficiencies found in schizophrenic populations (Lang & Buss, 1965; Payne, 1966), it is not surprising that several authors have noted the difficulties involved in implementing systematic desensitization procedures with schizophrenics. Cowden and Ford (1962) reported that schizophrenic patients have difficulty in selecting anxiety-related stimuli. Their patients appeared inattentive and lacked concentration during the experimental sessions, and they infrequently practiced relaxation exercises. Both Weinmann *et al.* (1972) and Serber and Nelson (1971) reported that their subjects had considerable difficulty in completing hierarchies and had limited imagery abilities. Zeisset (1968) suggested, "perhaps pessimistically," that the relaxation exercises themselves may be the only component helpful to this population. In summary, these results are not very encouraging. Besides the need for better-controlled research, two directives should be noted. First, future research should pay closer attention to specifically delineating a functional relationship between anxiety-related stimuli and apparently anxiety-motivated behavior. Second, more effort should be directed toward incorporating *in vivo* hierarchies into the procedure, obviating some of the cognitive components necessarily involved in imagery procedures.

Although very few behavioral interventions have been applied to other major "symptoms" associated with the diagnosis of schizophrenia, a few other interesting procedures have been directed at specific behavior problems of schizophrenic patients. One of these procedures, stimulus satiation, calls for the repeated presentation of a reinforcing stimulus. Presumably, the patient will become satiated and the reinforcing stimulus or reinforcing activity will become neutral or aversive. Although only a few reports of this procedure have appeared in the literature, most have appeared to be successful. Using this procedure, Ayllon (1963) successfully treated a patient who hoarded towels in her room, and Ayllon and Michael (1959) treated a patient who carried so much trash on his person that he eventually suffered skin rashes. Wolff (1971) also successfully applied this procedure to the delusional behavior of a patient by requiring her to voice her delusions for one hour a day. Liberman *et al.* (1974), however, had less success in reducing visual hallucinations using this technique.

Other researchers have combined elements of aversive conditioning with covert processes. Agras (1967) successfully eliminated glass breaking in a chronic patient by administering faradic shock whenever the patient reported ''visualizing'' this behavioral sequence. Royer, Flynn, and Osadca (1971) also reported success in treating a patient's persistent fire setting by having him light pieces of paper and throw them into a pail of water, simultaneously shocking the patient when he did so.

While these studies reflect the creative application of behavioral interventions in problem behaviors, future research is needed to systematically examine the application of these procedures to the symptomatology of schizophrenia.

Cognitive-Behavior Therapy

In recent years, cognitive-behavioral interventions have been successfully applied to a large variety of problem behaviors (Kendall & Hollon, 1979; Mahoney, 1974). The general popularity of these techniques has been prompted, in part, by an increased effort to obtain adequate generalization of treatment effects and also, in part, by the pragmatic intention of behavior therapists of providing their patients with methods of controlling their own behavior. Conceptually, cognitive interventions are founded on two independent assumptions. The first is that cognitive processes serve an important mediating role in controlling human behavior. The second major assumption is that these covert processes are subject to the same basic principles of learning (both classical and instrumental) that explain overt behavior. Although most behaviorally oriented researchers were initially hesitant to include nonobservable events in their behavioral paradigms, interest in these clinical procedures has grown geometrically in the last 10 years.

Meichenbaum (1969) reported one of the first attempts to utilize these cognitive procedures with a schizophrenic population. In a well-controlled design, Meichenbaum compared both token and reinforcement procedures in their ability to increase the relevant and logical use of proverbs in an interview setting. Ultimately, these procedures were designed to promote ''healthy talk.'' The results revealed that both treatment groups showed significantly more improvement than control groups. The token reinforcement procedure was more effective than social reinforcement. Meichenbaum also reported that the treatment effects were maintained at a follow-up interview and were generalized to other verbal skills. Unfortunately, his follow-up interval was only one week after posttest.

In attempting to better understand the processes of generalization, Meichenbaum rather serendipitously observed some of the patients talking aloud to themselves, apparently giving themselves instructions such as ''Be logical'' or ''Be coherent.'' He reasoned that these self-statements or self-instructions provided the patient with a useful aid in ignoring distractions (especially self-generated ones) and in increasng task-oriented attention.

To further examine the effects of what Meichenbaum coined as ''self-instructional training,'' he and Cameron (Meichenbaum & Cameron, 1973) specifically tried to train subjects to think to themselves in this fashion. By means of procedures such as modeling and social approval, patients were eventually shaped to internalize their thinking. Lastly, the subjects were trained to become more perceptive of this ordered speech in others. The results of two experiments showed that the patients receiving this cognitive training improved more in problem-solving skill and reduced their disordered speech more than yoked-practice control subjects who received similar reinforcement for correct performance but without self-instructional training.

Although Meichenbaum's procedure appears especially robust with respect to these target variables, little research has examined the general applicability of this technique to other schizophrenic symptomatology. In a case study, Meyers, Mercatoris, and Sirota (1976) applied a self-instructional procedure to reduce a chronic schizophrenic's psychotic speech. The results of their treatment showed a marked reduction of inappropriate verbalization. The results also showed good generalization of treatment effects as well as continued reduction of these inappropriate verbalizations at a six-month follow-up.

While these studies point to the potential benefits of cognitive interventions in general and self-instructional training in particular, at least one attempt to replicate Meichenbaum and Cameron's research has been unsuccessful. Margolis and Shemberg (1976) assigned a group of process schizophrenics and a group of reactive schizophrenics to either a self-instructional training procedure or a yoked-practice control group. Although these authors employed two half-hour sessions instead of a single one-hour session, both the treatment and the assessment procedures were modeled after Meichenbaum and Cameron's study. Although Margolis and Shemberg's study would appear to have greater statistical power (e.g., eight subjects per group as compared with only five subjects per group in the Meichenbaum study), they were hard-pressed to explain the absence of any significant treatment or interaction effects. In attempting to explain these findings, the authors noted that their subjects often described the treatment as "silly" or "babyish." Second, they found that most subjects had forgotten their training during posttesting. Third, the authors suggested that self-instructional training may be highly task-specific, detrimental, in fact, in those tasks with a speed component (e.g., digit symbol). In any case, the brief duration of treatment in both studies suggests a need for further research examining a more comprehensive and thorough training procedure.

Another applied research area using cognitive principles includes methods of increasing subjects' problem-solving ability. The major impetus in this area is D'Zurilla and Goldfried's (1971) premise that the basis for most abnormal behaviors is the person's inability to solve situational problems. When problems remain unresolved, they subsequently lead to both cognitive and behavioral deficits. The ultimate goal of problem-solving training is to initially delineate the problem, to develop alternative strategies, and to monitor the effectiveness of the chosen alternative. Although these techniques are particularly attractive at the theoretical or conceptual level, surprisingly little data exist to support their effectiveness in modifying schizophrenic behavior. Those studies that have specifically examined problem-solving procedures (Coche & Douglas, 1977; Coche & Flick, 1975; Siegel & Spivack, 1976) report positive changes on self-report data. Unfortunately, they fail to include behavioral measures.

As will be noted later in this chapter, several ambitious projects are currently under way that include an intensive "social-skill-training" approach to the treatment of schizophrenia (Brown, 1982; Liberman, 1982; Wallace, 1982). To say the least, these investigators have employed an extremely comprehensive treatment package, including components of problem-solving training. Although the preliminary data clearly pointed to a particularly promising treatment of schizophrenia (e.g., in reducing recidivism), further component research is needed to isolate the respective contribution of problem-solving processes *per se*.

In summary, the contribution of individual behavioral programs in the treatment of schizophrenia is extremely difficult to evaluate. Although early researchers should be commended for their ingenuity in applying behavioral principles to the treatment of schizophrenic symptomatology, attempts to assess *both* the maintenance (durability) and the generalization of treatment have appeared in only relatively recent literature. Moreover, investigators are often hard-pressed to demonstrate any generalization. Further research is especially needed to isolate those factors responsible for the promotion of generalization. Although common sense would dictate the potential utility and benefits of cognitive interventions (especially in promoting generalization), extremely few controlled studies have appeared in the literature. Research is needed to further examine these potentially viable procedures.

Token Economies

Establishment of a Token Economy: Problems and Suggestions

This section of the chapter is based largely upon the first author's experience as an intern on a research project directed by Gordon L. Paul (Paul & Lentz, 1977) and later consulting work with various institutionalized populations. The problems and issues addressed as well as the suggestions made are not meant to be comprehensive but merely illustrative of the complexities involved in establishing a token economy. Any and all the problems discussed, if not addressed, can severely diminish the effectiveness of such a program. The management of such a program requires a continual monitoring of all aspects of the program and a dedicated and knowledgeable staff.

Selecting and Defining Criterion Behaviors. Before establishing a token economy program, it is obviously imperative that one decide which criterion behaviors and their components are to be reinforced within the system. It is useful to view these criterion behaviors in a hierarchical fashion. For example, one major grouping of behaviors may be self-care (such as bathing, shaving, dressing, and feeding); occupational (good work habits such as promptness and staying on task); educational (basic rudiments of reading, writing, and arithmetic), and social (such as initiating conversations and participating in games and social activities). Deviant or crazy behavior is another category of behavior that must be attended to, but since these are behaviors we are wishing to eliminate rather than to reinforce, we will discuss them in a later section.

Under each of these four major headings one further has to stipulate an exhaustive list of those behaviors that are to be reinforced. For example, under self-care behaviors, one could include such things as appropriate eat-

ing, bathing, feeding, and dressing. Each of these behaviors must then be operationalized. For example, on Paul's (Paul & Lentz, 1977) research project, appearance checks were made in order to reinforce appropriate dressing patterns. The 11 subcomponents of appropriate appearance used were (1) proper use of makeup; (2) clean fingernails; (3) hair combed; (4) teeth brushed; (5) all appropriate clothing on; (6) clothing buttoned, zipped, and tucked in; (7) clothing clean and neat; (8) body clean; (9) no odor; (10) shaven; and (11) hair cut appropriately (Paul & Lentz, 1977). Each of these subcomponents was further operationalized (e.g., "teeth brushed" was defined as no food on teeth, no grit on teeth, breath that allowed one to stand within a few feet, nicotine stains acceptable, and dentures in).

It is extremely important to have each of the criterion behaviors well defined in order to prevent inconsistencies among those individuals responsible for dispensing the tokens. If the token dispensers are inconsistent, then the token program will appear arbitrary to the patients and produce resentment. It is also important when operationalizing these criterion behaviors that the capabilities of the residents (i.e., the individuals residing within the token economy) be given some consideration. For example, if residents are to receive tokens for engaging in recreational activities such as volleyball, some consideration must be given to their athletic talent. One would not expect a 50-year-old chronically institutionalized psychiatric patient to play volleyball as well as a well-coordinated college athlete. Hence, playing volleyball may be defined as standing mostly in one's assigned zone, attempting to hit the ball over the net, not kicking the ball or catching it and throwing it at another patient, etc.

One must always remain extremely vigilant so that the operationalized definitions of the criterion behaviors are consistent with the goals of the program. For example, when Paul's project was first started, residents received tokens for "on-task" behavior in a classroom. It became apparent after a short while that some residents were extremely ingenious at "looking as if they were busy" and doing classroom work, when in reality, they were producing only little work, which was of inferior quality given their capabilities. Consequently, a production criterion was built into the system whereby the teachers, based on their knowledge of the residents' capabilities, judged whether the person had performed acceptable work. One may also find that the operational definition of these criterion behaviors may have to be changed over a period of time because of numerous factors. For example, the absolute hair length of young male patients that was judged acceptable changed when long hair on males became fashionable in the late 1960s. A constant reevaluation of the criterion behaviors and their components is critical. If any changes are made, some means must be established by which these changes can be communicated to the staff. In addition, in all likelihood, new behaviors will have to be added because it is difficult if not impossible to conceive of all of the criterion behaviors that will prove useful to the resident after discharge. For example, it may not occur to one when first establishing a program that patients need to know how to write checks, use credit cards, etc., in order to facilitate their functioning in the natural environment.

Elicitation of Criterion Behaviors. As anyone knows who has worked with schizophrenic patients, it is highly inefficient to wait for a patient to exhibit the total criterion behaviors before reinforcing them. Chronic patients may never have exhibited these behaviors or may no longer be exhibiting them because of institutionalization, psychopathology, etc. Various activities must be arranged in which these behaviors are to be expected, and teaching devices must be employed in order to elicit and develop the criterion behaviors. For example, self-help classes can be arranged in which residents are shown how to shave, make their beds, bathe, wash their clothes, iron their clothes, etc. Other classes can be arranged wherein residents are taught how to make change, write checks, use a telephone, etc. Activities can be planned in which residents are expected to interact both with other residents and with treatment staff members. Residents can be taught how to initiate a social interaction, how to terminate one, how to make small talk, etc. Numerous learning techniques may be used to teach these target behaviors, including instruction, mod-

eling, verbal and physical prompts, fading procedures, response chaining, and response shaping.

Any and all of these techniques may be used to teach a skill, although some procedures may work best for a particular skill or for a given resident. For example, in teaching highly regressed residents to shave, we found the following procedures useful: modeling criterion behaviors; providing verbal prompts such as "Pick up the razor" and "Hold it up to your face"; using physical prompts such as holding the patient's wrist and pulling down on his wrist when the razor was adjacent to his face; fading these prompts with time; shaping better and better approximations to removing all whiskers; and chaining a series of behaviors such as washing the face and applying the shaving cream. Another example of the use of these procedures can be found in our attempts to get many of the mute residents to speak. Modeling and prompting procedures were first used to get the patient to imitate nonverbal behaviors. Physical prompts such as holding the patient's mouth in such a way as to make a particular sound were utilized. Chaining procedures were used to get residents to emit several sounds in sequence that corresponded to words, etc.

Shaping was the most common procedure utilized. Shaping was generally employed on either a time dimension or by reinforcing subcomponents of the criterion behaviors. As already mentioned, many criterion behaviors were broken down into subcomponents (e.g., appropriate appearance had 11 subcomponents). At each appearance check, a resident would have to maintain his/her previous gains (e.g., 3 out of 11 subcomponents) plus 1 additional subcomponent in order to receive a token. A set number of failures on the new criterion would result in a drop back to the previous criterion. Other criterion behaviors, such as participation in recreational activities, were shaped on a time dimension. For some residents, this meant 30 sec of participation and for other residents participation during the whole time period (e.g., 50 min). Careful recording of each resident's attainment of the various criteria set out for him/her that day is necessary in order to adequately shape criterion behaviors.

Promoting Transfer of Attained Skills to the Natural Environment. Skills are developed and behavior is shaped in a token economy in a much more systematic and direct fashion than is usually the case in the natural environment. Unless residents are gradually introduced back into the natural environment and extramural support systems are established, there is some likelihood that the skills developed within the token economy may deteriorate. A useful procedure for promoting transfer back into the natural environment is a concept of step levels within the token system. As a resident progresses through the step levels, he/she is "weaned" from the token system, and more time is spent in the natural environment. In the initial steps, reinforcement is immediate (e.g., a resident is given a token immediately after the appearance check), while on the more advanced step levels, residents may receive the tokens that they have earned only at the end of the week, much like a check. In the most advanced steps, a resident may essentially be given a credit card. He/she may also be working eight hours a day in the community and just sleeping in the residential unit at night. To advance to the upper step levels, a resident's behavior must become more and more appropriate. That is, a resident must meet more and more of the criterion behaviors established within the program. At the earliest step levels, a resident earns only enough tokens to purchase minimal and necessary reinforcers. As a resident progresses through the steps, more individualization of the treatment program can also occur. At more advanced levels, a resident can join a prerelease group, the goal of which is to prepare the resident for self-supporting functioning in the community. The leader of the prerelease group can serve as the liaison person for the resident between the community and the treatment staff within the residential treatment center. The leader of the prerelease group assists the resident in securing employment and a place to live. Previous research (Paul, 1969) would seem to indicate that an important factor in preventing recidivism is for a released resident to have established a good relationship with a "significant other" individual. A significant other may be a relative; however, great care must be exercised in choosing this significant other.

The research of Brown, Monck, Carstairs, and Wing (1962) demonstrated that residents returning to a home where relatives show a high degree of emotional involvement are more likely to relapse than those who do not return to such homes (Vaughn & Leff, 1976).

Several other methods may be employed to introduce residents to the community gradually. Once or several times a week, a community trip may be planned for those residents who meet individualized criteria. Trips to restaurants, bowling alleys, etc., may be arranged so that residents can gain valuable exposure to community facilities. The taking of day, night, and weekend passes should be encouraged. In fact, in order to maintain status at the upper step levels, residents may be required to take passes of various durations. Another means by which to give residents exposure to the community is to bring the community to them. For example, in the Paul program (Paul & Lentz, 1977), an off-unit evening activity program was run, mainly with volunteers from the community. These individuals generally volunteered for one night a week and engaged in various types of activities, such as teaching the residents to use makeup, serving as lifeguards at a swimming pool, and showing the residents how to bake a cake. These volunteers need to be extensively trained in the principles of a token economy system so that their interactions are consistent with the overall program. These volunteers often serve as valuable liaison persons in the community after a resident has been discharged.

Token Distribution. Individual staff members must be assigned specified times to distribute tokens and should be held responsible for their distribution. For example, one staff member may be assigned to room inspection from 6:30 A.M. to 7:00 A.M. and to appearance check at 7:00 A.M., while another staff member may be assigned to distribute tokens for appropriate eating behavior at breakfast, and so on. When the staff member distributes the token, verbal praise should be given, and the behavior that is being reinforced should be specified. In addition, staff individuals should also specify the criteria that the resident will have to meet in the next check. For example, the staff individual might say, "Here's your token, John, for working ten minutes during class today. You did a super job, and I'm really proud of you. Tomorrow, in order to earn your token, you'll have to be working twenty minutes.'' The staff member will then record that the resident has been given a token and specify the criterion for the next activity of a similar kind. When working with extremely low-functioning residents, it is important for them to receive direct, immediate, and constant reinforcement. Often, these residents need to be reinforced every 5 min or for even briefer periods of time. For logistical purposes, it is often useful to have what is called a *shaping chip* to distribute to these low-functioning residents. A shaping chip is similar in form to a token except that it has a different color. These chips may be distributed at frequent intervals during an activity and may be exchanged for a token at the end of the activity if the resident has met the criterion. For example, one resident might have to earn 10 shaping chips during an activity in order to receive 1 token, while another resident may have to earn only 4 chips.

Backup Reinforcers. In order to motivate low-functioning residents to earn tokens, it is essential to have control over their access to reinforcers. This control may have to include basic reinforcers such as cigarettes, clothing, and meals. It is important to have many and varied reinforcers available as backups to the token system. Though it may not be physically possible to have all these backups located in the residential treatment center, they can still be made available. For instance, catalogs from various department stores and other outlets may be available to the residents. Exchange rates can be established (i.e., *x* tokens equal *y* dollars), so that a patient may earn tokens for merchandise illustrated in these catalogs. Civic organizations such as Lions Clubs, Kiwanis, and Knights of Columbus are often willing to donate reinforcers if other funds are lacking.

It is important to determine what is reinforcing for any particular resident. Very often, quite idiosyncratic reinforcers are found, and determining these idiosyncratic reinforcers may make all the difference in the world. Numerous methods are available to determine what a resident may find reinforcing, including asking them and asking relatives, friends, etc.

It has been our experience that very often, many of these residents have been isolated for such long periods of time it is actually necessary to expose them to a wide variety of reinforcers and have them sample them in order to make a determination of what they find reinforcing.

A Balanced Economy. There is a very thin line between having a depressed or an inflated economy. Both depression and inflation must be avoided, or the functioning of the token economy may be jeopardized. Therefore, tokens should be dispersed only at scheduled times, by designated members of the staff, and only for specific behaviors. Minimal functioning should result in minimal token earnings and minimal reinforcement. As a resident passes through the various step levels, earning power should increase, and more and varied reinforcers should be made available. As in any community, individual residents may attempt to live outside the monetary system by such behaviors as stealing, black-marketeering, and counterfeiting. One manner of handling disruptions to the economy such as stealing would be to place an individual offender on a different-color token, so that stolen tokens become valueless because they cannot be spent.

Inappropriate and Intolerable Behaviors. A token economy is basically a rewarding system that reinforces individuals for appropriate behaviors. Residents are not forced to do anything; rather, they are free to choose within the token system to work for reinforcers. Inappropriate behaviors, such as ''crazy talk,'' are handled by a complete absence of reinforcement; that is, engagement in inappropriate behavior is often incompatible with earning tokens, and the staff are trained to ignore and not to socially reinforce inappropriate behaviors. Intolerable behaviors, such as striking another resident or a staff member, can be handled in a number of ways, including a response cost, time-out, restitution procedures, and demotion to a lower step level. However, it is important to note again that a token economy should be a rewarding system and should not be seen as a means of punishment.

Data Collection. Some form of data collection is absolutely necessary in order to maintain a token economy system. One needs to know how many tokens were dispensed and to what residents, how many tokens each resident spent, and on what reinforcers. The staff needs to know what the criterion is for any particular resident for any particular activity during the day. Summary recordings for each individual resident indicating their level of functioning with respect to the criterion behaviors must be recorded in order to determine the residents' status with respect to the various step levels. The amount of a fine for an intolerable behavior must be recorded because the fined residents then have to pay back the fine. Without these types of recordings, a token system could not operate. Forms may be developed to make these recordings extremely efficient, so that they require only a few seconds of staff time after each scheduled activity (Paul & Lentz, 1977). In addition to these necessary data recordings, other forms of data collection are desirable. Incidences of inappropriate behaviors can be recorded in order to determine the effectiveness of a token system in reducing inappropriate behavior. Staff behavior can also be periodically monitored in order to determine whether they are behaving in a fashion consistent with the program. If a staff member is behaving unprogrammatically, then direct and immediate feedback should be given.

Staff Training, Communications, and Morale. In order to establish an effective token economy, it is essential that the staff be thoroughly trained in its procedures so that their behavior is consistent with the goals of the program. There are numerous skills that the treatment staff must master. The staff must be able to judge reliably whether any resident has met a criterion behavior and all its subcomponents. They must learn to complete daily recording sheets accurately and efficiently. They need to learn how to administer verbal and nonverbal prompts, how to chain behavior, and how to shape it. Extensive training needs to be undertaken before a staff member should be allowed to operate as a member of the treatment team. Training can include reading instructional material, viewing videotapes emphasizing criterion behavior, and on-the-unit training with an experienced staff member.

The morale in any unit dealing with low-functioning chronic psychiatric patients can be a problem. Teaching low-functioning residents more appropriate behaviors is an extremely slow, painstaking process. Staff members need to be constantly informed of the patient's progress from the beginning to the end of the program. It helps to have members of the senior staff working on the "front lines" with junior staff members for morale purposes. In addition, senior members of the staff are more likely to voice opinions regarding the appropriateness of specific procedures for a particular resident. It is also important to have a representative from each treatment shift attend a weekly meeting to discuss potential problems and changes in the program.

Good communication among all staff members is extremely important in a token economy. All staff members need to know the present status of each resident with respect to step levels, whether anyone has been fined, changes in medication, who has been caught stealing, who has been promoted, which residents are working and what hours, and so on. This type of communication should be recorded in a log book, which is read by the incoming staff "out loud" in the presence of the outgoing staff so that all individuals may be informed and any difficulties cleared up. Because there will often be changes in how the token economy operates during the course of several months, it is important that all staff members be made aware of these changes via memos, etc., and periodically tested on the rules and regulations of the program.

Conclusions. It is the contention of the authors that all the above issues need to be addressed in some fashion in order to establish an efficient and effective token economy. Suggestions regarding each of these issues were largely based on the first author's experience in the use of token economies with severely psychotic, chronic mental patients. Token-economy treatment programs dealing with less debilitated patients may not require some of the features suggested. For example, programs focusing on less debilitated patients may not require such elaborate procedures for teaching patients various instrumental skills because these skills already exist in the patients' repertoire, and the contingency system alone will serve to attain the desired performance. Likewise, in working with less debilitated patients, it may not be necessary to depend on primary reinforcers as "backups" to the token system. However, although elaborate procedures may not be necessary to overcome each of these problems, they still need to be addressed in some sort of systematic fashion if the token economy is to be successful.

Problems in Evaluation

It is difficult to draw a firm conclusion regarding the outcomes of most of the token economy studies reported in the literature because they contain numerous flaws in experimental design (e.g., failure to equate subjects and failure to equate treatment staffs). It is even more difficult to compare results across studies because of differences in the patient populations used, differences in the dependent measures, and major differences in program components within the token economies. Some studies include severely debilitated patients, while others concern mildly debilitated patients or a mixture of mildly and severely debilitated patients. Even in those studies in which an attempt has been made to use a relatively homogeneous (with respect to one or several dimensions) group of residents, other patient characteristics may interact with treatment effectiveness. For example, Kowalski, Daley, and Gripp (1976) suggested that paranoid schizophrenic patients seem to improve more than other types of schizophrenics in a token economy.

The types of dependent variables used as outcome measures have varied greatly in the literature. In some studies, the focus is on measuring decreases in psychotic behaviors, such as delusions or bizarre repetitive motoric behaviors, while in other studies, the dependent measures focus on measuring increases in behavior such as socialization, and attendance at unit activities. Some studies employ discharge into the community as a major dependent variable, although discharge is more often a function of an administrative decision than a reflection of improved functioning on the part of the resident. Comparisons across studies are also made difficult by the lack of

specification of the details of the treatment program and/or the lack of attention paid to the components addressed in the previous section. As Paul and Lentz (1977) stated:

Reports of so-called token economy programs that do not articulate, let alone monitor, the specific classes of patient behavior of focus, the criterion for disbursing or withholding tokens and other sociable and tangible consequences, the range and control of backups, the nature of staff patient interaction, etc., may be no more related to other token economy programs than the action of heroin is related to that of penicillin, even though both are administered by injection. (p. 434)

The first author once had the experience of serving as a consultant to an already-established "token-economy" program in a state hospital. He was flabbergasted to discover that although tokens were dispensed, there were no backup reinforcers supplied within this system. Amusingly enough, the administrators were puzzled over the lack of success of their "token" program. While none of the reviewed studies contain such a glaring omission of a component of a token program, many of them do not appear to have paid sufficient detailed attention to all of the components addressed above. A brief review of token economy studies is contained in the next section. Single-case studies are not reviewed here because the use of operant procedures in a single-case format have been discussed elsewhere in this chapter.

Treatment

The pioneer research on token economies was conducted by Ayllon and Azrin (1968). Their research was directed at developing and testing operant procedures rather than evaluating the overall effectiveness of a token economy. Nevertheless, their findings, which indicated that an operant system could change certain types of psychotic behavior in a controlled setting, stimulated interest in the use of token economies for the treatment of chronic psychiatric patients.

Schaefer and Martin (1966) compared the relative effect of a contingent and a noncontingent token system on severely regressed psychiatric patients. The same treatment staff administered the contingent and noncontingent tokens, therefore controlling for staff attention and ward atmosphere. The results indicated significant decreases in apathy and increases in responsibility and general activity in the patients receiving contingent tokens when compared with the patients who were receiving noncontingent tokens. Baker, Hall, and Hutchinson (1974) also compared the effects of the use of contingent tokens. A group of seven schizophrenic patients were exposed to differential aspects of a token economy system in a sequential manner. The patients were first transferred to a smaller ward with a better standard of care. After 6 weeks of just ward exposure, a stimulating activity program was initiated. After the activity program had been in operation for 3 weeks, noncontingent tokens were disbursed for a 7-week period, followed by a contingent token program of 14 weeks. The patients improved in several areas; however, most of this improvement occurred before the application of contingent tokens. The authors concluded that token reinforcement components did not emerge as the critical therapeutic agent. In another study, Baker, Hall, Hutchinson, and Bridge (1977) compared patients in a contingent token program with patients in a noncontingent milieu-type program. The results suggested that the patients in the milieu noncontingent program improved more than the patients in the token program. However, in both of the Baker studies, there appeared to be little attempt within the token programs to teach and shape instrumental behaviors.

A number of investigators (Ellsworth, 1969; Foreyt, Rockwood, Davis, Desvousges, & Hollingsworth, 1975; Liberman, 1971) have reported higher discharge rates and lower readmission rates after token systems have been introduced for chronic patients who had been previously unaffected by other treatments. Heap, Boblitt, Moore, and Hord (1970) studied the effects on discharge of a treatment program that combined features of both a token economy and a milieu treatment. Significantly more patients treated in the combined token economy and milieu program were discharged from the hospital than patients in a control ward. Lower readmission rates were reported by Hollingsworth and Foreyt (1975) for patients who had been exposed to a token economy program in comparison with a hospital control group. However, there

were few differences between the discharged token-economy patients and the discharged control patients with respect to community functioning. Although, as mentioned previously, discharge is often the result of an administrative decision rather than improvement in a patient's behavior, the consistency of results obtained across different investigators is encouraging.

Token economies have been reported to affect many different types of behavior. Gorham, Green, Caldwell, and Bartlett (1970) found an initial increase in psychotic symptoms after a token economy had been introduced, but improved functioning after a short period of time. Gripp and Magaro (1971) compared the effects of a token economy program on chronic female patients with patients in three other units. The authors reported significantly more improvement for the residents of the token economy unit with respect to symptomatic behaviors (e.g., agitated depression, social withdrawal, and thought disorders). Residents on the token program were also seen as improving more with respect to social competence and self-care maintenance. Presly, Black, Gray, Hartie, and Seymour (1976) reported increases in social interaction among chronic male patients after the introduction of the token economy system, but no major changes in bizarre psychotic behavior. Neither the Presly et al. (1976) study nor the Gripp and Magaro (1971) study adequately equated patients in their treatment and control groups, and therefore, caution should be used in interpreting the results. Two studies, one of male psychiatric patients (Shean & Zeidberg, 1971) and one of female psychiatric patients (Maley, Feldman, & Ruskin, 1973), reported significant increases on measures of cooperation, communication, and social contact in patients in the token economy program when compared with control groups. Olson and Greenberg (1972) found that group contingencies resulted in increased attendance at activities by mildly disabled patients when compared with patients in control groups. Although each of these studies possesses some methodological flaws, the consistency of results would seem to suggest that token economies can modify a wide variety of behaviors.

In one of the better controlled studies in the

literature, Stoffelmayr, Faulkner, and Mitchell (1973) studied the differential effectiveness of four treatment programs with severely chronic male psychiatric patients over a one-year period. The patients were assigned to one of four groups: a hospital control, a token system group, and two different milieu groups, one of which was more structured and had more meetings than the other group. The residents in the token economy program, when compared with the hospital control group, evidenced significantly greater improvement in all areas of functioning measured. When compared with the residents in either of the milieu treatment programs, the residents in the token program demonstrated significantly more improvement in self-care skills, overall increases in activity, and decreases in apathy. The residents in either of the milieu programs demonstrated initial improvement over the hospital controls but these improvements were not maintained over time.

In what is recognized (by Gomes-Schwartz, 1979) as the most comprehensive and best-controlled study in the literature, Paul and Lentz (1977) compared the relative effectiveness of a token economy to an enriched milieu treatment and a hospital control treatment. This study evaluated the effects of four years of treatment on severely regressed, chronic schizophrenics. A multitude of assessment instruments were used to evaluate the relative effectiveness of these programs. In general, the results clearly indicate the superiority of the token economy system over either the milieu treatment program or the hospital control program. At the end of treatment, 89.3% of the token economy patients were significantly improved, in contrast with 46.4% of the milieu patients. Unfortunately, this program was prematurely ended after a four-year period (Paul & Lentz, 1977). At the termination of the program, all the residents capable of functioning in the community were placed in the community. Some of these residents were placed with their families, others in extended-care facilities, and others achieved independent functioning. After termination of the program, a six-month follow-up was conducted. The percentages of residents who had achieved a release and had evidenced a continuous community stay were 92.5% for the token economy unit, 71% for the milieu treatment unit, and 48.4% for the hospital comparison unit. Of the patients on the token economy unit, 10% were able to live independently and be self-supporting. Clearly, the results of this well-controlled study are both the dramatic and encouraging.

Conclusions

Although many of the studies reviewed have severe methodological flaws, the mostly consistent positive results seem to support the contention that token economies can be effective in treating chronic schizophrenics. Given the fact that many of the token programs reviewed "shortchanged" some of the components listed in the previous section (e.g., did little to develop the target behaviors or paid little attention to posthospital care), one would expect even more dramatic results if all these issues were clearly faced and effectively resolved.

It is our contention that the major advantage of a token economy is that it provides a structure and a motivational system wherein patients learn new skills and coping strategies through various therapeutic interventions. We agree with D'Zurilla and Goldfried's (1971) suggestion that abnormal behavior may be viewed as an inability (for whatever reason) on the part of the individual to resolve situational problems. Subsequently, the individual's ineffective attempts to resolve the problems results in an increase in or a maintenance of emotional, cognitive, and behavioral pathologies. Since schizophrenics do not possess adequate coping skills to handle the stresses in their lives effectively, it is essential in treating schizophrenics to teach them adequate coping strategies and instrumental skills.

It is interesting to note that in the Paul program (Paul & Lentz, 1977), there was little focus on psychopathology *per se*. Psychotic behaviors were ignored except when they presented a danger to either the residents or the treatment staff. The major focus was on training patients in instrumental behaviors. As the residents developed more instrumental behaviors, decreases in psychotic behaviors occurred (Paul & Lentz, 1977).

In the next section of this chapter, we review studies in which systematic attempts have been made to teach psychiatric patients social skills in order to increase their overall social functioning. Although previous research (Zigler & Phillips, 1961c,1962) has demonstrated the important role that patients' social skill level plays with respect to hospitalization, posthospital functioning, recidivism rate, etc., it has been only in the last decade that investigators have systematically attempted to increase the social functioning of psychiatric patients.

Social Skills Training

The many studies cited earlier in this chapter demonstrate that operant technology can be and has been successfully employed in modifying specific maladaptive behaviors of individuals who are labeled schizophrenic. The limitations of this technology have been discussed with regard to the issues of maintenance of behavior change and generalization of treatment effects. Durability and generalization of treatment effects have been especially poor in the treatment of deficit interpersonal behaviors (Paul, 1969). One reason may be that most operant approaches merely reinforce behaviors that exist in the patient's repertoire and do not teach patients how to cope with problems in interpersonal interactions. The problem is that many schizophrenic patients do not have appropriate social behaviors in their interpersonal repertoires that can be strengthened through reinforcement. Since interpersonal problem behaviors are especially severe among many schizophrenic patients, a more comprehensive intervention strategy is warranted.

Although recognition of the relationships between social competence and psychiatric disorder date as far back as 20 years ago (Strauss & Carpenter, 1974, Zigler & Phillips, 1960, 1961a,b), relatively few treatment strategies have been developed that systematically address the problem of social inadequacy among psychiatric patients. The significance of socially relevant treatment strategies for schizophrenics is reflected in a recent summary report of research on the psychosocial treatment of schizophrenia submitted to the Institute of Medicine, National Academy of Sciences. It concludes, "it is noteworthy that the positive findings from controlled studies are most consistent for those treatments that involve extensive attention to the individual patient's social environment" (Mosher & Keith, 1979, p. 629). No treatment has more directly or systematically attempted to influence patients' social environments than social skills training.

Definition and Patient Population

Social skills training consists of a comprehensive treatment package that usually includes the following components: behavior rehearsal, modeling, reinforcement, prompts, homework assignments, feedback, and instructions (Goldstein, 1973; Hersen & Bellack, 1976b). Although several conceptual definitions of social skills training have been offered, each having slightly different theoretical and treatment implications, we have found Goldsmith and McFall's (1975) description concise and useful:

A general therapy approach aimed at increasing performance competence in critical life situations. In contrast to therapies aimed primarily at the elimination of maladaptive behaviors, skill training emphasizes the positive, educational, aspects of treatment. It assumes that each individual always does the best he can, given his physical limitations and unique learning history, to respond as effectively as possible in every situation. Thus, when an individual's "best effort" behavior is judged to be maladaptive, this indicates the presence of a situation-specific skill deficit in that individual's repertoire. . . . Whatever the origins of this deficit (e.g., lack of experience, faulty learning, biological dysfunction) it often may be overcome or partially compensated for through appropriate training in more skillful response alternatives. (p. 51)

Although social skills training has been implemented with many psychiatric disorders (Hersen, 1979), our comments in this section are based on studies of patients who fall under the diagnostic category of schizophrenia. Before commenting on these studies, a major methodological-strategic problem regarding diagnosis deserves attention. Given the behavior therapist's general philosophy concerning diagnosis, it is not surprising to find that in most cases, little effort has been expended in securing reliably diagnosed schizophrenics. Indeed, it is questionable whether most patients labeled schizophrenic in social skills studies would fit the DSM III criteria for schizophrenia. This is unfortunate, since unreliable diagnoses make comparability across studies very difficult and make it almost impossible to explain contradictory findings (Wallace, Nelson, Liberman, Aitchison, Lukoff, Elder, & Ferris, 1980). Nevertheless, the studies that have been considered for the present section are those that have used the labels *schizophrenic* or *psychotic* to describe at least some of their patient population. Though such a pooling procedure makes interpretation difficult, consideration of only those reports describing their patient populations as *schizophrenic* would include only a small fraction of the studies available, and we feel that little information would be gained from such a review. Studies that have clearly excluded patient groups labeled *schizophrenic* or *psychotic* have not been drawn upon.

Social skills training for schizophrenic patients is based on the notion that poor social performance may be due to one or several of the following factors: (1) the individual may never have learned the appropriate social behavior; (2) if appropriate social behavior has been learned, it may not now be available because of disuse resulting from a lengthy psychiatric illness; (3) the individual may have a faulty cognitive-evaluative appraisal of the contingencies and consequences of a particular social interaction; and (4) the individual may have a high level of anxiety, which interferes with what otherwise might be adequate performance. It should be noted that the skills training approach is primarily focused on performance, not on hypotheses about why the deficits may or may not exist.

Treatment Protocols

A consideration of some of the major features of various social skills treatment protocols reveals that although many of the training packages utilize many of the same essential procedures, there is little precise consistency in protocols across treatment studies (Curran, 1979). This situation is similar to that mentioned earlier in relation to token economy programs. For example, although nearly all social-skills training protocols include the components of rehearsal, modeling, reinforcement, feedback, and instructions, some researchers (e.g., Hersen & Bellack, 1976a) employ these specifically to increase or decrease certain circumscribed target behaviors (e.g., eye contact or speech latency), whereas other researchers (e.g., Monti, Fink, Norman, Curran, Hayes, & Caldwell, 1979) apply the same treatment components to a much more global target (e.g., giving criticism). Another example may be found in the more recent interest in patients' "internal states." Once again, the level of emphasis has varied for different treatment protocols. For example, Bellack and Hersen (1978) have included components such as listening, identifying emotions, and getting clarification. Along similar lines, Trower, Bryant, and Argyle's (1978) protocol emphasizes training observational skills, meshing skills (timing and relevance), listening skills, and problem-solving skills. An even more cognitively oriented program is provided by the work being done by Wallace, Liberman, and their colleagues (Wallace, 1978; Wallace, Nelson, Lukoff, Webster, Rappe, & Ferris, 1978). These investigators reason that a skillful response is the result of an integrated chain of behaviors. This chain begins with the accurate "reception" of social stimuli, progresses to the "processing" of these stimuli, and results in the "sending" of an appropriate response. Wallace and his colleagues have identified sets of variables that are important for each of these behaviors. The assessment and treatment of schizophrenic patients is focused on each of these variables. Another significant aspect of this approach that differentiates it from others is the intensity of the treatment protocol. Liberman, Nuechterlein, and Wallace (1982) have suggested that a minimum of six months of intensive treatment may be necessary to establish clinically significant changes in schizophrenic patients.

Since space limitations preclude a detailed presentation of each of the treatment protocols that have been developed for schizophrenic patients, we present here a summary of the social-skills treatment protocol that we use in our treatment groups at the Behavior Training Clinic of the Providence Veterans Administration Medical Center. The reader is referred to Monti, Corriveau, and Curran (1982) for a more detailed presentation of this treatment package.

Treatment sessions led by co-therapists are usually conducted during the week on a daily basis for 60 min over a 4-week period (a total of 20 sessions). Groups usually consist of 7–10 patients. The treatment sessions are based on a 10-chapter treatment manual, which consists of the following topics: starting conversations, nonverbal behavior, giving and receiving compliments, self-instructional training, giving criticism, receiving criticism, feeling talk and listening skills, being assertive in business situations, close relationships, and intimate relationships. Each chapter is the focus of two sessions. The first session of a particular chapter is largely concerned with teaching the content of that chapter. A good deal of role playing and modeling is done by the co-therapists, who model appropriate behavior utilizing material in the text. Patients in the group are asked about their personal experiences as they might relate to examples mentioned in the text. Through this procedure, role-play situations are modified and developed, and the material is made more relevant to the specific needs of the members of any particular group. Patients are encouraged to rehearse and role-play material in the text during this session. This gives the co-therapists a sense of the group's baseline level of functioning regarding a particular area. The second session on a chapter is used for additional teaching and rehearsal. During this session, patients role-play their responses with each other as well as with the co-therapists. A good deal of coaching and instruction is provided by the co-therapists. Feedback and reinforcement are provided by both therapists and patients following each rehearsal. Videotape feedback is often used to provide more specific feedback. Care is taken not to emphasize the negative aspects of the patients' behavior. Rather, positive aspects are emphasized, and through gradual shaping procedures, appropriate behavior replaces inappropriate behavior. If after role playing, information, and feedback, members of the group are still deficient in certain behaviors, the cycle is repeated as time allows.

Homework assignments accompany both sessions of each chapter. Homework consists of having the patient practice outside of the group the behaviors discussed and learned during a particular session. For example, a homework assignment for the chapter on starting conversations might include instructions directing the patient to start a conversation with someone he/she knows and then to start a conversation with a stranger. Patients are given homework forms and are encouraged to write down the specifics of the situation (e.g., who the conversation was with and the difficulties encountered). Homework assignments are collected and discussed at the beginning of each session. The completion of homework assignments may be publicly charted, depending on the particular group. Patients are encouraged to bring problems they had in the homework into the group, where they can role-play the homework assignment and receive feedback from the group. Homework assignments are specifically used to promote extrasession generalization.

Generalization is also promoted through the use of adjunct role-players. These are staff members or trained students, usually unknown to the patients, who attend a group on occasion and serve as additional role-players. This procedure provides patients with opportunities to practice their new response repertoires with "strangers," in the context of support and encouragement from other group members.

Evidence of Treatment Effectiveness

It is not our purpose to provide an exhaustive review of the literature, since excellent recent reviews of the experimental evidence on social skills training with schizophrenic patients are available (Hersen, 1979; Wallace *et al.*, 1980). Rather, consistent with the theme of this chapter, we shall summarize the social-skills-treatment literature giving special emphasis to the maintenance and generalization of treatment effects. Since the experimental literature can be clearly divided, on methodological grounds, into single-case experimental design and group-design studies (Wallace *et al.*, 1980), a prototypical example of each study design is provided, accompanied by a summary of the most consistent findings obtained by each method. Next, the evidence for the generalization and durability of behavior change is reviewed. Finally, suggestions are made regarding possible ways of promoting or enhancing the effects of social skills training for schizophrenics.

Single-Case Experimental Design Studies. Single-case experimental methodology, usually employing multiple baselines across behaviors, patients, and/or situations, have contributed a great deal to our understanding of the effects of social skills training on the behavior of schizophrenics. Indeed, almost all of the studies reported to date that have carefully identified schizophrenic patients have been conducted in the single-case experimental design fashion. Most of these studies have employed laboratory-type procedures, such as the Behavioral Assertiveness Test (BAT; Eisler, Miller, & Hersen, 1973), to do both training and assessment. Nearly all single-case experimental design studies report positive treatment effects.

A good example of a single-case study that is particularly relevant to the present chapter is the Hersen, Turner, Edelstein, and Pinkston (1975) study. This investigation is especially pertinent since it considers a schizophrenic patient who, prior to social skills training, was on a general token-economy program as well as a combination of medications. After several weeks, it was clear that the general token economy was not therapeutic for this patient. At this point, an individualized token-economy program was designed and implemented, and within two days "remarkable improvement in the patient's appearance was noted" (p. 589). Next, a behavioral analysis of the patient's social interactions was conducted, and it revealed certain social skills deficits (e.g., poor eye contact and response latency). The BAT scenes served as both the training and the assessment instrument.

Training in this study consisted of instructions, behavioral rehearsal, feedback, and *in vivo* modeling of four of the eight BAT scenes. The remaining four scenes served as a measure of generalization. A multiple-baseline design was employed. Eye contact, response latency, and requests for new behavior were targeted and monitored, while the patient's verbal initiations during group therapy were unobtrusively monitored as an additional measure of generalization. A baseline and each of four experimental phases lasted approximately one week each. The results suggested that sequential treatment for eye contact, latency, and requests for new behavior showed improvement over baseline. Three other behaviors (overall assertiveness, voice trials, and speech disruptions), although not treated, improved, as did verbal initiations in group therapy sessions. Follow up interviews, conducted at 4-week intervals to 22 weeks postdischarge, indicated that the patient's progress had been maintained.

This single-case study emphasizes several important aspects of treating schizophrenic patients. First, medication was and should be regulated prior to experimental intervention (Hersen, 1979). This regulation is especially important when dealing with schizophrenics, since cognitive functions can be significantly affected by changes in psychotropic medications and, in turn, can interact with the effectiveness of social skills training. Second, the patient's participation in a token economy program as well as the social skills training program points to another important aspect of dealing with this patient population, namely, that often a response acquisition approach is needed in addition to a simple token-economy approach because the appropriate behavior may not exist in the patient's repertoire and may actually have to be taught.

The results of the Hersen *et al.* study have been replicated in other similarly designed studies conducted by Hersen, Bellack, and their colleagues (Eisler, Hersen, & Miller, 1974; Hersen & Bellack, 1976a; Williams, Turner, Watts, Bellack, & Hersen, 1977) as well as by other researchers (e.g., Matson & Stephens, 1978; Wood, Barrios, & Cohn, 1979). In general, the results of these studies indicate a definite improvement in specific behavioral components of social skill, such as eye contact, voice volume and tone, latency and duration of speech, and posture. Clearly, the short-term effects of social skills training on specific behavioral components of social skills are well documented in single-case experimental design studies.

Group-Design Studies. Studies that have examined the effect of social skills training on schizophrenics by means of group-comparison designs are particularly difficult to summarize since there is a great deal of variance in patient characteristics (e.g., rigor of diagnoses and severity of skills deficits) and assessment methodologies, both across and sometimes within studies. In addition, treatment methods vary considerably across studies (Wallace *et al.*, 1980). Nevertheless, group-design studies can be generally characterized as offering relatively few group treatment sessions and yet showing positive treatment effects. Such effects are typically measured by laboratory-based pre- and postassessment instruments (e.g., the BAT), which are given to both experimental group and control group patients.

A study conducted by Finch and Wallace (1977) is used here as an illustration of a group-comparison design study. This study compared the effectiveness of a social skills training program to an assessment-only control condition. The subjects in the study were 16 nonassertive male schizophrenic inpatients. The treatment, which was conducted in a group format, included 12 sessions of interpersonal skills training designed to "increase assertive behavior both in and out of the group and to decrease anxiety in interpersonal situations" (p. 887). The treatment effects were assessed by comparing pre–post differences on three role-playing and four spontaneously enacted interpersonal encounters, which were audiotaped. The role-play situations were initiating a conversation, offering an apology, and extending a social invitation. The spontaneous situations were expressing an opinion, receiving a compliment, refusing an unreasonable request, and accepting thanks. All situations were rated on loudness and fluency of speech, affect, latency, and content. All but latency, which was timed, were rated on 5-point scales. In addition, quality of eye contact was judged by the confederate. Compared with the control group, the skills training group significantly improved on all measures. The improvements were apparent across both role-played and spontaneously enacted situations and across trained and untrained situations. Finch and Wallace did not report any evidence of generalization outside their assessment situations, nor did they report any follow-up data.

The findings of Finch and Wallace (1977), that specific behavioral components of social skills do improve as a function of treatment when tested in situations similar to treatment situations, are consistent with those of almost all of the group-design studies reported in the literature (Field & Test, 1975; Goldsmith & McFall, 1975; Goldstein, Martens, Hubben, van Belle, Schaaf, Wiersma, & Goedhart, 1973). Other consistent findings in the group-design literature are that more global measures of social skill (e.g., overall social skill) improve as a function of treatment (Monti *et al.*, 1979; Monti, Curran, Corriveau, DeLancey, & Hagerman, 1980), as do self-report measures of social skill and social anxiety (Goldsmith & McFall, 1975; Monti *et al.*, 1980). Thus, there is good consistency across both single-case designs and group-design studies, suggesting that social skills training can change posttest performance on either specific behavioral components or more global measures of social skill when tested in laboratory-based situations similar in kind to the treatment situations. Clearly, at this level of analysis, social skills training does seem to be effective in modifying the social behavior of schizophrenic patients. We now turn to an examination of more clinically relevant issues, namely, the generalization and maintenance of behavior change resulting from social skills training.

Evidence of Generalization of Behavior Change

Although consistently positive treatment effects have been reported for nearly all single-case and group-design studies that utilize assessment instruments similar to training instruments (e.g., Finch & Wallace, 1977; Hersen *et al.*, 1975; Monti *et al.*, 1979), much less consistency is found when testing scenes or situations that are not similar to those presented in training (Wallace *et al.*, 1980). Several studies (Bellack, Hersen, & Turner, 1976; Frederiksen, Jenkins, Foy, & Eisler, 1976; Williams *et al.*, 1977) have shown little or no improvement on scenes dissimilar to those presented in training, whereas other studies (Finch & Wallace, 1977; Monti *et al.*, 1979) do show improved performance on untrained scenes as well as trained scenes. Finally, the results of both single-case and group-comparison studies typically show poor generalization of improvement as measured by assessment situations clearly different (i.e., non-laboratory-based) from those trained. For example, Gutride, Goldstein, and Hunter (1973) found only limited improvement in ward behavior, and Jaffe and Carlson (1976) found no improvement in ward behavior. Hence, treatment results typically form a kind of gradient of generalization, and treatment effects are more consistently demonstrated on measures that are similar to training situations and less consistently demonstrated on measures dissimilar to training situations.

In contrast to the general trend of poor generalization to situations dissimilar to training situations, Goldsmith and McFall (1975) demonstrated clear improvement in a situation different from situations presented in treatment. Goldsmith and McFall's study involved both the development and the evaluation of a social skills training program for schizophrenic inpatients. Perhaps the most significant feature of this study is that a behavioral-analytic approach was used to identify the problem behaviors of the patient population. Based on this analysis, a social skills training program was designed and compared with both a pseudotherapy control group and an assessment-only control group. The social skills training program involved training in initiating and terminating conversations, dealing with rejection, being more assertive and self-disclosing, etc. The results of this study indicated that the social skills training group proved superior to both the pseudotherapy control group and the assessment-only control group in producing significant pre–post therapeutic changes as measured by both self-report and behavioral instruments. Behavioral changes were obtained on both laboratory measures as well as on the Simulated Real-Life Behavior Test, which was based on a five-minute social interaction. The results were, for the most part, maintained at follow-up.

In another study where good generalization was obtained, Monti et al. (1979) compared the effectiveness of a systematic social skills group-training program with both a bibliotherapy program group and an assessment-only control group. In this study, 30 patients were randomly assigned to one of the three treatment conditions. The social skills treatment included modeling, role playing, coaching, rehearsal, and written homework assignments, which accompanied each session and which were thoroughly discussed both before and after they were completed. The results on a pre–post behavioral test (role-play performance on eight simulated social interactions) suggested that the patients in the social skills training group were more skillful after treatment than the control-group patients. Two unique aspects of this study are that follow-up data were collected across treatments at the longest interval (10 months) recorded in the group-design literature, and that measures of generalization were given at follow-up. The follow-up data suggested that the treatment effects were maintained and that the generalization effects were demonstrated in an analysis of trained versus untrained scenes, as well as on the Clinical Outcome Criteria Scale (Strauss & Carpenter, 1972) based on a clinical interview. The interview was conducted by a psychiatrist who was blind to the treatment conditions. Items on the scale reflected aspects of the patients' posthospital adjustment, such as job status and number of acquaintances seen. The findings on this measure showed that the patients who received social skills training were significantly improved as compared with the control-group patients.

Evidence of Durability of Behavior Change

Evidence of the durability of behavior change as a result of social skills training has been rather inconsistent. That is, some studies report the maintenance of treatment effects, while others report no treatment effects at follow-up. In addition, in many studies, no follow-up data are reported at all, and in others, only very short-term follow-up data are reported.

Let us first consider the status of follow-up data among the single-case experimental design studies. Most studies in this category that report positive treatment effects also report some follow-up data. These are usually for relatively brief, three- to five-month follow-up periods (e.g., Bellack et al., 1976; Hersen & Bellack, 1976a; Hersen et al., 1975). Although these follow-up results are usually positive, the follow-up data are sometimes merely impressions from a follow-up clinical interview.

The one single-case experimental design study in the literature (Liberman, Lillie, Falloon, Vaughn, Harpin, Leff, Hutchinson, Ryan, & Stoute, 1978) that reported a more extended one-year follow-up is perhaps the most ambitious study of social skills training and schizophrenia reported to date. This study treated three chronic schizophrenics who were at high risk for relapse with 300 hours of intensive skills training. A multiple-baseline design across areas of homework assignments (interactions with nursing staff, parents, and community agents) was utilized to demonstrate improvements in the patients' performance as a function of treatment. Improvements were measured by the number of homework assignments completed as reported by the patients and a validating staff member, parent, or community agent. One of the many significant features of this study was that the patients were diagnosed by means of the Present State Examination (Wing, Cooper, & Sartorius, 1974), one of the most reliable measures of schizophrenia available. Social skills training was judged to be effective as measured by completed homework assignments changing only when appropriate training was applied to each respective setting. Unfortunately, the one-year follow-up data indicated that the patients' levels of social competence returned to baseline after they had been discharged from treatment.

Relevant data on the maintenance of behavior change as a result of skills training are less available for group design studies than they are for single-case studies, as evidenced by the fact that only one-third of the group-design studies reviewed include any follow-up assessment whatsoever. Among those few group-design studies that do report follow-up data, nearly all report maintenance of treatment effects (e.g., Field & Test, 1975; Goldsmith & McFall, 1975; Monti *et al.*, 1979, 1980). However, some of these studies report incomplete follow-up data and/or no follow-up data for control subjects. For example, Field and Test (1975) reported follow-up data for four experimental patients, all of whom maintained their gains in three role-play test situations. Control-group patients were not tested at follow-

up, since many had received treatment during the follow-up interval. The absence of appropriate control-group follow-up data makes the interpretation of experimental data very difficult. Two studies (Monti *et al.*, 1979, 1980) reported follow-up data on appropriate control patients. Although both of these studies suggest relatively long-term treatment effects, neither study looked at schizophrenic patients exclusively. The need for more long-term follow-up data with schizophrenic patients is obvious.

Promoting Generalization and Maintenance of Behavior Change

Given the paucity of evidence for the generalization and maintenance of behavior change resulting from social skills training with schizophrenics, it is clear that we need more work directed at these problem areas. In this section, we consider possible avenues through which generalization and maintenance might be enhanced, in the hopes that such a discussion will prompt further thought on and empirical testing of some of these ideas. One treatment variable that might benefit from closer examination is the nature of the behaviors that are taught in social skills training protocols. Many of the single-case studies and some of the group-design studies have focused on circumscribed target behaviors (e.g., eye contact and speech latency). It is possible that such emphasis on specific components may be too simplistic, since it may omit other important aspects of social skill, such as timing, monitoring, sequencing, and other "process skills" (Trower, 1980). Experimental evidence provided by Fischetti, Curran, and Wessberg (1977) has pointed to the importance of some of these process variables in discriminating between groups of skilled and unskilled individuals. Since it is unlikely that we have identified all of the relevant variables involved in skillful responding, training on more global dimensions (so as to include both component and process variables) may be more profitable, given our present level of understanding of social skill.

A related variable that may be important and deserving of further empirical attention is the nature of the situations employed in training protocols. Most social skills training programs have selected their training material on the basis of clinicians' experience and intuition. Since most protocols have not employed much care in identifying those situations that are especially difficult for their patients, it may well be that we are using training situations that are not as relevant to patients as we assume they are. One notable exception is the painstaking, empirically based behavioral-analytic approach that Goldsmith and McFall (1975) employed in identifying the problem areas of their patients prior to treatment. Since Goldsmith and McFall's treatment results do seem to have generalized, it is possible that their empirically based treatment content was, in part, responsible for the generalization obtained. It is quite plausible that greater relevancy will facilitate learning and thereby influence the generalization and maintenance of behavior change. We are in agreement with Goldsmith and McFall's position that "content of a skill-training program is at least as critical to its ultimate success as the training methods it employs" (p. 51). We feel that more empirical work needs to be done in identifying relevant training material prior to embarking on treatment.

Yet another approach to facilitating learning and generalization might involve expanding on potential target areas for training. The recent interest on "internal states" (e.g., cognitive and emotional processes) is a step in this direction. An example of such an expended approach to the problems of social skills training and schizophrenia is provided by the work of Wallace (1978), which was discussed earlier. Wallace's approach emphasizes the receiving and processing as well as the sending components of social skill. The model proposed by Wallace and his colleagues is clearly more "cognitive" than many proposed to date. Given the well-documented cognitive deficits apparent in schizophrenia, Wallace's approach would seem to have particular promise for this patient population. Although no data were available at the time this chapter was written, Wallace and his colleagues are currently testing the adequacy of their model. Hopefully, the results of their innovative treatment work will show improvement in the durability and generalization of social-skills treatment effects with schizophrenic patients.

Another source for improving social skills training, generalization, and durability may be the existing literature on schizophrenia. As Liberman *et al.* (1982) have suggested, "It's as though the behavior therapists using social skills training and the experimentalists and psychopathologists studying the nature of schizophrenia live in two separate worlds" (p. 6). We feel that more integrated work is needed in studying the social skills training process and how it might interact with the known characteristics and deficits of schizophrenics. A study reported by Eisler, Blanchard, Fitts, and Williams (1978) provides an illustration of how a more integrated approach to the study of skills training and schizophrenia may prove useful. These authors reasoned that since schizophrenic patients suffer from increased thought and speech disturbances and more withdrawal than nonpsychotic patients, different training strategies might be necessary to teach these two different patient groups most effectively. In a 3×2 design, 24 schizophrenic and 24 nonpsychotic patients, all of whom had been preselected on the basis of their poor skill performance on the Behavioral Assertiveness Test-Revised (BAT-R), were randomly assigned to one of three experimental conditions: social skills training without modeling, social skills training with modeling, and a practice control ($n = 8$ per group). The treatment for each condition consisted of six 30-min rehearsal sessions, during which the patients role-played BAT-R training scenes. The patients in the social-skills training group without modeling received coaching, feedback, and practice on problem behaviors. The patients in the program of social skills training plus modeling received all of the above plus, prior to coaching, a videotape of a highly skilled model responding to a confederate. The results of pre–post BAT-R analyses and additional data obtained from a semistructured interpersonal conversation suggested that both social-skills training programs had positive effects. Tests of specific interaction effects suggested that modeling was essential in improving the performance of schizophrenics and "seemingly detrimental to non-psychotic individuals" (p. 167).

In this study, attention to the psychopathology of schizophrenia led to a different evaluation of training strategies for different patient groups. The obtained results emphasize the potential benefits of integrating knowledge from other areas of study on schizophrenia with our treatment approaches. We agree with the conclusion of Eisler *et al.* that "More effort is needed to design more specific training strategies for groups who share characteristic skill deficits and who are amenable to different sorts of learning experiences" (p. 170). In the absence of such specification, we may be inhibiting learning, and thus generalization and maintenance, by "turning off" our schizophrenic patients to our treatment because of deficiencies in our training procedures.

A factor that may influence the generalization and the durability of social skills training with schizophrenics is medication. Although many single-case studies have taken this possibility into some consideration (Hersen, Bellack, and their colleagues usually report that medication is regulated prior to beginning training), most group-design studies do not even mention medication, let alone control for its effects. Since psychotropic medications are apt to influence thought processes and behavior, it is likely that their effects influence treatment results and therefore should be carefully considered. An additional possible complication emerges when considering the literature on state-dependent learning in psychopharmacology. This literature suggests that learning under certain drugs may not readily transfer to drug-free states. Consequently, the issues of maintenance and generalization may be somewhat contingent on whether or not the schizophrenic patient continues on the same or similar medication (Paul, Tobias, & Holly, 1972). Experimental data that specifically examine the independent and interaction effects of social skills training and psychotropic medication, with well-diagnosed schizophrenics, are needed in order to address this important area adequately. Medication maintenance issues are especially important since a review of the literature outside the boundaries of social skills training suggests that in the long run, the most effective treatment for this patient population includes a combination of both pharmacological control and socioenvironmental interventions (Wing, 1978).

Another possible way to promote generalization and to maximize the long-term effects of our skills training programs may simply be to do more training. It is quite surprising to find that several group-design studies done on schizophrenics (e.g., Goldstein *et al.*, 1973; Goldsmith & McFall, 1975) have employed as few as 1, 3, or 4 sessions of social skills training. The studies reporting relatively good maintenance of behavior change have employed 10 or 20 intensive sessions (Monti *et al.*, 1979, 1980). Since these studies include relatively few schizophrenics, it is likely that much more training would be required when dealing exclusively with schizophrenics. Support for this argument may be found in the work of Shepherd (1978), who has recently demonstrated that increased frequency and duration of training have improved the generalization of behavior change with schizophrenics. Indeed, as mentioned previously, Liberman *et al.* (1982) suggested that at least 6 months and perhaps as much as two to four years of treatment are necessary for clinically significant and durable results with chronically and severely impaired schizophrenics. In addition to more extensive training, the inclusion of periodic "booster sessions" that extend well into follow-up periods may also enhance treatment effects. Since social skills training, like other therapeutic treatments, is rather expensive in terms of staff time and energy, we need research directed toward identifying what the optimal number of treatment and "booster sessions" might be for enhancing treatment effects.

Another factor that may contribute to generalization and maintenance is the attention given to the accurate completion and review of homework assignments during which the newly learned skills are practiced. This component was emphasized in the Monti *et al.* (1979) study, which produced relatively long-lasting and generalized treatment effects. Although Monti *et al.*'s use of extrasession homework assignments is not unique, few studies report as much emphasis on this component. Although the homework component was not formally tested in this study, it did provide patients with many opportunities to practice newly learned behaviors in different settings, and such procedures have been shown to promote generalization (Stokes & Bear, 1977).

At a different level of intervention, several recent innovative skills-training programs have utilized *in vivo* social skills training (Brown, 1982; Stein & Test, 1978) to further promote the generalization of treatment effects. Such *in vivo* treatment differs from typical homework assignments in that the therapist actually accompanies the patient into the real world and does "on-site" training. Several *in vivo* programs have placed schizophrenic patients in community-based living environments among ordinary people. On a rotating basis, trained staff provide *in vivo* treatment, which consists of performing day-to-day activities, such as cooking, shopping, and job hunting, along with the patient. The emphasis of such programs is on modeling, prompting, and shaping. Although too few relevant data are available regarding the generality of the effects of such comprehensive *in vivo* treatment approaches, it is probable that generalization will be maximized when it is so clearly programmed. As Brown (1982) suggested, it may well be time to pack up our cameras and begin to make the real world our training ground.

Summary

Although the relationship between social competence and psychiatric disorder has been known for quite some time, researchers have only recently begun to study the effect of social skills training on schizophrenic patients. In general, the studies that have been done have clearly demonstrated, on laboratory-based assessment tasks, the effectiveness of social skills procedures in improving specific behavioral components of social skill as well as more global measures of social skill.

When measuring the durability and generalization of behavior change, the results have been mixed. Most studies do not demonstrate a long-term maintenance of behavior change, nor have most studies adequately demonstrated the generalization of treatment effects. Several suggestions were offered for enhancing the generalization and/or the durability of behavior change. These include the development of a more empirically based training content; a possible expansion of the behaviors to be taught; movement toward a theoretically and practically more integrative approach; the control of medication; more extensive train-ing; more systematic use of homework assignments; and more *in vivo* skills training.

Although the treatment results obtained to date have been promising, the poor generalization of treatment effects and the absence of long-term follow-up data reflect the state of an area that is still in its infancy. We need to identify and integrate more of the relevant theoretical and practical variables before we embark on future treatment-outcome work. Indeed, only then can we expect clinically meaningful results that can be predictably obtained with this most challenging group of patients.

General Summary and Conclusions

In the introduction to this chapter, the gravity of the problem of schizophrenia was stressed. A brief review of the definitional problems revolving around schizophrenia led to a plea for the use of more objective criteria in defining schizophrenia, such as those endorsed by DSM III. The treatment section of this chapter is divided into three general sections. Two of these sections, the ones on token economies and on social skills training, involve attempts to make major, multiple, and comprehensive changes in the functioning of a schizophrenic patient. The first treatment section is in reality a "catchall" treatment section. Most of the procedures reviewed in this section are operant, although other behavioral procedures, such as desensitization and more cognitive-behavioral approaches, are also reviewed. In most cases, these treatment interventions are aimed at a rather circumscribed aspect of the schizophrenic's functioning. In general, these studies indicate that these procedures can be successfully employed in modifying specific maladaptive behaviors of schizophrenics. These studies are important because they demonstrate that schizophrenic symptomatology can be modified. However, in most cases, there are few data to support treatment maintenance and generalization and whether the treatment results in major changes in the clinical status of the individuals treated.

The section on token economies involves a discussion of some of the problems in establishing a token economy and presents some suggestions for the resolution of these problems. Some of the problems discussed were selecting, defining, and eliciting criterion behavior; developing procedures to handle inappropriate and intolerable behavior; establishing methods of token distribution; balancing the economy; and developing potent "back-ups." The crucial issue of promoting transfer was discussed, along with staff-related issues and the necessity for data collection. In reviewing the treatment outcome studies on token economies, we feel that many of these problems have not been adequately addressed; consequently, the effectiveness of token intervention programs has been limited. Nevertheless, the outcome studies still generally indicate positive, if limited, results. In those studies where these issues were adequately addressed, significant clinical changes appear to have occurred and to have generalized to the natural environment and to have been maintained. We feel that the major advantage of a token economy is that it provides a structure and motivational system wherein patients learn new skills and coping strategies that are instrumental in their functioning in the natural environment.

Social skills training is a systematic attempt to teach patients behaviors that will increase their social functioning. The training procedures generally include behavioral rehearsal, modeling, reinforcement, prompts, homework assignments, feedback, and instructions. Although most social-skills training programs utilize most of these procedures, there are numerous differences in the treatment protocols described in the literature. Consequently, making comparisons across studies is difficult at best. The evidence from both single-case studies and group-design studies indicates positive treatment effects, as measured by laboratory-based assessment procedures. However, the evidence with respect to the generalization of these behaviors to the natural environment and the maintenance of these positive changes over time is much less consistent. Several suggestions for enhancing generalization and maintenance included developing more empirically based training content; extending target behaviors; including more cognitive procedures; giving more extensive

training; and using more systematic homework and more *in vivo* skills training.

Although it is difficult to summarize the results of behavioral interventions with schizophrenics, some general conclusions can still be made. First, it is clearly possible to produce changes in the circumspect aspects of schizophrenic behavior. Unfortunately, these results often do not maintain or generalize very well, and hence, these changes are often of little clinical significance. Clinically significant changes appear to be found only when comprehensive and systematic procedures, such as token economies and social skills training, are applied in such a manner as to produce generalization and maintenance. These procedures involve teaching schizophrenics instrumental behaviors that will assist them in their functioning in the natural environment. The present status of our treatment of schizophrenia, which resembles a "revolving-door" approach (i.e., short stays, rapid turnover, and resulting high readmission rates), is not acceptable. Evaluations of intensive treatment programs are called for to determine whether they result in improved functioning of the schizophrenic patient.

While behavior therapists have made some strides in developing treatment procedures for use with schizophrenics, we have quite simply not met the challenge fully. Our immediate attention should now focus on the criteria we select to evaluate treatment success. While criteria such as "statistically significant reductions of delusional speech" have served a timely purpose in the development of a behavioral technology for schizophrenic patients, we must now attend to more clinically significant criteria, such as reducing the notoriously high readmission rates, promoting successful deinstitutionalization, and assisting schizophrenic patients to return to truly productive lives.

Before further strides can be made in this treatment area, we must first accept the reality that productive research will be difficult. Collectively, the studies reviewed in this chapter point to the need for comprehensive, long-term treatment programs for schizophrenic patients. Admittedly, this is not an easy task. Nonetheless, we are faced with an important challenge: to further develop treatment procedures for schizophrenic patients, a responsibility that must be accepted if we are to continue to point to the utility of behavioral technology with schizophrenics.

References

Agras, W. Behavior therapy in the management of chronic schizophrenia. *American Journal of Psychiatry*, 1967, *124*, 240–243.

Alford, G. S., & Turner, S. M. Stimulus interference and conditioned inhibition of auditory hallucinations. *Journal of Behavior Therapy and Experimental Psychiatry*, 1976, *7*, 155–160.

Alumbaugh, R. V. Use of behavior modification techniques towards reduction of hallucinating behavior: A case study. *The Psychological Record*, 1971, *21*, 415–417.

American Psychiatric Association, *Diagnostic and statistical manual of mental disorders*, III. Washington, D.C.: Author, 1980.

Anderson, L. R., & Alpert, M. Operant analysis of hallucination frequency in a hospitalized schizophrenic. *Journal of Behavior Therapy and Experimental Psychiatry*, 1974, *5*, 13–18.

Astrachan, B. M., Harrow, M., Adler, D., *et al.* A checklist for the diagnosis of schizophrenia. *British Journal of Psychiatry*, 1972, *121*, 529–539.

Ayllon, T. Intensive treatment of psychotic behavior by stimulus satiation and food reinforcement. *Behaviour Research and Therapy*, 1963, *1*, 53–61.

Ayllon, T., & Azrin, N. H. *The token economy*. New York: Appleton-Century-Crofts, 1968.

Ayllon, T., & Haughton, E. Modification of symptomatic verbal behaviour of mental patients. *Behaviour Research and Therapy*, 1964, *2*, 87–97.

Ayllon, T., & Michael, J. The psychiatric nurse as a behavioral engineer. *Journal of Experimental Analysis of Behavior*. 1959, *2*, 323–334.

Baker, R., Hall, J. N., & Hutchinson, K. A token economy project with chronic schizophrenic patients. *British Journal of Psychiatry*, 1974, *124*, 367–384.

Baker, R., Hall, J. N., Hutchinson, K., & Bridge, G. Symptom changes in chronic schizophrenic patients on a token economy: A controlled experiment. *British Journal of Psychiatry*, 1977, *131*, 381–393.

Bellack, A. S., & Hersen, M. Chronic psychiatric patients: Social skills training. In M. Hersen & A. S. Bellack (Eds.), *Behavior therapy in the psychiatric setting*. Baltimore: Williams & Wilkins, 1978.

Bellack, A. S., Hersen, M., & Turner, S. M. Generalization effects of social skills training with chronic schizophrenics: An experimental analysis *Behaviour Research and Therapy*, 1976, *14*, 391–398.

Brown, M. Maintenance and generalization issues in skills training with chronic schizophrenics. In J. P. Curran & P. M. Monti (Eds.), *Social skills training: A practical handbook for assessment and treatment*. New York: Guilford Press, 1982.

Brown, G. W., Monck, E. M., Carstairs, S. M., & Wing, J. K. Influence of family life on the course of schizophrenic illness. *British Journal of Preventive and Social Medicine*, 1962, *16*, 55–68.

Bucher, B., & Fabricatore, J. Use of patient-administered shock to suppress hallucinations. *Behavior Therapy*, 1970, *1*, 382–385.

Carpenter, W. T., Strauss, J. S., & Bartko, J. J. A flexible system for the identification of schizophrenia: A report from the International Pilot Study of Schizophrenia. *Science*, 1973, *182*, 1275–1278.

Coche, E., & Douglas, A. A. Therapeutic effects of problem-solving training and play-reading groups. *Journal of Clinical Psychology*, 1977, *33*, 820–827.

Coche, E., & Flick, A. Problem-solving training groups for hospitalized psychiatric patients. *The Journal of Psychology*, 1975, *91*, 19–29.

Coleman, J. C. *Abnormal psychology and modern life*. Glenview, Ill.: Scott, Foreman, 1976.

Cooper, J. E., Kendell, R. E., Gurland, B. J., Sharpe, L., Copeland, J. R., & Simon. *Psychiatric diagnosis in New York and London*. London: Oxford University Press, 1972.

Cowden, R. C., & Ford, L. Systematic desensitization of phobic schizophrenia. *American Journal of Psychiatry*, 1962, *119*, 241–245.

Curran, J. P. Social skills: Methodological issues and future directions. In A. S. Bellack & M. Hersen (Eds.), *Research and practice in social skills training*. New York: Plenum Press, 1979.

Davis, J. R., Wallace, C. J., Liberman, R. P., & Finch, B. E. The use of brief isolation to suppress delusional and hallucinatory speech. *Journal of Behavior Therapy and Experimental Psychiatry*, 1976, *7*, 269–275.

Davison, G. C. Appraisal of behavior modification techniques with adults in institutional settings. In C. M. Franks (Ed.), *Behavior therapy: Appraisal and status*. New York: McGraw-Hill, 1969.

D'Zurilla, T. J., & Goldfried, M. R. Problem solving and behavior modification. *Journal of Abnormal Psychology*, 1971, *78*, 107–126.

Eisler, R. M., Miller, P. M., & Hersen, M. Components of assertive behavior. *Journal of Clinical Psychology*, 1973, *29*, 295–299.

Eisler, R. M., Hersen, M., & Miller, P. M. Shaping components of assertive behavior with instructions and feedback. *American Journal of Psychiatry*, 1974, *131*, 1344–1347.

Eisler, R. M., Blanchard, E. B., Fitts, H., & Williams, J. G. Social skill training with and without modeling for schizophrenic and non-psychotic hospitalized psychiatric patients. *Behavior Modification*, 1978, *2*, 147–172.

Ellsworth, J. R. Reinforcement therapy with chronic patients. *Hospital and Community Psychiatry*, 1969, *20*, 238–240.

Endicott, J., Forman, J. B., & Spitzer, R. L. *Diagnosis of schizophrenia: Research criteria*. Paper presented at the 132nd Annual Meeting of the American Psychiatric Association, Chicago, 1979.

Feighner, J. P., Robins, E., Guze, S. B., Woodruff, R. A., Winokur, G., & Muñoz, R. Diagnostic criteria for use in psychiatric research. *Archives of General Psychiatry*, 1972, *26*, 57–63.

Field, G. D., & Test, M. A. Group assertive training for severely disturbed patients. *Journal of Behavior Therapy and Experimental Psychiatry*, 1975, *6*, 129–134.

Finch, B. E., & Wallace, C. J. Successful interpersonal skills training with schizophrenic inpatients. *Journal of Consulting and Clinical Psychology*, 1977, *45*, 885–890.

Fischetti, M., Curran, J. P., & Wessberg, H. Sense of timing: A skill deficit in heterosexual-socially anxious males. *Behavior Modification*, 1977, *1*, 179–194.

Foreyt, J. P., Rockwood, C. E., Davis, J. C., Desvousges, W. H., & Hollingsworth, R. Benefit-cost analysis of a token economy program. *Professional Psychology*, 1975, *6*, 26–33.

Frederiksen, L. W., Jenkins, J. O., Foy, D. W., & Eisler, R. M. Social skills training to modify abusive verbal outbursts in adults. *Journal of Applied Behavior Analysis*, 1976, *9*, 117–127.

Goldsmith, J. B., & McFall, R. M. Development and evaluation of an interpersonal skills training program for psychiatric inpatients. *Journal of Abnormal Psychology*, 1975, *84*, 51–58.

Goldstein, A. P. *Structured learning therapy: Toward a psychotherapy for the poor*. New York: Academic Press, 1973.

Goldstein, A. P., Martens, J., Hubben, J., van Belle, H. H., Schaaf, W., Wiersma, H., & Goedhart, H. The use of modeling to increase independent behaviors. *Behaviour Research and Therapy*, 1973, *11*, 31–42.

Gomes-Schwartz, B. The modification of schizophrenic behavior. *Behavior Modification*, 1979, *3*, 439–468.

Gorham, D. R., Green, L. W., Caldwell, L. R., & Bartlett, E. R. Effect of operant conditioning techniques on chronic schizophrenics. *Psychological Reports*, 1970, *27*, 223–224.

Gripp, R. F., & Magaro, P. A. A token economy program evaluation with untreated control ward comparisons. *Behaviour Research and Therapy*, 1971, *9*, 137–149.

Gunderson, J. G., & Mosher, L. R. The cost of schizophrenia. *American Journal of Psychiatry*, 1975, *132*, 1257–1264.

Gutride, M. E., Goldstein, A. P., & Hunter, G. F. The use of modeling and role-playing to increase social interaction among asocial psychiatric patients. *Journal of Consulting and Clinical Psychology*, 1973, *40*, 408–415.

Haynes, S. N., & Geddy, P. Suppression of psychotic hallucinations through time-out. *Behavior Therapy*, 1973, *4*, 123–127.

Heap, R. F., Boblitt, W. E., Moore, C. H., & Hord, J. G. Behavior-milieu therapy with chronic neuropsychiatric patients. *Journal of Abnormal Psychology*, 1970, *76*, 349–354.

Hersen, M. Modification of skill deficits in psychiatric patients. In A. S. Bellack & M. Hersen (Eds.), *Research and practice in social skills training*. New York: Plenum Press, 1979.

Hersen, M., & Bellack, A. S. A multiple-baseline analysis of social skills training in chronic schizophrenics. *Journal of Applied Behavior Analysis*, 1976, *9*, 239–245. (a)

Hersen, M., & Bellack, A. S. Social skills training for chronic psychiatric patients: Rationale, research findings, and future directions. *Comprehensive Psychiatry*, 1976, *17*, 559–580. (b)

Hersen, M., Turner, S. M., Edelstein, B. A., & Pinkston, S. G. Effects of phenothiazines and social skills training in a withdrawn schizophrenic. *Journal of Clinical Psychology*, 1975, *34*, 588–594.

Hollingsworth, R., & Foreyt, J. P. Community adjustment

of released token economy patients. *Journal of Behavior Therapy and Experimental Psychiatry*, 1975, *6*, 271–274.

Inglis, J. *The scientific study of abnormal behavior*. New York: Aldine, 1966.

Isaacs, W., Thomas, J., & Goldiamond, I. Application of operant conditioning to reinstate verbal behavior in psychotics. *Journal of Speech and Hearing Disorders*, 1960, *25*, 8–12.

Jaffe, P. G., & Carlson, P. M. Relative efficacy of modeling and instructions in eliciting social behaviors from chronic psychiatric patients. *Journal of Consulting and Clinical Psychology*, 1976, *44*, 200–207.

Keith, S., Gunderson, J., Reifman, A., Buchsbaum, S., & Mosher, L. R. Special report: Schizophrenia 1976. *Schizophrenic Bulletin*, 1976, *2*, 509–565.

Kendall, P. C., & Hollon, S. D. *Cognitive-behavioral interventions*. New York: Harcourt Brace, Jovanovich, 1979.

Kendell, R. E. Schizophrenia—The disease concept defined. *Trends in Neurosciences*, 1978, *July*, 24–26.

Kendell, R. E., Brockington, I. F., & Leff, J. P. Prognostic implications of sex alternative definitions of schizophrenia. *Archives of General Psychiatry*, 1979, *35*, 25–31.

Kowalski, P. A., Daley, G. D., & Gripp, R. P. Token economy: Who responds how? *Behaviour Research and Therapy*, 1976, *14*, 372–374.

Kraft, A., Binner, P., & Dickey, R. The community mental health program and the longer stay patient. *Archives of General Psychiatry*, 1967, *16*, 64–70.

Lambley, P. Behavior modification techniques and the treatment of psychosis: A critique of Alumbaugh. *The Psychological Record*, 1973, *23*, 93–97.

Lang, P. J., & Buss, A. H. Psychological deficit in schizophrenia. II: Interference and activation. *Journal of Abnormal Psychology*, 1965, *70*, 77–106.

Leitenberg, H., Agras, W. S., Thompson, L. E., & Wright, D. E. Feedback in behavior modification: An experimental analysis of two phobic cases. *Journal of Applied Behavior Analysis*, 1968, *11*, 131–137.

Liberman, R. P. Behavior modification with chronic mental patients. *Journal of Chronic Diseases*, 1971, *23*, 803–812.

Liberman, R. P., Nuechterlein, K., & Wallace, C. J. Social skills training and the nature of schizophrenia. In J. P. Curran & P. M. Monti (Eds.), *Social skills training: A practical handbook for assessment and treatment*. New York: Guilford Press, 1982.

Liberman, R. P., Teigen, J., Patterson, R., & Baker, V. Reducing delusional speech in chronic paranoid schizophrenics. *Journal of Applied Behavior Analysis*, 1973, *6*, 57–64.

Liberman, R. P., Wallace, C. J., Teigen, J., & Davis, J. Interventions with psychotic behaviors. In K. S. Calhoun, H. E. Adams, & K. M. Mitchell (Eds.), *Innovative treatment methods in psychopathology*. New York: Wiley, 1974.

Liberman, R. P., Lillie, F., Falloon, I., Vaughn, C., Harpin, E., Leff, J., Hutchinson, W., Ryan, P., & Stoute, M. *Social skills training for schizophrenic patients and their families*. Unpublished manuscript, Camarillo, Calif., 1978.

Lindsley, O. R. Operant conditioning methods applied to

research in chronic schizophrenia. *Psychiatric Research Reports*, 1956, *5*, 118–139.

Lindsley, O. R. Characteristics of the behavior of chronic psychotics as revealed by free-operant conditioning methods. Diseases of the Nervous System. *Monograph Supplement*, 1960, *21*, 66–78.

Mahoney, M. *Cognition and behavior modification*. Cambridge, Mass.: Ballinger, 1974.

Maley, R. F., Feldman, C. L., & Ruskin, R. S. Evaluation of patient improvement in a token economy treatment program. *Journal of Abnormal Psychology*, 1973, *82*, 141–144.

Margolis, R., & Shemberg, K. Cognitive self-instruction in process and reactive schizophrenics: A failure to replicate. *Behavior Therapy*, 1976, *7*, 668–671.

Matson, J. L., & Stephens, R. M. Increasing appropriate behavior of explosive chronic psychiatric patients with a social skills training package. *Behavior Modification*, 1978, *2*, 61–77.

May, P. R. A. *Treatment of schizophrenia*. New York: Science House, 1968.

Meichenbaum, D. The effects of instructions and reinforcement on thinking and language behavior of schizophrenics. *Behaviour Research and Therapy*, 1969, *7*, 101–114.

Meichenbaum, D. H., & Cameron, R. Training schizophrenics to talk to themselves: A means of developing attentional controls. *Behavior Therapy*, 1973, *4*, 515–534.

Meyers, A., Mercatoris, M., & Sirota, A. Case study: Use of covert self-instruction for the elimination of psychotic speech. *Journal of Consulting and Clinical Psychology*, 1976, *44*, 480–482.

Monti, P. M., Fink, E., Norman, W., Curran, J. P., Hayes, S., & Caldwell, H. Effect of social skills training groups and social skills bibliotherapy with psychiatric patients. *Journal of Consulting and Clinical Psychology*, 1979, *47*, 189–191.

Monti, P. M., Curran, J. P., Corriveau, D. P., DeLancey, A. L., & Hagerman, S. The effects of social skills training groups and social skills bibliotherapy with psychiatric patients. *Journal of Consulting and Clinical Psychology*, 1980, *48*, 241–248.

Monti, P. M., Corriveau, D. P., & Curran, J. P. Social skills training for psychiatric patients: Treatment and outcome. In J. P. Curran & P. M. Monti (Eds.), *Social skills training: A practical handbook for assessment and treatment*. New York: Guilford Press, 1982.

Mosher, L. R., & Keith, S. J. Research on the psychosocial treatment of schizophrenia: A summary report. *The American Journal of Psychiatry*, 1979, *136*, 623–631.

Mosher, L. R., Govera, L., & Menn, A. The treatment of schizophrenia as a developmental crisis. *American Journal of Orthopsychiatry*, 1972, *42*, 320.

Nydegger, R. U. The elimination of hallucinatory and delusional behavior by verbal conditioning and assertive training: A case study. *Journal of Behavior Therapy and Experimental Psychiatry*, 1972, *3*, 225–227.

Olson, R. P., & Greenberg, D. J. Effects of contingency contracting and decision-making groups with chronic mental patients. *Journal of Consulting and Clinical Psychology*, 1972, *38*, 376–383.

Patterson, R. L., & Teigen, J. R. Conditioning and posthospital generalization of non-delusional responses in a chronic psychotic patient. *Journal of Applied Behavior Analysis*, 1973, *6*, 65–70.

Paul, G. L. Chronic mental patient: Current status-future directions. *Psychological Bulletin*, 1969, *71*, 81–94.

Paul, G. L., & Lentz, R. J. *Psychosocial treatment of chronic mental patients: milieu vs. social learning programs*. Cambridge: Harvard University Press, 1977.

Paul, G. L., Tobias, L. L., & Holly, B. L. Maintenance psychotropic drugs in the presence of active treatment programs: A "triple-blind" withdrawal study with long-term mental patients. *Archives of General Psychiatry*, 1972, *27*, 106–115.

Payne, R. W. The measurement and significance of overinclusive thinking and retardation in schizophrenic patients. In P. H. Hock & J. Zubin (Eds.), *Psychopathology of schizophrenia*. New York: Grune & Stratton, 1966.

Presly, A. S., Black, D., Gray, A., Hartie, A., & Seymour, E. The token economy in the national health service: Possibilities and limitations. *Acta Psychiatrica Scandinavica*, 1976, *53*, 258–270.

Rickard, H. C., & Dinoff, M. A follow-up note on "Verbal manipulation in a psychotherapeutic relationship." *Psychological Reports*, 1962, *11*, 506.

Rickard, H. C., Digman, P. J., & Horner, R. F. Verbal manipulation in a psychotherapeutic relationship. *Journal of Clinical Psychology*, 1960, *16*, 364–367.

Rieder, R. O. The origins of our confusion about schizophrenia. *Psychiatry*, 1974, *37*, 197–208.

Royer, F. L., Flynn, W. F., & Osadca, B. S. Case history: Aversion therapy for fire setting by a deteriorated schizophrenic. *Behavior Therapy*, 1971, *2*, 229–232.

Rutner, I. T., & Bugle, C. An experimental procedure for the modification of psychotic behavior. *Journal of Consulting and Clinical Psychology*, 1969, *33*, 651–653.

Schaefer, H. H., & Martin, P. L. Behavior therapy for apathy of hospitalized schizophrenics. *Psychological Reports*, 1966, *19*, 1147–1158.

Serber, M., & Nelson, P. The ineffectiveness of systematic desensitization and assertive training in hospitalized schizophrenics. *Journal of Behavior Therapy and Experimental Psychiatry*, 1971, *2*, 107–109.

Shean, G. D., & Zeidberg, Z. Token reinforcement therapy: A comparison of matched groups. *Journal of Behavior Therapy and Experimental Psychiatry*, 1971, *2*, 95–105.

Shepherd, G. Social skills training: The generalization problem—Some further data. *Behaviour Research and Therapy*, 1978, *16*, 287–288.

Sherman, J. A. Use of reinforcement and imitation to reinstate verbal behavior in mute psychotics. *Journal of Abnormal Psychology*, 1965, *70*, 155–164.

Siegel, J., & Spivack, G. Problem-solving therapy: The description of a new program for chronic psychiatric patients. *Psychotherapy: Theory, Research, and Practice*, 1976, *10*, 368–373.

Slade, P. D. The effects of systematic desensitization on auditory hallucinations. *Behaviour Research and Therapy*, 1972, *10*, 85–91.

Slade, P. D. The psychological investigation and treatment of auditory hallucinations: A second case report. *British Journal of Medical Psychology*, 1973, *46*, 293–296.

Spitzer, R. L., Endicott, J., & Robins, E. *Research diagnostic criteria (RDC) for a selected group of functional disorders.* New York: Biometric Research, 1978.

Stahl, J. R., & Leitenberg, H. Behavioral treatment of the chronic mental hospital patient. In H. Leitenberg (Ed.), *Handbook of behavior modification and behavior therapy.* Englewood Cliffs, N.J.: Prentice-Hall, 1976.

Stein, L. I., & Test, M. A. *Alternatives to mental hospital treatment.* New York: Plenum Press, 1978.

Stoffelmayr, B. E., Faulkner, G. E., & Mitchell, W. S. *The rehabilitation of chronic hospitalized patients—A comparative study of operant conditioning methods and social therapy techniques.* Edinburgh: Scottish Home and Health Department, 1973.

Stokes, T. F., & Bear, D. M. An implicit technology of generalization. *Journal of Applied Behavior Analysis,* 1977, *10*, 349–367.

Strauss, J. S., & Carpenter, W. T. The prediction of outcome in schizophrenia. I: Characteristics of outcome. *Archives of General Psychiatry,* 1972, *27*, 739–746.

Strauss, J. S., & Carpenter, W. T. The prediction of outcome in schizophrenia. II: The relationship between prediction and outcome variables. *Archives of General Psychiatry,* 1974, *31*, 39–42.

Szasz, T. S. *The myth of mental illness—Foundations of a theory of personal conduct.* New York: Dell, 1961.

Szasz, T. S. *Schizophrenia.* New York: Basic Books, 1976.

Szasz, T. S. Schizophrenia—A category error. *Trends in Neurosciences,* July 1978, 26–28.

Thomson, N., Fraser, D., & McDougall, A. The reinstatement of speech in near-mute chronic schizophrenics by instructions, imitative prompts and reinforcements. *Journal of Behavior Therapy and Experimental Psychiatry,* 1974, *5*, 83–89.

Trower, P. Situational analysis of the components and processes of behavior of socially skilled and unskilled patients. *Journal of Consulting and Clinical Psychology,* 1980, *48*, 327–339.

Trower, P., Bryant, B., & Argyle, M. *Social skills and mental health.* Pittsburgh: University of Pittsburgh Press, 1978.

Tuma, A. H. Treatment of schizophrenia, an historical perspective. In P. R. A. May (Ed.), *Treatment of schizophrenia.* New York: Science House, 1968.

Ullman, L. P. *Institution and outcome: A comparative study of psychiatric hospitals.* New York: Pergamon Press, 1967.

Vaughn, C. E., & Leff, J. P. The influence of family and social factors on the course of psychiatric illness. A comparison of schizophrenic and depressed neurotic patients. *British Journal of Psychiatry,* 1976, *159*, 125–137.

Wallace, C. J. *The assessment of interpersonal problem solving skills with chronic schizophrenics.* Paper presented at the Annual Meeting of the American Psychological Association, New York, Sept. 1978.

Wallace, C. J. The social skills training project of the Mental Health Clinical Research Center for the Study of Schizophrenia. In J. P. Curran & P. M. Monti (Eds.), *Social skills training: A practical handbook for assessment and treatment.* New York: Guilford Press, 1982.

Wallace, C. J., Nelson, C., Lukoff, D., Webster, C.,

Rappe, S., & Ferris, C. *Cognitive skills training.* Paper presented at the Annual Meeting of the Association for the Advancement of Behavior Therapy, Chicago, Nov. 1978.

Wallace, C. J., Nelson, C. J., Liberman, R. P., Aitchison, R. A., Lukoff, D., Elder, J. P., & Ferris, C. A review and critique of social skills training with schizophrenic patients. *Schizophrenia Bulletin,* 1980, *6*, 42–64.

Weidner, F. In vivo desensitization of a paranoid schizophrenic. *Journal of Behavior Therapy and Experimental Psychiatry,* 1970, *1*, 79–81.

Weingaertner, A. H. Self-administered aversive stimulation with hallucinating hospitalized schizophrenics. *Journal of Consulting and Clinical Psychology,* 1971, *36*, 422–429.

Weinman, B., Gelbart, P., Wallace, M., & Post, M. Inducing assertive behavior in chronic schizophrenics: A comparison of socioenvironmental, desensitization, and relaxation therapies. *Journal of Consulting and Clinical Psychology,* 1972, *39*, 246–252.

WHO (World Health Organization). *International Pilot Study Of Schizophrenia,* Vol. 1. Geneva: World Health Organization, 1973.

Wilkins, W. Desensitization: Social and cognitive factors underlying the effectiveness of Wolpe's procedure. *Psychological Bulletin,* 1971, *76*, 311–317.

Williams, M. T., Turner, S. M., Watts, J. G., Bellack, A. S., & Hersen, M. Group social skills training for chronic psychiatric patients. *European Journal of Behavioral Analysis and Modification,* 1977, *1*, 223–229.

Wilson, F. S., & Walters, R. H. Modification of speech output of near mute schizophrenics through social learning procedures. *Behaviour Research and Therapy,* 1966, *4*, 59–67.

Wincze, J. P., Leitenberg, H., & Agras, W. S. The effects of token reinforcement and feedback on the delusional verbal behavior of chronic paranoid schizophrenics. *Journal of Applied Behavior Analysis,* 1972, *5*, 247–262.

Wing, J. K. *Schizophrenia: Towards a new synthesis.* London: Academic Press, 1978.

Wing, J. K., Cooper, J. E., & Sartorius, N. *The description and classification of psychiatric symptoms: An instruction manual for the PSE and CATEGO system.* London: Cambridge University Press, 1974.

Wolff, R. The systematic application of the satiation procedure to delusional verbiage. *Psychological Record,* 1971, *21*, 459–463.

Wolpe, J. *Psychotherapy by reciprocal inhibition.* Johannesburg: Witwatersrand University Press, 1958.

Wolpe, J. The systematic desensitization treatment of neurosis. *Journal of Nervous and Mental Disease,* 1961, *132*, 189–203.

Wood, D. D., Barrios, B. A., & Cohn, N. B. *Generalization effects of a cognitive rule in social skills training with hospitalized chronic schizophrenics.* Paper presented at the Annual Convention of the Association for the Advancement of Behavior Therapy, San Francisco, 1979.

Zeisset, R. M. Desensitization and relaxation in the modification of psychiatric patients' interview behavior. *Journal of Abnormal Psychology,* 1968, *73*, 18–24.

Zigler, E., & Phillips, L. Social effectiveness and symptomatic behaviors. *Journal of Abnormal and Social Psychology*, 1960, *61*, 231–238.

Zigler, E., & Phillips, L. Psychiatric diagnosis: A critique. *Journal of Abnormal and Social Psychology*, 1961, *63*, 607–618. (a)

Zigler, E., & Phillips, L. Psychiatric diagnosis and symptomatology. *Journal of Abnormal and Social Psychology*, 1961, *63*, 69–75. (b)

Zigler, E., & Phillips, L. Social competence and outcome in psychiatric disorders. *Journal of Abnormal and Social Psychology*, 1961, *63*, 264–271. (c)

Zigler, E., & Phillips, L. Social competence and the process-reactive distinction in psychopathology. *Journal of Abnormal and Social Psychology*, 1962, *65*, 215–222.

Zubin, J. Classification of the behavior disorders. *Annual Review of Psychology*, 1967, *18*, 373–406.

CHAPTER 8

Adult Medical Disorders

C. Barr Taylor

Introduction

Identification of Problem or Topic

Behavior, at long last, may be taking its proper place in Western medicine. The study of behavior in medicine has even spawned a new discipline, sometimes called *behavioral medicine*. In the broadest sense, *behavioral medicine* refers to the application of behavioral science knowledge and techniques to the understanding of physical health and illness and to prevention, diagnosis, treatment, and rehabilitation. In this chapter, we discuss behavioral medicine only in terms of the application of behavioral therapy and applied analysis to these same areas. An astonishing number of studies have been published in this area, mostly in the past 10 years, and the numbers are increasing exponentially.

Most of the behavior therapy techniques used in behavioral medicine are the same as those used to treat other problems: progressive muscle relaxation, systematic desensitization, positive reinforcement, and feedback, for example, have all been used extensively to treat medical problems. The methodologies for evaluating such techniques are also similar in behavioral medicine to those in behavior therapy; for example, single-case subject designs, direct measures of behaviors, and reversals have all been applied to medical problems.

But behavioral medicine differs from other areas of behavioral therapy because of its close connection with medicine, borrowing heavily from the knowledge of physiology, biochemistry, pathophysiology, pharmacology, epidemiology, and prevention to determine both the focus and the outcome of interventions. For instance, behavior therapy techniques designed to reduce dietary cholesterol intake do so because of the epidemiological data showing a correlation between serum cholesterol and increased risk for heart disease; biofeedback was derived in part from techniques and instruments developed by physiologists.

Although behavioral medicine relies on medicine, the relationship between them is an interactive one: behavioral techniques, which can be characterized in part by their specificity of measuring behavior, enhance medical methodology, technique, and science. For instance, few pharmacological studies measure a patient's direct drug use; they may monitor drug metabolites appearing in the urine or obtain a self-report of drug use, but both are indirect measures of actual use. A recent behavioral medicine paper described a technique for substantiating a subject's daily drug use, which

C. Barr Taylor • Department of Psychiatry, Stanford University Medical Center, Stanford, CA 94305.

could be used as a direct measure (Epstein & Masek, 1978). Or behavioral research, by examining classes of behavior, may show the important and otherwise unobserved impact of drugs on behavior. For instance, by monitoring a class of behaviors for five retarded adults, both on and off chlorpromazine, Marholin, Touchette, and Malcolm (1979) demonstrated that some desirable behaviors, such as eye contact, time out of bed, and proximity to others, increased when the subjects were taken off medication. Physicians frequently prescribe drugs for one problem and note the side effects on the physiological systems, but rarely note behavioral changes that may be critical, as in the case of the study reported above.

As a final example, behavioral medicine techniques may uncover close connections between behavior and morbidity. For instance, investigators have explored how eating behaviors relate to obesity (Adams, Ferguson, Stunkard, & Agras, 1978) or how Type A behavior relates to atherogenesis (Blumenthal, Williams, Wong, Schanberg, & Thompson, 1978).

Contemporary Importance

The preceding examples of interactions between behavioral medicine and branches of medicine indicate the mutual interaction that has already occurred between these two fields and suggest the clear importance of behavioral medicine to medicine in general. Because of the close connection between behavioral medicine and medicine, it is reasonable to assume that behavioral medicine researchers and practitioners will continue to make broad contributions to medicine. Thus, one important feature of behavioral medicine is that it focuses on the relationship between behavior and the development of health and disease and demands specific measurements to facilitate such discoveries. But behavioral medicine is important in other ways: (1) behavioral medicine has provided specific treatments for certain medical problems; and (2) it has potential for improving general patient care and healthy lifestyles.

Overview of the Chapter

In this chapter, we review the application of various behavior techniques to treat illnesses, to enhance health care, and to reduce disability. We then summarize the usefulness of the two techniques (relaxation and biofeedback) that have been most extensively studied in this literature. Before reviewing the application of behavioral medicine techniques, it is important to review the historical roots of behavioral medicine and to discuss some overall problems that affect the field.

Historical Perspective

Because behavioral medicine is an interface discipline, relating behavioral science to medicine, its history embodies many trends. Three disciplines are particularly important: the history of patient care, psychosomatic medicine, and behavioral approaches to medical problems.

Patient Care

Patient care involves two important aspects: how patients are cared for and who cares for them. As Benjamin Rush, one of the fathers of American medicine, noted, patients can be "cured" through four processes: first, from their own natural recuperative properties; second, from medicines and allied procedures; third, through surgery; and fourth, through nonspecific factors (Binger, 1966). The history of medical "cures" in this century is largely that of the second and third types. The advancement of technology in medicine and surgery has been nothing less than spectacular; many diseases previously fatal are now curable. But how well patients recover because of their own "natural properties" may, if anything, have taken a setback (Illich, 1976), and nonspecific factors continue to be viewed by physicians as a nuisance rather than a benefit (Goodwin, Goodwin, & Vogel, 1979).

Historically, technological medication has placed the care of sick individuals firmly in the hands of physicians. As a result, preventive care for adults has not achieved great importance in the health care system, and preventive practices for adults, except as they are prescribed by physicians, have not achieved widespread use. Physicians have come to expect large changes from their interventions, to recognize illness, and to consider clinical but not statistical significance. These attitudes reflect treatment practice. For instance, few physicians would bother prescribing a medication to reduce blood pressure by 2 mm. For a particular individual, a reduction of 2 mm of blood pressure may not be clinically significant, but for a society, 2 mm may mean a significant reduction in morbidity and mortality. Achieving the 2-mm change in a population requires attention to everybody's habits as they relate to blood pressure. Thus, statistical significance may be more important for the wellness of society than clinical significance, and behavioral approaches may be particularly important in facilitating these changes.

This ownership of who treats disease and the great financial benefits that accrue from it necessarily create conflicts of role and identity and reimbursement between medical and so-called nonmedical practitioners. Many major insurance carriers do not pay for "health education" or even many behavioral medicine procedures (e.g., Medicare will not reimburse for biofeedback). As more nonmedical practitioners enter the medical field, we can expect such conflicts and issues to be heightened.

Psychosomatic Medicine

The second field directly related to behavioral medicine is psychosomatic medicine. In part, psychosomatic medicine has arisen in the last 50 years as an attempt to care for the whole patient, who has been lost in an increasingly mechanistic and technological medical system. As Lipowski noted (1977), developments in psychosomatic medicine since its beginning in the 1920s have followed two major directions: first, attempts to identify specific psychological variables postulated to underlie specific somatic disorders; and second, attempts by experiment or epidemiological study to discover correlations between social stimulus situations, a subject's psychological and physiological responses, and/or changes in

health status. The first approach was largely directed by Franz Alexander, a psychoanalyst, who studied asthma, hypertension, peptic ulcer disease, ulcerative colitis, rheumatoid arthritis, hyperthyroidism, and headaches in particular (Alexander, French, & Pollock, 1968). Such disorders were viewed as symptoms of underlying intrapsychic conflicts and as being connected with certain personality types. But, as noted in several recent reviews, attempts to demonstrate that certain personalities correlate with specific disease states or that the procedures generated by these psychosomatic theoreticians and practices are effective in bringing about change has been disappointing (Weiner, 1977). No psychosomatic therapy has been demonstrated as having a specific effect on preventing or improving the outcome of any particular disease in carefully controlled group outcome studies. For instance, while some patients may exhibit reduced blood pressure in the course of psychotherapy, it has not been demonstrated that the psychotherapy *per se* brings about the reductions in blood pressure. Because of this lack of success and probably because psychosomatic theory has tended to be too abstruse for most general practitioners, it has not achieved a widespread impact in changing medical care or in influencing the practice of medicine. Nevertheless, behavioral medicine researchers continue to focus on many of the same diseases identified by early psychosomatic practitioners.

The second trend in psychosomatic medicine focused on the scientific study of the relationships among sociological, social, and biological factors in determining health and disease. Wolff and Goodell (1968) undertook many classic studies relating biological and interpersonal factors, and many of the studies are close in design to those now undertaken by behavioral medicine researchers.

Behavioral Medicine

Behavioral medicine as a discipline has a short history. A few early studies relevant to behavioral medicine can be found scattered throughout the medical literature. For example, Ferster, Nurnberger, & Levitt (1962) outlined many of the eating behaviors that would subsequently become the focus of behavioral interventions aimed at changing eating patterns; Yates (1958) used massed practice to treat tics; Raymond (1964) used aversive conditioning to change smoking behavior in a young boy; Jacobson, in the 1920s, used relaxation to effect change; and the 1960s provided EMG feedback for polio victims to restore muscle strength. The first collection of articles (focusing mostly on biofeedback) appeared only in 1973 (Birk, 1973). In 1975, when Katz and Zlutnick prepared a collection of behavioral medicine articles, they noted that although examples could be found in behavior therapy of interventions applicable to many medical disorders, the literature was neither broad nor deep. Since Katz and Zlutnick's (1975) publication, the field has exploded. Already three journals are devoted to behavioral medicine (*The Journal of Behavioral Medicine* and *Behavioral Medicine Update*), and one is in its second year, *Behavioral Medicine Abstracts*. There are now eight textbooks published or in preparation. Behavioral medicine articles appear throughout the behavioral medicine literature and throughout the medical literature as well. The field even has a society, the Society for Behavioral Medicine, which, in its first year, accepted 800 members, and an Academy of Behavioral Medicine devoted to the more scientific aspects of behavioral medicine. The direction and importance of the behavioral medicine explosion are yet to be determined. Because of the clear usefulness of behavioral approaches to medical practice, it is more curious why this explosion was so slow in coming rather than that it occurred at all.

Possible Adoption and Disillusionment

Unfortunately, behavioral medicine has grown so rapidly that already behavioral techniques have been "oversold" and greater promises made than the procedures can actually accomplish. A model of adaptation of new drugs described by Goodman (1966) is relevant to the practice and dispersal of behavioral techniques. According to Goodman, when a new drug is introduced, it tends to be widely used. As side effects are observed, as

some people fail to improve with the medication, or as the drug does not seem to be clearly superior to those already on the market, the drug may then be underutilized relative to its true effect. Eventually, perhaps over a period of years, the drug assumes a position more appropriate to its worth, assuming the usual promotional techniques by drug companies.

Behavioral procedures may follow the same course of early adoption, disillusionment (which has already occurred with weight programs), and then a more appropriate use. Here the analogy ends. Behavioral therapies become popular and are included in practice without the extensive animal and biochemical preparation that often precedes the development of a new drug. Furthermore, federal requirements are such that drugs must not only undergo such early animal and biological testing but must also be demonstrated to be harmless and efficacious in carefully controlled studies. Often, once a drug has been demonstrated to be potent and harmless (relative to the merits of its use), it is then tried on large populations over extensive periods before it becomes generally available to the public. Also, even if a drug is available to the public, it may be withdrawn if these trials fail to show that it is particularly efficacious.

There is no analogous testing of behavioral procedures, although a few techniques have undergone carefully controlled studies to determine their worth. Furthermore, a behavioral technique, unlike a drug, may fail not so much because of its biopotency, but because of insufficient attention to maintenance of the technique or incorrect application of the technique in the first place. Unfortunately, no procedures have been developed to monitor the usefulness of behavioral techniques or to establish any kind of quality control in the realm of practice.

Clinical versus Statistical Significance

The extent of changes in a particular variable achieved by behavioral techniques has been criticized in the medical literature as lacking clinical significance. Such criticism implies that there are clear standards as to when a particular problem needs to be treated.

In fact, in medicine, the decision to treat is often complex, varying from one physician to another and frequently changing. The case of blood pressure illustrates this point. Ten years ago it was not considered appropriate to treat blood pressures under 160/100. However, several large prospective studies proved that even lower blood pressures are associated with reduced morbidity and mortality (e.g., Hypertension Detection and Follow-Up Program Cooperative Group, 1979). Nevertheless, many physicians are reluctant to treat blood pressures below certain levels. Also, physicians are trained to think in a dichotomous fashion (e.g., that blood pressure is either normal or not) rather than in a progressive fashion (e.g., that as blood pressures are distributed on a curve, any reduction may, in fact, be beneficial). This ingrained notion among physicians that biochemical and physiological values are normal or not creates a gap between when and how physicians may use the emerging technology of behavioral medicine. It may be frustrating for nonmedically trained professionals to have treatment techniques that would be clearly useful to patients and not be able to use them because physicians refuse to recommend such treatment.

Side Effects

Behavioral interventions, like medical ones, may have side effects. Although there has been no systematic attempt to determine the side effects of behavioral procedures, the need is indicated by the evidence that some potentially harmful procedures, like rapid smoking, have already achieved extremely wide use. Lichtenstein and Glasgow (1977), for example, estimated that rapid puffing has been practiced by as many as 30,000 smokers. From a conceptual standpoint, the side effects of behavioral procedures, as of pharmacological agents, can occur from the direct effects of a procedure or may simply be associated with the procedure. Direct effects include such things as psychotic episodes occurring during prolonged meditation (which presumably could occur with relaxation) (French, Schmid, & Ingalls, 1976), ST segment changes during rapid puffing (Horan, Hackett, Nicholas, Linberg, Stone, & Lusaki, 1977), conditioning of un-

pleasant feelings about objects other than those intended during aversive conditioning (Raymond, 1964), or the development of undesirable behavior as another behavior is extinguished (Epstein, Doke, Sajwaj, Sorrell, & Rimmer, 1974). Indirect effects are those that occur secondarily to a behavioral procedure. Examples include adverse reactions occurring from an underlying disease or associated treatment of that disease changed by a behavioral approach, for example, relaxation leading to decreased insulin requirements in a diabetic who continues to use the same dosage of insulin; or failure to comply with a medical procedure because the patient prefers a behavioral treatment. For example, a patient stops hypertensive medication because she prefers to practice relaxation (Taylor, 1980). Since behavior techniques have already achieved mass acceptance without frequent problems being reported, we need not be overly alarmed or fearful of their use. However, behavioral researchers and practitioners need to pay more attention to the possible direct and indirect side effects of their procedures.

Current Empirical Status

Cardiovascular Disorders

Behavioral medicine researchers have made significant advances in understanding and treating cardiovascular disorders. Most of the work has focused on hypertension, arrhythmias, Type A behavior, cardiovascular risk reduction, and Raynaud's disease.

Hypertension. Hypertension is a major national health problem, affecting as many as 24 million Americans and leading to increased cardiovascular morbidity and mortality unless controlled (Smith, 1977a). There are many etiologies of hypertension, and some forms can be completely cured by surgery. The mainstay of treatment is, however, pharmacological. Unfortunately, as many as 10% of patients refuse to take medication because of drug intolerance, and many more adhere poorly to medication for this and other reasons (Smith, 1977b). In theory, behavioral techniques would be of value in patients (1) who have essential hypertension but are intolerant to medications or are poorly controlled on medication or (2) who have blood pressure levels not customarily treated by physicians but who might benefit from reduced blood pressure levels. Behavioral techniques might also be useful in all patients as an adjunct to other blood pressure therapies.

Methodological Problems. On the surface, blood pressure would seem to be the perfect measure for a behavioral intervention: easily and noninvasively obtained, it can frequently be sampled with minimal harm to the patient. Unfortunately, blood pressure levels are extremely labile, since they are controlled by a variety of interacting variables like peripheral resistance, blood volume, and cardiac output.

These variables are, in turn, influenced by one another and may in and of themselves be under complex control. For instance, peripheral resistance is controlled by interactions among at least six different hormones! Furthermore, the measurement of blood pressure itself is subject to much error: differences in sphygmomanometer size, the arm radius, the rate of deflation, the hearing acuity of the examiner, the position of the arm, and the stethoscope are all variables that affect the accuracy of a reading. Other noninvasive blood-pressure-measuring devices, like random zero sphygmomanometers (in which the examiner does not know the actual reading of the column until the measurement has been taken) or automatic cuffs that "listen" for the same heart sounds have advantages but are subject to many of the same measurement errors.

Finally, blood pressure levels are subject to a variety of nonspecific influences: instruc-tions, experimenter demands, placebos, and time of day have all been demonstrated to bring about considerable and sometimes long-lasting effects (Taylor, 1980). Thus, the inter- and intravariations in error in blood pressure measurement make this seemingly perfect measure less so. Furthermore, the extent of change from any treatment is greater the higher the initial blood pressure, so that the results of studies cannot be easily compared unless the initial blood pressures are the same. To overcome the problem, Jacob, Kraemer, and Agras (1977) have calculated a regression line that compares pretreatment systolic pressure with decreases in systolic pressure. An active treatment must produce significantly greater changes than would be predicted by the regression line alone. This procedure allows studies to be compared in terms of pre- and posttreatment (although a similar procedure has not been developed for long-term outcome studies). Kraemer, Jacob, Jeffery, and Agras (1979) have also described the most ideal designs for outcome research on hypertension.

Behavioral Interventions. The vast majority of studies on behavioral approaches to blood pressure have reported the effect of relaxation and related procedures or biofeedback on reducing blood pressure levels. In fact, behavioral approaches besides relaxation and biofeedback are of potential use. In Table 1 we have listed behavioral approaches (on the right), which might affect a physiological event (on the left) that influences blood pressures. For instance, relaxation may reduce peripheral catecholamine level (Davidson, Winchester, Taylor, Alderman, & Ingels, 1979; Stone

Table 1. Possible Mechanisms of Behavioral Intervention Aimed at Blood Pressure Reduction

Blood pressure pathophysiology	Behavioral intervention
Increased cardiac output	Reduced salt intake, pulse-transit time biofeedback, relaxation and related procedures, medication compliance, weight reduction, exercise
Increased fluid volume	Reduced salt intake, medication compliance
Increased vascular reactivity	Relaxation and related techniques
Increased catecholamine excretion and/or elevated renin	Caffeine reduction, relaxation and related techniques

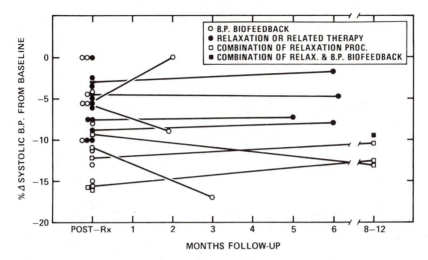

Figure 1. Immediate posttreatment systolic blood pressure changes from baseline in 41 studies using biofeedback, relaxation and related therapy, or combinations of these procedures. The follow-up results are for 11 of these studies. (Adapted from Taylor, 1980.)

& DeLeo, 1976), which may, in turn, reduce blood pressure. Adherence to a low-salt diet reduces blood volume and consequently blood pressure. As a final example, pulse-wave transit time, as measured by the R-wave and a peripheral pulse, may, in fact, reflect changes in cardiac output, which is elevated in some types of hypertension (Obrist, Light, Mc-Cubbin, Hutcheson, & Hoffer, 1979). Pulse-wave transit-time feedback may be used to reduce cardiac output. Thus, interventions aimed at increasing compliance with taking blood pressure medication, increasing exercise, and reducing weight and salt intake are relevant to blood pressure control. However, most studies have focused on only a few procedures: relaxation and related techniques, biofeedback, or combinations of these procedures.

Figure 1 shows the percentage of change in systolic blood pressure from baseline for 41 studies in which a behavioral treatment was compared with another treatment (Taylor, 1980). We will discuss each of these treatments independently.

Relaxation and Related Procedures. Many studies have compared relaxation and related procedures in terms of their effects on lowering blood pressure. Relaxation procedures have generally been modeled after Jacobson (1938) or Wolpe (1958), although Benson's

(1975) relaxation response has also been used. The posttreatment effects of relaxation have generally led to as much as a 10% reduction from baseline in systolic and diastolic blood pressure. Three studies with adequate controls and design have found the initial effects to be maintained at six months. There have been too few studies to make comparisons between procedures; simple relaxation procedures appear as effective as more elaborate ones.

Combination of Relaxation Procedures. Some studies have combined several relaxation procedures to reduce blood pressure. In the first large-scale application of relaxation therapy, Datey, Deshmukh, Dalvi, and Vinekar (1969) used *shavasan*, a yogic exercise in which patients assume a supine position while they practice a slow, rhythmic diaphragmatic breathing to lower blood pressure and at the same time practice relaxing thoughts. This procedure was combined with EMG-assisted biofeedback in the next major study (Patel, 1973). This combination of procedures has brought about the most significant long-term effects and greatest pre–post changes seen in Figure 1. However, these same studies also have the highest mean pretreatment systolic pressure and fall along the same regression line as the studies mentioned in the previous paragraph. Thus, the effects of combinations of procedures are not certain. Such procedures have brought about the greatest and most long-lasting changes, but they have not been compared directly with more simple procedures.

Biofeedback of Blood Pressure. Biofeedback has been used in several imaginative ways to lower blood pressure. Basically, three procedures have been used. The first procedure merely involves measuring the patient's blood pressure with a conventional sphygmomanometer and reporting blood pressure to the subject orally or visually. Unfortunately, this method requires frequent measurement, and the cuff needs to be inflated often and may cause discomfort to the patient. Another approach has been to use a constant cuff. With this procedure, a cuff is inflated to about the subject's average systolic pressure and held constant at that level. Whenever the systolic pressure rises to above the cuff pressure, a Korotkoff's sound is detected on a microphone (Shapiro, Mainardi, & Surwit, 1977). To lower blood pressure, patients are then instructed to eliminate the sounds, which can occur only when the blood pressure is decreased. The third approach is to measure blood pressure indirectly by using blood pressure velocity. Blood pressure velocity can be measured by using two pulses separated in space or by using the ECG R-wave (which represents the presystolic ejection period) and the peripheral pulse (Obrist, *et al.*, 1979). In general, as pulse wave velocity increases, so does blood pressure.

Blood pressure biofeedback using any of these mechanisms has not been demonstrated to be any more effective than relaxation at six months, and in some cases, it has been demonstrated to be less effective than relaxation. However, as can be seen in Figure 1, two studies have reported significant decreases in blood pressure from posttreatment to three and four months. In the three-month follow-up study, Kristt and Engel (1975) taught patients to control their blood pressure outside the clinical setting. This generalization training may be the crucial variable in producing long-term change.

Summary. The studies thus far reported in the behavioral medicine literature suggest that behavioral interventions, particularly relaxation and related techniques, may be of value

in the areas we mentioned in the beginning of this section, that is, in patients (1) who are intolerant to medications and are poorly controlled on medication and (2) who have blood pressures at levels not customarily treated by physicians but who might benefit from reduced blood pressure levels. Behavioral techniques might also be useful in all patients as an adjunct to other therapies.

Cardiac Arrhythmias. The treatment of cardiac arrhythmias has been widely studied in behavioral research, although mostly with single-case and single-group outcome studies.

Ectopic Beats. Ectopic beats (called *premature ventricular contractions*, or *PVCs*) represent beats that originate outside the usual conduction system of the heart and interfere with it. PVCs are often harmless but may, especially if they occur frequently, indicate cardiopathology.

Behavioral techniques have been most successful with single ectopic beats. In an early study, Pickering and Miller (1977) trained a 35-year-old male who had PVCs for one year to increase his heart rate. The patient wore a cardiac monitor to give him feedback on his heart rate. After five months of practice, he was able to increase his heart rate by 20–40 beats per minute with or without feedback and was able to suppress his PVCs approximately 50% of the time. By the end of a second training period, which followed five months of practice at home, he was able to suppress his PVCs 100% of the time. (The clinical importance of this study is not clear.) A second patient was unable to maintain a normal sinus rhythm without feedback. In a larger study, Weiss and Engel (1971) studied eight patients. All eight subjects learned some degree of heart-rate control; five were able to control the frequency of PVCs in the laboratory, and four subjects showed decreased PVCs at the time of follow-up visits up to 21 months after training. Benson, Alexander, and Feldman (1975) taught 11 subjects the "relaxation response." A significant reduction in PVCs occurred in 8 of the 11 patients. The absolute decrease was slight (from 2.5 to 2.2 PVCs per minute), but the decrease in 3 of these patients was over 85%.

A series of single-case studies suggests that similar procedures may be useful in reducing the frequency and type of multiple ectopic beats. No controlled-outcome study with multiple PVCs has been reported.

Other Arrhythmias. Behavioral procedures have been used with a variety of other arrhythmias. Biofeedback to reduce heart rate, as well as relaxation and related procedures, has been demonstrated in single cases to reduce the frequency of paroxysmal atrial tachycardia, a condition in which the heart rate periodically accelerates to potentially dangerous levels (Engel & Bleecker, 1974); sinus tachycardia (Scott, Blanchard, Edmundson, & Young, 1973; Engel & Bleecker, 1974), a condition in which heart rates are consistently elevated; and Wolff-Parkinson-White syndrome (Bleecker & Engel, 1973a). In most cases, improvement has been demonstrated. Two clients with chronic atrial fibrillation were able to reduce their ventricular rate during training, but neither client showed any reduction in day-to-day variability (Bleecker & Engel, 1973b). Biofeedback and other psychological therapies have not been found effective in third-degree heart block (Engel & Bleecker, 1974).

Summary. It appears that heart-rate control results in the elimination or reduction of the frequency of PVCs in some patients. The training procedure that appears to be most effective is one that includes sessions in heart-rate deceleration, acceleration, or a combination. The relaxation response has been successfully used to reduce PVCs. Deceleration through biofeedback also appears useful in reducing heart rate in stress-related tachycardia. Behavior interventions seem to be most useful in treating arrhythmias that are not caused by arteriosclerosis; however, interventions that may affect the development of arteriosclerosis are obviously relevant to preventing arrhythmias.

Type A Behavior. The third area of major focus in behavioral approaches to cardiovascular diseases has been with so-called Type A behavior. *Type A behavior* is a term used by Friedman and Rosenman (1974) to characterize the behavior of many patients they were seeing in their clinical cardiology practice. Type A patients suffer from a chronic sense of time urgency, impose unrealistic and frequent deadlines, interrupt, and, in general,

appear aggressive and hostile (Friedman & Rosenman, 1974). Type A patients have demonstrated significantly more coronary morbidity and mortality than patients without these characteristics. Recent studies have also shown that Type As suffer more physiological arousal under stress and have more serious arteriosclerosis in their angiograms (Blumenthal *et al.*, 1978; Dembroski, MacDougall, Shields, Petitto, & Lushene, 1978). However, it is not clear exactly how Type A behavior leads to coronary artery disease. One intriguing suggestion has been made by Henry and Stephens (1977): like dominant mice that show continued sympathetic arousal and are prone to develop cardiovascular disease, Type As exhibit marked catecholamine excretion under stress, whereas subordinate mice exhibit a different physiological profile of stress. They suggest that Type A patients may be under continual sympathetic arousal.

It is not clear if all Type A patients are at risk to develop coronary artery disease or what the critical links may be in humans between the various components of Type A behavior and their physiological properties and cardiovascular illness.

Because of the suggested connection between Type A behavior and cardiovascular illness, interventions have been developed directed at changing the lifestyle of Type A individuals. The procedures that have been used include relaxation, stress management techniques, improvement in interpersonal techniques, and general modification of Type A behaviors (Suinn, 1974). For instance, with stress management techniques, Type A individuals are taught to leave or avoid stressful areas, to improve time management, to change scheduling so that stressful interviews are interspersed with nonstressful ones, to delegate tasks, to refuse to take on overwhelming tasks, to increase the amount of recreation, to learn to rely on others for emotional support, to reduce their rate of speech, eating, and movements, etc.

In one study, a procedure that utilizes these techniques was applied to two groups in a cardiac rehabilitation program (Suinn, 1974). Both groups received the same exercise prescription, physiological stress testing, dietary assistance, and smoking management, but only the stress management group received behavioral training. This group showed significant reductions in serum cholesterol compared with controls (2.6% mg compared with 15.0% mg). In another study, on a paper-and-pencil test (the Jenkins Activity Survey), patients with Type A behavior were taught relaxation techniques to control anxiety (Suinn & Bloom, 1978). The treated group showed trends toward reductions in blood pressure (mean systolic reduction was 14 mm Hg, not significant compared with controls). Several large-scale studies are now under way to determine the impact of these procedures in reducing morbidity and mortality from heart disease in Type A individuals.

Cardiovascular Risk Reduction. The fourth and perhaps major area where behavioral approaches have contributed to the treatment of cardiovascul problems is the provision of techniques to reduce cardiovascular risk factors (Enelow & Henderson, 1975). Large prospective studies have shown that cigarette smoking, weight, blood pressure, and diet are related to cardiovascular morbidity and mortality, and that reducing or eliminating these risks is associated with decreased morbidity and mortality (Blackburn, 1978). Other data suggest that exercise and perhaps stress are also related to cardiovascular risk (Paffenbarger, Hale, Brand, & Hyde, 1977). Thus, interventions directed at smoking cessation and weight reduction are directly related to cardiovascular risk reduction. The effectiveness of such interventions is addressed in another section of this book. Similarly, interventions that encourage salt intake reduction, change in diet from high cholesterol to low cholesterol, increases in fiber in the diet, and exercise are directly important in cardiovascular disease. In another section, we review behavioral approaches to nutrition and exercise.

Raynaud's Disease. Patients with Raynaud's disease suffer from pain in the hands and feet. This disorder is thought to be secondary to extreme vasoconstriction. Two types of biofeedback for peripheral blood flow have been used to treat the disorder: direct training in peripheral vasodilation feedback and hand-warming feedback. Shapiro and Schwartz (1972) reported the only cases in which blood volume feedback has been used. One patient given this feedback improved; a second failed to show improvement. On the other hand, hand-warming feedback proved relatively more successful. Jacobson, Hackett, Surman, and Silverberg (1973), Blanchard and Haynes (1975), and Sunderman and Delk (1978) have all reported success with one client. Taub (1977) reported success in two cases.

May and Weber (1976) reported four case studies of patients with Raynaud's disease and four with Raynaud's phenomenon, caused by scleroderma or lupus. The treatment consisted of sixteen 50-minute temperature-feedback sessions over eight weeks. Five normal controls were also studied. The patients with Raynaud's phenomenon showed the most consistent and most effective control. The subjects with severe symptoms performed better and achieved more symptom reduction than those with mild symptoms, an effect the authors attributed to increased motivation. They commented that "the success of the training depends more on the subject achieving mental contact with his fingers (perhaps easier for a Raynaud's subject since his disease is a sign of a connection, albeit a maladaptive one) and on the motivation of the subject . . . than it depends on the degree of physiological pathology present" (p. 50).

One study compared the hand-warming feedback plus autogenic phrases with autogenic therapy phrases alone (Surwit, Pilon, & Fenton, 1978). Fifteen subjects were randomized to the two treatments. In addition, half of the subjects in each group were trained primarily in the laboratory, while the other half received most of their training at home. The results indicated that the laboratory and the home treatment groups showed equal improvement in their ability to warm their hands and equally significant clinical improvement. However, there were no group differences between subjects receiving hand-warming feedback plus autogenic phrases or autogenic phrases alone. Both groups demonstrated significant gains. Because thermal imagery, suggestion, and self-instruction can lead to vasodilation, the specific usefulness of biofeedback for the disorder remains unproved (Conners, 1980).

Respiratory Disorders

Asthma. Behavioral treatment approaches to respiratory disorders have focused primarily on bronchial asthma. Asthma would seem to be a condition amenable to behavioral interventions because (1) asthma attacks seem to occur during times of emotional stress or are made worse by such stress; (2) bronchial spasms may, in some cases, represent a classically conditioned response; and (3) the management of the illness requires considerable effort on the part of the patient and the family. Studies have been directed at developing interventions appropriate for each of these areas.

Stress Reduction. Many studies using systematic desensitization and relaxation suggest that such procedures produce an immediate effect on improving airway functioning (Alexander, 1972; Alexander, Cropp, & Chai, 1979; Alexander, Micklich, & Hershkoff, 1972). Unfortunately, the extent of these changes has been less than 15%, relative to baseline. Changes not exceeding 30% are required before a therapy appears to produce relief (in most patients).

Anxiety or fears that may alter lung function directly (and remember that sympathetic activity usually results in bronchodilation) are very different from the anxiety or stress that *results* from asthma. Stimuli associated with asthma (e.g., tightness and wheezing) are presumed to have become classically conditioned to trigger fear and anxiety responses (Walton, 1969). Eckert, McHugh, Philander, and Blumenthal (1979) used a desensitization technique to produce anxiety conditioned to increasing expiratory resistance in nine patients. Treatment was significantly more effective in the patients who received desensitization than in those who received relaxation control.

Biofeedback. Biofeedback of respiratory rate and airflow has been used to increase these variables in asthmatics. Vachon and Rich (1976) and Fieldman (1976) used forced-oscillation feedback to increase the respiratory rate in asthmatics, but its clinical usefulness was not evaluated. Khan and his associates (Khan, 1977; Khan & Olson, 1977; Khan, Staerk, & Bonk, 1973, 1974) have undertaken a series of studies to determine the effects of increasing bronchodilation using biofeedback of airflow in asthmatic children. The subjects receive verbal praise from the experimenter contingent on specified increases in airflow. Khan and Olson (1977) found the technique to be effective in reducing the number of asthma attacks, the amount of medication used, and the number of emergency room visits, effects that were maintained at 8- to 10-month follow-up. However, another investigation did not confirm Khan's findings (Danker, Miklich, Prott, & Creer, 1975).

Illness and Management. The third respiratory-illness area where behavioral techniques have been demonstrated to be useful involves problems that result from having asthma and the constant struggle to cope with and adapt to it (Creer, 1978). Disease-related problems include poor medication compliance, maladaptive behaviors, untoward specific emotional reactions, or the development of symptoms (like a cough) that begin to occur autonomously from the asthma itself. There have been many case reports indicating the usefulness of behavioral procedures in reducing these problems. The studies have been focused on children, but the techniques could be used equally with adults.

For example, Rene and Creer (1976) used operant conditioning techniques to teach four asthmatic children to correctly use an intermittent-positive-pressure breathing device. The authors documented that the training procedure significantly reduced the amount of drug required during the subsequent treatments and, furthermore, that the procedure could be used by nurses.

Summary. Behavioral approaches are useful for at least three aspects of asthma. First, relaxation and desensitization and daily relaxation practice invariably lead to statistical improvement in airway function, although the extent of changes may not bring much relief to the patient. The role of biofeedback in improving airway function remains uncertain. Second, behavioral techniques may make important contributions to reducing the anxiety secondary to the patient's asthma. Third, behavioral treatments are useful in reducing behavioral excesses or deficits involved in the ongoing management of the patient's asthma.

Other Disorders. Behavioral medicine has also had an impact on some other aspects of respiratory illness. Since respiratory disease is a major side effect of smoking, behavioral interventions designed to reduce and eliminate smoking behavior have obvious importance to respiratory disease. These interventions are reviewed in another chapter of this handbook.

Gastrointestinal System

Behavioral researchers have paid surprisingly little attention to the treatment of gastrointestinal disorders (excluding obesity and anorexia as gastrointestinal disorders). Gastrointestinal problems caused by stress or anxiety constitute as much as 50% of the disorders seen in gastrointestinal practice, and we would assume that stress reduction interventions would be of some use. In fact, the most extensive work in this area has focused on the control of esophageal and rectal sphincter control and not on more common problems, like irritable bowel and peptic ulcer disease.

Nausea. Persistent nausea without medical cause has received some attention from behavioral researchers. Ingersoll and Curry (1977) used social and activity reinforcers to alter (1) the amount of time food was retained and (2) the type of fluid in the drink of a patient with a persistent amount of vomiting and nausea. The treatment lasted for five days, after which the patient was no longer vomiting. Also, she was not vomiting at one-year follow-up according to her self-report. Alford, Blanchard, and Buckley (1972) used contingent social contact and reduced the tension to eliminate vomiting in a 17-year-old female. There was no report of a recurrence seven months after treatment stopped. In another case, Tasto and Chesney (1977) used emotive imagery to decondition nausea in a 25-year-old engineer. The patient reported no symptoms at the one-year follow-up. These three individual cases suggest that behavioral techniques could be very useful with persistent nausea and vomiting, but they have not been applied to nausea secondary to medications, one of the most common causes of nausea.

Diarrhea and Irritable Bowel. While diarrhea and the irritable bowel syndrome are often caused by different problems, both relate to increased gastric motility and are discussed together here. Diarrhea is often a symptom of irritable bowel syndrome, although abdominal pain with alternating diarrhea and constipation may be the presenting complaint. Stress has been clearly demonstrated to increase gastric motility (Almy & Tulin, 1947). Of the two general behavioral approaches to the irritable bowel syndrome, one is to provide biofeedback to decrease colonic motility; the second is to desensitize or to use relaxation procedures, presumably to reduce the amount of the patient's stress or anxiety. Cohen and Reed (1968) used systematic desensitization to treat two patients with diarrhea, exacerbated when the patients were required to travel. Using freedom of activity and frequency of self-report outcome measures, the patients described modest gains, which remained at 6- and 12-month follow-up. Hedberg (1973) also used systematic desensitization to treat a patient with chronic diarrhea. His patient averaged 10 bowel movements a day. Bowel control was achieved by the eighth session and was maintained at two-month follow-up.

Biofeedback has been used in several different ways. Furman (1973) had patients listen to their bowel sounds monitored with an electronic stethoscope. The patients were taught to increase or decrease their peristaltic activity. The author reported that within five training sessions, all patients showed some degree of control over their intestinal motility and apparently experienced symptomatic improvement. Weinstock (1976), however, had no success with 12 patients trained in this method, although 9 of the 12 later improved using a combination of EMG biofeedback and relaxation. Similarly, Tarler-Benlolo and Love (1977) successfully treated a patient with long-standing spastic colon with the same combination of EMG biofeedback and relaxation.

Another approach to reducing these symptoms has been to provide direct feedback of rectosigmoid distension to patients with irritable bowel syndrome, by using the same techniques that have been developed for biofeedback treatment of fecal incontinence. In a typical system, three balloons are inserted rectally. The uppermost is lodged in the rectosigmoid space. The next balloon is positioned in the internal sphincter, and the third balloon is in the external sphincter. Subjects are instructed both to increase and to decrease distension in the rectosigmoid space and thus gain control over sphincter tone. The procedure was tried with 21 patients (with an average duration of symptoms of seven years) (Bueno-Miranda, Cerulli, & Schuster, 1976). Of the 21 patients, 14 were able to increase distension by 34% and decrease distension by an average of 29%. The same patients were able to continue such suppression eight weeks later. The effects on the functional bowel syndrome were not reported, but the authors have used this procedure with some patients with irritable bowel syndrome and claim some success.

Fecal Incontinence. Biofeedback techniques have been successfully developed for treating fecal incontinence. This has been accomplished with feedback provided by changes in sphincter pressure, also measured with balloons (Engel, Nikoomanesh, & Schuster, 1974). Thus, subjects are able to gain control of their sphincter tone. In one study, 40 patients (6 to 96 years old) were treated with this procedure. Of these patients, 28 responded well as evidenced by the disappearance of incontinence or by a decrease in frequency of incontinence of at least 90%.

Peptic Ulcer Disease. Peptic ulcer disease is one of the most common human ailments. Although peptic activity is the ultimate damaging agent responsible for mucosal ulceration, many other factors influence the development of ulcers. Studies have shown that stress is one factor that contributes to the development of peptic ulcer disease in some patients. In several interesting studies, it has been demonstrated that gastric acid secretion can be altered by means of feedback techniques. For instance, in an early study, Welgan (1974) continuously aspirated gastric secretions and measured the pH. pH feedback and instruction led to significant reductions in acid secretion.

Whitehead, Renault, and Goldiamond (1975) developed an ingenious technique to provide direct feedback of acid secretion. Subjects swallowed a plastic tube that contained a pH detection tube and two other tubes. One tube was used to inject sodium bicarbonate and another drove an electric relay, signaling that the pH had dropped to certain levels. When the pH dropped to this level, sodium bicarbonate was used as the independent measure of gastric acid secretion. Four subjects underwent a design involving baseline, followed by instructions to increase gastric secretion, and then instructions to decrease acid secretion. During the increase or decrease secretion periods, the subjects were given visual feedback of their gastric acid secretion as determined from the sodium bicarbonate intake. Two subjects were able both to increase and to decrease gastric acid secretion, one subject was able to increase only, and one subject showed no changes in either condition. The authors suggested that the latter subject had been conditioned to gastric emptying rather than pH change. These two studies offer exciting directions for the possibility of operant conditioning of gastric acid secretion.

Pain Syndromes

Pain is one of the most common human experiences: at any one time, 10% of the population may, for instance, suffer from headache. In this section, we review the behavioral approaches to three important pain problems: chronic pain, migraine headaches, and tension headaches.

Chronic Pain. A few patients with acute pain eventually develop chronic pain, defined as pain of at least six months' continuous duration, with no organic base to explain its origin. Often these patients suffer from polysurgery, polymedication, and polyaddiction. There has been much speculation as to how an acute pain can develop into a chronic pain. Fordyce (1976), a pioneer in the development of treatment approaches to chronic pain, assumes that some patients develop chronic pain as a result of being reinforced for pain behavior in their environments. He differentiates between respondent pain, which represents a classically conditioned response to a particular stimulus, and operant pain, which results from reinforced pain behavior. Fordyce's program is significant in providing a comprehensive treatment approach that has now been applied to thousands of patients in many different settings.

Fordyce begins his treatment approach with a complete evaluation of the patient. The evaluation is designed to identify the relationship between the patient's behavior and the environmental events or consequences resulting from this behavior. Fordyce analyzes the time pattern of the pain, the environmental events that increase or diminish the pain, the effect of tension and relaxation on the pain, and the changes in activity level as a result of the pain. Patients who seem amenable to a behavioral program are then accepted into an inpatient program. The goals of the program are to reduce pain behavior, to increase activity, to retrain the family to provide appropriate environmental contingencies, to reduce excessive health-care utilization, and to establish and maintain well behavior. Patients addicted or habituated to medication are slowly withdrawn by means of a pain cocktail containing the patient's baseline medications mixed with a color- and taste-masking vehicle. The cocktail is first administered as needed. Then the active ingredients are slowly faded, and the cocktail is finally terminated when the active ingredients reach zero. To increase activity, subjects are given a selection of easily monitored exercises relevant to posttreatment activities. Patients work to quotas determined by previously achieved levels of exercise and the symptoms that may occur from excessive exercise. Quotas and the success in achieving these quotas are graphed, and verbal praise is given for achieving quotas. Patients may also be given vocation and career counseling as appropriate to increase general levels of activity.

Several studies have reported the effects of inpatient programs modeled after Fordyce's. Unfortunately, the outcome measures have varied so widely between these programs (the methodology has been fairly inadequate, and no controls were employed in any study) that it is hard to determine the effects of these various programs (Anderson, Cole, Gullickson, Hudgens, & Roberts, 1979; Cairns, Thomas, Mooney, & Pace, 1976; Fordyce, Fowler, Lehmann, DeLateur, Sand, & Trieschmann, 1973; Newman, Seres, Yospe, & Garlington, 1978; Sternbach, 1974; Swanson, Floreen, & Swenson, 1976). In general, inpatient programs have led to significant pre- and posttreatment reductions in chronic pain complaint and medication use, as well as significant increases in activity. Follow-up results of six months and longer have indicated that the increases in activity are maintained, that the disability claims have decreased, that employment has increased, and that the pain has usually decreased or increased slightly but has not returned to preadmission levels. Medication reduction is also maintained at follow-up. These studies are tantalizing but inconclusive. It is not clear, for instance, which components of the multicomponent programs that have evolved are necessary for treating patients or even if these programs could be successfully carried out in an outpatient setting.

Headache. Headaches account for much human suffering. At any one time, 10% of the adult population may be affected by headaches (Ogden, 1952). The two most common headache complaints are migraine and tension headaches. Although we discuss these two entities separately, the distinction between these two types of headaches is often unclear; in practice, patients often report symptoms compatible with both types of headache.

Migraine Headaches. Migraine headache is a vascular condition characterized by episodic and severe pain, usually occurring on one side of the head. Four behavioral treatments have been evaluated extensively: skin temperature biofeedback, cephalic vasomotor feedback, relaxation, and combinations (particularly of skin temperature and relaxation).

Skin Temperature Biofeedback. With skin temperature biofeedback, skin temperature is monitored at a peripheral site, such as an index finger, and the subjects receive continuous feedback of change in their finger temperature. The goal is to produce vasodilation at the local site and to redirect the blood flow from the cephalic beds, reducing blood volume in the temple arteries. The results of several studies have shown that skin temperature feedback generally leads to headache symptom reduction (Mullinix, Norton, Hack, & Fishman, 1978; Reading & Mohr, 1976; Sargent, Walters, & Green, 1973; Turin & Johnson, 1976; Wickramasekera, 1973b).

Other authors have combined hand warming with other procedures like psychotherapy (Adler & Adler, 1976), frontalis EMG (Medina, Diamond, & Franklin, 1976), and autogenic instructions (Mitch, McGrady, & Iannone, 1976).

Few studies have used control groups, but

a few clever strategies have been used to control for nonspecific factors. In one strategy, Turin and Johnson (1976) included an irrelevant feedback condition prior to the introduction of hand-warming feedback. The migraine clients first received training in reducing their hand temperature and were led to believe that *hand cooling* was an effective treatment. The hand-cooling condition proved ineffective in reducing symptoms, whereas the next phase of hand-warming feedback resulted in symptom reduction. This study provides some evidence that the effectiveness of hand-warming biofeedback is not totally the result of nonspecific factors.

A second strategy involved the use of false feedback (Mullinix *et al.*, 1978) and led to an opposite conclusion. Although the subjects in the group receiving true temperature feedback altered their skin temperatures significantly more than the false feedback group, both groups showed similar reductions in headache symptoms. These results suggest that nonspecific factors contribute to the success of hand-warming training. In a test of the basic assumption behind hand warming—that the procedure may reduce the flow to cephalic beds—Koppman, McDonald, and Kunzel (1974) found that feedback-influenced vasodilation of the temple artery was not correlated with digital blood-flow changes. Price and Tursky (1976) pointed out that skin temperature feedback may act to increase an overall state of relaxation and in this way may produce vasodilation in cephalic and digital sites together.

The relative effects of skin temperature biofeedback and relaxation were directly assessed in one controlled study (Blanchard, Theobald, Williamson, Silver, & Brown, 1978). The authors compared the effects of temperature biofeedback and progressive muscle relaxation to a waiting-list control group on multiple measures of migraine symptoms. The two treatment groups differed significantly from the waiting-list control group on all dependent measures except headache frequency, but there were no significant differences between the groups. Moreover, a one-year follow-up also showed no differences between the conditions (Blanchard & Ahles, 1979).

Cephalic Vasomotor Feedback. Cephalic vasomotor feedback (CVMF) has also been used to reduce migraine headaches. With the procedure, the patient is given visual or auditory feedback reflecting the momentary changes in blood volume pulse of the temporal artery. Feuerstein, Adams, and Beiman (1976) compared frontalis EMG feedback and CVMF in a single-case study of a mixed migraine–tension-headache client. CVMF was superior to EMG in the overall reduction of headache activity. In a well-controlled group-outcome study, Friar and Beatty (1976) gave feedback of the temporal artery to one group of migraine patients while a second group received feedback for peripheral vasoconstriction. Both groups showed criteria changes in vasoconstriction at the site of feedback. Cranial and peripheral vasomotor changes within the subject were uncorrelated. Statistically significant changes in headache activity were noted for the group receiving feedback for cranial vasoconstriction.

Relaxation. Relaxation has also been demonstrated to show some effectiveness in the treatment of migraine headaches. Two single-group uncontrolled-outcome studies indicate that about two-thirds of patients given a brief course of relaxation and related techniques improve (Hay & Madders, 1971; Warner & Lance, 1975), while about one-third improve from brief training in a passive meditation form of relaxation (Benson, Beary, & Carol, 1974a). Two controlled studies found that relaxation led to similar improvement as temperature biofeedback training combined with autogenic training and regular home practice at the three-month follow-up (Blanchard *et al.*, 1978) and posttreatment (Andreychuk & Skriver, 1975). Why CVMF (resulting in vasoconstriction) and relaxation (involving vasodilation) are both effective in reducing migraine frequency remains uncertain.

Other Approaches. Mitchell and Mitchell (1971) have reported on the use of a behavioral treatment package to reduce migraine headaches. In the first study, three students received a behavioral package including training in progressive relaxation, systematic desensitization, assertiveness training, and training in problem solving for daily living. Three other students only monitored headache activity. At the two-month follow-up, the treated subjects were significantly improved and the controls were unchanged. In the next study, the combined behavioral treatment ($n = 7$) was compared with relaxation alone ($n = 7$) and no treatment ($n = 3$). The combined behavioral treatment was superior to relaxation and to no treatment. In the next study, Mitchell and White (1977) gave 12 patients various parts of the treatment package. The total package, administered almost entirely from audiotapes and written instructions, resulted in significantly greater improvement than that found in a group receiving relaxation training and systematic desensitization. Of the patients treated with this package, 100% showed substantial improvement. These impressive results certainly bear repeating by other investigators and in other settings. Holroyd, Andrasik, and Westbrook (1977) compared EMG biofeedback with a cognitive therapy that focused on teaching clients more effective ways to cope with stress. The cognitive procedure was more effective than the biofeedback procedure, which was not more effective than the control—a finding inconsistent with most other studies.

Summary. In summary, skin temperature feedback and relaxation procedures are both effective in reducing the frequency and the intensity of migraine headache report. One procedure does not appear superior to the other. Cephalic vasomotor feedback may also be useful. Behavioral treatment packages have shown dramatic effectiveness in a few cases.

Tension Headaches. Headache pain is so common that 65% of nonclinical populations report periodic headache (Ogden, 1952). Tension headaches are typically assumed to be the result of sustained contraction of the facial, scalp, neck, or shoulder muscles. However, the available data do not support the assumption that changes in the level of muscular activity are the basis for the headaches (Epstein & Cinciripini, 1980; Phillips, 1977). This is important, of course, because EMG feedback is frequently used to treat tension headaches.

Biofeedback (EMG). The first treatment involving biofeedback and related procedures to treat tension headaches was reported by Budzynski, Stoyva, and Adler (1973). They illustrated that EMG changes could be influenced by analogue auditory stimuli and that the observed changes in muscle activity were a function of the relationship between contingent changes in the feedback signal. Three of five clients taught to reduce EMG levels reported

decreases in headaches. Wickramasekera (1973b) found similar results of biofeedback in a single-group outcome study. In a controlled-group outcome study, Budzynski, Stoyva, Adler & Mullaney (1973) compared the effects of analogue feedback plus self-instructed home relaxation to pseudobiofeedback plus relaxation instruction and to a no-treatment control group that received no relaxation. Both feedback groups had a decline in EMG activity, although during follow-up, the EMG activity was lower only for the biofeedback group. Headache frequency was significantly reduced for the biofeedback group and only slightly for the pseudobiofeedback group. That the controls were unchanged suggests that the biofeedback procedures and not the home relaxation instructions were the critical variable. Other authors have found significant reduction in headache activity with EMG feedback (Chesney & Shelton, 1976; Haynes, Griffin, Mooney, & Parise, 1975; Hutchings & Reinking, 1976; Peck & Kraft, 1977), although one study found no effect (Holroyd *et al.*, 1977). Epstein and Cinciripini (1980) reported on a single-case evaluation of the influence of biofeedback on EMG activity and headache pain using an A-B-A-B experimental control design. The authors showed that feedback had a controlling effect on EMG levels and the pain reports. Wickramasekera (1973a) and Kondo and Center (1977) used true and false feedback. In the latter study, during the false biofeedback condition, subjects were told that the feedback represented actual muscle tension. True but not false biofeedback led to reduction in headache intensity, although it is not certain that the subjects believed that the false biofeedback actually reflected reduced muscle tension.

Relaxation. Three single-group outcome studies (Fitchler & Zimmerman, 1973; Tasto & Hinkle, 1973; Warner & Lance, 1975) have shown substantial reductions in headache pain report. Cox, Freundlick, and Meyer (1975), Haynes *et al.* (1975), and Chesney and Shelton (1976) found that relaxation was superior to controls.

Comparison of Biofeedback and Relaxation. The three previously mentioned studies also compared relaxation with biofeedback. In all of these studies, relaxation was equal or superior to EMG biofeedback. One study has reported an advantage of biofeedback training over relaxation training (Hutchings & Reinking, 1976), although the authors used an amalgamation of several relaxation techniques for brief training periods. In a follow-up study, Hutchings and Reinking (1976) found that patients receiving EMG biofeedback, with or without relaxation training were significantly more improved (at one-month posttreatment) than those receiving relaxation training alone. By three months, those receiving the combined treatment were better than those in the other two conditions; at two months, six months, and one year, all differential treatment effects had vanished. Regular practice of relaxation was associated with significantly fewer headaches regardless of initial treatment.

Summary. Behavioral approaches have been extensively evaluated with three chronic pain problems. Behaviorally oriented inpatient units are effective in reducing much of the disability associated with chronic pain in some patients. Unfortunately, the methodology will have to be improved and long-term outcome studies will have to be undertaken before the specific usefulness of these packages has been demonstrated. Both relaxation and biofeedback (particularly of skin temperature) are useful in reducing the frequency and intensity of migraine headaches. Finally, relaxation appears to be the treatment of choice for reducing the frequency and the intensity of headaches due to chronic tension, although EMG biofeedback works equally well.

Other case reports have demonstrated the usefulness of a variety of behavioral approaches to other pain problems. For instance, relaxation was used to reduce the frequency of pain reported in patients with phantom limb pain (Sherman, Gall, & Gormly, 1979), a condition in which patients experience excruciating pain in a limb that has been amputated. EMG feedback has been demonstrated to reduce myofascial pain dysfunction symptom (Dohrmann & Laskin, 1978).

Central Nervous System

Hearing and Vision. Behavioral techniques have been used for some time in the assessment and modification of hearing and visual problems. As much of this work has occurred

with children, it is not reviewed in this section. However, with adults, several applications of behavioral principles have been applied to myopic subjects and are of both theoretical interest and perhaps practical importance. Epstein, Collins, Hannay, and Looney (1978) used a fading-plus-reinforcement project to modify acuity in myopic subjects. The technique involved gradually increasing the distance at which the myopic subjects could discriminate visual stimuli, and contingent approval was provided for correct discriminations. The fading-plus-reinforcement treatment was compared with a matched no-treatment control group on a measure of visual acuity. Discrimination improvement was shown for the experimental subjects. In a second study (Epstein, Greenwald, Hennon, & Hiedorn, 1981), four replications of a multiple-baseline design across stimuli were used to evaluate changes in visual acuity. Three of the four subjects showed changes appropriate for the fading-plus-reinforcement procedures. One subject given acuity training to pass the medical portion of a job screening showed changes in both eyes from 20/40, 20/50, to 20/20, 20/25.

Seizures. Several studies have clearly shown that the frequency of seizures can be reduced by means of various behavioral techniques. Biofeedback has been studied most extensively, although other techniques have also been used.

Biofeedback. Three different frequencies of electrocortical activity have been studied in attempts to provide feedback to a patient. The most extensively studied electrocortical activity is the so-called sensorimotor rhythm, a 12–15 Hz rhythm over the sensorimotor cortex (SMR). Interest in using the rhythm derived from basic science work with cats. When cats were taught to remain motionless (Roth, Sterman, & Clemente, 1967), this rhythm became more apparent. Furthermore, it was found that increases in SMR rhythm could be operantly conditioned in cats, resulting in a greater resistance to drug-induced seizures. In an early experiment, Sterman and Friar (1972) provided SMR feedback to a 23-year-old female with a history of major motor seizures since age 16. The subject observed a series of lamps, which successively became lit as she increased her SMR activity. The subject was able to increase her SMR activity and experienced only one seizure during the next four months of training. Several other clients have also experienced reduction in seizures with SMR training (Finley, Smith, & Etherton, 1975; Sterman, 1973), although the procedure has not been consistently effective (Kaplan, 1975; Kuhlman & Allison, 1977; Lubar, 1975) and may require continued practice (Sterman, 1973). Other researchers have used mu rhythm or somatomotor rhythm with varying success with several clients (Kaplan, 1975) and alpha, again with varying success.

Deconditioning. Parrino (1971) reduced the frequency of grand mal seizures in a 36-year-old male. Before therapy, the base rate of seizures was approximately 58 per day. Because the patient reported that his seizures were triggered by anxiety-producing stimuli, he was started on a course of systematic desensitization. Over a treatment period of three months, his seizure frequency dropped to 10 per day. When the patient returned to work, he experienced an increase in seizures but applied a self-desensitization system. At five-month follow-up, all medications had been withdrawn and the patient was seizure-free. Similar procedures have been reported with a 12-year-old boy with petit mal and grand mal seizures (Ince, 1976), but cue-controlled relaxation was added. Wells, Turner, Bellack, and Hersen (1978) conducted a single-case analysis of cue-controlled relaxation in the treatment of a 22-year-old female with psychomotor seizures. After baseline, the rates of seizure and anxiety level decreased when treatment was provided and increased when treatment was removed.

Forster (1967) developed various procedures based on classical conditioning to treat the so-called reflex epilepsies. In a typical procedure, he presented the conditioned stimuli repeatedly until the conditioned response no longer occurred. For instance, with a 21-year-old woman who experienced stroboscopically induced seizures, he repeatedly presented stroboscopic illumination until no response occurred. The seizures were subsequently eliminated in response to a 22 cps stroboscopic frequency but did not generalize to values either lower or higher than 11 cps; extinction trials had to be initiated at all frequencies from 15 to 35 cps. Forster (1967) also used fading and other techniques to similarly reduce dys-

rhythmia and seizures precipitated by many other types of stimuli.

Other Techniques. In a very early study, Efron (1956) reported on the case of a 41-year-old woman who had suffered from grand mal attacks for over 26 years. He assumed that the seizure was the end response of a chain of responses that went from feelings of depersonalization, to "forced thinking," to olfactory hallucinating, to auditory hallucinating, to right-direction head movement, and finally to a grand mal seizure. He found that the inhalation of fumes from a vial of hydrogen sulfide prior to the olfactory hallucination prevented the seizure. The patient was seizure-free at 14-month follow-up. Zlutnick, Mayville, and Moffat (1975) also developed a procedure to break chains associated with the development of major and minor seizures in five children. Other procedures used to control seizures in adults have included covert and operant conditioning (Daniels, 1975) and contingency management (Flannery & Cautela, 1973; Richardson, 1972). This has been reviewed recently by Mostofsky and Balaschak (1977).

Memory. An interesting area of importance to aging individuals and perhaps crucial to the survival of some is the development of techniques to improve memory. Many of these techniques are behavioral. Successful use of memory improvement, especially through techniques that use paired-association memory tasks, have been reported for community-dwelling elderly people (Patten, 1972; Robertson-Tchabo, Nausman, & Arenberg, 1976; Rowe & Schnore, 1971) and the brain-injured (Benton & Spreen, 1964; Jones, 1974; Lewinsohn, Danaher, & Kikel, 1977). Systematic applications of these techniques, especially incorporating principles that would enhance the maintenance of procedures of learning in the laboratory, are now being undertaken.

Peripheral Nerve Damage. Biofeedback has been used in the rehabilitation of individuals with nerve damage secondary to a variety of causes. In an early study, Marinacci and Horande (1960) reported on seven cases in which EMG biofeedback helped reverse various neuromuscular dysfunctions. For example, using needle electrodes and auditory EMG feedback, one patient with a complete right facial paralysis of six years' duration was able to bring some previously dysfunctional motor units under voluntary control. After two sessions per week for six months, motor-unit EMG activity in some muscles increased from 400 mico V to 1500 mico V, and the patient experienced a 40% return of function in both the orbicularis and the frontalis muscles. Jankel (1978) used a baseline–treatment–baseline reversal design to demonstrate the specific usefulness of EMG feedback. The patient was asked to match EMG levels obtained from the paralyzed side of her face with EMG from her unaffected side of her face. She increased her EMG significantly during the intervention phase, an effect that carried over during the reversal. Other case examples have shown similar effects in patients with peripheral nerve damage (Booker, Rubow, & Coleman, 1969; Kukulka, Brown, & Basmajian, 1975).

Since biofeedback can be useful in improving conditions secondary to severe peripheral nerve damage, it is not surprising that similar findings have been demonstrated in patients with hemiplegia and paraplegia. In one large study, Brudny, Korein, Grynbaum, Friedmann, Weinstein, Sachs-Frankel, and Belandres (1976) used biofeedback with 39 patients with upper extremity hemiparesis who participated in an 8- to 12-week training period that required accomplishing progressively more demanding muscle tasks. At the end of the study, 27 of 39 patients exhibited greatly improved upper extremity function. At follow-up from two to three years later, 20 of the 39 patients maintained this greatly improved function.

Several controlled-group outcome studies have also been undertaken. Basmajian, Kukulka, Narayan, and Takebe (1975) compared the effects of traditional physical therapy with a combined treatment of traditional therapy and EMG. Twenty subjects with dorsiflexion paralysis (foot drop) were randomly assigned to the two treatment groups. Both groups increased ankle range of movement and strength, with the combined-treatment group showing average increases in both measures that were nearly twice as great as those of the physical-therapy-only group. The second controlled-group outcome study was reported by Mroczek, Halpern, and McHugh (1978). Nine patients with upper-extremity hemiplegia for at least one year were first trained with instruc-

tional procedures to contract or inhibit the biceps. Following baseline, the patients were randomly assigned to four weeks of biofeedback followed by four weeks of physical therapy or four weeks of physical therapy followed by four weeks of biofeedback. EMG and range of measurement (ROM) were measured during the treatment sessions. Pooled group analysis revealed no significant differences in either average EMG activity or active ROM between biofeedback and physical therapy.

Spasmodic Torticollis. Spasmodic torticollis is a dysfunction characterized by sustained constriction of muscles that rotate the head to one side. Several single-case studies and small-group designs have reported reduction in spasm with EMG feedback (Brudny, Grynbaum, & Korein, 1974a; Brudny et al., 1976; Cleeland, 1973). Brudny, Korein, Levidow, Grynbaum, Lieterman, and Friedman (1974) have reported on the effect of the procedure with 48 torticollis patients. Over follow-up periods ranging from three months to three years, 19 (40%) of the patients maintained improvement. Improvement included large reductions in EMG activity in the formerly hypertrophied sternocleidomastoid muscles, and many subjects could return their heads to a normal position. Other behavioral approaches, like negative practice (Agras & Marshall, 1965; Meares, 1973), have shown inconsistent and equivocal results.

Tics. Tics are frequent and troublesome twitches of involuntary muscles. In an early study, Yates (1958) instructed patients to repeat the unwanted response until it became effortful and tiresome, a procedure he called "mass practice." The procedure produced encouraging results, but its effects have not been consistent (Agras & Marshall, 1965; Nicassio, Liberman, Patterson, & Ramirez, 1972). Other procedures that have been used include brief seclusion to eliminate an obscene tic (Lahey, McNees, & McNees, 1973); time-out from pleasant music to reduce multiple tics (Barrett, 1962); self-monitoring and systematic desensitization (Thomas, Abrams, & Johnson, 1971); self-monitoring alone (Hutzell, Platzek, & Logue, 1974); and so-called habit reversal (Azrin & Nunn, 1973).

Sleep. In a recent review, Bootzin and Nicassio (1978) concluded that relaxation has been clearly demonstrated to result in moderate improvement among mild to severe cases of insomnia. Unfortunately, these studies were conducted without EEG records substantiating these effects. Two studies have, however, demonstrated that progressive relaxation produces changes in EEG sleep parameters (Borkovec & Weerts, 1976; Freedman & Papsdorf, 1976). Borkovec, Grayson, O'Brien, and Weerts (1979) evaluated the effects of relaxation on subtypes of insomnia—those with pseudoinsomnia, who show little evidence of sleep deficit according to EEG criteria, and those with real insomnia, who show clear sleep retardation and deficits as measured by the EEG. Twenty-nine insomniacs participated in the study and were assigned to three conditions: progressive relaxation, a condition with progressive relaxation instructions but no muscle-tension releasing, and a no-treatment control condition. The tension release and progressive muscle relaxation were more effective than the other two conditions on subjective sleep measures, regardless of insomnia subtype, and on objective sleep measures only for idiopathic insomniacs. Subjective improvement was maintained for all treatment groups at 12-month follow-up. This study demonstrates the importance of objective measures of sleep and the possible interactions that may exist between treatments and the etiology of the condition.

Thoresen, Coates, Zarcone, Kirmil-Gray, and Rosekind (1980) have described a self-management procedure to manage a variety of behaviors associated with insomnia. The program includes relaxation training, self-monitoring, self-hypnosis, cognitive restruction, and problem solving as necessary.

Other Disorders. Behavioral procedures have been used with other neurological problems. Successful applications of biofeedback have been reported to increase function in patients with hemifacial spasms, dystonia, dysphagia, and muscle atrophy (Brudny *et al.*, 1976); to increase the facial expressiveness of blind patients (Webb, 1977); and to decrease chronic eye blinking (Peck & Kraft, 1977; Roxanas, Thomas, & Rapp, 1978). Nonbiofeedback procedures have been useful in reducing tardive-dyskinesia movement in at least one case of tardive dyskinesia (Taylor, Zlutnick, & Hoehle, 1979).

Health Care Behavior

Epidemiological studies have clearly demonstrated that our lifestyle contributes to our illnesses. What we eat, how we handle stress, how we sleep, how much we exercise, and the quality of our air (severely compromised in smokers) are major factors in determining what diseases we develop. It is also clear that changes in some aspect of our lifestyle, like reducing our cholesterol intake or stopping smoking, lead to reduced morbidity and mortality. It is less clear who is responsible for effecting these changes: certainly the traditional health-care system has shown little interest in prevention in well populations, although this may have changed in recent years. (For instance, the National Center for Disease Control, previously concerned mostly with infectious disease, has now established national prevention goals in all areas of lifestyle.) The technology for implementing such changes lags behind the obvious importance of making such changes, and it is perhaps in this area more than in any other—affecting lifestyle change—that behavioral medicine will make its greatest contribution. The most extensive work in behavioral medicine, in fact, has been directed at changing eating and smoking behavior (the present status of this work is reviewed in other chapters). But there has also been extensive work in four other areas: nutrition, adherence to medication, exercise, and stress reduction.

Nutrition. Large prospective studies have shown that reductions in serum cholesterol are associated with lower morbidity and mortality, at least with hyperlipidemic males, and other evidence is overwhelming that diet contributes to heart disease. Other evidence has demonstrated that increased salt intake is associated with increased blood pressure and, conversely, that reduction in salt intake is associated with lowered blood pressure. There is less convincing but still suggestive evidence that diet may also be related to such problems as colon cancer. Certainly, the majority of Americans consume a diet that is considerably out of line with that recently recommended by the American Select Commission on Nutrition. It is surprising that so few studies have looked at behavioral approaches to diet. An early study was conducted by Meyer and Henderson (1974), who treated 36 subjects at an industrial site with behavior modification, including modeling and token reward, individual counseling, or a single-physician consultation. At 11 weeks posttreatment and at three-month follow-up, all three groups showed a statistically significant reduction in cholesterol and triglycerides. At a follow-up three months later, the behavioral group was significantly different in cholesterol from the other two groups.

This same approach was incorporated and expanded in the intensive instruction portion of the Stanford Three Community Study. Comparisons involved the effects of media plus intensive instruction and media alone with a control in effecting nutrition change as measured by serum chemistries. This study was accomplished in a longitudinal cohort in three California towns of about 14,000 (Farquhar, Maccoby, Wood, Alexander, Breitrose, Brown, Haskell, McAlister, Meyer, Nash, & Stern, 1977). Significant reductions occurred in plasma cholesterol after two years in the towns provided with the media campaign. There were no significant differences in the high-risk group between those given intensive instruction and those exposed to media only.

Foreyt, Scott, Mitchell, and Giotto (1979) have reported on the success of three types of diet intervention programs: diet booklet only, nutrition education, and behavioral intervention with nutrition education for reducing plasma cholesterol and triglycerides. The results from 183 subjects showed that at 6 months, the subjects who received the behavioral intervention with nutrition education had a significantly greater reduction in cholesterol than those in the other two conditions. Both nutrition education and behavioral intervention groups had small but statistically significant cholesterol and triglyceride reduction at 12 months.

Finally, Foxx and Rubinoff (1979) reported on the effects of reducing caffeine ingestion in three habitual coffee addicts. Caffeine increases plasma catecholamines and is, in general, associated with increased blood pressure. The treatment involved a gradual reduction in caffeine to 600 mg per day (fewer than five cups of brewed coffee). The subjects deter-

mined their baseline rate of caffeine use, subtracted 600 mg from this figure, and divided the difference by 4 to determine the goals of reduction for each phase. The coffee drinkers were required to self-monitor and plot their daily intake of caffeine. They received monetary prizes for not exceeding the treatment phase criteria and forfeited a portion of the treatment deposits when they did. Coffee reduction averaged 69% during the four weeks of treatment and 67% at 10-month follow-up. Similar procedures could be applied to a variety of nutritional practices.

Adherence to Medication (and Medical Advice). The importance of this area is illustrated by the fact that 33%–82% of patients do not follow or err in following regimens (Becker & Morman, 1975; Stewart & Cluff, 1972).

A behavioral analysis of adherence to medication and interventions to improve adherence has been a small but exciting part of the behavioral medicine literature, as we noted in the introduction. Although behavioral studies have shown the superiority of simple over complex regimens, the instructional component has not been carefully studied. Such variables as prompts have been shown to improve adherence. Counseling in adherence by paraprofessionals has also been shown to improve adherence. In a recent study, 60 poor adherers from lipid research clinics were randomly allocated to one of three groups: a multicomponent procedure, an attention-control group, and a usual-care group (Dunbar, 1977). The multicomponent package consisted of scheduled phone calls for social reinforcement and individual analysis of medication. The multicomponent package was more effective in bringing a significantly greater proportion of patients above a preestablished adherence criterion than either of the other treatments.

Exercise. There has been surprisingly little attention paid to improving exercise. Exercise behaviors comprise a large number of overt motoric responses that differ in topography, intensity, frequency, and duration and thus are ideal for behavioral measurement techniques. Several studies have attempted to increase exercise adherence. In one study, Epstein and Wing (1980) compared the effects of three contract groups, a lottery group, and a no-treatment control group to increase exercise in 37 female college students. The contract groups differed according to exercise intensity. Subjects in the contract group deposited $5 prior to the study and were refunded $1 per week, contingent on attendance at four of the five exercise sessions. Subjects in the lottery condition deposited $3 prior to the study and were able to earn a chance in the lottery by attending four of the five exercise sessions for a given week. An analysis of the attendance data showed that the mean number of sessions attended by the three contract groups and the lottery group was equivalent or superior to the attendance in the control group.

Wysocki, Hall, Iwata, and Riordan (1979) demonstrated that behavioral contracting can increase physical activity among college students. The authors used aerobic points as outcome measures, which had the advantage that inexperienced observers could be quickly trained to observe exercise behavior and to translate these observations into their aerobic point equivalents. At follow-up some 12 months later, seven of the eight subjects reported that they were earning more aerobic points per week than had been the case during baseline.

Self-Management and Cognitive Strategies. Lifestyle changes have been the focus of self-management studies. Although some proponents of self-management apply the term to the application of behavior therapy principles to oneself, the term has come to refer to a variety of processes, and it is often used synonymously with *self-control* and *self-regulation*. With self-control, the external constraints are inconspicuous. Mahoney and Arnkoff (1979) recently articulated some of the problems and ironies of self-control. For instance, they noted, "We tend to attribute more self-control to the person who is just beginning a personal change . . . after ten years of abstinence, for example, an ex-smoker is not given as much credit when he or she turns down a cigarette" (pp. 79–80). Furthermore, the term *self-control* seems to be used when the change is motivated by noble ideals, involves sacrifice, and is socially desirable.

A number of procedures have emerged from this literature that have been applied to medical problems. These procedures include: self-monitoring, used for instance to record the number of cigarettes smoked or bites eaten; and cueing strategies, which involve a variety of stimulus control strategies like notes on a calendar reminding an individual who has been adhering to a diet change to record the cholesterol in his cupboards. Rehearsal is a strategy in which an individual practices a response in anticipation of a particular event (e.g., a patient learns an alternative response to her husband, which may reduce blood pressure rises during that condition). Self-punishment is a strategy in which an individual administers a punishment for a particular behavior (e.g., he obtains a slight shock when he removes a cigarette from a case). Self-reward is a strategy that provides the individual with a reward for a particular change. A related strategy is to incorporate these same principles into a cognitive strategy.

Although some studies have shown the effectiveness of self-management packages in reducing symptoms like migraine headache (Mitchell & White, 1977), Type A behavior (Suinn & Bloom, 1978), and insomnia (Thoresen *et al.*, 1980), their effectiveness has not been well established or evaluated, particularly as compared with other, simpler techniques.

Disability

Throughout the preceding two sections, we provided examples of the use of behavioral techniques to reduce the severity of a particular illness or symptom and to improve health-care behavior. But behavioral approaches are equally important in reducing the disability that results from a disease. From a behavioral standpoint, the procedures used to change the diet of a young person with minimal arteriosclerosis may be similar to those used to change the diet of a person with established arteriosclerosis, but most studies have focused on the prevention of disease rather than minimizing disability. From society's standpoint, the latter is critically important. The U.S. Department of Commerce estimates that as many as 30 million Americans suffer from some chronic disorder or disability. In this section, we focus on reducing the disabilities and improving the life of three types of disabled individuals: outpatients, inpatients, and shut-ins.

Outpatient Strategies. In the previous sections, we provided a few examples of behavioral approaches to minimizing the consequences of illness or to improving a patient's management of his/her illness. For instance, relaxation and desensitization may reduce the anxiety and fear conditioned to symptoms in patients with chronic asthma, and reinforcement with instructions facilitates the use of a respirator in chronic asthma patients.

An example of the use of behavioral techniques to facilitate the management of a patient's complex medical regimen to reduce disability was recently reported by Dapcich-Muria and Hovell (1979). They used a token reinforcement system to improve an elderly patient's adherence to a complex medical regimen. Using a multiple-baseline and reversal single-case design, the authors demonstrated that the reinforcement contingency was responsible for doubling walking, increasing orange juice consumption, and increasing pill taking.

Inpatient Management Strategies. The second area of treatment of chronic illnesses has been in the inpatient setting. We reviewed the results of Fordyce's inpatient treatment programs earlier. Other authors have described treatment programs designed to decrease patients' illness behavior and to increase their self-care. Wooley, Blackwell, and Winget (1978) reviewed the global outcomes of 300 patients treated on a "psychosomatic unit" employing a learning model of chronic illness behavior. The overall philosophy of the program requires independent action by the patient at each step of treatment in order to progress to the next. Before admission, patients must specify their goals in each of four areas: symptom management, social functioning, family interaction, and life plans. Current status, immediately accepted outcome, and ideal outcome in each are listed and given numerical values of 0–100. The treatment includes biofeedback, skill training, family therapy, and group sessions. In a series of studies, Wooley's group has shown that the program has altered the social contingencies supporting illness behavior, has reduced verbal complaint behavior, and has led to global improvement, maintained at one-year follow-up in the focus target areas for at least one subset of patients.

Shut-Ins. Programs have been developed to enhance the care of patients in institutional settings, like nursing homes, geriatric wards, or board-and-care facilities. For instance,

Baltes, Burgess, and Stewart (1978) have recently reported on techniques to measure self-care behaviors in a nursing home. Geiger and Johnson (1974) developed methods to measure and increase correct eating skills in elderly patients. The measurement procedures involved having observers watch each feeding response and record the type of action involved (scooping, cutting, drinking, etc.), the degree of independence, and any errors, such as spilling food or using the hands instead of the proper utensils. Other investigators have focused on methods of assessing and improving ambulation (McClannahan & Risley, 1974), reducing incontinence (McClannahan, 1973), and improving toileting in general (Pollock & Liberman, 1974; Risley, Spangler, & Edwards, 1978) and intellectual performance. The latter area is particularly exciting because it may be possible to improve intellectual performance in individuals with organic diseases.

A behavioral analysis of a patient's living environment may reveal obvious areas where simple changes may improve patients' functioning. For instance, Peterson, Knapp, Rosen, and Pither (1977) have demonstrated that furniture arrangement can affect the social interaction of geriatric residents in mental hospital wards. McClannahan and Risley (1974) improved social and leisure-time participation on the part of residents by creating a store in the lobby of a nursing home. In another study, they found that the level of leisure participation of severely disable nursing-home residents could increase significantly if they were provided with proper recreational equipment. The simple procedure of serving meals in large bowls (family style), as opposed to serving the food in individual plates, increased verbal interactions (Risley, Gottula, & Edwards, 1978).

Overview of Relaxation and Related Techniques and Biofeedback

Because of their extensive use in behavioral medicine, in this section we review the uses of biofeedback and relaxation.

Relaxation and Related Techniques

Relaxation-centered behavior therapy is an adjunct to systematic desensitization. Wolpe

(1958) shortened Jacobson's progressive muscle relaxation to provide an easy-to-learn procedure that presumably inhibited fear when paired with a fear-arousing situation. However, it became clear that relaxation was not necessary for systematic desensitization. Meanwhile, relaxation began to be used to treat a variety of problems in which anxiety or stress appeared to be the major factor. In fact, Jacobson (1938) had developed relaxation primarily to treat anxiety-related disorders. In a now classic paper, Benson, Beary and Carol (1974), building on work by Gellhorn (1970), observed that progressive muscle relaxation, hypnosis, many forms of meditation, and autogenic training shared several properties: the subject assumes a passive frame of mind in a relaxing position, repeats a simple phrase, and breathes in a deep, regular manner. They argued that this technique elicits the so-called relaxation response, which tends to reduce central-nervous-system sympathetic activity, which, in turn, reduces peripheral sympathetic activity. They noted that a variety of studies have demonstrated that these techniques elicit physiological changes, like decreased muscle tone, blood pressure, heart rate, and skin conductance, which are consistent with decreased sympathetic activity. Many of the treatment effects of relaxation are explained by this reduction in sympathetic activity, and there is even direct evidence of such changes (Davidson *et al.,* 1979). Because of the similarities among progressive relaxation, hypnotic relaxation instructions, autogenic training, many forms of meditation, and relaxation response technique, we classify them together as *relaxation and related techniques.*

Not all authors are convinced that relaxation induces a central trophotropic response. For instance, Henry and Stephens (1977) noted that the central response need not be hypothesized to explain the effects of relaxation. Sympathetic activity can be reduced simply by changing the level of input or response in midbrain regulatory centers. Furthermore, the findings of reduced sympathetic activity are not consistent across these procedures meant to induce the relaxation response (Lang, Dehof, Meurer, & Kaufmann, 1979). Some of the apparent effects of relaxation (like increased flow rates in asthmatics) are responses that are not under sympathetic control. Finally, it should be kept in mind that many forms of meditation, hypnotic procedures, and autogenic training induce increased, and not decreased, sympathetic activity (Corby, Roth, Zarcone, & Kopell, 1978). Nevertheless, it is clear that relaxation shares an illustrious history with procedures practiced in most cultures for all recorded history.

A variety of progressive-muscle-relaxation programs have been described in the literature, but the superiority of one over the other has not been demonstrated. Nor is it clear for how long, or under what circumstances, an individual should practice relaxation. In general, programs that use one session are less effective than longer ones. Taped sessions are usually as effective as live programs (but see Brauer, Horlick, Nelson, Farquhar, & Agras, 1979), and group sessions are as effective as individual sessions. Most clinicians have subjects practice at least five sessions and teach them how to generalize their relaxation to other settings. It is not clear for how long subjects should practice relaxation. Subjects who continue to practice seem to do better than those who stop, but the issue has never been empirically investigated in a long-term study.

In Table 2, we have listed the conditions in which relaxation has been demonstrated to be useful. To be classified as probably useful, relaxation in at least two controlled-group outcome studies must have demonstrated its superiority over control groups for at least three months (the paucity of carefully controlled outcome studies of six months or longer is shocking). Relaxation has been most extensively studied and demonstrated to be useful in treating patients with essential hypertension. It also appears to be useful to patients with migraine and tension headaches. The evidence also suggests that it is useful with sleep-onset insomnia. Relaxation may be useful in the other conditions listed in the table, although the studies are too few to justify any clear recommendations. Relaxation has been reported in single-case reports to be useful for literally hundreds of other problems, at least as an adjunct to different therapies. It does not appear to be useful in cases where structural disturbances have produced fixed abnormalities (e.g., in patients with conduction difficul-

Table 2. Summary of Usefulness of Relaxation

Probably useful	Possibly useful	Not useful
Essential hypertension	PVCs	Intrinsic conduction disturbance of heart
Migraine headaches	Paroxysmal atrial tachycardia	Muscle rehabilitation
Tension headaches	Asthma	
Sleep-onset insomnia	Nausea	
	Irritable bowel	
	Pain tolerance	
	Muscle spasm	

ties resulting from damage to the myocardium).

Biofeedback

One of the more extraordinary and exciting observations in recent times has been the systematic study of a person's ability to control her/his own physiology. Of course, voluntary control of physiological functions has been reported for centuries by religious mystics. But in recent times, the use of inexpensive technology has allowed the average person to achieve the same phenomenon. Shapiro and Surwit (1979) defined *biofeedback* as the "application of operant conditioning methods to the control of visceral, somatomotor, and central nervous system activities" (p. 45).

Uses of Biofeedback. Biofeedback can be conceptualized from three standpoints: (1) it provides an ideal method of enhancing unspecified (placebo) therapeutic effects; (2) it facilitates the relaxation response; and (3) it induces specific therapeutic effects.

Biofeedback as a Placebo. We have previously argued that unspecified therapeutic effects account for much of the success of many medical procedures. To say that biofeedback acts as a placebo is to say that for some people, it offers considerable help. From a clinical standpoint, biofeedback is appealing to many patients who might otherwise refuse to engage in some treatment of possible help to them. Biofeedback instrumentation—with flashing lights, noises, and other techniques to enhance a person's control of her/his physiology—may induce the same effect that Goldring (1956) elicited in his classic experiment on unspecified effects on hypertension. Goldring manu-

factured an elaborate electronic gun with flashing lights and complicated switches. He then aimed it at subjects and told them that it would reduce their blood pressures, as indeed it did (for as long as the subjects remained in the study). Stroebel and Glueck (1973) have even argued that biofeedback is the ultimate placebo in the sense that it "provides the patient with an effective means of preventing illness and/or potentially curing himself by helping him regulate the pace of his daily life-style . . . his habits etc." (p. 20). Also, the "word ultimate implies a self-individualized path with many different options where the person himself owns responsibility for achieving the goal of therapy" (p. 20).

Induction of the Relaxation Response. Another general use of biofeedback may be to elicit the relaxation response. Brener (1974), for instance, has shown that physiological functions are not entirely independent and that learned or instructed changes in one system may induce changes in others. Other authors have found that subjects are repeating words to themselves like "Heart rate still," a message similar to autogenic instructions when attempting to comply with feedback instructions to reduce blood pressure.

Specific Biofeedback Effects. Biofeedback may be a specific treatment for some disorders, when neither relaxation nor nonspecific factors result in significant changes. Single-case and group-outcome studies have shown the biofeedback is useful in treating fecal incontinence and encopresis (anal sphincter feedback) and for muscle retraining (EMG feedback), particularly for foot drop, torticollis, and stroke rehabilitation. In Table 3, we have listed the conditions in which biofeedback is probably useful.

Table 3. Summary of Usefulness of Biofeedback[a]

Probably useful	Possibly useful
Encophoresis, fecal incontinence (anal sphincter)	Blood pressure (Pulse Transit Time, actual BP)
Migraine headache (skin temperature)	PVCs (heart rate)
Tension headache (EMG)	Paroxysmal atrial tachycardia (heart rate)
Muscle retraining (EMG)	Sinus tachycardia (heart rate)
	Postural hypotension (actual BP)
	Wolff-Parkinson-White syndrome (heart rate)
	Asthma (respiratory flow rate)
	Irritable bowel (rectosigmoid pressure)
	Peptic ulcer disease (gastric pH)
	Raynaud's syndrome (skin temperature)
	Migraine headache (cephalic blood volume, EMG)
	Major motor seizures (SMR)
	Temporomandibular joint dysfunction (EMG)
	Torticollis (EMG)
	Back pain (EMG)

[a] The type of feedback is in parentheses.

Future Perspectives

The future of behavioral medicine is rosy. The interest of practitioners and researchers of behavior therapy and applied behavioral analysis in medical problems will greatly enhance our understanding of the relationship between health, disease, and behavior. In particular, a technology may be developed to improve self-care, to maintain health, and to minimize disability and discomfort from disease.

On a basic science level, we can anticipate that behavioral medicine researchers will continue to make important contributions to medical science. Medicine prides itself on the specificity of measurement, but rarely has behavior been included in this measurement. Such straightforward but critical behaviors, such as actual drug use in an experiment of the effects of a procedure on a class of behaviors, are rarely described in even the most sophisticated medical articles. As behavioral techniques are proved beneficial, it becomes important to determine the reasons for these effects, for instance, how relaxation may induce changes in blood pressure.

On a treatment level, more techniques will be developed and practiced. The success of the application of these techniques will be de-termined as much by political and social factors—like how adequately behavioral medicine practitioners are reimbursed and how easily they become incorporated into the medical system—as by scientific ones. We can anticipate that some techniques, currently oversold, will lose credibility, if not in the eyes of the public, then certainly in the practice of traditional medical practitioners, who currently seem infatuated with behavioral medicine techniques. But it may occur that physicians, who are used to dramatic changes in physiological variables and are trained to think in clinical and not statistical terms, will become discouraged by the immediate and sometimes small impact of a particular behavioral intervention. And how behavioral techniques may achieve widespread use of their most promising effects—prevention and rehabilitation—is an even more complicated question.

We can expect that behavioral medicine techniques will play an even more important part in prevention and rehabilitation. Programmed techniques will be developed to facilitate the management of complex regimens and to minimize disability. The impetus for adopting such changes and the philosophy for incorporating these changes may have to come from social and political forces, since commitment to prevention has been minimal on the part of traditional medical practitioners. On a more optimistic note, prevention has been designated as a very important national health goal and one we must strive to achieve.

Summary

In the last 10 years, behavior therapy techniques and practices have moved from being applied to a few medical problems to becoming a major new discipline. Hypertension, arrhythmias, Type A behavior, and risk reduction have been the most extensively studied areas of cardiovascular problems in behavioral medicine. Relaxation has been demonstrated to be of benefit in reducing blood pressure in some patients with essential hypertension. However, the role of biofeedback is less clear. Both relaxation and biofeedback may help in reducing the frequency of some types of arrhythmias. Self-management strategies are being developed for changing Type A behavior; their usefulness has yet to be determined. Management of a patient's illness and reducing the anxiety and stress accompanying it are helpful in the case of asthma.

There has been less work done specifically on gastrointestinal system disorders. Various behavioral techniques have shown promise in reducing the complaint of nausea and symptoms of the irritable bowel syndrome and the reducing gastric acid in peptic ulcer disease. Carefully controlled trials are urgently needed in this area.

Impressive treatment gains have been made in reducing the severity and the extent of migraine and tension headache complaints. Inpatient programs have been developed for the treatment of chronic pain but have not, as yet, been extensively evaluated. Behavioral techniques have been applied to a variety of health care behaviors. A few studies have shown that instructions and simple behavior therapy programs improve nutrition, increase exercise, and increase adherence to medication. Self-management and cognitive strategies may offer particular promise in this area.

Biofeedback has been demonstrated to be effective in reducing fecal incontinence, migraine and tension headache, and muscle re-

training. The evidence is less substantial but promising for many other conditions.

References

Adams, N., Ferguson, J., Stunkard, A. J., & Agras, S. The eating behavior of obese and nonobese women. *Behaviour Research and Therapy*, 1978, *16*, 225–232.

Adler, C., & Adler, S. Biofeedback-psychotherapy for the treatment of headaches: A five-year clinical follow-up. *Headache*, 1976, *16*, 189–191.

Agras, S., & Marshall, C. The application of negative practice to spasmodic torticollis. *American Journal of Psychiatry*, 1965, *122*, 579–582.

Alexander, A. B. Systematic relaxation and flow rates in asthmatic children: Relationship to emotional precipitants and anxiety. *Journal of Psychosomatic Research*, 1972, *16*, 405–410.

Alexander, A. B., Miklich, D. R., & Hershkoff, H. The immediate effects of systematic relaxation training on peak expiratory flow rates in asthmatic children. *Psychosomatic Medicine*, 1972, *34*, 388–394.

Alexander, A. B., Cropp, G. J. A., & Chai, H. Effects of relaxation training on pulmonary mechanics in children with asthma. *Journal of Applied Behavior Analysis*, 1979, *12*, 27–35.

Alexander, F., French, T. M., & Pollock, G. H. *Psychosomatic specificity*. Chicago: University of Chicago Press, 1968.

Alford, G. S., Blanchard, E. B., & Buckley, T. M. Treatment of hysterical vomiting by modification of social contingencies: A case study. *Journal of Behavior Therapy and Experimental Psychiatry*, 1972, *3*, 209–212.

Almy, T. P., & Tulin, M. Alterations in colonic function by men under stress: Experimental production of changes simulating the "irritable colon." *Gastroenterology*, 1947, *8*, 616–626.

Anderson, T. P., Cole, T. M., Gullickson, G., Hudgens, A., & Roberts, A. H. Behavior modification of chronic pain: A treatment program by a multidisciplinary team. *Journal of Clinical Orthopedics and Related Research*, 1977, *129*, 96–100.

Andreychuk, T., & Skriver, C. Hypnosis and biofeedback in the treatment of migraine headache. *International Journal of Clinical and Experimental Hypnosis*, 1975, *23*, 172–183.

Azrin, N., & Nunn, R. Habit reversal: A method of eliminating nervous habits and tics. *Behaviour Research and Therapy*, 1973, *11*, 619–628.

Baltes, M. M., Burgess, R. L., & Stewart, R. B. *Independence and dependence in nursing home residents: An operant ecological study*. Paper presented at the Nova Behavioral Conference on Aging, Port St. Lucie, Fla., 1978.

Barrett, B. Reduction in rate of multiple tics by free operant conditioning methods. *Journal of Nervous and Mental Disease*, 1962, *135*, 187–195.

Basmajian, J. V. *Muscles alive: Their functions revealed by electromyography* (3rd ed.). Baltimore: Williams & Wilkins, 1974.

Basmajian, J. V., Kukulka, C. G., Narayan, M. G., &

Takebe, K. Biofeedback treatment of footdrop after stroke compared with standard rehabilitation technique. Effects on voluntary control and strength. *Archives of Physical Medicine and Rehabilitation,* 1975, *56,* 231–236.

Becker, M. H., & Morman, L. A. Sociobehavioral determinants of compliance with health and medical care recommendations. *Medical Care,* 1975, *13,* 10–24.

Benson, H. *The relaxation response.* New York: William Morrow, 1975.

Benson, H., Beary, J. F., & Carol, M. P. The relaxation response. *Psychiatry,* 1974, *37,* 37.

Benson, H., Klemchuk, H. P., & Graham, J. R. The usefulness of the relaxation response in the therapy of headache. *Headache,* 1974, *14,* 14–52.

Benson, H., Alexander, S., & Feldman, C. L. Decreased premature ventricular contractions through use of the relaxation response in patients with stable ischaemic heart-disease. *Lancet,* 1975, *2,* 380–382.

Benton, A., & Spreen, O. Visual memory test performance in mentally deficient and brain damaged patients. *American Journal of Mental Deficiency,* 1964, *68,* 630–633.

Binger, C. *Revolutionary doctor: Benjamin Rush, 1746–1813.* New York: Norton, 1966.

Birk, L. *Biofeedback: Behavioral medicine.* New York: Grune & Stratton, 1973.

Blackburn, H. Diet and mass hyperlipidemia: Public health considerations. In R. Levy, B. Rifkind, B. Dennis, & N. Ernst (Eds.), *Nutrition and coronary heart disease.* New York: Raven Press, 1978.

Blanchard, E. B., & Ahles, T. A. Behavioral treatment of psychophysical disorders. *Behavior Modification,* 1979, *3,* 518–549.

Blanchard, E. B., & Haynes, M. R. Biofeedback treatment of a case of Raynaud's disease. *Journal of Behavior Therapy and Experimental Psychiatry,* 1975, *6,* 230–234.

Blanchard, E. B., Theobald, D., Williamson, D., Silver, B., & Brown, B. Temperature feedback in the treatment of migraine headaches. *Archives of General Psychiatry,* 1978, *35,* 581–588.

Bleecker, E. R., & Engel, B. T. Learned control of cardiac rate and cardiac conduction in the Wolff-Parkinson-White syndrome. *New England Journal of Medicine,* 1973, *288,* 560–562. (a)

Bleecker, E. R., & Engel, B. T. Learned control of ventricular rate in patients with atrial fibrillation. *Psychosomatic Medicine,* 1973, *35,* 161–170. (b)

Blumenthal, J. A., Williams, R. B., Wong, Y., Schanberg, S. M., & Thompson, L. W. Type A behavior pattern and coronary atherosclerosis. *Circulation,* 1978, *58,* 634–639.

Booker, H. B., Rubow, R. T., & Coleman, P. J. Simplified feedback in neuromuscular training: An automated approach using electromyographic signals. *Archives of Physical Medicine and Rehabilitation,* 1969, *50,* 621–625.

Bootzin, R. R., & Nicassio, P. M. Behavioral treatment for insomnia. In M. Hersen, R. M. Eisler, & P. M. Miller (Eds.), *Progress in behavior modification,* Vol. 6. New York: Academic Press, 1978.

Borkovec, T. D., & Weerts, T. C. Effects of progressive relaxation on sleep disturbance: An electroencephalic evaluation. *Psychosomatic Medicine,* 1976, *38,* 173–180.

Borkovec, T. D., Grayson, J. B., O'Brien, G. T., & Weerts, T. C. Relaxation treatment of pseudoinsomnia and idiopathic insomnia: An electroencephalographic evaluation. *Journal of Applied Behavior Analysis,* 1979, *12,* 37–54.

Brauer, A. P., Horlick, L., Nelson, E., Farquhar, J. W., & Agras, W. S. Relaxation therapy for essential hypertension: A Veterans Administration outpatient study. *Journal of Behavioral Medicine,* 1979, *2,* 21–29.

Brener, J. A general model of voluntary control applied to the phenomena of learned cardiovascular change. In P. A. Obrist, A. H. Black, J. Brener, & L. V. DiCara (Eds.), *Cardiovascular psychophysiology.* Chicago: Aldine, 1974.

Brudny, J., Grynbaum, B. B., & Korein, J. Spasmodic torticollis: Treatment by feedback display of the EMG. *Archives of Physical Medicine and Rehabilitation,* 1974, *55,* 403–408.

Brudny, J., Korein, J., Levidow, L., Grynbaum, B. B., Lieberman, A., & Friedman, L. W. Sensory feedback therapy as a modality of treatment in central nervous systems disorders of voluntary movement. *Neurology,* 1974, *24,* 925–932.

Brudny, J., Korein, J., Grynbaum, B. B., Friedman, L. W., Weinstein, S., Sachs-Frankel, G., & Belandres, P. V. EMG feedback therapy: Review of treatment of 114 patients. *Archives of Physical Medicine and Rehabilitation,* 1976, *57,* 55–61.

Budzynski, T., Stoyva, J., & Adler, C. Feedback-induced muscle relaxation: Application to tension headache. *Journal of Behavior Therapy and Experimental Psychiatry,* 1970, *1,* 205–211.

Budzynski, T. H., Stoyva, J. M., Adler, C. S., & Mullaney, D. EMG biofeedback and tension headache: A controlled-outcome study. *Psychosomatic Medicine,* 1973, *35,* 484–496.

Bueno-Miranda, F., Cerulli, M., & Schuster, M. M. Operant conditioning of colonic motility in irritable bowel syndrome (IBS). *Gastroenterology,* 1976, *70,* 867.

Cairns, D., Thomas, L., Mooney, V., & Pace, J. B. A comprehensive treatment approach to chronic low back pain. *Pain,* 1976, *2,* 301–308.

Chesney, M. A., & Shelton, J. L. A comparison of muscle relaxation and electromyogram biofeedback treatments for muscle contraction headache. *Journal of Behavior Therapy and Experimental Psychiatry,* 1976, *7,* 221–225.

Cleeland, C. S. Behavioral techniques in the modification of spasmodic torticollis. *Neurology,* 1973, *23,* 1241–1247.

Cohen, S. I., & Reed, J. L. The treatment of "nervous diarrhea" and other conditioned autonomic disorders by desensitization. *British Journal of Psychiatry,* 1968, *114,* 1275–1280.

Conners, C. K. Behavioral and psychophysiological aspects of Raynaud's disease. In J. M. Ferguson & C. B. Taylor (Eds.), *The comprehensive handbook of behavioral medicine.* Jamaica, N.Y.: SP Medical & Scientific Books, 1980.

Corby, J. C., Roth, W. T., Zarcone, V. P., Jr., & Kopell, B. S. Psychophysiological correlates of practice of Tantric Yoga meditation. *Archives of General Psychiatry,* 1978, *35,* 571–577.

Cox, D. J., Freundlick, A., & Meyer, R. G. Differential effectiveness of electromyograph feedback, verbal relaxation instructions, and medication placebo with tension headaches. *Journal of Consulting and Clinical Psychology*, 1975, *43*, 892–899.

Creer, T. L., Asthma: Psychological aspects and management. In E. Middleton, C. Reed, & E. Ellis (Eds.), *Allergy: Principles and practice*. St. Louis: Mosby, 1978.

Daniels, L. K. Treatment of grand mal epilepsy by covert and operant conditioning techniques. *Psychosomatics*, 1975, *16*, 65–67.

Danker, D. S., Miklich, D. R., Prott, C., & Creer, T. L. An unsuccessful attempt to instrumentally condition peak expiratory flow rates in asthmatic children. *Journal of Psychosomatic Research*, 1975, *19*, 209–215.

Dapcich-Miura, E., & Hovell, M. F. Contingency management of adherence to a complex medical regimen in an elderly heart patient. *Behavior Therapy*, 1979, *10*, 193–201.

Datey, L. K., Deshmukh, S. N., Dalvi, C. P., & Vinekar, S. L. "Shavasan": A yogic exercise in the management of hypertension. *Angiology*, 1969, *20*, 325–333.

Davidson, D. M., Winchester, M. A., Taylor, C. B., Alderman, E. A., & Ingels, N. B., Jr. Effects of relaxation therapy on cardiac performance and sympathetic activity in patients with organic heart disease. *Psychosomatic Medicine*, 1979, *41*, 303–309.

Dembroski, T. D., MacDougall, J. L., Shields, J. L., Petitto, J., & Lushene, R. Component of the Type A coronary-prone behavior pattern and cardiovascular responses to psychomotor performance challenge. *Journal of Behavioral Medicine*, 1978, *1*, 159–176.

Dohrmann, R. J., & Laskin, D. M. An evaluation of electromyographic biofeedback in the treatment of myofascial pain-dysfunction syndrome. *Journal of the American Dental Association*, 1978, *96*, 656–662.

Dunbar, J. *Adherence to medication: An intervention study for poor adherers*. Doctoral thesis, Stanford University, 1977.

Eckert, E., McHugh, R. B., Philander, D. A., & Blumenthal, M. N. Bronchial asthma: Improved lung function after behavior modification. *Psychosomatics*, 1979, *20*, 325–331.

Efron, R. The effect of olfactory stimuli in arresting uncinate fits. *Brain*, 1956, *79*, 267–277.

Efron, R. The conditioned inhibition of uncinate fits. *Brain*, 1957, *80*, 251–262.

Enelow, A. J., & Henderson, T. B. (Eds.), *Applying behavioral science to cardiovascular risk*. Dallas: American Heart Association, 1975.

Engel, B. T., & Bleecker, E. R. Application of operant conditioning techniques to the control of cardiac arrhythmias. In P. A. Obrist, A. H. Black, J. Brener, & L. V. DiCara (Eds.), *Cardiovascular psychophysiology*. Chicago: Aldine, 1974.

Engel, B. T., Nikoomanesh, P., & Schuster, M. M. Operant conditioning of rectosphincteric responses in the treatment of fecal incontinence. *New England Journal of Medicine*, 1974, *290*, 646–649.

Epstein, L. H., & Cinciripini, C. M. Behavioral control of tension headaches. In J. M. Ferguson & C. B. Taylor (Eds.), *The comprehensive handbook of behavioral medicine, Vol. 2*. Jamaica, N.Y.: SP Medical & Scientific Books, 1980.

Epstein, L. H., & Masek, B. J. Behavioral control of medicine compliance. *Journal of Applied Behavior Analysis*, 1978, *11*, 1–9.

Epstein, L. H., & Wing, R. Behavioral approaches to exercise habits and athletic performance. In J. M. Ferguson & C. B. Taylor (Eds.), *The comprehensive handbook of behavioral medicine*. Jamaica, N.Y.: SP Medical & Scientific Books, 1980.

Epstein, L. H., Doke, L. A., Sajwaj, T. E., Sorrell, S., & Rimmer, B. Generality and side effects of overcorrection. *Journal of Applied Behavior Analysis*, 1974, *7*, 385–390.

Epstein, L. H., Collins, F. L., Jr., Hannay, H. J., & Looney, R. L. Fading and feedback in the modification of visual acuity. *Journal of Behavioral Medicine*, 1978, *1*, 273–287.

Epstein, L. H., Greenwald, D. J., Hennon, D., & Hiedorn, B. The effects of monocular fading and feedback on vision changes in the trained and untrained eye. *Behavior Modification*, 1981, *5*, 171–186.

Farquhar, J. W., Maccoby, N. M., Wood, P. D., Alexander, J. K., Breitrose, H., Brown, B. W., Haskell, W. L., McAlister, A. L., Meyer, A. J., Nash, J. D., & Stern, M. P. Community education for cardiovascular health. *Lancet*, 1977, *1*, 1192–1195.

Ferster, C. B., Nurnberger, J. I., & Levitt, E. B. The control of eating. *Journal of Mathetics*, 1962, *1*, 87–109.

Feuerstein, M., Adams, H. E., & Beiman, I. Cephalic vasomotor and electromyographic feedback in the treatment of combined muscle contraction and migraine headaches in a geriatric case. *Headache*, 1976, *16*, 232–237.

Fieldman, C. M. The effect of biofeedback training on respiratory resistance of asthmatic children. *Psychosomatic Medicine*, 1976, *38*, 27–34.

Finley, W. W., Smith, H. A., & Etheron, M. D. Reduction of seizures and normalization of the EEG in a severe epileptic following sensorimotor biofeedback training: Preliminary study. *Biological Psychology*, 1975, *2*, 189–203.

Fitchler, H., & Zimmerman, R. R. Change in reported pain from tension headaches. *Perceptual and Motor Skills*, 1973, *36*, 712.

Flannery, R. B., Jr., and Cautela, J. R. Seizures: Controlling the uncontrollable. *Journal of Rehabilitation*, 1973, *39*, 34–36.

Fordyce, W. F. *Behavioral methods for chronic pain and illness*. St. Louis: Mosbey, 1976.

Fordyce, W., Fowler, R., Lehmann, J., DeLateur, B., Sand, B., & Trieschmann, R. Operant conditioning in the treatment of chronic pain. *Archives of Physical Medicine and Rehabilitation*, 1973, *54*, 399–408.

Foreyt, J., Scott, L. W., Mitchell, R. E., & Giotto, A. M. Plasma lipid changes in the normal population following behavioral treatment. *Journal of Consulting and Clinical Psychology*, 1979, *47*, 440–452.

Forster, F. M. Conditioning of cerebral dysrhythmia induced by pattern presentation and eye-closure. *Conditional Reflex*, 1967, *2*, 236–244.

Forster, F. M. *Reflex epilepsy, behavioral therapy and conditional reflexes*. Springfield, Ill.: Charles C Thomas, 1977.

Forster, F. M., Paulsen, W. A., & Baughman, F. A. Clinical therapeutic conditioning in reading epilepsy. *Neurology*, 1969, *19*, 717–723.

Foxx, R. M., & Rubinoff, A. Behavioral treatment of caffeinism: Reducing excessive coffee drinking. *Journal of Applied Behavior Analysis*, 1979, *12*, 315–324.

Freedman, R., & Papsdorf, J. D. Biofeedback and progressive relaxation treatment of sleep-onset insomnia: A controlled, all-night investigation. *Biofeedback and Self-Regulation*, 1976, *1*, 253–271.

French, A. P., Schmid, A. C., & Ingalls, E. Transcendental meditation, altered reality testing, and behavioral change: A case report. *Journal of Nervous and Mental Disease*, 1976, *161*, 55–59.

Friar, L. R., & Beatty, J. Migraine: Management by trained control of vasoconstriction. *Journal of Consulting and Clinical Psychology*, 1976, *44*, 46–53.

Friedman, M., & Rosenman, R. H. *Type A behavior and your heart.* New York: Knopf, 1974.

Furman, S. Intestinal biofeedback in functional diarrhea: A preliminary report. *Journal of Behavior Therapy and Experimental Psychiatry*, 1973, *4*, 317–321.

Geiger, O. G., & Johnson, L. A. Positive education for elderly persons: Correct eating through reinforcement. *The Gerontologist*, 1974, *14*, 432–436.

Goldring, W., Chasis, H., Schreiner, G. E., & Smith, H. W. Reassurance in the management of benign hypertensive disease. *Circulation*, 1956, *14*, 260–264.

Goodman, M. A., & Gilman, A. *The pharmacological basis of therapeutics* (3rd ed.). New York: Macmillan, 1966.

Goodwin, J. S., Goodwin, J. M., & Vogel, A. V. Knowledge and use of placebos by house officers and nurses. *Annals of Internal Medicine*, 1979, *91*, 106–110.

Hay, K. M., & Madders, J. Migraine treated by relaxation therapy. *Journal of the Royal College of General Practitioners*, 1971, *21*, 449–664.

Haynes, S. N., Griffin, R., Mooney, D., & Parise, M. Electromyographic biofeedback and relaxation instructions in the treatment of muscle contraction headaches. *Behavior Therapy*, 1975, *6*, 672–678.

Hedberg, A. G. The treatment of chronic diarrhea by systematic desensitization: A case report. *Journal of Behavior Therapy and Experimental Psychiatry*, 1973, *4*, 67–68.

Henry, J. P., & Stephens, P. M. The social environment and essential hypertension in mice: Possible role of the innervation of the adrenal cortex. In W. De Jong, A. P. Provost, & A. P. Shapiro (Eds.), *Hypertension and brain mechanisms: Progress in Brain Research*, 1977, *47*, 263–277.

Holroyd, K., Andrasik, F., & Westbrook, T. Cognitive control of tension headache. *Cognitive Therapy and Research*, 1977, *1*, 121–133.

Horan, J. J., Hackett, G., Nicholas, W. C., Linberg, S. E., Stone, C. I., & Lukaski, H. C. Rapid smoking: A cautionary note. *Journal of Consulting and Clinical Psychology*, 1977, *45*, 341–343.

Hutchings, D., & Reinking, R. Tension headaches: What form of therapy is most effective? *Biofeedback and Self-Regulation*, 1976, *1*, 183–190.

Hutzell, R., Platzek, D., & Logue, P. Control of Gilles de la Tourette's syndrome by self-monitoring. *Journal of Behavior Therapy and Experimental Psychiatry*, 1974, *5*, 71–76.

Hypertension Detection and Follow-Up Program Cooperative Group. Five-year findings of the hypertension detection and follow-up program. *Journal of the American Medical Association*, 1979, *242*, 2562–2577.

Illich, I. D. *Medical nemesis: The expropriation of health.* New York: Pantheon, 1976.

Ince, L. P. The use of relaxation training and a conditioned stimulus in the elimination of epileptic seizures in a child: A case study, *Journal of Behavior Therapy and Experimental Psychiatry*, 1976, *7*, 39–42.

Ingersoll, B. F., & Curry, F. Rapid treatment of persistence, vomiting in a 14-year-old female by shaping and time out. *Journal of Behavior Therapy and Experimental Psychiatry*, 1977, *8*, 305–307.

Jacob, R. G., Kraemer, H. C., & Agras, W. S. Relaxation therapy in the treatment of hypertension: A review. *Archives of General Psychiatry*, 1977, *34*, 1417–1427.

Jacobson, A. M., Hackett, T. P., Surman, O. S., & Silverberg, E. Raynaud phenomenon: Treatment with hypnotic and operant technique. *Journal of the American Medical Association*, 1973, *225*, 739–740.

Jacobson, E. *Progressive relaxation.* Chicago: University of Chicago Press, 1938.

Jankel, W. R. Bell palsy: Muscle reeducation by electromyographic feedback. *Archives of Physical Medicine and Rehabilitation*, 1978, *59*, 240–242.

Jones, M. K. Imagery as a mnemonic aid after left temporal lobectomy: Contrast between material-specific and generalized memory disorders. *Neuropsychologia*, 1974, *12*, 21–30.

Kaplan, B. J. Biofeedback in epileptics: Equivocal relationship of reinforced EEG frequency to seizure reduction. *Epilepsia*, 1975, *16*, 477–485.

Katz, R. C., & Zlutnick, S. (Eds.). *Behavior therapy and health care: Principles and applications.* New York: Pergamon, 1975.

Kentsmith, D., Strider, F., Copenhaver, J., & Jacques, D. Effects of biofeedback upon the suppression of migraine symptoms and plasma dopamine-B hydroxylase activity. *Headache*, 1976, *16*, 173–177.

Khan, A. V. Effectiveness of biofeedback and counterconditioning in the treatment of bronchial asthma. *Journal of Psychosomatic Research*, 1977, *21*, 97–104.

Khan, A. V., & Olson, D. L. Deconditioning of exercise-induced asthma. *Psychosomatic Medicine*, 1977, *39*, 382–392.

Khan, A. V., Staerk, M., & Bonk, C. Role of counterconditioning in the treatment of asthma. *Journal of Psychosomatic Research*, 1973, *17*, 389–394.

Khan, A. V., Staerk, M., & Bonk, C. Role of counterconditioning in the treatment of asthma. *Journal of Psychosomatic Research*, 1974, *18*, 89–93.

Kondo, C., & Canter, A. True and false electromyographic feedback: Effect on tension headache. *Journal of Abnormal Psychology*, 1977, *86*, 93–95.

Koppman, J. W., McDonald, R. D., & Kunzel, M. G. Voluntary regulation of temporal artery diameter in migraine patients. *Headache*, 1974, *14*, 133–138.

Kraemer, H. C., Jacob, R. G., Jeffery, R. W., & Agras, W. S. Empirical selection of matching factors in matched-pairs and matched-blocks small-sample research designs. *Behavior Therapy*, 1979, *10*, 615–628.

Kristt, D. A., & Engel, B. T. Learned control of blood

pressure in patients with high blood pressure. *Circulation*, 1975, *51*, 370–378.

Kuhlman, W. N., & Allison, T. EEG feedback training in the treatment of epilepsy: Some questions and answers. *Pavlovian Journal of Biological Science*, 1977, *12*, 112–122.

Kukulka, C. G., Brown, D. M., & Basmajian, J. V. A preliminary report on biofeedback training for early finger joint mobilization. *American Journal of Occupational Therapy*, 1975, *29*, 469–470.

Lahey, B., McNees, P., & McNees, M. Control of an obscene "verbal tic" through timeout in an elementary school classroom. *Journal of Applied Behavior Analysis*, 1973, *6*, 101–104.

Lang, R., Dehof, K., Meurer, K. A., & Kaufmann, W. Sympathetic activity and transcendental meditation. *Journal of Neural Transmission*, 1979, *44*, 117–135.

Lewinsohn, P. M., Danaher, B. G., & Kikel, S. Visual imagery as a mnemonic aid for brain-injured persons. *Journal of Consulting and Clinical Psychology*, 1977, *45*, 717–723.

Lichtenstein, E., & Glasgow, R. E. Rapid smoking: Side effects and safeguards. *Journal of Consulting and Clinical Psychology*, 1977, *45*, 815–821.

Lipowski, Z. J. Psychosomatic medicine in the seventies: An overview. *American Journal of Psychiatry*, 1977, *154*, 233–244.

Lipowski, Z. J., Lipsitt, D. R., & Whybrow, P. C. *Psychosomatic medicine*. New York: Oxford, 1977.

Lubar, J. F. Behavioral management of epilepsy through sensorimotor rhythm EEG biofeedback conditioning. *National Spokesman*, 1975, *8*, 6–7.

Mahoney, M. J., & Arnkoff, D. B. Self-management. In O. F. Pomerleau & J. P. Brady (Eds.), *Behavioral medicine: Theory and practice*. Baltimore: Williams & Wilkins, 1979.

Marholin, D., II, Touchette, P. E., & Malcolm, S. R. Withdrawal of chronic chlorpromazine medication: An experimental analysis. *Journal of Applied Behavior Analysis*, 1979, *12*, 159–172.

Marinacci, A. A., & Horande, M. Electromyogram in neuromuscular reeducation. *Bulletin of the Los Angeles Neurological Society*, 1960, *25*, 57–71.

May, D. S., & Weber, C. A. Temperature feedback training for symptom reduction in Raynaud's disease: A controlled study. *Proceedings of the 7th Annual Meeting of the Biofeedback Research Society*, 1976, p. 50.

McClannahan, L. E. Therapeutic and prosthetic living environments for nursing home residents. *The Gerontologist*, 1973, *13*, 424–429.

McClannahan, L. E., & Risley, T. R. Design of living environments for nursing home residents. *The Gerontologist*, 1974, *14*, 236–240.

Meares, R. Behavior therapy and spasmodic torticollis. *Archives of General Psychiatry*, 1973, *28*, 104–107.

Medina, J. L., Diamond, S., & Franklin, M. A. Biofeedback therapy for migraine. *Headache*, 1976, *16*, 115–118.

Meyer, A. J., & Henderson, J. B. Multiple risk factor reduction in the prevention of cardiovascular disease. *Preventive Medicine*, 1974, *3*, 225–236.

Mitch, P. S., McGrady, A., & Iannone, A. Autogenic feedback training in migraine: A treatment report. *Headache*, 1976, *15*, 267–270.

Mitchell, K. R., & Mitchell, D. W. Migraine: An exploratory treatment application of programmed behavior therapy techniques. *Journal of Psychosomatic Research*, 1971, *15*, 137–157.

Mitchell, K. R., & White, R. G. Behavioral self-management: An application to the problem of migraine headaches. *Behavior Therapy*, 1977, *8*, 213–221.

Mostofsky, D. I., & Balaschak, B. A. Psychobiological control of seizures. *Psychological Bulletin*, 1977, *84*, 723–750.

Mroczek, N., Halpern, D., & McHugh, R. Electromyographic feedback and physical therapy for neuromuscular retraining in hemiplegia. *Archives of Physical Medicine and Rehabilitation*, 1978, *59*, 258–267.

Mullinix, J., Norton, B., Hack, S., & Fishman, M. Skin temperature biofeedback and migraine. *Headache*, 1978, *17*, 242–244.

Newman, R., Seres, J., Yospe, L., & Garlington, B. Multidisciplinary treatment of chronic pain: Long-term follow-up of low-back pain patients. *Pain*, 1978, *4*, 283–292.

Nicassio, F., Liberman, R. P., Patterson, R., & Ramirez, E. The treatment of tics by negative practice. *Journal of Behavior Therapy and Experimental Psychiatry*, 1972, *3*, 281–287.

Obrist, P. A., Light, K. C., McCubbin, J. A., Hutcheson, J. S., & Hoffer, J. L. Pulse transit time: Relationship to blood pressure and myocardial performance. *Psychophysiology*, 1979, *16*, 292–301.

Ogden, H. D. Headache studies. Statistical data. I: Procedure and sample distribution. *Journal of Allergy*, 1952, *23*, 58–75.

Paffenbarger, R. S., Hale, W. E., Brand, R. J., & Hyde, R. T. Work energy level, personal characteristics and fatal heart attack: A birth-cohort effect. *American Journal of Epidemiology*, 1977, *105*, 200–213.

Parrino, J. J. Reduction of seizures by desensitization. *Journal of Behavior Therapy and Experimental Psychiatry*, 1971, *2*, 215–218.

Patel, C. H. Yoga and biofeedback in the management of hypertension. *Lancet*, 1973, *2*, 1053–1055.

Patten, B. M. The ancient art of memory—Usefulness in treatment. *Archives of Neurology*, 1972, *26*, 25–31.

Peck, C. L., & Kraft, G. H. Electromyographic biofeedback for pain related to muscle tension: Study of tension headache, back, and jaw pain. *Archives of Surgery*, 1977, *112*, 889–895.

Peterson, R. G., Knapp, T. J., Rosen, J. O., & Pither, B. F. The effects of furniture arrangement. *Behavior Therapy*, 1977, *8*, 464–467.

Phillips, C. The modification of tension headache pain using EMG biofeedback. *Behaviour Research and Therapy*, 1977, *15*, 119–129.

Pickering, T. G., & Miller, N. E. Learned voluntary control of heart rate and rhythm in two subjects with premature ventricular contractions. *British Heart Journal*, 1977, *39*, 152–159.

Pollock, D. D., & Liberman, R. P. Behavior therapy of incontinence in demented inpatients. *The Gerontologist*, 1974, *14*, 488–491.

Price, K. P., & Tursky, B. Vascular reactivity of migraineurs and nonmigraineurs: A comparison of responses to self-control procedures. *Headache*, 1976, *16*, 210–217.

Raymond, M. J. The treatment of addiction by aversion conditioning with apomorphine. *Behaviour Research and Therapy*, 1964, *1*, 287–291.

Reading, C., & Mohr, P. D. Biofeedback control of migraine: A pilot study. *British Journal of Social and Clinical Psychology*, 1976, *15*, 429–433.

Rene, C., & Creer, T. L. The effects of training on the use of inhalation therapy equipment by children with asthma. *Journal of Applied Behavior Analysis*, 1976, *9*, 1–11.

Richardson, R. A. *Environmental contingencies in seizure disorders.* Paper presented at the Association for Advancement of Behavior Therapy, New York, Oct. 1972.

Risley, T. R., Gottula, P., & Edwards, K. A. *Social interaction during family and institutional style meal service in a nursing home dining room.* Paper presented at the Nova Behavioral Conference on Aging, Port St. Lucie, Fla., 1978.

Risley, T. R., Spangler, P. F., & Edwards, K. A. *Behavioral care of nonambulatory geriatric patients.* Paper presented at the Nova Behavioral Conference on Aging, Port St. Lucie, Fla., 1978.

Robertson-Tchabo, E. A., Nausman, C. P., & Arenberg, D. A trip that worked: A classical mnemonic for older learners. *Educational Gerontology*, 1976, *1*, 216–226.

Roth, S. R., Sterman, M. B., & Clemente, C. D. Comparison of EEG correlates of reinforcement, internal inhibition, and sleep. *Electroencephalography and Clinical Neurophysiology*, 1967, *23*, 509–520.

Rowe, E. C., & Schnore, M. N. Item concreteness and reported strategies in paired-associate learning as a function of age. *Journal of Gerontology*, 1971, *26*, 470–475.

Roxanas, M. R., Thomas, M. R., & Rapp, M. S. Biofeedback treatment of blepharospasm with spasmodic torticollis. *Canadian Medical Association Journal*, 1978, *119*, 48–49.

Sargent, J. D., Walters, E. E., & Green, E. D. Psychosomatic self-regulation of migraine headaches. In L. Birk (Ed.), *Biofeedback: Behavioral medicine.* New York: Grune & Stratton, 1973.

Scott, R. W., Blanchard, E. B., Edmundson, E. D., & Young, L. D. A shaping procedure for heart rate control in chronic tachycardia. *Perceptual and Motor Skills*, 1973, *37*, 327–338.

Shapiro, D., & Schwartz, G. E. Biofeedback and visceral learning: Clinical applications. *Seminars in Psychiatry*, 1972, *4*, 171–184.

Shapiro, D., & Surwit, R. S. Biofeedback. In O. F. Pomerleau & J. P. Brady (Eds.), *Behavioral medicine: Theory and practice.* Baltimore: Williams & Wilkins, 1979.

Shapiro, D., Mainardi, J. A., & Surwit, R. S. Biofeedback and self-regulation in essential hypertension. In G. E. Schwartz & J. Beatty (Eds.), *Biofeedback: Theory and research.* New York: Academic Press, 1977.

Sherman, R. A., Gall, N., & Gormly, J. Treatment of phantom limb pain with muscular relaxation training to disrupt the pain anxiety tension cycle. *Pain*, 1979, *6*, 47–55.

Smith, W. M. Epidemiology of hypertension. *Medical Clinics of North America*, 1977, *61*, 467–486. (a)

Smith, W. M. Treatment of mild hypertension: Results of a ten-year intervention trial. *Circulation Research*, 1977, *40* (Suppl. 1), 98–105. (b)

Sterman, M. B. Neurophysiological and clinical studies of sensorimotor EEG biofeedback training: Some effects on epilepsy. In L. Birk (Ed.), *Biofeedback: Behavioral medicine.* New York: Grune & Stratton, 1973.

Sterman, M. B., & Friar, L. Suppression of seizures in an epileptic following sensorimotor EEG feedback training. *Electroencephalography and Clinical Neurophysiology*, 1972, *33*, 89–95.

Sternbach, R. A. *Pain patients: Traits and treatment.* New York: Academic Press, 1974.

Stewart, R. B., & Cluff, L. E. Commentary: A review of medication errors and compliance in ambulant patients. *Clinical and Pharmacological Therapy*, 1972, *13*, 463–468.

Stone, R. A., & DeLeo, J. Psychotherapeutic control of hypertension. *New England Journal of Medicine*, 1976, *294*, 80–84.

Stroebel, C. F., & Glueck, B. C. Biofeedback treatment in medicine and psychiatry: An ultimate placebo? In L. Birk (Ed.), *Biofeedback: Behavioral medicine.* New York: Grune & Stratton, 1973.

Suinn, R. M. Behavior therapy for cardiac patients. *Behavior Therapy*, 1974, *5*, 569–571.

Suinn, R. M., & Bloom, L. J. Anxiety management training for Pattern A behavior. *Journal of Behavioral Medicine*, 1978, *1*, 25–35.

Sunderman, R., & Delk, J. Treatment of Raynaud's disease with temperature biofeedback. *Southern Medical Journal*, 1978, *71*, 340–342.

Surwit, R., Pilon, R., & Fenton, C. Behavioral treatment of Raynaud's disease. *Journal of Behavioral Medicine*, 1978, *1*, 323–335.

Swanson, D., Floreen, A., & Swenson, W. Program for managing chronic pain. II: Short-term results. *Mayo Clinic Proceedings*, 1976, *51*, 409–411.

Swanson, D. W., Swenson, W. M., Huizenga, K. A., & Melson, S. J. Persistent nausea without organic cause. *Mayo Clinical Proceedings*, 1976, *51*, 257–262.

Tarler-Benlolo, L., & Love, W. A. *EMG-biofeedback treatment of spastic colon: A case report.* Presented at the meeting of the Biofeedback Society of America, Orlando, Fla., March 1977.

Tasto, D. K., & Chesney, M. A. The deconditioning of nausea and of crying by emotional imagery: A report of two cases. *Journal of Behavior Therapy and Experimental Psychiatry*, 1977, *8*, 139–142.

Tasto, D. L., & Hinkle, J. E. Muscle relaxation treatment for tension headaches. *Behaviour Research and Therapy*, 1973, *11*, 347–349.

Taub, E. Self-regulation of human tissue temperature. In G. Schwartz & J. Beatty (Eds.), *Biofeedback: Therapy and research.* New York: Academic Press, 1977.

Taylor, C. B. Behavioral approaches to essential hypertension. In J. M. Ferguson & C. B. Taylor (Eds.), *The comprehensive handbook of behavioral medicine*, Vol. 1. Jamaica, N.Y.: SP Medical & Scientific Books, 1980.

Taylor, C. B., Zlutnick, S. I., & Hoehle, W. The effects of behavioral procedures on tardive dyskinesias. *Behavior Therapy*, 1979, *10*, 37–45.

Thomas, E., Abrams, K., & Johnson, J. Self-monitoring and reciprocal inhibition in the modification of multiple tics of Gilles de la Tourette's syndrome. *Journal of Behavior Therapy and Experimental Psychiatry*, 1971, *2*, 159–171.

Thoresen, C. E., Coates, T. J., Zarcone, V. P., Kirmil-

Gray, K., & Rosekind, M. R. Treating the complaint of insomnia: Self-management perspectives. In J. M. Ferguson & C. B. Taylor (Eds.), *The comprehensive handbook of behavioral medicine*, Vol. 1. Jamaica, N.Y.: SP Medical & Scientific Books, 1980.

Turin, A., & Johnson, W. G. Biofeedback therapy for migraine headaches. *Archives of General Psychiatry*, 1976, *33*, 517–519.

U.S. Department of Commerce, U.S. Bureau of Census. *Statistical abstract of the United States, 1977*. Washington, D.C.: U.S. Government Printing Office, 1977.

U.S. Government Printing Office. *Dietary goals for the United States*. Washington, D.C.: U.S. Government Printing Office, 1978.

Vachon, L., & Rich, E. S. Visceral learning in asthma. *Psychosomatic Medicine*, 1976, *38*, 122–130.

Walton, D. The application of learning theory to the treatment of a case of bronchial asthma. In H. J. Eysenck (Ed.), *Behaviour therapy and the neuroses*. New York: Macmillan, 1969.

Warner, G., & Lance, J. W. Relaxation therapy in migraine and chronic tension headache. *Medical Journal of Australia*, 1975, *1*, 298–301.

Webb, N. C. The use of myoelectric feedback in teaching facial expression to the blind. *Biofeedback and Self-Regulation*, 1977, *2*, 147–160.

Weiner, H. M. *The psychobiology of human illness*. New York: Elsevier, 1977.

Weinstock, S. A. *The reestablishment of intestinal control in functional colitis*. Presented at the meeting of the Biofeedback Research Society, Colorado Springs, Feb. 1976.

Weiss, T., & Engel, B. T. Operant conditioning of heart rate in patients with premature ventricular contractions. *Psychosomatic Medicine*, 1971, *33*, 301–321.

Welgan, P. R. Learned control of gastric acid secretions in ulcer patients. *Psychosomatic Medicine*, 1974, *36*, 411–419.

Wells, K. C., Turner, S. M., Bellack, A. S., & Hersen, M. Effects of cue controlled relaxation on psychomotor seizures: An experimental analysis. *Behaviour Research and Therapy*, 1978, *16*, 51–53.

Whitehead, W. E., Renault, P. F., & Goldiamond, I. Modification of human gastric acid secretion with operant conditioning procedures. *Journal of Applied Behavior Analysis*, 1975, *8*, 147–156.

Wickramasekera, I. Application of verbal instructions and EMG feedback training to the management of tension headache: Preliminary observations. *Headache*, 1973, *13*, 74–76. (a)

Wickramasekera, I. Temperature feedback for the control of migraine. *Journal of Behavior Therapy and Experimental Psychiatry*, 1973, *4*, 343–345. (b)

Wolff, H. G., & Goodell, H. *Stress and disease* (2nd ed.). Springfield, Ill.: Charles C Thomas, 1968.

Wolpe, J. *Psychotherapy by reciprocal inhibition*. Stanford, Calif.: Stanford University Press, 1958.

Wooley, S. C., Blackwell, B., & Winget, C. A learning theory model of chronic illness behavior: Theory, treatment and research. *Psychosomatic Medicine*, 1978, *40*, 379–401.

Wysocki, T., Hall, G., Iwata, B., & Riordan, M. Behavioral management of exercise: Contracting for aerobic points. *Journal of Applied Behavior Analysis*, 1979, *12*, 55–64.

Yates, A. J. The application of learning theory to the treatment of tics. *Journal of Abnormal and Social Psychology*, 1958, *56*, 175–182.

Zlutnick, S., Mayville, W. J., & Moffat, S. Modification of seizure disorders: The interruption of behavioral chains. *Journal of Applied Behavior Analysis*, 1975, *8*, 1–12.

CHAPTER 9

Interpersonal Dysfunction

Alan S. Bellack and Randall L. Morrison

Introduction

It is a well-known truism that humans are "social animals." Social interactions are the hub of our existence, mediating work, leisure, the securing of food and shelter, and reproduction. The absence of quality interactions can have devastating consequences, ranging from retardation and autism in early infancy to the profound pattern of "institutionalization" found in many long-term residents of psychiatric hospitals. Consequently, it should not be surprising that social behavior has been a subject of great interest throughout history. Philosophers, theologians, and literary figures have long speculated on how and why people interact. More recently, social behavior has become a subject of scientific scrutiny. Social psychologists, linguists, sociologists, and anthropologists, among others, have devoted enormous energy to describing and understanding the rules, the content, and the structure of social encounters.

The relationship of social behavior to mental health and psychopathology was first lighlighted by the personality theories of Carl

Jung, Alfred Adler, and Harry Stack Sullivan. Their emphasis, naturally, was on the role of enduring, underlying traits, dispositions, and needs, which were thought to govern the form and quantity of interactions. Generally, the personality models made the tacit assumption that all people had the capability to interact effectively. Faulty interaction patterns were thought to result from problems in the personality structure (e.g., repressed hostility and anxiety). Hence, interpersonal difficulties were not viewed as problems in and of themselves. A strikingly different perspective was provided by the pioneering work of Zigler, Phillips, and their colleagues (Zigler & Levine, 1973; Zigler & Phillips, 1960, 1961, 1962). First, they emphasized the concept of *social competence*: the notion that effective social functioning depends on a set of abilities, which some people lack. Second, their work suggested that poor social functioning (i.e., low competence) could *lead to* psychopathology, rather than always resulting from it. While it is impossible to draw a direct connection from Zigler and Phillips to later behavioral work, their writings appear to have played an important role (cf. Bellack & Hersen, 1977a; Hersen & Bellack, 1976).

The primary stimulus for the behavioral interest in social functioning was the work of Wolpe and Lazarus (Wolpe, 1958; Wolpe &

Alan S. Bellack • Medical College of Pennsylvania at EPPI, 2900 Henry Avenue, Philadelphia, Pennsylvania 19129. Randall L. Morrison • Clinical Psychology Center, University of Pittsburgh, Pittsburgh, Pennsylvania 15260.

Lazarus, 1966). They highlighted the importance of assertiveness in a variety of "neurotic" problems, and they pioneered the use of assertiveness training to overcome social inhibitions and fears. Their early clinical work was followed up in the early 1970s by Michel Hersen, Richard Eisler, Richard McFall, and Arnold Goldstein, among others, who promulgated the *skills model* and developed empirically based training programs for alleviating skill deficits. In the ensuing years, behavioral interest in the area has mushroomed to staggering proportions. At least six behaviorally oriented books have been published on the topic in the last two years. Just about every recent issue of the *Journal of Consulting and Clinical Psychology*, as well as most behavioral journals, has at least one article on the behavioral assessment or treatment of interpersonal problems. Social-skills-training procedures have been applied or recommended for a wide variety of dysfunctions, including schizophrenia (Bellack, Hersen, & Turner, 1976); social isolation in children (Whitehill, Hersen, & Bellack, 1980); alcoholism (Miller & Eisler, 1977); depression (Bellack, Hersen, & Himmelhoch, 1981); hyperaggressivity (Fredericksen, Jenkins, Foy, & Eisler, 1976); sexual deviation (Barlow, Abel, Blanchard, Bristow, & Young, 1977); marital conflict (Birchler, 1979); drug addiction (Van Hasselt, Hersen, & Milliones, 1978); juvenile delinquency (Ollendick & Hersen, 1979); wife abuse (Rosenbaum & O'Leary, 1981); hysterical neurosis (Bellack & Hersen, 1978); heterosocial failure and shyness (Galassi & Galassi, 1979); and assertiveness deficits in women (Linehan & Egan, 1979). Either as a primary treatment or as a component of a treatment package, social skills training seems to have become a standard part of outpatient behavioral interventions. It is also widely accepted by society at large. Assertion training has become part of the "pop therapy" culture; assertion groups abound, and self-help books on the topic are big sellers. Interpersonal skills training is now a frequent curriculum component in elementary schools. Finally, skills training is one of the few psychosocial therapies generally recognized as effective with schizophrenics (Mosher & Keith, 1980).

Given the volume and diversity of material on this topic, it would be impossible to cover the literature in detail. Consequently, we present here an overview, highlighting the major issues. The interested reader is referred to the more specific review articles and book chapters that are cited throughout this chapter. We first consider just what the term *social skill* means: how it is defined and what elements comprise social skill. We also briefly examine how social skill develops and how it relates to psychopathology. Next, we discuss the assessment of social skill; this has been a problematic area. We describe the primary strategies that have been employed and highlight problems and limitations. The third major section deals with social-skill-training procedures. We describe the major strategies that are employed and give an overview of the literature on a number of behavioral dysfunctions, including depression, schizophrenia, dating skills, aggression, alcoholism, and unassertiveness. Finally, we briefly review some of the major problems confronting the field and consider research needs and future trends.

Nature of Social Skill

Definition

From a general perspective, everyone has a sense of what is meant by the term *social skill*, and there often is good agreement among friends and colleagues as to which acquaintances are unskilled. However, there has been remarkable difficulty in producing an acceptable definition of the term. Argyris (1965) referred to *social skill* as consisting of those behaviors that contributed to a person's effectiveness as part of a larger group of individuals. Weiss (1968) defined it in terms of communication, understanding, interest, and rapport between the speaker and the listener. According to Trower, Bryant, and Argyle (1978), "A person can be regarded as socially inadequate if he is unable to affect the behaviour and feelings of others in the way that he intends and society accepts. Such a person will appear annoying, unforthcoming, uninteresting, cold, destructive, bad-tempered, isolated or inept, and will generally be unrewarding to others" (p. 2). Libet and Lewinsohn (1973) defined *social skill* as "the complex ability both to emit behaviors which are positively or negatively reinforced and not to emit behaviors which are punished or extinguished by others'' (p. 304). Hersen and Bellack (1977) defined social skill as ''an individual's ability to express both positive and negative feelings in the interpersonal context without suffering consequent loss of social reinforcement. Such skill is demonstrated in a large variety of interpersonal contexts . . . and involve[s] the coordinated delivery of appropriate verbal and nonverbal responses. In addition, the socially skilled individual is attuned to the realities of the situation and is aware when he/she is likely to be reinforced for his/her efforts'' (p. 512).

Each of these definitions is effective in conveying a sense of what *social skill* connotes, but none is entirely satisfactory. The definitions tend to be too limited, omitting critical features. For example, the Trower *et al.* definition emphasizes society's response to the person and fails to specify what constitutes a skills repertoire. The other definitions are too inclusive, being so broad as to be functionally meaningless. Curran (1979) has explicated this point and highlighted one of the difficulties in arriving at an acceptable definition, using the Libet and Lewinsohn (1973) definition as an example: ''If a boxer ducks when an opponent throws him an overhand right, then the boxer is minimizing the strength of punishment from others, but is that an example of social skill? Why, on the other hand, do we not consider ducking as a social skill but regard eye contact as a component of social skill?'' (p. 321). Moreover, in some social contexts, physical violence is an acceptable response to conflict and thus might well be considered a social skill.

As indicated above, while no one definition has proved acceptable, there is general agreement on what the concept entails. First, the explicit use of the term *skills* signifies that interpersonal behavior consists of a set of learned performance abilities. The personality models presumed a more-or-less inherent capability to perform effectively. In contrast, the behavioral model emphasizes: (1) that response capability must be acquired, and (2) that it consists of an identifiable set of specific abilities, such as voice intonation and the use of social reinforcers (see below). The quality and the quantity of social behavior depend (to a great extent) on the individual's learned repertoire of social behaviors. By implication, some individuals have deficient learning histories, resulting in limited or faulty repertoires. They are defined as having *social skill deficits*. In keeping with a behavioral orientation, these deficits are presumed to be definable, measurable, and subject to remediation via education, practice, and reinforcement.

There are no definitive data on precisely how and when social skills are learned, but childhood is undoubtedly a critical period. For example, Kagan and Moss (1962) reported that ''passive withdrawal from stressful situations, dependency on the family, ease of anger arousal, involvement in intellectual mastery, social interaction anxiety, sex-role identification, and pattern of sexual behavior in adulthood were each related to reasonably analogous behavior dispositions during the early school years'' (p. 266). Case history reviews have demonstrated that the childhood years of adult schizophrenics were marked by interpersonal difficulties (cf. Roff & Knight, 1978). It has also been found that specific social-skill deficiencies could be identified in withdrawn and aggressive children as early as the third grade (Van Hasselt, Hersen, Whitehill, & Bellack, 1979).

The most likely explanation for this early learning of social behavior is offered by social learning theory (cf. Bandura, 1977; Sherman & Farina, 1974). The most critical factor appears to be modeling. Children observe their parents interacting with them as well as with others, and model parental style. Both verbal behavior (e.g., conversational topics, expression of emotion and use of ''I'' statements, question asking and information giving), and non-verbal behavior (e.g., smiles, voice intonation, interpersonal distance) can be learned in this manner. Direct tuition (i.e., instruction) is another important vehicle for learning. Statements such as: ''Say you're sorry,'' ''We don't talk with food in our mouths,'' ''Don't talk to your brother that way,'' and ''Wash your hands before dinner,'' all shape social behavior. Finally, social responses can be directly reinforced or punished. For example, apologizing might be praised, question asking might be reinforced by interest and approval, and appropriate play behavior with friends might be encouraged and rewarded. Anecdotal evidence suggests that chronic patients typically have maladaptive family histories, which provides convergent validity for a social learning explanation of their social skill deficits. There are also some empirical data which demonstrate a high correlation between the social adequacy of adults and their parents (e.g., Sherman & Farina, 1974). (Bellack & Hersen, 1978, pp. 171–172)

Of course, the onus for faulty social functioning in adulthood (or encomiums for high skill) does not lay entirely with parents. Peers are important role models and sources of reinforcement, especially during adolescence. Social mores and customs, fads and styles of dress, and language all change during a person's lifetime; hence, one must continually learn in order to remain socially skilled. In this regard, skills can also be lost through disuse, as after lengthy periods of social isolation. Social performance can also be inhibited or disrupted by affective and cognitive disturbance (e.g., anxiety and depression).

A second generally accepted aspect of social skill is that "socially skilled behavior is situationally specific. Few, if any, aspects of interpersonal behavior are universally or invariably appropriate (or inappropriate). Both cultural and situational factors determine social norms. For example, in American society physical contact is sanctioned within families and between females, but not between males. Direct expression of anger is more acceptable within families and when directed toward an employee than with strangers or toward an employer" (Bellack & Hersen, 1978, p. 172). The acceptable form of eye contact, interpersonal (spatial) distance, voice intonation, posture, etc., vary according to sex, age, status, degree of familiarity, and the culture background of the interpersonal partner, as well as with the context of the interaction. The appropriateness of specific responses even varies at different stages of the same interaction:

The socially skilled individual must know when, where, and in what form different behaviors are sanctioned. Thus, social skill involves the ability to perceive and analyze subtle cues that define the situation, as well as the presence of a repertoire of appropriate responses.

The *third* asepct [of social skills] involves the maximization of reinforcement. Marriage, friendship, sexual gratification, employment, service (e.g., in stores, restaurants, etc.), and personal rights are all powerful sources of reinforcement which hinge on social skills. The unskilled individual is apt to fail in most or all or these spheres, and consequently experience anxiety, frustration, and isolation; all of which can (do!) result in psychopathology. Social skills are, thus, vehicles for receiving reinforcement and, indirectly, avoiding or reducing other dysfunctional behavior. (Bellack & Hersen, 1978, p. 172)

Social skillfulness must be appraised with regard to a functional criterion: How well can the person meet his or her own needs?

Components of Social Skill

Social skill is a broad construct that incorporates a variety of interpersonal response dimensions, such as assertiveness, friendliness, warmth, conversational facility, and empathy. While these lower-level constructs are somewhat more specific, they are not objectively defined and have defied objective measurement. Consequently, there has been an effort to break them down further by identifying the specific response parameters of which they are comprised. That is, what precise behaviors constitute friendliness or assertiveness? Unfortunately, this has been a most difficult task, and there is no specific blueprint for each (or any!) of the broad dimensions. However, there is agreement about which response elements generally tend to be most important (cf. Harper, Wiens, & Matarazzo, 1978; Trower *et al.*, 1978). As shown in Table 1, they can be divided into three categories: expressive elements, receptive elements, and interactive balance.

Expressive elements consist of those response parameters that communicate information to the interpersonal partner. The most important of these elements is speech content: what the person says. By far, this element transmits the most information and is the central factor in social skill. However important

Table 1. Components of Social Skills

A. Expressive elements
  1. Speech content
  2. Paralinguistic elements
    a. Voice volume
    b. Pace
    c. Pitch
    d. Tone
  3. Nonverbal behavior
    a. Proxemics
    b. Kinesics
    c. Gaze (eye control)
    d. Facial expression
B. Receptive elements (social perception)
  1. Attention
  2. Decoding
  3. "Social intelligence"
C. Interactive balance
  1. Response timing
  2. Turn taking

speech content is, it carries only part of the information that the listener receives. The way something is said and the associated bodily activity play a vital role in communication. They generally qualify speech content and can sometimes change the meaning of a message entirely.

Paralinguistic elements consist of the non-verbal aspects of speech that determine *how* something is said. Table 1 lists representative examples. *Voice volume* refers to how loud the person speaks. *Pace* refers to how rapidly the person speaks, as well as the use of pauses, phrasing, and latency. Pitch and tone are important features of voice quality. In general, the paralinguistic aspects of speech play a vital role in communicating affect and nuance. For example, the word *no* can be stated to reflect hostility, polite disagreement or refusal, a question (e.g., "Are you sure?"), nonhostile authoritativeness, or reluctant refusal and ambivalence, as a function of the manner in which the word is uttered. Humor, sarcasm, joy, despondency, anger, and anxiety can all be transmitted by voice characteristics, even when the speech content presents an alternative meaning.

Nonverbal behavior is bodily movement and posture. The major elements are listed in Table 1. Proxemics is "the manner in which individuals use physical space in their interactions with others and how physical space influences behavior" (Harper *et al.*, 1978, p. 246). The most important proxemic factor is interpersonal distance, which is bound by precise rules that vary across cultures, age groups, and sexes. The term *kinesics* subsumes a wide variety of body movements, including hand and arm gestures, head nods, and posture. Some movements, such as trembling hands, tense posture, and bouncing legs, are communicative even without speech. Others, such as head nods and illustrative hand gestures, provide emphasis to speech. Frequently referred to as *eye contact*, gaze involves how a person looks and what the person looks at, as well as eye-to-eye contact: "The main function of gaze is the perception of non-verbal signals from others; in addition, the amount and type of gaze communicates interpersonal attitudes. Gaze is closely coordinated with speech, and serves to add emphasis, provide feedback and attention, and manage speaking turns" (Trower *et*

al., 1978, p. 12). Facial expression also plays an important role in giving emphasis to and/or qualifying speech content. Moreover, it is thought to be the most important single factor in the communication of affect (Harper *et al.*, 1978).

The behavioral literature on both assessment of social skill and skills training has placed almost exclusive emphasis on observable response dimensions like those described above: "But, motor response skill is only one of the factors affecting performance in interpersonal interactions. . . . Subjects must also know when and where to emit the various responses in their repertoires. The most polished assertion response will not be functional if the individual does not know when he/she has been treated unfairly, or when assertion is likely to be appropriate" (Bellack, 1979b, p. 171). This aspect of social skill, which involves a set of receptive features, is typically referred to as *social perception* (Morrison & Bellack, 1981). Specifically, the individual must first attend to the cues provided by the interpersonal partner; these include all of the expressive elements described above. The information so received must then be effectively decoded. This is a cognitive event that is probably beyond the scope of work on social skill. Both of these processes require extensive knowledge about cultural mores and the significance of a tremendous number of expressive cues and response patterns in diverse settings. This factor is generally called *social intelligence*. Little is known about how receptive skills develop, how they may be assessed, or how they may be modified. Considering how vital they are to the smooth and effective use of response skills, this is an important area for future research.

We should point out that there is some controversy about whether social perception and cognitive processes should be considered a part of "social skill." This issue is cogently raised by Curran (1979):

However, I am troubled by the expansion of the construct when we are still far from a definition of social skill with respect to motoric behaviors. If we do not restrain ourselves and put some limits on the construct of social skill, it will expand to include all human behavior, and social skills training will soon come to mean any process which is capable of producing changes in human behavior. . . . My bias, at this time, is to limit the construct . . . to motoric behavior. We should measure cognitive processes because these processes are important with respect to both theory and treatment. However, let us agree not to call these cognitive processes components of social skill. (p. 323)

The final aspect of social skill is interactive balance. This is not a specific response; it is a general parameter related to the flow of social encounters. Interpersonal behavior is not static. It is *interactive*, and effective performance requires a delicate give-and-take, or meshing. The absolute quantity, rate, or intensity of responses is often less important than their timing: when they are emitted in relation to the partner's behavior. For example, Fischetti, Curran, and Wessberg (1977) found no difference in the number of social reinforcers supplied to a female partner by heterosocially anxious and nonanxious males, but the two groups differed substantially in the *timing* of reinforcing responses. In the same context, Duncan and Fiske (1977) reported that when two people converse, smooth transitions from one speaker to the other depend on the proper placement of up to six discrete "turn-taking cues." Moreover, several of these cues involve *change* in a response rather than the simple emission of a particular behavior (e.g., initiating or breaking off eye contact, altering voice pitch or pace). When conversants do not use these signals and match their behavior to one another, the conversation is marred by interruptions, simultaneous talking, and long pauses.

Associated Factors

The discussion to this point seemingly implies that the quality of interpersonal performance depends entirely on the individual's skill repertoire (including expressive, receptive, and interactive elements). The repertoire does play a vital role and determines the outer limit of performance quality, but a number of other factors also have a major impact on how much and how well one interacts. Some of the primary influences are presented in Table 2.

The history of reinforcement (or punishment) for various interpersonal responses can determine the types of social situations the individual will enter and the specific behaviors

Table 2. Factors Affecting Social Behavior

1. Reinforcement history
2. Cognitive factors
   a. Goals
   b. Expectancies
   c. Values
   d. Etc.
3. Affect
   a. Anxiety
   b. Depression
   c. Anger
   d. Etc.
4. Psychopathology
   a. Thought disorder
   b. Alcohol–drug addiction
   c. Etc.

he or she will perform. For example, a woman might have all the skills required to be assertive with her husband but not use them because previous attempts have been unreinforced or punished. Cognitive factors play a related role. Social situations are likely to be avoided and behaviors are likely to be inhibited if they are thought to be socially inappropriate, immoral, unfair, or likely to lead to unpleasant consequences (Eisler, Frederiksen, & Peterson, 1978). Thus, Fiedler and Beach (1978) found that whether people act assertively is a function of the consequences they anticipate for such behavior. Anecdotal clinical data suggest that many clients are reluctant to express complaints and to stand up for their rights, as they associate such assertiveness with hostility and aggression. Shyness in college males is often more a function of inaccurate self-evaluation and expectations of rejection than of heterosocial skill deficits (Arkowitz, 1977; Galassi & Galassi, 1979).

Another factor that can have a dramatic impact on interpersonal behavior is affect. Anxiety and anger can disrupt the smooth performance of well-learned routines, causing stuttering, trembling, rapid speech, poverty of speech content, etc. (Bellack, 1980). High levels of emotional arousal can interfere with the receptive and cognitive processes required for effective performance. Of course, social anxiety can also lead to the avoidance of social situations. Depression is associated with reduced behavioral output, loss of the desire and energy to pursue relationships, and a variety of responses that elicit aversive reactions from others (Coyne, 1976; Hammen & Peters, 1978; Howes & Hokanson, 1979).

The final factor presented in Table 2 is psychopathology. We use this term in a generic manner to represent major syndromes or patterns of behavioral dysfunction (e.g., schizophrenia and alcoholism). Some of the specific symptoms associated with such syndromes can have a dramatic impact on social behavior. For example, the thought disorder and the behavioral disorganization associated with schizophrenia obviously prevent smooth social performance. Alcohol and heroin have a general debilitative affect, as well as disrupting ongoing behavior. The gross mood swings produced by manic-depressive disorder similarly produce anomalous behavior. Not only can these disturbances interfere with the use of social skills in the repertoire, but they can cause the erosion and the loss of skills.

The previous discussion indicates that negative affect and psychopathology can lead to poor social performance. This is only one of the ways in which these factors can interface with social skill. As is discussed further below, social skills deficits have been implicated in the genesis of a number of disorders, including depression (Bellack, Hersen, & Himmelhoch, 1980; Libet & Lewinsohn, 1973); alcoholism (Miller & Eisler, 1977); and hysterical neurosis (Blanchard & Hersen, 1976). The general model for this line of causation is that skill deficits lead to interpersonal failure and/or inability to achieve goals. In turn, this results in stress, negative affect, and the development of maladaptive behavior patterns to meet goals. A third pattern of interaction involves multiple determinism, in which skills deficits lead to disturbances in conjunction with some other factor. For example, skills deficits might lead to clinical depression only in conjunction with adverse life events, such as the loss of a significant other. Unassertiveness might contribute to alcoholism only in individuals who have a biochemical susceptibility. This "necessary but not sufficient" pattern is probably the most common, although there are no specific data in its support.

Assessment of Social Skill

In keeping with the behavioral emphasis on assessment, there is a voluminous literature on the assessment of social skill. Several review articles and book chapters have appeared on this topic in the past few years (Arkowitz, 1977, 1981; Bellack, 1979a,b; Curran & Mariotto, 1981; Eisler, 1976; Hersen & Bellack, 1977). The reader is referred to these sources for a detailed account of the literature. In this section, we describe the primary strategies that have been employed and identify some of the problems confronting the field.

Interviewing

The clinical interview is probably the most widespread strategy employed. The patient is the best and sometimes the only source of information about his or her interpersonal experience and associated thoughts, affect, etc. The interview provides the most convenient and the most broad-based strategy for securing this information. In addition to a description of current functioning, the interview also provides two other types of information: the interpersonal history and informal observational data. Historical information can provide important clues about the development of the current problem, whether the client ever performed effectively, etc. This information can be valuable in treatment planning (e.g., Is the interpersonal problem a by-product of other difficulties, or does it predate and underlie them?). The interview also affords the clinician an opportunity to observe the client interacting; it is, after all, an interpersonal encounter. The situation is unusual and some client behavior might be specific to it, but numerous important clues can be garnered: personal hygiene and grooming, use of social amenities, ability to perceive and respond to social cues, ease of establishing rapport, etc.

Unfortunately, interviewing is a highly inexact science, and there are few empirical data documenting its reliability and validity (Bellack & Hersen, 1977; Morganstern & Tevein, 1981). Patient reports are subject to the same bias, distortion, and faulty recollection associated with any self-report (cf. Bellack & Hersen, 1977). The interviewer is an imperfect observer and is another potential source of error. On the other hand, no objective assessment strategy has proved to be as sensitive in detecting the subtleties of performance quality as the subjective ratings of human observers (Curran, 1979). Hence, the standardization and the empirical evaluation of interview procedures is a high priority for future research.

Self-Monitoring

Self-monitoring (SM) has become one of the most widely used behavioral assessment procedures, yet it has been only a peripheral tool for the assessment of social skills. The only empirical literature which has regularly employed SM is research on heterosocial skills. . . . Subjects have frequently been asked to keep dating logs, recording information ranging from simple dating frequency to extensive self-evaluations of specific aspects of performance (Arkowitz, 1977). In addition to monitoring behavior, subjects have also been asked to rate subjective distress or anxiety and to note discriminative stimuli and environmental consequences to their behavior. Similar forms of SM would seem to be applicable for assessing other social skills as well, although anecdotal clinical reports outnumber research examples of this application. (Bellack, 1979a, p. 85)

The advantages and disadvantages of SM have been well-documented (Kazdin, 1974b; Nelson, 1977). It generally is more objective, reliable, and valid than other types of self-report data, but it is subject to reactivity and inconsistency. With regard to the recording of interpersonal behavior, SM has the special advantage of providing semiobjective data on behaviors that are not otherwise open to direct observation (e.g., intimate interactions, infrequent encounters and conflicts). Conversely, it is unlikely that people can accurately observe and evaluate molecular aspects of their performance (e.g., voice quality, gaze). It is difficult for trained observers to rate these responses from videotapes, let alone for subjects to recognize their fleeting occurrence during an interaction. Also, subjects often are unaware when they have misperceived a partner's behavior or have failed to identify the context of a situation correctly. Thus, SM is primarily useful for logging events, securing subject evaluations of performance, and developing a general picture of motor behavior categories (e.g., the general content of a conversation, the expression of praise).

Self-Report Inventories

Self-report scales and inventories comprise the most widely employed assessment strategy. In fact, almost every outcome study includes several overlapping scales measuring the central skill (e.g., assertiveness), as well as other scales that measure presumably related attributes (e.g., social anxiety). While such overkill guarantees breadth of coverage, it does not guarantee criterion validity, that is, an accurate picture of the subject's skill level and *in vivo* behavior.

Until recently, researchers in this area seemed to prefer to develop their own self-report instruments rather than to evaluate psychometrically and utilize existing devices. This "build-a-better-mousetrap" approach has produced a plethora of related instruments, but it has not provided a sound, consistently used battery. The existing instruments vary in reliability, validity, factorial structure, and item format. Several have been carefully constructed according to sound psychometric practice, but even the most sophisticated require further testing before they can be confidently recommended. In addition, even the best instruments are probably more useful for screening and gross categorization than for the precise evaluation of a specific subject's strengths and weaknesses. As stated above in regard to SM, subjects generally cannot report on much of their interpersonal behavior. In addition, the use of summative scores on these devices (e.g., adding up item scores to yield an overall score) masks the situational variability of performance. Thus, while self-report scales can be a valuable component of a comprehensive assessment package, they cannot be substituted for behavioral observation.

Behavioral Observation

One of the tenets of behavioral assessment is that direct observation is the most valid and desirable strategy. It should not be surprising that this approach has been widely employed in work on social skill. Three general strategies have been employed: observation in the natural environment, staged naturalistic interactions, and role-play enactments.

Observation in the Natural Environment. This is the most desirable strategy, but it has been extremely difficult to employ. Most interpersonal behaviors of interest (e.g., dating and assertion) occur in private circumstances and/or are infrequent and unpredictable. Hence, they are not readily accessible to the researcher or the clinician. The cost of sending observers into the community is another limiting factor. Given these difficulties, there are few examples of *in vivo* observation in the literature. King, Liberman, Roberts, and Bryan (1977) had chronic patients engage in a series of preplanned assertion situations with community residents. An observer escorted the patient to the setting and stood nearby during the interaction. Arkowitz and his colleagues have arranged dates for college students with heterosocial skill deficits and secured retrospective ratings from the dating partners (Christensen & Arkowitz, 1974; Royce & Arkowitz, 1976). The most systematic work on *in vivo* observation has been employed in research on family interaction (cf. Jacob, 1976; Patterson, 1974; Weiss & Margolin, 1977). Both live observers and automated tape recording systems have been stationed in the home. Observation is generally limited to circumscribed periods of high interaction, such as the dinner hour. This work has not generally been considered part of the social skill literature, but the focus on communication patterns makes it clearly relevant. The techniques employed (and their advantages and disadvantages) can be directly translated to work on social skill *per se*.

The *in vivo* observation strategies that have been employed have two primary limitations. First are the potential effects of reactivity (cf. Johnson & Bolstad, 1973). The presence of live observers would undoubtedly distort subject behavior in intimate situations and those associated with high affect arousal or socially undesirable behavior (e.g., wife abuse and intoxication). There is also the likelihood of reactivity on the part of the interpersonal partner, who is not a subject or a client. Thus, one is likely to observe the subject on his or her "best behavior" rather than exhibiting typical behavior. (Of course, this behavior does reflect some of the skills in the person's repertoire.) A second factor is restricted access to important situations. As previously stated, intimate interactions and infrequent events are generally not available for observation. *In vivo*

observation is most useful with "captive" populations, such as psychiatric inpatients or school-age children, and with highly public behaviors, such as play and casual conversation. Problems of reactivity and access are both limited in these contexts.

Staged Naturalistic Interactions. In response to the expense and the limited access of *in vivo* observation, many researchers have attempted to stage important interactions in the laboratory or clinic. Several different formats have been employed. Bellack, Hersen, and Lamparski (1979) surreptitiously observed male undergraduates interacting with a female confederate, who was introduced as another subject. The procedure was designed to assess the subject's ability to initiate a conversation with a potential dating partner. Arkowitz, Lichtenstein, McGovern, and Hines (1975) also used female confederates to assess dating skills. They avoided the use of deception by informing the subjects that the female partner was a research assistant. In one situation, the subjects were told to interact with the woman *as if* they had just met. In a second task, they engaged in a mock telephone conversation and responded as if they were trying to arrange a date with the confederate.

A third variation of this general strategy involves the use of so-called critical incidents. These are brief interchanges in which the subject is presented with a situation calling for an assertive response. For example, subjects have been deliberately shortchanged after participating in a study, pressured by confederates acting as magazine salespeople, asked to perform unreasonable favors, and denied earned privileges. In each case, the subject's skill in resisting social pressure or unfair treatment was assessed.

It is difficult to evaluate the utility and validity of these procedures on the basis of the existing literature. Most of the particular scenarios have been developed on an ad hoc basis in the context of specific research projects. They have each typically been orchestrated in an idiosyncratic fashion, according to face validity. In addition to content variations (e.g., waiting room versus prospective date), they also vary along a number of other potentially important dimensions. Durations have been arbitrarily varied from three minutes to 10 minutes, although behavior may well change at different points in the interaction. Confederates have been instructed to respond in a warm or neutral manner, to make comments after silences ranging from

5 seconds to 60 seconds, and to make only specified comments or to be more spontaneous. The effects of these variations are unknown, and warrant empirical evaluation. (Bellack, 1979b, p. 163)

A few conclusions can be drawn. The critical incident procedures generally tend to have anomalous stimulus elements and generally are not highly valid. The "act-as-if" format yields different results than interactions that employ deception. Subjects tend to perform better in the "as-if" context, but they report that the surreptitious format elicits more representative behavior (Higgins, Alonso, & Pendleton, 1979; Wessberg, Mariotto, Conger, Conger, & Farrell, 1979). There are also data to suggest that responses vary considerably when subjects are retested (Mungas & Walters, 1979). More general conclusions about reliability, validity, and format must await future research.

Role-Play Enactments. Role playing has been the most frequently employed strategy for assessing social skill. The basic procedure entails three steps: (1) an interpersonal scenario is described to the subject; (2) an experimental confederate, portraying someone in the scenario, delivers a prompt line; and (3) the subject responds to the confederate as if they were actually in the scenario. Numerous variations of this basic approach have been employed. Subjects have responded to audiotapes and videotapes as well as to live confederates. The interactions have been limited to one brief interchange or have been extended through varying numbers of retorts by the confederate. The number and content of the scenes have varied dramatically, as has the style of confederate behavior. Several features of role-play tests make them an attractive strategy. They are inexpensive and easy to employ, and the brief format makes it possible to present the subject with many different stimulus situations. Similarly, it is easy to construct a set of scenarios to fit each individual study or subject.

Unfortunately, the simplicity of constructing new items and the face validity of the procedure have proved to be disadvantages as well. There are widespread inconsistencies in format and content from study to study, making comparisons difficult. With few exceptions (cf. Freedman, Rosenthal, Donahoe, Schlundt,

& McFall, 1978; Perri & Richards, 1979), tests have been constructed solely on the basis of face validity and have uncertain psychometric adequacy. Moreover, many procedural variations that have been casually employed produce markedly different effects. There are substantial differences between brief and extended interactions, and between taped and live confederates (Galassi & Galassi, 1976). Subtle differences in scene content (e.g., the sex and the familiarity of the partner) produce dramatically different responses (Eisler, Hersen, Miller, & Blanchard, 1975; Hopkins, Krawitz, & Bellack, 1981). The effects of many other factors (e.g., the number of scenarios and the confederate's response style) are unknown but are probably meaningful as well.

Perhaps the greatest concern about role-play procedures pertains to the criterion validity of the entire strategy. That is, does performance on a role-play test correspond to the way subjects respond when actually confronted by the enacted situations? The answer to this question is a resounding *maybe not!* Primary support for the approach comes from studies in which "known groups" have been differentiated by role-play performance. For example, low-assertive psychiatric patients have performed more poorly than their high-assertive peers (Eisler *et al.*, 1975); low-frequency daters have been differentiated from high-frequency daters (Arkowitz *et al.*, 1975); and delinquent youths have been distinguished from nondelinquents (Freedman *et al.*, 1978). Numerous studies have also found that skill-deficient subjects who receive social skill training improve their performance on role-play tests more than similar subjects who do not receive such training. However, these data are not consistent, and they provide only convergent validational support.

Studies in which role-play behavior has been directly compared with performance in related criterion situations (Bellack, Hersen, & Lamparski, 1979; Bellack, Hersen, & Turner, 1978) or with identical situations *in vivo* (Bellack, Hersen, & Turner, 1979) have produced less positive results. The findings of these studies suggest that, at best, the traditional role-play procedure has modest validity. Furthermore, it appears to be differentially valid for males and females and for different specific behaviors. Much greater care is needed in the construction of role-play tests, and procedural modifications will be required if these devices are to prove useful.

The Focus of Assessment

The previous discussion pertains to *how* social skill can be assessed (e.g., self-report and role play). The question of *what* should be assessed is no less problematic. Two general strategies have been employed, singly or in combination: molecular and molar.

The molecular approach is closely tied to the behavioral model of social skill. Interpersonal behavior is broken down into specific component elements, such as the expressive features described above (e.g., eye contact and speech rate). These elements are then measured in a highly objective fashion (e.g., number of smiles and number of seconds of eye contact). Such measures are highly reliable and have good face validity. However, there are a number of serious problems with this approach. The most serious concern pertains to just how meaningful it is to measure such specific, static response characteristics. Social impact is determined not by the number of seconds of eye contact or by speech duration, but by a complex pattern of responses that occur in conjunction with the partner's behavior. Research suggests that the specific elements most commonly assessed do not account for much of the variance in response quality, either individually or when combined mathematically (cf. Romano & Bellack, 1980). Thus, the molecular measurement strategy might be yielding an elegant but trivial set of data. However, it must be emphasized that the behaviors commonly assessed have not been selected on an empirical basis. Only recently have researchers begun to analyze social skill systematically in an effort to determine precisely which response elements are critical (cf. Romano & Bellack, 1980; Royce & Weiss, 1975). The molecular approach might prove to be more useful when we learn more about what determines the impact of interpersonal behaviors and generate a socially validated assessment plan.

The molar approach to assessment eschews specific, objective ratings in favor of overall, subjective ratings. Judges employ Likert scales to rate overall skill, anxiety, assertiveness, etc. Their subjective impressions integrate the component response elements and provide a measure of how the subject impacts on others. These ratings tend to correspond better with meaningful external criteria, but they have somewhat lower reliability than molecular ratings. Their major disadvantage is that they fail to indicate what specifically the subject is doing well or poorly; hence, they do not provide information about which skills should be covered in training or which were improved in training. Nor do they specify whether the judges were focusing on the effectiveness or quality of the response (e.g., Did it get the job done?) or on their personal reaction to it (e.g., Do they like it, or would they respond in the same way?). Given that the purpose of assessment and training is ultimately tied to how the subjects affects others, qualitative ratings are vital. But it is important to break down such ratings and determine the cues that the judges use in making their judgments. Until problems with both the molar and the molecular approaches are resolved, the two procedures should be employed in conjunction with one another.

Two other issues pertaining to the focus of assessment also require brief comment. The first involves the assessment of receptive skills. As previously indicated, the importance of these elements has only recently been recognized; consequently, there are no acceptable instruments to assess them. This is a high priority for future work. The second issue concerns the role of social validation in the assessment process (cf. Kazdin, 1977). The primary criterion employed to identify targets for assessment and training and to evaluate outcome has been the researcher's own judgment about what is important and what is appropriate. It is now becoming apparent that much more attention must be paid to how the subject's environment evaluates his or her behavior. At one level, this can be accomplished by securing peer judgments about the importance and desirability of different behaviors. For example, several recent studies have investigated community reactions to different forms of assertion responses in order to determine the acceptability of various responses (Hollandsworth & Cooley, 1978; Hull & Schroe-der, 1979). At another level, peers and significant others (e.g., spouses) are being asked to evaluate the subject's performance. Thus, the judgment of the researcher (the expert) is supplemented by the judgment of people with whom the subject will actually interact. While these measures have some distinct limitations (Kane & Lawler, 1978), they are an important addition to our "in-house" criteria.

Social Skills Training

Models of Social Skills Training

Interest in social skills training has increased dramatically as documentation regarding the relationship between social competence and behavioral disorder has accumulated in both the psychiatric and the psychological literature. As specific social deficits that are critical to diverse forms of maladaptive behavior have been identified, social-skills-training programs have been instituted to ameliorate these deficits. Currently, there are four major viewpoints regarding the etiology and the maintenance of social disability. These can be labeled the *skills deficit model*, the *conditioned-anxiety model*, the *cognitive-evaluative model*, and the *faulty-discrimination model*. Each of the four concepts has given rise to different social-skills-training protocols.

Skills Deficit Model. The great majority of the social-skills-training studies that have been reported in the literature have been based on the skills deficit model (Bellack & Hersen, 1978; Hersen & Bellack, 1976). According to this model, the individual who evidences poor social skills lacks certain specific motor responses from his or her behavioral repertoire and/or uses inappropriate responses. The individual may never have learned the appropriate behavior (at least, to sufficient strength for smooth application) or may have learned inappropriate behavior. Given this inadequate repertoire, the individual does not handle the demands of various interpersonal situations appropriately.

The most common training paradigm based on the skills deficit model is the response ac-quisition approach. The treatment proceeds by training on each deficient response element (one at a time, in order of increasing difficulty) in a series of problem situations (sequentially, in order of increasing difficulty). The situation hierarchy must be determined for each patient. With regard to response elements, we have found it most effective to train the patient in conversational skills first, followed by perceptual skills and special problem areas. Within each of these areas, specific responses should be attacked in an order that maximizes the patient's success throughout the training (i.e., based on what the patient can most easily learn at each point). The strategy of focusing on the response elements one at a time and of ensuring continuous success throughout the treatment is especially important for patients with attentional difficulties (i.e., chronic schizophrenics). Training can be telescoped when the patient is less disturbed or when it has proceeded to a point where many responses are generalized across situations.

The training consists of five techniques: (1) instructions; (2) role play; (3) feedback and social reinforcement; (4) modeling; and (5) practice.

Instructions. The patient is first given specific instructions about the response at issue, including why and how it should be performed. For example, "If people are going to know you are serious, you must look at them when you speak. Try to look at my eyes or nose when you answer me."

Role Play. After instructions are given, the patient role-plays a scenario with the therapist or a role-model assistant. The format is analogous to the BAT-R, including a description of the situation and a prompt (or a series of prompts in an extended interaction).

Feedback and Social Reinforcement. Following the role play, the patient is given feedback about his or her performance. This feedback should be specific and should include positive social reinforcement for improved aspects of performance. Our clinical work suggests that social reinforcement, encouragement, and the frequent experience of some sucess play a vital role in maintaining the patient's interest and effort. An example of feedback is as follows: "You did much better that time. You told me that you wanted to go home in a clear manner, and you looked at me while you spoke. Let's try it again, and this time try to emphasize the word *no*. It will make your statement more convincing.'' This statement would be followed by further role-play.

Modeling. Some behaviors are relatively easy to learn (e.g., eye contact and response latency), and instructions, role play, and feedback will be sufficient. Similarly, higher functioning patients can master many of the responses with only these three techniques (cf. McFall & Twentyman, 1973; Rimm, Snyder, Depue, Haanstad, & Armstrong, 1976). However, more complex responses (e.g., most verbal content elements, intonation) and more regressed patients almost invariably require modeling (Edelstein & Eisler, 1976; Hersen, Eisler, Miller, Johnson, & Pinkston, 1973; Rimm *et al.*, 1976). Rather than simply instructing the patient in how to respond, the therapist or the role model actually performs (models) the appropriate response. The modeling display should focus on the particular response element at issue and should be prefaced and followed by a description of the relevant aspects of the display. The modeled response should also be based on the patient's previously role-played response. For example, ''That was better. This time let me try it. Listen to the way I make clear exactly what I want to do. 'I would like to help, but it's late, and I have to leave now.' See, I didn't simply say it was late, but I told him I had to leave right then.'' The patient would then be directed to role-play the response again. This sequence of instructions, role play, feedback and reinforcement, and modeling is repeated until the response is mastered. Training then shifts to the next response or, if the target situation has been mastered, to the next situation.

Practice. Regardless of how effectively the patient performs the requisite responses during the training sessions, there is little likelihood that her or his performance will generalize to the natural environment or be maintained in the absence of directed practice *in vivo*. The importance of practice is underscored by research in which success was achieved by practice alone (e.g., Christensen & Arkowitz, 1974; King *et al.*, 1977). Practice is encouraged both by giving general instructions to ''try things out'' and by giving specific homework assignments at the conclusion of each session (beginning after at least one response element has been mastered). The assignments should be relatively specific and should be geared to a level of difficulty and a situation that will maximize the probability of success (and reinforcement by the environment).

A second version of social skills training based on the skills deficit model is the use of covert modeling procedures in the assertion training protocol developed by Kazdin and his colleagues (Kazdin, 1974a, 1976; Hersen, Kazdin, Bellack, & Turner, 1979). Role-play scenarios again are used as the stimulus material, but they are rehearsed covertly (in imagination) rather than overtly. Each scene consists of three parts: (1) a description of the context and situation in which an assertive response is appropriate; (2) an imagined model who makes an assertive response (the model may be the individual undergoing assertion training); and (3) the favorable consequences that result from the model's response. During the training sessions, the subject is instructed to relax with his or her eyes closed and to imagine each scenario as it is presented by the therapist. Initially, the therapist presents the description of the situation. The subject signals by raising his or her index finger when he or she has a vivid image of the situation in mind. Next, the therapist presents the assertive response performed by the model for imagination by the subject. Finally, the therapist describes the positive consequences that are to be imagined by the subject. The training proceeds up a hierarchy of assertion scenarios as in the response acquisition approach. The covert modeling procedure is sometimes combined with behavior rehearsal. After covert imagery instructions, the subjects are asked to role-play the same situation. Homework assignments can be given for practicing the covert modeling procedure.

Conditioned-Anxiety Model. The conditioned-anxiety model assumes that the individual has the requisite skills in his or her repertoire but is inhibited from responding in a socially appropriate fashion because of conditioned-anxiety responses. Through aversive experiences or vicarious conditioning, previously neutral cues relating to social interactions have become associated with aversive stimuli. These conditioned reactions may develop regardless of the adequacy of the individual's repertoire of social skills.

Social dysfunction that results from conditioned anxiety may best be considered a form of anxiety disorder. As such, it is not included as a major focus of our discussion. According to the conditioned-anxiety model, the problem in social functioning can be eliminated only if the anxiety is extinguished, thereby permitting an opportunity for the expression of more appropriate behaviors. Anxiety reduction techniques, rather than social skills training, are treatments of choice (see Chapter 13 in this volume, by Emmelkamp).

Cognitive-Evaluative Model. The cognitive-evaluative model posits that the source of an individual's social inadequacy is faulty cognitive appraisal of social performance and the expectation of aversive consequences. Negative self-appraisals and negative self-statements are seen as mediating the social anxiety and/or the social avoidance of the interpersonally deficient individual. The social-skills-training procedures that follow from this model typically approximate the cognitive restructuring techniques outlined by Goldfried, Decenteceo, and Weinberg (1974). During training, the therapist provides instructions on how to restructure problem beliefs. The therapist also models a progression of thoughts to demonstrate the restructuring process. Third, the training sessions involve the practice of cognitive restructuring, using hierarchically presented imaginal situations during which the client searches for the rules and beliefs mediating his or her response and, if necessary, restructures the belief. Before each situation is practiced, the client is encouraged to verbalize one or more restructuring principles or adaptive beliefs that can guide the restructuring (self-instructions). After each practice sequence, the client self-evaluates and, if appropriate, self-reinforces the restructuring efforts. The therapist provides additional feedback, coaching, and response reinforcement. Also, homework is assigned involving *in vivo* practice of the cognitive restructuring procedures.

Faulty Discrimination Model. The faulty discrimination model assumes that the social disability is due to the individual's not knowing how to match specific social behaviors with specific social situations. Socially unskilled behavior may be the result of a failure on the part of the individual to discriminate adequately the situations in which a response already in the repertoire is likely to be effective. Therefore, the person may fail to respond or may respond inappropriately despite an adequate repertoire of interpersonal behaviors. This model suggests a therapy concerned with teaching the individual to discriminate which situations call for which behaviors.

Liberman, Wallace, and their colleagues (Wallace, 1978; Wallace, Nelson, Lukoff, Webster, Rappe, & Ferris, 1978) have developed such a package, which is intended to teach patients the "rules" or "language" of interpersonal interactions. As described by Wallace (1978), their program is an integrated assessment–treatment package for use with chronically relapsing schizophrenic patients. According to this program, social skills are considered problem-solving skills. Interpersonal communication is seen as the outcome of a three-part process. First, the individual has to correctly receive the "values" of all relevant situational parameters. These include the content of past and current messages, as well as the characteristics of the interpersonal partner, such as emotion, goals, and identity. Second, the individual must process the "values" of these parameters in order to generate potential responses, from which one is selected. The processing functions include the identification of one's own goals, the generation of response options, and the evaluation of the consequences of each option. Third, the individual must send the chosen response in a manner that will maximize the probability of attaining the goal that initially prompted the interpersonal communication. Sending involves numerous component behaviors, as specified in the skill deficit model.

The assessment–treatment package is implemented by means of a role-play format. After each situation is role-played with the patient, he or she is asked a series of questions designed to assess his or her knowledge of the receiving and processing variables. The questions used to assess accurate receiving might include (1) "Who spoke to you?" (2) "What was the main topic?'' (3) "What was ———— feeling?" The questions used to assess correct processing might be (1) "What was your short-term goal?" (2) "What was your long-term goal?" (3) "If you did ———— what would ———— feel? What would ———— do? Would you get your short-term goal? Would you get your long-term goal?"

The questions serve as the assessment devices. Incorrect answers result in the application of training techniques designed to elicit the correct answers. Sending skills are evaluated during the role play and are trained by means of the typical response-acquisition procedures (e.g., modeling and feedback).

Social Skills Training with Schizophrenic Patients

Deficiencies in social skills are currently considered as central to the development and continuation of schizophrenia as its more noticeable aspects, such as thinking disturbances, delusional systems, gross mood anomalies, and idiosyncratic mannerisms and language (e.g., Goldsmith & McFall, 1975; Hersen & Bellack, 1976; Zigler & Phillips, 1961, 1962). Many schizophrenic patients are socially isolated. They often fail to become integrated into a natural social network that might assist them in coping with social demands (Gleser & Gottschalk, 1967; McClelland & Walt, 1968). The schizophrenic's family is often the only natural network of which he or she is a part. However, the interaction patterns of families of schizophrenics may actually serve to increase the probability of relapse (Brown, Birley, & Wing, 1972; Vaughn & Leff, 1976). Furthermore, the schizophrenic patient often lacks the requisite skills to deal with stressful interpersonal interactions.

There have been numerous investigations of social skills training with schizophrenic patients. Single-subject experimental case studies conducted by Hersen, Bellack, Eisler, and their colleagues (Bellack *et al.*, 1976; Edelstein & Eisler, 1976; Hersen & Bellack, 1976; Hersen, Turner, Edelstein, & Pinkston, 1975; Williams, Turner, Watts, Bellack, & Hersen, 1977) provide strong evidence of the clinical efficacy of social skills training with this population.

As an example, Hersen and Bellack (1976) convincingly demonstrated the controlling effects of social skills training on targeted behaviors with two chronic schizophrenics. In one case, the treatment consisted of instructions and feedback. In the second case, instructions, feedback, and modeling were used. The targeted behaviors (eye contact, speech duration, speech disruptions, smiles, requests for new behavior, and compliances) were treated sequentially and cumulatively in a multiple-baseline design. The BAT-R (Eisler *et al.*, 1975) was used as both the assessment and the training vehicle. The training was directed toward improving both positive and negative assertiveness. The training began after each patient's phenothiazines were regulated, with drug dosage maintained at a constant level in baseline, training, and follow-up. The results were positive for both patients. Specific target behaviors improved when the treatment was specifically directed toward them, and gradual gains in overall assertiveness were recorded by independent observers. Additionally, the treatment gains remained at two-, four-, six-, and eight-week follow-ups.

Bellack *et al.* (1976) reported positive results for two of three schizophrenic patients. Improvements on topographical behaviors (such as eye contact) generalized to novel scenes on the BAT-R and were maintained at an 8- to 10-week follow-up. However, appropriate requests for behavioral change did not generalize as well to novel situations as did the "simpler" topographical behaviors.

Single-case experimental designs by Liberman and his colleagues have provided further demonstrations of the effectiveness of social skills training, based on the completion of homework assignments. Using a multiple-baseline design across areas of homework assignments, Liberman, Lillie, Falloon, Vaughn, Harper, Leff, Hutchinson, Ryan, and Stoute (1978) evaluated the effects of training on three subjects. There were three areas of homework assignments: specified interactions with (1) members of the nursing staff; (2) with parents; and (3) with social and vocational contacts in the community. The training was conducted over a 10-week period. During Weeks 1 and

2, performance on all assigned tasks was assessed. Training was then introduced for interactions with the nursing staff during Weeks 3–6. The training was shifted to interactions with parents as well as nursing staff during Weeks 7–8. Finally, during Weeks 9 and 10, the training was focused on interactions with community agents, family, and nursing staff. The results indicated that the completion of homework assignments did not change until the training was applied to that specific area. Thus, the results suggest that the training was responsible for the increase in the rate of completed assignments. However, it should be noted that while demonstrating the controlling effects of social skills training, the results also suggest that little or no generalization of training occurred. That is, training that was focused on interactions that took place in one setting, or with certain individuals, did not affect the subjects' behavior in other settings, or with other individuals. The findings therefore indicate that although social skills training is an effective behavior-change technique for schizophrenic patients, particular attention should be directed toward ensuring that generalization of training to novel situations in the natural environment is attained.

A number of researchers have examined the effectiveness of social skills training for schizophrenics in a group context (Field & Test, 1975; Lomont, Gilner, Spector, & Skinner, 1969; Percell, Berwick, & Beigel, 1974; Williams *et al.*, 1977). These studies have reported improvements on a variety of self-report and behavioral measures ranging from significant decreases on the D and Pt scales of the MMPI (Lomont *et al.*, 1969) to significant increases in eye contact, speech duration, intonation, smiles, and physical gestures (Williams *et al.*, 1977).

There have been few well-controlled comparisons of the efficacy of social skills training and other modes of psychotherapy with schizophrenic patients. Goldsmith and McFall (1975) compared the effects of interpersonal skills training, a pseudotherapy control, and an assessment-only control. The interpersonal skills training resulted in significantly greater pre–post changes than the two controls.

The effectiveness of social skills training was compared with the effectiveness of a sensitivity-group training program by Monti, Curran, Corriveau, DeLancey, and Hagerman (1980). In this study, 46 psychiatric patients were randomly assigned to one of the treatments for 20 daily 1-hr training sessions. It should be noted that only 16 of the patients had been diagnosed as psychotic. The 30 remaining patients were "neurotics." Patients in the social-skills-training group improved significantly more on self-report questionnaires and a role-play assessment measure than did the patients in the sensitivity training group. With the exception of group mean scores on the Rathus Assertiveness Schedule (Rathus, 1973b), significant differences were maintained at a six-month follow-up.

An earlier study by Monti and his colleagues (Monti, Fink, Norman, Curran, Hayes, & Caldwell, 1979) compared the effectiveness of social skills training with that of a bibliotherapy program and a typical hospital-treatment control group. The subjects were 30 psychiatric patients (7 psychotics and 23 neurotics) who were randomly assigned to groups. The results indicated that the social-skills-training group improved significantly more on a role-play assessment of social skills than the hospital-treatment control group. This difference was maintained at a 10-month follow-up. The effects of social skills training generalized to novel scenes on the role-play test. Finally, the social skills group also evidenced superior performance on the Rathus Assertiveness Schedule. Other comparative outcome investigations have obtained similar findings (Lazarus, 1966; Marzillier, Lambert, & Kellett, 1976).

The limited number of well-controlled outcome studies precludes making broad generalizations about overall efficacy. The issue is further complicated by the difficulty encountered when trying to make comparisons across studies. There are often minor variations in both independent and dependent variables from one investigation to the next. Large group studies are frequently further complicated by heterogeneity with regard to diagnostic groupings. Several studies have included patients with a wide variety of diagnoses, including many who are not diagnosed as schizophrenic (e.g., Monti *et al.*, 1979, 1980). These qualifications notwithstanding, the foregoing single-case and group comparison studies do suggest that social skills training is useful in promoting improvements in the interpersonal functioning of schizophrenic patients. The results of these studies further suggest that the generalization of the effects of such training to the patient's natural environment is not automatic. Instead, it should be systematically programmed as a component of the training process. Research into the most effective means of promoting both generalization and durability of gains must be conducted. In our own research, we are analyzing the effects of guided *in vivo* practice and booster sessions to accomplish these ends. Other possibilities include the application of self-control techniques, although cognitive interventions of this sort may prove to be of greater utility with nonpsychotic populations.

Depression

Social skills training is one of five principal behavioral treatments of depression (Rehm & Kornblith, 1979). Its use is based on etiological conceptualizations that regard depression as resulting from a loss of reinforcers because of various interpersonal-skills deficits. According to Lewinsohn (1975), the depressed patient is under a schedule whereby response-contingent positive reinforcement is diminished. As a result of specific skill deficits, the depressed person is unable to obtain the kind of gratification needed from the environment. However, he or she does obtain attention for complaints of depression in the form of sympathetic social response, usually from family and friends. Thus, depressed behavior is inadvertently reinforced and maintained. However, this behavior is aversive to others, and it tends gradually to alienate people. This alienation often results in the depressed individual's being deserted and leads to further loss of reinforcement, further social isolation, and increased depression.

As noted by Hersen, Bellack, and Himmelhoch (1982), Lewinsohn's "notions suggest that depressed individuals will emit fewer behaviors, elicit more behaviors from others than they emit, interact with fewer numbers of individuals, emit fewer positive reactions to others' behaviors, and have longer action latencies than nondepressed individuals" (p.

162). A number of these hypotheses have been confirmed by Lewinsohn and his colleagues (Lewinsohn & Shaffer, 1971; Libet & Lewinsohn, 1973). In a recent study, Sanchez and Lewinsohn (1980) provided additional experimental data in support of Lewinsohn's theoretical stance. Specifically, they found a $-.50$ correlation between assertiveness and depression over a 12-week period in 12 depressed patients. Moreover, on those days when assertiveness was more evident, the level of depression was decreased. Quite interestingly, the "rate of emitted assertive behavior predicted subsequent (next day) level of depression at statistically significant levels, whereas level of depression did not reliably predict subsequent rate of emitted assertive behavior" (Sanchez & Lewinsohn, 1980, p. 119).

Lewinsohn's (1975) treatment for depression centers on having the patient (1) engage in pleasant activities and (2) improve his or her social skills. This is done in a three-month time-limited program, which first is concerned with establishing the diagnosis, the depth of the depression, and the potential for suicide. A functional analysis of depressed and other critical behaviors is then conducted. Behaviors that need to be increased or decreased are clearly identified and targeted for modification. At times, the depressed patient's behavior is evaluated in a group setting or in the presence of a family member.

Although Lewinsohn's theoretical approach to depression appears to be basically sound, the actual treatment package he uses is not as well developed as the model or the associated assessment strategy. Nonetheless, portions of Lewinsohn's skill-training package have received positive confirmation in outcome studies conducted by McLean, Ogston, and Grauer (1973) and by McLean and Hakstian (1979). However, it should be recognized that the social skills training in these studies comprised only a portion of the total behavioral strategy.

Preliminary support for the effectiveness of social skills training independent of other procedures has been provided in the form of several uncontrolled clinical studies (Wells, Hersen, Bellack, & Himmelhoch, 1979; Zeiss, Lewinsohn, & Munoz, 1979). The preliminary results of a large-scale, well-controlled outcome project offer further support (Bellack *et al.*, 1980). Four treatments for unipolar (nonpsychotic) depression were contrasted: amitriptyline, social skills training plus amitriptyline, social skills training plus placebo, and psychotherapy plus placebo. The subjects were 72 female outpatients. The four treatments, conducted by experienced clinicians, were each found to be effective; all produced statistically significant and clinically meaningful changes in symptomatology and social functioning. However, they were not all equivalent. There was a significant difference in premature terminations across groups, from a high of 55.6% for amitriptyline to a low of 15% for social skills plus placebo. There was also a substantial difference across conditions in the proportion of patients who were significantly improved. Social skills plus placebo was also the most effective treatment on this dimension. These data suggest that social skills training is an effective strategy for the treatment of depression. However, until we know more about its long-term impact, a more definitive evaluation must be reserved.

Alcoholism

Social skills deficits have frequently been implicated as a major problem in alcoholism. Alcoholics have been found to be especially lacking in the interpersonal skills necessary to handle conflict situations. For example, Miller, Hersen, Eisler, and Hilsman (1974) reported that alcoholics tend to increase their consumption subsequent to interpersonal stress. The results of a study by Miller and Eisler (1977) indicated that the amount that alcoholics consumed on a laboratory drinking task was inversely correlated with ratings of their assertiveness on a behavioral role-playing test. Despite these findings, there have been relatively few studies in which the effects of social skills training on alcoholics have been evaluated.

Eisler, Hersen, and Miller (1974) evaluated the effects of social skills training on a 34-year-old, twice-divorced male with a history of alcoholism. A pretreatment role-play assessment involving six interpersonal encounters revealed four deficit behaviors: eye contact, compliance, affect, and behavioral requests. In a multiple-baseline design across behaviors, training resulted in marked improvements in all targets on both trained and untrained items on a posttreatment role-play assessment. However, a postdischarge follow-up was disappointing in that the patient was eventually arrested for drunken driving and admitted to a state hospital for further treatment.

Foy, Miller, Eisler, and O'Toole (1976) used social-skills-training procedures to teach alcoholics to effectively refuse drinks offered to them by others. The patients were two chronic alcoholics with 15- and 25-year drinking histories. A multiple-baseline design across behaviors was used in each case to evaluate the effects of the training. Based on a behavioral analysis, the behaviors that were targeted for training were (1) requests for change; (2) offering of alternatives to drinking; (3) changing the subject of conversation; (4) duration of looking; and (5) affect. The training consisted of modeling and instructions conducted in nine sessions over a two-week period. The results indicated that both men had improved ratings on all target behaviors at posttreatment. These improvements were maintained at a three-month follow-up. However, although one patient was abstinent at that time, the other had resumed heavy drinking and required "booster" treatments.

Several controlled-group outcome studies have included social skills training as components in comprehensive treatment packages. Hedberg and Campbell (1974) randomly assigned 49 outpatient alcoholics to behavioral family counseling, systematic desensitization, covert sensitization, or faradic aversion. The behavioral family counseling incorporated assertiveness training with behavior rehearsal as a means of improving the quality of verbal interaction between the patients and their family members. The results indicated that this group had the highest percentage of subjects achieving their goal of either abstinence or controlled drinking at a six-month follow-up.

Sobell and Sobell (1973) assigned 70 male inpatient alcoholics to a treatment goal of either abstinence or controlled drinking. The subjects assigned to each treatment goal were then further subdivided into two therapy conditions: (1) "conventional" therapy, consisting of group meetings, AA meetings, chemotherapy, psychotherapy, and industrial therapy; or (2) "conventional" therapy plus behavior therapy (stimulus control training, faradic aversion, and behavioral rehearsal). The behavioral rehearsal component involved the practice of socially appropriate responses to the interpersonal situations that typically precipitated heavy drinking. The alcoholics who underwent the behavior therapy program functioned significantly better (defined in terms of drinking dispositions at six-week and six-month intervals) than the alcoholics who received only the conventional therapy. This finding held true regardless of the initial treatment goals.

A short-term skill-training intervention that taught male alcoholics to generate appropriate behaviors in problem situations was evaluated by Chaney, O'Leary, and Marlatt (1978). Forty inpatient alcoholics were assigned to a skill training group, a discussion group, or a no-additional-treatment control group. The skill training incorporated instruction, modeling, behavioral rehearsal, and coaching for both overt behavior and the cognitive process for generating the response (using D'Zurilla and Goldfried's, 1971, stepwise analysis of problem solving). A role-play measure indicated significant improvement at posttreatment for the training group as compared with the control groups. A one-year follow-up indicated that the skill training had decreased the duration and the severity of relapse episodes.

Thus, social skills training appears to hold considerable promise for the treatment of problem drinking. However, in several of the investigations, adequate maintenance was not obtained. It appears to be vital to include specific techniques for promoting maintenance. Finally, it should be noted that these conclusions are based on a relatively small number of controlled research investigations, several of which involved only one or two subjects. Additionally, in several of the investigations, social skills training was one component of a comprehensive behavioral treatment package. Therefore, further research is needed to isolate the specific effects of such training.

Aggression

There has been considerable theoretical and empirical support regarding the etiological role of interpersonal skills deficits in aggressive or violent behavior. Bandura (1973) and Toch

(1969) have both concluded that many aggressive persons tend to be deficient in social skills. As a result, they have few options available in responding to stressful and/or aggression-eliciting situations. Aggression may be elicited or facilitated by arousal resulting from an inability to respond to interpersonal conflict in an effective (assertive) fashion.

Evidence suggests that both underassertiveness and aggression frequently occur among offenders and may be related to their antisocial behavior. Megargee (1966, 1971, 1973) reported a series of investigations concerned with the interpersonal skills repertoire of offenders convicted for violent aggressive acts. Both overcontrolled individuals (whose behavior would be predominantly unassertive) and undercontrolled individuals (whose behavior would be predominantly overassertive or aggressive) were found to be disproportionately represented in the offender group.

Anchor, Sandler, and Cherones (1977) compared men who had exhibited antisocial aggression with men from various control groups. One of the findings was that the aggressive subjects employed fewer outlets for self-disclosure—a behavior incorporated into most definitions of positive assertiveness (e.g., Eisler *et al.*, 1975; Hersen & Bellack, 1977; Galassi, DeLeo, Galassi, & Bastien, 1974; Lange & Jakubowski, 1976). Jenkins, Witherspoon, DeVine, deValera, Muller, Barton, and McKee (1974) observed that the best predictors of recidivism in incarcerated violent offenders were (1) fear of the environment outside the prison and (2) failure to maintain steady employment. Those individuals not likely to be steadily employed had difficulty establishing and maintaining relationships with fellow employees and supervisors.

Finally, Kirchner, Kennedy, and Draguns (1979) compared groups of convicted offenders and demographically similar participants in a publicly supported vocational rehabilitation program. The results of a role-play assessment of interpersonal skills indicated significantly higher aggressiveness among the offenders. Conversely, there was a significantly higher level of rated assertion among the nonoffenders.

A number of single-case experimental analyses and group-outcome studies have appeared in the literature in the last several years in which skills-training approaches have been applied to patients evidencing aggressive and explosive behaviors (Eisler *et al.*, 1974; Elder, Edelstein, & Narick, 1979; Foy, Eisler, & Pinkston, 1975; Frederiksen & Eisler, 1977; Frederiksen *et al.*, 1976; King *et al.*, 1977; Matson & Stephens, 1978; Rimm, Hill, Brown, & Stuart, 1974; Turner, Hersen, & Bellack, 1978). Foy, Eisler, and Pinkston (1975) reported one of the first studies describing the effects of modeled assertion in a case of explosive rage. The patient was a 56-year-old, twice-married carpenter who frequently responded to "unreasonable demand from others" with verbal abuse and assaultiveness. Although he was separated at the time of the investigation, the patient's marriage had been characterized by strife and repeated incidents of wife battering. The training was intended to teach the patient to respond appropriately to difficult interpersonal situations encountered at work. A pretreatment role-play assessment involving seven work-related situations led to the identification of specific behavioral excesses, and deficits. The training consisted of modeling, instructions, behavioral rehearsal, and feedback. The training procedures resulted in a marked improvement in all the targeted behaviors. The patient continued to exhibit his new repertoire of responses to role-played situations over a six-month follow-up period. Furthermore, the patient reported that his work-related aggressiveness and interpersonal discord had considerably decreased.

Social skills training was used by Frederiksen *et al.* (1976) in the modification of abusive verbal outbursts by two adult psychiatric inpatients. The training was conducted in a role-play format. Improved responding generalized to novel (untrained) role-play scenes at posttreatment. The only behavior showing incomplete generalization was appropriate requests. Also, there was evidence that socially appropriate responding generalized to those situations on the hospital ward that had previously elicited abusive behaviors. However, no follow-up data were reported.

Matson and Stephens (1978) employed social skills training with four severely debilitated female patients who had spent the previous 3–11 years in a psychiatric hospital. The four had been characterized as "loud, uncooperative, hostile, and combative" (Matson & Stephens, 1978, p. 64). Social skills training was evaluated in a multiple-baseline design across behaviors and subjects. Generalization of improved social behavior to the ward setting was observed at posttreatment. Furthermore, the treatment gains were maintained at a three-month follow-up. Similarly, Elder *et al.* (1979) modified the aggressive behavior of four adolescent psychiatric patients using social skills training. Generalization of the treatment effects to behavior on the psychiatric ward was demonstrated. These four patients showed a significant reduction in the need for seclusion and the number of token economy fines. Moreover, at a three-month follow-up, three of the four patients had been discharged to the community and subsequently remained there for nine months.

Using a group-trained format, Rimm *et al.* (1974) evaluated the effects of social skills training on male subjects who reported a history of expressing anger in an inappropriate or antisocial manner. The subjects were randomly assigned to either group assertion training or a placebo control group. The subjects in the assertion-training group showed greater improvement on a role-play test of assertiveness than the subjects in the placebo group. However, no follow-up data were obtained.

The results of the foregoing investigations appear promising. However, very limited information has been obtained regarding the impact of these training programs on the subjects' behavior outside the hospital setting. While laboratory and hospital ward observations of subjects' behavior have provided support for the efficacy of social skills training, we know little about the effect of these training programs on behavior in other environments. Such data are needed before firm conclusions can be reached regarding the merit of social skills training in the treatment of aggressivity.

Minimal Dating

One of the major hypotheses regarding impairment in heterosocial functioning is that the difficulty results from an inadequate or inappropriate behavioral repertoire (e.g., Curran, 1977; Galassi & Galassi, 1979; Twentyman

& McFall, 1975). An individual may never have learned appropriate heterosocial behavior or may have learned inappropriate behavior. The performance of competent males in heterosocial interactions has been differentiated from that of incompetent males on a number of dimensions. These include global ratings of skill (Arkowitz *et al.*, 1975; Borkovec, Stone, O'Brien, & Kaloupek, 1974); number of silences and amount of talk time (Twentyman, Boland, & McFall, 1978); quality of verbal content (Perri & Richards, 1979; Perri, Richards, & Goodrich, 1978); responses to positive female approach-cues (Curran, Little, & Gilbert, 1978); and response timing and placement (Fischetti *et al.*, 1977). These findings have stimulated numerous studies on the use of social skills training to increase the frequency and the quality of heterosocial interactions. The majority have been conducted with male undergraduates who report low frequencies of dating.

Twentyman and McFall (1975) evaluated the effects of social skills training on shy males who reported dating less than once a month and who scored at least one standard deviation below the mean on the Survey of Heterosexual Interactions (SHI). The three-session training program consisted of covert and overt rehearsal, coaching, modeling, and homework. In comparison with a no-treatment control group, the experimental subjects showed some indication of reduced physiological response in a heterosocial performance situation, significant increases on the SHI, and less avoidance responding during a role-play test. In a variety of performance situations, neither self-ratings nor the judges' ratings of anxiety consistently differentiated between the two groups. Only one of two global ratings of skill differentiated the experimental group from the control subjects. Finally, the experimental subjects reported more frequent, and longer, interactions at posttest than did the subjects in the control group. The treatment gains were not maintained at a six-month follow-up. However, subject attrition may have obscured between-group differences on the follow-up data.

Kramer (1975) found social skills training to be as effective as practice dating or practice dating with cognitive restructuring. Male and female subjects in all three treatment conditions reported increased heterosocial interactions and decreased heterosocial anxiety in comparison with a waiting-list control group. McGovern, Arkowitz, and Gilmore (1975) reported data comparing social skills training with a discussion therapy condition and a waiting-list control. The subjects were male low-frequency daters. The social skills training appeared to be no better than the discussion condition on self-reports of the frequency of heterosocial interactions and anxiety and skill during those interactions. However, no follow-up data were reported. Furthermore, the criteria for inclusion in the study were lenient (i.e., three or less dates in the month preceding the study).

Similarly, a study by Melnick (1973) is confounded by the subject selection procedures that were utilized as well as by the lack of follow-up data. In this investigation, low-frequency daters were defined as dating less than two times per week. Comparisons were made among six treatment conditions: video modeling, participant modeling, participant modeling and video feedback, participant modeling plus video feedback and analogue reinforcement, a discussion control, and a no-treatment control. The subjects in the two video feedback conditions appeared to benefit the most on global ratings of anxiety and skill in posttreatment analogue interaction-assessments. However, no differences were reported for any of the groups on dating frequency. This latter finding is confounded by the fact that the subjects in the study were not dating at a very low frequency to begin with.

Curran and his colleagues (Curran, 1975; Curran & Gilbert, 1975; Curran, Gilbert, & Little, 1976) have conducted a series of comparative-outcome investigations that provide support for the effectiveness of heterosocial skills training while rectifying some of the methodological shortcomings of the previous studies. In the first of these studies (Curran, 1975), social skills training was compared with systematic desensitization, an attention placebo condition (relaxation training), and a waiting-list control. Male and female subjects were recruited through a newspaper advertisement. The subjects who scored in the upper third of the distribution on the Situation Questionnaire (Rehm & Marston, 1968) were randomly assigned across treatments. Both social skills training and systematic desensitization resulted in significant pre–post changes in behavioral ratings of anxiety and skill during a simulated heterosocial interaction. The results thus provide support for the effectiveness of both social skills training and systematic desensitization in the treatment of heterosocial disability. However, no data were obtained regarding either pre or posttreatment dating frequencies, and no follow-up data were reported.

In the second investigation (Curran & Gilbert, 1975), social skills training was again compared with systematic desensitization and a waiting-list control. The subjects were male and female introductory psychology students who scored in the upper third of the distribution on both the Situation Questionnaire and the interpersonal items of the Fear Survey Schedule (Wolpe & Lang, 1964). Over 50% of the subjects had not dated during the eight weeks prior to the investigation. Social skills training and systematic desensitization resulted in significant posttreatment decreases on self-report measures of skill and anxiety and on behavioral ratings of anxiety in the simulated interaction. The subjects in the social-skills-training group scored significantly higher on the behavioral ratings of heterosocial skill than the subjects in the waiting-list control. At a six-month follow-up, the subjects in the social skills group received significantly higher skill ratings than the subjects in either the systematic desensitization or the waiting-list conditions. The subjects in both treatment conditions showed significant increases in dating frequency during and after treatment. Thus, both treatments appeared to effect changes in the subjects' heterosocial anxiety and dating frequency. However, only social skills training resulted in increases in the rated skill level.

The third study (Curran *et al.*, 1976) compared social skills training and sensitivity training for heterosocially anxious students. The subjects in the study had had a mean of 1.08 dates in the preceding two months. At posttreatment, the subjects in the skills training group rated themselves as significantly more skilled on a simulated heterosocial interaction than the subjects in either of the

other groups. Trained observers rated the subjects from the skills-training group as more skilled and less anxious than subjects in the sensitivity group. Indeed, there was no improvement from pre- to posttreatment for the sensitivity group. Finally, there were significant within group changes in dating frequency only for the skills-training group. Thus, in this and the previous study, skills training resulted in significant changes in the subjects' behavior in both laboratory assessment procedures and an indirect measure of transfer of training.

Similar improvements were noted in an outcome study by MacDonald, Lindquist, Kramer, McGrath, and Rhyne (1975). Comparisons were made among social skills training, social skills training with homework assignments, and attention-placebo therapy condition, and a waiting-list control. There were two groups of six persons in each condition. The subjects were male undergraduates who had dated four or fewer times during the past 12 months. The results indicated that three of the four skills-training groups showed significant increases in ratings of dating-skill level on a role-played dating-interaction measure. None of the attention-placebo or waiting-list control groups' improved significantly. No follow-up data were reported.

A study by Bander, Steinke, Allen, and Mosher (1975) compared social skills training, social skills training plus systematic desensitization, and sensitivity training. The subjects were recruited from a pool of volunteers from an introductory psychology class. They were selected on the basis of self-reports of dating behavior and anxiety. However, no data were provided as to their degree of anxiety or dating frequency. The social skills group was equivalent to the social skills plus systematic desensitization group on behavioral and self-report measures at posttreatment. Both social skills groups were superior to the sensitivity-training group on a behavioral measure. However, the results were confounded by the fact that the subjects were not assessed on the behavioral measure prior to treatment.

Finally, Glass, Gottman, and Shmurak (1976) studied the effects of social skills training in comparison with a cognitive self-statement approach, a combined skills-training–self-statement approach, and a waiting-list control in the treatment of shy males. The subjects were undergraduates who volunteered for a dating-skills-development program. The results at posttreatment and six-month follow-up indicated that all the treatment groups performed significantly better than the waiting-list control group on items from a role-play test on which they had received training. At posttreatment, both the skills-training and the combined treatment groups were significantly better on trained items than the self-statement group. The two groups that had received training in the modification of self-statements were the only groups to show improvement on the untrained items of the role-play test. This improvement was maintained at follow-up. The subjects' performance on a posttreatment phone-call task indicated that the self-statement modification group made more phone calls and were rated as more impressive than the other groups. Differences in the ratings of impressiveness were not maintained at follow-up. Finally, no significant between-group differences were observed at follow-up on a dating-frequency measure or on a measure of feelings of competency in dating situations. These findings suggest that while social skills training emphasizing behavior rehearsal may produce enhanced functioning in laboratory assessment procedures, the effects of training may fail to generalize to novel and/or more naturalistic measures of heterosocial competence. However, the findings are confounded by the fact that the only apparent qualification for inclusion in the study was a desire to participate in a dating-skills development program. Therefore, as with several other investigations in this area, it is questionnable whether the subjects who participated in the study experienced marked heterosocial dysfunction.

It is difficult to derive firm conclusions regarding the overall utility of heterosocial skills training. Many of the investigations that have appeared in the literature have been marked by serious methodological shortcomings. There have been critical variations across studies with regard to the specific skills-training paradigms that have been utilized. Furthermore, the outcome measures have differed across the studies. Finally, the subjects recruited for the

various investigations have differed greatly with regard to their degree of heterosexual dysfunction. Despite these issues, it does appear that heterosocial skills training can result in increased heterosocial competence as assessed by laboratory procedures. However, the effects of training have often failed to generalize to the natural environment. Future research is needed to develop and evaluate procedures that are intended to promote the transfer of training. The results of the studies by MacDonald et al. (1975) and Bander et al. (1975) suggest that homework assignments and/or cognitive training procedures may be useful in this regard. The durability of the effects of heterosocial skills training has yet to be adequately evaluated. In those studies where follow-up data have been reported, they have generally supported treatment effectiveness. However, follow-ups have frequently involved only self-report data gathered at disappointingly short intervals after the treatment was terminated. Further investigation is necessary before definitive conclusions regarding the maintenance of effects can be reached.

In closing this section, we should point out that our focus has been almost exclusively on the response acquisition approach. However, as we have suggested, the skills deficit hypothesis is only one of several models of social dysfunction. While considerable evidence exists to support the use of social skills training in the modification of minimal dating, there exists perhaps equally strong evidence supporting both the conditioned-anxiety and the cognitive-evaluative models of heterosocial failure. Positive results have been reported from the use of anxiety reduction strategies (e.g., Christensen, Arkowitz, & Anderson, 1975) and cognitive modification procedures (Glass et al., 1976). Another factor may be the physical attractiveness of the individual (Arkowitz, 1977; Curran, 1977; Galassi & Galassi, 1979). Of course, these are not mutually exclusive factors. For example, a given individual may be heterosocially inadequate as a result of skills deficits, or anxiety, or both. Careful assessment of the *nature* of the interpersonal dysfunction (e.g., skills deficit or conditioned anxiety) is necessary in order to determine what treatment is appropriate. Presumably, the effective matching of the subject and the treatment will produce the best results.

Unassertiveness

Assertion training has become one of the most popular techniques in the armamentarium of the clinical behavior therapist. For example, assertion training for women has become increasingly common as a result of the women's movement (e.g., Linehan & Egan, 1979). College students are a second population who frequently avail themselves of assertion-training programs (e.g., Galassi, Galassi, & Litz, 1974; McFall & Marston, 1970; McFall & Lillesand, 1971; McFall & Twentyman, 1973; Rathus, 1972, 1973b). Many clinicians routinely administer assertion training as part of a comprehensive treatment program.

Numerous controlled-outcome evaluations of assertion training have been reported. McFall and Marston (1970) conducted a study involving college students who reported significant difficulty in behaving assertively. The results indicated that the subjects exposed to behavior rehearsal (either with or without performance feedback) evidenced significantly greater pre–post changes on behavioral, self-report, and physiological measures than the subjects given placebo therapy or no treatment. The transfer of training was assessed during a two-week follow-up assessment in which the subjects' responses to a telephone salesperson's repeated requests were audiotaped. The results of the phone-call follow-up followed the patterns seen on the laboratory measures, but the differences between the experimental and the control groups were generally not significant.

McFall and Lillesand (1971) assigned unassertive college students to one of three different groups: (1) behavior rehearsal with overt performance; (2) behavior rehearsal with covert performance; or (3) a no-treatment control group. The posttreatment assessment consisted of a role-play task including trained and untrained items, as well as a one-item extended-interaction test in which a prerecorded confederate made increasingly insistent requests following a subject's refusal. A follow-up measure assessed the subjects' refusal of a telephone salesperson's repeated requests.

The subjects in the two experimental groups showed the most pronounced pre–post changes on the outcome measures. The experimental subjects showed some generalization to similar refusal situations in which they had received no training, including the extended interaction. However, the effects of the training did not generalize to the telephone follow-up. In a third report, comprised of four separate experiments, McFall and Twentyman (1973) again observed poor transfer. The effects of the training did not generalize to follow-up assessments involving the subjects' refusal of requests by a telephone salesperson.

Young, Rimm, and Kennedy (1973) compared modeling and modeling plus verbal reinforcement. Both modeling groups were superior to two control conditions in response to trained situations. However, the modeling-only condition resulted in greater generalization to untrained situations. Although reinforcement did not appear to supplement the effectiveness of modeling, the reinforcement procedures were general and poorly specified. There were no differences between the treatment groups on the self-report measures.

Kazdin (1974a) conducted a study with volunteer subjects recruited from a university community. Participation in the project was based on performance on self-report measures and a behavioral role-playing test. In four treatment sessions, both covert modeling and covert modeling plus model reinforcement resulted in considerable improvement on the self-report and behavioral measures of assertive responding. Model and model-reinforcement subjects were more assertive on a set of generalization situations included in the role-playing test than either a no-modeling (imagined scenes with neither an assertive model nor favorable consequences) or a delay-treatment control group. The model-reinforcement group tended to show greater assertiveness at posttreatment and at a three-month follow-up, during which self-report data were collected. On a two-week follow-up phone-call assessment, in which the subjects were phoned and asked to do volunteer work, the four groups did not differ on the majority of behavioral ratings that were made.

In a second study, using similar subject recruitment and selection criteria, Kazdin (1976) evaluated the effects of multiple models (imagining a single model versus several models performing assertively) and of model reinforcement (imagining favorable consequences following model behavior versus no consequences). Again, a nonassertive-model control group that imagined assertion-relevant scenes was included in the design. The results after four treatment sessions indicated that covert modeling produced significant increases in assertive behavior as reflected on self-report and behavioral measures. Imagining several models responding assertively and favorable consequences following the model's performance enhanced the treatment effects. The effects of the treatment generalized to novel role-playing situations and were maintained at a four-month follow-up on self-report measures.

In an application of his covert-modeling assertion-training paradigm to psychiatric patients, Kazdin and his colleagues (Hersen *et al.*, 1979) compared five training conditions: (1) test–retest; (2) live modeling plus rehearsal; (3) live modeling without rehearsal; (4) covert modeling plus rehearsal; and (5) covert modeling without rehearsal. In this study, 50 psychiatric patients who scored 19 or below on the Wolpe-Lazarus Assertiveness Scale were randomly assigned across groups. Live modeling and covert modeling effected improvements in the assertive responding of the patients on a role-play test. The two treatments were not differentially effective. Generally, the addition of rehearsal to live or covert modeling failed to enhance the treatment. There was evidence of a transfer of treatment effects on generalization scenes of the role-play test.

Modeling, behavioral rehearsal, and modeling plus behavioral rehearsal conditions were compared by Friedman (1969). Undergraduate subjects in all three treatment conditions responded more assertively on a behavioral measure than subjects who received "nonassertive readings." The modeling plus rehearsal condition was superior to the other two treatments. There were no differences between groups on self-report measures.

A number of investigators have developed comprehensive training protocols for use with nonassertive undergraduates. Galassi *et al.* (1974) reported on the use of a systematic,

short-term group assertion-training procedure comprising behavior rehearsal, videotaped modeling, videotape feedback, group feedback, trainer feedback, bibliotherapy, and homework assignments. A group of male and female college students were randomly assigned to either the assertion-training condition or an attention-control procedure. The subjects receiving assertion training were superior to the controls on a number of behavioral and self-report measures. The treatment gains were maintained at a one-year follow-up (Galassi, Kosta, & Galassi, 1975). Rathus (1972, 1973a) has conducted two studies investigating the efficacy of assertion training in groups with female college students. Although assertion training appeared superior to discussion or no-treatment control conditions in both studies, only self-report data were provided.

Several studies have been conducted to evaluate the effectiveness of treatment packages based on the cognitive-evaluative model of social skills deficits. As we have discussed, according to this model, maladaptive self-statements, beliefs, and expectations about assertive encounters are responsible for the individual's failure to respond effectively. Alden, Safran, and Weideman (1978) and Linehan, Goldfried, and Goldfried (1979) compared a cognitive-restructuring training procedure with a behavior rehearsal condition. With few exceptions, they observed no differences between the two treatments on behavioral measures of assertive responding and the subjects' reports of comfort in situations that required assertion. A study by Derry and Stone (1979) showed that a cognitive training procedure resulted in superior maintenance and generalization of assertive responses in comparison with a behavioral rehearsal condition. However, only two sessions of training were administered. Both the study by Linehan *et al.* (1979) and an earlier investigation by Wolfe and Fodor (1977) examined the combined effects of behavior rehearsal and cognitive restructuring. Although the findings suggest that the cognitive component may increase the effectiveness of behavior rehearsal, they are far from straightforward. In the study by Wolfe and Fodor, the combined training package was superior on self-reports of anxiety in situations requiring assertion, but not on behavioral outcome measures. However, the treatment consisted of only two sessions. Linehan *et al.* based their conclusion regarding the superiorty of the combined treatment on the comparison of each treatment with control conditions. They report that there were no significant differences between the two treatments themselves.

Other studies have examined the effects of variations in procedural aspects of assertion training. For example, Linehan, Walker, Bronheim, Haynes, and Yevzeroff (1979) found no significant differences between group and individual assertion training. Rakos and Schroeder (1979) reported the development and the empirical evaluation of a self-administered assertiveness-training program. The program resulted in superior performance on a role-play assessment in comparison with a procedurally parallel placebo program.

Overall, these data suggest that assertion-training techniques can effect durable improvements in assertive responding as assessed by self-report and laboratory behavioral measures. However, the effects of training have often failed to genealize to more naturalistic outcome measures, such as follow-up telephone-call assessment procedures. However, several methodological issues may be at least partly responsible for these failures to obtain generalization. The various studies that have relied on such naturalistic assessments have often involved analogue applications of assertion-training techniques. The treatments have often been of extremely short duration (e.g., Kazdin, 1974a) and have consisted of only one or two of the numerous techniques that have been identified as potentially important components of a comprehensive skills-training protocol (e.g., McFall & Lillesand, 1971; McFall & Marston, 1970; McFall & Twentyman, 1973). Second, the use of volunteer subjects (e.g., Kazdin, 1974a, 1976) may lead to outcomes that are not representative of those that would be obtained with clients or patients who actively seek help for assertiveness skill deficits. Certainly, the generalization of the effects of comprehensive assertion-training programs with persons who suffer clinically significant deficits warrants additional attention. Finally, the assessment

procedures themselves may not be valid indicators of *in vivo* performance.

Summary and Conclusions

In preparing our reference list, it was apparent that we reviewed an extensive literature. Yet in some respects we felt as if we had barely scratched the surface. There were many many studies that we did not cite. Some subareas, such as skills training for juvenile delinquency and sociometric assessment, were totally omitted or mentioned only in passing. As indicated at the beginning of this chapter, the area is simply too overwhelming to cover in a single review.

In a similar vein, it is difficult to make an overall appraisal of the area; it is too diverse and complex. Yet several points come up repeatedly. First, assessment is both a strength and a handicap. We have overcome our early naiveté and learned some hard lessons about the difficulty of appraising social skill. Many cherished beliefs and strategies have proved to be invalid. Others account for only a small portion of the variance. Yet, the baby must not be thrown out with the bathwater. Role play, staged interactions, and molecular analyses can all be useful. We simply must be aware of their limitations. Further research is needed to outline their utility clearly, as well as to develop new and better procedures.

A somewhat different problem must be faced in the area of skills training. We have also been overly enthusiastic about these techniques, but this overenthusiasm has not yet been widely recognized. Skills training clearly *works*, in the sense that it efficiently develops new behavioral skills in diverse populations. Yet, the clinical utility of the procedures is still uncertain in many respects. There are generalization and maintenance problems here, as there are in almost every other behavioral technique. We do not know how well and for how long people can transfer their newly learned response capabilities to their daily environments. Do they really use these responses on a day-to-day basis? No one knows. This is a vital area for research. Moreover, even if skills do transfer, do they make a significant impact on the person's life? In other words, are we teaching important responses? Does skills training make a difference?

The questions just raised lead to a final set of questions that pertain to the skills model. Earlier, we outlined several ways in which skills deficits can interface with psychopathology. Our training programs are based primarily on the notion that skills deficits are causal or maintaining factors. If not, such training may be a meaningless exercise. Yet, there are few solid data on this issue. We are operating mainly on the basis of a convincing model (otherwise known as "a wing and a prayer"!). This issue must be subjected to careful scrutiny. Skills training will clearly make no meaningful difference in the patient's life if skills deficits are not critical factors in the dysfunction.

References

Alden, L., Safran, J., & Weideman, R. A comparison of cognitive and skills training strategies in the treatment of unassertive clients. *Behavior Therapy*, 1978, *9*, 843–846.

Anchor, K. N., Sandler, H. M., & Cherones, J. H. Maladaptive antisocial aggressive behavior and outlets for intimacy. *Journal of Clinical Psychology*, 1977, *33*, 947–949.

Argyris, C. Explorations in interpersonal competence: I. *Journal of Applied Behavioral Science*, 1965, *1*, 58–83.

Arkowitz, H. Measurement and modification of minimal dating behavior. In M. Hersen, R. M. Eisler, & P. M. Miller (Eds.), *Progress in behavior modification*, Vol. 5. New York: Academic Press, 1977.

Arkowitz, H. The assessment of social skills. In M. Hersen & A. S. Bellack (Eds.), *Behavioral assessment: A practical handbook* (2nd ed). New York: Pergamon Press, 1981.

Arkowitz, H., Lichtenstein, E., McGovern, K., & Hines, P. The behavioral assessment of social competence in males. *Behavior Therapy*, 1975, *6*, 3–13.

Bander, K. W., Steinke, G. V., Allen, G. J., & Mosher, D. L. Evaluation of three dating-specific treatment approaches for heterosexual dating anxiety. *Journal of Consulting and Clinical Psychology*, 1975, *43*, 259–265.

Bandura, A. *Aggression: A social learning analysis.* Englewood Cliffs, N.J.: Prentice-Hall, 1973.

Bandura, A. *Social learning theory.* Englewood Cliffs, N.J.: Prentice-Hall, 1977.

Barlow, D. H., Abel, G. G., Blanchard, E. B., Bristow, A. R., & Young, L. D. A heterosocial skills behavior checklist for males. *Behavior Therapy*, 1977, *8*, 229–239.

Bellack, A. S. Behavioral assessment of social skills. In A. S. Bellack & M. Hersen (Eds.), *Research and practice in social skills training*. New York: Plenum Press, 1979. (a)

Bellack, A. S. A critical appraisal of strategies for assessing social skill. *Behavioral Assessment*, 1979, *1*, 157–176. (b)

Bellack, A. S. Anxiety and neurotic disorders. In A. E. Kazdin, A. S. Bellack, & M. Hersen (Eds.), *New perspectives in abnormal psychology*. New York: Oxford University Press, 1980.

Bellack, A. S., & Hersen, M. *Behavior modification: An introductory textbook.* New York: Oxford University Press, 1977. (a)

Bellack, A. S., & Hersen, M. The use of self-report inventories in behavioral assessment. In J. D. Cone & R. P. Hawkins (Eds.), *Behavioral assessment: New directions in clinical psychology*. New York: Brunner/Mazel, 1977. (b)

Bellack, A. S., & Hersen, M. Chronic psychiatric patients: Social skills training. In M. Hersen & A. S. Bellack (Eds.), *Behavior therapy in the psychiatric setting*. Baltimore: Williams & Wilkins, 1978.

Bellack, A. S., & Hersen, M. *Introduction to clinical psychology*. New York: Oxford University Press, 1979.

Bellack, A. S., Hersen, M., & Turner, S. M. Generalization effects of social skills training in chronic schizophrenics: An experimental analysis. *Behaviour Research and Therapy*, 1976, *14*, 391–398.

Bellack, A. S., Hersen, M., & Turner, S. M. Role play tests for assessing social skills: Are they valid? *Behavior Therapy*, 1978, *9*, 448–461.

Bellack, A. S., Hersen, M., & Lamparski, D. Role play tests for assessing social skills: Are they valid? Are they useful? *Journal of Consulting and Clinical Psychology*, 1979, *47*, 335–342.

Bellack, A. S., Hersen, M., & Turner, S. M. The relationship of role playing and knowledge of appropriate behavior to assertion in the natural environment. *Journal of Consulting and Clinical Psychology*, 1979, *47*, 670–678.

Bellack, A. S., Hersen, M., & Himmelhoch, J. M. Social skills training for depression: A treatment manual. *JSAS Catalog of Selected Documents in Psychology*, 1980, *10*, 92. (Ms. No. 2156.)

Bellack, A. S., Hersen, M., & Himmelhoch, J. M. Social skills training, pharmacotherapy, and psychotherapy for unipolar depression. *American Journal of Psychiatry*, 1981, *138*, 1562–1567.

Birchler, G. R. Communication skills in married couples. In A. S. Bellack & M. Hersen (Eds.), *Research and practice in social skills training*. New York: Plenum Press, 1979.

Blanchard, E. B., & Hersen, M. Behavioral treatment of hysterical neuroses: Symptom substitution and symptom return reconsidered. *Psychiatry*, 1976, *39*, 118–129.

Borkovec, T. D., Stone, N., O'Brien, G., & Kaloupek, D. Identification and measurement of a clinically relevant target behavior for analogue outcome research. *Behavior Therapy*, 1974, *5*, 503–513.

Brown, G. W., Birley, J. L. T., & Wing, J. K. Influence of family life on the course of schizophrenic disorders: A replication. *British Journal of Psychiatry*, 1972, *121*, 241–258.

Chaney, E. F., O'Leary, M. R., & Marlatt, G. A. Skill training with alcoholics. *Journal of Consulting and Clinical Psychology*, 1978, *46*, 1092–1104.

Christensen, A., & Arkowitz, H. Preliminary report on practice dating and feedback as treatment for college dating problems. *Journal of Counseling Psychology,* 1974, *21*, 92–95.

Christensen, A., Arkowitz, H., & Anderson, J. Practice dating as treatment for college dating inhibitions. *Behaviour Research and Therapy,* 1975, *13*, 321–331.

Coyne, J. C. Depression and the response of others. *Journal of Abnormal Psychology,* 1976, *85*, 186–193.

Curran, J. P. An evaluation of a skills training program and a systematic desensitization program in reducing dating anxiety. *Behaviour Research and Therapy,* 1975, *13*, 65–68.

Curran, J. P. Skills training as an approach to the treatment of heterosexual-social anxiety: A review. *Psychological Bulletin,* 1977, *84*, 140–157.

Curran, J. P. Social skills: Methodological issues and future directions. In A. S. Bellack & M. Hersen (Eds.), *Research and practice in social skills training.* New York: Plenum Press, 1979.

Curran, J. P., & Gilbert, F. S. A test of the relative effectiveness of a systematic desensitization program and an interpersonal skills training program with date anxious subjects. *Behavior Therapy,* 1975, *6*, 510–521.

Curran, J. P., & Mariotto, M. J. A conceptual structure for the assessment of social skills. In M. Hersen, R. M. Eisler, & P. M. Miller (Eds.), *Progress in behavior modification,* Vol. 10. New York: Academic Press, 1981.

Curran, J. P., Gilbert, F. S., & Little, L. M. A comparison between behavioral training and sensitivity training approaches to heterosexual dating anxiety. *Journal of Counseling Psychology,* 1976, *23*, 190–196.

Curran, J. P., Little, L. M., & Gilbert, F. S. Reactivity of males of differing heterosexual social anxiety to female approach and non-approach cue conditions. *Behavior Therapy,* 1978, *9*, 961.

Derry, P. A., & Stone, G. L. Effects of cognitive-adjunct treatments on assertiveness. *Cognitive Therapy and Research,* 1979, *3*, 213–221.

Duncan, S., Jr., & Fiske, D. *Face to face interaction: Research, methods, and theory.* New York: Lawrence Erlbaum, 1977.

D'Zurilla, T. J., & Goldfried, M. R. Problem-solving and behavior modification. *Journal of Abnormal Psychology,* 1971, *78*, 107–126.

Edelstein, B. A., & Eisle, R. M. Effects of modeling and modeling with instructions and feedback on the behavioral components of social skills of a schizophrenic. *Behavior Therapy,* 1976, *7*, 382–389.

Eisler, R. M. The behavioral assessment of social skills. In M. Hersen & A. S. Bellack (Eds.), *Behavioral assessment: A practical handbook.* New York: Pergamon Press, 1976.

Eisler, R. M., Hersen, M., & Miller, P. M. Shaping components of assertiveness with instructions and feedback. *American Journal of Psychiatry,* 1974, *131*, 1344–1347.

Eisler, R. M., Hersen, M., Miller, P. M., & Blanchard, E. B. Situational determinants of assertive behaviors. *Journal of Consulting and Clinical Psychology,* 1975, *43*, 330–340.

Eisler, R. M., Frederiksen, L. W., & Peterson, G. L. The relationship of cognitive variables to the expression of assertiveness. *Behavior Therapy,* 1978, *9*, 419–427.

Elder, J. P., Edelstein, B. A., & Narick, M. M. Social skills training in the modification of aggressive behavior of adolescent psychiatric patients. *Behavior Modification,* 1979, *3*, 161–178.

Fiedler, D., & Beach, L. R. On the decision to be assertive. *Journal of Consulting and Clinical Psychology,* 1978, *46*, 537–546.

Field, G. D., & Test, M. A. Group assertiveness training for severely disturbed patients. *Journal of Behavior Therapy and Experimental Psychiatry,* 1975, *6*, 129–134.

Fischetti, M., Curran, J. P., & Wessberg, H. W. Sense of timing: A skill deficit in heterosexual-socially anxious males. *Behavior Modification,* 1977, *1*, 179–195.

Foy, D. W., Eisler, R. M., & Pinkston, S. G. Modeled assertion in a case of explosive rage. *Journal of Behavior Therapy and Experimental Psychiatry,* 1975, *6*, 135–137.

Foy, D. W., Miller, P. M., Eisler, R. M., & O'Toole, D. H. Social skills training to teach alcoholics to refuse drinks effectively. *Journal of Studies on Alcohol,* 1976, *37*, 1340–1345.

Frederiksen, L. W., & Eisler, R. M. The control of explosive behavior: A skill-development approach. In D. Upper (ed.), *Perspectives in behaviour therapy.* Kalamazoo, Mich.: Behaviordelia, 1977.

Fredriksen, L. W., Jenkins, J. O., Foy, D. W., & Eisler, R. M. Social skills training in the modification of abusive verbal outbursts in adults. *Journal of Applied Behavior Analysis,* 1976, *9*, 117–125.

Freedman, B. J., Rosenthal, L., Donahoe, J. R., Schlundt, D. G., & McFall, R. M. A social-behavioral analysis of skill deficits in delinquent and nondelinquent adolescent boys. *Journal of Consulting and Clinical Psychology,* 1978, *46*, 1448–1462.

Friedman, P. H. The effects of modeling and roleplaying on assertive behavior. (Doctoral dissertation, University of Wisconsin, 1968). *Dissertation Abstracts International,* 1969, *29*, 4844B. (University Microfilms No. 69-912.)

Galassi, J. P., & Galassi, M. D. Modification of heterosocial skills deficits. In A. S. Bellack & M. Hersen (Eds.), *Research and practice in social skills training.* New York: Plenum Press, 1979.

Galassi, J. P., DeLeo, J. S., Galassi, M. D., & Bastien, S. The College Self-Expression Scale: A measure of assertiveness. *Behavior Therapy,* 1974, *5*, 165–171.

Galassi, J. P., Galassi, M. D., & Litz, M. C. Assertive training in groups using video-feedback. *Journal of Counseling Psychology,* 1974, *21*, 390–394.

Galassi, J. P., Kosta, M. P., & Galassi, M. D. Assertive training: A one-year follow-up. *Journal of Counseling Psychology,* 1975, *22*, 451–452.

Galassi, M. D., & Galassi, J. P. The effects of role playing variations on the assessment of assertive behavior. *Behavior Therapy,* 1976, *7*, 343–347.

Glass, C. R., Gottman, J. M., & Shmurak, S. H. Response-acquisition and cognitive self-statement modification approaches to dating-skills training. *Journal of Counseling Psychology,* 1976, *23*, 520–526.

Gleser, G. C., & Gottschalk, L. A. Personality characteristics of chronic schizophrenics in relationship to sex and current functioning. *Journal of Clinical Psychology,* 1967. *23,* 349–354.

Goldfried, M. R., Decenteceo, E. T., & Weinberg, L. Systemic rational restructuring as a self-control technique. *Behavior Therapy,* 1974, *5*, 247–254.

Goldsmith, J. B., & McFall, R. M. Development and evaluation of an interpersonal skill-training program for psychiatric patients. *Journal of Abnormal Psychology,* 1975, *84,* 51–58.

Hammen, C. L., & Peters, S. D. Interpersonal consequences of depression: Responses to men and women enacting a depressed role. *Journal of Abnormal Psychology,* 1978, *87,* 322–332.

Harper, R. G., Wiens, A. N., & Matarazzo, J. D. *Nonverbal communication: The state of the art.* New York: Wiley, 1978.

Hedberg, A. S., & Campbell, L. A. A comparison of four behavioral treatments of alcoholism. *Journal of Behavior Therapy and Experimental Psychiatry,* 1974, *5,* 251–256.

Hersen, M., & Bellack, A. S. Social skills training for chronic psychiatric patients: Rationale, research findings, and future directions. *Comprehensive Psychiatry,* 1976, *17,* 559–580.

Hersen, M., & Bellack, A. S. Assessment of social skills. In A. R. Ciminero, K. S. Calhoun, & H. E. Adams (Eds.), *Handbook for behavioral assessment.* New York: Wiley, 1977.

Hersen, M., Eisler, R. M., Miller, P. M., Johnson, M. B., & Pinkston, S. G. Effect of practive, instructions, and modeling on components of assertive behavior. *Behaviour Research and Therapy,* 1973, *11,* 443–451.

Hersen, M., Turner, S. M., Edelstein, B. A., & Pinkston, S. G. Effects of phenothiazines and social skills training in a withdrawn schizophrenic. *Journal of Clinical Psychology,* 1975, *34,* 588–594.

Hersen, M., Kazdin, A. E., Bellack, A. S., & Turner, S. M. Effects of live modeling, covert modeling, and rehearsal on assertiveness in psychiatric patients. *Behaviour Research and Therapy,* 1979, *17,* 369–377.

Hersen, M., Bellack, A. S., & Himmelhoch, J. M. Social skills training with unipolar depressed women. In J. P. Curran & P. M. Monti (Eds.), *Social skills training: A practical handbook for assessment and treatment.* New York: Guilford Press, 1982.

Higgins, R. L., Alonso, R. R., & Pendleton, M. G. The validity of role-play assessments of assertiveness. *Behavior Therapy,* 1979, *10,* 655–662.

Hollandsworth, J. G., Jr., & Cooley, M. L. Provoking anger and gaining compliance with assertive versus aggressive responses. *Behavior Therapy,* 1978, *9,* 640–646.

Hopkins, J., Krawitz, G., & Bellack, A. S. The effects of situational variations in role-play scenes on assertive behavior. *Journal of Behavior Assessment,* in press.

Howes, M. J., & Hokanson, J. E. Conversational and social responses to depressive interpersonal behavior. *Journal of Abnormal Psychology,* 1979, *88,* 625–634.

Hull, D. B., & Schroeder, H. E. Some interpersonal effects of assertion, nonassertion, and aggression. *Behavior Therapy,* 1970, *10,* 20–28.

Jacob, T. Assessment of marital dysfunction. In M. Hersen & A. S. Bellack (Eds.), *Behavioral assessment: A practical handbook.* New York: Pergamon Press, 1976.

Jenkins, W. O., Witherspoon, A. D., DeVine, M. D., deValera, E. K., Muller, J. B., Barton, M. C., & McKee, J. M. *The post-prison analysis of criminal behavior and longitudinal follow-up evaluation of institutional treatment.* Elmore, Ala.: Rehabilitation Research Foundation, 1974.

Johnson, S. M., & Bolstad, O. D. Methodological issues in naturalistic observation: Some problems and solutions for field research. In L. A. Hamerlynck, L. C. Handy, & E. J. Mash (Eds.), *Behavior change: Methodology, concepts, and practice.* Champaign, Ill.: Research Press, 1973.

Kagan, J., & Moss, H. A. *Birth to maturity: A study in psychological development.* New York: Wiley, 1962.

Kane, J. S., & Lawler, E. E., III. Methods of peer assessment. *Psychological Bulletin,* 1978, *85,* 555–586.

Kazdin, A. E. Effects of covert modeling and model reinforcement on assertive behavior. *Journal of Abnormal Psychology,* 1974, *83,* 240–252. (a)

Kazdin, A. E. Self-monitoring and behavior change. In M. J. Mahoney & C. E. Thoresen (Eds.), *Self-control: Power to the person.* Monterey, Calif.: Brooks/Cole, 1974. (b)

Kazdin, A. E. Effects of covert modeling, multiple models, and model reinforcement on assertive behavior. *Behavior Therapy,* 1976, *7,* 211–222.

Kazdin, A. E. Assessing the clinical or applied importance of behavior change through social validation. *Behavior Modification,* 1977, *4,* 427–452.

King, L. W., Liberman, R. P., Roberts, J., & Bryan, E. Personal effectiveness: A structured therapy for improving social and emotional skills. *European Journal of Behavioural Analysis and Modification,* 1977, *2,* 82–91.

Kirchner, E. P., Kennedy, R. E., & Draguns, J. G. Assertion and aggression in adult offenders. *Behavior Therapy,* 1979, *10,* 452–471.

Kramer, S. R. Effectiveness of behavior rehearsal and practice dating to increase heterosexual social interaction. (Doctoral dissertation, University of Texas, 1975.) *Dissertation Abstracts International,* 1975, *36,* 913B–914B. (University of Microfilms, No. 75-16, 693.)

Lange, A. J., & Jakubowski, P. *Responsible assertive behavior.* Champaign, Ill.: Research Press, 1976.

Lazarus, A. A. Behaviour rehearsal vs. non-directive therapy vs. advice in effecting behaviour change. *Behaviour Research and Therapy,* 1966, *4,* 209–212.

Lewinsohn, P. M. The behavioral study and treatment of depression. In M. Hersen, R. M. Eisler, & P. M. Miller (Eds.), *Progress in behavior modification,* Vol 1. New York: Academic Press, 1975.

Lewinsohn, P. M., & Shaffer, M. Use of home observations as an integral part of the treatment of depression: Preliminary report and case studies. *Journal of Consulting and Clinical Psychology,* 1971, *37,* 87–94.

Liberman, R. P., Lillie, F., Falloon, I., Vaughn, C., Harper, E., Leff, J., Hutchinson, W., Ryan, P., & Stoute, M. *Social skills training for schizophrenic patients and their families.* Unpublished manuscript, 1978.

Libet, J. M., & Lewinsohn, P. M. Concept of social skill with special reference to the behavior of depressed persons. *Journal of Consulting and Clinical Psychology,* 1973, *40,* 304–312.

Linehan, M. M., & Egan, K. J. Assertion training for women. In A. S. Bellack & M. Hersen (Eds.), *Research and practice in social skills training.* New York: Plenum Press, 1979.

Linehan, M. M., Goldfried, M. R., & Goldfried, A. P. Assertion therapy: Skill training or cognitive restructuring. *Behavior Therapy,* 1979, *10,* 372–388.

Linehan, M. M., Walker, R. O., Bronheim, S., Haynes, K. F., & Yevzeroff, H. Group versus individual assertion training. *Journal of Consulting and Clinical Psychology*, 1979, *47*, 1000–1002.

Lomont, J. F., Gilner, F. H., Spector, N. J., & Skinner, B. F. Group assertion training and group insight therapies. *Psychological Reports*, 1969, *23*, 463–470.

MacDonald, M. L., Lindquist, C. U., Kramer, J. A., McGrath, R. A., & Rhyne, L. D. Social skills training: Behavior rehearsal in groups and dating skills. *Journal of Counseling Psychology*, 1975, *22*, 224–230.

Marzillier, J. S., Lambert, C., & Kellett, J. A controlled evaluation of systematic desensitization and social skills for socially inadequate psychiatric patients. *Behaviour Research and Therapy*, 1976, *14*, 225–238.

Matson, J. L., & Stephens, R. M. Increasing appropriate behavior of explosive chronic psychiatric patients with a social-skills training package. *Behavior Modfication*, 1978, *2*, 61–76.

McClelland, D. C., & Walt, N. F. Sex role alienation in schizophrenia. *Journal of Abnormal Psychology*, 1968, *12*, 217–220.

McFall, R. M., & Lillesand, D. B. Behavior rehearsal with modeling and coaching in assertion training. *Journal of Abnormal Psychology*, 1971, *77*, 313–323.

McFall, R. M., & Marston, A. An experimental investigation of behavioral rehearsal in assertive training. *Journal of Abnormal Psychology*, 1970, *76*, 295–303.

McFall, R. M., & Twentyman, C. T. Four experiments on the relative contributions of rehearsal, modeling, and coaching to assertion training. *Journal of Abnormal Psychology*, 1973, *81*, 199–218.

McGovern, K. B., Arkowitz, H., & Gilmore, S. K. Evaluation of social skills training programs for college dating inhibitions. *Journal of Counseling Psychology*, 1975, *22*, 505–512.

McLean, P. D., & Hakstian, A. R. Clinical depression: Comparative efficacy of outpatient treatments. *Journal of Consulting and Clinical Psychology*, 1979, *47*, 818–836.

McLean, P. D., Ogston, K., & Grauer, L. A behavioral approach to the treatment of depression. *Journal of Behavior Therapy and Experimental Psychiatry*, 1973, *4*, 323–330.

Megargee, E. I. Undercontrolled and overcontrolled personality types in extreme antisocial aggression. *Psychological Monographs*, 1966, *80*, (Whole No. 611).

Megargee, E. I. The role of inhibition in the assessment and understanding of violence. In J. E. Singer (Ed.), *The control of aggression and violence: Cognitive and physiological factors*. New York: Academic Press, 1971.

Megargee, E. I. Recent research on overcontrolled and undercontrolled personality patterns among violent offenders. *Social Symposium*, 1973, *9*, 37–50.

Melnick, J. A. A comparison of replication techniques in the modification of minimal dating behavior. *Journal of Abnormal Psychology*, 1973, *81*, 51–59.

Miller, P. M., & Eisler, R. M. Assertive behavior of alcoholics: A descriptive analysis *Behavior Therapy*, 1977, *8*, 146–149.

Miller, P. M., Hersen, M., Eisler, R. M., & Hilsman, G. Effects of social stress on operant drinking of alcoholics and social drinkers. *Behaviour Research and Therapy*, 1974, *12*, 65–72.

Monti, P. M., Fink, E., Norman, W., Curran, J., Hayes, S., & Caldwell, A. Effect of social skills training groups and social skills bibliotherapy with psychiatric patients.

Journal of Consulting and Clinical Psychology, 1979, *47*, 189–191.

Monti, P. M., Curran, J. P., Corriveau, D. P., DeLancey, A. L., & Hagerman, S. M. Effects of social skills training groups and sensitivity training groups with psychiatric patients. *Journal of Consulting and Clinical Psychology*, 1980, *48*, 241–248.

Morganstern, K. P., & Tevein, H. E. Behavioral interviewing: The initial stages of assessment. In M. Hersen & A. S. Bellack (Eds.), *Behavioral assessment: A practical handbook* (2nd ed.). New York: Pergamon Press, 1981.

Morrison, R. L., & Bellack, A. S. The role of social perception in social skill. *Behavior Therapy*, 1981, *12*, 69–79.

Mosher, L. R., & Keith, S. J. Psychosocial treatment: Individual, group, family, and community support approaches. *Schizophrenia Bulletin*, 1980, *6*, 10–41.

Mungas, D. M., & Walters, H. A. Pretesting effects in the evaluation of social skills training. *Journal of Consulting and Clinical Psychology*, 1979, *47*, 216–218.

Nelson, R. O. Methodological issues in assessment via self-monitoring. In J. D. Cone & R. P. Hawkins (Eds.), *Behavioral assessment: New directions in clinical psychology*. New York: Brunner/Mazel, 1977.

Ollendick, T. H., & Hersen, M. Social skills training for juvenile delinquents. *Behaviour Research and Therapy*, 1979, *17*, 547–554.

Patterson, G. R. Interventions for boys with conduct problems.: Multiple settings, treatments and criteria. *Journal of Consulting and Clinical Psychology*, 1974, *42*, 471–481.

Percell, L. P., Berwick, P. T., & Beigel, A. The effects of assertive training on self-concept and anxiety. *Archives of General Psychiatry*, 1974, *31*, 502–504.

Perri, M. G., & Richards, C. S. Assessment of heterosocial skills in male college students: Empirical development of a behavioral role-playing test. *Behavior Modification*, 1979, *3*, 337–354.

Perri, M. G., Richards, C. S., & Goodrich, J. D. The heterosocial adequacy test (HAT): A behavioral role-playing test for the assessment of heterosocial skills in male college students. *JSAS Catalog of Selected Documents in Psychology*, 1978, *8*, 16 (MS. No. 1650).

Rakos, R. F., & Schroeder, H. E. Development and empirical evaluation of a self-administered assertiveness training program. *Journal of Consulting and Clinical Psychology*, 1979, *47*, 991–993.

Rathus, S. A. An experimental investigation of assertive training in a group setting. *Journal of Behavior Therapy and Experimental Psychiatry*, 1972, *3*, 81–86.

Rathus, S. A. Instigation of assertive behavior through videotape-mediated assertive models and directed practice. *Behaviour Research and Therapy*, 1973, *11*, 57–65. (a)

Rathus, S. A. A 30-item schedule for assessing assertive behavior. *Behavior Therapy*, 1973, *4*, 398–406. (b)

Rehm, L. P., & Kornblith, S. J. Behavior therapy for depression: A review of recent developments. In M. Hersen, R. M. Eisler, & P. M. Miller (Eds.), *Progress in behavior modification*, Vol. 7. New York: Academic Press, 1979.

Rehm, L. P., & Marston, A. R. Reduction of social anxiety through modification of self-reinforcement: An instigation therapy technique. *Journal of Consulting and Clinical Psychology*, 1968, *32*, 565–574.

Rimm, D. C., Hill, G. A., Brown, N. N., & Stuart, J. E. Group-assertive training in treatment of expression of inappropriate anger. *Psychological Reports,* 1974, *34,* 791–798.

Rimm, D. C., Snyder, J. J., Depue, R. A., Haanstad, M. J., & Armstrong, D. P. Assertive training versus rehearsal and the importance of making an assertive response. *Behaviour Research and Therapy,* 1976, *14,* 315–322.

Roff, J. D., & Knight, R. Young adult schizophrenics: Prediction of outcome and antecedent childhood factors. *Journal of Consulting and Clinical Psychology,* 1978, *46,* 947–952.

Romano, J. M., & Bellack, A. S. Social validation of a component model of assertive behavior. *Journal of Consulting and Clinical Psychology,* 1980, *48,* 478–490.

Rosenbaum, A., & O'Leary, K. D. Marital violence: Characteristics of abusive couples. *Journal of Consulting and Clinical Psychology,* 1981, *49,* 63–71.

Royce, W. S., & Arkowitz, H. *Multi-model evaluation of in vivo practice as treatment for social isolation.* Unpublished manuscript, University of Arizona, 1976.

Royce, W. S., & Weiss, R. L. Behavioral cues in the judgment of marital satisfaction: A linear regression analysis. *Journal of Consulting and Clinical Psychology,* 1975, *43,* 816–824.

Sanchez, V., & Lewinsohn, P. M. Assertive behavior and depression. *Journal of Consulting and Clinical Psychology,* 1980, *48,* 119–120.

Sherman, H., & Farina, A. Social adequacy of parents and children. *Journal of Abnormal Psychology,* 1974, *83,* 327–330.

Sobell, M. B., & Sobell, L. C. Individualized behavior therapy for alcoholics. *Behavior Therapy,* 1973, *4,* 49–72.

Toch, H. *Violent men.* Chicago: Aldine, 1969.

Trower, P., Bryant, B., & Argyle, M. *Social skills and mental health.* Pittsburgh: University of Pittsburgh Press, 1978.

Turner, S. M., Hersen, M., & Bellack, A. S. Social skills training to teach prosocial behavior in an organically impaired and retarded ambulatory patient. *Journal of Behavior Therapy and Experimental Psychiatry,* 1978, *9,* 253–258.

Twentyman, C. T., & McFall, R. M. Behavioral training of social skills in shy males. *Journal of Consulting and Clinical Psychology,* 1975, *43,* 384–395.

Twentyman, C. T., Boland, T., & McFall, R. M. *Five studies exploring the problem of heterosocial avoidance in college males.* Unpublished manuscript, 1978.

Van Hasselt, V. B., Hersen, M., & Milliones, J. Social skills training in alcoholics and drug addicts: A review. *Addictive Behaviors,* 1978, *3,* 221–233.

Van Hasselt, V. B., Hersen, M., Whitehill, M., & Bellack, A. S. Assessment and modification of social skills in children. *Behaviour Research and Therapy,* 1979, *17,* 413–438.

Vaughn, C. E., & Leff, J. P. The influence of family and social factors on the course of psychiatric illness: A comparison of schizophrenic and depressed neurotic patients. *British Journal of Psychiatry,* 1976, *129,* 125–137.

Wallace, C. J. *The assessment of interpersonal problem-solving skills with chronic schizophrenics.* Paper presented at the Annual Meeting of the American Psychological Association, New York, September 1978.

Wallace, C. J., Nelson, C., Lukoff, D., Webster, C., Rappe, S., & Ferris, C. *Cognitive skills training.* Paper presented at the Annual Meeting of the Association for Advancement of Behavior Therapy, Chicago, November 1978.

Weiss, R. L. Operant conditioning techniques in psychological assessment. In P. McReynolds (Ed.), *Advances in psychological assessment.* Palo Alto, Calif.: Science & Behavior, 1968.

Weiss, R. L., & Margolin, G. Marital conflict and accord. In A. R. Ciminero, K. S. Calhoun, & H. E. Adams (Eds.), *Handbook for behavioral assessment.* New York: Wiley, 1977.

Wells, K. C., Hersen, M., Bellack, A. S., & Himmelhoch, J. Social skills training in unipolar nonpsychotic depression. *American Journal of Psychiatry,* 1979, *136,* 1331–1332.

Wessberg, H. W., Mariotto, M. J., Conger, A. J., Conger, J. C., & Farrell, A. D. The ecological validity of role plays for assessing heterosocial anxiety and skill of male college students. *Journal of Consulting and Clinical Psychology,* 1979, *47,* 525–535.

Whitehill, M. B., Hersen, M., & Bellack, A. S. Conversation skills training for socially isolated children. *Behaviour Research and Therapy,* 1980, *18,* 217–225.

Williams, M. T., Turner, S. M., Watts, J. G., Bellack, A. S., & Hersen, M. Groups social skills training for chronic psychiatric patients. *European Journal of Behavioural Analysis and Modification,* 1977, *1,* 223–229.

Wolfe, J. L., & Fodor, I. G. A comparison of three approaches to modifying assertive behavior in women: Modeling-plus-behavior rehearsal, modeling-plus behavior rehearsal-plus-rational therapy, and consciousraising. *Behavior Therapy,* 1977, *8,* 567–574.

Wolpe, J. *Psychotherapy by reciprocal inhibition.* Stanford, Calif.: Stanford University Press, 1958.

Wolpe, J., & Lang, P. J. A fear survey schedule for use in behavior therapy. *Behaviour Research and Therapy,* 1964, *2,* 27–30.

Wolpe, J., & Lazarus, A. A. *Behavior therapy techniques.* New York: Pergamon Press, 1966.

Young, E. R., Rimm, D. C., & Kennedy, T. D. An experimental investigation of modeling and verbal reinforcement in the modification of assertive behavior. *Behaviour Research and Therapy,* 1973, *11,* 317–319.

Zeiss, A. M., Lewinsohn, P. M., & Muñoz, R. F. Nonspecific improvement effects in depression using interpersonal skills training, pleasant activity schedules, or cognitive training. *Journal of Consulting and Clinical Psychology,* 1979, *47,* 427–439.

Zigler, E., & Levine, J. Premorbid adjustment and paranoid-nonparanoid status in schizophrenia. *Journal of Abnormal Psychology,* 1973, *82,* 189–199.

Zigler, E., & Phillips, L. Social effectiveness and symptomatic behaviors. *Journal of Abnormal and Social Psychology,* 1960, *61,* 231–238.

Zigler, E., & Phillips, L. Social competence and outcome in psychiatric disorder. *Journal of Abnormal and Social Psychology,* 1961, *63,* 264–271.

Zigler, E., & Phillips, L. Social competence and the process-reactive distinction in psychopathology. *Journal of Abnormal and Social Psychology,* 1962, *65,* 215–222.

Childhood Disorders

Child behavior therapy has emerged as an important area within the field. The area is not merely the extension of behavioral techniques presented in previous chapters. Rather, childhood behavior problems raise their own set of issues. The behaviors to which interventions are applied may vary widely over the course of child development as the child matures, becomes more involved in activities and relationships outside the home, and so on. Also, the techniques themselves may be unique in the sense that parents, teachers, and peers may be involved in administration of treatment.

Behavior modification techniques with children have been applied to a diverse set of behaviors in the home, at school, and in the community, as well as traditional settings where treatment is provided such as outpatient clinics and institutions. The range of behaviors included in such programs has varied widely in the severity of problems they encompass. Many problems treated are those that emerge as part of normal development such as toileting and self-care skills. More frequently, behavioral techniques have been applied to address problem behaviors at home and at school that involve noncompliance, aggressive behavior, and poor academic performance. In addition, techniques have been applied to many serious problems where the child may be institutionalized because of behavioral and/or medical problems.

In the present section, we have selected chapters that represent the diversity of applications and convey the richness of the field. Different behavioral aproaches are illustrated, and evidence attesting to their efficacy is reviewed. The chapters convey how child behavior therapy is conducted and the range of approaches. In Chapter 10, Sulzer-Azaroff and Pollack discuss child behavior problems that emerge in the home. Techniques are reviewed that have been applied to alter fear and anxiety, various "nervous" habits, toileting, noncompliance, social isolation, mutism, and behaviors in the community. The chapter points to the important role that parents and teachers play in altering child behavior. Special topics in this chapter include parent-management training, self-control techniques, and ethical and legal aspects of child treatment.

In Chapter 11, Ruggles and LeBlanc focus on classroom procedures that have helped children at different educational levels. Reinforcement and punishment practices and instructional techniques with demonstrated effectiveness are evaluated. The authors discuss factors that contribute to child classroom behavior including teacher behavior, special features of the physical environment, and peers. Finally, the chapter reviews the impact of behavioral techniques on attentive child behavior and academic performance.

In Chapter 12, Neisworth and Madle examine behavioral techniques applied to the mentally retarded and adolescents. The mentally retarded represent a heterogeneous group that varies widely in age, deficits, and strengths. Neisworth and Madle review treatment approaches for many areas that have received rather extensive attention, including self-care skills, self-stimulatory behaviors, and speech and articulation problems. Applications are also discussed in novel areas such as preparing mentally retarded persons for community living, for jobs, and in developing positive social skills.

In Chapter 13, the final chapter, Doleys and Bruno examine behavioral techniques that are applied to the treatment of medical problems. Behavioral medicine, as the area is often referred, includes the use of behavioral techniques alone or in combination with medical treatments, to alter a wide range of medical problems. The chapter reviews applications in four areas, including asthma, convulsive (seizure) disorder, childhood obesity, and hyperactivity. The chapter covers many techniques including relaxation, systematic desensitization, biofeedback, reinforcement and punishment techniques, and self-instruction training. The chapter conveys the important role of behavioral techniques beyond the traditional areas that have been the focus of many psychological interventions.

Overall, this section points to several directions that go beyond the usual confines of treatment. The chapters convey the important role that behavioral techniques play in prevention, treatment, education, and rehabilitation. The areas extend well beyond the focus of traditional treatment approaches to children.

CHAPTER 10

The Modification of Child Behavior Problems in the Home

Beth Sulzer-Azaroff and Martin J. Pollack

Introduction

The problems created by children's troublesome behavior at home constitute one of the most serious sources of difficulty in our society. Children's problems may lead to dissatisfaction, to distress, or even to violence (Bell, 1979) among family members. Since its inception, the field of behavior modification has addressed children's home-based behavioral problems. Many problem areas have been addressed, from temper tantrums and other noxious social behaviors, to health-related behaviors, social skills, and many others. As the scope of the problems addressed broadens, new and effective treatment methods are being developed and research methodology is becoming more precise.

Over the years, one may begin to note the emergence of trends that characterize the field. There have been a number of specific problem areas that it has heavily emphasized. Other areas have either been overlooked, or perhaps effective treatment strategies have failed to be discovered. In the present chapter, it is our intention to (1) discuss the history of behavior modification with children at home; (2) elaborate on some of the more extensively addressed problem areas; (3) consider some of the trends that have characterized the development of the field and the underexplored areas of investigation; and (4) use a hopefully representative sample of reported findings to illustrate those points. Perhaps the general survey that we present will prompt refinements in methodology or new directions for research on the modification of children's problem behavior in the home.

The Historical Beginnings of Behavior Modification of Child Behavior Problems in the Home

The application of principles of operant and respondent conditioning to modify child behavior problems in the home goes back to the

Beth Sulzer-Azaroff • Department of Psychology, University of Massachusetts, Amherst, Massachusetts 01003. Martin J. Pollack • Department of Psychology, Mansfield Training School, Mansfield Depot, Connecticut 06251.

311

early years of the century. Kazdin (1978) has traced the development of the field from that time, citing early work in the conditioning of emotions (Jones, 1924) and other operant and respondent conditioning research with children. One important illustration is Mowrer's work on a conditioning treatment for enuresis: a pad with a buzzer that awakens the child at the onset of urination (Mowrer & Mowrer, 1938). In 1959, at a time when operant conditioning was beginning to be employed to treat adults (e.g., Ayllon & Michael, 1959), Williams (1959) conducted a now classic study. The parents of a child who exhibited severe temper tantrums at bedtime requested assistance. Noting that the tantrums accorded the child substantial attention, Williams counseled terminating the attention for that behavior. After consistently practicing the procedure, the tantrums did diminish substantially. A "natural reversal phase" was introduced when a concerned relative was a guest at the house. Her attention to the tantrums led to their rapid recovery. The noxious behavior again diminished when that attention was no longer forthcoming.

Perhaps one of the reasons that that particular case received so much notice was that it had several critical properties. First, the treatment approach was based on the operant conditioning principles of reinforcement and extinction. Second, data were recorded. Third, the natural reversal phase provided a source of experimental control, demonstrating that the behavior did appear to "turn on and off" as a function of the consequences.

In the early 1960s, Donald Baer and Sidney Bijou collaborated in developing some conceptual analyses of child development, from the perspective of operant and respondent conditioning (Bijou & Baer, 1961, 1965). Their colleagues and students also implemented various operant conditioning programs with children. Besides several school-based programs (e.g., Birnbrauer, Bijou, Wolf, & Kidder, 1965), a particularly fascinating case was undertaken with an autistic child (Wolf, Risley, & Mees, 1964). Although initially conducted in a hospital, the procedures were eventually transferred to the home. The child exhibited many of the extremely maladaptive behaviors that frequently characterize children who are called autistic: a lack of functional language, high rates of tantrums, failure to follow directions, and other deviant behaviors. Wolf et al. demonstrated that shaping and other operant procedures were amenable to the clinical treatment of these extreme behavior problems.

Among some of the early applications of behavior modification in the home were several studies with children who exhibited either very disturbing or very objectionable behavior (Hawkins, Peterson, Schweid, & Bijou, 1966; Bernal, Duryee, Pruett, & Burns, 1968); isolation and noncompliance (Patterson, McNeal, Hawkins, & Phelps, 1967); and oppositional behavior (Wahler, 1969a). Hawkins et al., (1966) argued for the value of the therapist's observing the child's problem behaviors and the interactions between child and parent in their natural surroundings in order to be able to make meaningful specific suggestions.

In the study conducted by Bernal et al. (1968), home observations and videotapes were used to identify the condition that appeared to maintain the child's problem behaviors. Modifying those conditions led to major reductions in the problems. Bernal continued this line of research, the next year publishing another study on the reduction of "brat" behaviors (Bernal, 1969) and reporting similar reductions in other noxious behaviors.

In the Patterson et al. study (1967), conditions in the home were reprogrammed through written and oral instructions and feedback based on clinic and home observations. This approach resulted in an increase in "warm" responding by a mother to her child and a reduction in the child's isolate behavior. In the study reported by Wahler (1969a), the parents were instructed and observed in the home. A combination of differential attention and time-out led to a reduction in the oppositional behavior of two children.

From those early beginnings, the field began to burgeon exponentially. So extensive is the collection of studies that it is no longer feasible to present a completely exhaustive review of the literature within the confines of a single chapter. We have elected instead to present summaries of a set of specific problem areas and then to discuss some of the critical aspects that characterize studies dealing with child behavior problems in the home.

Specific Problem Areas

The specific problem areas addressed by the field may be categorized in various ways. We have elected to start with individual problems (health, toileting problems, and nervous habits and fears) and then to move on to the more complex, family-related problems (noncompliance, sibling conflicts, and troublesome behavior while shopping). Next, we cover problems that involve the relations between home and school, such as the home-based management of school problems, attendance, and homework, followed by social isolation and elective mutism. Last, we focus on the positive: prosocial behaviors and social and conversational skills.

Health-Related Behavior of Children

The discipline of behavioral medicine has been evolving to such an extent that many medical schools and medical service facilities now incorporate behavior modification approaches within their assessment and therapy programs. Behavior modification methods are particularly relevant to the prevention and the treatment of the somatic disorders of children (Gentry, 1976).

Preventing and Treating. Parallel to its development in other disciplines, the modification of health-related behaviors initially tended to focus on those that were most serious and most resistant to treatment. Such serious conditions as chronic vomiting (Wolf, Birnbrauer, Williams, & Lawler, 1965); anorexia (Bachrach, Erwin, & Mohr, 1965); and excessive scratching to the point of inflicting tissue damage (Allen & Harris, 1966) were among the targets in studies reported initially. Since then, the kinds of behaviors that have been targeted for modification have broadened to include asthma (Neisworth & Moore, 1972); diet and nutrition (Fox & Roseen, 1977; Hebert-Jackson, & Risley, 1977; Tizard, 1977);

self-feeding and consuming nutritious table foods (Bernal, 1972); and other problems of food ingestion besides rumination and anorexia. Now, efforts are being made to treat children's obesity (Epstein, Masek, & Marshall, 1978; Aragona, Cassady, & Drabman, 1975) by working either with the children directly or with their parents.

Motivating compliance with prescribed regimens, such as special diets or the use of inhalation equipment by asthmatics (Renne & Creer, 1976), is another area of focus. Also, behaviors have been modified in order to prevent the development or the worsening of health problems; dental care (Horner & Keilitz, 1975) and cooperation with the dentist (Stokes & Kennedy, 1980); motor skill training (Hardiman, Goetz, Reuter, & LeBlanc, 1975); automobile safety (Christopherson, 1977); exercise such as swimming (McKenzie & Rushall, 1974); bathing a burn victim to prevent further complications (Weinstein, 1977); and foot care by a diabetic child (Lowe & Lutzker, 1979). Pain and complaints of pain are also being more effectively managed among children, as in studies by Miller and Kratochwill (1979) and Sank and Biglan (1974).

As is typical of the field, when behavior modification is applied to children's health behaviors, it tends to emphasize positive reinforcement heavily. Attention is often used as a reinforcer in conjunction with other procedures. It has been presented contingent on the absence of vomiting (Munford, 1979; Wright, Brown, & Andrews, 1978) or of complaints of abdominal pain (Miller & Kratochwill, 1979). Usually paired with praise, tokens or points exchangeable for backup rewards and privileges have been used to reduce scratching (Allen & Harris, 1966); to promote conforming to diet regimens (Fox & Roseen, 1977; Fox et al., 1977; Aragona et al., 1975); to reduce complaints of abdominal pain (Sank & Biglan, 1974); to reduce anorexia (Garfinkel, Kline, & Stancer, 1973); to improve nutrition (Epstein et al., 1978); and to promote dental cooperation (Stokes & Kennedy, 1980). Sometimes the backup reinforcers are contrived, selected solely for their powerful reinforcing quality, particularly when optimal compliance is of critical importance, while often reinforcers intrinsic to the situation are selected (e.g., Stokes & Kennedy, 1980).

Elements of stimulus control are incorporated within many of the procedures applied to modify children's health behaviors, as reinforcement is presented contingent on the response's occurring when paired with given antecedent stimuli. Rules and instructions are usually provided for nutritional and dieting regimens, as in the Aragona *et al.* (1975) study, in which parents were trained to treat their overweight children, and in that of Epstein *et al.* (1978), in which children were given reinforcement for selecting nutritious, low-calorie foods from among several offered. Often, too, complex tasks are analyzed for their subskills, and these are communicated to children, parents and/or care givers. For instance, Horner and Keilitz (1975) analyzed the task of tooth brushing, and Renne and Creer (1976) broke down the task of using inhalation therapy equipment into three specific subskills. Modeled prompts were provided by Stokes and Kennedy (1980), as they permitted clients to observe others behaving cooperatively in the dental situation. In many instances, the initial attempts to perform skills are fully guided or prompted. These prompts are then slowly faded. An illustration is Renne and Creer's (1976) manipulation of the patient's abdomen to guide the diaphragmatic breathing response. A program that effectively applied a complex combination of behavior procedures, feedback plus systematic desensitization or feedback plus cognitive restructuring, was conducted by Ollendick (1979) with a 16-year-old anorexic boy.

Issues. The moral and ethical justification of using negative reductive procedures, such as punishment, response cost, and time-out, is relatively less problematic when children's health is involved than it may be with less serious problems. Chronic rumination behavior is life-threatening, and the application of aversive stimuli contingent on the behavior or its precursors should meet with little opposition when less severe alternatives have a poor prospect of success. Among the noxious stimuli that have been applied in such cases have been electric shock (Lang & Melamed, 1969; Linscheid & Cunningham, 1977) and lemon juice (Becker, Turner & Sajwaj, 1978; Apolito

& Sulzer-Azaroff, 1981). Another form of punishment was used to interrupt the chain of behaviors that terminated in epileptic seizures (Zlutnick, Mayville, & Moffat, 1975). This consisted of a sharp "no" and grasping and shaking the child by the shoulder, contingent on the emission of the initiation of the chain. Response-cost in the form of loss of cash on deposit has been used to maintain parents' involvement in and implementation of weight reduction programs with their children (Aragona *et al.*, 1975), and time-out was used to reduce unwarranted complaints of pain (Miller & Kratochwill, 1979; Sank & Biglan, 1974). In most cases in which negative contingencies are arranged, either the program also provides for reinforcement of alternative behaviors, or reinforcement is intrinsic to improvement. Assuming they no longer earn reinforcement in the form of extensive attention, improvement in such distressing behaviors as seizures and vomiting is probably its own reward.

Other factors are particularly relevant to behavior modification and children's health. Often, initial interventions take place outside the home, which may limit transfer into the home (Wahler, 1969a). If anorexia is modified in the hospital (as in the program conducted by Garfinkel, Kline, & Stancer, 1973), it may reappear at home unless the procedures are transferred to that setting. One attempt to overcome that problem was described in a case by Azerrad and Stafford (1969), in which they trained the parents to implement their procedures. Recognizing the potential limitations of intervening outside the natural environment, Lowe and Lutzker (1979) left their offices to train their diabetic patient in her home, where she was expected to maintain the regimen. Their 10-week follow-up assessment supported the justifiability of that procedure.

Another problem is methodological. Often, problems are brought to the attention of the behavior modifier after they have become serious. Such methodological niceties as extended baselines, elaborate measures with demonstrated reliability, and within- or across-subject replications are luxuries that may not always prove feasible. Fortunately, some of these difficulties are not as serious as they might seem, since the medical field has developed many reliable and sophisticated instruments. Electromyograms, refined chemical analyses, and other methods have been utilized to assess changes in patients' behavior. For example, one of the measures used by Lowe and Lutzker (1979) to monitor their patient's compliance with her diet was the results of laboratory tests. When dependent measures are collected by objective, uninformed, analytically skilled technicians, potential confounds such as expectancy, bias, or observer drift are reasonably controlled in contrast to the direct collection of behavioral data by live observers.

As hospital costs rise and the trend continues toward maintaining children in the least restrictive environment possible, it is probable that the management of children's health behaviors will be based in the home more frequently. Improving technologies for training parents, as well as developing methods for promoting compliance and improvements in the precision of home-based data collection techniques, should permit increasingly effective methods for modifying children's health behaviors. It is probably not too farfetched to anticipate that medical-service-delivery organizations will increasingly seek the assistance of behavior modifiers to participate in the cooperative design, implementation, and evaluation of home-based programs for modifying children's health behaviors.

Toileting Problems

Soiling and wetting during the day or at night while asleep is a source of difficulty for children beyond the age of about 3 years and for their parents. Besides necessitating extra laundering chores, they cause embarrassment and may lead to social alienation. The behavioral treatment of these problems has a relatively long history, dating back to the invention of the bell-and-pad apparatus (Mowrer & Mowrer, 1938). Following a classical conditioning paradigm, a pad was devised that would set off an alarm bell (or buzzer) when urine came in contact with the pad. According to studies by Lovibond (1964) and Doleys (1977), the success rate has been found to range from 75% to 90%. Sacks and De Leon (1978) used the bell-and-pad method to successfully treat several emotionally disturbed children, although

the more severely disturbed children took longer to achieve a stable remission. Success with the apparatus has apparently been sufficient to establish the system as a standard method for treating nocturnal enuresis.

While the bell-and-pad system did make a major inroad toward the solution of bed wetting, problems remained. In addition to seeking further improvements in the treatment of nighttime enuresis, daytime enuresis and day and nighttime soiling required treatment. Also, a relapse rate of 40% (Lovibond, 1964; Doleys, 1977) suggested the need for methods that would produce more durable effects. Procedural and methodological questions also needed to be addressed: What components of the treatment procedures are critical for success? Who should conduct the interventions and how should those people be trained? Are outcome reports reliable? How can the reliability of reporting be improved? These are some of the questions that have been addressed by behavioral researchers within the recent past.

Procedures used to reduce incontinence have ranged from simple reinforcement for the successful use of the toilet or negative consequences for "accidents," to full cleanliness training. Among the reinforcers delivered contingent on successful toileting have been tokens exchangeable for weekend outings (Ayllon, Simon, & Wildman, 1975); money (Bach & Moylan, 1975), food and trinkets (Doley & Wells, 1975); and praise (Azrin, Sneed, & Foxx, 1974). Among the negative consequences that have been presented as a function of "accidents" have been overcorrection and positive practice (Crowley & Armstrong, 1977); full cleanliness training (Azrin et al., 1974; Doleys, McWhorter, Williams, & Gentry, 1977); and parental disapproval (Azrin et al., 1974; Doleys, McWhorter et al., 1977). In one study (Tough, Hawkins, McArthur & Ravensway, 1971), a brief cold bath was given as a consequence of a toileting accident. Other procedures have been tested recently. In a study by Azrin, Hontos, and Besalel-Azrin (1979), awareness training was used to heighten sensitivity to bladder sensations as one component of a program to eliminate enuresis. Discrimination training to establish stimulus control was successfully employed by using glycerine suppositories to stimulate bowel movements at times when parental supervision was possible (Ashkenazi, 1975). Behavioral rehearsal was found to be a helpful adjunct to a training program designed to teach parents and children to follow a prescribed set of procedures (Crowley & Armstrong, 1977). Several studies have included retention or bladder control training as an element of the program. Azrin *et al.* (1974) required positive practice and fluid intake before sleep and after periodic awakenings, in order to maximize the opportunities to practice appropriate urination. Once awake, the children were urged to retain urine for at least a few minutes, or until the next hourly awakening if possible, and were praised contingent on success. Doleys and Wells (1975) used a similar approach with a 42-month-old girl who received rewards for retaining her urine for gradually increasing intervals. Doleys, McWhorter *et al.* (1977) also supplemented their procedure with retention control training. In a more extensive application of retention control training, Harris and Purohit (1977) taught 18 children over five days, for 3 hr per day, to increase the duration of their retention intervals. Reinforcement was provided contingent on progressively longer intervals between drinking and urination and for releasing increasing volumes of urine at one time. The program was subsequently shifted to the home for maintenance by the parents.

Frequently, a variety of procedures are combined within a comprehensive package. The "dry-bed program" of Azrin *et al.* (1974), which has served as a model for many subsequent studies, has demonstrated its success repeatedly. Included in the package were: differential positive reinforcement, positive practice, cleanliness training, scheduled nighttime checks and awakenings, retention control training, and a urine alarm. The program maximized early success by using a trained therapist in the home for the first day of intensive training. Subsequent training was administered by the parents, who gradually faded out the urine alarm and the nightly awakenings as success was demonstrated. The program rapidly reduced rates of wetting for all children from a baseline median of seven per week to one per week during each of the first two weeks. Wettings were eliminated completely by the fourth week. The 14-dry-night criterion was reached with an average of only two accidents per child. The maintenance of these effects was demonstrated over a six-month period in which no relapses occurred. These results compared favorably with the exclusive use of a standard urine-alarm procedure, which served as a control. In the latter group, only 2 of 13 children attained similar success. The Azrin *et al.* (1974) results have been replicated by Doleys, Ciminero, Tollison, Williams, and Wells (1977), and while the degree of effectiveness was less striking than that achieved by Azrin *et al.* (1974), the mean number of wetting accidents was reduced considerably.

The dry-bed procedure has been modified by Bollard and Woodroffe (1977). Parents, rather than trained therapists, conducted the program, and for one group, the alarm apparatus was not used. In a comparison of three groups, the authors found that the parents functioned effectively as trainers and achieved a reduction in wetting accidents from a baseline of seven per week to zero in 3 weeks, with the exception of a single child, for whom 13 weeks were required. Two children relapsed, but their rate of accidents did not return to the high baseline level, and both were retrained. The group not using the apparatus achieved only a partial reduction in the rate of accidental wetting, changing from a baseline average of seven to an average of three over a 6-week period. No children achieved a perfect record. The study showed that parents could function as effective trainers, perhaps because of their ability to respond quickly and consistently, particularly when cued by the activation of the alarm.

Daytime enuresis has been successfully treated through incentives for appropriate urination (e.g., money in a study by Bach and Moylan, 1975). Incentives may and can be aided by combining them with other procedures: regular pants checks that permit frequent reinforcement for dryness, and cleanliness training or overcorrection for accidents. Azrin and Foxx (1974) have developed an intensive multicomponent program leading to successful toilet training in a single day. Although these procedures include the use of a therapist in the home for the day, they lend themselves quite well to use by parents alone.

A study by Butler (1976) showed that presenting the Azrin and Foxx materials in three brief lectures was sufficient to enable parents to implement the procedures with a success comparable to that achieved with the therapists.

Studies have begun to investigate the function of various components of procedural packages. Azrin and Thienes (1978) compared results with a buzzer-and-pad alarm to those of the dry-bed procedure. The rates of accidental wetting dropped from an average of 90% during baseline to 76% for the group using the alarm alone, compared with 15% for the group that was given the dry-bed training program without the alarm. The superior results were replicated when the buzzer-and-pad control group was then provided the dry-bed program. Comparing the results of this dry-bed program with earlier results (Azrin *et al.*, 1974), the authors concluded that the original dry-bed procedure, which included the alarm, was probably preferable, since the rates of reduction had been superior and had been achieved more quickly.

Another study (Catalina, 1976) compared success rates as a function of the people to whom the buzzer signal was directed: child only, parent only, both, or neither. (In the latter case, bed checks by the parents were scheduled.) The best results, a 90% reduction, were achieved with the two groups involving the parents. There was a 70% reduction when only the children were signaled, but just a 40% reduction for those not receiving any signal. Not only does this study underscore the importance of the alarm component in treating nocturnal enuresis, but it substantiates the findings of Azrin *et al.* (1974) in rejecting a classical conditioning explanation of the mechanism by which the alarm achieves its effectiveness. It seems more likely that an operant conditioning explanation is appropriate, the sound or being awakened by the parent functioning as an aversive consequence to beginning to urinate in bed, and also signaling that a continuation of the behavior is apt to result in negative consequences.

Does there have to be a one-to-one correspondence between wetting episodes and the sounding of the alarm? This question was addressed in a study by Finley, Wansley, and Blenkarn (1977). Rather than sounding every time, the buzzer was scheduled to sound 70% of the time. Under those conditions, 75 of 80 children achieved success within 14 nights. The one-year relapse rate was found to be 25%.

The degree of precision with which training strategies have been described in the literature has varied considerably. Additionally, it is often difficult to ascertain, from reading reports in this area, to what degree the instructions have been carried out. When such information is missing, the influence of the level of adherence to the program on the degree of success becomes an open question. Crowley and Armstrong (1977) conducted a study on three children with a lengthy history of encopresis. The report described the training methodology in precise detail. Additionally, weekly office visits by the clients and regular telephone contact served as a means of supplying additional information about the level of adherence and the results. Similarly, Azrin *et al.* (1979) have also used regular telephone contact in their attempt to attain more reliable data. These studies illustrate the kinds of efforts that are being made to overcome some of the deficiencies in reporting methods and outcomes within this problem area.

Many reports on this topic have consisted of case studies of the baseline (A)–treatment (B) variety. Unless the methodology is directly replicated across subjects, in a multiple-baseline fashion, the generality of findings must be questioned. Recently, however, instances of full experimental comparisons (e.g., Azrin & Thienes, 1978) are appearing more frequently in the literature. With such improvements in design strategies, confidence in the reliability of findings should continue to increase.

Also frequently absent from published reports on toilet training are data on convenience, preference, and other measures of consumer satisfaction. Such data would permit an assessment of the potential utilization of any given procedure. Preference for the dry-bed program was measured behaviorally in the Azrin and Thienes (1978) study by offering the parents of the children in the control group the option of having their children shift into the other group. The fact that 23 of the 29 subjects exercised the option served as evidence that the treatment was preferred. Verbal expressions of satisfaction with the dry-bed method provided additional supportive evidence.

The potential utilization rate may also depend on the side effects of a given course of treatment. Some studies have cited intitial resistance and aggression in response to the application of negative contingencies, such as cleanliness training and positive practice (Butler, 1976; Doleys, McWhorter, Williams, & Gentry, 1977) and to cold baths (Tough *et al.*, 1971). Other factors affecting the acceptability of a given method by consumers are frequently provided in reports: the number of days necessary to reach criterion; the amount of time required for training; the locus of training (at home or in the office); the necessity of professional or paraprofessional assistance; the costs of the services and the apparatus; and others.

In summary, although there are some areas of investigation remaining in this problem area, it is apparent that some very dramatic strides have been made. In a large number of instances, children with a variety of repertoires have been successfully taught appropriate toileting habits through the application of behaviorally based methods.

Nervous Habits and Fears

At various times, everyone engages in repetitive physical behaviors that have no discernible function: twiddling thumbs, pushing back hair, biting cuticles, and so on. It is only when those behaviors occur at a very high rate or so intensively that they are judged to be damaging or disfiguring or to impair personal or social functioning that they deserve to be identified as problem "nervous habits." Behavior modification approaches have been used to treat children for a variety of such habits: thumb sucking, tics, hair pulling or twirling, nail biting, stuttering, and others.

Children are also often fearful on appropriate occasions: when threatened or when coming in contact with objects or events that have, in their past experience, proved aversive. As with nervous habits, however, it is only when a fear is so severe that it interferes with normal functioning that it deserves to be called a problem. This may happen when a child reacts inordinately fearfully in a mildly threatening sit-

uation, such as attending school for the first time, or when the fear has no ground in reality. An example is a case reported by Waye (1979), in which a child was convinced that parts of her body were shrinking. Here we summarize some of the procedures that have been used to treat nervous habits and fears along with some special characteristics of those methods, and we discuss some of the issues that pertain specifically to this topic.

Treating Nervous Habits. Many standard behavior modification procedures have been used to treat children's nervous habits. These are generally combined into packages. Positive reinforcement, in the form of storytelling, token delivery, or simply attention contingent on intervals during which the behavior has been omitted, is one method that is frequently applied (Allen & Harris, 1966; Knight & McKenzie, 1974). Children have been given pennies (Lowitz & Suib, 1978) or food as reinforcers following intervals during which thumb sucking (Hughes, Hughes, & Dial, 1979) and scratching (Allen & Harris, 1966) were absent. Attention is systematically eliminated when it has been judged to have contributed to the maintenance of the nervous habit. This approach has been used to treat insomnia (Anderson, 1979) and multiple tics (Schulman, 1974). Another procedure has been labeled *vicarious learning*. The client observes as another child receives reinforcement for alternative acceptable behaviors. For example, Sanchez (1979) reported the case of a child who pulled her hair habitually. It was arranged that the mother would pay attention to a sibling's proper hair care, in the presence of the client.

Time-out is another procedure that has been used to reduce various nervous habits. Loss of free play time contingent on a tic response (Varni, Boyd, & Cataldo, 1978), loss of TV time for thumb sucking (Ross, 1975), and restriction to the child's room for hair pulling (Sanchez, 1979) are among the time-out procedures that have been successfully applied. Ross (1975) used access to TV as a contingency in a program that involved two sisters in an attempt to reduce their brother's thumb sucking. When the child was observed sucking his thumb, the TV was turned off for a period of time, thus both the child and his siblings were denied access to the TV. The siblings were also taught how to cue non-thumb-sucking.

Awareness training is a procedure that is reported to be an especially useful adjunct to modification programs designed to treat nervous habits (Azrin & Nunn, 1973). Awareness training consists of teaching clients to note when they are engaging in the habit. Various techniques have been used to teach clients to become more aware of their habitual responses: using a mirror to observe tic responses (Varni *et al.*, 1978); recording nail-biting and stuttering episodes (Azrin & Nunn, 1974, 1976); the therapist's demonstrating the behavior, such as barking and swearing by a child with Gilles de la Tourette's syndrome, and feedback to and rehearsal by the client (Hutzell, Platzek, & Logue, 1974). Lassen and Fluet (1978) reported using a glove during sleep to control thumb sucking. This probably assisted the child to be more aware of placing the thumb in her mouth. Vaseline was applied to a client's eyelids to draw attention to the fact that she was touching her lashes, and jangly bracelets and perfumed fingers cued awareness for arm and finger movements (McLaughlin & Nay, 1975). Naturally, the reduction in the rate of the response and increases in desirable alternatives must also be reinforced if the effect is to endure.

Relaxation training is another procedural component of many programs designed to treat nervous habits. The Azrin and Nunn habit-reversal program (1974, 1976) follows awareness training with training in relaxation. Sleep disturbances, such as insomnia (Anderson, 1979), have also been treated with relaxation training. In the latter study, although training was conducted in the therapist's office, the client was able to transfer its application to the home. Relaxation training may be facilitated by the use of audiotapes (Weil & Goldfried, 1973). The tape prompts may then be gradually faded by using a progression of shorter, more simplified tapes, eventually withdrawing them completely. Relaxation training was combined with covert reinforcement and response-cost procedures in treating a client's hair pulling in a study reported by McLaughlin and Nay (1975). For covert reinforcement, the client was instructed to fol-

low successful efforts to avoid hair pulling by imagining the desirable outcomes that accompany having a full head of hair. For the response-cost, the client was instructed to interrupt her ongoing activities, inspect her scalp in the bathroom mirror, and log the behavior in detail.

Relaxation is also an integral part of the systematic desensitization procedure (Wolpe, 1974). In this procedure, the client learns to relax in the presence of a hierarchy of successively more anxiety-producing situations. In one report (Bornstein & Rychtarik, 1978), systematic desensitization was used to treat hair pulling. The hierarchy consisted of an arrangement of anxiety-producing situations associated with the habit.

Programs designed to reduce nervous habits may involve training the client directly in the clinic, as in the 2-hr intensive session used by Azrin and Nunn (1973, 1974), or the parents may be instructed to carry out specific procedures or may be trained to conduct a program either in the laboratory (Lowitz & Suib, 1978) or at home (Knight & McKenzie, 1974). Successful transfer may thus become an issue, as treatment shifts from the therapist to the patient or to the parents, or from one setting and time to another. The impressive results reported by Azrin and Nunn (e.g., 1974) and others are probably a function of directly training the client in a set of habit reversal skills that could readily be transferred outside the clinic. Alternatively, training parents directly in the home with provision for reliability of measurement as in Hughes *et al.* (1979) is another promising approach.

Issues. There are several methodological issues that are especially pertinent to the modification of nervous habits. One is that most of the reported studies have been conducted with only one subject. (Exceptions have included those of Azrin and Nunn; 1974, 1976, and Knight and McKenzie, 1974. In these studies, multiple replications added support to an otherwise limited A-B design.) Also, since many of the programs involve procedures to be implemented at home, assessing for reliability becomes difficult. In that regard, it is perhaps fortunate that many nervous habits leave their own records. For example, hair pulling may leave bald spots; thumb sucking, raw skin, and the results of nail biting are apparent. In fact, before-and-after photographs are used to validate procedural effectiveness in the Azrin and Nunn studies of nail biting. Such enduring outcomes may thus mitigate the problem of validity and reliability of recording.

Many of the procedures designed to treat nervous habits include features that must be managed by clients, such as self-recording, relaxation, and covert procedures. Therefore, the success of those programs often depends on the client's ability and willingness to follow instructions. The client's learning history in regard to self-management may thus prove very critical for success. Fortunately, motivation to follow through presents less of a hindrance in this as opposed to other problem areas, because the habit is often a source of embarrassment or stress to the client. Even young children have successfully followed through with monitoring and other self-control procedures (Azrin & Nunn, 1974; Varni et al., 1978; Weil & Goldfried, 1973). But the very fact that self-management operations are often a major feature of programs for treating nervous habits also creates some confusion. It is difficult to identify exactly which features are functionally related to the change. For example, self-recording probably serves several functions: besides providing data on progress, it may heighten awareness and serve as a source of positive or negative feedback. These factors, in turn, may affect covert behaviors, which unless orally reported, remain obscure and inaccessible to functional analysis.

Treating Fears. Aside from school phobia, discussed below, childhood fears have been given relatively scant attention by researchers employing behavioral approaches. In a recent review of the literature, Graziano, DeGiovanni, and Garcia (1979) pointed out that research on childhood fears has almost exclusively involved mild to moderate fears as opposed to severe fears in which a significant disruption of daily routines is evident. In those studies in which fear reduction is the objective, three treatment approaches predominate: modeling (e.g., Bandura & Menlove, 1968), systematic desensitization plus contingency management packages (e.g., Mann, 1972), and cognitive or verbal-mediation approaches (e.g., Kanfer, Karoly, & Newman, 1975). In addition to being confined largely to fears that are not

debilitating, Graziano and his colleagues pointed out that the range of fears treated has been narrow. The bulk of the controlled studies, they found, have consisted of problems in medical and dental fears ($n = 9$), animal fears ($n = 7$), social interaction fears ($n = 5$), and fear of the dark ($n = 3$).

Of the major treatment approaches, modeling has provided by far the most extensive and consistently effective procedural option. The basic modeling paradigm consists of observation by the subject of a model approaching the feared stimuli, followed by attempts by the subject to approach the feared stimuli. Beneficial outcomes have been demonstrated by using live models (Bandura, Grusec, & Menlove, 1967) or symbolic models (e.g., via videotapes in Bandura & Menlove, 1968); by using single (Ritter, 1968) or multiple models (Bandura & Menlove, 1968); and by using modeling exclusively or in combination with a gradual active involvement with the models and the feared stimuli (Lewis, 1974; Murphy & Bootzin, 1973). Models have approached a single feared stimulus (Kornhaber & Schroeder, 1975) and multiple feared stimuli (Bandura & Menlove, 1968) introduced in a graduated sequence. Some evidence suggests that the similarity between the model and the subject may enhance fear reduction (Kornhaber & Schroeder, 1975). To be effective, symbolic modeling may require multiple trials, multiple models, and varied fear stimuli (see Bandura & Menlove, 1968), but symbolic modeling has important implications for prevention as well as treatment. Melamed and Siegel (1975) and Melamed, Yurchison, Fleece, Hutcherson, and Hawes (1978) used film models to reduce anxiety among children scheduled for surgical and dental procedures. Interestingly, it has been observed that models who themselves initially show fear when approaching the feared stimulus are more effective than models who exhibit no fear (see Meichenbaum, 1971; Rachman, 1972). Modeling has only infrequently been used to treat fears involving social stimuli. In one such study (O'Connor, 1969), nursery-school children exposed to social models successfully overcame their social withdrawal.

While Graziano et al., (1979) suggested that desensitization and contingency management approaches have yet to demonstrate their effectiveness, there is some evidence that these approaches hold promise. In one study, a 4-year-old child had a fear of water. The treatment included *in vivo* modeling of the desensitization hierarchy by a paraprofessional and, later, the parent. As the child began to imitate, physical affection, praise, and edibles were provided contingently as he progressed through a 12-step hierarchy (Pomerantz, Peterson, Marholin, & Stern, 1977). The child reached the final step in the hierarchy by the eighth day of treatment.

In another study employing contingency management, Waye (1979) treated a child with a fear that her thumbs were shrinking by arranging for her parents to attend to her when she played appropriately. A cardboard tracing of the thumb was also presented in response to complaints of shrinking, to provide a realistic form of visual feedback and to dispel the fearful response.

Cognitive approaches are the least commonly reported in the treatment of children's fears. Recently, Graziano, Mooney, Huber, and Ignasiak (1979) described a verbal mediation technique combined with relaxation, self-monitoring, and the delivery of exchangeable tokens for "bravery." Children with severe fears of the dark were taught exercises in which they used self-directed statements of competence and courage. With some parental assistance in structuring times for the exercises, the children were able to reduce the frequency and the intensity of their fearful responses.

In summary, a variety of children's fears and nervous habits have been effectively modified. Treatment may be conducted directly by therapists, or the parents or the children themselves may, with therapeutic supervision, implement the package of procedures. Methodological problems include insufficient replications, the need for more reliable and valid measures, and the difficulty of separating the critical components of the program.

Noncompliance

Noncompliance is one of the behavior problems that parents cite most frequently (e.g., Karoly & Rosenthal, 1977; Patterson & Reid, 1973; Forehand, 1977). The child's response may consist of simply not performing the re-

quested behavior, doing it too slowly, stating a refusal to comply, promising to do it later but not following through on the commitment, engaging in a competing response, and others. Children might respond differentially to parental requests as a function of the way in which the request is given. For instance, a request posed in a tentative tone may occasion quite a different response than one stated firmly and decisively. Sometimes parents alter their requests, communicating conflicting messages, and the child is confused about which to follow. Parents may ask the impossible of their children at times. For instance, the child may not be capable of doing what is asked. There are apparently other conditions that evoke noncompliance as well.

Treatment Procedures. A consideration of the conditions that may control noncompliance is important if treatment strategies are to be planned. Suppose the requested behavior is part of the child's repertoire. Then, a modification of the consequences, such as reinforcing compliance and/or punishing noncompliance, or placing it on extinction, may be the most appropriate procedure. In a study by Schutte and Hopkins (1970), when the child followed instructions, attention by the teacher led to a major increase in instruction following. In a case reported by Fjellstedt and Sulzer-Azaroff (1973), the subject had been placed in a special class for emotionally disturbed children. Systematically decreasing latencies—the interval between the instructions and the response—led to a reinforcement with tokens. Improvement was sufficient to permit the child to return to a regular class. A case study reported by Wiltz and Gordon (1974) described a particularly difficult problem. A 9-year-old child was facing institutionalization for his extremely disturbing and often bizarre behaviors, among which was a very low rate of complying with parental instructions. Using an experimental residential apartment as the training site, the parents were successfully taught to combine points exchangeable for toys for compliance, and time-out for noncompliance or other inappropriate behaviors. A similar case reported by Ayllon, Garber, and Allison (1977) yielded comparable outcomes.

In some cases, low compliance rates are a function of particular antecedent conditions, such as the way in which the request is delivered. Then, the treatment of choice would be a modification in the manner of making the request. Many parent-training programs include portions that involve methods of effectively delivering instructions to children (e.g., Patterson, Cobb, & Ray, 1973). In one study (Peed, Roberts, & Forehand, 1977), positive treatment effects were observed in the home when the parents were instructed to give clear commands. They were also asked to avoid interrupting the children and to resist the temptation to carry out the requests themselves. In a study of four children who failed to reduce their oppositional behavior under a social-play-contracting contingency, Wahler and Fox (1980) altered the contract to a solitary-play-plus-time-out contingency, with dramatic improvement.

Forehand (1977) has extensively surveyed a series of outcome studies of behavioral treatments of noncompliance. The survey analyzed the results of studies conducted and assessed in the clinic, studies conducted in the clinic and assessed in both the clinic and the home, and those conducted and measured in the home. Studies in the laboratory have permitted the identification of some variables that control noncompliance. Among these are the consequences of responding, such as reinforcement for compliance or time-out for noncompliance (e.g., Forehand & King, 1974). But the generality of conclusions may be limited when findings have been isolated within the laboratory only. In contrast, in-home observations do permit an assessment of the transfer of treatment effects to the natural setting. Mixed results have been found when parents are trained in the clinic and assessment takes place in the home. Sometimes, as in Peed *et al.* (1977) and Reisinger and Ora (1977), generality into the home is demonstrated. In the latter case, parents were taught in a clinic setting to attend to their toddler's cooperative behavior and to withhold their attention when the child failed to follow instructions. The measures of change in the clinic resembled changes measured via live and taped observations. At other times, observations in the home show inconsistent transfer. An example is the study by Bizer, Sulzer-Azaroff, and Fredrickson (1978). Four pairs of children and their parents were taught to problem-solve by using Blechman's (1974) family contract game. Noncompliance was one of the behaviors addressed. In some instances, measures from home observations closely matched those found in the laboratory. In others, there was no apparent match between laboratory and home problem-solving.

According to Forehand (1977), "Comparing across treatment and assessment settings, one would conclude that decreases in noncompliance in the home can best be affected by training parents in the home" (p. 141). His conclusion is supported by a set of research studies conducted by Wahler (1969b, 1975) and others. Patterson's (1976) research also supports that conclusion. Such studies have shown that when parents were trained in the home to modify their child's noncompliance, the changes tended to endure in that setting.

As in other problem areas, research on noncompliance has begun assessing collateral effects. In addition to examining transfer from the clinic to the home, several studies have examined the generality of effects from the training setting to the school or the application by parents across siblings. Wahler (1975) measured a child's noncompliance at home and in school. While the rate of noncompliance was reduced at home, a similar reduction did not take place in the school. In fact, at school, where it was not directly treated, it increased. An earlier study by Wahler (1969b) had shown that introducing treatment with the teacher subsequent to a home intervention did result in reducing noncompliance at school. Several experiments directly assessed the question of whether treatment would transfer from the treated to the untreated sibling (Arnold, Levine, & Patterson, 1975; Lavigueur, Peterson, Sheese, & Peterson, 1973; Humphreys, Forehand, McMahon, & Roberts, 1978). For example, Humphreys *et al.* (1978) arranged to have target children treated in the clinic, and both the parents' and the untreated siblings' behaviors were observed in the home. They found that the parents did transfer their newly acquired techniques to effectively handling the noncompliance of untreated siblings. Lavigueur *et al.* (1973) found similar results.

Issues. Any discussion of modifying children's noncompliance would be incomplete without some consideration of a prime philosophical issue: Is it ethically defensible to train compliance? Studies on obedience, such as those by Milgram (e.g., 1963), have raised some fundamental concern in that regard. (See Staub, 1978, Chapter 4, for an extensive discussion on this topic.) Training children to follow any and all instructions is indeed a questionable practice, which may have frightening results. Rather, children need to be taught to discriminate reasonable instructions from those that if followed would damage or harm themselves and others.

Within the field of behavior modification, targeting behaviors designed to teach children to be still, quiet, and docile has been questioned by Winett and Winkler (1972). Those authors have argued that the focus should be on behaviors that are to the advantage of the children themselves rather than to the teachers and other care givers. Certainly, there should be at least a reasonable balance between the two. Referring specifically to the control exerted by parents over their children's behavior, Peterson (1976) questioned whether parents might be overcontrolling their children. He dismissed arguments such as the natural reciprocity of control between children and parents by asserting that even though all members in a family may exert an influence on one another, the person in primary control is the one with the larger number of skills and responses, and thus with the broadest array of alternatives to bring to bear to the situation. Interpersonal power is based on the reinforcers, punishers, and other stimuli that one can manage over the behavior of the other. Overcontrol may exist when the distribution of contingency control is one-sided.

From the opposite perspective, one could provide a convincing argument for the importance of teaching children to comply with reasonable instructions. (In fact, the U.S. Supreme Court traditionally supports the family's ultimate right, if not responsibility, to manage their children.)

Few would argue with the need to require compliance with treatment regimens for such life-threatening behavior problems as anorexia or rumination, or with diets prescribed for children with kidney failure. A parent who failed to teach a child to follow the instruction to stop at a busy street corner or when reaching for poisonous or hazardous materials would surely be labeled negligent. Compliance with instructions to behave according to certain social mores permits children to attain reinforcement from the social setting as well as preventing their interference with others' attainment of reinforcement. There would probably be general agreement that compliance with instructions would be a justifiable goal for a child who refuses to stop running and screaming, throwing objects about, and generally interfering with the well-being of others.

When one begins to deal with behaviors in the gray area—for example, when it is unclear that compliance will further the well-being of the child or help avoid danger or disruption—the issue becomes more clouded. How important is it to teach a young man to rise when a woman enters a room? Is it essential that a child comply with instructions to button her coat or to turn in only perfect papers, or to sit with her hands folded, or to be quiet in class? Do the required behaviors reflect an unduly restrictive value system?

Also, other factors need to be considered: Is compliance being taught for the convenience of adults, and might it work eventually to the child's and the parents' disadvantage? A child who is never permitted to make decisions may remain continually dependent. How mature is the child? Is the child capable of entering into negotiation? Are the requisite negotiating and alternative skills part of the child's repertoire? Can they be taught? What are the "natural" baselines of child compliance under the given circumstances? Regarding the latter question, research data are providing a clearer picture of natural compliance rates and the factors that may influence them. Often these data are obtained from an analysis of preintervention baselines; at other times, they are discovered via naturalistic obervations in the clinic or the home. Forehand, King, and Yoder (1975) considered normative data in interpreting the results of a study in which they compared the compliance rates of clinical and nonclinical samples of children. They cited findings from their own research program (e.g., Forehand & King, 1974) and from the work of others (Johnson & Lobitz, 1974). Forehand et al. (1975) found that the rates of compliance by nonclinical children in the sample was about 62%, similar to that found by Johnson and Lobitz (1974). The clinical children's compliance rate of about 41% in Forehand *et al.* (1975) was similar to that found during the preintervention baseline phase of a treatment program for problem children in Forehand and King's study.

Forehand (1977) has summarized the current research on compliance norms, identifying those parameters that appear to control their rates: clinical versus nonclinical population, number and type of parental commands, consequences of noncompliance, other presenting problems, age, socioeconomic status, and sex. (Interestingly, in contrast with the other factors, there are no differences in rates of compliance between boys and girls, nor is there a difference when commands are delivered by the mother or by the father.)

Reference to normative information on compliance rates has been used to guide some designers of therapeutic interventions. Patterson (1976) and Eyberg and Johnson (1974) are among several who have utilized such information in analyzing their program outcomes. Forehand's (1977) citation of a range of rates of compliance to parental commands from 60% to 80% for nonclinical samples provides a rough basis for deciding if compliance rates are inadequate or excessive.

Peterson (1976) discussed several tactics for avoiding overcontrol by parents. Citing Hively and Duncan (1972), he endorsed their conviction that parents and children should mutually select the behaviors to be changed and that the child should be involved in recording and in negotiating motivational circumstances to bring about the change. Peterson also suggested that the setting conditions may be altered to avoid overcontrol: the physical environment might be altered, as in removing poisons from access. Natural consequences might be allowed to take over control, for example, letting the child learn to button her coat because she will get cold if she does not. Parents may be counseled against the use of overcontrol. Children may be taught techniques for managing the behavior of others and their own behavior. Children may set their own performance standards; administer their own reinforcers to themselves; operate self-government systems; and participate in self-re-

porting, evaluation, and recording. (See also the section on self-control elsewhere in this chapter.) Hopefully, such suggestions will be heeded by parents and those who provide them consultation.

Problems in Everyday Family Living

Often, no single behavior is the cause of family conflict. Rather, various behaviors combine to constitute a source of irritation among family members: whining, complaining, failing to perform assigned chores, or else doing them but not satisfactorily, dawdling, lateness, interrupting, demanding attention and unnecessary assistance, creating clutter, standing, climbing, kicking and screaming in the car, and so on. Such individual behaviors may not occur frequently enough to merit the designation "problem behavior," but combined, they can create difficulty within a family.

Some of these nuisance behaviors are targeted for change as components of other treatment programs (e.g., noncompliance; Forehand, 1977). Some of the irritating verbal behaviors, such as interrupting, are approached in some of the social (e.g., Bornstein, Bellack, & Hersen, 1977) or conversational skills programs (Lysaght & Burchard, 1975) discussed below. But an alternative method is to identify each of the behaviors in the cluster, define them operationally, and then manage contingencies to increase or decrease their rates.

The completion of household chores and the reduction of noxious social behaviors were targeted for change in a study by Christophersen, Arnold, Hill, and Quilitch (1972). Two different families were involved as subjects. In each case, specific behaviors were identified, and the parents collected baseline data on the rates of the behaviors. Occasionally, the experimenters made unannounced visits to the home to demonstrate the reliability of the measurement system. Using a multiple-baseline design, the authors demonstrated that the point system (a combination of points exchangeable for privileges and fines) effectively increased chore completion and decreased bickering, whining, and teasing. Christophersen (1977) found that not only standing and climbing but also kicking and screaming were dramatically reduced when young children were restrained in car seats.

Treating Sibling Conflict. Conflict among siblings has been reported as one of the more frequent behavior problems encountered in the home. Several procedures have been attempted to reduce that problem, including a combination of time-out for conflict and reinforcement for cooperative play (O'Leary, O'Leary, & Becker, 1967) and time-out alone (Allison & Allison, 1971).

Attempting to utilize positive rather than punitive contingencies, Leitenberg, Burchard, Burchard, Fuller, and Lysaght (1977) compared two positive reductive procedures: differential reinforcement of other behavior (DRO, also called *omission training*) and the reinforcement of alternative behaviors (Alt-R), in this case appropriate interactions.

The interventions were implemented in the homes of six families, and data were collected by the mothers and via direct or taped observations by the experimenters. In the DRO condition, the children were given pennies for not engaging in conflict during designated one-minute intervals. The Alt-R condition involved presenting a penny to each of the children who engaged in appropriate interactions during one-minute intervals. Both procedures were effective in suppressing conflict, while the Alt-R condition promoted higher rates of positive interactions than the DRO procedure. The DRO procedure, requiring simply the consequation of the elapsed time period in which conflict was absent, was simpler for the mothers to employ. Thus, that is the procedure they maintained following the formal intervention phases. Since DRO would permit children to attain reinforcers by isolating themselves from one another, parents probably should be guided to utilize the Alt-R procedure, at least intermittently, so that the siblings can acquire the skills required to interact appropriately with one another.

Treating Troublesome Behavior during Shopping. Shopping is another frequently cited source of family conflict. Children who are too young to remain at home alone must accompany their parents. Research into the specific nature of the difficulties encountered during family shopping expeditions has in-

cluded reviews of parenting texts, interviews with parents and store personnel, and direct observation. (See Barnard, Christophersen, & Wolf, 1977, and Clark, Greene, Macrae, McNees, Davis, & Risley, 1977, for summaries of that research.) The child behaviors that have been identified as particularly troublesome are running around the store and otherwise being out of the proximity of the parent, bumping into people and objects, touching merchandise, and distracting parents in various ways: asking questions not relevant to the activity, whining or asking for items, and other forms of aversive verbal behavior.

The two studies on shopping cited above (Barnard *et al.*, 1977, and Clark *et al.*, 1977) were directed toward the amelioration of troublesome child behaviors while shopping. Each showed that contingency management programs could lead to dramatic improvements in children's behavior. The focus of the Barnard *et al.* (1977) study was the child's proximity to the mother and the disturbance of products. Since all three subjects in the study had been functioning under token economies at home, the same procedures were then utilized in the supermarket. The mothers were instructed to present points to their sons at the rate of two to three per aisle traversed without any rule violations. Two points were to be deducted for each rule transgression. Verbal interactions between the mother and the child were tape-recorded so that their quality could be assessed, for example, whether what the mother said was positive, negative, or neutral. Findings monitored directly in the supermarket indicated that the procedures were strikingly effective, with the irritating behaviors almost completely eliminated. These improvements generally persisted over an extensive follow-up interval. Similarly, the quality of the mother's verbal interactions with the child became less negative and more positive or neutral. The evaluations by the consumers of the training package were very positive.

In a more extensive project (Clark *et al.*, 1977), a parent-advice package for family shopping trips was developed, distributed in written form, and validated. Specific rules on proximity, product disturbance, and the distraction of parents were communicated to the parents and three children in two "teaching families" (foster-care family groupings for neglected dependent children). Using nickels as reinforcers, the parents were instructed during the first intervention to permit each child 50 cents for each shopping trip. Nickels were deducted from this amount for specific rule infractions. During that phase, the aversive child behaviors diminished substantially, but so did their positive social and educational comments. In the third phase, then, the parents were instructed to increase their rates of engaging in relevant social and educational conversation with the children, and thé rates of the children's social and educational comments increased accordingly. Thus, the shopping activity became far less aversive and more reinforcing to both parents and children.

In the second phase, the written advice package was accompanied by quiz materials consisting of academic questions and multiple-choice questions about hypothetical family conversations. Also included was a shopping-list form that guided the parents to tally the nickels earned and lost and to use self-feedback checks. During this phase, the parents were directly guided by the experimenter to implement procedures according to the advice package. Initial trips were kept short: 15 min the first two times, 30 min the subsequent two. Interspersed within the first 15-min sessions were three 5-min feedback intervals in which the parents and the children checked on their adherence to the rules. Those self-check intervals were later extended to once each 10 min and ultimately to once at the end of the shopping event. The impressive improvement in the parents' implementation of the program and the children's behavior led to the last phase, an attempt to validate the revised written package as a completely independent program. The experimenter was involved only in collecting data and not in assisting in the intervention. Apparently, the written package was able to stand on its own, as the six families with which it was tested showed improvements comparable to those gained in the earlier phases. The package is currently available as a paperback book entitled *Shopping with Children* (1978)[1] and represents, along with

[1] Academic Therapy Publications, P.O. Box 899, San Raphael, Calif.

Azrin and Foxx's manual on toilet training (1974), one of the few extensively evaluated, specific parent-training packages available.

Home–School Relations

Events that occur in school may influence the child's behavior at home, while those at home may reflect on what the child does in school. Behavior modification has addressed some of the problems that fall within the realm of home–school relations. Examples are home-based systems of contingency management of school behaviors, methods for reducing absenteeism and for increasing the completion of homework, and the treatment of elective mutism. The first three problem areas are discussed here, while the last topic is discussed along with other social skills.

Managing School Behavior through Home-Based Contingencies. When behavior modification first began to be applied in schools, it was recognized that it would be sensible to involve parents in programs introduced to improve their children's school behavior (e.g., McKenzie, Clark, Wolf, Kothera, & Benson, 1968; Thorne, Tharp, & Wetzel, 1967). Parents control many of the important reinforcers in a young child's life and probably have the strongest investment in their child's development. Periodic progress reports have traditionally been used by schools. Thus, the progress reported could be modified and utilized as a relatively unobtrusive device. Reports have been completed by teachers daily (e.g., Bailey, Wolf, & Phillips, 1970); weekly (McKenzie, Clark, Wolf, Kothera, & Benson, 1968; Besalel-Azrin, Azrin, & Armstrong, 1977); or even following each class period (Thoresen, Thoresen, Klein, Wilbur, Becker-Haven, & Haven, 1977; Blackmore, Rich, Means, & Nally, 1976). These reports have permitted frequent reinforcement with minimal delay, two basic principles of effective reinforcement.

Barth (1979) and Atkeson and Forehand (1979) have recently presented detailed reviews of the operation of systems of home-based reinforcement of school behavior. Among the topics on which Barth has elaborated are the frequency of the report, the extent of differential feedback, parents' responses to the feedback, the use of the program by and its function for teachers, methods of enlisting parents' and teachers' involvement, types of home consequation, the use of home-based systems as an adjunct to school-based programs, the involvement of pupil personnel workers, and others. In general, parental involvement is attained via conferences (Karraker, 1972) or notes sent home (Lahey, Gendrich, Gendrich, Schnelle, Gant, & McNee, 1977). School reports are usually mailed or sent home with the child and are received by the parents, who are instructed to deliver prespecified consequences. The consequences are almost uniformly positive other than the simple withholding of unearned reinforcers. Typical home consequences are usually privileges, such as permission to go out on a date or to use the phone (Thorne *et al.*, 1967) or to go backpacking (Blackmore *et al.*, 1976), or material rewards such as allowances (McKenzie *et al.*, 1968).

Usually, the initial schedule of reporting is very frequent, for example, each day. As the targeted behaviors improve, the frequency of reporting is gradually faded, until it eventually begins to resemble the regular school system's reporting schedule, such as a six-week report-card interval. In some cases (e.g., Thoresen *et al.*, 1977), the students themselves gradually take over the responsibility of rating their own behavior. (Procedures for the fading of reinforcement in home reporting systems are detailed in a manual by Schumaker, Hovell, and Sherman, 1977. General procedures for promoting maintenance via the fading of reinforcement frequency are included in Sulzer-Azaroff and Mayer, 1977, Unit 24.)

Home-based reinforcement systems have been used successfully to modify a variety of school behaviors, from truancy (Thorne *et al.*, 1967) and school phobia (MacDonald, Gallimore, & MacDonald, 1970) to disruption (Hawkins, Sluyter, & Smith, 1972; Ayllon, Garber, & Pisor, 1975); rule following (Besalel-Azrin *et al.*, 1977); aggression (O'Leary & Kent, 1974; Budd & Leibowitz, 1976); quality and completion of work in school (Schumaker *et al.*, 1977; McKenzie *et al.*, 1968) or at home (Dougherty & Dougherty, 1977); and many others. According to Atkeson and Forehand (1979), there have been methodological flaws in many of the studies, particularly the omission of multiple outcome measures and follow-up data. Nevertheless, their evaluation of 21 studies of home-based reinforcement indicated that *all* reported that the system was effective.

Parents may participate in *school-based* reinforcement systems, as well as carrying out reinforcement procedures in the home. One way this might be accomplished is through their contribution of reinforcing materials or events. In an unpublished study, Whitley and Sulzer (1970) asked the parents to provide a reward for their son's school performance. The child earned gift certificates for bicycle parts for accomplishing specified criterion levels, until the whole bike was assembled. Parents may also provide reinforcing activities directly, as in the case of one of the present author's school programs (Sulzer, Hunt, Ashby Koniarski, & Krams, 1971). Parents brought and showed films, gave talks, presented musical activities in school, and accompanied the class on trips and outings, all of which activities served as backup reinforcers for tokens earned by the students for academic performance.

Mentioned in the reports of various behavior modification studies are incidents suggesting that the relationship between the school and the family has improved along with the targeted behavior. Communication presumably becomes more regular and attitudes more positive.

It stands to reason that if a program focuses on the improvement of positive, adaptive behaviors, such behaviors will be closely scrutinized by teachers and parents. Just the heightened awareness of the occurrence of those behaviors may thus serve to cue the parents and the teachers to deliver praise or to pay more attention when the behavior is observed. As with other effectively programmed reinforcement systems, parents, teachers, and, in particular, students should thus find their relationships becoming increasingly positive. Since punishment and extinction are reduced, their side effects, such as aggression and withdrawal, should lessen, along with rates of vandalism and truancy. (See Mayer & Butterworth, 1979.) Research on such strategies as home-based reinforcement systems (and systems that involve parents in school reinforcement activities) should include the gathering of evidence of any such collateral effects.

Failing to Attend School. Irregular attendance can become a problem. When a child refuses to attend school at all, the behavior pattern may be considered pathological and may be assigned the label *school phobia*. Regardless of the label, when children fail to attend school regularly, it is assumed that their learning suffers. The family is often inconvenienced and may be concerned about violation of compulsory attendance laws.

Several studies have dealt with school attendance (e.g., Ayllon, Smith, & Rogers, 1970; Copeland, Brown, Axelrod, & Hall, 1972; Hersen, 1970; Barber & Kagey, 1977). Often, the parents are involved. An illustrative example is the study by Copeland *et al.* (1972). The principal played an active role, calling the child's parents and praising them for their child's attendance. Increases in attendance rates resulted.

Sometimes, the process of traveling to school is the link in the chain that influences school attendance. Some children are reluctant to ride a school bus, and if other transportation is unavailable, obviously the child does not reach school. A case study reported by Luiselli (1978) described the treatment of an autistic child who exhibited severe emotional behavior when he was asked to board the school bus. The procedure followed was essentially "backward chaining." The first training step was initiated on the school bus, which was at the school and parked outside. With the mother on the bus and the therapist to assist, the child successfully boarded the bus, with no major emotional distress. Gradually, in small steps, the program moved backward. The child spent more and more time on the bus, with the mother and the therapist eventually fading out their presence.

Completing Homework. Another way that parents have been traditionally involved in their child's education has been in the supervision or tutoring of their child's homework. Several studies have addressed this problem. For instance, Broden, Beasley, and Hall (1978) showed how a child's spelling performance in school improved as a function of home tutoring by the mother. Hunt and Sulzer-Azaroff (1974) reported a study in which severely handicapped children were assigned, as a homework exercise, a prewriting activity that required parental supervision. Although all parents saw to it that the homework was attempted on some occasions, only when graphic feedback and notes acknowledging the parents' help were delivered regularly to the parents was the homework consistently returned to the teacher.

A third example (Pollack, Sulzer-Azaroff, & Williams, 1972) involved a predelinquent high-school boy who was progressing poorly. Completion of homework in two subjects, arithmetic and spelling (areas of particular difficulty), was targeted for modification. When the boy earned points exchangeable for on-the-job training in auto mechanics contingent on completing his homework, the rate increased as a function of the schedules of reinforcement employed.

Social Isolation

The time that severe social isolation becomes manifest is when the child is placed in a group situation, as in school or in a day-care setting. Rarely does the problem occur at home. As a result, the literature on that topic generally reports treatment within the out-of-the-home setting (e.g., Hart, Reynolds, Baer, Brawley, & Harris, 1968; O'Conner, 1969; Ragland, Kerr, & Strain, 1978; Strain, Shores, & Timm, 1977).

Treatment Procedures. Among the procedures that have been found to facilitate social interactions have been teacher attention (Hart *et al.*, 1968); approaches by confederate peers (Ragland *et al.*, 1978; Strain *et al.*, 1977); "symbolic modeling" in the form of a film in which social consequences are the result of interactions (O'Conner, 1969); and reinforcement of peers for interacting with the child (Kandel, Ayllon, & Rosenbaum, 1977).

Kandel *et al.* (1977) worked with a 4-year-old boy with a complexity of behavioral problems, including talking only to himself and to no one else. Fifteen children were selected as social stimuli, according to a "flooding paradigm," during which the other children received reinforcement for playing with the target child. There were dramatic and enduring changes. Self-talk decreased, and communication with others increased dramatically. A second case involved a 7-year-old autistic child. A similar flooding approach with seven children serving as social stimuli resulted in strong resistance by the subject and had to be terminated in favor of interaction with only two children. Interaction levels were shown to increase substantially from the baseline level of zero. In order to validate the criterion levels of interaction achieved with these children, the authors conducted naturalistic observations of "normal" children and demonstrated that the experimental subjects were within 10% of mean normal interaction levels. Collateral behaviors previously described as bizarre were noted to decrease as the interaction levels increased.

Elective Mutism

Occasionally, the literature has reported cases in which children communicate effectively and appropriately at home but fail to speak in school or sometimes anywhere outside the home (Reid, Hawkins, Keutzer, McNeal, Phelps, Reid, & Mees, 1967). The child is not mute, since normal speech is part of the repertoire, but exhibits mutism in school, where normal verbal behavior is critical for academic and social development. This pattern is called *elective* or *selective mutism*.[2]

Treatment Procedures. Generally, elective mutism is analyzed as a problem in stimulus control. Wulbert, Nyman, Snow, and Owen (1973), Richards and Hansen (1978), and Sanok and Streifel (1979) are among those who have assumed that there are some stimuli that occasion "normal" speaking and some that fail to occasion (or that "inhibit") it. Apparently, stimuli at home are discriminative for speaking; those at school exert the opposite influence. If that is the case, stimulus fading should solve the problem. The challenge is to identify those critical stimulus dimensions that control

both classes of behavior. The stimuli that evoke speaking are employed exclusively during the initial stages. Gradually, these are faded out, while those that previously occasioned nonresponding are faded in. Combined with the fading steps are strong reinforcing (and occasionally aversive) consequences for progress or lack of progress.

Emma, a 6-year-old girl, had not spoken in Sunday school or preschool for a period of 3 years. Wulbert *et al.* (1973) selected experimenters, presumably adults who were strangers to her, as the "stimuli" to be faded in as substitutes for those adults (initially the mother, later other adults) who reliably occasioned verbal responding. Following compliance with requests to perform motor and verbal tasks, Emma was given praise and candy. Later, time-out for noncompliance was added to the procedure. Fading was accomplished over approximately 25 steps, starting with the mother and Emma alone and ending with the experimenter and Emma alone. Although during the early stages of treatment, hundreds of trials were required for the verbal responses to occur in the presence of new experimenters, as treatment progressed fewer and fewer trials were required. Eventually, strangers began to occasion verbal responses just as Emma's mother had.

The success of the Wulbert *et al.* (1973) study probably encouraged others to attempt similar approaches. An illustrative case study, reported by Conrad, Delk, and Williams (1974), involved an 11-year-old American Indian girl who lived on a reservation. Since she had been observed to speak with her family and friends, cultural characteristics were one dimension included in the fading steps. Candy, grooming aids, and other material rewards were provided as a consequence of the girl's giving oral answers to flash card questions. An indigenous American Indian mental-health worker was faded into the situation on the initial day of training. As the training sessions progressed, the mother absented herself, and the teacher and classmates were faded in. The setting was also gradually changed: from the home, to the clinic, to, eventually, the classroom. A one-year follow-up indicated that the girl continued to answer questions in school but did not speak

---

[2] Since both these terms suggest "volition," preferable terms might be "discriminated" or "differential mutism," to reflect the control by discriminative stimuli.

spontaneously (probably because she had not received training in spontaneous speech).

Several stimulus-and-response dimensions were systematically varied in another case study, reported by Richards and Hansen (1978). The setting shifted from the home, to the school route, to the school playground, and ultimately to the classroom. The number of children progressed from none to: a close friend, a group, and finally the entire class. Response requirements involved stepwise increases in the volume and length of utterance: from a whisper to normal volume, from a single-word response ultimately to spontaneous speech. Perhaps it was the inclusion of several carefully programmed stimulus-and-response dimensions that accounted for the durability of the modified behavior over a 5-year follow-up period.

Several other studies have used similar approaches (e.g., Ayllon & Kelly, 1974; Sanok & Streifel, 1979). Ayllon and Kelly (1974) used shaping procedures to restore a retarded child's speech outside the classroom and later in the classroom, within a single four-hour session. The results were maintained over a one-year follow-up. Sanok and Streifel (1979) varied response requirements across five categories, shifted training settings, and introduced new adults into the training site. Their procedures included using pennies and praise as reinforcers for correct responses, plus response-cost (removal of pennies for inappropriate responding) and corrective feedback. Once the training criteria were achieved, praise and corrective feedback alone were substituted for the more contrived contingencies. A 10-month follow-up demonstrated the durability of the effect.

Bauermeister and Jemail (1975) reported the case of an electively mute child who had returned to Puerto Rico from the mainland United States. Response requirements were varied across two settings: homeroom and English class. Gold stars earned for meeting daily requirements were brought home. When he accumulated a sufficient number, he earned a bicycle.

In general, then, research has demonstrated that, as with other forms of language, children's oral communication may be modified or extended outside the home via operant techniques. The next section discusses social skills that enhance the amount of reinforcement that children receive.

Recruiting Reinforcement

When children use effective social skills, they are more likely to receive reinforcement from members of their social environment. There is an alternative method for attaining such reinforcers, that is, for the child to influence directly the behavior of the adults and the other children in his or her environment who control valuable sources of reinforcement. Contractual arrangements between children and parents often involve the parents' expression of satisfaction with the child's performance (Dardig & Heward, 1976). The child may identify the nature of the response to be required of the parent, just as the parent requires specific criteria in the child's behavior: "Whenever possible, let a child participate in choosing a reward. Let him know what is required to earn it, and discuss what you each consider reasonable. Participation will give children an added interest in and commitment to completing their part of the bargain. And that helps both of you" (Graubard, 1977, p. 19).

Such advice is frequently found in behavior modification texts for parents or other service personnel.

Treatment Procedures. Other than such general advice, it does not appear that children have been specifically involved in programs designed to teach them to recruit parental reinforcement at home. Again, studies conducted outside the home may have direct relevance. Several programs have involved teaching children to attain more reinforcement from adults. Graubard, Rosenberg, and Miller (1971) specifically taught schoolchildren methods for attaining reinforcement from their teachers. The methods resembled the types of interventions that teachers are instructed to use when attempting to reinforce their students' behaviors. Another method, suggested by the results of a study by Sherman and Cormier (1974), is to find the means to assist students to improve in their school performance. Sherman and Cormier found that when students' behavior became more appropriate, teachers began to increase their rates of praising.

One more alternative method for teaching children to enhance the reinforcement they receive is to teach them directly to cue praise from adults, as in a study by Seymour and Stokes (1976). Delinquent girls were directly instructed in methods for cuing praise from the staff of the institution in which they resided. The generality of that finding was tested by Stokes, Fowler, and Baer (1978), who replicated the procedures with preschool children. In a series of two experiments, they taught normal preschoolers to elicit praise for correct academic production. Then, several "deviant" children were taught to do the same. In the first experiment, the evidence showed that not only did the children learn how to elicit the praise effectively, but the praise, in turn, operated reciprocally to increase their rates of correct academic performance. The authors stressed the point that if such procedures are to be used, it is essential that the children learn accurately to assess their own performance and that they solicit praise only when deserving. Nor should they solicit it too often, as that might be a nuisance to teachers.

Positive Social Behavior

As we have noted in our historical recounting of the evolution of behavior modification applied to children's problems in the home, noxious or distressing social behaviors have tended to be frequently targeted for change. Frequently, reductive procedures, such as time-out (Forehand, 1977) or extinction (Williams, 1959), have been the primary method of treatment. Often the reductive procedures are paired with procedures designed to reinforce alternative behaviors, judged acceptable by parents and others (e.g., Patterson & Reid, 1973).

Another strategy is to focus on positive social behavior, either primarily or exclusively, and to operate under the assumption that positive and noxious social behaviors are incompatible with one another. Thus, as the former increase, the latter decrease. That such strategies may prove effective has been demonstrated in several instances (e.g., Sulzer *et al.*, 1971). Consider the problem of "selfishness."

Research has identified some of the critical variables that affect children's learning to help, share, and donate (see Staub, 1978), and some of these may be applied to modify a child's behavior.

Another advantage of focusing on the positive is that productive or prosocial behavior, such as helping, smiling, or complimenting, are usually reinforcing to others. Thus, increases in the rates of such behaviors may enrich the relationships between children and others in their lives.

As with other classes of behavior, prosocial behaviors have been shown to be modifiable through operant conditioning. Sharing and donating have been modified in laboratories (Azrin & Lindsley, 1956; Gelfand, Hartmann, Cromer, Smith, & Page, 1975; Hake & Vukelich, 1972; Hartmann, Gelfand, Smith, Paul, Cromer, Page, & Lebenta, 1976) and in the nursery-school settings (Rogers-Warren, & Baer, 1976; Serbin, Tonick, & Sternglanz, 1977); with schizophrenic children (Hingtgen, Sanders, & DeMyer, 1965); with hearing-impaired children (Barton & Ascione, 1979); and with severely retarded children (Whitman, Mercurio, & Caponigri, 1970). Retarded clients' rates of smiling were increased through social reinforcement (Hopkins, 1968). Children with social-emotional problems increased their rates of sharing, smiling, positive physical contact, and verbal complimenting when instructed via modeling, instructions, and verbal praise (Cooke & Apolloni, 1976).

Self-instruction has been used frequently to teach children to manage their social behaviors (see Karoly, 1977). As Karoly concluded, self-control training has been conducted mainly in the laboratory. This fact is also true of other forms of social skills training. In the research literature, one does not see studies in which social skills, as a general cluster, are taught directly in the home setting. Rather, there tends to be an emphasis on teaching general problem-solving strategies outside the home to parents alone (see for example, the survey by Berkowitz & Graziano, 1972) or to parents and children (Blechman, 1974; Robin, 1979). The assumption is that those skills should transfer back into the home (Bizer *et al.*, 1978; Blechman, Olsen, & Hellman, 1976; Robin, Kent, O'Leary, Foster, & Pritz, 1977). Also, although many texts written for parents do focus on the promotion of effective social skills, rarely are the outcomes of such training evaluated. (See Bernal and North, 1978, for a survey of parent training manuals, including information on evaluations.) Here, let us turn to summaries of two of the areas of social behavior that have been researched primarily outside the family but that do have particular relevance to children's behavioral problems at home: social and conversational skills.

Social Skills. Effective social-interactional skills must be acquired if a child is to develop satisfactorily. Children who suffer from social isolation, who are avoided or ignored or punished by peers, have a much poorer prognosis for future adjustment than children who are accepted and who interact freely and assert themselves positively (Kagan & Moss, 1962). Recognizing that fact, the field has leaned toward studying methods for promoting effective social interactions.

Treatment Procedures. Recently, Van Hasselt, Hersen, and Bellack (1979) prepared a review designed to evaluate the adequacy of strategies for assessing and modifying social skills. In particular, attention was given to evidence of the durability and the generality of effects.

Van Hasselt *et al.* surveyed definitions of social skills and found them to contain various components: the skills were situation-specific (i.e., were utilized under some conditions and not others), and they consisted of learned verbal responses; they would not harm others and would maximize reinforcement. Self-expression, agreeing with and praising others; assertiveness in the form of making requests, disagreeing with another's opinions, and denying unreasonable requests; communication; and interpersonal problem-solving—all were among the specific skills mentioned. Other important ingredients of social skills might include the ability to dispense positive reinforcers, to approach peers and respond positively when they approach, to discriminate and label emotions, to communicate accurately and effectively to others, to assume the perspective of another on perceptual tasks, and to consider simultaneously one's own and others' views. The assessment of social skills has been based

primarily on self-reports, sociometrics, and motoric responses.

According to Van Hasselt *et al.* (1979) research on social skills *training* has focused on individual case reports, single-case studies, and group comparisons. The latter approach has tended to emphasize modeling as an intervention strategy and has pointed to the importance of considering developmental variables in assessing and designing intervention programs, since the components of socially effective behavior at one age may be quite different from those at another. (We would also add the need to consider social-milieu group factors, socioeconomic status, and cultural characteristics as critical variables in designing intervention programs for individuals.) Single-case studies have proved particularly valuable in identifying effective stategies for promoting social skills. Besides focusing on individuals, they have attempted to select the training procedures and settings that most closely resemble natural conditions. Reports of effective social-skills training have cited the use not only of verbal instructions but of behavioral rehearsal, imitation of modeled behavior, reinforcement of appropriate modeling or approximations to increasingly more skilled responding, and feedback (e.g., Bornstein *et al.*, 1977; Goldstein, Sherman, Gershaw, Sprafkin, & Glick, 1978). To illustrate, Bornstein *et al.* (1977) used such techniques to teach hyperactive children to maintain eye contact while communicating, to speak at an adequate volume (or duration), and to make requests for new behavior. It is reported that training of this kind has produced results that have endured for several weeks. Some studies also have reported evidence of generalization into the natural setting.

Issues. It appears that social skills have begun to be adequately defined, assessed, and modified. There do, however, seem to be some issues that might well be addressed in this realm. Self-report and sociometrics are often used for assessment purposes. From our own perspective, such data should be supplementary to those obtained through direct observation, for although the results on one sociometric scale may serve as a good predictor of similar assessments in the future, they are not necessarily correlated with behavioral data assessed in the natural setting. Self-report measures are similarly limited.

It is likely that the most valid form of social skills assessment is that conducted in the natural setting, although as Van Hasselt *et al.* (1979) noted, even direct *in vivo* observation is fraught with difficulties. Naturalistic observational data may be biased by such conditions as expectancies and variables that affect the reliability of scoring, such as consensual drift, the complexity of the system, and knowledge that reliability is being assessed. We would add the critical issue of reactivity in cases where the observers' presence is not easily camouflaged. The validity of assessment through direct *in vivo* observation, however, can be improved by means of several tactics (attributed to Gottman, 1977): Observing all, not just target children (thus obscuring the influence of expectancies of change for just some); sequential time-sampling (which distributes observation intervals over a more representative time interval); and spot checks rather than scheduled checks for reliability.

Van Hasselt *et al.* (1979) also emphasize the need for techniques for promoting generalization from the training to the natural setting and for promoting (and assessing) the durability of trained skills. We would also add that other procedures may accomplish what social skills training is intended to accomplish. For instance, simple positive reinforcement may be the procedure of choice for children who have acquired the skills but may not be practicing them.

Progress is clearly being made in the realm of social skills assessment and training. Let us now turn to the recent research on training in conversational skills, which is particularly relevant to an analysis of social skills as they relate to child behavior problems in the home.

Conversational Skills: Treatment Procedures. Conversational skills are often taught as components of social-skills-training packages (e.g., Reese, 1979a). Specific skills such as attending without interrupting and reflecting the content of the speaker's conversation are stressed. For example, Arnold, Sturgis, and Forehand (1977) taught the mother of a 15-year-old retarded girl different categories of

active conversational responses: encouraging, acknowledging, and questioning. Besides acquiring the general conversational skills, the girl increased her total rate of verbalizing.

At a much simpler level, behavioral programs have been designed to teach conversational skills to language-deficient children (e.g., Garcia, 1974). Presumably such procedures could readily be applied in the home with children deficient in conversational ability. Prompting, shaping, and reinforcement were used by Stokes, Baer, and Jackson (1974) to teach four retarded children to respond to others with a simple greeting, a hand wave. More importantly, they showed how to promote generalization across a large number of people by involving a second trainer. Luiselli, Colozzi, Donellon, Helfen, and Pemberton (1978) modeled the responses to be incorporated with a fairly complex verbal greeting exchange: "Hi," "Hi," "How are you today?" "I'm fine," and so on. Levels of complexity were shaped, and modeling prompts were faded as their moderately retarded, language-deficient subject began to acquire the appropriate response repertoire.

Conversational style becomes a different sort of a problem, though, when it is characterized not by insufficient skills but by qualities that interfere with positive social interactions. In that case, rather than simply teaching adaptive conversational skills, the task becomes one of teaching novel alternative behaviors, such as conflict resolution (Martin & Twentyman, 1976); negotiating skills (Kifer, Lewis, Green, & Phillips, 1974); or prosocial statements. This was the situation tackled by Sanson-Fisher, Seymour, Montgomery, & Stokes (1978). The subjects in their study were institutionalized delinquent girls who displayed very low rates of prosocial statements and of positive attention to statements made by peers and staff. The subjects were taught to say and to identify instances of prosocial comments and also to present positive attention to others. They were also shown how to record their own practice of those behaviors and were given tokens for meeting specific criteria. Although they did not learn to discriminate pro- and antisocial peer statements, they did substantially increase their rates of making prosocial comments and giving positive attention to others. Anecdotal reports indicated a simultaneous reduction in aggression and other negative social problems during the time that the self-recording phase was in effect.

In a similar study, conversations between a mother and a predelinquent 12-year-old boy were modified in a study by Lysacht and Burchard (1975). The youngster, who lived in a group home, was visited by his mother once a week. It was found that during baseline, the mother criticized twice as often as she praised and that she focused on inappropriate behaviors. Audiotapes of the conversations were used to provide the mother with feedback regarding her use of praise and criticism. During the treatment, her frequency of criticism diminished to zero. Alexander and Parsons (1973) compared several different family-intervention strategies to assess their impact on delinquent family process. The short-term behavioral treatment resulted in more equality among family members in talk time, silence, and interruptions. Also, recidivism rates were lower for that group.

Negative conversational interactions probably account for a substantial amount of difficulty experienced within families. Children may make negative, hostile, or antisocial remarks, thereby prompting negative reactions by parents and siblings. Extrapolating from the Sanson-Fisher *et al.* (1978) study, it should be possible to modify this form of behavior by teaching individual family members (1) to self-record accurately; (2) to discriminate their own and others' prosocial and other forms of positive and adaptive conversational content; and (3) to make such statements themselves. Contractual arrangements would be one way to increase both rates of recording and rates of the occurrence of the identified behaviors themselves.

Further Research on Positive Social Skills. Further research on techniques that parents can use to teach specific classes of prosocial behaviors would permit a heavier focus on preventing than on curing child behavior problems. The methods cited by Cooke and Apolloni (1976) and by Barton and Ascione (1979)—modeling, instructions, and contingent praise to teach specific social behaviors such as smil-

ing, sharing, and positive physical contact—should lend themselves readily to application in the home. There are probably several advantages to such an approach: Since the behaviors are discrete and specific, they should be easy for parents to demonstrate; they should be readily discriminable, so that the consequences may be presented at the appropriate time; and they should be readily quantified by parents. Generalization to the home should not be an issue, since that would be the base of training, and the behaviors should occasion not only programmed but also natural reinforcement. Instances of smiling, sharing, and positive physical contact would tend to stimulate in-kind responses from others, thereby introducing additional sources of reinforcement within the social environment.

Characteristics of Behavior Modification with Children in the Home

We have seen the breadth of children's home-based problem behaviors that have been addressed by the field of behavior modification. We have also had a chance to examine some of the behavioral approaches that have been applied to the treatment of those problems and to consider some issues that are specifically relevant to each area. Now, we turn to a discussion of the various issues that relate to the modification of children's behavior problems in the home in general. Included among them are the nature of the problems that have been addressed; behavioral assessment methods; the settings in which programs are conducted; the providers and targets of treatment; parent-training methods; self-management; the behavior modification procedures being applied; ethics and the law; and methodology.

The Nature of the Problem

As we have seen, the child behavior problems addressed by behavior modification have varied widely. Seriously disruptive behaviors such as noncompliance (Forehand, 1977), tantrums (Williams, 1959), oppositional responding (Wahler, 1969a), and aggression have received much attention, as have behaviors that are distressing or upsetting to family functioning. Relatively less attention has been devoted to the promotion of specific positive behaviors, such as assertiveness, creativity, helping and sharing, and honesty. However, outside the home, in laboratory and school settings, progressively more attention has been given to those areas.

The degree of *specificity* of the behavior targeted for change varies from case to case. Treatment may be directed toward changing a very discrete response, such as smiling (Hopkins, 1968) or reducing the initial link in a chain that terminates in a seizure (Zlutnick, Mayville, & Moffat, 1975); or more complex behaviors, such as a set of specific conversational skills (Sanson-Fisher *et al.*, 1978) or acceptable behavior while shopping (Barnard *et al.*, 1977), may be treated. Functional response classes (those behaviors that tend to covary as a function of the modification of any of the class members), such as imitative responding (Baer, Peterson, & Sherman, 1967), comprise yet another category in the specificity–generality dimension, while clusters of behaviors, often grouped together in common parlance, constitute an even more complex set: "Problem solving" (e.g., Blechman, 1974) is one such cluster. Other examples are "brat" (Bernal, 1969), "oppositional" (Wahler, 1969a), "noncompliant" (Forehand, 1977), "coercive" (Patterson, 1976), or "objectionable" (Hawkins *et al.*, 1966) behaviors, on the socially noxious side, and "nonassertiveness" (Bornstein *et al.*, 1977) on the side of social insufficiency. Each of those general terms actually consist of sets of discrete behaviors, such as failing to follow instructions, negating requests, and making derogatory comments. When research is conducted on such general behavioral categories, it is necessary to refine, operationalize, and specify precise measures for each component.

On the most comprehensive end of the continuum is child behavior in general, grouped into broad subcategories, such as those in need of increasing, decreasing, teaching, and so forth. Textbooks for providers of services to children and for parents, such as Sulzer-Azaroff and Mayer's (1977) and many in the group

reviewed by Bernal and North (1978), are intended to permit adults and children themselves to target the behaviors to be modified.

The desirability of involvement at one particular level of specificity appears to depend on a few factors. If transfer from one setting to another is of major concern, or if busy parents or teachers are to observe, record, and implement a program, it seems that very specific, clearly discrete behaviors are the most appropriate. (See Johnson, Bolstad, & Lobitz, 1976). Professionals, however, should be capable of analyzing and pinpointing the components of broad classes of behavior.

Assessing Behavior

In the early years of behavior modification, there was a definite trend away from the use of diagnostic instruments, other than direct observational recordings. The major emphasis was on improving and refining observational procedures (e.g., Reese, 1979b). Discovering critical contingency relationships was the prime objective of the field, since their discovery would permit management of the contingencies to set things right.

As the field has developed, however, other issues have emerged in relation to assessment. How does one decide whether a particular goal is reasonable for a particular child? What is the "normal" range of distribution of the behavior among children? Are the component or the prerequisite behaviors contained in the child's repertoire of behaviors? Will the environment support the projected change? The development of instruments that address such issues is on the increase.

One emphasis has been on observing "normal children" in natural settings, to permit an assessment of the appropriateness of the goals and the measurement of the behavior before, during, and following interventions. Examples are the work done by Twardosz, Schwartz, Fox, and Cunningham (1979), who developed and demonstrated the reliability and validity of a system designed to measure affectionate behavior, and by Peterson (1979), who used an interaction record to measure interpersonal relationships.

The development of observational forms and behavioral checklists has also been emphasized. These generally consist of a set of specific, clearly defined behaviors to be measured according to precisely specified criteria. Behavioral checklists are used by clients themselves, such as the Fear Survey Schedule (Scherer & Nakamura, 1968), or by trained observers conducting ecological assessments (Wahler, House, & Stambaugh, 1976).

As this area of focus in the field continues growing, one can anticipate a broader scope of application and methodological refinements. However, in contrast with more traditional child assessment, it can be predicted that behavioral assessment will focus on identifying "meaningful response units and the controlling variables for the purposes of understanding and altering behavior" (Nelson & Hayes, 1979, p. 13).

Settings

The programs described above have been located in various settings. Sometimes, training has taken place totally in the clinic, with the therapist initially treating the child and later shifting over the conduct of the therapy to the parent, as in the early phases of the Patterson *et al.* (1967) study. Frequently, the clinic or the community center has served as the training site. Sometimes, training conducted in the clinic has been shifted back to the home (e.g., Bernal, 1969), and frequently, treatment has taken place directly in the home throughout (e.g., Hawkins *et al.,* 1966).

The selection of settings for intervention and parent training has probably been based on convenience and practicality as much as on a consideration of empirical evidence for or against enduring effectiveness. For a trained therapist to expend considerable time traveling to homes, one would have to offer very convincing evidence of the superiority of that approach. Logic and informal observations of effective training in the home may not be as convincing as hard comparative data. Definitive studies that compare training and intervention sites remain to be conducted.

Providers and Targets of Treatment

Behavior modification programs are more frequently being incorporated within the child's natural social environment. We have seen how key individuals in the child's life have been trained to function as paraprofessional change agents: mothers (e.g., Shoemaker & Paulson, 1976), fathers (Rasbury, 1974), or both parents (e.g., Johnson & Lobitz, 1974); siblings (Steward & Steward, 1976), peers (Nelson, Worell, & Polsgrove, 1973), or even the children themselves (Benassi & Larson, 1976).

Sometimes the full family unit is treated (e.g., Alexander & Parsons, 1973), and individual members sometimes assume the role of change agents for specific purposes (e.g., Mealiea, 1976). This approach reflects the influence of the current focus on ecology (e.g., Rogers-Warren & Warren, 1977). The parent–child relationship is seen as reciprocal (Bell, 1979), or the family may be viewed as an "ecosystem." The Achievement Place teaching family (Phillips, Phillips, Fixsen, & Wolf, 1972) is a community-based group-home program for predelinquent youth. The program incorporates a sophisticated sequence of contingency arrangements for "family members." No single family member is the target of change. Rather, change is seen as a function of adjustments in the interaction among family members (e.g., Christophersen, Barnard, Ford, & Wolf, 1976). Studies of transfer and maintenance highlight the importance of incorporating support from within the natural setting (Conway & Bucher, 1976), especially if contrast effects are to be avoided (e.g., Wahler, 1969; Forehand *et al.,* 1975; Johnson, Bolstad, & Lobitz, 1976). Thus, depending on the nature of the problems of concern, the most responsible and effective strategy may be to direct treatment toward the total family as a functional ecosystem.

Instances in which full families are treated are becoming more frequent (e.g., Engeln, Knutson, Laughy, & Garlington, 1968; Mash, Hamerlynck, & Handy, 1976; Mash, Handy, & Hamerlynck, 1976). But usually such treatment incorporates training the parents, rather than all family members, to apply behavior modification procedures. In fact, very frequently, when children are to be treated at home, at least one parent, if not both parents, is given formal training, so that she or he may effectively conduct the modification program. Since there has been such a heavy emphasis on parent training, the next section is devoted to a summary of activities in that area.

Parent Training

Training should teach parents how their practices affect their children's behavior and how change may be supported: "the behavior modifier should focus efforts upon altering the social environment in which the child lives rather than directly with the deviant child. Within such a framework, alterations in the reinforcement schedules being used by the parents . . . would produce changes in the behavior of the child" (Patterson *et al.*, 1967, p. 181). Professional time can be saved by involving parents instead of professional change agents. Also, parents do have the ultimate responsibility for their (minor) children's behavior in our society. Most compelling, however, would be clear demonstrations that child behavior problems are better prevented or ameliorated when the parents are involved in the modification program.

Parents are becoming increasingly involved in programs with their children and probably will continue to be so. Thus, the challenge is to discover those variables that influence their effectiveness. Potentially critical variables have been identified in several review articles (Berkowitz & Graziano, 1972; Johnson & Katz, 1973; O'Dell, 1974; Reisenger, Ora, & Frangia, 1976), and by the editors and researchers in texts on the topic (e.g., Mash, Hamerlynck, & Handy, 1976; Mash, Handy, & Hamerlynck, 1976). Here, a sampling of some of the important variables is identified and discussed from the perspective of efficacy, practicality, and other considerations.

Complexity of Problems and Training. There has been a range in the level of the complexity of the problems targeted and in the procedures that parents have been trained to use. Examples of the very specific target behaviors are child behavior in a supermarket (Clark *et al.*, 1977) and proper use of the toilet (Azrin & Foxx, 1974). Somewhat more general are *sets* of behaviors, such as noncompliance (Forehand, 1977) or sibling conflict (Leitenberg *et al.*, 1977), and parents are taught specific strategies for treating them. For example, Resick, Forehand, and McWhorter (1976)

taught a mother to praise compliance or to use time-out for noncompliance. Patterson (e.g., Patterson & Reid, 1973) has developed a program to train parents to modify a broad range of "coercive" child behaviors by applying various reinforcing and punishing conditions. Still more general are the sorts of skills involved in family contracting (Blechman, 1974) or problem-solving communication training (Robin, 1979). Many textbooks written specifically for parents, such as some of those reviewed by Bernal and North (1978), or for any of a variety of managers of child behavior change (e.g., Sulzer-Azaroff & Mayer, 1977) teach general behavior-modification strategies almost in a cookbook fashion. Parents or other consumers of the books are expected to be able to apply a general model and then to select, implement, and evaluate the specific procedures appropriate to the problem at hand.

If a particular problem is the only one identified and tends to occur at a particular time and place, a specific set of instructions may be sufficient. But if parents are to be expected to practice effective behavioral skills across behaviors and conditions, it is probably preferable to instruct them in general as well as specific methods. This conclusion is supported on the basis of a study by Glogower and Sloop (1976), who compared those two treatment strategies among two small groups of mothers. They found that the group of mothers who were instructed in both general and specific procedures attained more stable and general change. Other relevant factors might be the history and background of the parents, particularly their ability to abstract and generalize; the amount of consultation they receive, and the number and type of examples that are supplied and that they are asked to generate themselves. These latter factors remain to be studied.

Where and with Whom Training Takes Place. Parents may receive their training individually or in groups; in a community setting, such as a clinic or school; or right at home. Sometimes the child or other family members are present; sometimes not. Where and with whom the training takes place may depend on the nature of the problem as well as on logistical and practical issues. It seems that target behaviors that are relatively independent of the setting are often treated outside the natural environment. For example, if the problem is in oral communication (Robin, 1979) or contracting (Blechman, 1974), it is probably readily transferable outside the training setting.

When the problem behavior has been firmly tied to conditions of the natural physical or social environment, home-based programs are often used. Bedtime tantrums (Williams, 1959), bed-wetting (Azrin & Thienes, 1978), completing chores (Phillips *et al.*, 1972), and other behaviors depend in part on physical stimuli of the natural environment. The most concrete form of parent training would involve those objects—the bed, the cleaning implements, the items to be cleaned, and so on.

Whether other family members (particularly the child with the identified problem) are present seems to depend on the trainer's assumption about the parent's ability to transfer knowledge and skills into the family setting. Various programs have involved parents and their children, and sometimes other family members, directly in the training setting. The initial training may begin with the therapist and be gradually shifted over to the parent (Engeln *et al.*, 1968), or it may involve parents throughout (Hawkins *et al.*, 1966).

The decision about where training should take place and who should be present must rest on other factors as well. Cost factors, such as the time available to the trainer and the parent, commuting expenses, the comfort parents feel in receiving trainers in the home, and the physical facilities, may influence the value of a given program. Sometimes training may be conducted both in the clinic and in the home. Parents may be instructed intensively in the clinic, with a series of booster sessions to promote both generalization into the family constellation and long-term maintenance. Not all contacts need to be personal, either. Telephone calls (Holden & Sulzer-Azaroff, 1972) or notes (Hunt & Sulzer-Azaroff, 1974) may bridge the time gap between in-person communications. The issues of cost for parents and therapists have been discussed in detail by Kovitz (1976) and in various review articles (e.g., Johnson & Katz, 1973; O'Dell, 1974).

Problems Targeted for Change by Parents. A general review of the literature on parent training indicates that behavioral reduction is frequently the selected goal. Parents are trained in how to use time-out (Flanagan, Adams, & Forehand, 1979), response-cost (Miller, 1975), and other reductive procedures effectively. Often, but not always, training does involve techniques for increasing the rate of positive, constructive behaviors. Noncompliance may simply be punished, or noncompliance punished and compliance reinforced. In the latter case, a more acceptable behavior is being strengthened simultaneously with the reduction in the less acceptable one (Leitenberg, Burchard, Burchard, Fuller, & Lysaght, 1977).

An alternative approach would be to train parents to teach their children behaviors that are either incompatible with or that prevent the development of deviant behaviors in the first place. An example of the former is the general problem-solving communication approaches that Robin (1979), Weathers and Liberman (1975), and others have used. A step further is the strictly preventive method of teaching parents how to guide their children to avoid the development of problems. Presumably, if parents are trained to arrange the physical and the social environment to support their children's positive adaptive behaviors, there should be less need for therapeutic intervention.

Risley, Clark, and Cataldo (1976) have emphasized the importance of identifying critical problem areas in normal family life. Specific intervention packages may then be designed, tested, and disseminated (e.g., the family shopping package, by Risley *et al.*, 1976, designed to promote not only compliance by the children but also important incidental learning).

Procedures Parents Are Trained to Use. The types of procedures that parents have been taught to use are mentioned throughout various sections of this chapter. When the problem is noxious, the parent is usually taught to use some form of reductive procedure: time-out (Flanagan *et al.*, 1979); response-cost (Miller, 1975); punishment, such as a spanking (Bernal, 1969); or extinction (Engeln *et al.*, 1968). Usually, those procedures are to be paired with the positive reinforcement of alternative behaviors. These might include attention (Wahler, 1969a); access to preferred activities (Hopkins, Schutte, &

Garton, 1971); money (Clark *et al.*, 1977); or other material rewards (Wiltz & Gordon, 1974). Training parents to use differential attention may backfire, however. Herbert, Pinkston, Hayden, Sajwaj, Pinkston, Cordua & Jackson (1973) found that when parents systematically withheld attention following their children's deviant behavior, those behaviors *increased*.

When the problem is a skill deficit, such as dressing, toileting, or following a health routine (such as using an inhalator), parents are taught to reinforce successive approximations and segments of the chain of responses. Many of the complex training packages also contain strategies for establishing effective stimulus control. For instance, parents are taught how to present instructions and, depending on the child's response, what consequences to deliver and when (Peed *et al.*, 1977).

Training manuals for parents often include the procedures cited above (e.g., Clark, 1975; Patterson, Reid, Jones, & Conger, 1975; Miller, 1975), as do textbooks designed for training professionals, paraprofessionals, and parents in the concepts (e.g., Sulzer-Azaroff & Mayer, 1977) and skills (e.g., Sulzer-Azaroff & Reese, 1982) of applying behavior analysis. Occasionally, a training manual is designed to teach one specific class of behaviors. An example is Markel and Greenbaum's (1979) *Parents Are to Be Seen and Heard,* a programmed text designed to teach parents to be assertive in the planning of their handicapped children's education.

It seems that if serious problem behaviors are to be prevented, there should be a wide dissemination of procedures for increasing positive behaviors. More parents will need to be taught how to use reinforcement effectively and how and when to reinforce differentially, when to withhold reinforcers, and how and when to apply reductive procedures. They would then be more apt to provide the conditions that enhance positive family interactions: cooperation, altruism, responsibility, creativity, and other socially desirable classes of behavior.

Procedures for Training Parents. The training of parents ranges from lectures and readings to more active involvement, such as observing models (e.g., Flanagan *et al.*, 1979; O'Dell, Mahoney, Horton, & Turner, 1979),

either in filmed form (O'Dell *et al.*, 1979) or with a live demonstration (Johnson & Brown, 1969). Parents may be encouraged to imitate the modeled behavior, rehearsing it repeatedly until a particular level of performance is met. Often, their children are also involved, and the parents are given immediate feedback via a bug-in-the-ear device (Green, Forehand, & McMahon, 1979) or a tone (Bernal, 1969). Videotapes are often used to provide specific feedback, permitting parents to analyze their own performance *vis-à-vis* their children (Bizer *et al.*, 1978). Sometimes simulated problem situations are presented so that the trainer can assess how effectively the parent solves the problem (Nay, 1975). In one case (O'Dell *et al.*, 1979), boys recruited by the trainers were rehearsed to exhibit problem and nonproblem behavior. Their behavior was used to test how effectively a group of parents had learned to apply time-out.

In general, it appears that those procedures that train skills in the home and that most closely resemble those to be ultimately applied are the most effective. For instance, Nay (1975) found that although all of the parents he trained acquired knowledge, it was only when written material and lectures were supplemented with a videotaped model or with role playing that the simulation test performance was superior. O'Dell *et al.* (1979) concluded that their training film enhanced performance, while Flanagan *et al.* (1979) found that in-home modeling procedures produced performance that was superior to that trained by lectures, written materials, and role playing outside the home.

Self-Management

Children are also being trained to manage their own behavior. The assumption (e.g., Brownell, Coletti, Ersner-Hershfield, & Wilson, 1977) is that their involvement should promote enduring change in the absence of externally imposed control. There are also the pragmatic advantages of saving the time and the effort of significant others in the child's life.

The topic of self-control among children has been studied most extensively in the laboratory (e.g., Weiner & Dubanowski, 1975) or in applied settings outside the home. (See Karoly, 1977; O'Leary & Dubey, 1979, and Rosenbaum & Drabman, 1979, for extensive reviews of the topic.) Those studies have yielded information on several facets of self-control: self-instruction, self-determined criteria, self-assessment, and self-reinforcement. In general, according to O'Leary and Dubey (1979), if children adhere to instructions to self-instruct, if they have a history of reinforcement for successful adherence, and if they are skilled in the required behavior, self-instruction can be very effective. Children may also be involved in setting the criteria for their successful performance. According to Brownell *et al.*'s (1977) finding, children achieved more by using stringent criteria than lenient ones. Children can be taught to assess their own behavior accurately. When they do so, the assessment may improve an already effective reward system. Children may reward their own behavior with as much effectiveness as when others deliver the rewards, and they may learn general or comprehensive procedures that can promote transfer across settings and maintained performance.

Examples of the use of self-control procedures by children are being seen increasingly in the literature. For example, various facets of self-control are integral to the "habit reversal" system developed by Azrin and his colleagues (e.g., Azrin & Nunn, 1974; Nunn & Azrin, 1976). Lowe and Lutzker (1979) taught their diabetic client to record the results of her own urine tests. In training conversational skills, Sanson-Fisher *et al.* (1978) taught their clients, delinquent girls, to assess and record the types of comments that they made. Further, Karoly (1977) has offered several useful suggestions for methods of teaching children self-control skills.

Parents are also being trained to make use of various self-control components to manage those of their own behaviors that may influence the behavior of their children (i.e., self-reinforcement; Brown, Gamboa, Birkimer, & Brown, 1976). Herbert and Baer (1972) trained parents to self-record their use of contingent attention with their children. In that instance, the self-recording alone was sufficient to promote more effective parenting skills.

Procedural Trends

Regardless of who manages the contingencies, some general procedural trends in the modification of children's behavior problems may be noted. (These are only briefly summarized here, as other sections in the chapter refer to procedures as well.) First, in treating children's behavior problems, rarely is one procedure implemented in its "pure" form. Rather, procedural "packages" (combinations of various procedures) tend to be used. Not only, for example, is good behavior while shopping reinforced, but prompting, conditioned reinforcement, and many other procedural features are incorporated into the program (Barnard *et al.*, 1977). Relaxation training was combined with a number of other components in the habit reversal program of Azrin and Nunn (1973). In addition, one sees an increased reliance on procedures validated in the applied setting, trends away from contrived material rewards and painful punishers and toward managing antecedents to simple and complex behaviors.

As the field continues to develop, procedures are more apt to be selected on the basis of research evidence than on the basis of logic alone. The earliest behavior-modification procedures were based on principles derived from basic laboratory-based operant research (e.g., Williams, 1959). More recently, it has been increasingly possible to test procedures in the natural setting and, accordingly, to modify principles derived from that evaluation. For example, differential attention has been used effectively with a variety of child behaviors (e.g., Harris, Wolf, & Baer, 1964), but it may be limited to certain subject populations (Herbert *et al.*, 1973).

There appears to be a trend away from the use of highly contrived material-reward systems. Perhaps this is a reaction to a series of studies based on the "overjustification theory." Data from laboratory studies indicated that some children may reduce their rates of engaging in a previously preferred activity following the termination of a phase in which they were given material rewards contingent on that behavior (e.g., Greene & Lepper, 1974). More recent research (e.g., Fisher, 1979; Ramey & Sulzer-Azaroff, 1977) suggests that the generality of those findings is probably limited. But as Fischer (1979) has demonstrated, it does seem that maintenance under extinction conditions is superior following minimal rather than very dense reinforcement conditions. Or perhaps the move away from contrived material rewards is a reaction to the legal restrictions placed on the withholding of material goods (*Wyatt* v. *Stickney,* 1972). At any rate, one is more apt to see preferred activities, social events, or more "natural" material rewards, such as allowances (Fredricksen, Jenkins, & Carr, 1976), used as reinforcers, rather than the more contrived material reward. Exceptions, of course, are made when the behavior must be modified rapidly, as in life-threatening situations (e.g., Magrab & Papadopoulou, 1977), or when the less contrived rewards are not sufficiently effective.

Another trend has been toward the increasing use of stimulus control procedures to modify children's behavior. Such antecedent conditions as rules (Stuart, 1971), self-instructions (Monahan & O'Leary, 1971), visual cues (Gold, 1972), and physical guidance (Striefel & Wetherby, 1973) are being paired with reinforcing consequences, as youngsters learn both simple response patterns and complex behaviors.

Sometimes antecedent cues are paired with shaping and chaining procedures, as young people begin to acquire the subskills identified via a task analysis. Unless the cues are intrinsic to the situation, they are usually gradually faded. An example is a study by Cronin and Cuvo (1979), in which retarded adolescents were taught mending skills. Each of the steps in their task analysis was prompted, if need be, according to a prompt sequence that involved progressively less assistance. The combination of task analyses, prompting, and the fading of prompts holds much promise for teaching children many complex skills that might serve to prevent the development of certain behavior problems altogether. A child might respond to his or her repeated failure to perform a particular skill by throwing a temper tantrum. This could be avoided by breaking the skill down into component tasks so that success is more likely (see Sulzer-Azaroff, Brewer, & Ford, 1978 for a manual designed to teach such instructional skills).

There appears to have been a gradual trend away from the use of punishers that induce pain. Spankings (Bernal, 1969) and electric shock (e.g., Linscheid & Cunningham, 1977) have tended to be replaced by the application of punishing stimuli that seem more benign, such as overcorrection (Foxx & Azrin, 1973); lemon juice (Apolito & Sulzer-Azaroff, 1981); a water mist (Dorsey, Iwata, Ong, & McSween, 1981); and requiring the child to engage in low-preference activities such as contingent running (Luce, Delquadri, & Hall, 1980). Although much attention has been paid to the ethical aspects of punishment by the behavior modification practitioners who have used painful stimuli (Lovaas & Simmons, 1969), it is probable that the experimenters themselves have been punished by the reactions of partially informed critics. Additionally, many constraints have been placed on the use of aversive procedures via agency and governmental policies (see, e.g., May, Risley, Twardosz, Friedman, Bijou, Wexler *et al.,* 1976). The issue of whether a very rapidly effective aversive procedure, such as electric shock, is or is not more humane than one that is less painful but slower to produce effective results remains unsettled. Nevertheless, any recommendation that physical forms of punishment be administered to modify children's behavior problems at home must be cautiously presented. Careful supervision must be provided, and procedures must be acceptable within current laws, policies, and ethical principles. (For a full discussion on this topic, see Carr & Lovaas, 1980).

Ethical and Legal Aspects

There has been a trend in all human service areas toward increasing concern about ethical and legal issues. The Education for All Handicapped Children Act (Public Law 94.142) epitomizes how these aspects have been incorporated within U.S. federal policy. The law includes a variety of provisions for ensuring due process and requires the specification of an individual educational plan to meet the child's special needs. Objective assessment and monitoring of progress toward meeting the goals of the educational program are also required. Children eligible to receive special services may also receive programs directed toward social and other problem areas that do not fall strictly under the heading of academic performance. Behavioral services would be among them (see Pollack & Sulzer-Azaroff, 1981). Thus, those behavior modification programs that are meeting the requirements of the law are conducted with parental approval, and the treatment setting is selected from the least restrictive alternative available for providing an appropriate program.

Integral to behavior modification is the recording of behavioral data. Thus, practitioners must meet the provisions of professional ethics codes related to both service and research (i.e., the *Ethical Principles in the Conduct of Research with Human Participants* by the American Psychological Association, 1973, and the American Psychological Association's *Ethical Standards of Psychologists,* 1979). Thus, the child's participation in the research should be voluntary, and informed consent should be obtained. (When children are too young or disabled to give their consent, a parent or an advocate often serves that function.) State, local, or agency laws and policies may also apply further constraints.

Although behavior modification with children has tended to adhere to legal and ethical requirements, it is only recently that such adherence has been cited or documented. Illustrative of such documentation is the following quote, taken from a study of recording methodology. Family interactions were taped at times known and times unknown to family members: "Three means of censorship were provided to protect the families' privacy. (1) The family could activate a censor switch located on the outside of the trunk to disconnect the receiver for 15 min. (b) The family could listen to and erase any part of the tapes before their coding by observers. (c) The family could listen to and erase any part of the tapes after their coding by observers. Confidentiality of all assessment materials was assured, and censorship was not discouraged" (Johnson *et al.,* 1976, p. 214).

Perhaps as a function of Public Law 94.142 and the trend toward maintaining children in their own homes rather than placing them in institutions, there has been an increasing focus on promoting developmental functioning. Par-

ent-training efforts have recently begun to include not only methods for getting rid of noxious behaviors but also methods for enhancing self-care (Bucher & Reaume, 1979) and other constructive activities for children. Efforts are also continually being made to discover optimal levels of stimulation to be applied to reduce undesirable behaviors. Examples are the trend toward using as brief a time-out period as may be effective (see Risley & Twardosz, 1974) or shorter positive-practice durations within the overcorrection procedure (Harris & Romanczyk, 1976).

Methodology

The methodological rigor with which child behavior problems in the home have been studied seems to vary considerably, particularly in the precision with which behavior has been observed and in the experimental designs of the studies. Many of the early studies relied, at least in part, on parental reporting. Later, along with the development of more precise observational technology (e.g., Bijou, Peterson, & Ault, 1968) within the behavior modification field in general, more precision could be seen in the study of the home-based problems of children. Observers began to receive more training, were kept as uninformed as possible about the interventions being used and the outcomes expected, and learned to avoid interacting with the families, and the *reliability* of their observational recording was estimated regularly. More recently, the *validity* of selected behavioral measures has begun to be assessed by referring to multiple sources, including interviews, case records, naturalistic observations, behavioral checklists, normative data, and standardized observations and tests (see, e.g., Johnson, Bolstad, & Lobitz, 1976.)

Another methodological problem that is particularly relevant here is reactivity to the measurement of behavior in the home. The behavior modification field has relied heavily on the use of live observers or in their stead, video or audio recorders. In a home, the presence of a noninteracting stranger is particularly obtrusive, and presumably, the observer's presence influences the data (Johnson & Bolstad, 1975). Audio recordings or radio transmitters (Johnson, Christensen, & Bellamy, 1976)—either activated by the parents, as in Bizer *et al.* (1978), or programmed by the experimenter to turn on at preset random times (Johnson, Christensen, & Bellamy, 1976)—have been used in attempts to minimize reactivity to observation. Another option is the involvement of family members in validating self-recording (Azrin & Nunn, 1973). Studies of the latter options suggest that reactivity can probably be reduced substantially. However, continued research on this problem is clearly needed.

The precision with which studies of child behavior problems in the home are experimentally designed also continues to vary. The range of designs covers individual and replicated case studies, reversal, within- and across-subject–multiple-baseline replications (according to the rules of single-subject research design), program reports, and group designs. In general, the studies that control for passage of time, variation of conditions from day to day, and other potentially confounding variables are those from which principles can most confidently be drawn.

There are situations in which the luxury of a highly sophisticated experimental design is not feasible. Occasionally, an infrequently observed condition requires modification (e.g., the modification of Gilles de la Tourette's syndrome might be difficult to replicate across subjects, as it is so rare a problem). Sometimes a behavior is so dangerous that sufficient baseline recording would not be feasible. A two-day unstable baseline prior to the treatment of a seriously debilitated infant for chronic rumination was judged in one case to be about as long as responsible ethics would permit (Lang & Melamed, 1969).

Future Perspectives

The field of behavior modification has demonstrated that parents, siblings, and other family members may take an active part in remediating children's problems. In many instances, the young clients themselves may effectively involve themselves in the treatment of their own problems. Success seems to depend on adequate training, supervision, con-sultation, monitoring, and follow-up. But much of the research on family and client involvement in the management of the treatment process has been conducted with select groups: people who have answered advertisements in the newspapers, people who have responded to cash incentives for participation, people who have sought assistance voluntarily, or people who have responded favorably to referrals for assistance. And so, the generality of research findings is of necessity limited.

It is very likely that many families who could profit from acquiring problem prevention and treatment skills are not being reached either as research subjects or as clients or trainees. Methods need to be devised to assist families to seek out services and to acquire the skills that will permit a more positive family life. Kazdin (1979) has discussed the problems of disseminating information about behavior modification to the public and of reaching those families that are most at risk. As more information about behavior modification is being included in the curriculum offerings of institutions of higher education, presumably more young adults will acquire knowledge of the model, and perhaps some skills, that they may apply later on with their own children. But again, such audiences are relatively restricted. One possible alternative is to turn to the social institution that does reach the large majority of potential parents: the secondary school. The high-school teaching of psychology is becoming increasingly prevalent. It should be possible to include content on effective parenting skills within, or in addition to, the general psychology course.

Regardless of how families are reached, simply teaching a chain of verbal behavior is insufficient. Active participation is essential. The literature on the training of clients, parents, family members, and professionals and paraprofessionals has demonstrated that behavior modification skills may be acquired by means of various innovative techniques: modeling and imitation of skilled demonstrators, behavior rehearsal–role playing, guided practice and other simulated practice, and practice *in vivo* under supervision and with appropriate feedback (e.g., Sulzer-Azaroff & Reese, 1982). Additionally, monitoring and feedback may be necessary if the acquired skills are to maintain and transfer. Research on the broad-scale dissemination of knowledge and skills and on training and management techniques for promoting the enduring practice of effective skills would contribute to the eventual improvement of family life.

In addition to efforts to promote the dissemination of information about effective preventive strategies, much remains to be accomplished in the realm of research. Within the sections on specific problem areas and on trends and issues, we have mentioned topics in need of further investigation. From the broad perspective, regardless of the problem area, some general research questions are especially timely.

What are the conditions that support the long-term maintenance of change in the behavior of parents and children? The assumptions about long-term maintenance need to be tested for extensive trial periods spanning several years. What conditions support the transfer of parental modification skills across different behaviors within the same child or across siblings or settings? What are the collateral effects of different child-management strategies *vis-à-vis* the child's behavior outside the home? Do some strategies promote positive spin-offs? Do others tend to produce antisocial reactions? Such questions call not only for effective training and supervision strategies but also for some fairly extensive ecological assessments.

There is a continuing need to seek procedural refinements that save funds and time, without sacrificing benefit. What strategies can be designed to allow power to be distributed fairly among family members? Studies in that realm should promote situations in which neither parents nor children wield excessive control over one another.

Then, there is the more traditional development of intervention strategies designed to resolve specific problems. Many family problems remain particularly difficult to treat: substance abuse, theft, and others that yield children rapid and powerful reinforcement, as well as neglect and physical abuse by their parents. Other family problems are just beginning to be recognized as being heavily influenced by environmental events: various health problems, activity level, affective "state," and others.

Undoubtedly, the scope of the problem areas addressed will continue to grow.

Finally, there is the whole area of how research findings might interface with public policy. Issues such as legal restrictions on the use of punishment, policies on the provision of behavioral services to children and families, school curricula, and others should increasingly reflect cognizance of research results in promoting policies to serve both individual children and the common good.

References

Alexander, J. F., & Parsons, B. V. Short-term behavioral intervention with delinquent families: Impact on family process and recidivism. *Journal of Abnormal Psychology*, 1973, *81*, 219–225.

Allen, K. E., & Harris, F. R. Elimination of a child's excessive scratching by training the mother in reinforcement procedures. *Behaviour Research and Therapy*, 1966, *4*, 79–84.

Allison, T. S., & Allison, S. L. Time-out from reinforcement: Effect on sibling aggression. *The Psychological Record*, 1971, *21*, 81–86.

American Psychological Association. *Ethical principles in the conduct of research with human participants.* Washington, D.C.: Author, 1973.

American Psychological Association. *Ethical standards of psychologists.* Washington, D.C.: Author, 1979.

Anderson, D. R. Treatment of insomnia in a 13 year old boy by relaxation training and reduction of parental attention. *Journal of Behavior Therapy and Experimental Psychiatry*, 1979, *10*, 263–265.

Apolito, P. M., & Sulzer-Azaroff, B. Lemon juice therapy: The control of chronic vomiting in a twelve year old profoundly retarded female. *Education and Treatment of Children*, 1981, *4*, 339–347.

Aragona, J., Cassady, J., & Drabman, R. S. Training overweight children through parental training and contingency contracting. *Journal of Applied Behavior Analysis*, 1975, *8*, 269–278.

Arnold, J. E., Levine, A. G., & Patterson, G. R. Changes in sibling behavior following family intervention. *Journal of Clinical and Consulting Psychology*, 1975, *43*, 683–688.

Arnold, S., Sturgis, E., & Forehand, R. Training a parent to teach communication skills: A case study. *Behavior Modification*, 1977, *1*, 259–276.

Ashkenazi, Z. The treatment of encopresis using a discriminitive stimulus and positive reinforcement. *Journal of Behavior Therapy and Experimental Psychiatry*, 1975, *6*(2), 155–157.

Atkeson, B. M., & Forehand, R. Home based reinforcement programs to modify classroom behavior: A review and methodological evaluation. *Psychological Bulletin*, 1979, *86*, 1298–1308.

Ayllon, T., & Kelly, K. Reinstating verbal behavior in a functionally mute retardate. *Professional Psychology*, 1974, *5*, 385–393.

Ayllon, T., & Michael, J. The psychiatric nurse as a behavioral engineer. *Journal of the Experimental Analysis of Behavior*, 1959, *2*, 323–334.

Ayllon, T., Smith, D., & Rogers, M. Behavior management of school phobia. *Journal of Behavior Therapy and Experimental Psychiatry*, 1970, *1*, 125–138.

Ayllon, T., Garber, S., & Pisor, K. The elimination of discipline problems through a combined school-home motivational system. *Behavior Therapy*, 1975, *6*, 616–626.

Ayllon, T., Simon, S. J., & Wildman, R. W. Instructions and reinforcement in the elimination of encopresis: A case study. *Journal of Behavior Therapy and Experimental Psychiatry*, 1975, *6*, 235–238.

Ayllon, T., Garber, S. W., & Allison, M. G. Behavioral treatment of childhood neurosis. *Psychiatry*, 1977, *40*, 315–322.

Azerrad, J., & Stafford, R. L. Restoration of eating behavior in anorexia nervosa through operant conditioning and environmental manipulation. *Behaviour Research and Therapy*, 1969, *7*, 165–171.

Azrin, N. H., & Foxx, R. M. *Toilet training in less than a day*. New York: Simon & Schuster, 1974.

Azrin, N. H., & Lindsley, O. R. The reinforcement of cooperation between children. *Journal of Abnormal and Social Psychology*, 1956, *52*, 100–102.

Azrin, N. H., & Nunn, R. G. Habit reversal: A method of eliminating nervous habits and tics. *Behaviour Research and Therapy*, 1973, *11*, 619–628.

Azrin, N. H., & Nunn, R. G. A rapid method of eliminating stuttering by a regulated breathing approach. *Behaviour Research and Therapy*, 1974, *12*, 279–286.

Azrin, N. H., & Nunn, R. G. Eliminating nail biting by the habit reversal procedure. *Behaviour Research and Therapy*, 1976, *14*, 65–67.

Azrin, N. H., & Thienes, P. M. Rapid elimination of enuresis by intensive learning without a conditioning apparatus. *Behavior Therapy*, 1978, *9(3)*, 342–354.

Azrin, N. H., Sneed, T. J., & Foxx, R. M. Dry Bed: Rapid elimination of childhood enuresis. *Behaviour Research and Therapy*, 1974, *12*, 147–156.

Azrin, N. H., Hontos, P. T., & Besalel-Azrin, V. Elimination of enuresis without a conditioning apparatus: An extension by office instruction of the child and parents. *Behavior Therapy*, 1979, *10*, 14–19.

Bach, R., & Moylan, J. J. Parents administer behavior therapy for inappropriate urination and encopresis: A case study. *Journal of Behavior Therapy and Experimental Psychiatry*, 1975, *6(13)*, 239–241.

Bachrach, H. J., Erwin, W. J., & Mohr, J. P. The control of eating behavior in an anorexic by operant conditioning techniques. In L. P. Ullmann & L. Krasner (Ed.), *Case studies in behavior modification*. New York: Holt, Rinehart & Winston, 1965.

Baer, D. M., Peterson, R. F., & Sherman, J. A. The development of imitation by reinforcing behavioral similarity to a model. *Journal of Experimental Analysis of Behavior*, 1967, *10*, 405–417.

Bailey, J. S., Wolf, M. M., Phillips, E. L. Home-based reinforcement and the modification of predelinquents' classroom behavior. *Journal of Applied Behavior Analysis*, 1970, *3*, 223–233.

Bandura, A., & Menlove, F. L. Factors determining vicarious extinction of avoidance behavior through symbolic modeling. *Journal of Personality and Social Psychology*, 1968, *8*, 99–108.

Bandura, A., Grusec, J. E., & Menlove, F. L. Vicarious extinction of avoidance behavior. *Journal of Personality and Social Psychology*, 1967, *5*, 16–23.

Barber, R. M., & Kagey, J. R. Modification of school attendance for an elementary population. *Journal of Applied Behavior Analysis*, 1977, *10*, 41–48.

Barnard, J. D., Christophersen, E. R., & Wolf, M. M. Teaching children appropriate shopping behavior through parent training in the supermarket setting. *Journal of Applied Behavior Analysis*, 1977, *1*, 45–59.

Barth, R. Home-based reinforcement of school behavior: A review and analysis. *Review of Educational Research*, 1979, *49*, 436–458.

Barton, E. J., & Ascione, E. R. Sharing in preschool children: Facilitation, stimulus generalization, response generalization, and maintenance. *Journal of Applied Behavior Analysis*, 1979, *12*, 417–430.

Bauermeister, J. J., & Jemail, J. A. Modification of "elective mutism" in the classroom setting: A case study. *Behavior Therapy*, 1975, 246–250.

Becker, J. V., Turner, S. M., & Sajwaj, T. E. Multiple behavioral effects of the use of lemon-juice with a ruminating toddler-age child. *Behavior Modification*, 1978, *1*, 267–278.

Bell, R. Q. Parent, child and reciprocal influences. *American Psychologist*, 1979, *34*, 821–826.

Benassi, V. A., & Larson, K. M. Modification of family interaction with the child as the behavior-change agent. In E. J. Mash, L. C. Handy, & L. A. Hamerlynck (Eds.), *Behavior modification and families*. New York: Brunner/Mazel, 1976.

Berkowitz, B. P., & Graziano, A. M. Training parents as behavior therapists. *Behaviour Research and Therapy*, 1972, *10*, 297–317.

Bernal, M. E. Behavioral feedback in the modification of brat behaviors. *The Journal of Nervous and Mental Disease*, 1969, *148*, 375–385.

Bernal, M. E. Behavioral treatment of a child's eating problem. *Journal of Behavior Therapy and Experimental Psychiatry*, 1972, *3*, 43–50.

Bernal, M. E., & North, J. A. A survey of parent training manuals. *Journal of Applied Behavior Analysis*, 1978, *11*, 533–544.

Bernal, M. E., Duryee, J. S., Pruett, H. L., & Burns, B. J. Behavior modification and the brat syndrome. *Journal of Consulting and Clinical Psychology*, 1968, *32*, 447–455.

Besalel-Azrin, V., Azrin, N. H., & Armstrong, P. M. The student-oriented classroom: A method of improving student conduct and satisfaction. *Behavior Therapy*, 1977, *8*, 193–204.

Bijou, S. W., & Baer, D. M. *Child development, Vol. 1: A systematic and empirical theory*. New York: Appleton-Century Crofts, 1961.

Bijou, S. W., & Baer, D. M. *Child development, Vol. II: Universal state of infancy*. New York: Appleton-Century Crofts, 1965.

Bijou, S. W., Peterson, R. F., & Ault, M. H. A method to integrate descriptive and experimental field studies at the level of data and empirical concepts. *Journal of Applied Behavior Analysis*, 1968, *1*, 175–191.

Birnbrauer, J. S., Bijou, S. W., Wolf, M. M., & Kidder, J. D. Programmed instruction in the classroom. In L. P. Ullmann & L. Krasner (Eds.), *Case studies in behavior modification*. New York: Holt, Rinehart & Winston, 1965.

Bizer, L. S., Sulzer-Azaroff, B., & Frederickson, R. H. *Parent child problem solving training—Generality from laboratory to home*. Paper presented at the annual meeting of the Association for the Advancement of Behavior Therapy; Chicago, December, 1978.

Blackmore, M., Rich, N., Means, Z., & Nally, M. Summer therapeutic environment program—STEP: A hospital alternative for children. In E. Mash, L. Hamerlynck, & L. Handy (Eds.), *Behavior Modification Approaches to Parenting*. New York: Brunner/Mazel, 1976.

Blechman, E. A. The family contract game: A tool to teach interpersonal problem solving. *Family Coordinator*, July 1974, 269–280.

Blechman, E. A., Olson, D. H. L., & Hellman, I. D. Stimulus control over family problem-solving behavior. *Behavior Therapy*, 1976, *7*, 686–692.

Bollard, R. S., & Woodroffe, P. The effect of parent-administered dry-bed training on nocturnal enuresis in children. *Behaviour Research and Therapy*, 1977, *15*(2), 159–166.

Bornstein, M. R., Bellack, A. S., & Hersen, M. Social-skills training for unassertive children: A multiple baseline analysis. *Journal of Applied Behavior Analysis*, 1977, *10*, 183–195.

Bornstein, P. H., & Rychtarik, R. G. Multi-component behavioral treatment of trichotillomania: A case study. *Behaviour Research and Therapy*, 1978, *16*, 217–220.

Broden, M., Beasley, A., & Hall, R. V. In-class spelling performance: Effects of home tutoring by a parent. *Behavior Modification*, 1978, *2*, 511–530.

Brown, J. H., Gamboa, A. M., Birkimer, J., & Brown, R. Some possible effects of parent self-control training on parent-child interactions. In E. J. Mash, L. C. Handy, & L. A. Hamerlynck (Eds.), *Behavior modification approaches to parenting*. New York: Brunner/Mazel, 1976.

Brownell, K. D., Colletti, G., Ersner-Hershfield, R., Hershfield, S. M., & Wilson, G. T. Self-control in school children: Stringency and leniency in self-determined and externally imposed performance standards. *Behavior Therapy*, 1977, *8*, 442–455.

Bucher, B., & Reaume, J. Generalization of reinforcement effects in a token program in the home. *Behavior Modification*, 1979, *3*, 63–72.

Budd, K. S., & Liebowitz, J. M. *Programmed Activities for School Success (PASS): Modification of disruptive classroom behavior in young children through home-based contingencies*. Paper presented at the second annual convention of the Midwestern Association for Behavior Analysis, Chicago, May 1976.

Butler, J. F. The toilet training success of parents after reading *Toilet Training in Less Than a Day*. *Behavior Therapy*, 1976, *7*, 185–191.

Carr, E. G., & Lovaas, O. I. Contingent electric shock as a treatment for severe behavior problems. In S. Axelrod & J. Apsche (Eds.), *Punishment: Its effects on human behavior*. Lawrence, Kans.: H. & H. Enterprises, 1980.

Catalina, D. *Enuresis: Parent mediated modification*. Paper presented at the Eastern Psychological Association Meeting, New York, 1976.

Christophersen, E. R. Children's behavior during automobile rides: Do car seats make a difference? *Pediatrics*, 1977, *60*, 69–74.

Christophersen, E. R., Arnold, C. M., Hill, D. W., & Quilitch, H. R. The home point system: Token reinforcement procedures for application by parents of children with behavior problems. *Journal of Applied Behavior Analysis*, 1972, *5*, 485–497.

Christophersen, E. R., Barnard, J. D., Ford, D., & Wolf, M. M. The family training program: Improving parent-child interaction patterns. In E. J. Mash, L. C. Handy, & L. A. Hamerlynck (Eds.), *Behavior modification approaches to parenting*. New York: Brunner/Mazel, 1976.

Clark, H. B., Greene, B. F., Macrae, J. W., McNees, M. P., Davis, J. L., & Risley, T. R. A parent advice package for family shopping trips: Development and evaluation. *Journal of Applied Behavior Analysis*, 1977, *10*, 605–624.

Clark, M. L. *Responsive Parent Training Manual*, Box 4792, Overland Park, Kans., 1975.

Conrad, R. D., Delk, J. L., & Williams, C. Use of stimulus fading procedures in the treatment of situation specific mutism: A case study. *Behavior Therapy and Experimental Psychiatry*, 1974, *5*, 99–100.

Conway, J. B., & Bucher, B. D. Transfer and maintenance of behavior change in children: A review and suggestions. In E. J. Mash, L. A. Hamerlynck, & L. C. Handy (Eds.), *Behavior modification and families*. New York: Brunner/Mazel, 1976.

Cooke, T. P., & Apolloni, T. Developing positive social-emotional behaviors: A study of training and generalization effects. *Journal of Applied Behavior Analysis*, 1976, *9*, 65–78.

Copeland, R. E., Brown, R. E., Axelrod, S., & Hall, R. V. Effects of school principals praising parents for school attendance. *Educational Technology*, 1972, *12*(7), 56–59.

Cronin, K. A., & Cuvo, A. J. Teaching mending skills to mentally retarded adolescents. *Journal of Applied Behavior Analysis*, 1979, *12*, 401–406.

Crowley, C. P., & Armstrong, P. M. Positive practice, overcorrection and behavior rehearsal in the treatment of three cases of encopresis. *Journal of Behavior Therapy and Experimental Psychology*, 1977, *8*(4), 411–416.

Dardig, J. C., & Heward, W. L. *Sign here: A contracting book for children and their parents*. Kalamazoo, Mich.: Behaviordelia, 1976.

Doleys, D. M. Behavioral treatments for nocturnal enuresis in children: A review of the recent literature. *Psychological Bulletin*, 1977, *84*, 30–54.

Doleys, D. M., & Wells, K. C. Changes in functional bladder and bed-wetting during and after retention control training: A case study. *Behavior Therapy*, 1975, *6*, 685–688.

Doleys, D. M., Ciminero, A. R., Tollison, J. W., Williams, S. C., & Wells, K. C. Dry-bed training and retention control training: A comparison. *Behavior Therapy*, 1977, *8*, 541–548.

Doleys, D. M., McWhorter, A. Q., Williams, S. C., & Gentry, W. R. Encopresis: Its treatment and relation to nocturnal enuresis. *Behavior Therapy*, 1977, *8*, 77–82.

Dorsey, M. F., Iwata, B. A., Ong, P., & McSween, T. E. Treatment of self-injurious behavior using a water mist: Initial response suppression and generalization. *Journal of Applied Behavior Analysis*, 1980, *13*, 343–354.

Dougherty, E., & Dougherty, A. The daily report card: A simplified and flexible package for classroom behavior management. *Psychology in the Schools*, 1977, *14*, 191–195.

Engeln, R., Knutson, J., Laughy, L., & Garlington, W. Behaviour modification techniques applied to a family unit: A case study. *Journal of Child Psychology and Psychiatry*, 1968, *9*, 245–252.

Epstein, L. H., Masek, B. J., & Marshall, W. R. A nutritionally based school program for control of eating in obese children. *Behavior Therapy*, 1978, *9*, 766–788.

Eyberg, S., & Johnson, S. Multiple assessment of behavior modification with families: Effects of contingency contracting and order of treated problems. *Journal of Consulting and Clinical Psychology*, 1974, *42*, 594–606.

Finley, W. W., Wansley, R. A., & Blenkarn, M. M. Conditioning treatment of enuresis using a 70% intermittent reinforcement schedule. *Behaviour Research and Therapy*, 1977, *15*, 419–428.

Fisher, E. B. Overjustification effects in token economies. *Journal of Applied Behavior Analysis*, 1979, *12*, 407–415.

Fjellstedt, N., & Sulzer-Azaroff, B. Reducing the latency of a child responding to instructions by means of a token system. *Journal of Applied Behavior Analysis*, 1973, *6*, 125–130.

Flanagan, S., Adams, H. E., & Forehand, R. A comparison of four instructional techniques for teaching parents to use timeout. *Behavior Therapy*, 1979, *10*, 94–102.

Forehand, R. Child noncompliance to parental requests: Behavior analysis and treatment. In M. Hersen, R. M. Eisler, & P. M. Miller (Eds.), *Progress in behavior modification*. New York: Academic Press, 1977.

Forehand, R., & King, H. E. Pre-school children's noncompliance: Effects of short term behavior therapy. *Journal of Community Psychology*, 1974, *2*, 42–44.

Forehand, R., King, H. E., Peed, S., & Yoder, P. Mother-child interactions: Comparison of a non-compliant clinic group and a non-clinic group. *Behaviour Research and Therapy*, 1975, *13*, 79–84.

Fox, R. A., & Roseen, D. L. A parent administered token program for dietary regulation of phenylketonuria. *Journal of Behavior Therapy and Experimental Psychiatry*, 1977, *8*, 441–444.

Foxx, R. M., & Azrin, N. H. The elimination of autistic self-stimulatory behavior by overcorrection. *Journal of Applied Behavior Analysis*, 1973, *6*, 1–14.

Fredriksen, L. W., Jenkins, J. O., & Carr, C. R. Indirect modification of adolescent drug abuse using contingency contracting. *Journal of Behavior Therapy and Experimental Psychiatry*, 1976, *7*, 377–378.

Garcia, E. The training and generalization of a conversational speech form in nonverbal retardates. *Journal of Applied Behavior Analysis*, 1974, *7*, 137–149.

Garfinkel, P. E., Kline, S. H., & Stancer, H. C. Treatment of anorexia nervosa using operant conditioning techniques. *Journal of Nervous and Mental Disease*, 1973, *6*, 428–433.

Gelfand, D. M., Hartmann, D. P., Cromer, C. C., Smith, C. L., & Page, B. C. The effects of instructional prompts and praise on children's donating rates. *Child Development*, 1975, *40*, 980–983.

Gentry, W. D. Parents as modifiers of somatic disorders. In E. J. Mash, L. C. Handy, & L. A. Hamerlynck (Eds.), *Behavior modification approaches to parenting*. New York: Brunner/Mazel, 1976.

Glogower, F., & Sloop, E. W. Two strategies of group training of parents as effective behavior modifiers. *Behavior Therapy*, 1976, *7*, 177–184.

Gold, M. W. Stimulus factors in skill training of retarded adolescents on a complex assembly task: Acquisition, transfer, and retention. *American Journal of Mental Deficiency*, 1972, *76*, 517–526.

Goldstein, A. P., Sherman, B., Gershaw, N. J., Sprafkin, R. P., & Glick, B. Training aggressive adolescents in pro-social behavior. *Journal of Youth and Adolescence*, 1978, *7*, 73–92.

Gottman, J. M. Toward a definition of social isolation in children. *Child Development*, 1977, *48*, 513–517.

Graubard, P. S. *Positive parenthood: Solving parent-child conflicts through behavior modification*. New York: Bobbs-Merrill, 1977.

Graubard, P. S., Rosenberg, H., & Miller, M. B. Student applications of behavior modification to teachers and environment or ecological approaches to social deviancy. In E. A. Ramp & B. L. Hopkins (Eds.), *A new direction for education: Behavior analysis*. Lawrence: University of Kansas, 1971.

Graziano, A. M., DeGiovanni, I. S., & Garcia, K. A. Behavioral treatment of children's fears: A review. *Psychological Bulletin*, 1979, *86*, 804–830.

Graziano, A. M., Mooney, K. C., Huber, C., & Ignasiak, D. Self-instruction for children's fear reduction. *Journal of Behavior Therapy and Experimental Psychiatry*, 1979, *10*, 221–227.

Green, K. D., Forehand, R., & McMahon, R. J. Parental manipulation of compliance and non-compliance in normal and deviant children. *Behavior Modification*, 1979, *3*, 245–266.

Greene, D., & Lepper, M. R. Intrinsic motivation: How to turn play into work. *Psychology Today*, 1974, *8*, 49–54.

Hake, D. F., & Vukelich, R. A classification and review of cooperation procedures. *Journal of the Experimental Analysis of Behavior*, 1972, *18*, 333–343.

Hardiman, S. A., Goetz, E. M., Reuter, K. E., & LeBlanc, J. M. Primes, contingent attention, and training: Effects on a child's motor behavior. *Journal of Applied Behavior Analysis*, 1975, *8*, 399–409.

Harris, F. R., Wolf, M. M., & Baer, D. M. Effects of adult social reinforcement on child behavior. *Young Children*, 1964, *20*, 8–17.

Harris, L. S., & Purohit, A. P. Bladder training and enuresis: A controlled trial. *Behaviour Research and Therapy*, 1977, *15*, 485–490.

Harris, S. L., & Romanczyk, R. G. Treating self-injurious behavior of a retarded child by overcorrection. *Behavior Therapy*, 1976, *7*, 235–239.

Hart, B. M., Reynolds, N. J., Baer, D. M., Brawley, E. R., & Harris, F. R. Effect of contingent and non-contingent social reinforcement on the cooperative play of a preschool child. *Journal of Applied Behavior Analysis*, 1968, *1*, 73–76.

Hartmann, D. P., Gelfand, D. M., Smith, C. L., Paul, S. C., Cromer, C. C., Page, B. C., & Lebenta, D. V. Factors affecting the acquisition and elimination of children's donating behavior. *Journal of Experimental Child Psychology*, 1976, *21*, 328–338.

Hawkins, R. P., Peterson, R. F., Schweid, E., & Bijou, S. W. Behavior therapy in the home: Amelioration of problem parent-child relations with the parent in a therapeutic role. *Journal of Experimental Child Psychology*, 1966, *4*, 99–107.

Hawkins, R. P., Sluyter, D. J., & Smith, C. D. Modification of achievement by a simple technique involving parents and teachers. In M. B. Harris (Ed.), *Classroom uses of behavior modification*. Columbus, Ohio: Charles E. Merrill, 1972.

Herbert, E. W., & Baer, D. M. Training parents as behavior modifiers: Self-recording of contingent attention. *Journal of Applied Behavior Analysis*, 1972, *5*, 139–149.

Herbert, E. W., Pinkston, E. M., Hayden, M. L., Sajwaj, T. E., Pinkston, S., Cordua, G., & Jackson, C. Adverse effects of differential parental attention. *Journal of Applied Behavior Analysis*, 1973, *6*, 15–30.

Herbert-Jackson, E., and Risley, T. R. Behavioral nutrition: Consumption of foods of the future by toddlers. *Journal of Applied Behavior Analysis*, 1977, *10*, 407–414.

Hersen, M. Behavior modification approach to a school phobic case. *Journal of Clinical Psychology*, 1970, *26*, 128–132.

Hingtgen, J. N., Sanders, B. J., & DeMyer, M. K. Shaping cooperative responses in early childhood schizophrenics. In L. P. Ullmann and L. Krasner (Eds.), *Case studies in behavior modification*. New York: Holt, Rinehart & Winston, 1965.

Holden, B., & Sulzer-Azaroff, B. Schedules of follow-up and their effect upon the maintenance of a prescriptive teaching program. In G. Semb (Ed.), *Behavior analysis and education*. Lawrence: University of Kansas, Dept. of Human Development, 1972.

Hopkins, B. L. Effects of candy and social reinforcement, instructions, and reinforcement schedule learning on the modification and maintenance of smiling. *Journal of Applied Behavior Analysis*, 1968, *1*, 121–130.

Hopkins, B. L., Shutte, R. C., & Garton, K. L. The effects of access to a playroom on the rate and quality of printing and writing of first and second-grade students. *Journal of Applied Behavior Analysis*, 1971, *4*, 77–88.

Horner, R. D., & Keilitz, I. Training mentally retarded adolescents to brush their teeth. *Journal of Applied Behavior Analysis*, 1975, *8*, 301–309.

Hughes, H., Hughes, A., & Dial, H. Home-based treatment of thumbsucking: Omission training with edible reinforcers and a behavioral seal. *Behavior Modification*, 1979, *3*, 179–186.

Humphreys, L., Forehand, R., McMahon, R., & Roberts, M. Parent behavioral training to modify child noncompliance: Effects on untreated siblings. *Behavior Therapy and Experimental Psychiatry*, 1978, *9*, 235–238.

Hunt, S., & Sulzer-Azaroff, B. *Motivating parent participation in home training sessions with pre-trainable retardates*. Paper presented at the meeting of the American Psychological Association, New Orleans, September 1974.

Hutzell, R. R., Platzek, D., & Logue, P. E. Control of

symptoms of Gilles de la Tourette's syndrome by self-monitoring. *Journal of Behavior Therapy and Experimental Psychiatry*, 1974, *5*, 71–76.

Johnson, C. A., & Katz, R. C. Using parents as change agents for their children: A review. *Journal of Child Psychology and Psychiatry*, 1973, *14*, 181–200.

Johnson, S. A., & Brown, R. A. Producing behavior change in parents of disturbed children. *Journal of Child Psychology and Psychiatry*, 1969, *10*, 107–121.

Johnson, S. M., & Bolstad, O. D. Reactivity to home observation: A comparison of audio recorded behavior with observers present or absent. *Journal of Applied Behavior Analysis*, 1975, *8*, 181–185.

Johnson, S. M., & Lobitz, G. K. Parental manipulation of child behavior in home observations. *Journal of Applied Behavior Analysis*, 1974, *7*, 23–31.

Johnson, S. M., Bolstad, O. D., & Lobitz, G. K. Generalization and contrast phenomena in behavior modification with children. In E. J. Mash, L. A. Hamerlynck, & L. C. Handy (Eds.), *Behavior modification and families*. New York: Brunner/Mazel, 1976.

Johnson, S. M., Christensen, A., & Bellamy, G. T. Evaluation of family intervention through unobtrusive audio recordings: Experiences in "bugging" children. *Journal of Applied Behavior Analysis*, 1976, *9*, 213–219.

Jones, M. C. The elimination of children's fears. *Journal of Experimental Psychology*, 1924, *7*, 382–390.

Kagan, J., & Moss, H. A. *Birth to maturity*. New York: Wiley, 1962.

Kandel, H. J., Ayllon, T., & Rosenbaum, M. S. Flooding or systematic exposure to extreme social withdrawal in children. *Journal of Behavior Therapy and Experimental Psychiatry*, 1977, *8*, 75–81.

Kanfer, F. H., Karoly, P., & Newman, A. Reduction of children's fear of the dark by competence-related and situational threat-related verbal cues. *Journal of Consulting and Clinical Psychology*, 1975, *43*, 251–258.

Karoly, P. Behavioral self-management in children: Concepts, methods, issues and directions. In M. Hersen, R. M. Eisler, & P. M. Miller (Eds.), *Progress in behavior modification, Vol. 5*. New York: Academic Press, 1977.

Karoly, P., & Rosenthal, M. Training parents in behavior modification: Effects on perceptions of family interactions and deviant children. *Behavior Therapy*, 1977, *8*, 406–410.

Karraker, R. Increasing academic performance through home managed contingency programs. *Journal of School Psychology*, 1972, *10*, 173–179.

Kazdin, A. E. *History of behavior modification*. Experimental Foundation of Contemporary Research. Baltimore: University Park Press, 1978.

Kazdin, A. E. Advances in child behavior therapy. *American Psychologist*, 1979, *34*, 981–987.

Kifer, R. E., Lewis, M. A., Green, D. R., & Phillips, E. L. Training pre-delinquent youths and their parents to negotiate conflict situations. *Journal of Applied Behavior Analysis*, 1974, *7*, 257–364.

Knight, M. F., & McKenzie, H. S. Elimination of bedtime thumbsucking in home settings through contingent reading. *Journal of Applied Behavior Analysis*, 1974, *7*, 33–38.

Kornhaber, R. C., & Schroeder, H. E. Importance of

model similarity on the extinction of avoidance behavior in children. *Journal of Consulting and Clinical Psychology,* 1975, *43,* 601–607.

Kovitz, K. E. Comparing group and individual methods for training parents in child management techniques. In E. J. Mash, L. C. Handy, & L. A. Hamerlynck (Eds.), *Behavior modification approaches to parenting.* New York: Brunner/Mazel, 1976.

Lahey, B., Gendrich, J., Gendrich, S., Schnelle, L., Gant, D., & McNee, P. An evaluation of daily report cards with minimal teacher and parent contacts as an efficient method of classroom intervention. *Behavior Modification,* 1977, *3,* 381–394.

Lang, P. J., & Melamed, B. G. Case report: Avoidance conditioning therapy of an infant with chronic ruminative vomiting. *Journal of Abnormal Psychology,* 1969, *74,* 1–8.

Lassen, M. K., & Fluet, N. R. Elimination of nocturnal thumbsucking by glove wearing. *Journal of Behavior Therapy and Experimental Psychiatry,* 1978, *9,* 85.

Lavigueur, H., Peterson, R. F., Sheese, J. G., & Peterson, L. W. Behavioral treatment in the home: Effects on an untreated sibling and long term follow-up. *Behavior Therapy,* 1973, *4,* 431–441.

Leitenberg, H., Burchard, J. D., Burchard, S. N., Fuller, E. J., & Lysaght, T. V. Using positive reinforcement to suppress behavior: Some experimental comparisons with sibling conflict. *Behavior Therapy,* 1977, *8,* 168–182.

Lewis, S. A comparison of behavior therapy techniques in the reduction of fearful avoidance behavior. *Behavior Therapy,* 1974, *5,* 648–655.

Linscheid, T. R., & Cunningham, C. E. A controlled demonstration of the effectiveness of electric shock in the elimination of chronic infant rumination. *Journal of Applied Behavior Analysis,* 1977, *10,* 500.

Lovaas, O. I., & Simmons, J. Q. Manipulation of self-destruction in three retarded children. *Journal of Applied Behavior Analysis,* 1969, *2,* 143–157.

Lovibond, S. H. *Conditioning and enuresis,* Oxford, England: Pergamon Press, 1964.

Lowe, K., & Lutzker, J. F. Increasing compliance to a medical regimen with a juvenile diabetic. *Behavior Therapy,* 1979, *10,* 57–64.

Lowitz, G. H., & Suib, M. R. Generalized control of persistent thumbsucking by differential reinforcement of other behaviors. *Journal of Behavior Therapy and Experimental Psychiatry,* 1978, *9,* 343–346.

Luce, S., Delquadri, J., & Hall, R. V. Contingent exercise: A mild but powerful procedure for suppressing inappropriate verbal and aggressive behavior. *Journal of Applied Behavior Analysis,* 1980, *13,* 583–594.

Luiselli, J. K. Treatment of an autistic child's fear of riding a school bus through exposure and reinforcement. *Journal of Behavior Therapy and Experimental Psychiatry,* 1978, *9,* 169–172.

Luiselli, J. K., Colozzi, G., Donellon, S., Helfen, C. S., and Pemberton, B. W. Training and generalization of a greeting exchange with a mentally retarded, language deficient child. *Education and Treatment of Children,* 1978, *1,* 23–29.

Lysaght, T. V., & Burchard, J. D. The analysis and modification of a deviant parent-youth communication pattern. *Journal of Behavior Therapy and Experimental Psychology,* 1975, *6,* 339–342.

MacDonald, W., Gallimore, R., & MacDonald, G. Contingency counseling by school personnel: An economical model of intervention. *Journal of Applied Behavior Analysis,* 1970, *3,* 175–182.

Magrab, P. R., & Papadopoulou, Z. L. The effect of a token economy on dietary compliance for children on hemodialysis. *Journal of Applied Behavior Analysis,* 1977, *10,* 573–578.

Mann, R. A. The behavior-therapeutic use of contingency contracting to control an adult behavior problem: Weight control. *Journal of Applied Behavior Analysis,* 1972, *5,* 99–109.

Markel, G. P., & Greenbaum, J. *Parents are to be seen and heard: Assertiveness in educational planning for handicapped children.* San Luis Obispo, Calif.: Impact Publishers, 1979.

Martin, B., & Twentyman, C. Teaching conflict resolution skills to parents and children. In E. J. Mash, L. C. Handy, & L. A. Hamerlynck (Eds.), *Behavior modification approaches to parenting.* New York: Brunner/Mazel, 1976.

Mash, E. J., Hamerlynck, L. A., & Handy, L. C. *Behavior modification and families.* New York: Brunner/Mazel, 1976.

Mash, E. J., Handy, L. C., & Hamerlynck, L. A. *Behavior modification approaches to parenting.* New York: Brunner/Mazel, 1976.

May, J. G., Risley, T. R., Twardosz, S., Friedman, P., Bijou, S. W., Wexler, D., et al. *Guidelines for the use of behavioral procedures in state programs for retarded persons.* Arlington, Texas: National Association for Retarded Citizens, 1976.

Mayer, G. R., & Butterworth, T. W. A preventive approach to school violence and vandalism: An experimental study. *Personnel and Guidance Journal,* 1979, *57,* 436–441.

McKenzie, H., Clark, M., Wolf, M., Kothera, R., & Benson, C. Behavior modification of children with learning disabilities using grades as tokens and allowances as back-up reinforcers. *Exceptional Children,* 1968, *34,* 745–752.

McKenzie, T. L., & Rushall, B. S. Effects of self-recording on attendance and performance in a competitive swimming training environment. *Journal of Applied Behavior Analysis,* 1974, *7,* 199–206.

McLaughlin, J. G., & Nay, W. R. Treatment of trichotillomania using positive coverants and response cost: A case report. *Behavior Therapy,* 1975, *6,* 87–91.

Mealiea, W. L. Conjoint-behavior therapy: The modification of family constellations. In E. J. Mash, L. C. Handy, & L. A. Hamerlynck (Eds.), *Behavior modification approaches to parenting.* New York: Brunner/Mazel, 1976.

Meichenbaum, D. Examination of model characteristics in reducing avoidance behavior. *Journal of Personality and Social Psychology,* 1971, *17,* 298–307.

Melamed, B. G., & Siegel, L. J. Reduction of anxiety in children facing hospitalization and surgery by use of filmed modeling. *Journal of Consulting and Clinical Psychology,* 1975, *43,* 511–521.

Melamed, B. G., Yurchison, R., Fleece, E. D., Hutcherson, S., & Hawes, R. Effects of film modeling on the reduction of anxiety-related behaviors in individuals varying in level of previous experience in the stress situation. *Journal of Consulting and Clinical Psychology*, 1978, *46*, 1357–1367.

Milgram, S. The behavioral study of obedience. *Journal of Abnormal and Social Psychology*, 1963, *67*, 371–378.

Miller, A. J., & Kratochwill, T. R. Reduction of frequent stomach ache complaints by timeout. *Behavior Therapy*, 1979, *10*, 211–218.

Miller, W. H. *Systemic Parenting Training*. Champaign, Ill.: Research Press, 1975.

Monahan, J., & O'Leary, K. D. Effects of self-instruction on rule breaking behavior. *Psychological Reports*, 1971, *29*, 1059–1066.

Mowrer, O. H., & Mowrer, W. M. Enuresis: A method for its study and treatment. *American Journal of Orthopsychiatry*, 1938, *8*, 436–459.

Munford, P. Outpatient contingency management of operant monitoring. *Journal of Behavior Therapy and Experimental Psychiatry*, 1979, *10*, 135–137.

Murphy, C. M., & Bootzin, R. R. Active and passive participation in the contact desensitization of snake fear in children. *Behavior Therapy*, 1973, *4*, 203–211.

Nay, W. R. A systematic comparison of instructional techniques for parents. *Behavior Therapy*, 1975, *6*, 14–21.

Neisworth, J. T., & Moore, F. Operant treatment of asthmatic responding with the parent as therapist. *Behavior Therapy*, 1972, *3*, 95–99.

Nelson, C. M., Worell, J., & Polsgrove, L. Behaviorally disordered peers as contingency managers. *Behavior Therapy*, 1973, *4*, 270–276.

Nelson, R. O., & Hayes, S. C. Some current dimensions of behavioral assessment. *Behavioral Assessment*, 1979, *1*, 1–16.

Nunn, R. G., & Azrin, N. H. Elimination of nailbiting by the habit reversal procedure. *Behaviour Research and Therapy*, 1976, *14*, 65–67.

O'Connor, R. D. Modification of social withdrawal through symbolic modeling. *Journal of Applied Behavior Analysis*, 1969, *2*, 15–22.

O'Dell, S. Training parents in behavior modification. *Psychological Bulletin*, 1974, *81*, 418–433.

O'Dell, S. L., Mahoney, N. D., Horton, W. G., & Turner, P. E. Media assisted parent training: Alternative models. *Behavior Therapy*, 1979, *10*, 103–110.

O'Leary, K. D., & Kent, R. N. *A behavioral consultation program for parents and teachers of children with conduct problems*. Paper presented at the meeting of the American Psycho-pathological Association, Boston, December 1974.

O'Leary, K. D., O'Leary, S., & Becker, W. C. Modification of deviant sibling interaction patterns in the home. *Behaviour Research and Therapy*, 1967, *5*, 113–120.

O'Leary, S. G., & Dubey, D. R. Applications of self-control procedures by children: A review. *Journal of Applied Behavior Analysis*, 1979, *12*, 449–465.

Ollendick, T. H. Behavioral treatment of anorexia nervosa: A 5 year study. *Behavior Modification*, 1979, *3*, 124–135.

Patterson, G. R. The aggressive child: Victim and architect of a coersive system. In E. J. Mash, L. A. Hamerlynck, & L. C. Handy (Eds.), *Behavior modification and families*. New York: Brunner/Mazel, 1976, pp. 267–316.

Patterson, G. R., & Reid, J. B. Intervention for families of aggressive boys: A replication study. *Behaviour Research and Therapy*, 1973, *11*, 383–394.

Patterson, G. R., McNeal, N., Hawkins, N., & Phelps, R. Reprogramming the social environment. *Journal of Child Psychology and Psychiatry*, 1967, *8*, 181–195.

Patterson, G. R., Cobb, J. A., & Ray, R. S. A social engineering technology for retraining the families of aggressive boys. In H. E. Adams & I. P. Unikel (Eds.), *Issues and trends in behavioral therapy*. Springfield, Ill.: Charles C Thomas, 1973.

Patterson, G. R., Reid, J. B., Jones, R. R., & Conger, R. E. *A social learning approach to family intervention*. Eugene, Ore.: Castalia Publishing, 1975.

Peed, S., Roberts, M. W., & Forehand, R. Evaluation of the effectiveness of a standardized parent training program in altering the interaction of mothers and their noncompliant children. *Behavior Modification*, 1977, *1*, 323–350.

Peterson, D. R. Assessing interpersonal relationships by means of interaction records. *Behavioral Assessment*, 1979, *1*, 221–236.

Peterson, R. F. Power, programming, and punishment: Could we be overcontrolling our children? In E. J. Mash, L. A. Hamerlynck, & L. C. Handy (Eds.), *Behavior modification and families*. New York: Brunner/Mazel, 1976, pp. 338–352.

Phillips, E. L., Phillips, E. M., Fixsen, D., & Wolf, M. M. The teaching family handbook. Lawrence: Department of Human Development, University of Kansas, 1972.

Pollack, M. J., & Sulzer-Azaroff, B. Protecting the educational rights of the handicapped child. In J. T. Hannah, H. B. Clark, & W. P. Christian (Eds.), *Preservation of client rights: A handbook for practitioners providing therapeutic, educational and rehabilitative services*. New York: Free Press, 1981.

Pollack, M. J., Sulzer-Azaroff, B., & Williams, R. The experimental analysis of a homeward educational program with a pre-delinquent juvenile. In G. Semb (Ed.), *Behavior analysis and education*. Lawrence: Department of Human Development, University of Kansas, 1972.

Pomerantz, P. B., Peterson, N. T., Marholin D., Stern, S. The *in vivo* elimination of a child's water phobia by a para-professional at home. *Journal of Behavior Therapy and Experimental Psychiatry*, 1977, *8*, 417–422.

Rachman, S. Clinical applications of observational learning, imitation and modeling. *Behaviour Research and Therapy*, 1972, *3*, 379–397.

Ragland, E. U., Kerr, M. M., & Strain, P. S. Behavior of withdrawn autistic children: Effects of peer social initiations. *Behavior Modification*, 1978, *2*, 565–578.

Ramey, G., & Sulzer-Azaroff, B. *Effects of extrinsic rewards on the subsequent choice behavior of academically delayed children*. Paper presented at the 1977 meeting of the American Educational Research Association, April 4–8, New York, N.Y.

Rasbury, W. C. Behavioral treatment of selective mutism: A case report. *Journal of Behavior Therapy and Experimental Psychiatry*, 1974, *5*, 103–104.

Reese, E. P. Interviewing for jobs or graduate programs.

South Hadley, Mass.: Mount Holyoke College, 1979. (a)

Reese, E. P. Observing, defining and recording. South Hadley, Mass.: Mount Holyoke College, 1979. (b)

Reid, J. B., Hawkins, N., Keutzer, C., McNeal, S. A., Phelps, R. E., Reid, K. M., and Mees, H. L. A marathon behavior modification, *Psychiatry*, 1967, *8*, 27–30.

Reisinger, J. J., & Ora, J. P. Parent-child and home interaction during toddler management training. *Behavior Therapy*, 1977, *8*, 771–786.

Reisinger, J. J., Ora, J. P., & Frangia, G. W. Parents as change agents for their children: A review. *Journal of Community Psychology*, 1976, *4*, 103–123.

Renne, C. M., & Creer, T. L. Training children with asthma to use inhalation therapy equipment. *Journal of Applied Behavior Analysis*, 1976, *9*, 1–12.

Resick, P. A., Forehand, R., & McWhorter, A. Q. The effect of parent treatment with one child on an untreated sibling. *Behavior Therapy*, 1976, *7*, 544–548.

Richards, C. S., & Hansen, M. K. A further demonstration of the efficacy of stimulus fading treatment of elective mutism. *Journal of Behavior Therapy and Experimental Psychiatry*, 1978, *9*, 57–60.

Risley, T. R., & Twardosz, S. *Suggested guidelines for the humane management of the behavior problems of the retarded.* Unpublished document, State of Florida, Department of Health and Rehabilitative Services, Division of Retardation, 1974.

Risley, T. R., Clark, H. B., & Cataldo, M. F. Behavioral technology for the normal middle-class family. In E. J. Mash, L. A. Hamerlynck, & L. C. Handy (Eds.), *Behavior modification and families.* New York: Brunner/Mazel, 1976.

Ritter, B. The group treatment of children's snake phobias using vicarious and contact desensitization procedures. *Behaviour Research and Therapy*, 1968, *6*, 1–6.

Robin, A. L. Problem-solving communication training: A behavioral approach to the treatment of parent-adolescent conflict. *American Journal of Family Therapy*, 1979, *7*, 69–82.

Robin, A. L., Kent, R., O'Leary, K. D., Foster, S., & Prinz, R. An approach to teaching parents and adolescents problem-solving communication skills: A preliminary report. *Behavior Therapy*, 1977, *8*, 639–643.

Rogers-Warren, A., & Baer, D. M. Correspondence between saying and doing: Teaching children to share and praise. *Journal of Applied Behavior Analysis*, 1976, *9*, 335–354.

Rogers-Warren, A., & Warren, S. F. (Eds.) *Ecological perspectives in behavior analysis.* Baltimore: University Park Press, 1977.

Rosenbaum, M. S., & Drabman, R. S. Self-control training in the classroom: A review and critique. *Journal of Applied Behavior Analysis*, 1979, *12*, 467–485.

Ross, J. Parents modify thumbsucking: A case study. *Journal of Behavior Therapy and Experimental Psychiatry*, 1975, *6*, 248–249.

Sacks, S., & De Leon, G. Training the disturbed enuretic. *Behaviour Research and Therapy*, 1978, *16*, 296–299.

Sanchez, V. Behavioral treatment of chronic hair pulling in a 2 year old. *Journal of Behavior Therapy and Experimental Psychiatry*, 1979, *10*, 241–245.

Sank, L. I., & Biglan, A. Operant treatment of a case of recurrent abdominal pain in a 10 year old boy. *Behavior Therapy*, 1974, *5*, 677–681.

Sanok, R. L., & Streifel, S. Elective mutism: Generalization of verbal responding across people and settings. *Behavior Therapy*, 1979, *10*, 357–371.

Sanson-Fisher, B., Seymour, F., Montgomery, W., & Stokes, T. Modifying delinquents' conversation using token reinforcement of self-recorded behavior. *Journal of Behavior Therapy and Experimental Psychiatry*, 1978, *9*, 163–168.

Scherer, M. W., & Nakamura, C. Y. A fear survey schedule for children: A factor analytic comparison with manifest anxiety. *Behaviour Research and Therapy*, 1968, *6*, 173–182.

Schulman, M. Control of tics by maternal reinforcement. *Journal of Behavior Therapy and Experimental Psychiatry*, 1974, *5*, 95–96.

Schumaker, J. B., Hovell, M. F., & Sherman, J. A. An analysis of daily report cards and parent managed privileges in the improvement of adolescents' classroom performance. *Journal of Applied Behavior Analysis*, 1977, *10*, 449–464.

Schutte, R. C., & Hopkins, B. L. The effects of teacher attention on following instructions in a kindergarten class. *Journal of Applied Behavior Analysis*, 1970, *3*, 117–122.

Serbin, L. A., Tonick, I. J., & Sternglanz, S. H. Shaping cooperative cross-sex play. *Child Development*, 1977, *48*, 924–929.

Seymour, F. W., & Stokes, T. F. Self-recording in training girls to increase work and evoke staff praise in an institution for offenders. *Journal of Applied Behavior Analysis*, 1976, *9*, 41–54.

Sherman, T. M., & Cormier, W. H. An investigation of the influence of student behavior on teacher behavior. *Journal of Applied Behavior Analysis*, 1974, *7*, 11–22.

Shoemaker, M. E., & Paulson, T. L. Group assertion training for mothers: A family intervention strategy. In E. J. Mash, L. C. Handy, & L. A. Hamerlynck (Eds.), *Behavior modification approaches to parenting.* New York: Brunner/Mazel, 1976.

Staub, E. *Positive social behavior and morality*, Vol. 1. New York: Academic Press, 1978.

Steward, M., & Steward, D. Parents and siblings as teachers. In E. J. Mash, L. C. Handy, & L. A. Hamerlynck (Eds.), *Behavior modification approaches to parenting.* New York: Brunner/Mazel, 1976.

Stokes, T. F., & Kennedy, S. H. Reducing child uncooperative behavior during dental treatment through modeling and reinforcement. *Journal of Applied Behavior Analysis*, 1980, *13*, 41–50.

Stokes, T. F., Baer, D. M., & Jackson, R. L. Programming the generalization of a greeting response in four retarded children. *Journal of Applied Behavior Analysis*, 1974, *7*, 599–610.

Stokes, T. F., Fowler, S. A., & Baer, D. M. Training preschool children to recruit natural communities of reinforcement. *Journal of Applied Behavior Analysis*, 1978, *11*, 285–303.

Strain, P. S., Shores, R. E., & Timm, M. A. Effects of peer social initiations on the behavior of withdrawn preschool children. *Journal of Applied Behavior Analysis*, 1977, *10*, 289–298.

Striefel, S., & Wetherby, B. Instruction-following behavior of a retarded child and its controlling stimuli. *Journal of Applied Behavior Analysis,* 1973, *6,* 663–670.

Stuart, R. B. Behavioral contracting within the families of delinquents. *Journal of Behavior Therapy and Experimental Psychiatry,* 1971, *2,* 1–11.

Sulzer, B., Hunt, S., Ashby, E., Koniarski, C., & Krams, M. Increasing rate and percentage correct in reading and spelling in a class of slow readers by means of a token system. In E. A. Ramp & B. L. Hopkins (Eds.), *New directions in education: Behavior analysis.* Lawrence: Department of Human Development (Follow Through Project), University of Kansas, 1971, pp. 5–28.

Sulzer-Azaroff, B., & Mayer, G. R. *Applying behavior analysis procedures with children and youth.* New York: Holt, Rinehart & Winston, 1977.

Sulzer-Azaroff, B., & Reese, E. P. *Applying behavior analysis: A program for developing professional competence.* New York: Holt, Rinehart & Winston, 1982.

Sulzer-Azaroff, B., Brewer, J., & Ford, L. *Making educational psychology work: Carrying concepts into action.* Santa Monica, Calif.: Goodyear Publishing, 1978.

Thoresen, K., Thoresen, C., Klein, S., Wilbur, C., Becker-Haven, J., & Haven, W. Learning house: Helping troubled children and their parents change themselves. In J. Stumphauzer (Ed.), *Progress in behavior therapy,* Vol. 2. Springfield, Ill.: Charles C Thomas, 1977.

Thorne, G. L., Tharp, R. G., & Wetzel, R. J. Behavior modification techniques: New tools for probation officers. *Federal Probation,* 1967, *31,* 21–27.

Tizard, J. Nutrition and human development. In B. C. Etzel, J. B. LeBlanc, & D. R. Baer (Eds.), *New developments in behavioral research.* Hillsdale, N.J.: Lawrence Erlbaum, 1977, pp. 111–118.

Tough, J. H., Hawkins, R. P., McArthur, M. M., & Ravensway, S. V. Modification of enuretic behavior by punishment: A new use for an old device. *Behavior Therapy,* 1971, *2,* 567–574.

Twardosz, S., Schwartz, S., Fox, J., & Cunningham, J. L. Development and evaluation of a system to measure affectionate behavior. *Behavioral Assessment,* 1979, *1,* 177–190.

Van Hasselt, V. B., Hersen, M., Whitehall, M. B., & Bellack, A. S. Social skill assessment and training for children: An evaluative review. *Behaviour Research and Therapy,* 1979, *17,* 413–438.

Varni, J. W., Boyd, E. F., & Cataldo, M. F. Self-monitoring, external reinforcement and timeout procedures in the control of high rate tic behaviors in a hyperactive child. *Journal of Behavior Therapy and Experimental Psychology,* 1978, *9,* 353–358.

Wahler, R. G. Oppositional children: A quest for parental reinforcement control. *Journal of Applied Behavior Analysis,* 1969, *2,* 159–170. (a)

Wahler, R. G. Setting generality: Some specific and general effects of child behavior therapy. *Journal of Applied Behavior Analysis,* 1969, *2,* 239–246. (b)

Wahler, R. G. Some structural aspects of deviant child behavior. *Journal of Applied Behavior Analysis,* 1975, *8,* 27–42.

Wahler, R. G., & Fox, J. J. Solitary toy play and time out: A family treatment package for children with aggressive and oppositional behavior. *Journal of Applied Behavior Analysis,* 1980, *13,* 23–39.

Wahler, R. G., House, A. E., & Stambaugh, E. E. *Ecological assessment of child problem behaviors.* Elmsford, N.Y.: Pergamon Press, 1976.

Waye, M. F. Behavioral treatment of a child displaying comic-book mediated fear of hand shrinking: A case study. *Journal of Pediatric Psychology,* 1979, *4,* 43–47.

Weathers, L., & Liberman, R. P. Contingency contracting with families of delinquent adolescents. *Behavior Therapy,* 1975, *6,* 356–366.

Weil, G., Goldfried, M. R. Treatment of insomnia in an eleven year old child through self-relaxation. *Behavior Therapy,* 1973, *4,* 282–284.

Weiner, H. R., & Dubanowski, R. A. Resistance to extinction as a function of self- or externally determined schedules of reinforcement. *Journal of Personality and Social Psychology,* 1975, *31,* 905–910.

Weinstein, D. J. Imagery and relaxation with a burn patient. *Behaviour Research and Therapy,* 1976, *14,* 481.

Whitley, A. D., & Sulzer, B. *Increasing reading response rate and accuracy through token reinforcement.* Unpublished paper. Southern Illinois University, Carbondale, 1970.

Whitman, T. L., Mercurio, J. R., & Caponigri, V. Development of social responses in two severely retarded children. *Journal of Applied Behavior Analysis,* 1970, *3,* 133–138.

Williams, C. D. The elimination of tantrum behavior by extinction procedures. *Journal of Abnormal and Social Psychology,* 1959, *59,* 269.

Wiltz, N. A., & Gordon, S. B. Parental modification of a child's behavior in an experimental residence. *Behavior Therapy and Experimental Psychiatry,* 1974, *5,* 107–109.

Winett, R. A., & Winkler, R. C. Current behavior modification in the classroom: Be still, be quiet, be docile. *Journal of Applied Behavior Analysis,* 1972, *5,* 499–504.

Wolf, M., Risley, T. R., & Mees, H. Application of operant conditioning procedures to the behaviour problems of an autistic child. *Behaviour Research and Therapy,* 1964, *1,* 305–312.

Wolf, M. M., Birnbrauer, J. S., Williams, T., & Lawler, J. A note on apparent extinction of the vomiting behavior of a retarded child. In L. P. Ullmann & L. Krasner (Eds.), *Case studies in behavior modification.* New York: Holt, Rinehart & Winston, 1965.

Wolpe, J. *The practice of behavior therapy.* Elmsford, N.Y.: Pergamon Press, 1974.

Wright, D. F., Brown, R. A., & Andrews, M. E. Remission of chronic ruminative vomiting through a reversal of social contingencies. *Behaviour Research and Therapy,* 1978, *16,* 134–136.

Wulbert, M., Nyman, B. A., Snow, D., & Owen, Y. The efficacy of stimulus fading and contingency management in the treatment of elective mutism: A case study. *Journal of Applied Behavior Analysis,* 1973, *6,* 435–442.

Wyatt v. Stickney, 344 F. Supp. 387 (M.D. Ala. 1972).

Zlutnick, S., Mayville, W. J., & Moffat, S. Modification of seizure disorders: The interruption of behavioral chains. *Journal of Applied Behavior Analysis,* 1975, *8,* 1–12.

CHAPTER 11

Behavior Analysis Procedures in Classroom Teaching

Ted R. Ruggles and Judith M. LeBlanc

Behavioral research conducted in classroom settings has analyzed behaviors contributing to the maintenance of order in the classrooms as well as behaviors involved in the actual learning of academic concepts. The procedures used to change these behaviors include those involving the manipulation of consequent stimuli and those involving the manipulation of antecedent stimuli. These delineations of procedures and behaviors provide essentially four general categories into which classroom behavioral research can be meaningfully divided: (1) research analyzing the effects of contingent relationships on the behaviors involved in maintaining order in the classroom; (2) research analyzing the effects of discriminative stimuli on behavior involved in maintaining order in the classroom; (3) research analyzing the effects of contingent relationships on the amount and correctness of

work produced by the children in the classroom; and (4) research analyzing the effects of manipulating teachers' instructions and discriminative stimulus materials on children's learning academic concepts and skills.

Applied behavior-analysis research of the first type, involving the manipulation of consequent events in order to develop procedures to keep children orderly, working, and attentive in the classroom, is broad and varied. Some critics feel that this research supports questionable educational goals (Winnett & Winkler, 1972), that is, that its goal is keeping children quiet rather than enhancing their learning. It cannot be denied, however, that procedures are now available that can change the behaviors of problem children so that they may remain inside the classroom to learn rather than being sent outside the classroom to be disciplined. The breadth of the research included in this category is sufficient, in terms of populations, behaviors, settings, and procedures, to allow the production of entire books outlining procedures that teachers may use to maintain order (cf. O'Leary & O'Leary, 1972; Clark, Evans, & Hamerlynck, 1972; Hall, 1970; Kazdin, 1975).

Research of the second type, investigating the effects of antecedent stimuli on maintain-

_____

Ted R. Ruggles and Judith M. LeBlanc • Department of Human Development, University of Kansas, Lawrence, Kansas 66045. Preparation of this manuscript and portions of the research described were supported by one or more of the following sources: The National Institute for Child Health and Human Development (HD 07066, HD 002528, 1-T32-HD-07173 and 1-T01-HD-00247) and the United States Department of Education, Bureau for the Education of the Handicapped (USOE 300-77-0308).

ing order in the classroom, is not nearly as common as that manipulating the consequences of this behavior. Studies of the relationship of behavior to environmental settings (Barker, 1968; Proshansky, Ittleson, & Rivlin, 1970) and findings reported within the generalization literature (Stokes & Baer, 1977) suggest that discriminative stimuli may be powerful determinants of the probability of certain behaviors. The few existing studies that are relevant to these considerations, in combination with studies still to emerge, may provide valuable information regarding how the physical arrangement of the classroom might best be programmed.

The third type of research, which seeks methods to increase the rate, accuracy, and performance of academic behavior in the classroom, is also not abundant but is becoming more so as researchers begin to attend to what children are actually learning in the classroom. This body of research indicates that it is the children who are experiencing difficulty learning who are frequently also those who create disturbances in the classroom. Thus, the emphasis in the research conducted in this category is on increasing the motivational level of children through reinforcement of productivity and correctness. Results from this type of research indicate that for some children, such procedures are quite adequate to increase and maintain productivity. For others, however, the procedures are not sufficient to increase academic learning. Thus, the fourth category of research includes those instances in which researchers have begun to analyze how and under what circumstances children can best learn.

In addition to analyzing how and under what conditions children learn, research involved in the fourth category seeks the best methods for teaching children who do not learn under ordinary circumstances. This research assumes that questions regarding motivation have been resolved and that therefore, something involved in the presentation of the stimulus materials and/or the instructions must be the factor limiting learning for the child having difficulty. Chronologically, this area of research closely parallels (but occurs about 10 years later in time) the development of the contingent relationships that are effective in

maintaining classroom order. That is, this research is being initially conducted with mentally handicapped and very young children, perhaps because the environment of these children is simpler and thus easier to operationally define, measure, and analyze. For example, it is easier to identify effective reinforcers for young and/or mentally handicapped children than for adolescents or adults. Similarly, concepts to be learned by young and/or handicapped children are simpler, and thus, techniques for teaching these children effectively can be more readily identified. As occurred in the sequential development of the application of contingent relationships, it is expected that techniques developed from research on instructional and stimulus control variables will ultimately be applied across various populations, handicaps, and ages.

Contingent Relationships and the Behavior Involved in the Maintenance of Classroom Order

The procedures effective in increasing desired classroom behavior (i.e., response-increment procedures) range from simple adult attention for desired behavior, through access to preferred activities, to many different types of token-reinforcement systems. Also varied are those procedures that have been demonstrated to effectively reduce undesired behavior in the classroom (i.e., response-decrement procedures). They include time-out, removal of tokens, reprimands, extinction, and differential reinforcement of low-rate behavior (DRL). Much of the classroom research analyzing the effectiveness of contingently applied procedures deals primarily with the maintenance of order in the classroom. Its focus of application has been primarily on sitting quietly and working in the classroom. Thus, the behaviors dealt with in this type of research may be, but are not necessarily, related to the academic performance of the children in the classroom. The research is, however, designed to develop a classroom atmosphere in which children's learning need not be disrupted by either their own behavior or that of others. Without the development of such procedures, it would be most difficult to begin to analyze the other factors that might be involved in children's academic learning in the classroom.

Response-Increment Procedures

Adult Attention as a Reinforcer. Prior to the use of behavior analysis in any classroom, operant principles were primarily implemented with infrahuman subjects, or occasionally with institutionalized populations (e.g., Ayllon & Michael, 1959; Ayllon & Haughton, 1962). The earliest applications of behavior analysis in the classroom seem to have evolved from concern for the social development of preschool children and depended on adult attention to manipulate children's social interaction. This preschool classroom research demonstrated that behavior analysis techniques could be successfully applied by classroom teachers to change specific undesirable behavior of children who usually were otherwise considered normal. Much of this early research involved procedures sometimes referred to as *praise-and-ignore* (i.e., reinforcement and extinction). Essentially, the overall amount of adult attention was usually not increased but was redistributed, so that most of the attention that a child received followed the occurrence of desired behaviors and little, if any, followed undesirable behavior. That is, desired behavior was reinforced and undesired behavior was ignored or extinguished.

Research involving praise-and-ignore procedures can be distinguished by whether the emphasis was on increasing desired behavior or decreasing undesired behavior. Some research was designed to increase a particular behavior through reinforcing that behavior and ignoring or extinguishing an incompatible class of behaviors. Other research using these procedures was designed to decrease a particular behavior through ignoring it when it occurred and reinforcing (with adult attention) incompatible or desired behaviors. (This procedure is a form of differential reinforcement of other behavior, i.e., DRO.)

An early study by Allen, Hart, Buell, Harris, and Wolf (1964) emphasized increasing the peer interaction of a preschool child through systematically presenting adult attention contingent on that behavior and ignoring attempted interaction with adults. In subsequent studies, this procedure was effective in increasing cooperative play (Hart, Reynolds, Baer, Brawley, & Harris, 1968); attending to play materials (Allen, Henke, Harris, Baer, & Reynolds, 1967), playing vigorously on playground equipment (Johnson, Kelley, Harris, & Wolf, 1966); and other social behaviors (Harris & Miksovic, 1972; Scott, Burton, & Yarrow, 1967). Hall and Broden (1967) also applied these procedures with brain-injured children in a special education setting to change their manipulation of materials, their physicial activity, and their social interactions. Hart, Allen, Buell, Harris, and Wolf (1964) emphasized decreasing operant crying in two preschoolers by ignoring it when it occurred and reinforcing (with adult attention) those incompatible behaviors considered appropriate responses to minor injuries, arguments with peers, etc. Similar procedures have been used by Brown and Elliot (1965), by Allen, Turner, and Everett (1970), and by Hall, Panyan, Rabon, and Broden (1968). These latter studies also extended the application of praise-and-ignore to change the disruptive behavior of all children in a classroom.

Although adult attention was a functional reinforcer in the research thus far described, such may not always be the case. As a function of a child's history, adult attention may not acquire reinforcing properties, either because adults have not been sufficiently paired with more "basic" reinforcers (e.g., food and warmth) or because an adult's attention is consistently paired with aversive or neutral consequences and thus acquires punishing or neutral qualities. If children do not discriminate between adults, these pairings can affect the potency of the attention of all adults.

Tangible Reinforcement

Because adult attention is not always sufficiently powerful to produce behavior change, a number of studies have relied on the presentation of tangible reinforcers to increase the occurrence of specific social behaviors. Since tangible reinforcers are expensive to maintain for an extended period of time or with a large group of students, access to special activities or free time has been frequently used as a behavioral consequence. Wasik (1970), for example, increased the amount of playtime children were allowed contingent on such appropriate behaviors as sharing materials and following directions. In addition, the amount of playtime was *reduced* contingent on the occurrence of inappropriate behaviors. Thus, this procedure combined elements of both reinforcement and punishment. A similar combination was used by Dickinson (1968) for a student in a regular classroom and by Osborne (1969) in a classroom of deaf students.

The use of procedures employing tangible reinforcement in classroom settings has been greatly facilitated through the use of token reinforcement (see review by Kazdin, 1977). A token, to the extent that it is associated with the delivery of a desired event (a factor largely determined by the success of the token exchange procedure), bridges the time between behavior and reinforcement since it can be delivered much more temporally approximate to the behavior than can those reinforcers for which it may be exchanged. In addition, the token can signal the availability of a variety of reinforcers, thus assuring the potency of the reinforcement procedure across many subjects and/or across extended periods of time. Finally, the delivery of token reinforcement is not likely to disrupt ongoing sequences of behavior in the same way as immediate access to special activities or free play.

The earliest demonstration of procedures roughly equivalent to present token systems was accomplished with primates. For example, Wolfe (1936) taught chimpanzees to obtain grapes by inserting tokens into a slot. The chimps were then taught to obtain tokens by pressing a lever and, finally, to obtain a specific number of tokens before an exchange was possible. The conditioned reinforcing function of tokens with primates has also been the focus of research by Smith (1939) and by Kelleher (1958).

An early investigation of the use of token reinforcement to manipulate students' classroom behavior in a special education setting was conducted by Birnbrauer and Lawler (1964). Teachers conducted classes of 6–13 pupils, in which tokens, exchangeable for candy and trinkets, were delivered for working

on tasks, entering the classroom quietly, hanging up coats, and sitting at desks attentively. These procedures improved the behavior of 37 of 41 students. However, the direct delivery of candy and trinkets occurred in a portion of the study, making a firm conclusion regarding the effective elements of the token system impossible. Therefore, in a replication conducted by Birnbrauer, Wolf, Kidder, and Tague (1965), a reversal was conducted to compare performance when tokens were not presented with performance when they were. Of the 15 subjects in the study, 10 evidenced decreases in some aspects of academic productivity or increases in disruptive behavior when tokens were not presented.

Tokens for Individuals. Tokens have frequently been used for individual children in private sessions to teach behaviors that should be exhibited in the classroom. Walker and Buckley (1968) used a token system for increasing the proportion of time a 9-year-old boy spent attending to assigned problems. The subject in this experiment participated in treatment sessions conducted outside the regular classroom. The subject earned points exchangeable for a model by meeting a criterion for attending. After attending increased in the experimental setting, the child returned to the regular classroom, where intermittent reinforcement and a resulting increase in attending in that setting occurred.

Patterson, Jones, Whittier, and Wright (1965) extended the use of individually implemented token systems to a hyperactive child in a special classroom. One of the primary aims of this study was to demonstrate whether an increase in attending would generalize across settings. The subject wore an earphone during the training sessions from which a tone was heard contingent on the passage of 10 sec of "attention." It was found that once conditioning in the experimental setting was complete, the subject was more attentive in another (unmanipulated) class period than a control child.

A unique method for individualizing a token system to modify the social behavior of a single subject in a classroom setting was presented by Schwarz and Hawkins (1970). In this procedure, a 12-year-old child's classroom behavior was videotaped and later viewed by the child and a therapist. The therapist gave the child tokens (which were accumulated and exchanged for such items as jewelry and a dress) whenever the child's videotaped behavior met a predetermined criterion for reinforcement. This private, delayed-reinforcement procedure successfully decreased the target behaviors in the classroom setting and, in addition, resulted in behavioral changes during other periods of the day as well as in other, unmanipulated, behavior. Such procedures are especially useful in situations in which it is not possible (or advisable) to reinforce behavior at the actual time it occurs.

Token systems for individual children have also been used in the classroom, and in some cases, access to reinforcement for all members of the class has been dependent on the performance of the target child. In these procedures, referred to by Litlow and Pumroy (1975, p. 342)[1] as "dependent group-oriented contingencies," the target child earns rewards that are distributed across the classroom. Group systems are potentially quite powerful, since the probability is great that peer pressure for the target child to perform will occur. Although designing procedures to promote such pressure might be considered unethical, contingencies of this type no doubt will effect immediate and possibly more lasting behavioral change. In addition, these dependent group-oriented contingencies provide a vehicle for changing the behavior of one child without implementing a token system for all members of the class, an alternative that would be realistic if most of the class members did not demonstrate the types of behavioral problems that were addressed.

Patterson (1965) designed such a token system to decrease the disruptive behavior of a 9-year-old second-grade student who was "hyperactive" and "academically retarded" (p. 371). A light, placed on the child's desk, flashed whenever the child had not exhibited any disruptive behavior for a specific period of time. A counter next to the light counted the number of light flashes that had occurred during the observation period. Candy or pennies, in an amount indicated by the counter, were distributed to *all* members of the class at the end of each session. Patterson *et al.* (1965) reported using the same procedure to change essentially the same behavior. Other studies have utilized such procedures to modify off-task behavior (Coleman, 1970) and to change aspects of social behavior or academic productivity (Walker & Buckley, 1972).

Tokens with Groups. Token systems have often been used to change the behavior of whole groups of children in classroom settings. A common method for arranging the contingencies, referred to by Litlow and Pumroy (1975) as "independent group-oriented contingency systems," involves all members of a group's being simultaneously exposed to the same contingencies, with individual access to reinforcement determined by each child's performance. That is, if an individual child earns enough tokens, the backup reinforcement is forthcoming, and if not, the backup reinforcement is withheld.

Bushell, Wrobel, and Michaelis (1968) demonstrated the effectiveness of such independent group-oriented contingency systems in one of the earliest studies of token reinforcement used to modify the behavior of a group of children in a regular classroom. Attending and working by each of 12 preschool children was consequated independently of their classmates. It was demonstrated that a higher level of attending occurred when tokens, redeemable for access to a variety of special activities, were presented contingently rather than noncontingently.

In another examination of the effects of a token system on the behavior of a group of children, O'Leary, Becker, Evans, and Saudargas (1969) isolated the functions of classroom rules, structure, teacher praise, and tokens on the occurrence of disruptive behavior in the classroom. The subjects in this study were 7 members of a second-grade class of 21 economically disadvantaged children. The various contingencies examined were (1) no consequences for disruptive behavior; (2) daily explanations by the teacher of the rules for

---

[1] Litlow and Pumroy's brief review provides an excellent listing of group contingency studies not included in the present review. It should be noted that their classification includes not only those studies utilizing token procedures but also those using various other contingencies. We have utilized their classification in discussing token procedures with groups, since it provides a suitable framework within which to discuss these varied procedures.

classroom behavior; (3) rules plus structure or reorganization of the classroom schedule into 30-min periods in which specific activities occurred (spelling, reading, arithmetic, and science); (4) rules, structure, and praise for appropriate behavior and ignoring of inappropriate behavior; and (5) the previous conditions with the addition of tokens, exchangeable for a variety of small toys, for appropriate classroom behavior. For 6 of the 7 children, "rules, structure, praise, and ignore" did not appreciably lower disruptive behavior. The addition of the contingent delivery of tokens with the accompanying backup reinforcement, however, reduced disruptive behavior for 5 of the remaining subjects.

Independent group-oriented contingencies have been used in conjunction with tokens in a number of other classroom studies (Ayllon & Roberts, 1974; Bijou, Birnbrauer, Kidder, & Tague, 1966; Birnbrauer, Bijou, Wolf, & Kidder, 1965; Broden, Hall, Dunlap, & Clark, 1970; Drabman, 1973; Chadwick & Day, 1971; Drabman, Spitalnik, & O'Leary, 1973; Kuypers, Becker, & O'Leary, 1968; O'Leary & Becker, 1967). Independent group-oriented contingencies have been used for arranging access to activities (Homme, de Bacca, Devine, Steinhorst, & Rickert, 1963; Hopkins, Schutte, & Garton, 1971; Osborne, 1969; Wasik, 1970) and teacher attention (Hall, Panyan, Rabon, & Broden, 1968; Kazdin & Klock, 1973; Madsen, Becker, Thomas, Koser, & Plager, 1968; McAllister, Stachowiak, Baer, & Conderman, 1969).

Besides those systems in which access to reinforcement is based on the performance of selected individuals, Litlow and Pumroy (1975) described another category referred to as "interdependent group-oriented procedures," in which contingencies are specified in terms of group performance. In one of these procedures, the contingencies are specified in terms of the behavior of each student, but access to reinforcement is dependent on all children's meeting some behavioral criterion. Graubard (1969) used such a procedure to increase the appropriate behavior of a group of delinquent youths. In this study, points were given to each group member for appropriate conduct and academic output. The acquisition of backup reinforcement, however, was dependent on

each group member's receiving a minimum number of points. Such procedures rely heavily on peer influence. In describing the study, Graubard reported that "subjects would spontaneously remind transgressors that inappropriate behavior affected them all" (p. 269). The reason for the paucity of research on such procedures is perhaps that in most cases, requiring the entire group to meet certain expectations simultaneously is not only unrealistic but perhaps not ethical.

In a second form of interdependent group-contingency arrangement, reward is dependent on the entire class's meeting some criterion without regard to the behavior of individual class members. Packard (1970) experimentally manipulated all members of a classroom as a unit by illuminating a red light mounted on the teacher's desk whenever *one or more* of the members of a classroom were attending. In comparison to no contingencies associated with the light illumination, access to play materials and privileges contingent on the class's reaching a criterion of attending resulted in increased attending. This research was replicated in kindergarten, third, fifth, and sixth grade. It is conceivable in this system that only one child could be attending for the entire class period and thus obtain reinforcement for all.

In addition to those procedures that base interdependent contingencies on the class as a whole, reinforcement has been based on the average, the highest, the lowest, or a randomly selected performance (Hamblin, Hathaway, & Wodarski, 1971; Drabman, Spitalnik, & Spitalnik, 1974). These procedures differ from the dependent group-oriented contingencies to the extent that the student, or students, on whose behavior the contingencies are based vary from day to day, and thus the criterion is not predictable prior to evaluation.

A variation on the use of the entire class as the group is to divide the class into smaller groups or "teams." Barrish, Saunders, and Wolf (1969) developed a "good-behavior game" for working with a group of 24 students, 7 of whom had been referred for problems such as being out of their seats, making noise, and other disruptive behaviors. The class was divided into two teams, and the number of "rule violations" for each team was recorded on the chalkboard. (Rules prohibited getting out of one's seat, talking without permission, making noise, sitting on desks, etc.). If one team got fewer marks than the other, or if both teams got fewer than 5 marks in a session, the team was allowed to participate in an extra 30-min free period, line up early, put stars by the team members' names on a chart, etc. In addition, if a team got fewer than 20 marks in a week, that team was allowed 4 min of extra recess time for a week.

Maloney and Hopkins (1973) extended the use of the good-behavior game to the manipulation of compositional variables with fourth-, fifth-, and sixth-grade children. They awarded points for the use of different adjectives, action verbs, etc. The members of the team who received the most points (or both teams, if they reached a predetermined point criterion) received candy and 5 min of extra recess. Harris and Sherman (1973) also utilized a version of the good-behavior game in fifth- and sixth-grade classrooms and analyzed the contributions of the various components of the procedure across a series of manipulations. Early dismissal from school, the criterion established for "winning" the game, and the division of the class into teams each seemed to contribute somewhat to the overall effectiveness of the procedure. Removal of any one component, however, did not drastically decrease the procedure's effectiveness. Other versions of the good-behavior game have been implemented by Medland and Stachnik (1972), Robertshaw and Hiebert (1973), and Wilson and Williams (1973).

The arrangement of contingencies based on the behavior of all or some portion of the children in a classroom represents a potentially substantial advance in the implementation of these procedures by classroom teachers. Further evidence supporting this contention is found in the fact that several comparisons of the relative effectiveness of group-oriented interdependent and group-oriented independent procedures suggest that the interdependent procedures are at least as effective as the independent procedures. Litlow and Pumroy (1975) reported that of 14 studies that have compared these two approaches, 7 have found no differences between the two (Axelrod, 1973; Drabman et al., 1974; Grandy, Madsen & DeMersseman, 1973; Herman & Tramon-

tana, 1971; Levin, 1971; Prentice, 1970; Turknett, 1971), and 6 have reported that interdependent procedures are more effective (Graubard, Lanier, Weisert, & Miller, 1970; Hamblin et al., 1971; Jacobs, 1970; Long & Williams, 1973; McNamara, 1971; Witte, 1971).

Although powerful, the fact that group-contingency procedures are, to a large extent, based on the occurrence of social processes seems to demand that they be implemented with some degree of caution. O'Leary and Drabman (1971) have noted that problems may arise when particular children are unable to perform the required behavior, when such procedures result in undue pressure on individual children, or when one or more children subvert the program.

Token systems are efficient behavioral-change systems for teachers to use in classrooms. They provide an opportunity to make the delivery of reinforcement quite discriminable, and thus, behavior change is likely to occur more rapidly. In addition, the systems provide an opportunity for teachers to use a variety of reinforcers, which results in a greater potential for a reinforcer to be available for each child. There are, however, some drawbacks to token systems that must not be overlooked. The very discriminability that makes token systems immediately effective can also work to the ultimate detriment of the system. That is, once tokens are used with children, it is difficult, although not impossible, to "wean" them from the system. Such weaning is necessary, since the real world is not based on token systems.

As already indicated, the effectiveness of token systems lies somewhat in the opportunity to choose a reinforcer from among a variety of items. Thus, a teacher must either be extremely creative in development reinforcing items that are of low cost, or money must be available to purchase such items. A possible method for overcoming the cost problem lies in implementing a token system that has its backup basis in the home rather than in the classroom. Bailey, Wolf, and Phillips (1970) developed and successfully used such a procedure with predelinquent boys who lived in a special home with parents trained in behavior analysis skills. Schumaker, Hovell, and Sherman (1977) extended the use of such procedures to the natural parents of children who were experiencing difficulties in school.

Finally, token systems are more cumbersome and burdensome to use than teacher attention, grades, etc. Token systems require a much more elaborate "bookkeeping" system than more traditional classroom procedures. Even for token systems that are based in the home, it still remains for the teacher to assume the burden of the evaluation and bookkeeping system. Rather than assume the additional work involved, many busy teachers refuse to use the system until the disruptive behaviors of children reach totally unbearable levels.

Response-Decrement Procedures

There has been much public discussion regarding the use of punishment in school settings. Because of societal concerns and ethical issues, however, research involving the application of aversive stimuli in school settings is almost nonexistent. As Gardner (1969) remarked, punishment is often avoided "not on the basis of an objective evaluation of scientific data but on the basis of ethical, philosophical and sociopolitical considerations" (p. 88).

Among the popular arguments aimed at punishment is that all or many of the stimuli that accompany its occurrence may assume "conditioned punishing" qualities. Thus, it would follow that teachers who administer punishment, the classroom in which punishment is administered, and education in general may occasion avoidance of or escape from school by the child. Although there is no direct evidence to support or dispel this contention, examination of analogous positive reinforcement situations suggests that such generalization of effects probably does not occur as a matter of course.

A second argument against the use of punishment is that its effects are not considered long-lasting. This is not surprising, since positive reinforcement effects are similarly short-lived if the overall environmental arrangement of contingencies is not carefully programmed. Without careful planning, it is a rare bit of luck when a reinforcement procedure can be discontinued without a resulting reversal in behavior. It should, however, be possible to maintain the presence or absence of behavior through arranging the transfer of behavioral control from contrived punishing or reinforcing stimuli to stimuli that occur in the "natural community" (Stokes & Baer, 1977) of consequences.

While many generally held notions of punishment may not be empirically sound, there are reasons to avoid the use of such procedures whenever possible. Behavior analysts must respect, if not empirically agree with, societal restrictions on the use of punishment. Additionally, punishment is likely to be applied in situations in which desperation, anger, and lack of rational planning occur. Thus, it requires more careful planning and justification than does the use of positive reinforcement. Additionally, it should be remembered that response-decrement procedures should be used only in conjunction with response-increment procedures. Obviously, a reduction or elimination of an undesirable behavior does not ensure that more appropriate behavior will fill the behavioral void.

Not all punishment involves inflicting physical pain on the child (in fact, very few currently prescribed, applied procedures do). For example, MacMillan, Forness, and Trumbull (1973) noted that "teacher frowns, glances, reprimands, withdrawal of privileges" (p. 89) may be punishers. These authors suggested two points that should be considered in selecting a punishment procedure. First, the procedure should correspond to the "functional maturity of the child" (p. 89). If children operate at an extremely low developmental level, physically painful stimuli may be necessary, at least initially. If children develop normally and are socially adjusted, however, verbal reprimands may be sufficient. Second, a stimulus is punishing only if it results in a decrease in the behavior it consistently follows, or if the child avoids or chooses to get away from that stimulus.

In 1938, Skinner differentiated two types of punishment: first, the contingent presentation of an aversive event, and second, the contingent withholding or removal of a positive reinforcer. Since that time, much has been written regarding the operational definitions of punishment (cf. Azrin & Holz, 1966), and basic experimental punishment procedures continue to be divided into categories similar to those defined by Skinner. There is little research, however, involving the contingent application of aversive stimuli in applied settings. In fact, the response-decrement procedures most frequently used in applied settings involve both punishment and reinforcement, as well as other, less readily categorized, procedures. Thus, to divide *applied* response-decrement procedures into distinct punishment categories such as those found in the basic experimental literature is almost impossible.

One of the most frequently used response-decrement procedures in applied behavior analysis has been time-out from reinforcement or social isolation. Because of society's increasing resistance to the use of social isolation to decrease behavior, however, other, less aversive procedures have been developed. One of these, response-cost, is limited to those situations in which a token economy or a point system is in operation in the classroom. Other response-decrement procedures often used in classroom settings include reprimands, differential reinforcement of other (DRO) behavior, differential reinforcement of low-rate (DRL) behavior, paced instructions, and shifting a teacher's attention from a target child to another child contingent on an inappropriate aggressive behavior emitted by the target child.

Time-Out and Social Isolation. In describing the use of social isolation to decrease undesirable behavior, Wolf, Risley and Mees (1964) indicated that the procedure resembled Ferster and Appel's (1961) use of time-out from positive reinforcement as an aversive stimulus (Wolf *et al.*, 1964, p. 306). Subsequently, Drabman and Spitalnik (1973) attributed to them the popularization of the use of the term *time-out* to describe any situation in which a child is temporarily removed from ongoing activities as a consequence of some (undesired) behavior.

The term *time-out* implies that (1) the child is temporarily denied access to some positively reinforcing event, and (2) the denial is responsible for an observed decrease in behavior. Thus, for time-out to be effective, a reinforcing contingency to which the child can be temporarily denied access must be present in the environment. Also, as with all behavior-change procedures, there must be a demon-

stration that it is the denial and not some concurrently operating contingency that is responsible for the decrease in behavior. In many cases, time-out includes social isolation or other, possibly aversive, consequences. Changes in behavior that occur as a result of such ancillary procedures cannot usually be attributed solely to time-out. As Drabman and Spitalnik indicated, only when the reinforcing aspects of the environment have been directly manipulated is it possible to assess directly the individual contributions of time-out and social isolation.

Perhaps the largest difference between social isolation (also referred to as *room time-out*) and other time-out procedures is that social isolation involves removing the child from the classroom to an isolated area. Drabman and Spitalnik (1973), for example, placed institutionalized children in social isolation rooms for 10 min each time that disruptive behavior, aggression, and out-of-seat occurred. In a reversal design, the social isolation procedure was shown to be effective for reducing all three target behaviors in nearly all subjects. Clark, Rowbury, Baer, and Baer (1973) also used the removal of a mongoloid child from a preschool classroom to reduce severely disruptive behaviors. In addition to demonstrating the effectiveness of the procedure, it was indicated that "some schedules of intermittent punishment may be as effective as continuous punishment, at least in the case of the continued suppression of a response that has already been reduced to a low frequency" (p. 454).

Another type of time-out involves placing the child in a chair, apart from the ongoing activities in the classroom. LeBlanc, Busby, and Thomson (1973) used this chair time-out procedure to change the disruptive and aggressive behaviors of a preschool child. In this procedure, the child was placed on a chair, away from the center of activity, whenever a disruptive or aggressive behavior occurred. If the child refused to remain in the chair for the duration of the time-out period, a backup, (room time-out) was used for further isolation. The use of this backup room time-out appeared to strengthen the effectiveness of the chair time-out across the conditions of the experiment. That is, in the final manipulation of a three-component multiple-baseline design, the chair time-out alone was sufficient to eliminate the aggressive behavior, whereas in the prior two components, the room time-out was required on occasion to back up the chair time-out.

Another version of chair time-out was labeled "contingent observation" by Porterfield, Herbert-Jackson, and Risley (1976). The label *contingent observation* was used because when inappropriate behavior occurred, the children were told what they did wrong and what the appropriate alternative would be, and they were then separated from the group to *observe* the appropriate behavior of the other children. After indicating an understanding of what the appropriate behavior should be, a child was returned to participation in the group. In this chair time-out procedure, a backup room time-out was also used. This procedure was compared with a more traditional redirection of behavior and found to be more effective. However, it is not clear whether it was the contingent observation or the backup room time-out that made the contingent observation procedure more effective.

Chair time-out procedures remove the child from an activity that can still be observed, whereas social isolation procedures remove the child from all but the "memory" of the ongoing activity. Thus, in social isolation, it is doubtful, once isolation begins, that the procedure can accurately be labeled *time-out*. For very young and small children, chair time-out is probably as aversive and effective as room time-out, in that both remove the child from ongoing activities. Unlike the social isolation involved in room time-out, however, chair time-out does not seem to conflict with legal, ethical, and other societal points of view. For older and larger children, however, isolation may be the only effective treatment available because of the difficulties involved in keeping them seated.

Some time-out procedures do not involve the removal of the child from the setting in which reinforcement occurs; rather, they remove the opportunity to respond for reinforcement. Foxx and Shapiro (1978), for example, described a procedure in which each of five special-education students wore a ribbon indicating that the child was eligible to receive periodic teacher attention and to be allowed to participate in activities. If a child behaved inappropriately, the teacher removed the child's ribbon for 3 min. The procedure successfully reduced the occurrence of misbehavior without necessitating removal of the child from the setting.

In another procedure, Plummer, Baer, and LeBlanc (1977) removed materials, and the teacher turned away from the child to constitute a time-out for disruptive, aggressive and inappropriate behaviors that functionally retarded children emitted in response to the teacher's instructions in a one-to-one teaching situation. Although this time-out procedure was successful with many other children in the same teaching laboratory, it did not decrease the undesirable behaviors of these children. Plummer *et al.* indicated that removing the opportunity to obtain reinforcement might produce a negative rather than a positive reinforcement effect if other variables in the environment were aversive. That is, the children might be disruptive so that the teacher would remove the academic materials and the children would then not have to continue working. It was theorized that working on the tasks to obtain the available reinforcers was less reinforcing than it was to emit inappropriate behavior, which resulted in the removal of the sometimes difficult academic work. Thus, negative reinforcement may operate even though demonstrated positive reinforcers exist in the time-in environment, if the latter environment is relatively aversive in other ways.

Solnick, Rincover, and Peterson (1977) also used the removal of the reinforcers and the reinforcing agent as a time-out procedure. These procedures were ineffective for decreasing the tantrums of an autistic child and for decreasing the spitting and self-injurious behavior of a severely retarded child. With the autistic child, however, when the opportunity to engage in the self-stimulatory behaviors that occurred during time-out was made contingent on tantrums, the tantrums increased. In the case of the severely retarded child, enriching the time-in environment was sufficient to reduce spitting and self-injurious behavior; that is, when new toys and other interesting, stimulating objects were used rather than the typical activities, such as putting blocks in cans and sorting colors, the inappropriate behaviors decreased. It was concluded that the effectiveness of time-out is influenced by the nature of the behaviors that a child engages in while in time-out and by the characteristics of the time-in setting.

Paced Instructions. Plummer *et al.* (1977) worked with two subjects who often responded to instructions by emitting inappropriate behaviors. Consistent instruction was necessary, however, because the children would not engage in academic tasks without them. When time-out for inappropriate behaviors proved ineffective, a paced-instruction procedure was designed in which instructions were repeatedly given at 1-min intervals, regardless of the subject's behavior, until the subject complied. Since the subject was not allowed to escape from the instructions (through being timed out or by preventing instruction through disruption), compliance with instructions increased and inappropriate behavior decreased. The paced-instruction procedure used by Plummer *et al.* had an additional unexpected side effect. Teachers who had previously avoided instructing the children because they did not want disruptive behavior to occur were now willing to interact with the children. It was only at this point that academic learning could begin to occur.

Goldstein, Cooper, Ruggles, and LeBlanc (1980) implemented paced instructions at 10-sec intervals and increased rather than decreased a child's aggressive and destructive behaviors that accompanied the teacher's instruction. When paced reprimands for the occurrence of inappropriate behaviors were combined with paced instructions, there was an increase in task-related behavior and a decrease in inappropriate behavior. Possibly reprimands were a necessary addition to the paced-instruction procedure because the child was sophisticated enough to engage in self-reinforcing behavior. Apparently, the pacing procedures did not become aversive until paced reprimands were added. Only then did the child engage in task-related behavior to avoid the aversiveness of pacing.

Reprimands. Doleys, Wells, Hobbs, Roberts, and Cartelli (1976) examined the influence of loud verbal reprimands on noncompliance. In this study, conducted in a laboratory setting, developmentally handicapped children were reprimanded for not complying with instructions. The level of noncompliance during this condition was lower than in comparison conditions in which time-out and positive practice were used. Other researchers have variously demonstrated that reprimands from teachers may function as punishers or reinforcers for inappropriate behavior. This variability of results may stem from differences in style of reprimand presentation. O'Leary and Becker (1968) and O'Leary, Kaufman, Kass, and Drabman (1970) compared soft reprimands heard only by the children to whom they were directed with louder reprimands that could be heard by several other children in the class. The effects of soft versus loud reprimands on out-of-seat, talking out, off-task, aggression, etc., were analyzed by O'Leary *et al.* with 10 children (2 in each of five classes) who were selected on the basis of a high rate of such disruptive behaviors. In general, soft reprimands resulted in less disruptive behavior than loud reprimands.

Thomas, Becker, and Armstrong (1968) suggested that a teacher's disapproval may function as a reinforcer for maintaining the occurrence of inappropriate classroom behavior. The research by O'Leary *et al.* supports this contention; that is, disapproval heard only by the reprimanded student seemed to have less of a reinforcing value and more of a behaviorally depressing effect than loud reprimands that drew the attention of others to the child being reprimanded. It is also possible that the reinforcing effect is in the target subject's apparent control over the teacher in these situations. That is, when the teacher delivers loud reprimands, the target child's classmates may find it amusing that the teacher lost control of the target. If this is the case, then teachers who wish to use reprimands to change behavior should elect the quieter approach.

Response-Cost. Response-cost involves the contingent removal of an environmental stimulus that results in a decrease in the probability of the behavior on which the removal is contingent. Response-cost differs from extinction in that it generally involves the contingent removal of some object or activity that is assumed to function as a reinforcer, while extinction simply precludes the delivery of that reinforcer. Many token and point systems (previously described) have included response-cost components.

The effectiveness of response-cost procedures in changing human behavior was convincingly demonstrated in a series of basic experimental studies by Weiner (1962). This research alternated periods of positive reinforcement with periods of response-cost. Most applied research incorporating response-cost does not utilize alternating periods; instead, it implements the response-cost contingency concurrently with reinforcement contingencies. It is not clear whether these procedural differences would seriously limit the effectiveness of response-cost. What is a definite limitation is that response-cost, of whichever type, cannot be implemented unless previously earned reinforcers are present in the behavior change setting. In token systems, for example, the subject must always have some "reserve" tokens on which response-costs can be levied. In addition, the size and the frequency of response-cost must be sufficient to change behavior while allowing the subject access to reinforcement. This becomes obvious in token systems, since, in order to retain their reinforcing function, tokens must be regularly paired with existing (backup) reinforcers.

In a number of cases, the effectiveness of response-cost has been compared with that of reward procedures for reducing inappropriate classroom behavior. The results of this research indicated that reward systems are equal to (Hundert, 1976; Iwata & Bailey, 1974; Kaufman & O'Leary, 1972) or more effective than (McLaughlin & Malaby, 1972) response-cost procedures. These findings, in combination with the difficulties involved in maintaining the bookkeeping system (which are similar to those in maintaining token systems), may account for the limited use of response-cost procedures for changing classroom behavior.

Differential Reinforcement of Low-Rate Behavior. Procedures employing differential reinforcement of low rates of behavior (DRL) may be especially useful when the complete elimination of a behavior is not desirable or necessary, or when it is not reasonable to require that a behavior not occur for some time before reinforcement can be delivered. Dietz and Repp (1973, 1974) utilized such procedures to lower the rate of verbalizations of students in special and regular classrooms. In one experiment, free play was contingent on maintaining a rate of talk-outs equal to or less than .06 per minute. Reinforcement was contingent on the occurrence of fewer than a specified number of responses in a time period rather than the passage of a specific period of time with no responding. The results of this study suggested that the student's behavior was controlled by the parameters of the DRL schedule. In addition, the 1973 study demonstrated that the DRL rate limits could be gradually reduced until the behavior was eliminated. Thus, DRL could be a valuable response-elimination procedure in settings in which abrupt behavioral change might cause disruptions in other children's behavior and/or in the classroom routine.

Differential Reinforcement of Other Behavior. Reynolds (1968) defined DRO as a procedure in which reinforcement is delivered when a particular response has *not* occurred for a specified period of time. Thus, reinforcement can be delivered contingent on *any* behavior, appropriate or inappropriate, that is occurring when the specified time period elapses. It was suggested by Uhl and Garcia (1969) that this type of DRO be referred to as "omission training" and that the term *DRO* be used only when reinforcement is delivered contingent on the occurrence of a *specific* other behavior or behaviors. Most applied research has implemented this latter type of DRO, primarily because it is difficult to implement the time-based DRO in applied settings and because it is frequently considered neither ethical nor functional to reinforce *any* behavior that occurs when a specified time period elapses. Time-based DRO has been used in one-to-one therapeutic settings in which the subjects have few responses in their repertoires other than the target responses, for example, self-stimulatory behavior (Corte, Wolf, & Locke, 1971), or in which there is only one other behavior that can be emitted and it is incompatible with the target response, for example, screaming (Bostow & Bailey, 1969). Research using DRO to change behavior in classroom situations is limited and, as with the research conducted by Twardosz and Sajwaj (1972), usually has not involved a time base. Their research indicated the usefulness of DRO to increase the amount of time a 4-year-old preschool child spent sitting in a chair. Increases in collateral behaviors, such as proximity to other children and use of toys, were also noted.

Differential reinforcement of other behavior is frequently used in classroom research as a reversal control procedure (Osborne, 1969; Peterson, Cox, & Bijou, 1971, Reynolds & Risley, 1968). Goetz, Holmberg, and LeBlanc (1975) compared the effectiveness of DRO and noncontingent reinforcement as reversal control procedures. DRO resulted in a faster, less variable, and more persuasive reversal of behavior than did noncontingent reinforcement. Even though DRO as a reversal control involves the ethically questionable procedure of reinforcing inappropriate behavior, it may be justified by the applied experimenter since it allows one to demonstrate experimental control quickly and to return to increasing desirable behavior.

Shifting the Teacher's Attention. While extinction has been a component of almost all procedures designed to modify classroom behaviors through reinforcement, its use in reducing aggression in classrooms has been uncommon. The most obvious reason for this fact is that it is not generally acceptable to allow a child's classmates to endure abuse while the gradual extinction of the behavior occurs. A procedure designed by Pinkston, Reese, LeBlanc, and Baer (1973) introduced a partial solution to this problem. In this study, aggressive behavior was followed by the teacher ignoring the aggressive child while attending to the child who had been attacked. This procedure reduced aggression without allowing further harm to come to the victim. In addition to extinction, the authors suggest that giving attention to the victim may have punished the aggressive act.

Summary

The breadth and scope of research analyzing the effects of contingent relationships on behavior involved in maintaining order in the classroom are currently sufficient to allow teachers to be knowledgeably advised regarding what to do with behavior-problem chil-

dren. It should therefore no longer be acceptable for teachers to indicate that they cannot deal with problem children in the classroom. With the availability of the various teacher-attention and token-reinforcement systems, as well as response-cost, time-out, and other response-decrement procedures, it is possible to handle the majority of behavior problems that occur in most classroom settings. There is currently a need to impart the knowledge of behavior-analysis procedures to the practitioners in the field so that the use of these procedures can become more widespread. As this occurs, perhaps there will be more of an emphasis in classrooms on what and how we are teaching children rather than on how their behavior can be controlled so that the classroom can continue in operation.

The research emphasis in this area appears to be beginning to focus on refinements and combinations of the more general procedures used for many years, as evidenced in the research involving DRO, DRL, paced instructions, and the shifting of the teacher's attention from the target child to another child. Perhaps, in the future, this type of research will yield information regarding more efficient and less intrusive procedures that can be used in classroom settings to change inappropriate behavior.

Effects of Environmental Discriminative Stimuli on Behavior Involved in Maintaining Order in the Classroom

To the extent that a stimulus or a stimulus complex is consistently associated with a specific behavior and its consequences, it can control the future occurrence of similar responses. In applied behavior analysis, the control of behavior by discriminative stimuli has been most often considered in the context of the generalization of behavior across settings and/or experimenters or teachers. Researchers have frequently noted the failure to maintain or transfer behavior change across stimulus conditions (cf. Lovaas & Simmons, 1969; Meddock, Parsons, & Hill, 1971; Peterson & Whitehurst, 1971: Redd & Birnbrauer, 1969;

Tate & Baroff, 1966). This failure to transfer is often attributed to inconsistencies between controlling stimuli across settings (Marholin, Siegel, & Phillips, 1976; Marholin & Steinman, 1977). Failures to produce across-setting generalization demonstrate the power that discriminative stimuli can exert over the occurrence of a variety of behaviors.

Most applied behavioral research addressing the role of discriminative stimuli has emphasized procedures for facilitating the occurrence of a newly trained or manipulated behavior across settings. The direct manipulation of discriminative stimuli as a procedure for effecting behavior change occurs relatively infrequently in the literature. In fact, reviewers tend to dismiss this area of analysis by stating that there are few studies that have systematically manipulated antecedent conditions (Klein, 1979; O'Leary & O'Leary, 1976). Some researchers, however, have addressed issues that are either directly or indirectly related to developing an understanding of the role of discriminative stimulus variables in designing procedures to change classroom behavior. In general, research analyzing the role of discriminative stimuli in applied research can be categorized according to variables relating to the physical environment, to the behavior or presence of the teacher, and to the behavior or presence of a child's peers.

The Role of Physical Environment Characteristics as Discriminative Stimuli

The relationship between classroom characteristics and children's behavior has, at times, been examined in studies in which researchers have simply quantified the different behaviors that occurred in various stimulus settings. For example, parallel play in preschools most often occurs in the art and the play areas (Hartup, 1970), and social interaction seems to be controlled by dramatic play (Charlesworth & Hartup, 1967) and dolls (Shure, 1963). More direct analyses of the effects of the physical arrangement of the classroom on behavior have consisted of observing and recording behavior before and after some rearrangement of the physical environment. Using this tactic, Twardosz, Cataldo, and Ris-

ley (1974) demonstrated the effect of arranging an "open" classroom environment on the activities of infants and toddlers in a day-care setting, and Weinstein (1977) showed that the one-task behavior of second- and third-grade children was related to the location, the nature, and the quantity of classroom furniture.

In a study in which the manipulation of discriminative stimuli within the classroom was specifically designed to remediate social deficits, Mitaug and Wolfe (1976) increased the verbalizations of special-education pupils by presenting them with tasks that required the verbal response of peers before materials for completing the task could be received. Mitaug and Wolfe indicated that environmental restructuring becomes the procedure of choice for remediating behavior when the desired behaviors do not occur or occur too infrequently for reinforcement procedures to be optimally effective.

The Role of Teacher Verbalizations and Presence as Discriminative Stimuli

Just as aspects of the physical environment control the occurrence of behavior, aspects of teacher verbal behavior or even teacher presence can, depending on a child's history of reinforcement, function as stimuli that control behavior. For most children, compliance with instruction develops through experiencing instructions paired with consequences for responding or not responding. For these children, verbal instructions provide teachers with a means of evoking behavior that can, if desired, be strengthened through the concurrent application of consequent events.

In research designed to increase a child's involvement with large motor activities (Hardiman, Goetz, Reuter, & LeBlanc, 1975) and social interaction (Strain, Shores, & Kerr, 1976), a combination of teacher prompts and contingent attention was used. Hardiman *et al.* demonstrated that teacher prompts plus contingent attention were more effective than contingent attention alone in increasing the subject's involvement in motor activities. In describing their results, Hardiman *et al.* pointed out that during conditions using only attention, if the subject did not independently engage in an activity, there was no behavior to reinforce and thus behavioral change could not be effected. The manipulation of discriminative stimuli (instructions) to produce behaviors that could then be reinforced undoubtedly circumvented the arduous process of shaping successive approximations or simply waiting for a reinforceable instance of the behavior to occur.

In one study (Wulbert, Nyman, Snow, & Owen, 1973), manipulations of discriminative stimuli were used to teach a child to respond to verbal instructions given by many different people. Since the child responded only to verbalizations from her family members, the authors employed a fading procedure in which the child's mother initially administered the training items that required a verbal or motor response. Across trials, a stranger gradually entered the room, sat with mother and child, administered items simultaneously with the mother, and finally administered items to the child alone. After the child began to follow the stranger's instructions, the mother was gradually moved out of the room. Several other experimenters were subsequently faded into the setting in the same way. Finally, a similar stimulus-control procedure was implemented to move the child into the regular classroom, to establish verbal control by the classroom teacher, and to begin to produce interaction with classmates. While this procedure employed consequence manipulations (time-out and verbal reinforcement) in addition to the fading procedure, reinforcement alone would not have been effective, since the desired behavior never occurred and thus could not be reinforced.

Most young children have a reinforcement history that results in a certain amount of their behavior being controlled by an adult's presence. This is most evident in the differences found in children's behavior when the teacher is absent or present in the room. In one of the few studies to demonstrate such discriminative control, Marholin and Steinman (1977) showed that academic productivity and on-task behavior deteriorated less in the teacher's absence when reinforcement was contingent on academic productivity than when it was contingent on on-task behavior. These results seem to be attributable to the different amounts of discriminative control acquired by the teacher

in the two procedures. Since the teacher's presence was necessary for evaluation of the children's behavior in terms of the on-task contingency, there was a lack of powerful controlling stimuli in the teacher's absence. On the other hand, when the contingencies were placed on academic productivity, some portion of the functional discriminative stimulus complex (i.e., the academic materials themselves) remained present and functional even in the teacher's absence.

The Role of Peer Behavior as Discriminative Stimuli

It seems almost obvious that the behavior of students within the classroom may, like the physical environment and the teacher's behavior, acquire discriminative properties and affect the behavior of other students within the setting. Teachers often report, for example, that disruptive behavior by one or a few students in the classroom "sets off" disruption by others. The inverse, in which consequences directed to one or a few subjects in a group are accompanied by changes in the behavior of other children, is also common. Thus, it seems that the social process sometimes described as *observational learning* (see Whitehurst, 1978, for a review) may play an important role in the occurrence of some behavior within the classroom and could be important in the development of successful, economical classroom intervention strategies.

Whitehurst (1978) said that observational learning occurs when "the topography, functional outcome, and/or discriminative context of one organism's behavior controls a related characteristic of another's behavior" (p. 150). Thus, the meaning of observational learning is expanded from including only those instances in which the observer's behavior is topographically similar or identical to that of the model to include also those instances in which the behavior of the model and the observer is controlled by the same discriminative stimuli or context or the outcomes of those behaviors are functionally the same. Vicarious reinforcement, a process sometimes seen as separate from observational learning, is viewed by Whitehurst as one of a variety of contextual stimuli that determine which, if any, aspects of a model's behavior come to control the observer's behavior. Also included as contextual stimuli are the observer's past history with regard to reinforced imitation, verbal or other instructions, etc.

Perhaps the area of observational learning that has received the most attention by behavior analysts is vicarious consequences. Broden, Bruce, Mitchell, Carter, and Hall (1970), for example, reported that teacher attention delivered to one child for attending resulted in an increase in the attending of a child at an adjacent desk. The authors stated that the effects might be attributable to imitation, to the reinforcing aspects of the teacher's proximity, or to the possibility that increased attending by the target child resulted in fewer disruptions of the peer's study. Unfortunately, there were no controls that would dismiss such direct reinforcement (in the form of teacher proximity) as a cause for the increase in the child observer's behavior. Thus, any statement regarding the role of observation learning in this study is prohibited.

In a study conducted by Kazdin (1973), the target subjects of pairs of retarded children received adult praise for attending, and the attending of adjacent peers increased along with that of the target subjects. Of additional interest in this research was the fact that the observer subjects' behavior remained at the increased level even when the target subjects were praised for inappropriate behavior.

Several extensions of research on vicarious effects have been reported. Drabman and Lahey (1974), for example, reported that the behavior of the subject, a 10-year-old girl, as well as of her classmates, became less disruptive when feedback to the subject was given in the form of occasional teacher ratings. Strain *et al.* (1976) demonstrated that "spillover" effects were partially the function of the behavior and reinforcement history of peers and that such effects were greater when treatment was consistently applied to two children (as opposed to a single child). Finally, Kazdin, Silverman, and Sittler (1975) examined the use of prompts to enhance the effect of nonverbal approval on nontarget peers. It was reported that nonverbal reinforcement was sufficient to increase the target subject's attentive behavior, but vicarious effects were produced only when nonverbal plus verbal attention occurred or when the nonverbal approval was accompanied by a verbal prompt to classmates to look at the target subject when nonverbal approval occurred.

Summary

Relatively few researchers have directly investigated the manipulation of discriminative stimulus events to produce changes in the behaviors that allow children to function effectively in the classroom. Further study of this topic might shed light on the optimal arrangement of the physical environment for facilitating the emergence as well as the maintenance of desired behavior patterns. Such manipulations could be less costly in terms of time and money as well as simpler to implement in classroom settings than the procedures that are currently employed. In addition, a better understanding of the controlling relationships that exist between a child's behavior and that of the child's peers may allow the development of classroom maintenance procedures, based on observational learning, that could have broader effects across children.

Contingent Relationships and Attention, Rate, Accuracy, and Amount of Responding on Academic Tasks

The rationale for conducting applied behavior-analysis research that emphasizes the maintenance of classroom order is based on the assumption that children who engage in behaviors that are not obviously academically related disrupt their own learning process as well as that of their classmates. While most educators agree that some level of classroom decorum is necessary for learning to occur, the exact nature of the relationship between learning and classroom order has not been adequately demonstrated. The most outspoken criticism of applied behavior-analysis research that concentrates on decreasing disruptive behavior and on increasing on-task behavior was provided by Winett and Winkler (1972). They quoted Silberman's assessment (p. 10; Winett

& Winkler, p. 499) of public-school classrooms as "grim, joyless places" and suggested that behavior analysts (by developing the technology for accomplishing these goals) were "instruments of the *status quo*, unquestioning servants of a system of law and order to the apparent detriment of the educational process itself" (Winett & Winkler, p. 501). Winett and Winkler were also subject to criticism because they included only a limited and somewhat biased sample of behavior-analysis research in their survey (O'Leary, 1972). Their article, however, provoked a great deal of thought regarding the functional connection between disruptive or on-task behavior and academic productivity.

Not all researchers who investigated the development of academic productivity prior to the publication of the Winett and Winkler article were deserving of such criticism. In fact, a number of investigations had previously demonstrated the effectiveness of placing consequences directly on academic responding. For example, in some of this research, children were reinforced for work completion (Wolf, Giles, & Hall, 1968); correct responding on spelling tests (Lovitt, Guppy, & Blattner, 1969); the rate and accuracy of their printing (Hopkins *et al.*, 1971; Salzberg, Wheeler, Devar, & Hopkins, 1971); and the accuracy and/or the rate of various other academic tasks (Evans & Oswalt, 1968; Haring & Hauck, 1969; Lovitt & Curtiss, 1969; Tyler & Brown, 1968).

These early studies and some that followed approached the manipulation of academic productivity through reinforcing various aspects of academic production rate or accuracy. In addition, some of this research was designed to allow comparisons of the efficacy of targeting either or both of these variables as an alternative to or in combination with the reinforcement of on-task behavior.

Reinforcement of On-Task Behavior

In reviewing the literature dealing with on-task behavior, Klein (1979) included the research of O'Leary *et al.* (1969), Main and Munro (1977), Hall, Lund, and Jackson (1968), and Broden, Hall, and Mitts (1971). The behaviors targeted by O'Leary *et al.* and Main

and Munro included behaviors that the authors referred to as disruptive (wandering around the room, hitting, kicking, striking, clapping hands, stomping feet, etc.). Thus, so long as children were in their seats and quiet, they were not considered disruptive and were, according to Klein's distinction, on-task. The definitions used by Hall *et al.* and Broden *et al.*, on the other hand, specified that in order to be scored as on-task, children had to be facing the teacher, a peer, or the task material (depending on what activity was occurring at the time).

It might be argued that this latter type of definition requires that, to be scored as on-task, a child must be emitting behaviors that are likely to bring that child into contact with academic materials and teacher instruction, while such is not necessarily the case with the first type. At the same time, however, it is important to realize that in neither case should a consistent relationship between on-task behavior and academic productivity be expected; instances in which children meet the definitions for being on-task but fail to be academically productive (and vice versa) are common.

Included in research using reinforcement to increase on-task behavior are those studies demonstrating the effectiveness of verbal praise from teachers in normal (Hall, Lund, & Jackson, 1968; Main & Munro, 1977; Lobitz & Burns, 1977; Warner, Miller, & Cohen, 1977) as well as special (Broden *et al.*, 1970; Lewis & Strain, 1978) classrooms. In addition, at least one study (Darch & Thorpe, 1977) demonstrated that attention from the school principal increased on-task behavior when attention from the classroom teacher was not successful. Some critics feel that teacher praise directed to individual children may disrupt the work of nontarget children. In response, Kazdin and Klock (1973) developed a procedure involving nonverbal approval from the teacher (smiles and physical contact) that increased the attending of a group of moderately retarded children.

As would be expected, token-reinforcement systems have also been effectively administered to increase on-task behavior. Ascare and Axelrod (1973) demonstrated that tokens delivered for teacher ratings of on-task behavior increased that behavior. Alexander and Apfel (1976) further demonstrated that on-task behavior could be increased by changing the schedule of token delivery from once per hour to a variable- or fixed-interval of 3 min. Comparisons of the effects of token reinforcement with those of teacher attention (Broden *et al.*, 1970; Main & Munro, 1977) suggested that teacher attention combined with token delivery was more effective in increasing on-task behavior than teacher attention alone. Glynn, Thomas, and Shee (1973) demonstrated that the behavioral assessment of on-task behavior could be shifted from the teacher to the children, who engaged in self-assessment on which tokens were awarded. Thomas (1976) and Epstein and Goss (1978) have also shown self-assessment procedures in combination with token systems effectively maintain on-task behavior.

A combination of self-assessment and self-reinforcement was used by Bornstein and Quevillon (1976) to control on-task behavior. Broden *et al.* (1971) made a study of the effects of self-assessment and self-recording of on-task behavior paired with praise from a junior-high-school counselor in comparison with the same procedures *not* paired with praise. In both cases, on-task behavior increased, but the increase for the nonreinforced child was short-lived.

From this brief review, it is apparent that numerous procedures have effectively influenced that group of behaviors called *on-task*. Teacher attention can enhance the effectiveness of token procedures, and self-assessment procedures, especially in combination with token procedures, offer a powerful alternative to more time-consuming interventions controlled solely by the teacher. Conclusions regarding the literature involving the manipulation of on-task behavior are, of course, clouded by the controversy advanced by Winett and Winkler (1972). Perhaps their criticism can be aimed only at the research that does *not* require that children be actually engaged in task-related activities in order to be recorded as on-task. Put another way, a methodology currently exists to produce changes in academic behavior through direct intervention. Thus, manipulations of off-task or on-task behaviors that are not directly related to the academic requirements of the task do not represent the most efficient use of the techniques of behavior analysis.

Reinforcement of Rate of Academic Responding

On a few occasions, academic response rate alone has been measured and manipulated. Lovitt and Curtiss (1969), for example, compared the rate of completion of various academic tasks when the teacher determined the ratios of the amount of work to the points received, to the rate when the student determined this relationship. Performance on all tasks was better in the pupil-determined condition. In this study, however, no mention was made of whether the responses that the student made were correct or incorrect. The problem illustrated by this study is that procedures that measure and reinforce the rate of production without an accuracy criterion may functionally reinforce incorrect responses. Thus, most research involving the manipulation of rate have maintained some measure of work quality as well.

In a study by Lovitt and Esveldt (1970), for example, only the rate of *correct* responses was considered. Measures of error rate revealed that incorrect responding remained at a low level across experimental conditions. Saudargas, Madsen, and Scott (1977) compared the effects of two schedules of home reports indicating number of academic tasks completed and specified that only those assignments completed to a criterion of 85% accuracy were counted and reported as completed. In this study, the students completed a larger number of assignments when the home reports occurred on a variable as opposed to a fixed schedule.

Increases in the number of correct responses may not always reflect an increase in overall accuracy. Klein (1975) indicated that increases in the number of correct responses may reflect changes in the number of items attempted when the number of items assigned or attempted is variable. Brigham, Finfrock, Breunig, and Bushell (1972) had earlier demonstrated this possibility in a study that compared contingent with noncontingent tokens on accuracy on a handwriting task. In one condition of the study, accuracy did not increase when a contingency was placed on accurate responses. An analysis showed that a high rate of responding was sufficient to produce a number of tokens even though overall accuracy was low. The authors pointed out that children in this situation could increase the number of tokens received for accurate responses by increasing either accuracy or rate.

Reinforcement of Correct Academic Responding

Since the nature of the tasks used in the research just reported was generally such that the number of responses made within a given period of time could vary widely, rate was the primary variable of interest. When the number of responses is somewhat restricted by the nature of the task (e.g., completing a specified number of problems), the primary variable of interest becomes the proportion of a discrete number of responses that are correct. The academic tasks that have been manipulated by reinforcing correct responses include spelling (Evans & Oswalt, 1968; Foxx & Jones, 1978; Lovitt *et al.*, 1969); math (Johnson & Bailey, 1974; Harris & Sherman, 1974; Fink & Carnine, 1975; Evans & Oswalt, 1968); handwriting (Salzberg *et al.*, 1971; Trap, Milner-Davis, Joseph & Cooper, 1978); reading (Copeland, Brown, & Hall, 1974; Wolf *et al.*, 1968; Lahey & Drabman, 1974); social studies (Harris & Sherman, 1974); and retention of information from televised newscasts (Tyler & Brown, 1968).

The consequences that teachers have used to manipulate the proportion of correct responses have also been varied. In a number of studies, praise from teachers (Hasazi & Hasazi, 1972), peer tutors (Johnson & Bailey, 1974), or school principals (Copeland *et al.* 1974) has been shown to be effective in increasing the proportion of correct student responses. In addition, contingent free time (Salzberg *et al.*, 1971; Harris & Sherman, 1974; Lovitt *et al.*, 1969; Evans & OSwalt, 1968) has been a popular consequence for accurate responding.

A few studies have compared the effectiveness of various consequences. Some, for example, have suggested that a teacher's feedback regarding the correctness of responses is not, in itself, an effective consequence. Salzberg *et al.* (1971), for example, compared the

effect of intermittent grading with that of intermittent grading plus contingent free time. The authors reported that intermittent feedback alone failed to produce increased accuracy, but when free time was made contingent on accuracy, accuracy increased. Fink and Carnine (1975) compared a condition in which the teacher provided feedback regarding the correctness of math problems with a condition that included feedback and having the children graph their performance. Again, the feedback condition was the less effective intervention. In one other study, Trap *et al.* (1978) compared feedback with a condition that included feedback, praise, and rewriting incorrectly printed words. In this comparison, feedback, praise, and rewriting seemed to be more effective. Even this combination, however, did not seem to be as effective as a condition that included praise, feedback, and rewriting plus the opportunity to win a ''handwriting certificate.'' The results of the comparisons across conditions of this study must be considered tentative, however, since there was no experimental control for the order of treatments.

At least three studies have reported programs in which contingent tokens for correct responses have been compared with other procedures. Tyler and Brown (1968) compared a procedure in which tokens were awarded for correct answers on quizzes about newscast content with a procedure in which tokens were provided noncontingently. The authors reported that the contingent relationship was necessary for enhancing responding on the quizzes. Dalton, Rubino, and Hilsop (1973) compared the performance of two groups of Down's syndrome children who received either verbal praise or verbal praise plus tokens for correct responses on Distar Math and Language. The group who received tokens and praise showed achievement test gains in both language and math, while the group who received only verbal praise showed improvement only in language. A one-year follow-up showed that the token group maintained both gains, while the praise-only group lost the language gain shown on the earlier test. In another comparison, Lahey and Drabman (1974) compared token reinforcement with verbal reinforcement for the retention of sight words. Again, the token system proved to be more powerful.

Foxx and Jones (1978) compared procedures that included only weekly tests and combinations of weekly tests and positive practice procedures for incorrect responses. The combination of positive practice following pretest and weekly tests was the most effective. The use of positive practice, which operates primarily on the principle of negative reinforcement (avoidance), however, is ethically questionable in situations in which more positive procedures have been shown to be equally effective. In addition, the time and the teacher effort required to carry out the positive practice regimen would seem to be prohibitive in most applied settings.

The body of research that has demonstrated procedures through which correct responding may be increased is, for the most part, immediately applicable. Sufficient knowledge exists at this time so that we can make a number of observations and recommendations with respect to traditional educational practice. First, it seems safe to say that teacher feedback alone is not sufficient to increase correct responding. Therefore, it is unlikely that merely indicating that answers are correct or incorrect would have a consistent positive effect. There would seem to be some uncertainty with respect to the exact point at which teacher feedback may, if descriptive and positive, come to function as praise. Perhaps the obvious point is that when a great deal of teacher feedback centers on what the child has done incorrectly, its instructional role, in terms of what response should have been made, is minimal. Positive consequences, on the other hand, serve to inform the child immediately of the nature of the response that is, in that context, desired. Self-assessment and self-reinforcement also appear to serve such a positive function, in addition to having the potential of teaching children to be self-reliant.

Comparisons of Reinforcement of On-Task Behavior with Reinforcement of Productivity

Although research analyzing the various functions of reinforcement on on-task behavior, as well as on accuracy and rate, has added much to the development of techniques for increasing children's academic performance in the classroom, criticisms, such as those of Winett and Winkler (1972), have prompted questions regarding the most efficient and effective techniques to use in given situations. Perhaps the major empirical issue raised by Winett and Winkler was whether there is a relationship between on-task or disruptive behavior and academic productivity. A number of studies have addressed this issue by manipulating either on-task or academic productivity while measuring changes in both of these variables, or by systematically manipulating both variables.

In an early study by Birnbrauer, Wolf *et al.* (1965), the abrupt removal of token reinforcement for correct responses had no effect on the academic productivity or disruptiveness of 5 of 15 retarded subjects. For the remaining subjects, the manipulation resulted in decreased accuracy (6 subjects) or decreased accuracy and increased disruptive behavior (4 subjects). Following this study, other research has implemented reinforcement for academic productivity and measured the effects of this manipulation on on-task or disruptive behavior. Ayllon and Roberts (1974) delivered tokens for accuracy on reading workbook assignments and measured a decrease in off-task behavior such as out-of-seat and talking, while academic behaviors increased. Felixbrod and O'Leary (1973) compared the effectiveness of delivering tokens for correct math problems when the pupils determined the number of problems to be completed for each point in a point system with a yoked condition in which the children had no control over this relationship. Both procedures were equally effective in increasing academic productivity and in producing accompanying decreases in off-task behavior. Ballard and Glynn (1975) differentially reinforced various composition elements to produce changes in the composition of stories written by elementary-school children. This reinforcement, based on the children's self-assessment of their compositions, increased on-task as well as academic behavior.

Other research reporting concurrent decreases in off-task behavior with increases in academic performance has used reinforcement other than token systems. An adjusting ratio of teacher praise, used by Kirby and Shields

(1972), produced increases in the rate of the math problems completed and the proportion of time spent attending. Contingent free time or access to activities has also been demonstrated to result in similar concomitant changes in academic performance and time spent on-task (Aaron & Bostow, 1978; Morraco & Fasheh, 1978). In examining the effects of a package of procedures including timing, feedback, and the public posting of writing rate on writing rate and on-task behavior, Van Houten, Hill, and Parsons (175) reported that each contributed to the increases that resulted from the contingent application of the package.

Investigations manipulating accuracy and measuring on-task behavior suggest that reinforcing accuracy produces increases in accuracy as well as on-task behavior. Such research does not, however, indicate whether the reinforcement of attending results in increased attending as well as increased accuracy. Occasionally, researchers have arranged such consequences. For example, while comparing token reinforcement for compliance with classroom rules and token removal (response-cost) for rule violations, Iwata and Bailey (1974) found that each was equally effective in reducing rule violations but that neither affected the accuracy of the math problems worked during that period. This lack of effect may have been attributable to the fact that correct math problems were 80%–90% of the total completed throughout the study. To show further increases in accuracy would be difficult unless procedures were employed to remediate the errors that the students were producing. Conflicting with the no-effect conclusions drawn from the Iwata and Bailey research, a series of studies that reinforced on-task behavior resulted, although sometimes inconsistently, in increases in achievement test scores (Greenwood, Hops, & Walker, 1977; Hops & Cobb, 1973; Walker & Hops, 1976).

From the research that reinforced only academic accuracy, it appears that both accuracy and on-task behavior are increased, and from that reinforcing only on-task behavior, it appears that on-task behavior and achievement test scores are increased, but this has little effect on accuracy. These studies have manipulated only one or the other type of behavior and have simply observed the behavior that was not manipulated for concurrent changes. There has been, however, some research in which these concomitant changes have been compared through directing reinforcement first to either on-task behavior or accuracy and subsequently shifting the contingencies to the other behavior while recording both. McLaughlin and Malaby (1972), for example, first delivered tokens for the completion of a variety of academic tasks and then shifted the contingencies to reinforcement for being quiet. The shift resulted in some decrement in academic productivity. It is not possible to determine whether quiet behavior was similarly affected when academic productivity was reinforced, since there were no data presented on this variable. It was observed, however, that the productivity of a student who normally completed most assignments was much less affected by the shift in contingencies than was the productivity of a student who usually did not complete assignments.

Hay, Hay, and Nelson (1977) and Marholin and Steinman (1977) found that when on-task behavior was reinforced, only that behavior improved, but when contingencies were directed at academic productivity, increases in productivity and on-task behavior occurred. Marholin and Steinman also found that on-task behavior was much more affected by the teacher's presence than accuracy–rate measures. This finding suggests that the teacher acquired discriminative stimulus properties that controlled the occurrence of on-task behaviors when they were reinforced, but when academic productivity was reinforced, the academic materials apparently began to control the occurrence of the behaviors related to that productivity. Such findings have many implications for producing school environments in which academic learning could become reinforcing in itself. Ferritor, Buckholdt, Hamblin, and Smith (1972) produced findings somewhat contrary to those of Marholin and Steinman and of Hay *et al.* As expected, token reinforcement for attending decreased disruption but did not affect accuracy, but reinforcement for accuracy increased accuracy as well as disruption; a *decrease* in disruption had been expected. Only when reinforcement was contingent on both accuracy and attending did both behaviors increase. In discussing these results, the authors stated that "speculation of change in other than targeted behaviors may be misleading" (p. 16). They further stressed the importance of designing contingencies specifically for each target behavior.

Summary

The research that has compared the reinforcement of on-task behavior with the reinforcement of academic performance seems clearly to favor manipulations of rate or correctness as a means of increasing classroom productivity. Such procedures have been referred to as *parsimonious* (Broughton & Lahey, 1978) because they eliminate at least some off-task behavior while increasing the probability that the student's productive behavior will come under the control of the academic materials rather than the teacher's presence. The commonly advanced alternative—reinforcing on-task behavior—does not reliably result in concomitant increases in productivity and accuracy. Furthermore, this latter practice has come under some degree of ethical scrutiny in recent years.

Even with the application of the most ideal reinforcement procedures for academic productivity and accuracy and with off-task behavior held to reasonable levels in the learning environment, there will be children in the classroom who do not learn. Thus, it remains for educators not only to be mindful of optimal contingent relationships for producing academic productivity and accuracy but also to assess, under these optimal conditions, whether the children are progressing. If not, then alternative procedures, usually those involving the manipulation of discriminative stimuli in the curriculum, must be implemented.

Effects of Manipulating Discriminative Stimulus Materials and Teaching Procedure on Children's Learning of Academic Concepts and Skills

Although some reviewers have indicated the possible influence of antecedent events on children's academic behavior (e.g., LeBlanc,

Etzel, & Domash, 1978), relatively few studies have examined the role of discriminative stimuli (such as teacher instructions or curriculum materials) in the learning process. The paucity of research in these areas continues, although teachers continually seek better teaching methods, especially for children experiencing difficulty in learning.

Etzel and LeBlanc (1979) pointed out that many children can learn irrespective of the nature of the curriculum materials or the instructions provided for them. For these children who learn easily, the major concern is that teaching be organized so that the skills are learned in some logical sequence, in which new components are introduced only when the necessary prerequisite skills have been acquired. Such sequencing allows learning to occur with optimal ease for both teacher and child. Task analyses, such as those which Resnick, Wang, and Kaplan (1973) presented for teaching mathematics to children, provide teachers with "an organized set of progressive learning objectives around which instructional programs of many types can be organized" (p. 700). The objective of such analyses is not to provide information regarding *how* each component should be taught but to indicate a sequence in which component skills can be taught. For children who do not experience problems in learning, such an approach would be appropriate and seems to follow what Etzel and LeBlanc (1979) referred to as the selection of the "simplest treatment alternative." In other words, in most cases, simply organizing the progression of task presentation into some logical sequence will result in children's acquiring the desired skills.

When children have difficulty learning in even well-organized instructional programs, an analysis of *how* teachers teach becomes critical. In such situations, intervention strategies are usually necessary. Perhaps the simplest of these derives from an analysis of the motivational system used in the teaching process. However, motivation through reinforcement may not always be sufficient, since some component of a to-be-learned skill must be emitted by the child for reinforcement to occur. If increased motivational levels do not enhance the learning process, according to the parsimonious "simplest treatment alternative" proposed by Etzel and LeBlanc, the next step is to analyze the effectiveness of the teacher's instructions and/or the method by which the curriculum materials are presented to the children. If altering the instructional mode does not effect learning in some children, it is proposed that arrangements of the stimulus materials themselves will be necessary to reduce errors and to allow learning to begin to occur.

Teacher Presentation of Materials and Instructions

Some children who are motivated, who are orienting to the task, and who possess the prerequisite skills for learning a new task still do not learn. In these situations, the learning environment must be analyzed for variables, such as instructions, feedback, sequence of task presentation, or other environmental stimuli, that may be impeding the learning process. In the last five years, some researchers have begun to analyze the learning environment from this viewpoint. Because of the paucity of research in this area, however, conclusions are, at best, limited.

Manipulations of Teacher Prompts and Instructions. Sometimes, it is possible to manipulate children's academic responding through the use of simple verbal prompts. Two studies, for example, have examined the relationship of question asking by teachers or students to other aspects of academic responding. When Broden, Copeland, Beasley, and Hall (1977) required teachers of junior-high special-education students to increase the number of questions they asked as well as the proportion of questions that required multiple-word answers, the students responded with answers of increased length. These authors also found that an increase in the proportion of complete sentence answers occurred when teachers instructed the children to answer in this fashion and ignored all nonsentence answers. Knapczyk and Livingston (1974) found that when teachers prompted question asking by educable mentally retarded students, the number of questions asked as well as the levels of reading comprehension and on-task behavior increased. Using a slightly different procedure, Lovitt and Curtiss (1968) demonstrated that a child's accuracy and rate of working mathematics problems could be en-

hanced by simply instructing the child to verbalize the problem before writing the answer. The authors stated that such memory aids may add a second stimulus dimension (oral recitation) to the learning process or may simply make the child more deliberate. A related but somewhat different explanation is that requiring the child to read the problem increased the probability that the child would attend to each part of that problem.

In another area of research, the content of teacher's verbal instructions has been shown to influence the academic learning of preschool children. Miller and LeBlanc (1973) compared instructions that merely stated what the children were to do in a visual discrimination task with instructions that added exemplar details to the basic statement. Thus, for example, the detailed instructions in one part of the experiment were: "This is the word 'dig.' You dig with a shovel. You dig in the sand. It's fun to dig. Point to 'dig' and say 'dig.'" The minimal instructions were merely: "This is the word 'dig.' Point to 'dig' and say 'dig.'" Discrimination acquisition between two three-letter words of similar configuration (e.g., *dig* and *dog*) occurred more rapidly with the minimal than with the detailed instructions.

Hass, Ruggles, and LeBlanc (1979) noted that the examples provided in the detailed instructions used by Miller and LeBlanc were not related to the critical (visual) differences between the two stimuli involved in the discrimination. To determine if this were essential to obtaining the differences that occurred, they compared the effects of minimal instructions (similar to those used by Miller and LeBlanc) with those of detailed instructions that focused the child's attention on the differences between the words that were most relevant to the discrimination. Thus, the detailed instructions were changed to "This is the word 'dig.' The word 'dig' has the letter 'i' in it. The letter 'i' looks like a shovel and you can dig with a shovel. Point to the 'i' in 'dig' and say 'dig.'" These criterion-related instructions were at least as effective, if not more so, than minimal instructions for enhancing discrimination acquisition. Further analyses also indicated that the discrimination acquisition effects of the non-criterion-related instructions originated by Miller and LeBlanc were enhanced when criterion-related detailed instructions were concurrently used to teach a separate discrimination. This research, which analyzed the differential effects of differing instructional content, demonstrates that manipulations as simple as changing the content of a teacher's instructions can substantially change the rate of discrimination acquisition.

Manipulation of Sequential Aspects of Task Presentations. Some research has indicated that the sequence in which stimulus materials are presented to individuals or groups of children may determine the efficacy of the teaching process. Neef, Iwata, and Page (1977), for example, studied acquisition in spelling and sight-reading tasks when previously learned items were interspersed with unknown items in comparison with that which occurred when only unknown items were presented. For six, individually trained, mentally retarded adolescents, acquisition and retention were enhanced for both tasks when known items were interspersed with unknown items. These differences could be partially due to the degree to which each of the procedures included consequences for attending to each stimulus presentation. That is, in the interspersed procedure, the intermittent appearance of a previously learned item on which the child could easily answer correctly may have reinforced the child for attending. Such would not be the case if only unknown items were presented.

Britten, Ruggles, and LeBlanc (1980) compared the effects of massed presentation of stimulus items to those that were intermixed. In a task involving the concurrent presentation of two visual stimuli, massed stimulus presentations involved requiring a response to one stimulus for 10 consecutive trials and then requiring a response to the other stimulus for another 10 trials. For the intermixed stimulus presentation, responses to the two different stimuli were randomly required. Although the preschool children generally performed better during recognition training with massed training, their performance on periodic probes of recognition and recall was better following intermixed training, possibly because the children could respond correctly on all but the initial trial in massed training by simply pointing to or saying the stimulus, which resulted

in reinforcement on the previous trial. Thus, the teacher's instructions were not required as a discriminative stimulus for making a particular choice. Intermixed training, on the other hand, did necessitate utilizing the teacher's instructions as a discriminative stimulus for choosing the correct stimulus or applying the proper label.

Other researchers examining the effects of the sequential presentation of stimuli on learning are Cuvo, Klevans, Borakove, Borakove, Van Landuyt, and Lutzker (1980) and Panyan and Hall (1978). Cuvo *et al.* compared the effects of massed, intermixed, and combined massed and intermixed stimulus presentations on the labeling of objects by college students, retarded children and adolescents, and normal preschool children. In massed (called *successive*) presentations, one stimulus was presented consecutively until the subject correctly responded 15 times. In intermixed (called *simultaneous* stimulus presentations, the five stimuli were put before the subject, who was required to label them in random order until the subject made 15 correct responses on each stimulus. The combined procedure involved aspects of both of the other procedures. Performance was better with the intermixed (or simultaneous) and combined procedures. Panyan and Hall compared concurrent training in which training on one task continued for 5 min, followed by 5 min of training on a second task and then a return to the first task, etc., with serial training in which one task was presented for an entire 15-min period. Concurrent training of tracing and vocal imitation by retarded students was as effective as serial training for acquisition, but concurrent training also produced more transfer to untrained items in generalization testing.

The research discussed to this point has shown that the sequence in which tasks are presented may determine the success with which children acquire discriminations. By strategically designing the sequence in which discriminations are trained, children who are trained in groups may not only acquire those discriminations that are directly taught to them but also those that are taught to others in the group or with which they have had little or no direct training. Sabbert, Holt, Nelson, Domash, and Etzel (1976a), for example, designed a near-errorless program to teach simple mathematics to preschool children. Although the program was originally designed, as are most errorless programs, to be presented to inividual children, Sabbert *et al.* analyzed the effects of presenting each of the steps in the program to different children, in a group. The 14-trial program was presented to groups of two, three, four, and five children, as well as to individual children. When the program was presented to five children, each child responded to only two or three trials from the entire program. Since the program was designed so that the information required to respond to each trial came from previous trials, the children were encouraged to attend to the training trials of the children who preceded them. Attending was also enhanced by randomly selecting the order in which the children were to answer. It was found that groups of two, three, four, and five children could be taught the mathematics concepts in the same number of total training trials as were required to teach one child individually, because the children were able to learn from the responses of the other children in the group.

The occurrence of learning without direct training has been demonstrated in several investigations. Sidman and Cresson (1973), for example, first trained individuals on the correspondence between a dictated word and a symbol and then on the correspondence between the same dictated word and its printed counterpart. Following this training, the subjects could match the picture to the printed word, a relationship on which the subject had received no direct training. Subsequent researchers have reported similar findings on variations of Sidman's original procedure (Barmeier, 1978, 1979; Gast, vanBiervliet, & Spradlin, 1979; Sidman, Cresson, & Willson-Morris, 1974; vanBiervliet, 1977).

A technique developed by Ruggles and LeBlanc (1979) combined the beneficial effects of learning through observation (as shown in the Sabbert *et al.* procedure) with a variation of Sidman and Cresson's procedure to teach discriminations to children in a group setting. In this study, two students in a preacademic group were trained to choose international agricultural symbols that corresponded to the teacher's instructions (e.g.,

point to the picture of the "cow"). Concurrently, the other two children were taught to choose the printed words that corresponded to the symbols taught to the first two children (e.g., point to the word "cow"). After training, a mediation test was conducted in which the children (in a match-to-sample format) were asked to match symbols to corresponding printed words. On the match-to-sample test, the children were able to use the information on which they were directly trained, in combination with the information learned through observing the other children's responses, to make the transfer response. A variation of the procedure by Ruggles and LeBlanc was subsequently used to increase the efficiency with which the academic concepts of *fruit* and *vegetable* could be trained to a group of preschool children (Fallows, Cooper, Etzel, LeBlanc, & Ruggles, 1980).

The mediated transfer research of Sidman and his colleagues demonstrated that through the proper arrangement of training, one untrained relationship would be learned when two were trained directly. The research by Ruggles and LeBlanc and by Fallows *et al.* demonstrated the practical implications of these findings for classroom teaching by showing that through the arrangement of training and a reliance on the occurrence of learning through observation, the acquisition of three or more relationships may occur when each group member is directly taught only one relationship.

Manipulation of the Temporal Parameters of Task Presentation or Responding. Some researchers have manipulated the temporal relationship between successive trial presentations, or between trial presentation and the child's response, to determine if timing influences learning. Busby and LeBlanc (1972), for example, compared a 4-sec time limit with no limit on a preschooler's responding for reinforcement on a picture bingo task. Response latencies during the time-limit conditions were, in general, shorter and less variable than those in the no-time-limit conditions. In a systematic replication of the Busby and LeBlanc research, Kramer, Ruggles, and LeBlanc (1979) found no consistent relationship between the time-limit condition and response latencies. Thus, exact conclusions regarding the effects of imposing time limits on responding in a discrete trial task are not clear.

Ayllon, Garber, and Pisor (1976) investigated the effect of a gradual reduction in the amount of time that educably retarded students were given to complete mathematics problems. During the first condition, the subjects were given 20 min to complete 20 problems. Following a condition in which the time allowed to complete the problems was abruptly decreased to 5 min, the time limit was gradually reduced, across four conditions, from 20 min to 5 min (20, 15, 10, and 5 min). The rate of correct problems per minute gradually increased from the abrupt imposition of the 5-min limit across the gradual reduction of the time limit to 5 min. While the results of the Ayllon *et al.* study are impressive, the possible influence of practice cannot be ignored. The same pool of math problems was apparently used throughout, and experimental controls in the form of control subjects or interspersed probes with the 5-min time limit were lacking.

Carnine (1976) has demonstrated that temporal manipulations involving the pace of teacher instructions influence responding. During a slow-rate condition, the teacher waited approximately 5 sec between each child's response and the presentation of the next trial. During the fast-rate condition, the teacher immediately proceeded to the next trial after a response from the child. For both experimental subjects (low-achieving first-graders), more correct responding and participation, as well as less off-task behavior, were evident in the fast-rate condition than in the slow-rate condition. Koegel, Dunlap, and Dyer (1980) also investigated the influence of the length of the intertrial interval on autistic children's learning on verbal-imitation, object-discrimination, object-labeling, and other tasks. Intertrial intervals of 1 sec produced a higher proportion of correct responding than intertrial intervals of 4 sec.

Research examining the pacing of stimulus presentations generally favors teaching sessions that move as quickly as possible. These findings counter more traditional notions that children must not be rushed but must be given as much time as possible to respond to academic materials. Empirically, it appears that extra time may not be necessary and, in fact,

may allow the development of behaviors that are incompatible with academic learning.

Temporal relationships between instructions and feedback have also been shown to influence learning. Touchette (1971), for example, trained three retarded subjects to select a red versus a white response key. On the first trial of the next phase of training, two forms were superimposed on the colored key, and the subject was reinforced for selecting the key with the form on the red background. On subsequent trials, the two forms were presented on the key, and the onset of the colored background was delayed. The length of the delay gradually increased across trials. Eventually, as the delay increased, the subjects began to select the correct form before the colored background was illuminated. Following Touchette's sample, Radgowski, Allen, Schilmoeller, Ruggles, and LeBlanc (1978) taught English-speaking preschool children to respond receptively and productively in French. In the early receptive training trials, the teacher gave an instruction in French and immediately modeled the response. Following the model, the child imitated the teacher's response. Across successive trials, the delay between the instruction and the model became progressively longer. As the delay increased, there came a point when most children began to respond with the correct answer before the model. Productive training was similar, except that the teacher demonstrated the motor response, then, following a delay, said the phrase. For most children, the delayed-cue procedure produced rapid learning with few or no errors.

Manipulating Curriculum Material Stimuli

Not all of the research related to teachers' presentation of curriculum materials and instructions has been conducted in applied settings (i.e., classrooms). The importance of such research to teachers who are faced with selecting the best procedures to use with children who have difficulty learning is, however, obvious. Such procedures as prompting children at strategic times, pacing the teaching, controlling the content of the instructions, setting time limits on responding, altering the sequences of task presentations, and arranging groups so that optimal learning can occur are a few among many potentially potent methods that teachers could use if research outcomes more clearly dictated when and how these procedures should be used. Even the most optimally arranged learning environments, however, are apparently not sufficient for some children to learn some tasks. Nevertheless, teachers are faced with the increasing demand from parents and government agencies that all children be educated. In response to such demands, researchers and teachers are becoming interested in errorless learning procedures and optimal arrangements of curriculum material stimuli.

Because of a particular theoretical bias in the experimental analysis of behavior, most early applied behavior-analysis researchers emphasized the reinforcement rather than the discriminative stimulus part of the three-term contingency $(S^d - R - S^{r+})$ on which operant psychology is based. For example, Skinner (1963) strongly cautioned against the use of instructional control procedures in learning experiments on the grounds that they circumvent and obscure the functional analysis of behavior. This theoretical bias was further supported by the immediacy of the need for the development of procedures that professionals could use to change the behaviors of persons who were not considered acceptable in society. The strength of reinforcement of such purposes cannot be denied. Applied researchers were attracted to reinforcement analyses because reinforcement is a powerful tool, and they provided immediate, dramatic results in both clinical and classroom settings. Thus, it was only after reinforcement procedures were well analyzed that a few researchers began to look at the behavioral effects that might emanate from manipulations of discriminative stimuli.

In classroom research, it is becoming obvious that educators need more information regarding what procedures they should use when children have difficulty learning. When reinforcement is functioning and learning is not occurring, only an analysis of discriminative stimulus functions can provide such information. In addition, if the precise rearrangement of instructions and material presentations does not result in learning for these children, then the visual and auditory stimuli directly involved in the learning process must be arranged so that they can learn. This requirement usually involves developing materials that will produce learning without errors. Materials designed to produce errorless learning involve discriminative stimulus manipulations that allow a child initially to make correct responses on a simple discrimination and to continue responding with few or no errors as the stimulus control is gradually transferred from the simple discrimination to a more complex one.

Errorless Learning. In the late 1950s and the early 1960s, some behavior-analysis researchers concentrated on programmed learning and automated self-instructional procedures (cf. Holland, 1960; Skinner, 1961). The emphasis in this research was learning with few or no errors and resulted in programmed texts designed primarily for higher education. The field of programmed instruction did not, however, reach down the educational ladder to public-school classroom research. Perhaps this was because the programmed instruction techniques were dependent on an already acquired reading ability, but in the first years of public school, reading is a central part of the curriculum rather than a tool of learning.

Information regarding the processes involved in visual errorless-discrimination learning was initially forthcoming from research with pigeons conducted by Terrace (1963a,b, 1966). Errorless learning was subsequently demonstrated with other infrahuman organisms, such as sea lions (Schusterman, 1967) and monkeys (Leith & Haude, 1969). During this period of the late 1960s, other researchers began to examine the feasibility and the implications of errorless learning in humans (cf. Bijou, 1968; Moore & Goldiamond, 1964; Sidman & Stoddard, 1966, 1968; Stoddard & Sidman, 1967; Touchette, 1969). This early research was conducted primarily with retardates in laboratory settings and on tasks involving simple discriminations. Only now, almost a decade later, are researchers beginning to focus on the implications of errorless-learning procedures for classroom teaching. Much of the support and the development of functional errorless-learning procedures that can be used by teachers are found in the work of Etzel and her colleagues (cf. Etzel & LeBlanc, 1979; Etzel, LeBlanc, Schilmoeller, & Stella, 1981). As indicated by Etzel and LeBlanc (1979), designing programs to teach children with few or no errors is a difficult task. However, they also indicated, "if simpler procedures are not effective for teaching difficult-to-teach children, then . . . the most complex procedure becomes the procedure of choice" (pp. 380–381).

Implications of Errorless-Learning Techniques for Classroom Teaching. Research involved in the development of errorless learning has, for the most part, been conducted in laboratory settings. One exception is the research conducted by Sabbert, Holt, Nelson Domash, and Etzel (1976a,b), which demonstrated that five children could learn as successfully as one in the same number of trials if errorless-learning procedures are used and if contingencies are arranged that require the children to observe the responses of the other children in the program. In another study using errorless-learning procedures in a classroom setting, Nelson, Holt, and Etzel (1976a,b) demonstrated that the prerequisite skills needed to learn math skills could be empirically determined (rather than being determined through guessing) while teaching small groups of children with procedures designed to preclude or reduce errors. Procedures were developed for identifying these skills and for teaching them (if necessary) before teaching more complex skills. The limited use of this new technology of stimulus-control procedures to solve applied educational problems historically parallels the limited applications of reinforcement procedures when operant psychology was moving from the laboratory into applied settings. That is, research was first conducted in infrahuman laboratories, interest was then sparked in human laboratory research, and finally research involving the application of procedures in applied settings was forthcoming. As occurred with the application of reinforcement procedures, it is expected that as the technology of applied stimulus-control procedures becomes better formulated, more direct applications of such procedures will be found in classroom settings.

There are essentially two methods for pro-

ducing the errorless learning of visual discriminations: stimulus fading and stimulus shaping. These two methods are sometimes used in conjunction with the superimposition of one stimulus on the other, and the superimposed stimulus is either faded or shaped into the criterion stimulus involved in the discrimination being taught (Etzel & LeBlanc, 1979). Stimulus fading involves a gradual shift of discriminative control from a dominant stimulus element to a different, criterion stimulus. This shift is produced by fading along some physical dimension (e.g., intensity, size, or color) that changes the basis of the discrimination from one stimulus dimension to another one (which is usually more difficult for the learner). Stimulus shaping, attributed to Sidman and Stoddard (1966) by Etzel and LeBlanc (1979), involves a change in the topography (configuration) of the stimulus. That is, the initial stimulus on which a discrimination can be easily made (which does not resemble the ultimate stimulus) is topographically altered (changed in shape) until it resembles the stimulus on which the criterion (usually more difficult) discrimination is to be made.

Some research has indicated that fading is not always a successful learning procedure (cf. Cheney & Stein, 1974; Gollin & Savoy, 1968; Guralnick, 1975; Koegel & Rincover, 1976; Schwartz, Firestone, & Terry, 1971; Smith & Filler, 1975). Research conducted by Schilmoeller and Etzel (1977) and by Schilmoeller, Schilmoeller, Etzel, and LeBlanc (1979) indicates that these failures could be attributed to fading dimensions of the stimuli that were not related to the stimuli involved in the final criterion discrimination. That is, when the last discernable stimulus element that was being faded was removed, the subjects did not shift their discrimination from that stimulus element to the criterion stimulus. Doran and Holland (1979) demonstrated the importance of the criterion stimulus's controlling responding *before* the fading cue is completely removed.

The research of Schilmoeller and Etzel (1977) emphasized the need for manipulating only criterion-related stimuli and has obvious implications for the technology of developing curriculum materials for classroom use. Based on the assumption, introduced by Bijou (1968), that one should manipulate the part of a stimulus on which the ultimate or criterion discrimination will be made, Schilmoeller and Etzel developed a program that taught preschool children to discriminate between exceedingly complex stimuli with few or no errors. To demonstrate the importance of manipulating *only* those stimulus elements that are related to the criterion discrimination, the authors put a red square around the sample and the correct match on the initial trial of the successful program, and they gradually eliminated the red boxes across trials until the boxes were no longer visible at the end of the program. Thus, the red boxes (similar to those used in many children's workbooks) were used to cue the child to respond to the correct stimulus. The boxes apparently cued the child to attend only to the red boxes, however, and not to the stimuli that were gradually changing in the program that was demonstrated to be successful without the boxes. The children were unable to make the criterion discrimination when the red boxes were superimposed on the correct stimuli but were able to learn the discrimination with the same errorless-learning program when the red boxes were not used as cues.

Stimulus fading and stimulus shaping have been used to teach a variety of simple and complex concepts to preschool and elementary-school children. For example, the very difficult left–right relational abstraction has been programmed for retarded and preschool children (Bijou, 1968; Bybel & Etzel, 1973; Schreibman, 1975). Sidman and Stoddard (1966) developed a program for teaching a discrimination between a circle and an ellipse to retardates, and Powers, Cheney, and Agostino (1970) taught color discriminations to preschool children. A variety of simple and complex relational concepts, such as under, over, behind, top-left-back, and top-right-front, have been taught with few errors to preschool children by means of a three-dimensional house that they could manipulate (Dial & Etzel, (1972). Dixon, Spradlin, Girardeau, and Etzel (1974) taught severely retarded children an in-front discrimination using complex two-dimensional pictures with few or no errors, and this training generalized to other similar stimuli. Symmetrical and asymmetrical abstractions have and also been taught to young children by Schwartz *et al.* (1971) and by Barrera and Schilmoeller (as reported by Etzel & LeBlanc, 1979). Conditional discriminations have been programmed for preschool children by Gollin (1965, 1966), by Gollin and Savoy (1968), and by Schilmoeller *et al.* (1979). One of the first applied stimulus-control programs to produce errorless learning was a shoe-tying program developed for retarded and developmentally delayed children (Cooper, LeBlanc, & Etzel, 1968). The oddity concept (i.e., indicating a stimulus that is different from an array of stimuli) was programmed by Etzel and Mintz (1970).

Along more academic lines, reading has been the target of several programs using errorless-learning techniques. For example, Corey and Shamow (1972) studied the effects of fading on reading acquisition; Guralnick (1975) examined the effects of fading on letter and form discriminations; Dorry and Zeaman (1975) compared fading and nonfading procedures while teaching a simple reading vocabulary to retarded children; Griffiths and Griffiths (1976), Egeland and Winer (1974), Karraker and Doke (1970), and Rincover (1978) established errorless-learning procedures to teach children letter discriminations; and Parr, Stella, and Etzel (reported in LeBlanc *et al.*, 1978) used stimulus shaping to teach children sight-word vocabularies with few errors.

Other academic concepts that have had errorless-learning procedures applied to them include simple addition (Sabbert *et al.*, 1976a,b); rote counting, number labeling, number writing, match-to-sample, and one-to-one correspondence (Nelson *et al.*, 1976a,b); addition, subtraction, and multiplication (Haupt, Van Kirk, & Terraciano, 1977); handwriting (Holt & Etzel, 1976); and the number of beats of musical notes (Stella & Etzel, 1977).

One reason that researchers may have begun to analyze the effects of errorless-learning procedures for purposes of application is that the autistic (Schreibman, 1975), the retarded, and other children experiencing learning problems often do not observe the cues that are relevant to making the discriminations being taught. Zeaman and House (1963) and Covill and Etzel (1976) both documented this fact with two very different groups of children. Stella and Etzel (1979a,b) indicated that this problem sometimes arises when children do not look at the stimulus materials. These authors developed a stimulus-shaping procedure to assess and to shape the children's attention so the opportunity to focus on the relevant stimulus dimension is at least available. Covill and Etzel (1976) further demonstrated that slow-learning children utilize inappropriate cues, such as the position of a stimulus, rather than the critical cues that allow discriminations to be made. Errorless-learning procedures, such as criterion-related fading, shaping, and the superimposition of stimuli, appear to help difficult-to-teach children to observe the relevant cues in learning. Thus, this technology can perhaps provide the avenue for behavior analysis to begin to deal with the problems of *educating* children rather than only modifying inappropriate behavior so as to maintain orderly behavior in the classroom.

Summary. There is a beginning technology of discriminative stimulus manipulations that appears to have implications for the use of behavior analysis not only to remediate behavioral problems but also to educate children. Etzel (1978) indicated that retarded and autistic children have waited for generations for scientists to find methods of teaching them. Perhaps the turning of scientific attention to the functions of discriminative stimuli and how they can best be manipulated to change and control behavior will provide these children with the learning programs they need. For years, classroom teachers have sought research outcomes that indicate what to do with children who experience learning difficulties. As more research is produced that analyzes the discriminations involved in the educational process, it is possible that some of the answers will come forth even before the beginning of the twenty-first century.

Summary

The most often heard complaints regarding public-school education are that there is no discipline in the classrooms and that the children are not learning anything other than how to misbehave. The current technology available for maintaining order in the classroom is vast and stems primarily from behavior-analysis research. However, there is sometimes a resistance to the application of behavior-analysis procedures in the classroom to maintain sufficient order for learning to occur. The rationale for such resistance is that children's creativity and openness should not be stifled in the name of education. It cannot be denied that creativity should be fostered in classrooms. Bedlam in classrooms is, however, frequently sufficient to preclude opportunities to foster such creativity. In this case, teachers should be encouraged to use reinforcement and even mild forms of punishment or response-decrement procedures to control the social climate of the classroom so that learning can occur and creativity can be enhanced. Research outcomes that indicate optimal procedures for controlling classroom behavior are currently sufficient for prescriptions to be developed for teachers to use when problems develop. It needs only to be done.

Once classroom order is maintained, teachers can then turn their attention to what and how much children are learning. The behavior-analysis technology for increasing children's motivation to learn and to produce at an acceptable rate is rapidly increasing. Currently, there are functional procedures that can be used for this purpose, and we, as a society, need only to begin to demand their implementation.

The available techniques that show teachers how to *teach* (in addition to how to discipline) are few. Such techniques would indicate how to arrange the learning environment so that all children can learn, starting from where they are and proceeding at a pace commensurate with their abilities. Research analyzing the effects of the manipulation of discriminative stimuli, such as teachers' instructions and curriculum materials, is beginning to provide information that is sorely needed by teachers who are faced with the education of all children, regardless of their learning ability. This research emanates primarily from the experimental laboratory, but it shows much promise in application for children who experience difficulty in learning.

When the behavior analysis technology of how to teach reaches the current level of sophistication of the technology of discipline and motivation, teachers will then be able to concentrate on the true issue of the profession, that is, teaching. There should, at that point, be few limitations on the learning progress that all children will be able to make. Then, education can become a pleasant affair rather than a laborious process for students, teachers, and parents alike.

References

Aaron, B. A., & Bostow, D. E. Indirect facilitation of on-task behavior produced by contingent free-time for academic productivity. *Journal of Applied Behavior Analysis*, 1978, *11*, 197.

Alexander, R. N., & Apfel, C. H. Altering schedules of reinforcement for improved classroom behavior. *Exceptional Children*, 1976, *43*, 97–99.

Allen, K. E., Hart, B. M., Buell, J. C., Harris, F. R., & Wolf, M. M. Effects of adult social reinforcement on isolate behavior of a nursery school child. *Child Development*, 1964, *35*, 511–518.

Allen, K. E., Henke, L. B., Harris, F. R., Baer, D. M., & Reynolds, N. J. Control of hyperactivity by social reinforcement of attending behavior. *Journal of Education Psychology*, 1967, *58*, 231–237.

Allen, K. E., Turner, K. D., & Everett, P. M. A behavior modification classroom for Head Start children with problem behaviors: Experiments 1–3. *Exceptional Children*, 1970, *37*, 119–127.

Ascare, D., & Axelrod, S. Use of a behavior modification procedure in four "open" classrooms. *Psychology in the Schoolds*, 1973, *10*, 249–252.

Axelrod, S. Comparison of individual and group contingencies in two special classes. *Behavior Therapy*, 1973, *4*, 83–90.

Ayllon, T., & Haughton, E. Control of the behavior of schizophrenic patients by food. *Journal of the Experimental Analysis of Behavior*, 1962, *5*, 343–352.

Ayllon, T., & Michael, J. The psychiatric nurse as a behavioral engineer. *Journal of the Experimental Analysis of Behavior*, 1959, *2*, 323–334.

Ayllon, T. A., & Roberts, M. D. Eliminating discipline problems by strengthening academic performance. *Journal of Applied Behavior Analysis*, 1974, *7*, 71–76.

Ayllon, T., Garber, S., & Pisor, K. Reducing time limits: A means to increase behavior of retardates. *Journal of Applied Behavior Analysis*, 1976, *9*, 247–252.

Azrin, N. H., & Holtz, W. C. Punishment. In W. K. Honig (Ed.), *Operant Behavior: Areas of Research and Application*. New York: Appleton-Century-Crofts, 1966.

Bailey, J. S., Wolf, M. M., & Phillips, E. L. Home-based reinforcement and the modification of pre-delinquents' classroom behavior. *Journal of Applied Behavior Analysis*, 1970, *3*, 223–233.

Ballard, K. D., & Glynn, T. Behavioral self-management in story writing with elementary school children. *Journal of Applied Behavior Analysis*, 1975, *8*, 387–398.

Barker, R. G. *Ecological psychology*. Stanford, Calif.: Stanford University Press, 1968.

Barmeier, A. A. *Mediated transfer in deaf reading instruction: A sign language model*. Paper presented at the meeting of the American Psychological Association, Toronto, August 1978.

Barmeier, A. A. *Mediated transfer in deaf reading instruction: A sign language model*. Paper presented at the meeting of the Association for Behavior Analysis, Dearborn, 1979.

Barrish, H. H., Saunders, M., & Wolf, M. M. Good behavior game: Effects of individual contingencies for group consequences on disruptive behavior in a classroom. *Journal of Applied Behavior Analysis*, 1969, *2*, 119–124.

Bijou, S. W. Studies in the experimental development of left-right concepts in retarded children using fading techniques. In Norman R. Ellis (Ed.), *International review of research in mental retardation*, Vol. 3. New York: Academic Press, 1968.

Bijou, S. W., Birnbrauer, J. S., Kidder, J. D., & Tague, C. E. Programmed instruction as an approach to the teaching of reading, writing and arithmetic to retarded children. *Psychological Record*, 1966, *16*, 505–522.

Birnbrauer, J. S., & Lawler, J. Token reinforcement for learning. *Mental Retardation*, October 1964, *2*, 275–279.

Birnbrauer, J. S., Bijou, S. W., Wolf, M. M., & Kidder, J. D. Programmed instruction in the classroom. In L. P. Ullmann & L. Krasner (Eds.), *Case studies in behavior modification*. New York: Holt, Rinehart & Winston, 1965, pp. 358–363.

Birnbrauer, J. S., Wolf, M. M., Kidder, J. D., & Tague, C. E. Classroom behavior of retarded pupils with token reinforcement. *Journal of Experimental Child Psychology*, 1965, *2*, 219–235.

Bornstein, P. H., & Quevillon, R. P. The effects of a self-instructional package on over-active preschool boys. *Journal of Applied Behavior Analysis*, 1976, *9*, 179–188.

Bostow, D. E., & Bailey, J. B. Modification of severe disruptive and aggressive behavior using brief timeout and reinforcement procedures. *Journal of Applied Behavior Analysis*, 1969, *2*, 31–38.

Brigham, T. A., Finfrock, S. R., Breunig, M. K., & Bushell, D. The use of programmed materials in the analysis of academic contingenecies. *Journal of Applied Behavior Analysis*, 1972, *5*, 177–182.

Britten, K., Ruggles, T. R., & LeBlanc, J. M. *A comparison of massed and intermixed stimulus presentations*. Paper presented at the meeting of the Association for Behavior Analysis, Dearborn, 1980.

Broden, M., Bruce, C., Mitchell, M. A., Carter, V., & Hall, R. V. Effects of teacher attention on attending behavior of two boys at adjacent desks. *Journal of Applied Behavior Analysis*, 1970, *3*, 199–203.

Broden, M., Hall, R. V., Dunlap, A., & Clark, R. Effects of teacher attention and a token reinforcement system in a junior school special education class. *Exceptional Children*, 1970, *36*, 341–349.

Broden, M., Hall, R. V., & Mitts, B. The effect of self-recording on the classroom behavior of two eighth-grade students. *Journal of Applied Behavior Analysis*, 1971, *4*, 191–199.

Broden, M., Copeland, G., Beasley, A., & Hall, R. V. Altering student responses through changes in teacher verbal behavior. *Journal of Applied Behavior Analysis*, 1977, *10*, 479–488.

Broughton, S. F., & Lahey, B. B. Direct and collateral effects of positive reinforcement, response cost and mixed contingencies for academic performance. *Journal of School Psychology*, 1978, *16*, 126–136.

Brown, P., & Elliot, R. The control of aggression in a nursery school class. *Journal of Experimental Child Psychology*, 1965, *2*, 103–107.

Busby, K., & LeBlanc, J. M. *Response latency as a function of reinforcement and temporal contingencies*. Paper presented at the meeting of the American Psychological Association, Honolulu, 1972.

Bushell, D., Wrobel, P. A., & Michaelis, M. L. Applying "group" contingencies to the classroom study behavior of preschool children. *Journal of Applied Behavior Analysis*, 1968, *1*, 55–61.

Bybel, N. W., & Etzel, B. C. *A study of pretraining procedures for establishing cue relevance in the subsequent programming of a conceptual skill*. Paper presented to the Society for Research in Child Development, Philadelphia, March 1973.

Carnine, D. W. Effects of two teacher-presentation rates on off-task behavior, answering correctly, and participation. *Journal of Applied Behavior Analysis*, 1976, *9*, 199–206.

Chadwick, B. A., & Day, R. C. Systematic reinforcement: Academic performance of underachieving students. *Journal of Applied Behavior Analysis*, 1971, *4*, 311–320.

Charlesworth, R., & Hartup, W. W. Positive social reinforcement in the nursery school peer group. *Child Development*, 1967, *38*, 993–1002.

Cheney, T., & Stein, N. Fading procedures and oddity learning in kindergarten children. *Journal of Experimental Child Psychology*, 1974, *17*, 313–321.

Clark, F. W., Evans, D. R., & Hamerlynck, L. A. *Implementing behavioral programs for schools and clinics*. Proceedings of the Third Banff International Conference on Behavior Modification. Champaign, Ill.: Research Press, 1972.

Clark, H. B., Rowbury, T., Baer, A. M., & Baer, D. M. Timeout as a punishing stimulus in continuous and intermittent schedules. *Journal of Applied Behavior Analysis*, 1973, *6*, 443–456.

Coleman, R. A. Conditioning technique applicable to elementary school classrooms. *Journal of Applied Behavior Analysis*, 1970, *3*, 293–297.

Cooper, M. L., LeBlanc, J. M., & Etzel, B. C. *A shoe is to tie* (16mm color, 10-min film depicting a programmed sequence for teaching shoe-tying to preschool children). Available from Edna A. Hill Child Development Preschool Laboratory, Department of Human Development, University of Kansas, January 1968.

Copeland, R. E., Brown, R. E., & Hall, R. V. The effects of principal-implemented techniques on the behavior of pupils. *Journal of Applied Behavior Analysis*, 1974, *7*, 77–86.

Corey, J. R., & Shamow, J. The effects of fading on the acquisition and retention of oral reading. *Journal of Applied Behavior Analysis*, 1972, *5*, 311–315.

Corte, H. E., Wolf, M. M., & Locke, B. J. A comparison of procedures for eliminating self-injurious behavior of retarded adolescents. *Journal of Applied Behavior Analysis*, 1971, *4*, 201–214.

Covill, J. L., & Etzel, B. C. *Effects of errorless learning on problem-solving skills*. Presented at the 84th annual convention of the American Psychological Association, Washington, D.C., 1976.

Cuvo, A. J., Klevans, L., Borakove, S., Borakove, L. S., Van Landuyt, J., & Lutzker, J. R. A comparison of three strategies for teaching object names. *Journal of Applied Behavior Analysis*, 1980, *13*, 249–258.

Dalton, A. J., Rubino, C. A., & Hilsop, M. W. Some effects of token rewards on school achievement of children with Down's syndrome. *Journal of Applied Behavior Analysis*, 1973, *6*, 251–260.

Darch, C. B., & Thorpe, H. W. The principal game: A group consequence procedure to increase classroom on-task behavior. *Psychology in the Schools*, 1977, *14*, 341–347.

Dickinson, D. J. Changing behavior with behavioral techniques. *Journal of School Psychology*, 1968, *6*, 278–283.

Dietz, S. M., & Repp, A. C. Decreasing classroom misbehavior through the use of DRL schedules of reinforcement. *Journal of Applied Behavior Analysis*, 1973, *6*, 457–463.

Dietz, S. M., & Repp, A. C. Differentially reinforcing low rates of misbehavior with normal elementary school children. *Journal of Applied Behavior Analysis*, 1974, *7*, 622.

Dixon, L. S., Spradlin, J. E., Girrardeau, F. L., & Etzel, B. C. Facilitating the acquisition of an *in front* spatial discrimination. *ACTA Symbolica*, 1974, *5*, 1–21.

Doleys, D. M., Wells, K. C., Hobbs, S. A., Roberts, M. W., & Cartelli, L. M. The effects of social punishment on noncompliance: A comparison with timeout and positive practice. *Journal of Applied Behavior Analysis*, 1976, *9*, 471–482.

Doran, J., & Holland, J. G. Control by stimulus features during fading. *Journal of the Experimental Analysis of Behavior*, 1979, *31*, 177–187.

Dorry, G. W., & Zeaman, D. Teaching a simple reading vocabulary to retarded children: Effectiveness of fading and nonfading procedures. *American Journal of Mental Deficiency*, 1975, *79*, 711–716.

Drabman, R. S. Child- versus teacher-administered token programs in a psychiatric hospital school. *Journal of Abnormal Child Psychology*, 1973, *1*, 68–87.

Drabman, R. S., & Lahey, B. B. Feedback in classroom behavior modification: Effects on the target and her classmates. *Journal of Applied Behavior Analysis*, 1974, *7*, 591–598.

Drabman, R. S., & Spitalnik, R. Social isolation as a punishment procedure: A controlled study. *Journal of Experimental Child Psychology*, 1973, *16*, 236–249.

Drabman, R. S., Spitalnik, R., & O'Leary, K. D. Teaching self-control to disruptive children. *Journal of Abnormal Psychology*, 1973, *82*, 10–16.

Drabman, R., Spitalnik, R., & Spitalnik, K. Sociometric and disruptive behavior as a function of four types of token reinforcement programs. *Journal of Applied Behavior Analysis*, 1974, *7*, 93–101.

Egeland, B., & Winer, K. Teaching children to discriminate letters of the alphabet through errorless discrimination training. *Journal of Reading Behavior*, 1974, *2*, 191–194.

Epstein, R., & Goss, C. M. A self-control procedure for the maintenance of nondisruptive behavior in an elementary school child. *Behavior Therapy*, 1978, *9*, 109–117.

Etzel, B. C. *Errorless stimulus control in the modification of conceptual behavior.* Invited presentation, Midwest Association for Behavior Analysis, Chicago, 1978.

Etzel, B. C., & LeBlanc, J. M. The simplest treatment alternative: The law of parsimony applied to choosing appropriate instructional control and errorless-learning procedures for the difficult-to-teach child. *Journal of Autism and Developmental Disorders,* 1979, *9,* 361–382.

Etzel, B. C., & Mintz, M. S. *Stimulus control procedures to preclude or greatly decrease errors during the acquisition of the oddity abstraction with three- and four-year-old children.* Presented at the American Psychological Association, Miami, 1970.

Etzel, B. C., LeBlanc, J. M., Schilmoeller, K. J., & Stella, M. E. Stimulus control procedures in the education of young children. In S. W. Bijou & R. Ruez (Eds.), *Contributions of behavior modification to education.* Hillsdale, N.J.: Lawrence Erlbaum, 1981.

Evans, G., & Oswalt, G. Acceleration of academic progress through the manipulation of peer influence. *Behavior Research and Therapy,* 1968, *6,* 189–195.

Fallows, R. P., Cooper, A. V., Etzel, B. C., LeBlanc, J. M., & Ruggles, T. R. *The use of a stimulus equivalency paradigm, and observational learning in teaching concepts to preschool children.* Paper presented at the meeting of the American Psychological Association, Montreal, September 1980.

Felixbrod, J. J., & O'Leary, K. D. Effects of reinforcement on children's academic behavior as a function of self-determined and externally imposed contingencies. *Journal of Applied Behavior Analysis,* 1973, *6,* 241–250.

Ferritor, D. E., Buckholdt, D., Hamblin, R. L., & Smith, L. The noneffects of contingent reinforcement for attending behavior on work accomplished. *Journal of Applied Behavior Analysis,* 1972, *5,* 7–17.

Ferster, C., & Appel, J. Punishment of S responding in match to sample by timeout from positive reinforcement. *Journal of The Experimental Analysis of Behavior,* 1961, *4,* 45–46.

Fink, W. T., & Carnine, D. W. Control of arithmetic errors using informational feedback and graphing. *Journal of Applied Behavior Analysis,* 1975, *8,* 461.

Foxx, R. M., & Jones, J. R. A remediation program for increasing the spelling achievement of elementary and junior high students. *Behavior Modification,* 1978, *2,* 211–230.

Foxx, R. M., & Shapiro, S. T. The timeout ribbon: A nonexclusionary timeout procedure. *Journal of Applied Behavior Analysis,* 1978, *11,* 125–136.

Gardner, W. I. Use of punishment with the severely retarded: A review. *American Journal of Mental Deficiency,* 1969, *74,* 86–103.

Gast, D. L., vanBiervliet, A., & Spradlin, J. E. Teaching number-word equivalences: A study of transfer. *American Journal of Mental Deficiency,* 1979, *83,* 524–527.

Glynn, E. L., Thomas, J. D., & Shee, S. M. Behavioral self-control of on-task behavior in an elementary classroom. *Journal of Applied Behavior Analysis,* 1973, *6,* 105–113.

Goetz, E. M., Holmberg, M. C., & LeBlanc, J. M. Differential reinforcement of other behavior and noncontingent reinforcement as control procedures during the modification of a preschooler's compliance. *Journal of Applied Behavior Analysis,* 1975, *8,* 77–82.

Goldstein, D. R., Cooper, A. Y., Ruggles, T. R., & LeBlanc, J. M. *The effects of paced instructions, reprimands and physical guidance on compliance.* Paper presented the annual meeting of the Association for Behavior Analysis, Dearborn, Michigan, June 1980.

Gollin, E. S. Factors affecting conditional discrimination in children. *Journal of Comparative and Physiological Psychology,* 1965, *40,* 422–427.

Gollin, E. S. Solution of conditional discrimination problems in young children. *Journal of Comparative and Physiological Psychology,* 1966, *62,* 454–456.

Gollin, E. S., & Savory, P. Fading procedures and conditional discrimination in children. *Journal of the Experimental Analysis of Behavior,* 1968, *11,* 443–451.

Grandy, G. S., Madsen, C. H., & DeMersseman, L. M. The effects of individual and interdependent contingencies on inappropriate classroom behavior. *Psychology in the Schools,* 1973, *10,* 488–493.

Graubard, P. S. Utilizing the group in teaching disturbed delinquents to learn. *Exceptional Children,* 1969, *36,* 267–272.

Graubard, P. S., Lanier, P., Weisert, H., & Miller, M. B. *An investigation into the use of indigenous grouping as the reinforcing agent in teaching maladjusted boys to read: Final report.* Yeshiva University, School of Education and Community Administration, June, 1970, Project No. 8-0174, Grant No. CEG-8-08174-4353, USOE Bureau of Education for the Handicapped.

Greenwood, C. R., Hops, H., & Walker, H. M. The program for academic survival skills (PASS): Effects on student behavior and achievement. *Journal of School Psychology,* 1977, *15,* 25–35.

Griffiths, K., & Griffiths, R. Errorless establishment of letter discrimination with a stimulus fading procedure in preschool children. *Perceptual and Motor Skills,* 1976, *42,* 387–396.

Guralnick, J. J. Effects of distinctive feature training and instructional technique on letter and form discrimination. *American Journal of Mental Deficiency,* 1975, *80,* 202–207.

Hall, R. V., & Broden, M. Behavior changes in brain-injured children through social reinforcement. *Journal of Experimental Child Psychology,* 1967, *5,* 463–479.

Hall, R. V., Lund, D., & Jackson, D. Effects of teacher attention on study behavior. *Journal of Applied Behavior Analysis,* 1968, *1,* 1–12.

Hall, R. V., Panyan, M., Rabon, D., & Broden, M. Instructing beginning teachers in reinforcement procedures which improve classroom control. *Journal of Applied Behavior Analysis,* 1968, *1,* 315–322.

Hamblin, R. L., Hathaway, C., & Wodarski, J. S. Group contingencies, peer tutoring and accelerating academic achievement. In E. A. Ramp & B. L. Hopkins (Eds.), *A new direction for education: Behavior analysis,* Vol. 1. lawrence: University of Kansas, 1971.

Hardiman, S. A., Goetz, E. M., Reuter, K. E., & LeBlanc, J. M. Primes, contingent attention, and training: Effects on a child's motor behavior. *Journal of Applied Behavior Analysis,* 1975, *8,* 399–409.

Haring, N. G., & Hauck, M. A. Improved learning conditions in the establishment of reading skills with disabled readers. *Exceptional Children,* 1969, *35,* 341–352.

Harris, M. B., & Miksovic, R. S. Operant conditioning of social interaction in preschool children. In M. B.

Harris (Ed.), *Classroom uses of behavior modification.* Columbus, Ohio: Charles E. Merrill, 1972.

Harris, V. W., & Sherman, J. A. Use and analysis of the "good behavior game" to reduce disruptive classroom behavior. *Journal of Applied Behavior Analysis,* 1973, *6,* 405–418.

Harris, V. W., & Sherman, J. A. Homework assignments, consequences, and classroom performance in social studies and mathematics. *Journal of Applied Behavior Analysis,* 1974, *7,* 505–519.

Hart, B. M., Allen, K. E., Buell, J. S., Harris, F. R., & Wolf, M. M. Effects of social reinforcement on operant crying. *Journal of Experimental Child Psychology,* 1964, *1,* 145–153.

Hart, B. M., Reynolds, N. J., Baer, D. M., Brawley, F. R., & Harris, F. R. Effect of contingent and non-contingent social reinforcement on the cooperative play of a preschool child. *Journal of Applied Behavior Analysis,* 1968, *1,* 73–76.

Hartup, W. W. Peer interaction and social organization. In Paul H. Mussen (Ed.), *Carmichael's manual of child psychology.* New York: Wiley, 1970.

Hasazi, J. E., & Hasazi, S. E. Effects of teacher attention on digit-reversal behavior in an elementary school child. *Journal of Applied Behavior Analysis,* 1972, *5,* 157–162.

Hass, S. L., Ruggles, T. R., & LeBlanc, J. M. *Minimal vs. criterion-related detailed instructions.* Paper presented at the Biennial meeting of the Society of Research in Child Development, San Francisco, March 1979.

Haupt, E. J., Van Kirk, M. J., & Terraciano, T. An inexpensive fading procedure to decrease errors and increase retention of number facts. In E. Ramp & G. Semb (Eds.), *Behavior analysis: Areas of research and application.* Englewood Cliffs, N.J.: Prentice-Hall, 1977.

Hay, W. M., Hay, L., & Nelson, R. O. Direct and collateral changes in on-task and academic behavior resulting from on-task versus academic contingencies. *Behavior Therapy,* 1977, *8,* 431–441.

Herman, S. H., & Tramontana, J. Instructions and group versus individual reinforcement in modifying disruptive group behavior. *Journal of Applied Behavior Analysis,* 1971, *4,* 113–119.

Holland, J. G. Teaching machines: An application of principles from the laboratory. *Journal of the Experimental Analysis of Behavior,* 1960, *3,* 275–287.

Holt, W. J., & Etzel, B. C. *Cognitive by-products of motor training.* Paper presented at the meeting of the American Psychological Association, Washington, D.C., 1976.

Homme, L. E., deBacca, P., Devine, J. V., Steinhorst, R., & Rickert, E. J. Use of the Premack principle in controlling the behavior of school children. *Journal of the Experimental Analysis of Behavior,* 1963, *6,* 544.

Hopkins, B. L., Schutte, R. C., & Garton, K. L. The effects of access to a playroom on the rate and quality of printing and writing of first and second-grade students. *Journal of Applied Behavior Analysis,* 1971, *4,* 77–87.

Hops, H., & Cobb, J. A. Survival behaviors in the educational setting: Their implications for research and intervention. In L. A. Hamerlynck, L. C. Handy, & E. J. Mash (Eds.), *Behavior change: Methodology, con-*

cepts and practice. Champaign, Ill.: Research Press, 1973.

Hundert, J. The effectiveness of reinforcement, response cost, and mixed programs on classroom behaviors. *Journal of Applied Behavior Analysis,* 1976, *9,* 107.

Iwata, B. A., & Bailey, J. S. Reward versus cost token systems: An analysis of the effects on students and teacher. *Journal of Applied Behavior Analysis,* 1974, *7,* 567–576.

Jacobs, J. F. *A comparison of group and individual rewards in teaching reading to slow learners: Final report.* University of Florida, College of Education, June 1970, Project No. 9-0257, Grant No. OEG-49-190257-0045 (010), USOE Bureau of Research.

Johnson, M. S., & Bailey, J. S. Cross-age tutoring: Fifth graders as arithmetic tutors for kindergarten children. *Journal of Applied Behavior Analysis,* 1974, *7,* 223–232.

Johnston, M. K., Kelley, C. S., Harris, F. R., & Wolf, M. M. An application of reinforcement principles to development of motor skills of a young child. *Child Development,* 1966, *37,* 379–387.

Karraker, J., & Doke, L. A. Errorless discrimination of alphabet letters: Effects of time and method of introducing competing stimuli. *The Journal of Experimental Education,* 1970, *38,* 4.

Kaufman, K. F., & O'Leary, K. D. Reward, cost, and self-evaluation procedures for disruptive adolescents in a psychiatric hospital school. *Journal of Applied Behavior Analysis,* 1972, *5,* 293–310.

Kazdin, A. E. The effect of vicarious reinforcement on attentive behavior in the classroom. *Journal of Applied Behavior Analysis,* 1973, *6,* 71–78.

Kazdin, A. E. *Behavior modification in applied settings.* Homewood, Ill.: Dorsey, 1975.

Kazdin, A. E. *The token economy: A review and evaluation.* New York: Plenum Press, 1977.

Kazdin, A. E., & Klock, J. The effect of nonverbal teacher approval on student attentive behavior. *Journal of Applied Behavior Analysis,* 1973, *6,* 643–654.

Kazdin, A. E., Silverman, N. A., & Sittler, J. L. The use of prompts to enhance vicarious effects of nonverbal approval. *Journal of Applied Behavior Analysis,* 1975, *8,* 279–286.

Kelleher, R. Fixed-ratio schedules of conditioned reinforcement with chimpanzees. *Journal of the Experimental Analysis of Behvior,* 1958, *3,* 281–289.

Kirby, F. D., & Shields, F. Modification of arithmetic response rate and attending behavior in a seventh-grade student. *Journal of Applied Behavior Analysis,* 1972, *5,* 79–84.

Klein, R. D. A brief research report on accuracy and academic performance. *Journal of Applied Behavior Analysis,* 1975, *8,* 121–122.

Klein, R. D. Modifying academic performance in the grade school classroom. In M. Hersen, R. M. Eisler, & P. M. Miller (Eds.), *Progress in behavior modification,* Vol. 8. New York: Academic Press, 1979.

Knapczyk, D., & Livingston, G. The effects of prompting question-asking upon on-task behavior and reading. *Journal of Applied Behavior Analysis,* 1974, *7,* 115–121.

Koegel, R. L., & Rincover, A. Some detrimental effects of using extra stimuli to guide learning in normal and autistic children. *Journal of Abnormal Child Psychology,* 1976, *4,* 59–71.

Koegel, R. L., Dunlap, G., & Dyer, K. Intertrial interval duration and learning in autistic children. *Journal of Applied Behavior Analysis*, 1980, *13*, 91–99.

Kramer, S., Ruggles, T. R., & LeBlanc, J. M. *The effects of imposing time limits on the responses of preschool children*. Paper presented at the meeting of the Association for the Advancement of Behavior Therapy, San Francisco, 1979.

Kuypers, D. S., Becker, W. C., & O'Leary, K. D. How to make a token system fail. *Exceptional Children*, October 1968, *11*, 101–109.

Lahey, B. B., & Drabman, R. S. Facilitation of the acquisition and retention of sight-word vocabulary through token reinforcement. *Journal of Applied Behavior Analysis*, 1974, *7*, 307–312.

LeBlanc, J. M., Busby, K. H., & Thomson, C. Functions of timeout for changing aggressive behavior of a preschool child. In R. E. Ulrich, T. S. Stachnik, & J. E. Mabry (Eds.), *Control of human behaior: In education*, Vol. 3. Glenview, Ill.: Scott, Foresman, 1973.

LeBlanc, J. M., Etzel, B. C., & Domash, M. A. A functional curriculum for early intervention. In K. E. Allen, V. A. Holm, & R. L. Schiefelbush (Eds.), *Early intervention—A team approach*. Baltimore: University Park Press, 1978.

Leith, N. J., & Haude, R. H. Errorless discrimination in monkeys. *Proceedings of 77th Annual Convention*. American Psychological Association, 1969, 799–800.

Levin, L. A comparison of individual and group contingencies with third and fourth-grade children. *Probe*, 1971, *1*, 101–107.

Lewis, B. L., & Strain, P. S. Effects of feedback, timing and motivational content on teachers' delivery of contingent social praise. *Psychology in the Schools*, 1978, *15*, 423–429.

Litlow, L., & Pumroy, D. K. A brief review of classroom group-oriented contingencies. *Journal of Applied Behavior Analysis*, 1975, *8*, 341–347.

Lobitz, W. C., & Burns, W. J. The "least intrusive intervention" strategy for behavior change procedures: The use of public and private feedback in school classrooms. *Psychology in the Schools*, 1977, *14*, 89–94.

Long, J. D., & Williams, R. L. The comparative effectiveness of group and individually contingent free time with innercity junior high school students. *Journal of Applied Behavior Analysis*, 1973, *6*, 465–474.

Lovaas, O. I., & Simmons, J. Q. Manipulation of self-destruction in three retarded children. *Journal of Applied Behavior Analysis*, 1969, *2*, 143–157.

Lovitt, T. C., & Curtiss, K. A. Effects of manipulating an antecedent event on mathematics response rate. *Journal of Applied Behavior Analysis*, 1968, *1*, 329–334.

Lovitt, T. C., & Curtiss, K. A. Academic response rate as a function of teacher- and self-imposed contingencies. *Journal of Applied Behavior Analysis*, 1969, *2*, 49–53.

Lovitt, T. C., & Esveldt, K. A. The relative effects on math performance of single versus multiple-ratio schedules: A case study. *Journal of Applied Behavior Analysis*, 1970, *3*, 261–270.

Lovitt, T. C., Guppy, T. E., & Blattner, J. E. The use of a free-time contingency with fourth-graders to increase spelling accuracy. *Behavior Research and Therapy*, 1969, *7*, 151–156.

MacMillan, D., Forness, S. R., & Trumball, B. M. The role of punishment in the classroom. *Exceptional Children*, 1973, *40*, 85–96.

Madsen, C. H., Becker, W. C., Thomas, D. R., Koser, L., & Plager, E. An analysis of the reinforcing function of "sit down" commands. In R. K. Parker (Ed.), *Readings in educational psychology*. Boston: Allyn & Bacon, 1968.

Main, G. C., & Munro, B. C. A token reinforcement program in a public Junior High School. *Journal of Applied Behavior Analysis*, 1977, *10*, 93–94.

Maloney, K. B., & Hopkins, B. L. The modification of sentence structure and its relationship to subjective judgments of creativity in writing. *Journal of Applied Behavior Analysis*, 1973, *6*, 425–434.

Marholin, D., & Steinman, W. M. Stimulus control in the classroom as a function of the behavior reinforced. *Journal of Applied Behavior Analysis*, 1977, *10*, 465–478.

Marholin, D., Siegel, L. J., & Phillips, D. Treatment and transfer: A search for empirical procedures. In M. Hersen, R. M. Eisler, & P. M. Miller (Eds.), *Progress in behavior modification*, Vol. 3. New York: Academic Press, 1976.

McAllister, L. W., Stachowiak, J. G., Baer, D. M., & Conderman, L. The application of operant conditioning techniques in a secondary school classroom. *Journal of Applied Behavior Analysis*, 1969, *2*, 277–285.

McLaughlin, T. F., & Malaby, J. Intrinsic reinforcers in a classroom token economy. *Journal of Applied Behavior Analysis*, 1972, *5*, 263–270.

McNamara, J. R. Behavioral intervention in the classroom: Changing students and training a teacher. *Adolescence*, 1971, *6*, 433–440.

Meddock, T. D., Parsons, J. A., & Hill, K. T. Effects of an adult's presence and praise on young children's performance. *Journal of Experimental Child Psychology*, 1971, *12*, 197–211.

Medland, M. B., & Stachnik, T. J. Good-Behavior Game: A replication and systematic analysis. *Journal of Applied Behavior Analysis*, 1972, *5*, 45–51.

Miller, R. M., & LeBlanc, J. M. *Experimental analysis of the effect of detailed and minimal instructions on the acquisition of preacademic skills*. Paper presented at the meeting of the American Psychological Association, Montreal, August 1973.

Mitaug, D. E., & Wolfe, M. S. Employing task arrangements and verbal contingencies to promote verbalizations between retarded children. *Journal of Applied Behavior Analysis*, 1976, *9*, 301–314.

Moore, R., & Goldiamond, I. Errorless establishment of visual discrimination using fading procedures. *Journal of the Experimental Analysis of Behavior*, 1964, *7*, 269–272.

Morraco, J. C., & Fasheh, V. Effects of contingency management on academic achievement and conduct of mentally retarded Arab students. *American Journal of Mental Deficiency*, 1978, *82*, 487–493.

Neef, N. A., Iwata, B. A., & Page, T. J. The effects of known-item interspersed on acquisition of spelling and sightreading words. *Journal of Applied Behavior Analysis*, 1977, *10*, 738.

Nelson, A. L., Holt, W. J., & Etzel, B. C. *A description of programs to teach beginning math skills*. Invited symposium on preparing atypical preschool children for future academic work. Presented at the Council for Exceptional Children, Chicago, 1976. (a)

Nelson, A. L., Holt, W. J., & Etzel, B. C. *Empirical analysis of essential skills in a complex task.* Presented at the American Psychological Association, Washington, D.C., 1976. (b)

O'Leary, K. D. Behavior modification in the classroom: A rejoinder to Winett and Winkler. *Journal of Applied Behavior Analysis,* 1972, *5,* 505–511.

O'Leary, K. D., & Becker, W. C. Behavior modification of an adjustment class: A token reinforcement program. *Exceptional Children,* 1967, *33,* 637–642.

O'Leary, K. D., & Becker, W. C. The effects of a teacher's reprimands on children's behavior. *Journal of School Psychology,* 1968, *7,* 8–11.

O'Leary, K. D., & Drabman, R. Token reinforcement programs in the classroom. *Psychological Bulletin,* 1971, *75,* 379–398.

O'Leary, K. D., & O'Leary, S. G. (Eds.) *Classroom management: The successful use of behavior modification.* New York: Pergamon Press, 1972.

O'Leary, S. G., & O'Leary, K. D. Behavior modification in the school. In H. Leitenberg (Ed.), *Handbook of behavior modification and behavior therapy.* New York: Prentice-Hall, 1976.

O'Leary, K. D., Becker, W. C., Evans, M. B., & Saudargas, R. A. A token reinforcement program in a public school: A replication and systematic analysis. *Journal of Applied Behavior Analysis,* 1969, *2,* 3–13.

O'Leary, K. D., Kauffman, K. F., Kass, R. E., & Drabman, R. S. The effects of loud and soft reprimands on the behavior of disruptive students. *Exceptional Children,* 1970, *37,* 145–155.

Osborne, J. G. Free time as a reinforcer in the management of classroom behavior. *Journal of Applied Behavior Analysis,* 1969, *2,* 113–118.

Packard, R. G. The control of "classroom attention": A group contingency for complex behavior. *Journal of Applied Behavior Analysis,* 1970, *3,* 13–28.

Panyan, M. C., & Hall, R. V. Effects of serial versus concurrent task sequencing on acquisition maintenance and generalization. *Journal of Applied Behavior Analysis,* 1978, *11,* 67–74.

Patterson, G. R. An application of conditioning techniques to the control of a hyperactive child. In L. P. Ullmann & L. Krasner (Eds.), *Case studies in behavior modification.* New York: Holt, Rinehart & Winston, 1965.

Patterson, G. R., Jones, R., Whittier, J., & Wright, M. A. A behavior modification technique for the hyperactive child. *Behavior Research and Therapy,* 1965, *2,* 217–226.

Peterson, R. F., & Whithurst, G. J. A variable influencing the performance of generalized imitation. *Journal of Applied Behavior Analysis,* 1971, *4,* 1–9.

Peterson, R. F., Cox, M. A., & Bijou, S. W. Training children to work productively in classroom groups. *Exceptional Children,* March 1971, *14,* 491–500.

Pinkston, E. M., Reese, N. M., LeBlanc, J. M., & Baer, D. M. Independent control of a preschool child's aggression and peer interaction by contingent teacher attention. *Journal of Applied Behavior Analysis,* 1973, *6,* 115–124.

Plummer, S., Baer, D. M., & LeBlanc, J. M. Functional

considerations in the use of procedural timeout and an effective alternative. *Journal of Applied Behavior Analysis,* 1977, *10,* 689–706.

Porterfield, J. K., Herbert-Jackson, E., & Risley, T. R. Contingent observation: An effective and acceptable procedure for reducing disruptive behavior of young children in a group setting. *Journal of Applied Behavior Analysis,* 1976, *9,* 55–64.

Powers, R. B., Cheney, C. D., & Agostino, N. R. Errorless training of a visual discrimination in preschool children. *The Psychological Record,* 1970, *20,* 45–50.

Prentice, B. S. *The effectiveness of group versus individual reinforcement for shaping attentive classroom behavior.* Unpublished doctoral dissertation, University of Arizona, 1970.

Proshansky, H. M., Ittleson, W. H., & Rivlin, L. G. (Eds.), *Environmental psychology.* New York: Holt, Rinehart & Winston, 1970.

Radgowski, T. A., Allen, K. E., Schilmoeller, G. L., Ruggles, T. R., & LeBlanc, J. M. *Delayed presentation of feedback in preschool group foreign language training.* Paper presented at the meeting of the American Psychological Association, Toronto, 1978.

Redd, W. H., & Birnbrauer, J. S. Adults as discriminative stimuli for different reinforcement contingencies with retarded children. *Journal of Experimental Child Psychology,* 1969, *7,* 440–447.

Resnick, L. B., Wang, M. C., & Kaplan, J. Task analysis in curriculum design: A hierarchically sequenced introductory mathematics curriculum. *Journal of Applied Behavior Analysis,* 1973, *6,* 679–709.

Reynolds, G. S. *A primer of operant conditioning.* Glenview, Ill.: Scott, Foresman, 1968.

Reynolds, N. J., & Risley, T. R. The role of social and material reinforcers in increasing talking of a disadvantaged preschool child. *Journal of Applied Behavior Analysis,* 1968, *1,* 253–262.

Rincover, A. Variables affecting stimulus fading and discriminative responding in psychotic children. *Journal of Abnormal Psychology,* 1978, *87,* 541–553.

Robertshaw, C. S., & Hiebert, H. D. The astronaut game: A group contingency applied to a first grade classroom. *School Applications of Learning Theory,* 1973, *6,* 28–33.

Ruggles, T. R., & LeBlanc, J. M. *Variables which affect the effectiveness of group training procedures designed for children with learning problems.* Paper presented at the 12th Annual Gatlinburg Conference on Research in Mental Retardation and Developmental Disabilities, Gulf Shores, Alabama, 1979.

Sabbert, J. K., Holt, W. J., Nelson, A. L., Domash, M. A., & Etzel, B. C. *Functional analysis of teaching different sizes of groups.* Presented at the American Psychological Association, Washington, D.C., 1976. (a)

Sabbert, J. K., Holt, W. J., Nelson, A. L., Domash, M. A., & Etzel, B. C. *Programming simple addition problems.* Invited symposium on preparing atypical preschool children for future academic work, Council on Exceptional Children, Chicago, 1976. (b)

Salzberg, B. H., Wheeler, A. J., Devar, L. T., & Hopkins, B. L. The effects of intermittent feedback and intermittent contingent access to play on printing of kindergarten children. *Journal of Applied Behavior Analysis,* 1971, *4,* 163–171.

Saudargas, R. W., Madsen, C. H., & Scott, J. W. Differential effects of fixed and variable-time feedback on production rates of elementary school children. *Journal of Applied Behavior Analysis*, 1977, *10*, 673.

Schilmoeller, K. J., & Etzel, B. C. An experimental analysis of criterion- and noncriterion-related cues in "errorless" stimulus control procedures. In B. C. Etzel, J. M. LeBlanc, & D. M. Baer (Eds.), *New developments in behavioral research: Theory, method and application. In honor of Sidney W. Bijou.* Hillsdale, N.J.: Lawrence Erlbaum, 1977.

Schilmoeller, G. L., Schilmoeller, K. J., Etzel, B. C., & LeBlanc, J. M. Conditional discrimination responding after errorless and trial-and-error training. *Journal of the Experimental Analysis of Behavior*, 1979, *31*, 405–420.

Schreibman, L. Effects of within-stimulus and extra-stimulus prompting on discrimination learning in autistic children. *Journal of Applied Behavior Analysis*, 1975, *8*, 91–112.

Schumaker, J. B., Hovell, M. F., & Sherman, J. A. An analysis of daily report cards and parent-managed privileges in the improvement of adolescents' classroom performance. *Journal of Applied Behavior Analysis*, 1977, *10*, 449–464.

Schusterman, R. J. Attention shift and errorless reversal learning by the California sea lion. *Science*, 1967, *156*, 833–835.

Schwartz, S. H., Firestone, I. J., & Terry, S. Fading techniques and concept learning in children. *Psychonomic Science*, 1971, *25*, 83–84.

Schwarz, M. L., & Hawkins, R. P. Application of delayed reinforcement procedures to the behavior of an elementary school child. *Journal of Applied Behavior Analysis*, 1970, *3*, 85–96.

Scott, P. M., Burton, R. V., & Yarrow, M. R. Social reinforcement under natural conditions. *Child Development*, 1967, *38*, 53–63.

Shure, M. B. Psychological ecology of a nursery school. *Child Development*, 1963, *34*, 979–992.

Sidman, M., & Cresson, O. Reading and cross-modal transfer of stimulus equivalences in severe retardation. *American Journal of Mental Deficiency*, 1973, *77*, 515–523.

Sidman, M., & Stoddard, L. T. Programming perception and learning for retarded children. In N. R. Ellis (Ed.), *International review of research in mental retardation*, Vol. 2. New York: Academic Press, 1966.

Sidman, M., & Stoddard, L. T. The effectiveness of fading in programming a simultaneous form discrimination for retarded children. *Journal of the Experimental Analysis of Behavior*, 1968, *10*, 3–15.

Sidman, M., Cresson, O., & Willson-Morris, M. Acquisition of matching to sample via mediated transfer. *Journal of the Experimental Analysis of Behavior*, 1974, *22*, 261–273.

Skinner, B. F. *The behavior of organisms.* New York: Appleton-Century, 1938.

Skinner, B. F. *Why we need teaching machines: Cumulative Record.* New York: Appleton-Century-Crofts, 1961.

Skinner, B. F. Operant behavior. *American Psychologist*, 1963, *18*, 503–515.

Smith, M. F. The establishment and extinction of the token reward habit in the cat. *Journal of General Psychology*, 1939, *20*, 475–486.

Smith, R. A., & Filler, J. W. Effects of a modified fading procedure on two-choice discrimination performance of toddler-age children. *Child Development*, 1975, *46*, 583–587.

Solnick, J. V., Rincover, A., & Peterson, C. R. Some determinants of the reinforcing and punishing effects of timeout. *Journal of Applied Behavior Analysis*, 1977, *10*, 415–424.

Stella, E. M., & Etzel, B. C. *The effects of daily criterion level probes on acquisition.* Presented at the American Psychological Association, San Francisco, 1977.

Stella, M. E., & Etzel, B. C. *A case for training eye orientations of difficult-to-educate children: Visual scanning differences between normal and retarded children.* Presented at the Association for Advancement of Behavior Therapy, San Francisco, 1979. (a)

Stella, M. E., & Etzel, B. C. *Manipulation of visual fixation on correct (S +) stimuli during acquisition.* Presented at the Society for Research in Child Development, San Francisco, 1979. (b)

Stoddard, L. T., & Sidman, M. The effects of errors on children's performance on a circle-ellipse discrimination. *Journal of the Experimental Analysis of Behavior*, 1967, *10*, 261–270.

Stokes, T. F., & Baer, D. M. An implicit technology of generalization. *Journal of Applied Behavior Analysis*, 1977, *10*, 349–368.

Strain, P. S., Shores, R. E., & Kerr, M. M. An experimental analysis of "spillover" effects on the social interaction of behaviorally handicapped preschool children. *Journal of Applied Behavior Analysis*, 1976, *9*, 31–40.

Tate, B. G., & Baroff, G. S. Aversive control of self-injurious behavior in a psychotic boy. *Behaviour Research and Therapy*, 1966, *4*, 281–287.

Terrace, H. S. Discrimination learning with and without "errors." *Journal of the Experimental Analysis of Behavior*, 1963, *6*, 1–27. (a)

Terrace, H. S. Errorless transfer of a discrimination across two continua. *Journal of the Experimental Analysis of Behavior*, 1963, *6*, 223–232. (b)

Terrace, H. S. Stimulus control. In W. K. Honig (Ed.), *Operant behavior: Areas of research and application.* New York: Meridith Corporation, 1966.

Thomas, J. D. Accuracy of self-assessment of on-task behavior by elementary school children. *Journal of Applied Behavior Analysis*, 1976, *9*, 209–210.

Touchette, P. E. The effects of graduated stimulus change on the acquisition of a simple discrimination in severely retarded boys. *Journal of the Experimental Analysis of Behavior*, 1969, *12*, 211–214.

Touchette, P. E. Transfer of stimulus control: Measuring the moment of transfer. *Journal of the Experimental Analysis of Behavior*, 1971, *15*, 347–354.

Trap, J. J., Milner-Davis, P., Joseph, S., & Cooper, J. O. The effects of feedback and consequences on transitional cursive letter formation. *Journal of Applied Behavior Analysis*, 1978, *14*, 381–394.

Turknett, R. L. *A study of the differential effects of individual versus group reward conditions on the creative productions of elementary school children.* Unpublished doctoral dissertation, University of Georgia, 1971.

Twardosz, S., & Sajwaj, T. Multiple effects of a procedure to increase sitting in a hyperactive retarded boy. *Journal of Applied Behavior Analysis*, 1972, *5*, 73–78.

Twardosz, S., Cataldo, M. F., & Risley, T. R. An open environment design for infant and toddler day care. *Journal of Applied Behavior Analysis*, 1974, *7*, 529–546.

Tyler, V., & Brown, G. Token reinforcement of academic performance with institutionalized delinquent boys. *Journal of Educational Psychology*, 1968, *59*, 164–168.

Uhl, C. N., & Garcia, E. E. Comparison of omission with extinction in response elimination in rats. *Journal of Comparative and Physiological Psychology*, 1969, *69*, 554–562.

vanBiervliet, A. Establishing words and objects as functionally equivalent through manual sign training. *American Journal of Mental Deficiency*, 1977, *82*, 178–186.

Van Houten, R., Hill, S., & Parsons, M. An analysis of a performance feedback system: The effects of timing and feedback, public posting, and praise upon academic performance and peer interaction. *Journal of Applied Behavior Analysis*, 1975, *8*, 449–457.

Walker, H. M., & Buckley, H. K. The use of positive reinforcement in conditioning attending behavior. *Journal of Applied Behavior Analysis*, 1968, *1*, 245–250.

Walker, H. M., & Buckley, N. K. Programming generalization and maintenance of treatment effects across time and across settings. *Journal of Applied Behavior Analysis*, 1972, *5*, 209–224.

Walker, H. M., & Hops, H. Increasing academic achievement by reinforcing direct academic performance and/or facilitative non-academic responses. *Journal of Educational Psychology*, 1976, *68*, 218–225.

Warner, S. P., Miller, F. D., & Cohen, M. W. Relative effectiveness of teacher attention and the "good behavior game" in modifying disruptive classroom behavior. *Journal of Applied Behavior Analysis*, 1977, *10*, 737.

Wasik, B. H. The application of Premack's generalization on reinforcement to the management of classroom be-havior. *Journal of Experimental Child Psychology*, 1970, *10*, 33–43.

Weiner, H. Some effects of response cost upon human operant behavior. *Journal of the Experimental Analysis of Behavior*, 1962, *5*, 201–208.

Weinstein, C. S. Modifying student behavior in an open classroom through changes in physical design. *American Educational Research Journal*, 1977, *14*, 249–262.

Whitehurst, G. J. Observational learning. In A. C. Catania & T. A. Brigham (Eds.), *Handbook of applied behavior analysis: Social and instructional processes*. New York: Irvington Publishers, 1978.

Wilson, S. H., & Williams, R. L. The effects of group contingencies on first garders' academic and social behaviors. *Journal of School Psychology*, 1973, *11*, 110–117.

Winett, R. A., & Winkler, R. C. Current behavior modification in the classroom. Be still, be quiet, be docile. *Journal of Applied Behavior Analysis*, 1972, *5*, 499–504.

Witte, P. H. *The effects of group reward structure on interracial acceptance, peer-tutoring, and academic performance*. Unpublished doctoral dissertation, Washington University, 1971.

Wolf, M. M., Risley, T. R., & Mees, H. L. Application of operant conditioning procedures to the behavior problems of an autistic child. *Behaviour Research and Therapy*, 1964, *1*, 305–312.

Wolf, M. M., Giles, D. K., & Hall, R. V. Experiments with token reinforcement in a remedial classroom. *Behaviour Research and Therapy*, 1968, *6*, 51–64.

Wolfe, J. B. Effectiveness of token rewards for chimpanzees. *Comparative Psychology Monograph*, 1936, *11* (5, Series No. 60).

Wulbert, M., Nyman, B. A., Snow, D., & Owen, Y. The efficacy of stimulus fading and contingency management in the treatment of elective mutism: A case study. *Journal of Applied Behavior Analysis*, 1973, *6*, 435–441.

Zeaman, D., & House, B. J. The role of attention in retardate discrimination learning. In N. R. Ellis (Ed.), *Handbook of mental deficiency: Psychological theory and research*. New York: McGraw-Hill, 1963.

CHAPTER 12

Retardation

John T. Neisworth and Ronald A. Madle

Defining retardation is a complicated task. The problems exhibited by individuals who have been labeled retarded can be extensive, affecting many areas of human functioning. In fact, one problem encountered in surveying behavior modification and therapy in the field of retardation is that *retardation* is a diagnostic term. As such, it identifies a category of people rather than a specific set of behaviors—the real domain of behavior modification. To align things appropriately, this chapter emphasizes, as have Bijou (1963) and Lindsley (1964), that behaviors, as opposed to individuals, are retarded. This perspective raises an issue about the term *mental retardation* when used by a behaviorist. Whatever is retarded when viewed from the standpoint of behaviorism is not "mentality." Some individuals in the field have advocated replacing the term *mental* with either *developmental* or *behavioral* (cf. Bijou, 1966). Neither of these alternatives appears to have met with widespread acceptance.

John T. Neisworth • Department of Special Education, The Pennsylvania State University, University Park, Pennsylvania 16802. Ronald A. Madle • Director of Training and Evaluation, Laurelton Center, Laurelton, Pennsylvania 17835 and Division of Individual and Family Studies, The Pennsylvania State University, University Park, Pennsylvania 16802. The contributions of the authors were equal with authorship order being arbitrarily selected.

An alternative approach, as used in this chapter, is simply to use the term *retardation* to refer to a condition in which there is a generalized delay in a wide range of behavioral domains (Neisworth & Smith, 1974). While this type of definition allows individuals labeled with other traditional diagnoses, such as autism, to be included, it is highly consistent with many other contemporary definitions of mental retardation as well as the term *developmental disabilities* (Public Law 95.517, 1970), which is gradually becoming more dominant than the large number of traditional diagnostic labels for severe disorders that manifest themselves during the early part of the lifespan. Most current definitions outside the field of medicine emphasize the severity of the delays in various behavioral domains rather than the etiology of the delays.

Traditional Definitions of Mental Retardation

Although there have been a number of historically significant definitions of retardation, the most commonly accepted one today was developed by the American Association on Mental Deficiency (Grossman, 1977). This definition indicates that *mental retardation* "refers to significantly subaverage intellectual functioning existing concurrently with deficits in adaptive behavior and manifested during the developmental period" (Grossman, 1977, p. 13). It should be noted that this definition refers to a delayed or deficient level of behavioral performance without reference to actual or presumed causes.

As far as intellectual performance is concerned, *significantly subaverage* is operationally defined as two or more standard deviations below the mean (IQ 69 or 70, depending on the test employed). While intellectual performance is still the most salient criterion used in identifying retardation, the concept of adaptive behavior has greatly changed the manner in which intervention is approached. In essence, adaptive behavior consists of the large set of behaviors that an individual must possess to "make it in society." These include behaviors typically grouped under behavioral domains such as self-care, motor ability, communication, socialization, and self-governance. Measures of these behaviors have not impacted significantly on practices in labeling individuals as retarded, since there are no simple cutoff points and scores for measures of adaptive behavior. These measures are usually put in the form of checklists enumerating the various significant capabilities. This measure, however, has significantly affected intervention practices. It has resulted in a sharper focus on changing adaptive behaviors rather than "mental" functioning. Therefore, most current approaches to intervening with the retarded more closely resemble behavioral approaches than they did a decade ago.

Given the great range and diversity of human functioning represented by the term *retardation*, individuals are typically classified into one of four levels of functioning. These levels are mild, moderate, severe, and profound retardation.

Mild retardation involves the least delay. The level of functioning differs little from that of other individuals of the same chronological age. Usually, the primary areas of delay are in academic and interpersonal skills. Most typically, people who display mild retardation are not even diagnosed or identified until they enter elementary school and begin having trouble academically. Once the person with mild retardation leaves school, he or she also is frequently able once again to "blend into" society and escape the "retarded" label that was acquired during school.

At the more impaired levels of functioning, individuals need some kinds of services throughout their lives. At the moderately retarded level, individuals show increased difficulty in doing tasks that are taken for granted by others. In addition to academic and interpersonal deficits, which are markedly more severe, the individual encounters difficulty with simple daily tasks, such as self-dressing, performing simple household chores, using money, and using leisure time effectively.

At the severely and profoundly retarded levels, the deficits become pronounced in all areas. Such simple tasks as toilet training, attending to people, and following instructions are learned only through systematic and intensive training. It is with this level that behavior modification will meet its greatest challenge in the near future. Legal mandates to provide education and training for the severely and profoundly retarded are now a fact. While behavioral techniques have been shown to be effective with these individuals in highly controlled settings, the task will now be to demonstrate that they can be effective in situations using parents, teachers, and other paraprofessionals as change agents.

Retardation is a problem of major social significance, as prevalence estimates range from 1% to as high as 11% or 12%, based on projections from the normal distribution of intelligence scores and from empirical studies. Dingman and Tarjan (1960) indicated that the actual prevalence may, in fact, be higher. Of course, the actual factors contributing to prevalence make this figure vary across geographic regions, sexes, ages, and so forth. For example, countries that are more tolerant of minor deviations from the norm, such as the Scandinavian countries, generally show a lower prevalence of retarded individuals, since their cutoff point for identifying this condition is lower than in many other countries. Whatever the criteria, however, retardation is a universal and significant social problem.

Behavioral Models of Retardation

Behavioral models of retardation have been discussed by a number of individuals (Bijou, 1963, 1966; Lindsley, 1964; Neisworth & Smith, 1973). Most current theoretical models are extensions of the model initially advanced by Bijou (1963). Basically, this analysis was derived from Skinner's (1953) objections to inferring personal traits from observed behavior and then, in turn, using the trait as an explanation of the behavior itself. Instead of viewing the cause of retardation as a theoretical construct such as mentality, or as a biological phenomenon such as impairment of the brain, Bijou suggested that retardation be conceived of as a *behavioral* deficiency generated by adverse reinforcement histories or as failures of stimulus-and-response functions. This form of functional analysis suggests a search into learning variables such as intermittent reinforcement and extinction, inadequate reinforcement history, severe punishment, and other factors such as extreme satiation and deprivation. A major advantage of this approach is that the variables suggested as causing regarded behaviors are all subject to objective definition and are all manipulable or potentially manipulable, a feature that is obviously desirable for empirical research and application. In addition, Bijou's theory requires not a special theory of retardation but an extension of the principles of operant learning theory to both the explanation and the modification of retarded behavior. Bijou's (1963) 4-point system of explaining the development and the maintenance of retarded behavior is described below.

Biological and Physiological Factors

While biological factors are included in this model of retardation, we will present it in such a way as to link them clearly to the development of behavior. This model specifies three specific ways in which biological apparatus can affect the development of behavior. First, essential response equipment may be impaired. A child is not able to perform tasks that require responses that are impossible to execute because the necessary biological

structures are absent or deficient. The child is not able to perform the task regardless of the amount of stimulation or exposure or training provided. Other responses that serve the same function and that compensate for this impairment *may* be learned, however. An excellent example has been the development of nonspeech methods of communication for individuals who are unable to speak.

The second way in which biological factors may limit the development of behavioral repertoires is the restriction of the stimuli that ordinarily are available to human beings. The child who can see, hear, smell, and feel objects and events can have infinitely more experiences than the child whose sensory mechanisms are impaired. Many times, this type of restriction can also be compensated for by other people and events in the child's environment. Some approaches to this problem are evident in Lindsley's (1964) statement about retardation, to be discussed shortly.

The third way in which biological impairment might restrict developmental opportunities is related to the way the person appears to others. Physical attractiveness, in part, controls opportunities for learning. The ugly child or one with certain repelling characteristics is deprived of the usual positive social stimulation provided to the "cute," normal child (see Neisworth, Jones, & Smith, 1978, for an expansion of this topic).

Intermittent Reinforcement and Extinction

Bijou (1963) discussed several ways in which intermittent reinforcement and extinction may operate to delay progressive changes in behavior. First, it is possible that for some parents, it is reinforcing to see their child remain helpless, ineffective, and infantile. Under these circumstances, they are likely to reinforce dependent behavior and systematically extinguish, or even punish, independent behaviors. Research on parent–child interactions with their handicapped and nonhandicapped children have confirmed these speculations (Campbell, 1973). The second possibility is that intermittent reinforcement is too lean and actual extinction may operate to weaken the development of classes of behavior that depend on frequent and consistent parental reinforcement. These especially include the social and language behaviors so necessary to early development.

Inadequate Reinforcement History

When an environment is dull, routine, unvaried, and limited in range, interactions are also restricted. Conditions of this sort would most likely limit repertoires in self-care, emotional-social reactions, and preacademic and academic skills. This type of reinforcement history may be expected, since retarded children are frequently raised under conditions that are less than optimal. These include being raised in isolated communities, in institutions where the conditions for good family living are not present, and in families with disturbed or deficient parenting.

Severe Punishment

The last factor that would be likely to retard development is *severe* punishment. Consequences of this sort may operate in several ways. For example, if a child is punished by his or her parents for saying negative things about a younger sibling, he or she may react by eventually garbling words in such a fashion that they do not elicit punishment. Such a change prevents the punishment but certainly does not lead to adequate language growth. Second, there is a large body of evidence (Azrin & Holz, 1966) indicating that severe punishment stops ongoing behavior. If such punishment is mild, it may well be possible to reestablish the behavior, but, if the punishment is severe, it may have long-lasting suppressing effects that would be extremely resistive to change. In addition, these effects become very disruptive when either response or stimulus generalization occurs. In this case, not only are the punished behaviors suppressed, but related behaviors in similar settings are suppressed. Additionally, previously neutral stimuli, such as the situation in which the punishment occurred, may become aversive. The prepotent response becomes one of avoiding the punishing situation, in which many skills are learned normally, and consti-

tutes negative reinforcement for avoiding potential learning situations.

While Bijou's (1963) analysis is now almost two decades old, it is nonetheless still current. Little systematic effort has been put into further developing an overall behavioral model of retardation or into systematically developing a comprehensive and coherent system of behavioral technology with the retarded that encompasses assessment, prescription, intervention, and evaluation.

The one possible extension of Bijou's theory occurred when Lindsley (1964) posited that *children* are not retarded, only their behavior in average environments is sometimes retarded. The primary emphasis of Lindsley's work was oriented to dealing with the biological conditions that Bijou discussed. His basic premise was that various forms of prostheses were available, including devices that could be carried about by an individual, training that could overcome behavioral handicaps, and the construction of prosthetic environments where the performance of the child would be more normal than in the average environment.

Probably the most influential aspect of Lindsley's work was his pointing out the fallacy of *similia similibus curantur,* or the "like-cures-like" doctrine. Lindsley pointed out that treatment need not be dictated by the alleged cause of a dysfunction. Even practitioners who do not accept a behavioral model of retarded development are likely to be able to employ behavioral procedures in modifying retarded development. Subsequent applied research on behavior modification with the retarded and a rapidly expanding literature clearly support either the adequacy of a behavioral model or at least the relevance of Lindsley's formulations.

Historical Perspectives on Treatment

In the more than 25 centuries that retardation has been recognized as a problem, there have been four major eras in approaches to the treatment of the retarded. During primitive times, the basic approach was survival. The retarded, like many other handicapped individuals, were simply not fit to exist and were allowed to die. As the fight for survival became less pressing, a somewhat humanitarian trend emerged. While not as frequently destroyed, the retarded were often ridiculed. Some became slaves; others were taken in by beggars and deliberately maimed so that they could solicit alms. Some of the more fortunate were taken in by wealthy families and kept as a source of amusement for family members and guests. Some were employed as court jesters or companions for the wealthy. While no longer eliminated, the retarded did not yet fare well.

During the Middle Ages, the religious movements brought increased humanitarianism. Retarded individuals were often taken in as wards of the church and cared for in monasteries and asylums. Of course, during the same era, there were some throwbacks to earlier times as, for example, when Martin Luther advocated throwing the retarded into the River Themes to perish, since he thought they were possessed by demons. The last era in the treatment of the retarded did not begin until around the seventeenth century and arose in the theories of John Locke (who was also a prominent figure in the development of behavioral approaches). Since Locke felt that the capabilities of human beings are primarily a function of the environment, this viewpoint brought a new optimism that the mentally retarded could be educated and trained rather than simply cared for.

The current era is one of treatment and training. Perhaps one of the earliest forms of treatment during this era was "moral treatment," in which it was felt that both the retarded and the mentally ill could be cured or at least improved through humane treatment. Unfortunately, the relative ineffectiveness of this approach to treatment, as well as the prevailing sociopolitical conditions (Sarason & Doris, 1969), resulted in a backlash and the establishment of the eugenics movement. The basic theme of this movement is that retardation is a genetic or biological problem that is not amenable to treatment. During this period, the retarded were segregated from society and in many cases sterilized to prevent the propagation of defective organisms. Even when this overall policy of segregation and sterilization

ended, the continued reliance on biological models resulted in the dominance of the medical profession in the care and treatment of the retarded. As is true in general, we appear to be recycling at this point and are now in an era close to moral treatment, that is, the philosophy of normalization. Once again, there are signs that this phase may be coming to a close and a backlash may be occurring. There is one primary difference between this point in the cycle and the late 1800s, when the last era of moral treatment ended: the presence of behavioral technology and its demonstrated effectiveness in training and habilitating the retarded.

Behavioral work with the mentally retarded began, for all practical purposes, with the work of Jean Itard, a physician and educator in the eighteenth century. It was Itard who, upon hearing the stories about a "wolf-child" found in the forests of France, decided to work with the child and attempt to train him to live in society. While Itard emphasized the sensory aspects of his techniques, it has become clear from an examination of the detailed records that he kept that many of the methods he used were in fact similar to those employed by current behavior modifiers. Given the lack of a coherent behavioral model in Itard's work, subsequent applications of his procedures were conducted by Maria Montessori, who again emphasized the sensory training aspects of his methodology. It was not until the middle of the twentieth century that behavioral techniques were once again applied to the training of the mentally retarded.

In an isolated report, Fuller (1949) demonstrated that the arm movement of a profoundly retarded adult could be brought under reinforcement control with the application of operant procedures. In 1963, Ellis produced a theoretical account of how the toilet training of the retarded might be accomplished through the systematic application of learning principles. Basic research in learning with the retarded began in earnest during the 1950s with the purpose of demonstrating that operant principles were applicable to the behavior and the learning of the mentally retarded. It was at this point that prominent behavioral researchers such as Sidney Bijou, Norman Ellis, Beatrice Barrett, Ogden Lindsley, Joseph

Spradlin, and Edward Zigler were prominent. They set the foundation for applied behavior analysis with the retarded. At this point began the vigorous work in applying and validating behavioral procedures to changing the practical behaviors of the retarded.

A survey of the current status of behavior modification and therapy with the retarded is presented in the next section. This survey of the literature is organized around three major areas. The first of these is the reporting of significant work related to *targets for change*, such as toileting, dressing, and social behaviors. Then we move on to the various *behavioral tactics* that have been applied with the retarded. Last, there is discussion of the overall *strategies* by which the behavioral tactics are applied.

Current Empirical Status and Developments

Targets for Change

Much of the early application of behavior modification with the retarded was to the development of such self-care behaviors as toilet training, dressing, grooming, and feeding among the severely and profoundly retarded individuals living in institutions. Operant techniques have been particularly well-suited to dealing with these groups because of the relatively little emphasis placed on the verbal skills of such clients.

Toilet Training. Toileting of the retarded has received a great deal of attention. One of the first theoretical analyses of applying behavior modification to the retarded was Ellis's (1963) analysis of how operant principles might be used in toilet training. Early applications of this suggested approach included work by Dayan (1964), Hundziak, Maurer, and Watson (1965), Minge and Ball (1967), Giles and Wolf (1966), and Watson (1968). Toilet training offers an excellent example of the progressive refinement of behavioral techniques.

Early work concentrated primarily on the use of positive reinforcement and punishment, and there was little application of other behavioral techniques. For example, Dayan (1964) had severely retarded children placed on the

toilet every two hours. Reinforcement was then delivered for elimination during these periods of time. The only real refinement came about when Watson (1968) developed an automated toilet trainer, which administered reinforcement when the child eliminated into the toilet. The primary advantage of these methods over traditional toilet training was the addition of appropriate consequences for toileting behavior to the toileting schedule procedure that already existed in most institutions.

At this point, a significant increase in the effectiveness of toileting programs occurred when Azrin and Foxx (1971) recognized the need for multiple intensive procedures. In addition to using an apparatus to signal when toileting occurred and providing appropriate consequences, the Azrin–Foxx procedure included modeling, priming to increase urination frequency, food and social reinforcement for urinating correctly or staying dry, reprimands and time-out for soiling, and shaping self-initiation of toileting. While previous behavioral and nonbehavioral approaches to toilet training the retarded required months of training and statistical tests to demonstrate their effectiveness, Azrin and Foxx (1971) trained nine profoundly retarded adults in a median time of four days. The longest training time for these nine individuals was 12 days. Procedures were also included in the program to ensure the long-term maintenance of toileting behaviors. While other toilet training programs have been effective, studies have demonstrated that a combination of procedures, including at least reinforcement, the chaining and shaping of responses, prompting, and punishment, are necessary (Baumeister & Klosowski, 1965; Kimbrell, Luckey, Barbuto, & Love, 1967; Mahoney, Van Wagenen, & Meyerson, 1971; Van Wagenen, Meyerson, Kerr, & Mahoney, 1969). Little further progress has occurred in the area of toilet training. The Azrin–Foxx program has virtually become a standard against which other techniques are assessed. In spite of the effectiveness of the procedure as reported by Azrin and Foxx, some individuals (e.g., Birnbrauer, 1976) have questioned the effectiveness of the procedure, since no independent replications have been reported. In addition, it has been the experience of one of the authors of this chapter (Madle) that many attempts to apply the Azrin–Foxx method have been halfhearted and have used only those components that the individual practioners have felt were necessary. Unpublished work currently going on has indicated, however, that the consistent and precise application of the method has resulted in an effectiveness comparable with that of Azrin and Foxx. This work, however, has had to employ eight separate trainers working with each individual resident, somewhat decreasing the overall efficiency of the procedure.

While most work on toileting has emphasized skill development, other studies have dealt with related toileting problems. For example, Luiselli (1977) reported a case of toileting phobia in a 15-year-old retarded male who manifested an intense fear of urinating in a toilet. As a result, he wet his pants at a frequent rate. Through a combination of various response-contingent consequences and the gradual introduction of structured contingencies, a steady reduction in the frequency of wetting was noted. By the end of a follow-up phase, the individual was self-initiating toileting in an appropriate manner.

A second related area has been the reduction of enuretic behaviors. One of the most prominent methods of accomplishing this is the pad-and-buzzer technique, developed by Mowrer and Mowrer (1938). Sloop and Kennedy (1973) conducted a study on two groups of individuals to evaluate the effectiveness of this procedure. In this study, the subjects treated with the pad-and-buzzer method had significantly more success than the control group in meeting the criterion of 13 dry nights. Unfortunately, 4 of the 11 successful subjects relapsed within 36–72 days. In the long run, only one-third of the treated group remained dry. It would seem that this technique may benefit from the addition of supplemental techniques, much as the early toilet training was improved by Azrin and Foxx. A second method of dealing with enuresis has been developed by Kimmel and Kimmel (1970) and consists of simply prompting the child to report when he or she needs to urinate during the day and instructing him or her to wait, briefly at first and then for longer periods. A controlled study by Paschalis, Kimmel, and Kimmel (1972) showed impressive results.

Feeding. Another behavior receiving early attention in the literature was self-feeding. Like other self-care behaviors, this was frequently given high priority since the ability of retarded individuals to care for themselves drastically reduces the amount of individualized attention necessary to maintain the individual and allows greater amounts of time to be spent on active training to become more self-sufficient and competent in other areas. Gorton and Hollis (1965) described the steps used to shape feeding skills in a task analysis of the various steps involved in filling a spoon from a tray or dish and moving the spoon toward and into the mouth. The basic technique employed was backward chaining and manual guidance, and the individual's hand was guided in filling the utensil, bringing the spoon to the mouth, and releasing the subject's hand just prior to the spoon's going into the mouth. As progress occurred at each stage, the hand was released further and further from the mouth, until eventually, the child was able to fill the spoon and feed herself or himself. Repeated demonstrations of these techniques (Henriksen & Doughty, 1967; Barton, Guess, Garcia, & Baer, 1970; Martin, McDonald, & Omichinski, 1971; Zeiler & Jervey, 1968) showed that this technique could be effective. Again, the primary innovation during this period of time was simply the addition of aversive contingencies, such as food removal for inappropriate behavior occurring in the training situation. This contingency somewhat increased the efficacy of the procedure.

Azrin's group at Anna State Hospital (O'Brien, Bugle, & Azrin, 1972) once again developed a superior procedure by combining a number of behavioral tactics into a coherent package. Later, Azrin (Azrin & Armstrong, 1973; O'Brien & Azrin, 1972) further developed the technology of feeding programs for the adult institutionalized person by using "minimeals" served regularly throughout a nine-hour training period. This increase in the number of training sessions, combined with the procedures of continuous reinforcement, graduated guidance, mastery of each utensil separately, multiple trainers, correction of errors, and positive practice, resulted in the rapid acquisition of feeding skills in previously unmanageable adult retarded persons.

An independent replication by Stimbert, Minor, and McCoy (1977) demonstrated that all the individuals in their study achieved correct eating responses to nearly optimal levels, that incorrect eating responses were reduced to minimal levels, and that inappropriate or disruptive behaviors were virtually eliminated. In addition, follow-up data at intervals of up to one year indicated that the effects of the program were quite durable and justified the effort expended during the training period. Nelson, Cone, and Hanson (1975) compared two techniques for training correct utensil use in retarded children: modeling and physical guidance. This study demonstrated that physical guidance was effective while modeling only was not. While much of the work on mealtime behavior with the retarded has been conducted in one-to-one settings using staff trainers, Mercatoris, Hahn, and Craighead (1975) used higher-functioning retarded residents of an institution to train 30 residents of another living unit in appropriate mealtime behaviors.

Dressing. Normally, children learn to dress with no special training; moderately to profoundly retarded individuals are unlikely to learn even minimal dressing skills unless special training has been provided. Initial behavior-modification programs, such as Bensberg's (1965) early effort, offered hope that low-functioning retarded persons could be taught to dress themselves. The procedures that were developed appeared to be effective for higher-functioning individuals; however, there was little or no evidence of success with low-functioning persons. Minge and Ball (1967) trained six profoundly retarded girls for 30 hours and found some improvement in undressing but virtually no improvement in the development of dressing skills. In 1970, Horner provided dressing training to 83 severely and profoundly retarded persons and found that one-third did not benefit from the training. The other individuals required approximately 70 sessions to reach criterion. Ball, Seric, and Payne (1971) found only slight improvement in the dressing skills of retarded boys after 90 days of training. Watson (1972) estimated that with this procedure, 8–12 months would be required to teach the profoundly retarded to dress themselves.

Several reinforcement procedures for teaching dressing skills have been described in detail along with the overall rationale (Ball *et al.*, 1971; Bensberg, Colwell, & Cassell, 1965; Bensberg & Slominski, 1965; Horner, 1970; Minge & Ball, 1967; Watson, 1972). Virtually all of these procedures have the following common characteristics: food or praise as reinforcers; reinforcement given at the completion of the act of taking off or putting on a specific garment; instructions given to start each trial for a given garment; backward chaining for each garment, whereby the instructor puts on or takes off the garment, allowing the subject to do only the final portion; instruction provided on one article of clothing before proceeding to the next; and finally, fading of the instructions and reinforcers. Brief training sessions of about 15 minutes' duration were used over a period of many weeks or months.

The status of dressing training indicates that another procedure developed by Azrin, Schaeffer, and Wesolowski (1976) is currently the most effective procedure for teaching low-functioning individuals to dress themselves. In contrast to prior programs, this technique includes rather lengthy and intensive training sessions, a forward sequence of steps rather than backward training, graduated and intermittent manual guidance, continuous talking and praising, graduated-sized clothing, and an emphasis on reinforcers natural to the dressing process. In the process of validating their program, Azrin *et al.* (1977) were able to train seven out of seven profoundly retarded adults both to dress and to undress themselves in an average of 12 hours distributed over three or four training days.

Other Self-Care Behaviors. While toileting, feeding, and dressing have been the most common areas of interest in self-care, a number of other areas have been touched on. Token reinforcement has been employed to a significant degree. Girardeau and Spradlin (1964) used this method with severely and moderately retarded women. Tokens were delivered for a variety of self-care, grooming, and social behaviors, including making beds, washing hair, and being on time for activities. For a few children, individualized contingencies were used to develop persistence at a task, cooperative play, and academic skills. This program emphasized individual improvement in behaviors rather than the performance of a predetermined response. Marked gains were reported 4½ months after the inception of the program.

Hunt, Fitzhugh, and Fitzhugh (1968) used token reinforcement to improve the personal appearance of 12 retarded individuals. Initially, continuous reinforcement was given when the subjects met the criterion for personal appearance. Subsequently, reinforcement was given intermittently. The individuals improved under the reinforcement program and showed the highest gains under the intermittent reinforcement condition. When reinforcement was totally withdrawn, their personal appearance deteriorated.

Barry, Apolloni, and Cooke (1977) assessed the effects of a contingency-contracting procedure on the personal hygiene skills of three retarded adults. These skills included such areas as clean hair, combed hair, clean teeth, and the absence of an objectionable body odor. In a reversal design, Barry *et al.* (1977) demonstrated that low levels of baseline responding could be increased significantly by providing rewards through a contingency-contracting procedure.

Horner and Keilitz (1975) developed a comprehensive toothbrushing program that included task analysis and training procedures specific to each component of the task analysis. Eight mentally retarded adolescents in two groups received individual acquisition training that included scheduled opportunities for independent performances, verbal instruction, modeling, demonstration, and physical assistance. Four of the subjects received tokens plus social reinforcement, while the other four received social reinforcement alone. All eight subjects showed improved toothbrushing when compared with baseline. Six of the eight subjects correctly performed all toothbrushing steps in two of three consecutive sessions. While other researchers (e.g., Abramson & Wunderlich, 1972; Lattal, 1969) have reported on toothbrushing programs, the results of Horner and Keilitz (1975) appear to be the most effective to date.

Language and Communication. The dysfunctions of the retarded within the communication domain include a large variety of behaviors, such as basic language skills, receptive and productive language, conversational skills, and various speech and articulation problems. The initial problem encountered in communication skills is usually a rate problem. The individual must first be made to emit various verbal operants at a satisfactory rate. Later, the primary issue becomes one of stimulus control, that is, training the client to emit the proper response to an appropriate stimulus.

Increasing Verbalization Rates. In the case of very severe communication disorders, the first step in working with the client is to begin by teaching simple vocal imitation skills. This typically has been accomplished by prompting behaviors in response to a modeled behavior and then reinforcing the imitative response (e.g., Garcia, Baer, & Firestone, 1971; Sloane, Johnston, & Harris, 1968). Before using vocal responses as imitative stimuli, it has generally been necessary to begin with simple motor-response imitation (e.g., Baer, Peterson, & Sherman, 1967) to build the basic imitative skills needed for early language training. While in early training only those imitations that are reinforced are imitated, soon the client begins to imitate all modeled behaviors at a high rate—a phenomenon referred to as *generalized imitation.*

Establishing Stimulus Control of Verbalizations. Once the client is able to imitate vocal stimuli, the next task is to bring these verbalizations under the stimulus control of appropriate stimuli, such as objects and pictures. The usual procedure for training basic labeling skills has been to show the client a picture or an object and to ask, "What is this?" Through a combination of prompting and reinforcement procedures, the client learns to label objects correctly (e.g., Risley & Wolf, 1967), and the prompts and reinforcement are gradually faded.

After labeling has been established, the client is taught generative speech, whereby she or he can emit a large number of possible phrases and sentences without specific training for each one. This training is the logical extension of generalized imitation training. Generative speech is produced by training the individual to respond to a selected number of individual elements of a given response class in order to establish a larger use of that class. As an example, Lutzker and Sherman (1974) established the appropriate use of sentences involving plural and singular subject–verb agreement by providing training in selected subject–verb combinations. As an increasing number of these sentences were taught, the individuals also began to use correct subject–verb combinations that had never been taught. Various syntactic aspects of communication, such as the use of plurals, have been taught in this manner.

Training in the receptive portion of communication skills has typically included establishing generalized instruction-following responses, including pointing to pictures and following action instructions. For example, Striefel, Wetherby, and Karlan (1976) trained retarded children to respond correctly to various verb–noun instructions that were recombined into new combinations. As the training increased, the children increasingly became able to respond correctly to novel noun–verb combinations on the first trial. Baer and Guess (1971) were also able to train the correct receptive use of the comparative and the superlative forms of various adjectives, such as *big, bigger, biggest,* through similar procedures. In each of the above cases of language training, the primary task was to train the retarded person to respond to a given stimulus with the "correct" response—a problem in establishing appropriate stimulus control.

Numerous investigators have trained instruction-following skills in retarded children and adults (Kazdin & Erickson, 1975; Striefel & Wetherby, 1973; Zimmerman, Zimmerman, & Russell, 1969) through procedures similar to those for teaching imitation. A command or an instruction is given, and the response is prompted, usually through physical guidance. Once emitted, the response is then reinforced. Over time, the individual becomes able to respond to a large number of commands without specific training on each one. In fact, both generalized imitation and instruction following appear to be in the same response class. The only difference is that the first is an exact reproduction of behavior, while the second is a generation of the behavior based on a topographically dissimilar command.

While the majority of studies in the communication area have been concerned with narrowly defined parts of the communication process, Keilitz, Tucker, and Horner (1973) concentrated on teaching three retarded males increased verbalization about current events. Each of the men individually viewed a videotape of a brief televised newscast and then received tokens for correct responses about the content of the materials. This training subsequently increased verbalizations about current events.

Speech. Other commonly encountered communication problems in the retarded individual include various dysfunctions in speech rather than in the language components of the process. One common problem has been voice volume. Some retarded individuals speak either too softly or too loudly. Jackson and Wallace (1974), for example, worked with a girl whose speech was barely audible. Through a microphone system in which the volume could be quantified, the girl received reinforcement for speech that exceeded a criterion. Her voice volume increased in the training sessions and eventually generalized to the classroom setting. Other topographical aspects of speech that have been worked with include articulation (Griffiths & Craighead, 1972; Murdock, Garcia, & Hardman, 1977); perseveration (Butz & Hasazi, 1973), echolalia (Palyo, Schuler, Cooke, & Apolloni, 1979); and dysfluencies (Kazdin, 1973).

Nonvocal Communication. Since many retarded individuals have structural abnormalities in their speech apparatus that limit normal speaking, a number of investigators have trained them to communicate either through sign language or a more recent technique: the communication board. Some investigators have used manual signs or gestures as aids in teaching a variety of language skills to normally hearing children (Bricker, 1972; Miller & Miller, 1973). A recent study by VanBiervliet (1977) demonstrated that six institutionalized retarded males were able to learn manual sign training to establish words and objects as functionally equivalent. The teaching of sign language to retarded children is still fraught with many difficulties, given the motor skills that are involved.

The use of communication boards has become much more widespread and is more easily taught. Reid and Hurlbut (1977) evaluated a training program for teaching communication skills to nonvocal retarded adults. Each of the four subjects was severely physically disabled and had never demonstrated functional speech. Each person was taught either to use a prosthetic head pointer or to point with the hand in using a communication board for expressive language. This study consisted of a series of three experiments. The first implemented coordination training, consisting of instructions, manual guidance, praise, feedback, and practice. Each person demonstrated a higher frequency of accurate pointing to the designated areas on the board during the coordination training than during baseline. In the second experiment, using identification training, instructions, praise, feedback, and practice, it was demonstrated that the subjects pointed more frequently to specific word–photograph combinations that corresponded to descriptive verbal labels after the introduction of identification training. Social validation was accomplished in the third experiment, which indicated that the communication board skills were functional in providing a method of expressing a choice of leisure activity to people who previously could not understand the subject's communication attempts. The acquired skills were maintained through a seven-week follow-up period.

Social Skills. Adequate social behavior is often cited as a major behavioral deficit of retarded persons, particularly those who are institutionalized. While the research in this area has been somewhat limited, Mayhew, Enyart, and Anderson (1978) indicated that three different basic strategies can be utilized in developing the social behavior of the retarded: (1) overall enrichment of the living environment; (2) direct training of specific cooperative tasks; and (3) direct training of specific response components of social behavior.

Enrichment programs are aimed at improving or at least maintaining the existing social-skill levels. Individuals in such programs generally engage in a higher frequency of informal and formal training situations in comparison with the regular ward routine and enjoy a more favorable staff-to-client ratio (Mitchell & Smeriglio, 1970). Most reports of this type have been anecdotal, although some research indicates that there may be drawbacks to enrichment programs. Harris, Veit, Allen, and Chinsky (1974) provided data suggesting that certain activities often reported as enriching, such as the improving of physical conditions and more favorable staff-to-client ratios, have only a minimal beneficial impact. In addition, a study by Wheeler and Wislocki (1977) demonstrated that peer conversation was differentially affected by the presence or absence of ward attendants. Interestingly, peer conversation decreased rather drastically when aides were present on the ward, certainly an undesirable condition. These authors also demonstrated, however, that the systematic removal of these aides and fading them back into the situation allowed high levels of social behavior to continue.

The second approach to social response development is the direct training of a few specific kinds of behaviors, such as ball rolling or block passing, that involve cooperation among a small number of individuals (Morris & Dolker, 1974; Samaras & Ball, 1975; Whitman, Mercurio, & Caponigri, 1970). While studies have generally shown that the development of these behaviors is not particularly difficult, an issue arises when the responses must be generalized to new settings and/or new individuals. An example of this type of approach is the study by Samaras and Ball (1975), in which seven dyads of retarded children and adults were placed in an environment where the cooperative operation of a task apparatus yielded reinforcement. During this period of time, cooperative behavior among the experimental subjects increased radically.

The third approach to training social responses involves direct training in specific response components, such as hand waving and playing with others (Stokes, Baer, & Jackson, 1974). An early attempt of this type (Hopkins, 1968) used candy and social reinforcement to develop smiling in two retarded boys. For both children, candy reinforcement was shown to control the frequency of smiling. After the initiation of a maintenance and generalization procedure, the children continued to show high rates of appropriate smiling on termination of the program. This approach has become more popular in recent years, especially with higher-functioning retarded persons, witness the development of structured learning therapy (Goldstein, 1973) and social-skills-training packages (Hersen & Bellack, 1976).

Perry and Cerreto (1977) reported on a prescriptive teaching approach that utilized modeling, role playing, and social reinforcement in a group to teach social skills to 10 retarded young adults. At the same time, 10 matched subjects were taught the same social skills in a discussion format, and 10 others received no treatment. The structured approach was considerably more effective in changing the social skills, both in a structured situation test that measured social interaction and in observation during the normal mealtime period. Matson and Stephens (1978) reported on the use of a social-skills-training package to increase the appropriate social behavior of explosive, chronic psychiatric patients, some of whom were mentally retarded. After targeting behaviors within each training session for individual subjects, the training involved instructions, modeling, role playing, and feedback. Using a multiple-baseline design, these authors demonstrated the effectiveness of this approach in strengthening the target behaviors. The trained skills also generalized to the ward setting, and the number of antisocial behaviors, such as arguing and fighting, was markedly reduced, indicating that many problem behaviors demonstrated by the retarded may, in fact, be due to their inability to emit appropriate social behaviors.

Whatever approach is taken, the problem of the generalization and maintenance of social behaviors continues to exist. The study by Mayhew *et al.* (1978) was designed to determine if the deficit in social behavior of retarded persons might be due in part to the failure of their environment to maintain that behavior. In a reversal design, a group of severely and profoundly retarded institutionalized adolescents were alternately ignored or given social reinforcement for appropriate social behaviors. Social behavior decreased during the nonreinforcement conditions and increased during reinforcement conditions. These data suggest that deficits in the social behavior of retarded persons may be due to the failure of their environment to maintain such behavior rather than to a lack of the skills needed.

Community and Vocational Preparation. The community and vocational preparation of the retarded has taken on increasing importance in recent years, largely because of the current emphasis on placing retarded individuals in the community rather than segregating them in specialized residential services (Wolfensberger, 1972). Both of these areas are typically considered developmental tasks during the adult portion of the life span. The American Association on Mental Deficiency (Grossman, 1977) has pointed out that living and working in the community are the primary adaptive behaviors developed during adulthood.

Community Preparation. While the literature on community preparation is somewhat sketchy, there are several studies indicating increased activity in this area. Iwata and his associates (Page, Iwata, & Neef, 1976; Neef, Iwata, & Page, 1978) conducted two studies on increasing the mobility of the retarded person in the community. In the first of these (Page *et al.*, 1976), five retarded males were taught basic pedestrian skills in a classroom setting. The training was conducted on a model built to simulate city traffic conditions. Each of the subjects was taught the specific skills involved in street crossing, including intersection recognition, pedestrian light skills, traffic light skills, and skills for two different stop-sign conditions. Before, during, and after the training, the subjects were tested on generalization probes on a classroom model and under actual city-traffic conditions. The results of the multiple-baseline design across both subjects and behaviors indicated that after receiving classroom training on the skills, each subject exhibited appropriate pedestrian skills under city traffic conditions. In addition, training in some skills appeared to facilitate performance skills not yet trained.

In the second study (Neef *et al.*, 1978), a classroom program was developed to teach bus-riding skills. Five retarded males were taught each component derived from a task analysis (locating, signaling, boarding, riding, and leaving a bus). The skills were taught sequentially by means of role playing, manipulating the actions of a doll on a simulated model, and responding to questions about slide sequences. Before, during, and after training, the subjects were tested on generalization both in the classroom and in the natural environment. The results indicated that up to 12 months after training, the subjects exhibited appropriate bus-riding skills on actual city buses. Interestingly, Neff *et al.* (1978) also trained two additional subjects *in vivo* on city buses. They found that both the classroom and the *in vivo* procedures were equally effective, but that the *in vivo* procedure was considerably more time-consuming and costly.

A second community-preparation area is clothing selection. This has traditionally been ignored, even though the importance of clothing to a handicapped person's lifestyle and acceptance has been emphasized for decades (Newton, 1976). Following this lead, Nutter and Reid (1978) taught clothing selection skills to five institutionalized retarded women. After observing women's apparel in a local community, a training program was developed using a puzzle simulation of a woman with alternative pieces of colored clothing. The color-coordination training was conducted using modeling, instruction, practice, praise, and feedback to teach popular selections of color combinations. The training was accompanied by large increases in the percentages of popular color selections in both the puzzle situation and actual clothing usage during generalization probes. These increases were maintained over seven 14-week follow-up periods. As in the earlier study on public transportation skills, Nutter and Reid (1978) concluded that the simulation approach resulted in considerable efficiency over an approach relying on the use of actual clothing.

Marholin, O'Toole, Touchette, Berger, and Doyle (1979) trained four retarded adult males to ride a bus to a specific destination, purchase an item, and order and pay for a meal. The training was conducted in the community and included graduated prompting, modeling, corrective feedback, social reinforcement, behavioral rehearsal, and occasional brief time-outs administered on a multiple-baseline across subjects. Correct performance increased during training and was transferred to a novel environment.

One additional community preparation area that is important is leisure-time behavior. The importance of appropriate leisure-time skills for the retarded individual should not be underemphasized. Many studies of the reasons for returning to an institutional setting have indicated that the most common reason is the inability to use discretionary leisure time appropriately. Rarely are persons returned because of their inability to work or to care for themselves adequately. Johnson and Bailey (1977) investigated the effect of the availability of materials, prizes for participation, and instruction on the leisure behavior of 14 retarded adults in a halfway house. A leisure program was conducted on weekday evenings, during which the residents could choose to participate in any of six activities offered: puzzles, card games, play, painting, weaving, and rug making. Instruction in weaving and rug making significantly increased the percentage of residents participating in these activities, and following instruction, prizes were not necessary to maintain high levels of participation. In contrast, prizes were more effective than the mere availability of materials in maintaining participation in the other activities. Interestingly, a point not raised by Johnson and Bailey (1977) is the choice of the six activities. A careful look at the six activities shows that weaving and rug making, which did not require prizes for maintenance, are more typical of adult discretionary activities, whereas the remaining items are more typically child-oriented, requiring special incentives to maintain participation.

Additional work in the area of community preparation includes problem solving and planning (Ross & Ross, 1973); making correct change (Lowe & Cuvo, 1976); cooking (Bellamy & Clark, 1977); housekeeping (Bauman & Iwata, 1977); using the telephone (Leff, 1974, 1975); and completing biographical information forms (Clark, Boyd, & Macrae, 1975).

Vocational Preparation. In 1973, Gold published a comprehensive and provocative review of the research in the vocational habilitation of the retarded. It would be difficult to improve on this review because of the brief time since then. Therefore, only some highlights of research on vocational habilitation are presented here.

Much of the vocational preparation of the retarded takes place in either a sheltered-workshop setting or in a specifically designed, task-analyzed program for teaching job skills. Some early studies are briefly reviewed here.

Zimmerman, Stuckey, Garlick, and Miller

(1969) used token reinforcement to increase the productivity of 16 multiply handicapped retarded individuals. After baseline rates were gathered on production, the subjects were trained in the use of tokens and could practice earning tokens without actually receiving them. Feedback was given by explaining how many tokens would have been earned. Eventually, the tokens were given for improvements in production. Practice alone was effective in increasing production over baseline; however, even greater improvements were seen when tokens were provided. The elimination of tokens at the end of the study resulted in a significant decrease in productivity.

Zimmerman, Overpeck, Eisenberg, and Garlick (1969) reported a different procedure, which resulted in long-lasting behavioral change after the contingencies were removed. In this case, an avoidance procedure was used in which the subjects worked at a table with other trainees. An individualized criterion was set for each person, and if his or her production goal was not met on a given day, the trainee had to work the next day isolated from the group. The avoidance procedure consistently improved performance, and when the contingency was finally withdrawn, the gains in production were maintained for up to two weeks and did not return to initial baseline levels. Most other studies in sheltered workshops (e.g., Brown & Pearce, 1970; Evans & Spradlin, 1966; Hunt & Zimmerman, 1969) have typically employed various incentive conditions to increase productivity and have found similar results.

Most of the work in teaching specific jobs to retarded individuals outside the sheltered-workshop setting has consisted of anecdotal case studies. Cuvo, Leaf, and Borakove (1978), however, described empirical research on teaching janitorial skills to the retarded. A task analysis of the janitorial skills required for cleaning a restroom was developed. A total of six subtasks, consisting of 181 component responses, was identified. The subjects were required to progress through a series of four prompt levels, ordered generally from more to less direct assistance, for 20 of the most difficult component steps. Another series of four prompts, ordered from less to more direct assistance, was used to teach the other 161

responses. The subjects progressed to the next, more-intense prompt level contingent on their failure to respond appropriately with less assistance. Six moderately retarded adolescents were trained in their public school. The results showed rapid response acquisition, skill generalization to a second restroom, and maintenance of the newly learned behaviors. Hopefully, future research in this area will employ as systematic and effective procedures as the Cuvo *et al.* (1978) study.

Academic Skills. Research with the mildly retarded has emphasized deceleration targets or, at best, the acquisition of prerequisite or "readiness" skills. This emphasis is apparently based on the presumption that a reduction of competing behaviors (such as out-of-seat behavior and impulsiveness) will automatically pave the way for academic improvement (Kazdin, 1978). Actually, the weight of evidence does not support such a presumption. A focus on prerequisite skills, such as paying attention and being in one's seat, does not result, *ipso facto,* in academic improvement (Ferritor, Buckholdt, Hamblin, & Smith, 1972). On the other hand, reinforcement for specified academic improvement does boost academic performance and prerequisite skills such as attentiveness and work-related conduct (e.g., Ayllon & Robert, 1974; Haubrich & Shores, 1976; Marholin, Steinman, McInnis, & Heads, 1975). With the movement toward specific academic targets, progress has been demonstrated among the mildly retarded in arithmetic, reading, writing, spelling, and vocabulary (Kazdin, 1978) and students who receive positive reinforcement in school generally show improvement in achievement test performance. Incidentally, it also appears that reinforcement provided *during* achievement testing also raises scores (Ayllon & Kelly, 1972; Edlund, 1972).

There are a number of curricula and programs emerging for use with mildly retarded students. Among the more successful appears to be the Ross and Ross (1972, 1974) program, which includes students with measured IQs of 40–80. The program is based on the assumption of a "central mediational process deficit." Regardless of the theoretical bases of learning problems, the program is basically behavioral, emphasizing active child involvement, explicit reinforcement, and observational learning. It appears to be successful in promoting academic progress in mildly retarded students. Thus, it appears that appropriate reinforcement procedures applied directly to academic behaviors can improve both academic learning and performance. The preoccupation with getting rid of competing behaviors before academic progress is attempted seems unwarranted.

Among the moderately and severely retarded, research itself has been retarded. Evidently, the continuing assumption has prevailed that academic progress is simply not possible by reason of constitutional deficit and/or that there are better things to teach the retarded. Kirk's (1972) assertion still seems to set the parameters of research attempts: "In general, trainable children do not learn to read from even first grade books. Some trainable children with special abilities can learn to read. Most who learn to read, however, are probably educable mentally retarded children" (p. 231).

Indeed, over the past several decades, the little research there has been aimed at teaching "the three R's" to moderately and severely retarded students has, for the most part, met with little or no success. Reynolds and Kiland (1953) provided an account of an unsuccessful program in academics, and Warren (1963) reported that a highly structured reading program failed to produce any significant results in children of IQ 50 or below. Tobias (1963) did offer some success in a program designed to teach telling time by five-minute intervals.

Because of past failures and the prevailing notion of "limited potential," most recent curricula for the moderately to severely retarded do not include academics. Of notable exception are several research efforts in reading during the 1970s. Brown, Fenrick, and Klemme (1971) taught basic sight vocabulary through reinforcement and modeling. Successful students then taught other students, although generalization outside the classroom was, alas, a problem. Emphasizing prerequisite word-recognition skills (discrimination, recall, sequencing, and association), Duffy and Sherman (1977) reported success in teaching functional reading to moderately retarded persons. The look–say approach of Sidman (1971; Sidman & Cresson, 1973) also has yielded some success. Nevertheless, the picture is generally dim, and there is no pervasive use of materials or methods for teaching academics to moderately and severely retarded students. It appears that what we do know about learning principles has not become a part of the materials for teaching. The learning materials are, for the most part, haphazard and devoid of a systematic use of learning principles (Coleman, 1970). With the exceptions cited above, the picture has not changed substantially to the present.

Maladaptive Behaviors. Contrary to the opinion of many people, exhibiting retarded behavior does not rule out various forms of maladaptive behavior, such as hitting, biting, scratching, and fears. In fact, there is considerable evidence that the retarded may be more likely to encounter these problems because of their limited ability to cope with various forms of environmental stimulation (Robinson & Robinson, 1976). The fact that these same problems are frequently found among groups of individuals who have not been labeled retarded means that the substantial literature on the behavioral treatment of maladaptive behavior is equally applicable to a retarded population. However, specific modifications of techniques may be necessary to adjust for appropriate developmental levels. Given this state of affairs, we do not attempt here to review fully the available literature that could be used in treating maladaptive behaviors; rather, we highlight some specific studies and trends in this area of application to the retarded.

Self-Injurious and Self-Stimulatory Behaviors. Retarded persons, especially those who have been institutionalized, frequently engage in stereotypical acts and self-stimulatory behaviors that appear to have no functional value (Berkson & Davenport, 1962). While often viewed as unusual, stereotypical behaviors are shared by many populations, ranging from the retarded and the autistic to the so-called normal population. Most frequently, the problem in deviant populations is one not of rate but of form and intensity. Stereotypical behaviors can be relatively innocuous, such as hand waving and rocking, or they can be self-injurious, such as slapping, biting, and head banging.

Eliminating self-injurious and self-stimulatory behaviors has been the focus of a large literature on retardation. Work in this area is covered in detail in several excellent reviews (Baumeister & Forehand, 1973; Forehand & Baumeister, 1976; Frankel & Simmons, 1976). Some highlights are provided here, as well as some updating of these earlier reviews.

The most common approach to self-stimulatory and self-injurious behavior, at least in the early literature, has been punishment. Aversive events such as shock, lemon juice in the mouth, and ammonia vapors have been used frequently and with great effect; a major advantage has been their relatively rapid impact on the targeted behavior. Shock has effectively eliminated behaviors such as rocking, head banging, and face slapping in a number of studies (e.g., Baumeister & Forehand, 1972; Corte, Wolf, & Locke, 1971; Lovaas & Simmons, 1969; Tate & Baroff, 1966; Young & Wincze, 1974).

Baumeister and Baumeister (1978) successfully used contingent inhalation of aromatic ammonia to decrease extremely high rates of severely self-injurious behaviors in two severely retarded institutionalized children. Other aversive stimuli that have been used include hair pulling (Griffin, Locke, & Landers, 1975); slapping (Foxx & Azrin, 1973); a loud noise (Sajwaj & Hedges, 1971); and reprimands (Baumeister & Forehand, 1972). While shock and other severely aversive stimuli can be extremely effective in the suppression of these behaviors, a major problem is that in many settings such procedures are now prohibited, and even if they were not prohibited, many people find them reprehensible. In fact, a survey of psychologists in facilities for the mentally retarded has shown that they would be hesitant to employ aversive stimuli such as shock in the treatment of self-injurious and self-stimulatory behavior, even if such treatment were not prohibited (Wallace, Burger, Neal, van Brero, & Davis, 1976). In fact, it has been the experience of one of the authors (Madle) that electric shock equipment purchased nearly 10 years ago has not yet been used because other effective means of dealing with these behaviors do exist.

Another procedure that has been employed frequently in institutions for this type of behavior has been some form of physical restraint. Typically, in the past, these restraints were used purely as a control measure, and little attention was paid to making physical restraint into an effective behavior-change procedure. Several recent studies have indicated an increased attention to developing restraint as an effective procedure (Barkley & Zupnick, 1976; Bucher, Reykdal, & Albin, 1976; Favell, McGimsey, & Jones, 1978; Schroeder, Peterson, Solomon, & Artley, 1977). For example, Schroeder et al. (1977) investigated the effects of contingent restraint with and without EMG feedback on head-banging behavior. The contingent restraint decreased the head-banging behavior and, when it was combined with EMG feedback, was even more effective: little head banging occurred during periods of deep-muscle relaxation.

Favell et al. (1978) reaffirmed the need to analyze functionally the consequences being employed when they determined that for three profoundly retarded persons, physical restraint, which had been used to prevent self-injury, appeared to be functioning as a positive reinforcer. By rearranging the contingencies and requiring increasing periods without self-injurious behavior to gain access to physical restraint, Favell et al. (1978) were able to decrease self-injurious behavior drastically.

Several investigations using time-out procedures have shown that self-injurious behavior can be decreased through this means (Hamilton, Stephens, & Allen, 1967; Nunes, Murphy, & Ruprecht, 1977; Tate & Baroff, 1966; Wolf, Risley, & Mees, 1964). While time-out procedures have shown relatively rapid suppression of the behaviors, they typically required a detailed analysis of contingencies and may be severely impeded if the individual's environment includes few positive reinforcers. Nunes et al. (1977), however, demonstrated a procedure for using time-out by providing a vibratory stimulus to the subjects and then withdrawing it contingent on self-injurious behavior. This approach was effective in decreasing the behavior. An alternative approach to using stimulation was reported by Evans (1979), who demonstrated that increas-

CHAPTER 12 • RETARDATION

ing the overall level of stimulation in the environment successfully resulted in decreases in self-stimulatory behavior.

Extinction procedures have been moderately successful in decreasing self-injurious behavior (Bucher & Lovaas, 1968; Corte *et al.,* 1971; Lovaas & Simmons, 1969). The major problem with the use of extinction is determining exactly what the reinforcers are that maintain the self-injurious or self-stimulatory behavior. In many cases, this is virtually impossible.

Recently, the most commonly employed punishment procedure has been overcorrection and positive practice. Positive practice consists of requiring the individual to practice forms of acceptable behavior that are incompatible with the stereotyped or self-injurious acts, contingent on the occurrence of these acts. For example, Azrin, Kaplan, and Foxx (1973) reduced rocking and head weaving in severely and profoundly retarded adults using positive practice and reinforcement of incompatible behaviors. The combined practice and reinforcement procedures rapidly reduced self-stimulation to almost zero. Measel and Alfieri (1976) demonstrated similar effects of overcorrection and reinforcement for incompatible behavior on head-slapping and head-banging behaviors in two profoundly retarded boys. Additional research on the effectiveness of overcorrection and positive practice has been reported by DeCatanzaro and Baldwin (1978), Harris and Romanczyk (1976), Ollendick, Matson, and Martin (1978), and Kelly and Drabman (1977). The generalizability of the results obtained from overcorrection is still in question. Kelly and Drabman (1977) reported generalization across settings, while Coleman, Whitman, and Johnson (1979) indicated that there was no evidence of generalized changes in self-stimulatory behavior across teachers and settings when an overcorrection procedure had been used.

Various reinforcement techniques, such as differential reinforcement of other behavior (DRO), of incompatible behavior (DRI), and of low rates (DRL), have been employed for self-stimulatory and self-injurious behavior (Repp & Deitz, 1974; Tarpley & Schroeder, 1979; Repp, Deitz, & Speir, 1974). Differential

reinforcement procedures have generally been found to be effective when consistently applied. Typically, studies have shown that DRI, in which a specific incompatible response is reinforced, produces superior effects to DRL or DRO (e.g., Tarpley & Schroeder, 1979).

Disruptive and Aggressive Behavior. The elimination of disruptive and aggressive behaviors has also been a popular and frequently attended-to area. In essence, the methods used with these types of behaviors in nonretarded populations show similar results with the retarded. In a recent review, Harris and Ersner-Hershfield (1978) dealt with the available research on the behavioral suppression of severely disruptive behavior in both psychotic and retarded individuals, with special attention to the use of punishment. This section highlights some of the techniques and behaviors that have been used for treatment.

As with self-injurious and self-stimulatory behavior, electric shock has been used a number of times to reduce disruptive behavior, particularly during the 1960s. Electric shock has been used to modify such hazardous behaviors as stereotyped screaming (Hamilton & Standahl, 1969); chronic ruminative vomiting (Luckey, Watson, & Musick, 1968); and dangerous climbing (Risley, 1968). Other forms of direct punishment that have been used with disruptive and aggressive behaviors include physical restraint (O'Brien, Bugle, & Azrin, 1972); slapping (Marshall, 1966; Morrison, 1972); shaking (Stark, Meisel, & Wright, 1969); aversive tickling (Greene & Hoats, 1971); and unpleasant-tasting or -smelling liquids (Sajwaj, Libet, & Agras, 1974).

Overcorrection has been extremely effective in reducing a number of aggressive behaviors. These have included hitting, biting, and throwing objects (Foxx & Azrin, 1972; Matson & Stephens, 1977); recurrent vomiting (Duker & Seys, 1977); public disrobing (Foxx, 1976); and noncompliance (Doleys, Wells, Hobbs, Roberts, & Cartelli, 1976).

Generally, overcorrection has been shown to be more effective than several alternative modes of intervention. Overcorrection has been shown to be superior to simple correction (Azrin, & Wesolowski, 1974, 1975); contingent social isolation and physical restraint (Foxx,

1976); DRO (Foxx & Azrin, 1973); and verbal warnings with response-cost procedures (Azrin & Powers, 1975). Only Doleys *et al.* (1976) found overcorrection less effective than another procedure, verbal scolding.

Extinction has been found of relatively little use in the suppression of severely disruptive behaviors in the retarded. Occasionally, it has been effective. For example, Duker (1975) reported that ignoring the self-biting and other disruptive behaviors of a retarded boy led to a decline in biting, but not in head banging. Martin and Foxx (1973) also demonstrated the use of extinction to reduce the aggressive behavior of a retarded woman. Other studies have demonstrated no decrease in behavior when extinction procedures were initiated (Ross, Meichenbaum, & Humphrey, 1971; Sajwaj, Twardosz, & Burke, 1972; Wolf, Birnbrauer, Williams, & Lawler, 1965). The ineffectiveness of extinction in these cases may possibly be attributable to difficulty in identifying the reinforcers maintaining the behavior (this finding is not unlike that of the operant laboratory). Extinction frequently fails to weaken behavior in simple operant tasks in a retarded population (Cairns & Paris, 1971; Madle, 1976).

Generally, the contingent removal of reinforcement (as in time-out and response-cost procedures) has proved moderately effective in dealing with aggressive and disruptive behavior in the retarded. These procedures have been used effectively to reduce inappropriate eating (Barton *et al.,* Baer, 1970; O'Brien & Azrin, 1972); escape from living quarters (Husted, Hall, & Agin, 1971); obscene speech (Lahey, McNees, & McNees, 1973); crying (Stark *et al.,* 1969); and inappropriate attention-seeking (Wiesen & Watson, 1967).

DRO and DRI should be seen as the first choice of techniques for dealing with inappropriate behavior, since it does not rely on aversive procedures that raise ethical issues. DRO increased sitting behavior in a hyperactive boy (Twardosz & Sajwaj, 1972), improved a retarded child's interaction with other youngsters (Wiesen & Watson, 1967), and decreased ward disruption by four retarded people (Mulhern & Baumeister, 1969). Frankel, Moss, Schofield, and Simmons (1976) reported dramatic decreases in aggression and head banging through the differential reinforcement of other behavior, whereas two different time-out procedures had failed previously. Repp and his associates (Deitz, Repp, & Deitz, 1976; Repp & Deitz, 1974) reported the successful use of DRO for both aggressive behavior and inappropriate classroom behaviors.

Occasionally, other techniques have been used to deal with aggressive and disruptive behavior. Jackson, Johnson, Ackron, and Crowley (1975) used food satiation to decrease vomiting in profoundly retarded adults. One of the most recent approaches has been the application of structured learning and assertion training to retarded populations. Fleming (1976) reported the effectiveness of using structured learning to teach assertive behaviors to both passive and aggressive mentally retarded children. The results indicated that the children were able to learn the skills involved in the training, but the results did not transfer to real-life situations. On the other hand, Matson and Stephens (1978) reported on social skills training with four inpatients with mixed schizophrenic and retarded diagnoses. The training consisted of instructions, modeling, role playing, and feedback and was effective in developing assertive behaviors. In addition, the trained skills generalized to the ward, and arguing and fighting were reduced markedly, a reduction maintained over a three-month follow-up period.

Anxiety. Only a few studies have dealt with anxiety or fear in the retarded. Freeman, Roy, and Hemmick (1976) and Mansdorf (1976) reported using operant techniques such as extinction and token rewards in eliminating the behavioral fears of physical examinations and riding in a car, respectively. Reisinger (1972) reported the use of extinction, positive reinforcement, and response-cost to eliminate severe disabling anxiety-based crying in a retarded woman. Silvestri (1977) investigated the effectiveness of implosive therapy with emotionally disturbed retarded individuals. Following the treatment, the implosive therapy group showed significantly more improvement than a pseudotherapy group and a no-treatment control group, although these gains were considerably lessened at a follow-up measurement. Desensitization procedures were used to eliminate phobias in 20 midly retarded subjects (Peck, 1977). The greatest effectiveness was found with a contact desensitization procedure, which did not rely on symbolic imagery in the subjects.

Seizure Disorders. Several studies have been reported in which seizures have been effectively dealt with by means of behavioral procedures. Zlutnick, Mayville, and Moffat (1975) investigated the effects of interruption and differential reinforcement on seizures. Seizures were conceptualized as the last link in a behavioral chain. This strategy attempted to identify and modify behaviors that reliably preceded the seizure climax. The seizure frequency was reduced in four of five subjects, whereas the frequency of preseizure behavior was reduced in only three. Iwata and Lorentzson (1976) were able successfully to reduce long-standing seizurelike behavior in a 41-year-old retarded male using a program of increased daily activities, DRO, and time-out. By the end of the 10th week of treatment, a gradual fading procedure was begun, and the decrease in seizure activity was maintained. Wells, Turner, Bellack, and Hersen (1978) were able to decrease the seizure activity of a retarded female through the use of cue-controlled relaxation by teaching the individual to relax herself when a seizure was imminent.

Behavioral Tactics

Other sections of this handbook cover specific behavioral tactics and the factors that determine their effectiveness; here, we highlight specific observations about the use of these techniques with retarded populations. By far, the majority of work on retardation has been done by individuals adhering to an operant orientation. Operant techniques have been particularly useful in developing the specific skills needed to overcome the severe response deficits present in retardation. In addition, they are particularly useful in eliminating the high frequency of inappropriate or problem behavior seen in a retarded population.

Positive Reinforcement. Since the beginning of behavioral work with the retarded, the manipulation of positive and negative consequences has received the greatest attention of any technique. Following responses with consequences that strengthen behavior has overcome specific response deficits where behaviors are not performed and has also developed responses that are capable of competing with and eliminating undesirable behaviors. Since the early work by Fuller (1949) demonstrating the conditioning of the arm movement of a profoundly retarded adolescent using reinforcement, the introduction of positive consequences to increase varied behaviors has remained a highly popular and frequently used technique.

Food Reinforcement. Food and other consumables have effectively altered a variety of behaviors. The effects of food are often great because it is a primary reinforcer and does not require preparatory conditioning to be effective. In many cases, entire meals or portions of meals, cereal, cookies, ice cream, soft drinks, and other similar items have been used as reinforcement. Sometimes food has been a natural consequence of the task being taught, as in the case of teaching self-feeding. In this case, food in the mouth is the logical reinforcement for the proper use of the spoon. However, in other cases, food has been introduced into a situation that would normally not contain it, for example, when it is used as a reinforcement in a toilet-training program (Azrin & Foxx, 1971).

While food has frequently been a very effective consequence, several limitations have restricted its use. First of all, it is difficult to deliver food immediately after a response, since there is some manipulation involved in using it. In addition, it is difficult to carry quantities of food around so that it may be used as needed. While neither of these factors is very important when food is naturally present, they limit the use of food to reinforce other types of responses. Another reason that food is difficult to use except in a one-to-one training program is that different types of food are reinforcing to different individuals. It would be impossible to carry the relatively large variety needed in daily situations. A fourth factor is that, in other than natural situations, eating can actually interfere with conditioning by interrupting the behavioral response patterns. The last major factor, which has become increasingly important, is that individuals cannot be deprived of food to the extent necessary to make it an effective reinforcer. Such deprivation raises ethical issues that are difficult to deal with. Therefore, much of the use of food as a reinforcer is actually the use of food preference, which creates many of the above-noted problems.

Feedback Reinforcement. The use of feedback as a reinforcer with the retarded can often be effective, especially with the mildly retarded, although uses have been noted at the more severe levels of impairment. Feedback can be particularly important with retarded individuals, since they frequently have difficulty evaluating the appropriateness of their own behaviors (Robinson & Robinson, 1976). The potential of feedback as a reinforcer has been minimally explored with retarded populations. It has primarily been used in vocational settings (Jens & Shores, 1969).

The use of feedback had advantages since it is relatively easy to provide in written or verbal forms and need not interfere to any great extent with ongoing response chains. While feedback has been quite variable in its effectiveness with retarded individuals, this is certainly also true of its effects on nonretarded populations. Feedback procedures can probably be developed that will have more consistent effects on behavior. It is important that feedback be developed as a method of working with retarded individuals, since it is a necessary first step in the development of adequate behavioral self-control procedures (Thoreson & Mahoney, 1974).

Social Approval. Forms of social approval such as verbal praise, attention, and physical contact have been used effectively in working with retarded individuals. As an example, Reisinger (1972) increased smiling behavior in a retarded woman, who exhibited many depressive behaviors, by providing her with both tokens and social approval for smiling. After the intervention was complete, he found that social approval alone effectively maintained the target behavior. Numerous other applications of social reinforcement have been reported in studies using aides, parents, and teachers (Panda & Lynch, 1972).

The use of social approval as a consequence has numerous advantages, including ease of administration and immediacy of delivery to the individual or group. Satiation is also not commonly found when social reinforcement is employed. Perhaps one of the greatest advantages, however, is that social reinforcement is a "naturally occurring" form of reinforcement, so that behaviors developed through this means are more readily generalized. Since social approval is frequently initially not reinforcing to the individual, additional procedures must be undertaken to establish its reinforcement value. In fact, with retarded individuals, some unusual phenomenon may be present. For example, Madle (1976) found that low-functioning retarded individuals who had been institutionalized for significant periods of their life responded well to social reinforcement that was delivered with inappropriate affect. That is, social reinforcement delivered in a "flat" tone of voice actually resulted in greater behavior change than that delivered in an appropriately and positively intoned manner.

Tokens. When a reinforcement system is based on the delivery of tokens, it is referred to as a *token economy.* Such methods have been used extensively in the treatment, habilitation, and educational programming of the retarded (cf. Kazdin, 1977). One of the earliest publicized programs for institutionalized retarded persons provided tokens for a wide range of behaviors, such as making one's bed, dressing for meals, taking showers, cleaning, and attending assignments (Girardeau & Spradlin, 1964; Lent, 1968; Spradlin & Girardeau, 1966). In this program, a rather sophisticated token economy was set up with numerous backup reinforcers, such as food, clothes, cosmetics, and equipment rental. An overall evaluation of this program after several years indicated a rather significant degree of success in programming for a population that had previously been considered essentially unchangeable. After this demonstration, numerous other reports of token economies for the retarded (see Kazdin, 1977, for a more thorough review) were reported.

Several advantages accrue from the use of tokens over other types of reinforcers. One is that tokens are often more effective because they are typically backed up by a large number of potential reinforcers, and at any one time, a retarded individual is highly unlikely to be satiated with all the available backup reinforcers. It should be noted that this advantage applies only when there is indeed a wide array of backup reinforcers.

Tokens can also be used merely as a substitute for a primary reinforcer. In some cases, token reinforcers are used primarily as a convenience and are exchangeable only for consumable reinforcers, often of one type. In this case, the use of tokens has many of the same disadvantages as the use of the original backup reinforcer. In fact, there may be some decrement in the power of the backup reinforcer because of its delayed delivery.

A third advantage is that tokens can be provided without overly disrupting ongoing response sequences and therefore do not interfere with behaviors in progress.

One of the last and most important advantages is that token reinforcers can provide a common medium of exchange; therefore, they can be used for a large number of individuals for whom different backup reinforcers have been identified.

Perhaps the most outstanding disadvantage of the use of tokens is that they are highly artificial reinforcers and require systematic generalization programs for transferring the learned behaviors from the original token-based setting to the natural situation. Kazdin (1977) has also pointed out a number of practical obstacles particular to token programs, such as the stealing or hoarding of tokens, the loss of tokens, and the need to maintain an effective record-keeping system of token earning and exchange.

It would appear that token economies are, at present, somewhat underutilized in the field of retardation. While the early work in the field stimulated a great number of token economies, these programs were generally conducted with mild to moderate retardates. A scanning of the current literature on retardation shows very little use of tokens with the severely and profoundly retarded. Such a phenomenon is difficult to understand, given the apparent power of token economies. One of the most likely reasons is the failure to employ procedures for establishing neutral objects as tokens with this group of low-functioning people. It is possible, however, to establish token use with very low-functioning individuals, as evidenced by the early work on tokens (Baer & Sherman, 1964).

Another possible reason might be the criticism of the early token economies (Subcommittee on Constitutional Rights, 1974), which attacked their nonindividualized approach to a given client group. Unfortunately, these problems have contributed to the current underutilization of this type of program.

Activity Reinforcers. The last major class of positive reinforcers used with the retarded is activity reinforcers. These reinforcers are generally implemented by allowing individuals access to highly preferred activities contingent on the completion of expected target behaviors. This ability of high-frequency, preferred activities to reinforce lower-frequency, non-preferred activities was initially described by Premack (1959) and is referred to as the *Premack principle.*

Preferred behaviors are often useful reinforcers since they are readily available in most settings. For example, engaging in recreational activities, going on field trips, and talking to friends at meals can be made contingent on the desired performances. Even being physically restrained (Favell, McGimsey, & Jones, 1978) has been shown to function as a reinforcer for other behaviors. One of the major limitations of Premack-type reinforcers is that they are frequently not available immediately on the emission of the target behavior and, if available, disrupt the ongoing response chain. Such limitations, however, are relatively easily overcome by using activity reinforcers as backups in a token-based reinforcement system.

Differential Reinforcement Procedures. Positive reinforcement can also be used to reduce the rates of undesirable behavior through procedures known as differential reinforcement of low rates (DRL), differential reinforcement of other behavior (DRO), and differential reinforcement of incompatible behavior (DRI).

In DRL, certain responses must be reduced but not necessarily eliminated, and the contingency is set up so that the reinforcement is received only when a low rate of behavior is exhibited. Deitz and Repp (1973) reported the successful use of DRL with a group of 10 moderately retarded children who engaged in frequent "talk-out" behavior (talking, singing, and humming). The contingency was set so that when the group made five or fewer talk-outs in 15 minutes, each member would receive two pieces of candy of their own choice. Talking-out behavior immediately declined to an average of 3.1 instances per session, from a baseline of 32.7.

In DRO, the procedure consists of reinforcing the omission or absence of a specified target behavior. Baer *et al.* (1967) reported a study in which they taught profoundly retarded children to imitate. First, the children were reinforced with food and praise for engaging in imitative behaviors; such behaviors increased substantially. In order to demonstrate that the reinforcing contingencies were responsible for the change, a DRO schedule was instituted. Reinforcement was then delivered after a period of time in which the imitative behavior was not emitted. Imitative behavior plunged rapidly under DRO. Repp and Deitz (1974) reported the successful combining of DRO with other procedures to reduce aggressive and self-injurious behavior in institutionalized retarded children.

The last method, DRI, consists of identifying a behavior that will compete with an undesirable behavior. Reinforcement is then provided for exhibiting the incompatible behavior, and there is a corresponding decrease in the undesirable one. An example was reported by Allen, Henke, Harris, Baer, and Reynolds (1967), who decreased hyperactivity in a preschooler. Moving from one activity to another at a high rate brought the child low reinforcement, but engaging in one activity for predetermined periods of time was socially reinforced. As a result, the hyperactive behavior was substantially reduced.

Negative Reinforcement. Negative reinforcement (i.e., the removal of an aversive event after a behavior, thus increasing the probability of that response) has been used infrequently in retardation. It has been difficult to justify ethically the use of aversive procedures when positive reinforcement programs can be effective (Repp & Dietz, 1978). Even so, several instances of negative reinforcement have been reported. Whaley and Tough (1970) increased a retarded child's use of toys through a negative reinforcement procedure. A toy truck was placed in front of the child, and a buzzer and a shock were presented. When the boy's hands touched the truck, the buzzer and shock were eliminated. Eventually, both events were avoided if the boy continued to hold the truck, as well as other toys. The increase in this response was considered valuable since it was incompatible with the boy's high frequency of head banging. Negative reinforcement, however, need not utilize aversize events that cause physical discomfort. Greene and Hoats (1969) found that television distortion could be used as an aversive event to control the work behavior of a mildly retarded adult. In order to remove the distortion of the television picture, the individual had to maintain acceptably high rates of work production.

Punishment. Punishment is operationally defined as the presentation or withdrawal of an event after a behavior that decreases that behavior. If the decrease in response strength is accomplished through the presentation of an aversive event, it is typically called *punishment by application* (or *positive punishment*). If, on the other hand, a procedure is used in which a positive event is removed contingent on a response, the procedure goes by the designation of *punishment by removal* (or *negative punishment*).

Punishment by Application. Punishment by application is used less frequently than punishment by removal for several reasons. First, punishment by application has been shown frequently to produce highly undesirable emotional side effects. Second, and even more importantly, current ethical standards (Sajwaj, 1977) in the field of retardation have severely curtailed the use of aversive stimulation. While the use of a strong aversive event such as an electric shock has not been completely ruled out, it is limited to areas where a response is highly dangerous either to the retarded individual or to other people. Lovaas and Simmons (1969), for example, eliminated the self-destructive behavior of both retarded and autistic children by using electric shock contingent on self-destructive behavior. After a few sessions and a small number of shocks, the behavior was completely eliminated. The most common approach taken today is that highly aversive procedures can be employed only after properly applied, less aversive procedures have been demonstrated to be ineffective.

Milder forms of aversive events have been used with somewhat more frequency. These include noxious liquids, reprimands, threats and warnings, and disapproval. While these forms of punishment have been effective at times in removing undesirable behaviors, their effects are by no means as consistent as those of more powerful forms of punishment, such as electric shock.

Punishment by Removal. The two primary techniques of punishment by removal are response-cost and time-out from positive reinforcement. Time-out from reinforcement can be effective even when used with brief time-out periods. Nunes *et al.* (1977) found that the brief withdrawal of a vibratory stimulus was successful in suppressing the self-abusive behavior of profoundly retarded individuals. In this case, vibratory stimulation was used as a reinforcer and was withdrawn whenever the self-abusive behaviors occurred.

One of the major conditions of the effective use of time-out is that the environment from which the individual is removed must be more reinforcing than the time-out environment (Solnick, Rincover, & Peterson, 1977). Unfortunately, the settings for working with severely and profoundly retarded children are frequently extremely impoverished. Without additional enrichment, such circumstances will not lead to the effective use of time-out procedures. In the above example (Nunes *et al.,* 1977), a new reinforcer (vibratory stimulation) had to be added to the environment before an effective time-out contingency could be used. Another consideration in the use of time-out is that the operating reinforcer in the situation must be identified. Lucero, Frieman, Spoering, and Fehrenbacher (1976) compared the effects of food withdrawal, attention withdrawal, and combined food–attention withdrawal on the rate of self-injurious behavior of three profoundly retarded girls during mealtime. Both the withdrawal of food and the withdrawal of food and attention combined led to a marked reduction of self-injurious behavior. The withdrawal of attention alone, however, resulted in an increased rate of two sub-

jects' self-injurious behavior and had little effect on the rate of self-injurious behavior of the third.

In more recent usage, two forms of time-out have been identified. The first of these is exclusionary time-out, in which the individual is actually removed from a reinforcing environment. The second is nonexclusionary time-out in which access to a reinforcer is denied, although the individual is not removed from the situation. Foxx and Shapiro (1978) explored the use of a time-out ribbon; the child wore a colored ribbon and received snacks and praise every few minutes for good behavior and for wearing the ribbon. When the time-out contingency was added, the child's ribbon was removed for any instance of misbehavior. The teacher's attention and participation activities ceased for three minutes or until the misbehavior stopped. Reinforcement continued at other times for appropriate behavior. The results indicated that the ribbon procedure is a viable form of time-out, provided the disruptive behaviors during the time-out can be tolerated within the setting or a backup procedure, such as exclusionary time-out, is available when needed.

The need to develop nonexclusionary procedures has been generated by frequent criticism of the misuse of time-out procedures. In many cases, children or adults who are displaying disruptive behavior are removed from a situation under a time-out contingency and left out of the environment for too long a period. In many cases, exclusionary time-out can cause staff members to operate a program on a passive-avoidance contingency, where they no longer need to respond to the disruption that the child displays. Under these conditions, time-out generally lasts too long. An alternative is an apparatus described by Neisworth and Madle (1976) which cast the staff's avoidance response into an active-avoidance paradigm: the period for which the child was to remain in time-out was predetermined and set on a timer; at the end of the interval, the door to the time-out room automatically opened and allowed the child to rejoin the others. If additional time-out was required, the staff actively had to avoid the reentry of the child by resetting the timer.

In response-cost, a positive reinforcer is taken away, or there is a penalty involving some work or effort after an undesired response. Typically, response-cost involves the loss of a privilege or a token. Response-cost has been applied in different forms with the retarded. As usually applied, response-cost is implemented by withdrawing tokens for performance. Kazdin (1971) reduced the bizarre statements of a 20-year-old adult in a sheltered-workshop setting by following frequent outbursts of irrational statements with the loss of reinforcers. A dramatic reduction in irrational verbalizations was maintained through a four-week follow-up period.

Overcorrection. A relatively new punishment procedure, called *overcorrection*, was developed by Foxx and Azrin (1972). It is particularly useful in situations in which extinction, positive reinforcement, response-cost, and time-out have little chance of succeeding. Overcorrection is a specific type of mild punishment designed to minimize the negative reactions caused by intense punishment. Essentially, there are two components in an overcorrection procedure. The first is to overcorrect the environmental effects of an inappropriate act, and the second is to require of the individual an intensive practice of overly correct forms of relevant behavior (Foxx & Azrin, 1973). The first component is referred to as *restitutional overcorrection*, and the second is called *positive practice.* An example of this procedure was reported by Azrin and Wesolowski (1974), in which they attempted to teach retarded clients not to steal one another's food. In the overcorrection procedure, the individuals were required not only to return the snacks that they stole (restitution) but also to practice the positive action of giving their own snacks to the victims (positive practice). Overcorrection has been particularly effective in toilet training (Azrin & Foxx, 1971) and the elimination of self-injurious and self-stimulatory behaviors (Foxx & Azrin, 1972, 1973).

Extinction. *Extinction* means withholding reinforcement for a response in order to decrease the frequency of that response. Often, this means no longer providing attention for inappropriate responses that have been inadvertently reinforced. Extinction has been found to be effective in reducing a wide variety of behaviors, especially when used in combination with other procedures. These behaviors include throwing glasses, disruptive classroom behavior, aggressive behavior, tantrums, and excessive classroom noise.

If extinction is used with maximum effectiveness, its results can be enduring. Unfortunately, the use of extinction in the natural setting is often difficult. It may be difficult to identify the reinforcers maintaining the behavior, and when the reinforcers have been identified, it may be difficult actually to remove them from the setting. An example of this problem was encountered by Neisworth, Madle, and Goeke (1975) when the contingent attention maintaining a preschooler's crying behavior on the mother's departure was difficult to remove from the setting. Student teachers in the classroom found it very difficult to ignore the crying of the 4-year-old and, in spite of well-intentioned contingencies, provided attention after a period of time. As an alternative, a fading procedure was used in which the mother was gradually faded out of the setting, with successful elimination of the behavior and little crying during the treatment phase. Another problem that has typically plagued attempts to use extinction procedures is the exhibition of the "extinction burst," in which the individual undergoing extinction displays higher rates of behavior immediately after the reinforcer has been removed. Often, this reaction is interpreted as a worsening of behavior, and the extinction contingency is removed too quickly. Extinction procedures often do require perseverance before any major success can be noted.

Other Behavioral Tactics. A number of other behavioral tactics, such as prompting, fading, modeling, behavioral rehearsal, systematic desensitization, implosion, assertion training, and self-control procedures have been used with the retarded.

Prompting and Fading. Prompting and fading have typically been employed in work with the retarded in combination with various reinforcement procedures. They have often, however, been ignored in critical settings where they could be effective. Most of the effective use of prompts has occurred in educational settings, particularly in teaching academic skills. One major application has been the use of prompting and fading in teaching sight vocabulary to retarded individuals (Dorry, 1976; Gamache & Madle, 1976; Walsh & Lamberts, 1979). Generally, in these situations, a word to be read is paired with a stimulus that already evokes the desired vocal response, such as a picture. While reinforcement is provided for saying the word in response to the picture, the picture is gradually, rather than abruptly, removed. The individual is able to "read" the word without the prompt by the end of the training sequence. There appears to be relatively little use of prompting and fading procedures outside the teaching of academic skills. In the earlier study by Neisworth *et al.* (1975) already mentioned, prompting and fading were systematically applied to eliminate a preschooler's crying. In another application by Petersen, Austin, and Lang (1979), prompts were used to increase the rate of social behavior of three severely and profoundly retarded adolescents.

Modeling. Modeling, which is also known as *observational learning* or *vicarious learning*, means developing behaviors by providing other individuals, or models, who perform the behavior. Modeling, a critical means by which individuals increase their behavioral repertoires, has been somewhat ignored in the area of retardation, especially with the severely and profoundly retarded. The importance of this technique was recognized early when Baer *et al.* (1967) developed a procedure for teaching profoundly retarded individuals to imitate. The successful development of the imitative response resulted in a substantial increase in the rate at which the individual could learn new motor and verbal behaviors. Modeling has been much used in teaching language skills to the retarded (Snyder, Lovitt, & Smith, 1975). In addition, modeling has been used in conjunction with a number of other techniques, such as positive reinforcement, to develop new behaviors, for example, telephone use (Stephan, Stephano, & Talkington, 1973).

Behavioral Rehearsal and Role Playing. Behavioral rehearsal and role playing involve practicing an overt behavior under simulated or real-life conditions. These approaches contrast with modeling, where learning is based primarily on observation rather than on active practice. The two procedures are often combined by having individuals rehearse an appropriate response under simulated conditions after it has been modeled.

An example of role playing was provided by Strain (1975), who increased the social play of severely retarded preschool children by having them act out storybook characters as the teacher read various stories. After story time, the children were observed in free play. Social play for all eight children increased during the free-play period.

Rehearsal and role playing are also used extensively in combination with other operant procedures. Overcorrection and positive practice include the rehearsal of behaviors that are incompatible with the responses to be suppressed. In these procedures, rehearsal is part of a much larger training package that utilizes prompts, reinforcing consequences, modeling, and other tactics. The primary advantage of rehearsal is that appropriate responses can be prompted with a high enough frequency to be reinforced and installed in an individual's repertoire.

Recent work in the area of retardation has been aimed toward the development of various social-skills-training packages for the retarded. Perry and Cerreto (1977) reported on a prescriptive teaching approach that used modeling, role playing, and social reinforcement to teach social skills to a group of 10 mentally retarded young adults. At the same time, 10 matched subjects were taught the same social skills in a discussion format, and another 10 controls received no treatment. The structured role-play training was significantly superior to either of the alternatives in producing appropriate social skills. Matson and Stephens (1978) used social skill training with four inpatients. Behaviors were targeted individually for each subject based on pretreatment observation. Instructions, modeling, role playing, and feedback were effective as shown with a multiple-baseline design. The trained skills generalized to the ward, resulting in markedly reduced arguing and fighting that was maintained during postcheckups three months following training.

Relaxation Training and Systematic Desensitization. While employed widely with a number of other dysfunctions, relaxation techniques have received minimal use with the retarded (Harvey, 1979), in spite of Bijou's (1966) suggestion that the behavior of the retarded is frequently characterized by escape and avoidance patterns triggered by anxiety-related, specific, aversive environmental consequences.

Perhaps one of the earliest applications of densitization to the retarded was by Guralnick (1973). In this study, tension–release relaxation training, in conjunction with desensitization procedures, was used with a severely retarded male. Little data were presented, however, to support the utility of relaxation with this type of individual. Peck (1977) used densensitization procedures with 20 mildly retarded subjects who exhibited a fear of either heights or rats. She randomly assigned the subjects to contact densensitization, vicarious symbolic desensitization, systematic densensitization, placebo attention control, and no treatment. The subjects were provided with up to 15 sessions of treatment. Contact desensitization proved the most effective approach. Peck reported that the subjects in the systematic and vicarious densensitization groups were able to respond to relaxation instructions and generally to learn realxation without undue difficulty; they were also able to report on their feeling state and to discriminate between feelings of anxiety and relaxation.

Harvey, Karan, Bhargava, and Morehouse (1978) reported the use of relaxation training with a moderately retarded female exhibiting violent temper tantrums. The relaxation was used to reduce her overall anxiety level and to permit an ongoing, appropriate coping response for dealing with social and vocational stress. In addition, a cue-conditioning procedure was added after deep relaxation was achieved. The subject was finally able to eliminate the tantrums both at work and at home.

Wells *et al.* (1978) employed cue-controlled relaxation for psychomotor seizures in a 22-year-old borderline retarded female. The study suggested that cue-controlled relaxation contributed significantly to minimizing her psychomotor seizures. In addition, the treatment effects were maintained across a three-month follow-up period although little contact with the therapist occurred during this period.

Implosive Therapy. In the only available study of implosive therapy with the retarded, Silvestri (1977) randomly assigned 24 retarded subjects to one treatment and two control groups. The treatment group received 10 sessions of implosive therapy, while the control groups received either no treatment or 10 sessions of pseudotreatment discussions. While the subjects in the implosive therapy group showed significantly more improvement across all indexes than those in either of the other two groups, the superiority was considerably less at a follow-up.

Self-Control Techniques. Like relaxation training, self-control procedures have been subject to increasing experimentation with other dysfunctions yet have been virtually ignored in the field of retardation. Kurtz and Neisworth (1976) reported on a number of possible adaptations of self-control procedures for use with the retarded, and Mahoney and Mahoney (1976) indicated that such procedures were, in fact, effective if appropriately structured. While self-control procedures have been attempted with the retarded (e.g., Long & Williams, 1976), they have typically employed higher-functioning subjects who deviated little from normal levels.

Overall, it would appear that a great deal of work has been accomplished in the field of retardation by applying tactics consisting of positive and negative reinforcement and punishment. Other forms of behavioral treatment (e.g., relaxation training, self-control, and behavioral rehearsal) have received far less attention and need considerable expansion to determine their potential effectiveness with retarded persons.

Strategies for Applying Behavioral Tactics

In addition to the behavioral tactics discussed above, one must consider overall strategies in delivering behaviorally based services. Essentially, three models have been used in delivering behavioral services to the retarded: professionally administered individualized programs, group-based programs, and programs mediated by paraprofessionals and parents.

Professionally administered individual programs have been used widely in areas such as the teaching of imitative skills and have been successful in demonstrating the power of behavioral tactics; however, such a delivery model restricts the number of clients who can be helped. Professional time spent on a one-to-one basis limits both the scope and the efficiency of the behavioral intervention.

Essentially, two strategies can be employed to extend the delivery of behavioral programs. The first is the use of group-based programs. The most common of these group-based programs have been those employing token economies, such as the work of Lent (1968), and the classroom delivery of services in special education. Typically this strategy has been employed with mildly and moderately retarded individuals. The consensus once was that behavioral programs for the severely and profoundly retarded required intensive one-to-one program delivery. Recently, Storm and Willis (1978) and Favell, Favell, and McGimsey (1978) compared group and individualized training methods in teaching severely and profoundly retarded individuals. In both studies, small-group training was determined to be at least as effective as one-to-one training. In addition, other advantages (such as increased activity and socialization levels for the clients) suggested that group instruction may actually be a preferred method for teaching some skills to severely and profoundly retarded individuals.

While the use of small-group programs increases the number of clients that can be worked with by an individual, the other major alternative is to increase the number of individuals who are available to carry out behavioral programming for retarded persons. This strategy has been employed extensively through the use of parents and paraprofessionals for the application of behavioral tactics (Madle, 1975). The available literature strongly suggests that paraprofessionals and parents can effectively modify retarded behaviors, given adequate training and supervision (e.g., Greene, Willis, Levy, & Bailey, 1978). To be effective, however, programs must employ systematic monitoring, feedback, and incentives for the paraprofessional staff (Iwata, Bailey, Brown, Foshee, & Alpern, 1976; Repp & Deitz, 1979; Favell, Favell, Seals, & Risley 1978).

In addition to adequate monitoring and supervision, training must be provided for paraprofessionals and parents so that they can properly carry out the procedures being used. The available evidence indicates that to be effective, such training programs must themselves employ behavioral tactics in developing behavior modification skills. Generally, the programs that have been successful have employed structured training and such techniques as modeling, feedback, prompting, and fading (Gardner, 1973; Nay, 1975; Parsonson, Baer, & Baer, 1974). Overall the literature suggests that in the absence of such behaviorally based training programs, parents and paraprofessionals can acquire the necessary terms for discussing behavior modification tactics but cannot actually apply them (Gardner, 1972; Lindsley, 1966).

The increased emphasis on teaching parents to apply behavioral technology with their children has allowed for the possibility of an effective early intervention and preventive strategy. An excellent example is the recent work in teaching the parents of Down's syndrome infants (Hanson, 1977) to use behavioral tactics in developing skills in their retarded children. Research on such projects has demonstrated that Down's syndrome children, who frequently function at severely and profoundly low levels by school age, may be able to function in the mildly retarded range when their parents have been trained and supervised in the application of behavioral tactics.

Future Perspectives and Directions

Before examining the directions that behavior modification with the retarded may or should take, it is appropriate to examine the trends over the past several years. In Table 1, a comparison is made of the pre-1973 behavioral literature on the retarded and the literature that appeared from 1976 to 1978. Approximately 100 articles that appeared from 1976 to 1978 were coded on the following variables: the ages of the clients, their level of retardation, the tactics used, and the intervention setting. A similar coding was also done on the studies appearing in the mental retardation section of Kazdin and Craighead's (1973) review.

Table 1. Comparison of the Pre-1973 with the 1976–1978 Behavioral Literature on Selected Variables

Category	Value	Pre-1973[a]		1976–1978	
		n	*%*	*n*	*%*
Age	Birth–21	36	87.8	104	79.5
	Over 21	5	12.2	27	20.5
Level of retardation	Mild	9	19.2	44	32.4
	Moderate	14	29.8	34	25.0
	Severe/profound	24	51.0	58	42.6
Setting	Institutional	38	92.7	59	39.3
	Community	3	7.3	91	60.7
Tactics	Reinforcement	21	48.8	96	69.5
	Punishment	6	14.6	18	13.7
	Time-out	10	24.4	13	9.9
	Response-cost	4	9.8	7	5.3
	Overcorrection	0	0.0	11	8.4
	Extinction	2	4.9	4	3.1
	DRO–Alt R	1	2.4	7	5.3
	Prompting	11	26.8	43	32.8
	Fading	4	9.8	15	11.5

[a] Kazdin and Craighead (1973).

Several trends are evident in this comparison. The setting in which the intervention occurred has been gradually shifting from institutions to the home and the community. Somewhat surprisingly, the level of retardation being dealt with in the literature has not shifted from the mild to the severe and the profound as much as current legislation and regulations would suggest. Instead, there has been somewhat of an increase in studies reporting on the mildly retarded. The reason, however, becomes obvious when it is noted that the studies are taking place at an increasing rate in community agencies. That is, the mildly retarded person is being placed in the community and therefore is becoming used increasingly in behavioral research.

While there have been no major shifts in the techniques reported, there does appear to have been some reduction in the use of punishment techniques and a corresponding increase in the use of reinforcement. The one exception is the use of overcorrection, which was very new in 1973. Studies also seem currently to be beginning to increase their attention to antecedent variables, as in prompting. Unfortunately, much of the early behavioral research relied heavily on the consequation of behavior, which is effective in increasing or decreasing existing behaviors but has little effect on teaching the new behaviors that are so needed by the retarded.

In looking at an overall view of the literature, we can detect weaknesses or problems of both a conceptual (or philosophical) and a methodological nature. A critique from the conceptual or philosophical perspective concerns dealing with the scope, the appropriateness, and the social relevance of the literature. These, of course, shift with changing social values, legislation, and litigation.

Of primary concern to us was the seeming preoccupation with behavioral *reduction* or *elimination*. A majority of reported studies focused on the use of techniques for weakening or narrowing problem behaviors. This is not surprising since most agencies and facilities are concerned, first, with maintaining order, discipline, and nondisruption. This preoccupation is perhaps also evident in the general behavior-modification literature addressed to regular classroom use and even self-management. The reasons for such a preoccupation may be administrative convenience (and staff sanity!) as well as the alleged therapeutic position that constructive changes (i.e., behavior building) depends on the elimination of interfering responses. Whatever the reasons, we see a picture of devotion to behavior *management* in a custodial sense; behavior modification, then, becomes a substitute for chains and/or drugs. The immediate aim is to subdue, "civilize," or discipline the subject rather than to install or strengthen adaptive skills. This "zombie" model for the use of behavior modification does not constitute much in the way of progress in a conceptual or philosophical sense. Therapists, educators, and care givers must have more progressive goals for their clients than mere management. The production of persons who *do not* do this or that is certainly not in keeping with the more comprehensive social goals of normalization, mainstreaming, and civil rights.

A second need would appear to be increased attention to the development of generalized social skills in the same manner that programs have been developed to create generalized imitation and language skills. The behavioral literature in other areas of dysfunction has increasingly reported the use of structured social-skills training as a means of increasing the interpersonal and social capabilities of the clients. Much of the work in retardation, however, still concentrates on the development of discrete, individually trained social behaviors. Given that interpersonal and social skills are one of the major lacks in retarded persons that prevents their placement in the community, this would appear to be a priority need for future development.

Another consideration is the need for validated disseminable packages that can be used by parents and paraprofessionals. For behavior modification to realize its potential impact on the field, a series of carefully developed, valid programs that can be consistantly applied by trained paraprofessional-level personnel is also needed (Azrin, 1977). Too much of the reported work in retardation still examines fundamental principles and isolated techniques that must be applied by individual practitioners.

The last apparent need is for the development of practical extensions of Bijou's (1966) behavioral model of retardation to assist practitioners in the systematic selection of appropriate techniques for dealing with specific target behaviors. It seems, at the present, that most applications of behavioral technology to the retarded have been derived from one of three sources: (1) the percolation of behavioral programs from other areas, as in systematic social skills training; (2) fads in behavioral technology, that is, "Here's a new technique that hasn't been tried with the retarded"; and (3) the trial-and-error approach, in which a practitioner tries various tactics until she or he finds one that works.

The need in the area of model development is to move practitioners back to the basics of the functional rather than the topographical analysis of problems. A functional analysis of behavior must consider both antecedent and consequent events, as well as measures of the appropriateness or the inappropriateness of behaviors. An initial concern is to determine if the overall *rate* of behavior shown by the individual is deficient or excessive. That is, certain behaviors, such as expressive language skills, can be absent or deficient. On the other hand, a behavior such as head banging or self-stimulation can be considered excessive, regardless of the situation in which it occurs. In addition to the rate of behavior, the *setting* in which it occurs must be considered. That is, the behavior itself may not be inappropriate, but its timing or place of occurrence may be the problem. For example, when teaching retarded persons to dress themselves, the behavior of dressing oneself may occur at an appropriate rate; however, the behavior may occur only in response to the verbal command "Dress yourself" or "Get dressed," rather than in response to the typical cues that prompt dressing. In this case, there is still a problem that requires behavioral intervention. The types of interventions selected are different, however, from those needed for dealing with rate problems. A second aspect of the prevailing stimulus conditions that may cause a problem is that a behavior may occur in response to the wrong cues. Again, the individual may undress at a typical frequency per day, but if the undressing occurs in public, a problem exists that is related to the antecedent conditions of the behavior.

The topographical classification of behavior may be more familiar to individuals working with the retarded, but it is not appropriate to a behavioral perspective of retardation. Problems such as inarticulate speech, bed wetting, fighting, rocking, tardiness, and failure to carry out duties are typically encountered among persons with retarded behavior. These terms, however, are not tied to a behavioral model, nor do they particularly suggest intervention strategies based on behavioral principles. The labeling of problem behaviors in terms of contingent variables does offer both theoretical and heuristic leverage in classifying and dealing with problems. Many times, the selection of an inappropriate behavioral tactic may occur without attention to the functional analytical considerations. In many cases, the tactic selected may, in fact, effectively modify the behavior. The problem, however, will be seen in the maintenance of the behavior. In order to develop an effective and systematic approach to the selection and application of behavioral tactics, a new practical model must be developed in which specific measures or guidelines can be used to assess the functional "cause" of the behavior and then to provide for the selection of appropriate tactics for dealing with the situation. The development and the validation of such a model may deal with the often-reported difficulty of generalizing the effects of behavioral programs across settings (Kazdin, 1978).

Summary

It seems clear that progress in our understanding of retardation and its treatment and the refinement of behavioral approaches is reciprocal. Trends in each influence the other. The recent shifts to natural settings and the use of paraprofessionals and parents are en-

couraging. The preoccupation with "management" and the paucity of research on the programmatic use of developmental objectives to expand the retarded individual's repertoire are not so encouraging. The most pressing need appears to be for an inclusive behavioral model of retarded development that systematically delineates targets, settings, strategies, tactics, and evaluation procedures. As was mentioned, Bijou's (1966) model may provide the basis for a comprehensive and programmatic guide to behavioral interventions for remediation, therapy, and education in the personal development of our retarded citizens.

ACKNOWLEDGMENTS

The authors would like to acknowledge the assistance of the following students in reviewing the literature: Sue Devenney, Sharon Harrity, Chris Hanneman, Betsy Llewellyn, Audrey Matty, Art Pentz, Sue Reinhard, Patti Skelly, and Dave Snell.

References

Abramson, E. E., & Wunderlich, R. A. Dental hygiene training for retardates: An application of behavioral techniques. *Mental Retardation,* 1972, *10,* 6–8.

Allen, K. E., Henke, L. B., Harris, F. R., Baer, D. M., & Reynolds, N. J. Control of hyperactivity by social reinforcement of attending behavior. *Journal of Educational Psychology,* 1967, *58,* 231–237.

Ayllon, T., & Kelly, K. Effects of reinforcement on standardized test performance. *Journal of Applied Behavior Analysis,* 1972, *5,* 447–484.

Ayllon, T., & Robert, M. D. Eliminating discipline problems by strengthening academic performance. *Journal of Applied Behavior Analysis,* 1974, *7,* 71–76.

Azrin, N. H. A strategy for applied research: Learning based but outcome oriented. *American Psychologist,* 1977, *32,* 140–149.

Azrin, N. H., & Armstrong, P. M. The "mini-meal"—A method of teaching eating skills to the profoundly retarded. *Mental Retardation,* February 1973, *11,* 9–13.

Azrin, N. H., & Foxx, R. M. A rapid method of toilet training the institutionalized retarded. *Journal of Applied Behavior Analysis,* 1971, *4,* 89–99.

Azrin, N. H., & Holz, W. C. Punishment. In W. K. Honig (Ed.), *Operant behavior: Areas of research and application.* New York: Appleton-Century-Crofts, 1966.

Azrin, N. H., & Powers, M. A. Eliminating classroom disturbances of emotionally-disturbed children by positive practice procedures. *Behavior Therapy,* 1975, *6,* 525–534.

Azrin, N. H., & Wesolowski, M. D. Theft reversal: An

overcorrection procedure for eliminating stealing by retarded persons. *Journal of Applied Behavior Analysis,* 1974, *7*, 577–581.

Azrin, N. H., & Wesolowski, M. D. The use of positive practice to eliminate persistant floor sprawling by profoundly retarded persons. *Behavior Therapy,* 1975, *6*, 627–631.

Azrin, N. H., Kaplan, S. J., & Foxx, R. M. Autism reversal: Eliminating stereotyped self-stimulation of retarded individuals. *American Journal of Mental Deficiency,* 1973, *78*, 241–248.

Azrin, N. H., Schaeffer, R. M., & Wesolowski, D. A rapid method of teaching profoundly retarded persons to dress by a reinforcement-guidance method. *Mental Retardation,* 1976, *14*, 29–33.

Baer, D. M., & Guess, D. Receptive training of adjectival inflections in mental retardates. *Journal of Applied Behavior Analysis,* 1971, *4*, 129–139.

Baer, D. M., & Sherman, J. A. Reinforcement control of generalized imitation in young children. *Journal of Experimental Child Psychology,* 1964, *1*, 37–49.

Baer, D. M., Peterson, R. F., & Sherman, J. A. The development of imitation by reinforcing behavioral similarity to a model. *Journal of the Experimental Analysis of Behavior,* 1967, *10*, 405–416.

Ball, T. S., Seric, K., & Payne, L. E. Long-term retention of self-help skill training in the profoundly retarded. *American Journal of Mental Deficiency,* 1971, *76*, 378–382.

Barkley, R. A., & Zupnick, S. Reduction of stereotypic body contortions using physical restraint and DRO. *Journal of Behavior Therapy and Experimental Psychiatry,* 1976, *8*, 167–170.

Barry, K., Apolloni, T., & Cooke, T. P. Improving the personal hygiene of mildly retarded men in a community-based residential training program. *Corrective and Social Psychiatry and Journal of Behavior Technology Methods and Therapy,* 1977, *23*, 65–68.

Barton, E. S., Guess, D., Garcia, E., & Baer, D. M. Improvement of retardates' mealtime behaviors by timeout procedures using multiple baseline techniques. *Journal of Applied Behavior Analysis,* 1970, *3*, 77–84.

Bauman, K. E., & Iwata, B. A. Maintenance of independent housekeeping skills using scheduling plus self-recording procedures. *Behavior Therapy,* 1977, *8*, 554–560.

Baumeister, A., & Klosowski, R. An attempt to group toilet train severely retarded patients. *Mental Retardation,* December 1965, *3*, 24–26.

Baumeister, A. A., & Baumeister, A. A. Suppression of repetitive self-injurious behavior by contingent inhalation of aromatic ammonia. *Journal of Autism and Childhood Schizophrenia,* 1978, *8*, 71–77.

Baumeister, A. A., & Forehand, R. Effects of contingent shock and verbal command on body rocking of retardates. *Journal of Clinical Psychology,* 1972, *28*, 586–590.

Baumeister, A. A., & Forehand, R. Stereotyped acts. In N. R. Ellis (Ed.), *International review of research in mental retardation,* Vol. 6. New York: Academic Press, 1973.

Bellamy, A. T., & Clark, G. Picture recipe cards as an approach to teaching severely and profoundly retarded adults to cook. *Education and Training of the Mentally Retarded,* 1977, *12*, 69–73.

Bensberg, G. J. (Ed.). *Teaching the mentally retarded.* Atlanta: Southern Regional Education Board, 1965.

Bensberg, G. J., & Slominski, A. Helping the retarded learn self-care. In G. J. Bensberg (Ed.), *Teaching the mentally retarded: A handbook for ward personnel.* Atlanta: Southern Regional Education Board, 1965.

Bensberg, G. J., Colwell, C. N., & Cassel, R. H. Teaching the profoundly retarded self-help activities by behavior shaping techniques. *American Journal of Mental Deficiency,* 1965, *69*, 674–679.

Berkson, G., & Davenport, R. K. Stereotyped movements in mental defectives: I. Initial survey. *American Journal of Mental Deficiency,* 1962, *66*, 849–852.

Bijou, S. W. Theory and research in mental (developmental) retardation. *Psychological Record,* 1963, *13*, 95–110.

Bijou, S. W. A functional analysis of retarded development. In N. R. Ellis (Ed.), *International review of research in mental retardation.* New York: Academic Press, 1966.

Birnbrauer, J. S. Mental retardation. In H. Leitenberg (Ed.), *Handbook of behavior modification and behavior therapy.* Englewood Cliffs, N.J.: Prentice-Hall, 1976.

Bricker, D. D. Imitative sign training as a facilitator of word-object association with low-functioning children. *American Journal of Mental Deficiency,* 1972, *76*, 509–516.

Brown, L., & Pearce, F. Increasing the production rates of trainable retarded students in a public school simulated workshop. *Education and Training of the Mentally Retarded,* 1970, *5*, 15–22.

Brown, L., Fenrick, N., & Klemme, H. Trainable pupils learn to teach each other. *Teaching Exceptional Children,* 1971, *4*, 18–24.

Bucher, B., & Lovaas, O. I. Use of aversive stimulation in behavior modification. In M. R. Jones (Ed.), *Miami Symposium on the Prediction of Behavior, 1967: Aversive stimulation.* Coral Gables, Fla.: University of Miami Press, 1968.

Bucher, B., Reykdal, B., & Albin, J. Brief physical restraint to control Pica in retarded children. *Journal of Behavior Therapy and Experimental Psychiatry,* 1976, *7*, 137–140.

Butz, R. A., & Hasazi, J. E. The effects of reinforcement on perseverative speech in a mildly retarded boy. *Journal of Behavior Therapy and Experimental Psychiatry,* 1973, *4*, 167–170.

Cairns, R. B., & Paris, S. G. Informational determinants of social reinforcement effectiveness among retarded children. *American Journal of Mental Deficiency,* 1971, *76*, 362–369.

Campbell, S. B. Mother-child interaction in reflective, impulsive, and hyperactive children. *Developmental Psychology,* 1973, *8*, 341–349.

Clark, H. B., Boyd, S. B., & Macrae, J. W. A classroom program teaching disadvantaged youths to write biographic information. *Journal of Applied Behavior Analysis,* 1975, *8*, 67–75.

Coleman, E. B. Collecting a data base for reading technology. *Journal of Educational Psychology Monograph,* 1970, *61*(4, Pt. 2), 1–23.

Coleman, R. S., Whitman, T. L., & Johnson, M. R. Suppression of self-stimulatory behavior of a profoundly retarded boy across staff and settings: An assessment of situational generalization. *Behavior Therapy*, 1979, *10*, 266–280.

Corte, H. E., Wolf, M. M., & Locke, B. J. A comparison of procedures for eliminating self-injurious behavior of retarded adolescents. *Journal of Applied Behavior Analysis*, 1971, *4*, 201–213.

Cuvo, A. J., Leaf, R. B., & Borakove, L. S. Teaching janitorial skills to the mentally retarded: Acquisition, generalization, and maintenance. *Journal of Applied Behavior Analysis*, 1978, *11*, 345–355.

Dayan, M. Toilet training retarded children in a state residential institution. *Mental Retardation*, 1964, *2*, 116–117.

DeCatanzaro, D. A., & Baldwin, G. Effective treatment of self-injurious behavior through a forced arm exercise. *American Journal of Mental Deficiency*, 1978, *82*, 433–439.

Deitz, S. M., & Repp, A. C. Decreasing classroom misbehavior through the use of DRL schedules of reinforcement. *Journal of Applied Behavior Analysis*, 1973, *6*, 457–463.

Dietz, S. M., Repp, A. C., & Dietz, D. E. Reducing inappropriate classroom behavior of retarded students through three procedures of differential reinforcement. *Journal of Mental Deficiency Research*, 1976, *20*, 155–170.

Dingman, H. F., & Tarjan, G. Mental retardation and the normal distribution curve. *American Journal of Mental Deficiency*, 1960, *64*, 991–994.

Doleys, S. M., Wells, K. C., Hobbs, S. A., Roberts, M. W., & Cartelli, L. M. The effects of social punishment on noncompliance: A comparison with timeout and positive practice. *Journal of Applied Behavior Analysis*, 1976, *9*, 471–482.

Dorry, G. W. Attentional model for the effectiveness of fading in training reading-vocabulary with retarded persons. *American Journal of Mental Deficiency*, 1976, *81*, 271–279.

Duffy, G. G., & Sherman, G. B. *Systematic reading instruction* (2nd ed.). New York: Harper & Row, 1977.

Duker, P. C. Behaviour control of self-biting in a Lesch-Nyhan patient. *Journal of Mental Deficiency Research*, 1975, *19*, 11–19.

Duker, P. C., & Seys, D. M. Elimination of vomiting in a retarded female using restitutional overcorrection. *Behavior Therapy*, 1977, *8*, 255–257.

Edlund, C. V. The effect on the test behavior of children, as reflected in the IQ scores, when reinforced after each correct response. *Journal of Applied Behavior Analysis*, 1972, *5*, 317–319.

Ellis, N. R. Toilet training the severely defective patient: An S-R reinforcement analysis. *American Journal of Mental Deficiency*, 1963, *68*, 98–103.

Evans, G. W., & Spradlin, J. E. Incentives and instructions as controlling variables of productivity. *American Journal of Mental Deficiency*, 1966, *71*, 129–132.

Evans, R. G. The reduction of hyperactive behavior in three profoundly retarded adolescents through increased stimulation. *AAESPH Review*, 1979, *4*, 259–263.

Favell, J. E., Favell, J. E., & McGimsey, J. F. Relative effectiveness and efficiency of group vs. individual training of severely retarded persons. *American Journal of Mental Deficiency*, 1978, *83*, 104–109.

Favell, J. E., Favell, J. E., Seals, E., & Risley, T. R. *The evaluation-feedback system: Getting services to the people.* Unpublished manuscript, 1978.

Favell, J. E., McGimsey, J. F., & Jones, M. L. The use of physical restraint in the treatment of self-injury and as positive reinforcement. *Journal of Applied Behavior Analysis*, 1978, *11*, 225–241.

Ferritor, D. E., Buckholdt, D., Hamblin, R. L., & Smith, L. The non-effects of contingent reinforcement for attending behavior on work accomplished. *Journal of Applied Behavior Analysis*, 1972, *5*, 7–17.

Fleming, E. R. Training passive and aggressive educable mentally retarded children for assertive behaviors using three types of structured learning training. (Doctoral dissertation, Syracuse University.) *Dissertation Abstracts International*, 1976, *37A*, 235.

Forehand, R., & Baumeister, A. A. Deceleration of aberrant behavior among retarded individuals. In M. Hersen, R. M. Eisler, & P. M. Miller (Eds.), *Progress in behavior modification*. New York: Academic Press, 1976.

Foxx, R. M. The use of overcorrection to eliminate the public disrobing (stripping) of retarded women. *Behaviour Research and Therapy*, 1976, *14*, 53–67.

Foxx, R. M., & Azrin, N. H. Restitution: A method of eliminating aggressive-disruptive behavior of mentally retarded and brain damaged patients. *Behaviour Research and Therapy*, 1972, *10*, 15–27.

Foxx, R. M., & Azrin, N. H. The elimination of autistic self-stimulatory behavior by over-correction. *Journal of Applied Behavior Analysis*, 1973, *6*, 1–14.

Foxx, R. M., & Shapiro, S. T. The timeout ribbon: A nonexclusionary timeout procedure. *Journal of Applied Behavior Analysis*, 1978, *11*, 125–136.

Frankel, F., & Simmons, J. Q. Self-injurious behavior in schizophrenic and retarded children. *American Journal of Mental Deficiency*, 1976, *80*, 512–522.

Frankel, F., Moss, D., Schofield, S., & Simmons, J. Q. Case study: Use of differential reinforcement to suppress self-injurious and aggressive behavior. *Psychological Reports*, 1976, *39*, 843–849.

Freeman, B. J., Roy, R. R., & Hemmick, S. Extinction of a phobia of physical examination in a seven-year-old mentally retarded boy: A case study. *Behavior Research and Therapy*, 1976, *14*, 63–64.

Fuller, P. R. Operant conditioning of a vegetative human organism. *American Journal of Psychology*, 1949, *62*, 587–590.

Gamache, R. F., & Madle, R. A. Word discrimination in institutionalized mentally retarded adults utilizing a fading procedure. *Research and the Retarded*, 1976, *3*, 14–23.

Garcia, E., Baer, D. M., & Firestone, I. The development of generalized imitation within topographically determined boundaries. *Journal of Applied Behavior Analysis*, 1971, *4*, 101–112.

Gardner, J. M. Teaching behavior modification to nonprofessionals. *Journal of Applied Behavior Analysis*, 1972, *5*, 517–521.

Gardner, J. M. Training the trainers: A review of research on teaching behavior modification. In C. M. Franks & R. Rubin (Eds.), *Advances in behavior therapy: Proceedings, 1971*. New York: Academic Press, 1973.

Giles, D. K., & Wolf, M. M. Toilet training institutionalized, severe retardates: An application of operant behavior modification techniques. *American Journal of Mental Deficiency*, 1966, *70*, 766–780.

Girardeau, F. L., & Spradlin, J. E. Token rewards in a cottage program. *Mental Retardation*, 1964, *2*, 345–351.

Gold, M. W. Research on the vocational habilitation of the retarded: The present, the future. In N. R. Ellis (Ed.), *International review of research in mental retardation*, Vol. 6. New York: McGraw-Hill, 1973.

Goldstein, A. P. *Structured learning therapy: Toward a psychotherapy for the poor.* New York: Academic Press, 1973.

Gorton, C. E., & Hollis, J. H. Redesigning a cottage unit for better programming and research for the severely retarded. *Mental Retardation*, 1965, *3*, 16–21.

Greene, B. F., Willis, B. S., Levy, R., & Bailey, J. S. Measuring client gains from staff-implemented programs. *Journal of Applied Behavior Analysis*, 1978, *11*, 395–412.

Greene, R. J., & Hoats, D. L. Reinforcing capabilities of television distortion. *Journal of Applied Behavior Analysis*, 1969, *2*, 139–141.

Greene, R. J., & Hoats, D. L. Aversive tickling: A simple conditioning technique. *Behavior Therapy*, 1971, *2*, 389–393.

Griffin, J. C., Locke, B. J., & Landers, W. F. Manipulation of potential punishment parameters in the treatment of self-injury. *Journal of Applied Behavior Analysis*, 1975, *8*, 458.

Griffiths, H., & Craighead, W. E. Generalization in operant articulation therapy. *Journal of Speech and Hearing Disorders*, 1972, *37*, 485–494.

Grossman, W. J. (Ed.). *Manual on terminology and classification in mental retardation.* Washington, D.C.: American Association on Mental Deficiency, 1977.

Guralnick, M. J. Behavior therapy with an acrophobic mentally retarded young adult. *Journal of Behavior Therapy and Experimental Psychiatry*, 1973, *4*, 263–265.

Hamilton, J. W., & Standahl, J. Suppression of stereotyped screaming behavior in a 24 year old profoundly retarded girl. *Journal of Experimental Child Psychology*, 1969, *7*, 114–121.

Hamilton, J. W., Stephens, L. Y., & Allen, P. Controlling aggressive and destructive behavior in severely retarded institutionalized residents. *American Journal of Mental Deficiency*, 1967, *71*, 852–856.

Hanson, M. *Training your Down's syndrome infant: A guide for parents.* Eugene: University of Oregon Press, 1977.

Harris, J. M., Veit, S. W., Allen, A. J., & Chinsky, J. M. Aide-resident ratio and ward population density as mediators of social interaction. *American Journal of Mental Deficiency*, 1974, *79*, 320–326.

Harris, S. L., & Ersner-Hershfield, R. Behavioral suppression of seriously disruptive behavior in psychotic and retarded patients: A review of punishment and its alternatives. *Psychological Bulletin*, 1978, *85*, 1352–1375.

Harris, S. L., & Romanczyk, R. Treating self-injurious behavior of a retarded child by overcorrection. *Behavior Therapy*, 1976, *7*, 235–239.

Harvey, J. R. The potential of relaxation training for the mentally retarded. *Mental Retardation*, 1979, *17*, 71–76.

Harvey, J. R., Karan, O. C., Bhargava, D., & Morehouse, N. *Relaxation training and cognitively oriented behavioral procedures to reduce violent temper outbursts in a moderately retarded woman.* Unpublished manuscript, 1978.

Haubrich, P. A., & Shores, R. Attending behavior and academic performance of emotionally disturbed children. *Exceptional Children*, 1976, *42*, 337–338.

Henriksen, K., & Doughty, R. Decelerating undesirable mealtime behavior in a group of profoundly retarded boys. *American Journal of Mental Deficiency*, 1967, *72*, 40–44.

Hersen, M., & Bellack, A. S. Social skills training for chronic psychiatric patients: Rationale, research findings, and future directions. *Comprehensive Psychiatry*, 1976, *42*, 559–580.

Hopkins, B. L. Effects of candy and social reinforcement, instructions, and reinforcement schedule learning on the modification and maintenance of smiling. *Journal of Applied Behavior Analysis*, 1968, *1*, 121–129.

Horner, R. D. *Detailed progress report: Behavior modification program to develop self-help skills.* Final report. Wheat Ridge, Colo.: State Home and Training School, 1970.

Horner, R. D., & Keilitz, I. Training mentally retarded adolescents to brush their teeth. *Journal of Applied Behavior Analysis*, 1975, *8*, 301–309.

Hundziak, M., Maurer, R. A., & Watson, L. S., Jr. Operant conditioning in toilet training of severely mentally retarded boys. *American Journal of Mental Deficiency*, 1965, *70*, 120–124.

Hunt, J. G., & Zimmerman, J. Stimulating productivity in a simulated sheltered workshop setting. *American Journal of Mental Deficiency*, 1969, *74*, 43–49.

Hunt, J. G., Fitzhugh, L. C., & Fitzhugh, K. B. Teaching "exit-ward" patients appropriate personal appearance by using reinforcement techniques. *American Journal of Mental Deficiency*, 1968, *73*, 41–45.

Husted, J. R., Hall, P., & Agin, B. The effectiveness of time-out in reducing maladaptive behavior of autistic and retarded children. *Journal of Psychology*, 1971, *79*, 189–196.

Iwata, B. A., & Lorentzson, A. M. Operant control of seizure-like behavior in an institutionalized retarded adult. *Behavior Therapy*, 1976, *7*, 247–251.

Iwata, B. A., Bailey, J. S., Brown, K. M., Foshee, T. J., & Alpern, M. A performance-based lottery to improve residential care and training by institutional staff. *Journal of Applied Behavior Analysis*, 1976, *9*, 417–431.

Jackson, D. A., & Wallace, R. F. The modification and generalization of voice loudness in a fifteen-year-old retarded girl. *Journal of Applied Behavior Analysis*, 1974, *7*, 461–471.

Jackson, G. M., Johnson, C. R., Ackron, G. S., & Crowley, R. Food satiation as a procedure to decelerate vomiting. *American Journal of Mental Deficiency*, 1975, *80*, 223–227.

Jens, K. E., & Shores, R. E. Behavioral graphs as reinforcers for work behavior of mentally retarded adolescents. *Education and Training of the Mentally Retarded*, 1969, *4*, 21–28.

Johnson, M. S., & Bailey, J. S. The modification of leisure behavior in a half-way house for retarded women. *Journal of Applied Behavior Analysis*, 1977, *10*, 273–282.

Kazdin, A. E. Toward a client administered token reinforcement program. *Education and Training of the Mentally Retarded*, 1971, *6*, 52–55.

Kazdin, A. E. The effect of response cost and aversive stimulation in suppressing punished and nonpunished speech disfluencies. *Behavior Therapy*, 1973, *4*, 73–82.

Kazdin, A. E. *The token economy: A review and evaluation.* New York: Plenum Press, 1977.

Kazdin, A. E. Behavior modification in retardation. In J. T. Neisworth & R. M. Smith (Eds.), *Retardation: Issues, assessment, and intervention.* New York: McGraw-Hill, 1978.

Kazdin, A. E., & Craighead, W. E. Behavior modification in special education. In L. Mann & D. A. Sabatino (Eds.), *The first review of special education*, Vol. 2. Philadelphia: Buttonwood Farms, 1973.

Kazdin, A. E., & Erickson, L. M. Developing responsiveness to instructions in severely and profoundly retarded residents. *Journal of Behavior Therapy and Experimental Psychiatry*, 1975, *6*, 17–21.

Keilitz, I., Tucker, D. J., & Horner, R. D. Increasing mentally retarded adolescents' verbalizations about current events. *Journal of Applied Behavior Analysis*, 1973, *6*, 621–630.

Kelly, J. A., & Drabman, R. S. Generalizing response suppression of self-injurious behavior through an overcorrection punishment procedure: A case study. *Behavior Therapy*, 1977, *8*, 468–472.

Kimbrell, D. L., Luckey, R. E., Barbuto, P. F. P., & Love, J. G. Operation dry pants: An intensive habit-training program for severely and profoundly retarded. *Mental Retardation*, February 1967, *5*, 32–36.

Kimmel, H. D., & Kimmel, E. An instrumental conditioning method for the treatment of enuresis. *Journal of Behavior Therapy and Experimental Psychiatry*, 1970, *1*, 121–123.

Kirk, S. A. *Educating exceptional children* (2nd ed.). New York: Houghton-Mifflin, 1972.

Kurtz, P. D., & Neisworth, J. T. Self-control possibilities for exceptional children. *Exceptional Child*, 1976, *42*, 212–217.

Lahey, B. B., McNees, M. P., & McNees, M. C. Control of an obscene "verbal tic" through time-out in an elementary classroom. *Journal of Applied Behavior Analysis*, 1973, *6*, 101–104.

Lattal, K. A. Contingency management of toothbrushing in a summer camp for children. *Journal of Applied Behavior Analysis*, 1969, *2*, 195–198.

Leff, R. B. Teaching the TMR to dial the telephone. *Mental Retardation*, 1974, *12*, 12–13.

Leff, R. B. Teaching use of phone. *Mental Retardation*, 1975, *13*, 9–12.

Lent, J. R. Mimosa Cottage: Experiment in hope. *Psychology Today*, 1968, *2*(1), 50–58.

Lindsley, O. R. Direct measurement and prosthesis of retarded behavior. *Journal of Education*, 1964, *147*, 62–81.

Lindsley, O. R. An experiment with parents handling behavior in the home. *Johnstone Bulletin*, 1966, *9*, 27–36.

Long, J. D., & Williams, R. L. The utility of self-management procedure in modifying the classroom behaviors of mentally retarded adolescents. *Adolescence*, 1976, *11*, 29–38.

Lovaas, O. I., & Simmons, J. Q. Manipulation of self-destruction in three retarded children. *Journal of Applied Behavior Analysis*, 1969, *2*, 143–157.

Lowe, M. L., & Cuvo, A. J. Teaching coin summation to the mentally retarded. *Journal of Applied Behavior Analysis*, 1976, *9*, 483–489.

Lucero, W. J., Frieman, J., Spoering, K., & Fehrenbacher, J. Comparison of three procedures in reducing self-injurious behavior. *American Journal of Mental Deficiency*, 1976, *80*, 548–554.

Luckey, R. E., Watson, C. M., & Musick, J. K. Aversive conditioning as a means of inhibiting vomiting and rumination. *American Journal of Mental Deficiency*, 1968, *73*, 139–142.

Luiselli, J. K. Case report: An attendant-administered contingency management programme for the treatment of a toileting phobia. *Journal of Mental Deficiency Research*, 1977, *21*, 283–288.

Lutzker, J. R., & Sherman, J. Producing generative sentence usage by imitation and reinforcement procedures. *Journal of Applied Behavior Analysis*, 1974, *7*, 447–460.

Madle, R. A. *Issues in research on paraprofessional training in behavior modification.* Paper presented at the Meeting of the Mideastern Region of the American Association on Mental Deficiency, Buckhill Falls, Pennsylvania, November 1975.

Madle, R. A. Intonation and instructions as factors in discrimination learning of institutionalized retarded adults. (Doctoral dissertation, The Pennsylvania State University.) *Dissertation Abstracts International*, 1976, *37A*, 189.

Mahoney, M. J., & Mahoney, K. Self-control techniques with the mentally retarded. *Exceptional Children*, 1976, *42*, 338–339.

Mahoney, K., Van Wagenen, R. K., & Meyerson, L. Toilet training of normal and retarded children. *Journal of Applied Behavior Analysis*, 1971, *4*, 173–182.

Mansdorf, I. J. Eliminating fear in a mentally retarded adult by behavioral hierarchies and operant techniques. *Journal of Behavior Therapy and Experimental Psychiatry*, 1976, *7*, 189–190.

Marholin, D., II, Steinman, W. M., McInnis, E. T., & Heads, T. B. The effect of a teacher's presence on the classroom behavior of conduct-problem children. *Journal of Abnormal Child Psychology*, 1975, *3*, 11–25.

Marholin, D., O'Toole, K., Touchette, P., Berger, P., & Doyle, D. "I'll have a Big Mac, large fries, large coke, and apple pie" . . . or teaching adaptive community skills. *Behavior Therapy*, 1979, *10*, 236–248.

Marshall, G. R. Toilet training of an autistic eight-year-old through conditioning therapy: A case report. *Behaviour Research and Therapy*, 1966, *4*, 242–245.

Martin, G. L., McDonald, S., & Omichinski, M. An operant analysis of response interactions during meals with severely retarded girls. *American Journal of Mental Deficiency*, 1971, *76*, 68–75.

Martin, P. L., & Foxx, R. M. Victim control of the aggression of an institutionalized retardate. *Journal of Behav-*

ior Therapy and Experimental Psychiatry, 1973, *4*, 161–165.

Matson, J., & Stephens, R. Overcorrection of aggressive behavior in a chronic psychiatric patient. *Behavior Modification*, 1977, *1*, 559–564.

Matson, J. L., & Stephens, R. M. Increasing appropriate behavior of explosive chronic psychiatric patients with a social-skills training package. *Behavior Modification*, 1978, *2*, 61–76.

Mayhew, G. L., Enyart, P., & Anderson, J. Social reinforcement and the naturally occuring social responses of severely and profoundly retarded adults. *American Journal of Mental Deficiency*, 1978, *83*, 164–170.

Measel, C. J., & Alfieri, P. A. Treatment of self-injurious behavior by a combination of reinforcement for incompatible behavior and overcorrection. *American Journal of Mental Deficiency*, 1976, *81*, 147–153.

Mercatoris, M., Hahn, L. G., & Craighead, W. E. Mentally retarded residents as paraprofessionals in modifying mealtime behavior. *Journal of Abnormal Psychology*, 1975, *84*, 299–302.

Miller, A., & Miller, E. E. Cognitive-developmental training with elevated boards and sign language. *Journal of Autism and Childhood Schizophrenia*, 1973, *3*, 65–85.

Minge, M. R., & Ball, T. S. Teaching of self-help skills to profoundly retarded patients. *American Journal of Mental Deficiency*, 1967, *71*, 864–868.

Mitchell, A. C., & Smeriglio, V. Growth in social competence in institutionalized mentally retarded children. *American Journal of Mental Deficiency*, 1970, *74*, 666–673.

Morris, R. J., & Dolker, M. Developing cooperative play in socially withdrawn retarded children. *Mental Retardation*, 1974, *12*, 24–27.

Morrison, D. Issues in the application of reinforcement theory in the treatment of a child's self-injurious behavior. *Psychotherapy: Theory, Research and Practice*, 1972, *9*, 40–45.

Mowrer, O. H., & Mowrer, W. M. Enuresis: A method for its study and treatment. *American Journal of Orthopsychiatry*, 1938, *8*, 436–459.

Mulhern, T., & Baumeister, A. A. An experimental attempt to reduce stereotypy by reinforcement procedures. *American Journal of Mental Deficiency*, 1969, *74*, 69–74.

Murdock, J. Y., Garcia, E. E., & Hardman, M. L. Generalizing articulation training with trainable mentally retarded subjects. *Journal of Applied Behavior Analysis*, 1977, *10*, 717–733.

Nay, W. R. A systematic comparison of instructional techniques for parents. *Behavior Therapy*, 1975, *6*, 14–21.

Neef, N. A., Iwata, B. A., & Page, T. J. Public transportation training: In vivo versus classroom instruction. *Journal of Applied Behavior Analysis*, 1978, *11*, 331–344.

Neisworth, J. T., & Madle, R. A. Time-out with staff accountability: A technical note. *Behavior Therapy*, 1976, *7*, 261–263.

Neisworth, J. T., & Smith, R. M. *Modifying retarded behavior*. Boston: Houghton Mifflin, 1973.

Neisworth, J. T., & Smith, R. M. Analysis and redefinition of "developmental disabilities." *Exceptional Children*, 1974, *40*, 345–347.

Neisworth, J. T., Madle, R. A., & Goeke, K. E. "Errorless" elimination of separation anxiety: A case study. *Journal of Behavior Therapy and Experimental Psychiatry*, 1975, *6*, 79–82.

Neisworth, J. T., Jones, R. T., & Smith, R. M. Body-behavior problems: A conceptualization. *Education and Training of the Mentally Retarded*, October 1978, *13*, 265–271.

Nelson, G. L., Cone, J. D., & Hanson, C. R. Training correct utensil use in retarded children: Modeling vs. physical guidance. *American Journal of Mental Deficiency*, 1975, *80*, 114–122.

Newton, A. Clothing: A positive part of the rehabilitation process. *Journal of Rehabilitation*, 1976, *42*, 18–22.

Nunes, D. L., Murphy, R. J., & Ruprecht, M. L. Reducing self-injurious behavior of severely retarded individuals through withdrawal of reinforcement procedures. *Behavior Modification*, 1977, *1*, 499–516.

Nutter, D., & Reid, D. H. Teaching retarded women a clothing selection skill using communicaty norms. *Journal of Applied Behavior Analysis*, 1978, *11*, 475–487.

O'Brien, F., & Azrin, N. H. Developing proper mealtime behaviors of the institutionalized retarded. *Journal of Applied Behavior Analysis*, 1972, *5*, 389–399.

O'Brien, F., Bugle, C., & Azrin, N. H. Training and maintaining a retarded child's proper eating. *Journal of Applied Behavior Analysis*, 1972, *5*, 67–72.

Ollendick, T. H., Matson, J. L., & Martin, J. E. Effectiveness of hand overcorrection for topographically similar and dissimilar self-stimulatory behavior. *Journal of Experimental Child Psychology*, 1978, *25*, 396–403.

Page, T. J., Iwata, B. A., & Neef, N. A. Teaching pedestrian skills to retarded persons: Generalization from the classroom to the natural environment. *Journal of Applied Behavior Analysis*, 1976, *9*, 433–444.

Palyo, W. J., Schuler, A. L., Cooke, T. P., & Apolloni, T. Modifying echolalic speech in preschool children: Training and generalization, *American Journal of Mental Deficiency*, 1979, *83*, 480–489.

Panda, K. C., & Lynch, W. W. Effects of social reinforcement on retarded children: A review and interpretation for classroom instruction. *Education and Training of the Mentally Retarded*, 1972, *7*, 115–123.

Parsonson, B. S., Baer, A. M., & Baer, D. M. The application of generalized correct social contingencies: An evaluation of a training program. *Journal of Applied Behavior Analysis*, 1974, *7*, 427–437.

Paschalis, A., Kimmel, H. D., & Kimmel, E. Further study of diurnal instrumental conditioning in the treatment of enuresis nocturna. *Journal of Behavior Therapy and Experimental Psychiatry*, 1972, *3*, 253–256.

Peck, C. L. Densensitization for the treatment of fear in the high level adult retardate. *Behavior Research and Therapy*, 1977, *18*, 137–148.

Perry, M. A., & Cerreto, M. C. Structured learning training of social skills for the retarded. *Mental Retardation*, 1977, *15*, 31–34.

Peterson, G. A., Austin, G. J., & Lang, R. P. Use of teacher prompts to increase social behavior: Generalization effects with severely and profoundly retarded adolescents. *American Journal of Mental Deficiency*, 1979, *84*, 82–86.

Premack, D. Toward empirical behavior laws: I. Positive reinforcement. *Psychological Review,* 1959, *66,* 219–233.

Public Law 91.517, 91st Congress, S.2846, October 30, 1970.

Reid, D. H., & Hurlbut, B. Teaching nonvocal communication skills to multihandicapped retarded adults. *Journal of Applied Behavior Analysis,* 1977, *10,* 591–603.

Reisinger, J. J. The treatment of "anxiety depression" via positive reinforcement and response cost. *Journal of Applied Behavior Analysis,* 1972, *5,* 125–130.

Repp, A. C., & Deitz, S. M. Reducing aggressive and self-injurious behavior of institutionalized retarded children through reinforcement of other behaviors. *Journal of Applied Behavior Analysis,* 1974, *7,* 313–325.

Repp, A. C., & Dietz, D. E. Ethical issues in reducing responding of institutionalized mentally retarded persons. *Mental Retardation,* 1978, *16,* 45–46.

Repp, A. C., & Dietz, D. Improving administrative-related staff behaviors at a state institution. *Mental Retardation,* 1979, *17,* 185–188.

Repp, A. C., Deitz, S. M., & Speir, N. C. Reducing stereotypic responding of retarded persons by the differential reinforcement of other behavior. *American Journal of Mental Deficiency,* 1974, *79,* 279–284.

Reynolds, M. C., & Kiland, J. R. *A study of public school children with severe mental retardation.* St. Paul, Minn.: State Department of Education, 1953.

Risley, T. R. The effects and side effects of punishing the autistic behaviors of a deviant child. *Journal of Applied Behavior Analysis,* 1968, *1,* 21–34.

Risley, T. R., & Wolf, M. M. Establishing functional speech in echolalic children. *Behaviour Research and Therapy,* 1967, *5,* 73–88.

Robinson, N. M., & Robinson, H. B. *The mentally retarded child: A psychological approach* (2nd ed.). New York: McGraw-Hill, 1976.

Ross, D. M., & Ross, S. A. The efficacy of listening training for educable mentally retarded children. *American Journal of Mental Deficiency,* 1972, *77,* 137–142.

Ross, D. M., & Ross, S. A. Cognitive training for the EMR child: Situational problem solving and planning. *American Journal of Mental Deficiency,* 1973, *78,* 20–26.

Ross, D. M., and Ross, S. A. *Pacemaker primary curriculum.* Belmont, Calif.: Fearon Publishers, 1974.

Ross, R. R., Meichenbaum, D. H., & Humphrey, C. Treatment of nocturnal head banging by behavior modification techniques: A case report. *Behaviour Research and Therapy,* 1971, *9,* 151–154.

Sajwaj, T. Issues and implications of establishing guidelines for the use of behavioral techniques. *Journal of Applied Behavior Analysis,* 1977, *10,* 531–540.

Sajwaj, T., & Hedges, D. "Side-effects" of a punishment procedure in an oppositional, retarded child. Paper presented at a meeting of the Western Psychological Association, San Francisco, April 1971.

Sajwaj, T., Twardosz, S., & Burke, M. Side effects of extinction procedures in a remedial preschool. *Journal of Applied Behavior Analysis,* 1972, *5,* 163–175.

Sajwaj, T., Libet, J., & Agras, S. Lemon-juice therapy: The control of life-threatening rumination in a six-month-old infant. *Journal of Applied Behavior Analysis,* 1974, *7,* 557–563.

Samaras, M. S., & Ball, T. S. Reinforcement of cooperation between profoundly retarded adults. *American Journal of Mental Deficiency,* 1975, *80,* 63–71.

Sarason, S. B., & Doris, J. *Psychological problems in mental deficiency.* New York: Harper & Row, 1969.

Schroeder, S. R., Peterson, C. R., Solomon, L. J., & Artley, J. J. EMG feedback and the contingent restraint of self-injurious behavior among the severely retarded: Two case illustrations. *Behavior Therapy,* 1977, *8,* 738–741.

Sidman, M. Reading and auditory-visual equivalences. *Journal of Speech and Hearing Research,* 1971, *14,* 5–13.

Sidman, M., & Cresson, O., Jr. Reading and cross modal transfer of stimulus equivalences in severe retardation. *American Journal of Mental Deficiency,* 1973, *77,* 515–523.

Silvestri, R. Implosive therapy treatment of emotionally disturbed retardates. *Journal of Consulting and Clinical Psychology,* 1977, *45,* 14–22.

Skinner, B. F. *Science and human behavior.* New York: Macmillan, 1953.

Sloane, H. N., Jr., Johnston, M. K., & Harris, F. R. Remedial procedures for teaching verbal behavior to speech deficient or defective young children. In H. N. Sloane, Jr., & B. D. MacAulay (Eds.), *Operant procedures in remedial speech and language training.* Boston: Houghton Mifflin, 1968.

Sloop, E. W., & Kennedy, W. A. Institutionalized retarded nocturnal enuretics treated by a conditioning technique. *American Journal of Mental Deficiency,* 1973, *77,* 717–721.

Snyder, L. K., Lovitt, T. C., & Smith, J. O. Language training for the severely retarded: Five years of behavior analysis research. *Exceptional Children,* 1975, *42*(1), 7–15.

Solnick, J. V., Rincover, A., & Peterson, C. R. Some determinants of the reinforcing and punishing effects of time-out. *Journal of Applied Behavior Analysis,* 1977, *10,* 415–424.

Spradlin, J. E., & Girardeau, F. L. The behavior of moderately and severely retarded persons. In N. Ellis (Ed.), *International review of research in mental retardation,* Vol. 1. New York: Academic Press, 1966.

Stark, J., Meisel, J., & Wright, T. S. Modifying maladaptive behavior in a non-verbal child. *British Journal of Disorders of Communication,* 1969, *4,* 67–72.

Stephan, C., Stephano, S., & Talkington, L. W. Use of modeling in survival social training with educable mentally retarded. *Training School Bulletin,* 1973, *70,* 63–68.

Stimbert, V. E., Minor, J. W., & McCoy, J. F. Intensive feeding training with retarded children. *Behavior Modification,* 1977, *1,* 517–530.

Stokes, T. F., Baer, D. M., & Jackson, R. L. Programming the generalization of a greeting response in four retarded children. *Journal of Applied Behavior Analysis,* 1974, *7,* 599–610.

Storm, R. M., & Willis, J. H. Small-group training as an alternative to individual programs for profoundly retarded persons. *American Journal of Mental Deficiency,* 1978, *83,* 283–288.

Strain, P. Increasing social play of severely retarded preschoolers with socio-dramatic activities. *Mental Retardation,* 1975, *13,* 7–9.

Striefel, S., & Wetherby, B. Instruction-following behavior of a retarded child and its controlling stimuli. *Journal of Applied Behavior Analysis,* 1973, *6,* 663–670.

Striefel, S., Wetherby, B., & Karlan, G. R. Establishing generalized verb-noun instruction-following skills in retarded children. *Journal of Experimental Child Psychology,* 1976, *22,* 247–260.

Subcommittee on Constitutional Rights. *Individual rights and the federal role in behavior modification.* Washington, D.C.: U.S. Government Printing Office, 1974.

Tarpley, H. D., & Schroeder, S. R. Comparison of DRO and DRI on rate of suppression of self-injurious behavior. *American Journal of Mental Deficiency,* 1979, *84,* 188–194.

Tate, B. G., & Baroff, G. S. Aversive control of self-injurious behavior in a psychotic boy. *Behaviour Research and Therapy,* 1966, *4,* 281–287.

Thoreson, C. E., & Mahoney, M. J. *Behavioral self-control.* New York: Holt, Rinehart & Winston, 1974.

Tobias, J. *Training for independent living: A three year report of occupation day center for mentally retarded adults.* New York: Association for Retarded Children, 1963, (Mimeographed.)

Twardosz, S., & Sajwaj, T. Multiple effects of a procedure to increase sitting in a hyperactive, retarded boy. *Journal of Applied Behavior Analysis,* 1972, *5,* 73–78.

VanBiervliet, A. Establishing words and objects as functionally equivalent through manual sign training. *American Journal of Mental Deficiency,* 1977, *82,* 178–186.

Van Wagenen, R. K., Meyerson, L., Kerr, N. J., & Mahoney, K. Field trials of a new procedure for toilet training. *Journal of Experimental Child Psychology,* 1969, *8,* 147–159.

Wallace, J., Burger, D., Neal, H. C., van Brero, M., & Davis, D. E. Aversive conditioning use in public facilities for the mentally retarded. *Mental Retardation,* 1976, *14,* 17–19.

Walsh, B. F., & Lamberts, F. Errorless discrimination and picture fading as techniques for teaching sight words to TMR students. *American Journal of Mental Deficiency,* 1979, *83,* 473–479.

Warren, S. A. Academic achievement of trainable pupils with five or more years of schooling. *Training School Bulletin,* 1963, *60,* 75–88.

Watson, L. S. Applications of behavior shaping-devices to training severely and profoundly retarded children in an institutional setting. *Mental Retardation,* 1968, *6,* 21–23.

Watson, L. S. *How to use behavior modification with mentally retarded and autistic children: Programs for administrators, teachers, parents, and nurses.* Libertyville, Ill.: Behavior Modification Technology, 1972.

Wells, K. C., Turner, J. M., Bellack, A. S., & Hersen,

M. Effects of cue-controlled relaxation on psychomotor seizures: An experimental analysis. *Behaviour Research and Therapy,* 1978, *16,* 51–53.

Whaley, D. L., & Tough, J. Treatment of a self-injuring mongoloid with shock-induced suppression and avoidance. In R. Ulrich, R. Stachnik, & J. Mabry (Eds.), *Control of human behavior,* Vol. 2. Glenview, Ill.: Scott, Foresman, 1970.

Wheeler, A. J., & Wislocki, E. B. Stimulus factors effecting peer conversation among institutionalized retarded women. *Journal of Applied Behavior Analysis,* 1977, *10,* 283–288.

Whitman, T. L., Mercurio, J. R., & Caponigri, V. Development of social responses in two severely retarded children. *Journal of Applied Behavior Analysis,* 1970, *3,* 133–138.

Wiesen, A. E., & Watson, E. Elimination of attention-seeking behavior in a retarded child. *American Journal of Mental Deficiency,* 1967, *72,* 50–52.

Wolf, M. M., Risley, T. R., & Mees, H. Application of operant conditioning procedures to the behaviour problems of an autistic child. *Behaviour Research and Therapy,* 1964, *1,* 305–312.

Wolf, M. M., Birnbrauer, J. S., Williams, T., & Lawler, J. A note on apparent extinction of the vomiting behavior of a retarded child. In L. Ullmann & L. Krasner (Eds.), *Case studies in behavior modification.* New York: Holt, Rinehart & Winston, 1965.

Wolfensberger, W. *Normalization: The principle of normalization in human services.* Toronto: National Institute on Mental Retardation, 1972.

Young, J. A., & Wincze, J. P. The effects of the reinforcement of compatible and incompatible alternative behaviors on the self-injurious and related behaviors of a profoundly retarded female adult. *Behavior Therapy,* 1974, *5,* 614–623.

Zieler, M. D., & Jervey, S. S. Development of behavior: Self-feeding. *Journal of Consulting and Clinical Psychology,* 1968, *32,* 164–168.

Zimmerman, J., Overpeck, C., Eisenberg, H., & Garlick, B. Operant conditioning in a sheltered workshop. *Rehabilitation Literature,* 1969, *30,* 326–334.

Zimmerman, J., Stuckey, T. E., Garlick, B. J., & Miller, M. Effects of token reinforcement on productivity in multiply handicapped clients in a sheltered workshop. *Rehabilitation Literature,* 1969, *30,* 34–41.

Zimmerman, E. H., Zimmerman, J., & Russell, D. Differential effects of token reinforcement on instruction-following behavior in retarded students instructed as a group. *Journal of Applied Behavior Analysis,* 1969, *2,* 101–118.

Zlutnick, S., Mayville, W. J., & Moffat, S. Modification of seizure disorders: The interruption of behavioral chains. *Journal of Applied Behavior Analysis,* 1975, *8,* 1–12.

CHAPTER 13

Treatment of Childhood Medical Disorders

Daniel M. Doleys and Jan Bruno

Introduction

This chapter contains a discussion of four medical problems found in children: seizures, asthma, obesity, and hyperactivity. Although there is no common etiological thread for these four disorders, they are linked by the following: (1) they are prevalent among children; (2) the first line of therapy is generally through the pediatrician; (3) each problem can affect the child academically, socially, and medically; and (4) one of the first lines of treatment is generally the use of some pharmacological agent.

The intention of this chapter is to provide a selective rather than an exhaustive review of various behavioral approaches that have been attempted with these four disorders. Examples of various procedures from the literature are provided to illustrate the application of a particular technique or approach. The intent is to provide the reader with an overview of the status of behavioral therapies in these various areas, rather than a detailed or in-depth analysis of any one technique or procedure.

Asthma

Introduction

Bronchial asthma is a reversible obstructive lung disorder that occurs in approximately 30 of every 1,000 persons in the United States (Department of Health, Education, and Welfare, 1973). Asthmatic attacks can be characterized by means of five categories of symptoms (Kinsman, Luparello, O'Banion, & Spector, 1973; Kinsman, Spector, Shucard, & Luparello, 1974). In decreasing frequency, these are bronchial constriction, fatigue, panic–fear, irritability, and hyperventilation–hypocapnia. To the patient, an asthma attack represents respiratory distress involving labored breathing, wheezing, tightness of the chest, anxiety, and coughing or gasping (Mathison, 1975). Physiologically, the asthmatic attack is characterized by a constriction of the

Daniel M. Doleys and Jan Bruno • Department of Psychology, University of Alabama Medical School, Birmingham, Alabama 35294. Preparation of this manuscript was supported in part by Project 910, U.S. Maternal and Child Health, H.S.M.S.A., Department of Health, Education and Welfare, as awarded to the Center for Developmental and Learning Disorders, University of Alabama in Birmingham School of Medicine, Birmingham, Alabama.

smooth muscles of the bronchioles, mucosal edema, and hypersecretion of viscus sputum, all resulting in increased airway resistance. The asthma attacks occur intermittently and vary in severity. Freedman and Pelletier (1970) suggested that asthma could be described as mild, persistent, or severe, and explosive. Eggleston (1976) employed a system of four categories, including sporadic attacks, continuous mild asthma, frequent episodes, and chronic or severe asthma. Asthma may be causally related to allergic hypersensitivity, psychological conflict, or some combination of the two (Blanchard & Aheles, 1970).

Behavioral treatments of asthma have generally adopted one of two approaches (Knapp & Wells, 1978). The first focuses on the asthmatic attacks themselves in an attempt to assess the antecedent stimulus conditions that come to be associated with the attacks. The second approach emphasizes an examination of reinforcing stimuli, which through operant conditioning, have come to maintain and/or exacerbate attacks.

Treatment

Relaxation and Systematic Desensitization. Relaxation training and systematic desensitization have been used with great regularity in the treatment of asthmatic patients. Such techniques can be applied to alter abnormal pulmonary functions in a direct or an indirect manner and to alter maladaptive emotional concomitants (Alexander, 1977; Phillip, Wilde, & Day, 1972). Through these procedures, it is suggested that the asthmatic's sensitivity and anxiety levels regarding asthmatic attacks and the stimuli that produced them can be lessened. Many of the studies in this area have used the peak expiratory flow rate (PEFR) as a measure of the maximum rate of airflow from the lungs during forced expiration. It is inversely correlated with the degree of airway constriction or obstruction. FEV_1 is the amount of forced air exhaled in one second. In order to be accurate, both measures require the cooperation of the asthmatic, who must attempt to produce maximum expiratory effect (Schaefer, Millman, & Levine, 1979).

Relaxation procedures have typically relied on the often-used tense–relax approach intro-

duced by Jacobson (1938). This may be accompanied by autogenic training (Schultz & Luthe, 1959). Alexander (1977) provided an excellent description of the application of these two procedures in relaxation with asthmatic children. In one of the earlier studies utilizing relaxation, Alexander, Miklich, and Hershkoff (1972) examined the effects of systematic relaxation on the PEFR of asthmatic children. Twenty-six children were divided equally according to demographic features and asthmatic severity. The subjects were then assigned to one of two groups. One group participated in three sessions of modified Jacobsonian systematic-relaxation training (tensing and relaxing hands, forearms, biceps, upper face, calves, and feet), while the second group was instructed to sit quietly during three sessions of equal duration. PEFR measures were obtained prior to and following each session. The results revealed a significant increase in PEFR over sessions for the relaxation group, while there was a nonsignificant decrease for the control subjects. Alexander (1972) replicated this procedure and confirmed the initial finding.

A variation of this relaxation training procedure was utilized by Sirota and Mahoney (1974), who utilized a portable timer that the subject set for various intervals and then relaxed on cue whenever it sounded. Other modifications included requiring the subject to briefly postpone the use of a bronchodilator by setting a timer for 3–4 min, during which time relaxation would be practiced, followed by the use of the bronchodilator if it was needed. Decreases in the inhalation of medication, the termination of corticosteroid therapy, a reduction of the use of an ephedrine bronchodilator, and the reduction or elimination of all asthmatic medications were noted.

Hock, Rodgers, Reddi, and Kennard (1978) compared relaxation training with assertion training involving role playing, the expression of positive and negative emotions, and the combination of these two procedures with asthmatic male adolescents. The treatment sessions occurred weekly for approximately one hour for seven to nine weeks. Relaxation was of the tense–relax type utilizing guided imagery. Pulmonary functions studies (FEV_1) and weekly attack-frequency measures were taken. The relaxation group and the relaxation and assertiveness training group showed significant decreases in the frequency of attacks and improved pulmonary function. The assertiveness-training-alone group and the untreated controls were unimproved. However, the frequency of attacks returned to pretreatment levels for each of the groups within four weeks after the end of the treatment, although pulmonary functions studies continued to be improved for those who received relaxation training alone or in combination with assertiveness training.

In summary, it would appear that relaxation is a potentially useful technique in reducing the frequency of asthmatic attacks and in promoting significant improvements in respiratory functions as measured by PEFR and FEV_1 (Alexander, 1972; Alexander et al., 1972; Davis, Saunders, Creer, & Chai, 1973; Hock et al., Scherr, Crawford, Sergent, & Scherr, 1975, 1978). The application of relaxation, however, may be limited to the older child and to the child who can concentrate for the length of training time needed and can follow the sequence of directions provided.

Once a relaxation response has been developed in the child, systematic desensitization can be added to the procedure. Under systematic desensitization, the child is exposed, usually imaginally, to a hierarchy of stimuli or situations generally known to be associated with asthmatic attacks. Moore (1965) compared relaxation, relaxation with suggestion, and relaxation with systematic desensitization. Systematic desensitization was found to be most effective in terms of improved PEFR, even though beneficial changes were noted for each of the three groups. Significant reductions in self-reported asthmatic attacks were also noted, but the differences were not statistically significant for the three groups.

Alexander (1977) described the use of in vivo as well as imaginal systematic desensitization. In the case of in vivo desensitization, a child who experienced anxiety any time she or he wheezed was first exposed to relaxation training. After this, the child was instructed to relax for a progressively longer period of time during wheezing, prior to the use of a nebulized bronchodilator.

Systematic desensitization appears to be somewhat more effective than relaxation training (Moore, 1965; Yorkston, McHugh, Brady, Serber, & Sergent, 1974). However, its application with younger children may be limited by the attentional capacities and imaginal abilities of the child. It is clear that more work is needed if we are to better evaluate the effective parameters of systematic desensitization, particularly in the in vivo type.

Biofeedback and Related Procedures. In some instances, relaxation has been facilitated by the use of EMG biofeedback (Davis et al., 1973; Kotses, Glaus, Crawford, Edwards, & Scherr, 1976; Scherr et al., 1975). Davis et al. (1973), for example, compared EMG feedback plus relaxation in one group to relaxation training alone in another; a control group was given reading materials and told to relax for a specific period of time. Frequency of asthmatic attacks and changes in PEFR were used as dependent measures. The outcome revealed that the EMG-biofeedback–assisted relaxation group produced the greatest positive change in the dependent measures. Relaxation training alone, however, was also noted to be effective. Interpretation of these data must be tempered by the fact that no differences were found for the severe steroid-dependent subjects and that the effects were not maintained at a one-week follow-up. In a similar study, Scherr et al. (1975) compared relaxation with EMG feedback to no treatment in a control group. The subjects were 44 children ranging in age from 6 to 15 years. The relaxation–EMG-feedback procedure was superior to no treatment on behavior ratings, changes in PEFR, reduction in number of asthmatic attacks, and reduction in medications.

Utilizing a slightly different approach, Khan and his associates (Khan, 1977; Khan & Olson, 1977; Khan, Staerk, & Bonk, 1974) employed operant shaping and counterconditioning in the treatment of asthmatics. Generally, asthmatic subjects were instructed to increase bronchodilation using a biofeedback apparatus that monitored airflow. A red light and praise were contingent on the subject's demonstrating an experimenter-specified FEV_1. Bronchial constriction was then experimentally induced, and the asthmatic attempted to overcome the constriction with the aid of the biofeedback apparatus. In one study (Khan,

1977), 80 asthmatic children (8–15 years old) were divided into "reacters" and "nonreacters" on the basis of whether they demonstrated significant bronchospasms after inhaling saline, which they were told contained allergens that would probably stimulate an attack. Half of each group then received treatment. Across the first eight, 50-min sessions, the treatment subjects were reinforced for gradually increasing their FEV_1. During the next 10 sessions, bronchial constriction was induced by any one of several procedures (saline vapors, tapes of wheezing children, etc.). The subjects were instructed to relax and to reduce airflow resistance when a bronchospasm was created. Isoproterenol (a bronchodilator) was given after 10 min to those who could not reduce resistance. The results showed a reduction in the frequency and the severity of attacks for the treated and the untreated "nonreacters" and for the treated "reacters." In another study, Kahn and Olson (1977) examined the effects of using inhaled isoproterenol on exercise-induced bronchial constriction (EIB). The subjects inhaled a mixture of .5 ml isoproterenol and 2.5 ml saline. The concentration of isoproterenol was reduced by .1 ml in each subsequent session for seven days. The mixture effectively prevented EIBs, even as the dose was gradually withdrawn and then eliminated. The effects were maintained at a three and six month follow-up.

Danker, Miklich, Pratt, and Creer (1975) replicated the Khan procedure in attempting to shape respiratory functions. In one study, none of the subjects showed evidence of increased PEFR. Three to five subjects in the second group showed significant increases in a comparison of baseline to treatment. However, when intersession data were analyzed, only one subject demonstrated a consistent increase following the beginning of treatment.

Feldman (1976) and Vachon and Rich (1976) employed total respiratory resistance (TRR) as a dependent measure. TRR is the total of several resistances involving the respiratory system, including upper and lower airway resistance and the viscous tissue resistance of the lung and the chest wall. Feldman (1976) selected four severe asthmatics whose conditions were considered primarily functional in nature. In a single-subject experimental design, the subjects were given a series of 30-min sessions in the biofeedback of inhaled isoproterenol. During biofeedback, the subjects were asked to synchronize their breathing rate with a signal heard over a set of earphones. A feedback signal in the form of a tone was provided to them based on the TRR levels. Pulmonary function studies were done before and after each session. Biofeedback was shown to be as effective as isoproterenol in reducing the TRR. Control subjects, who rested for 30 min, and normal subjects showed no significant changes in pulmonary functions.

Except for the study by Danker *et al.* (1975), there appears to be reason to believe that operant conditioning procedures can be effectively utilized to modify respiratory functioning. These procedures are somewhat confined by the necessity of employing instruments that may not be readily available.

Operant Conditioning Procedures. Several different operant-conditioning techniques have been used effectively in the management of maladaptive behavior patterns found in asthmatic children. Some studies have viewed asthmatic attacks as being induced and maintained by "secondary gains" and have focused on modifying the child's behavior and the consequences provided in the environment (Creer, 1970; Creer & Miklich, 1970; Creer, Weinberg, & Moulk, 1974; Gardner, 1968). Creer (1970), for example, modified the behavior of two asthmatic boys by manipulating the available reinforcers in a hospital setting. An A-B-A-B withdrawal design was used. Each subject had an extended history of repeated hospitalizations for asthmatic attacks. The children were attending a residential treatment center for severe asthmatics. During the first six weeks of the study, each subject was exposed to the usual hospital routine. Hospital admissions during the second six weeks resulted in exposure to the "time-out" condition: (1) each boy was placed alone in a room; (2) no visitors were allowed except medical or nursing personnel; (3) no visiting was allowed with other patients; (4) the child was allowed no TV or comic books, only schoolbooks; (5) the child could leave the room only to go to the bathroom with a nurse escort, and (6) all meals were eaten in the room alone. This treatment phase was followed by a 3-week return to baseline conditions and then another eight weeks of "time-out." The records showed a significant decrease in the frequency and duration of hospitalization during the time-out period for each of the subjects.

A similar approach was used by Creer *et al.* (1974) to reduce the frequency and the duration of the hospitalization in a 10-year-old male asthmatic. In this instance, time-out in the form of restriction of reinforcers was used, along with social reinforcement for improved school attendance and performance.

A variety of other procedures have been applied in studies utilizing one or two subjects. Gardner (1968) modified the disruptive and inappropriate behavior of a 6-year-old asthmatic by withdrawing attention contingent on the negative behavior and reinforcing appropriate behaviors, which were outlined to the child through instructions presented in stories. Creer and Miklich (1970) utilized videotape feedback in a self-modeling fashion to modify the inappropriate behaviors (temper tantrums, inappropriate social behavior, acting out) of a 10-year-old asthmatic child. Miklich (1973) reinforced quiet, relaxed sitting and then the calm acceptance of anxiety-provoking statements about asthma in a hyperactive 6-year-old boy to help reduce panic reactions to acute asthmatic attacks. Extinction has been used by Neisworth and Moore (1972) to reduce the frequency of excessive coughing displayed by a 7-year-old asthmatic child. Response cost has been applied (Creer & Yoches, 1971), as a means of increasing attending behaviors. Finally, Renna and Creer (1976) reported on the successful application of token reinforcement in the multiple-baseline design across four subjects (age 7–12 years) in teaching the proper use of inhalation therapy equipment.

Aversive conditioning procedures have been applied to control chronic coughing. Two studies (Alexander, 1977; Alexander, Chai, Creer, Miklich, Reane, & Cardoso, 1973) utilized an avoidance paradigm in which coughing had to be suppressed for gradually increasing periods of time in order for the subjects to avoid the onset of a brief electric shock to the forearm. In both cases, this approach was shown to be effective in suppressing coughing. In the latter study, a one-year follow-up supported the long-term maintenance of treatment effects.

Creer, Chai, and Hoffman (1977) used punishment to suppress coughing in a 14-year-old asthmatic boy. Unlike the avoidance paradigm, the punishment procedure resulted in the presentation of an uncomfortable electric shock (5 mA) to the forearm contigent on each cough. Quite dramatically, coughing was suppressed after only one application of the punishing stimulus. The effects were maintained at a 3-year follow-up, with no other maladaptive respiratory behaviors being demonstrated.

Convulsive Disorders

Introduction

Convulsive disorders occur in about 2% of the general population and are characterized by a variety of types of seizures. The most common types of seizures are grand mal, petit mal, and focal seizures of Jacksonian and psychomotor epilepsy. Seizures tend to be paroxysmal (sudden) events marked by a burst of cortical activity resulting from lesions or biochemical disruptions. Seizures are usually noticed as brief (1–2 min) interruptions in motor, sensory, cognitive, or conscious functions (Mostofsky & Iguchi, 1982). Whether "organic" in nature (i.e., associated with physical pathology) or "psychogenic," seizures can come under the control of environmental stimuli and can be evoked by stress and emotional factors (Schaefer *et al.,* 1979).

Treatment for seizure disorders consists primarily of medication. However, effective forms of treatment need to be developed for use when chemotherapy has not proved beneficial. Although increasing in number, the attempts to control or moderate seizure problems by any form of psychotherapy or behavior modification have been relatively infrequent (Mostofsky & Balaschak, 1977). An attempt is made here to review some of the behavioral treatment strategies that have been used. For convenience, the techniques have been categorized as (1) positive reinforcement, (2) aversive conditioning, (3) relaxation, (4) biofeedback, and (5) extinction (habituation). This system is similar to that used by Mostofsky and Balaschak (1977).

Treatment

Positive Reinforcement. Differential positive reinforcement involves the reinforcement of behavior other than, and preferably incompatible with, the target response, in this case seizures. Gardner (1967) utilized this strategy in the treatment of a 10-year-old girl who displayed "psychogenic" seizures. The child's parents were instructed to ignore their daughter's seizures and other inappropriate behavior. The parents were also instructed to utilize attention as a reinforcer whenever the child manifested appropriate behavior. Parent training was carried in over three weekly one-hour sessions. Ethical and practical considerations prevented the collection of adequate baseline data. However, within two weeks of discharge from the hospital and following the implementation of the treatment program, the frequency of seizure behavior dropped to zero, tantrum behavior increased in frequency to about three per week and then dropped, and the child's somatic complaints decreased and then increased to approximately one-half pretreatment level. Follow-up contact by phone every 2 weeks for 26 weeks revealed no resumption of seizure behavior.

Balaschak (1976) employed a contingency management program implemented by the teacher of an 11-year-old epileptic girl. A chart divided the school day into three periods, during which time the child received one check mark for each seizure-free time period. If the child accumulated a specified number of check marks by the end of the week, she received a reinforcer. The estimated baseline seizure rate was 60% of school days. For the 52 days during which the behavioral program was in effect, seizures were recorded on only 21% of the days. Following a lengthy absence due to illness, the teacher was unwilling to continue the program. During the remainder of the school year (40 days), the child had seizures on 62.5% of the days.

Zlutnick, Mayville, and Moffat (1975) described a case study wherein the seizures of a 17-year-old retarded female were decreased by the use of differential reinforcement for the cessation of preseizure behavior. Seizures were noted to be preceded by the girl's raising her arms. When the subject was observed raising her arms during treatment, her arms were placed at her side or in her lap. The subject was reinforced verbally and with candy if she kept them in that position for 5 sec. The use of an A-B-A-B withdrawal design revealed that there was a rapid decrease in daily seizure activity and that the decrease was a function of the treatment procedure. The effects were maintained through a 9-month follow-up.

Aversive Conditioning. Numerous aversive techniques, including punishment, escape–avoidance, and overcorrection, have been employed to reduce seizure behavior. Punishment reduces the rate of a target behavior as a function of the contingent presentation of an aversive stimulus. Wright (1973, 1976) used faradic stimulation as an aversive event to reduce seizure behavior in a 5-year old retarded boy and in a 14-year-old boy. The 5-year-old retarded child was observed to engage in self-induced seizures (Sherwood, 1962) at the rate of several hundred per day. He induced the seizures by waving his hand back and forth in front of his eyes and blinking while looking at a light. The treatment initially consisted of the application of .6 sec of 3 mA electric shock at approximately 60 V, contingent on hand waving. The shock was applied to the medial portion of the left midthigh. The treatment consisted of five 1-hr sessions over a three day period. Hand waving as a means of inducing seizures was totally eliminated, and a zero rate was maintained at a 7-month follow-up. Some five months after the initial treatment, the child was hospitalized for a second course of treatment as a result of self-inducing seizures by blinking. The same treatment protocol was utilized. The seizures were reduced from a base rate of 407 per hour to 36. At the month follow-up, seizures produced by blinking had increased over the frequency observed at the end of treatment but continued to be significantly less than pretreatment rates.

A similar procedure was used with the 14-year-old boy, who received mild electric shock contingent on his initiation of observable seizure-related behavior (Wright, 1976). The procedure was effective in reducing clinical and subclinical seizures. In both of these studies, punishment was attempted only after medically oriented treatments had been exhausted and with the approval of appropriate medical consultants.

Zlutnick *et al.* (1975) conceptualized seizures as the terminal behavior in a chain of events. Therefore, they reasoned that seizure frequency could be reduced by interrupting preseizure behaviors. Teachers and parents were trained to apply punishment contingent on observing preseizure behavior in four children (4–14 years old). Punishment included shouting "No" loudly and sharply, and grasping the child by the shoulders and shaking him or her vigorously. Three of the four children showed a significant, stable reduction in the frequency of seizures as a result of this procedure. Preseizure behavior, however, was reduced in only three of the four subjects, and two of the three responded to treatment.

Ounstead, Lee, and Hunt (1966) employed an escape–avoidance training paradigm to decrease seizures in an epileptic child. After determining that a 5-sec burst of photic stimulation was aversive to the child, it was programmed to occur contingent on spike-and-wave paroxysms in EEG activity. The aversive stimulus could be avoided if such EEG activity did not occur and was terminated as soon as it ceased. Caution must be used with this paradigm, as increased seizure activity and gastrointestinal disorders due to stress have been noted in epileptic monkeys during nontraining days when exposed to operant avoidance training (cf. Mostofsky & Iguchi, 1982).

Isolation, or time-out (Adams, Klinge, & Keiser, 1973), and overcorrection (Ashkenazi & Wisdom, 1957) have received some attention. Adams *et al.* (1973) used isolation from ward meetings, free periods, and eating with peers to reduce the self-injurious falling behavior of a 14-year-old mentally retarded female with a history of grand mal and petit mal seizures. Ashkenazi and Wisdom (1957) employed overcorrection to eliminate the preseizure head rolling and thus the frequency of seizures during treatment; these effects were not sustained in follow-up.

Relaxation. The role of anxiety in seizure activity has not been clearly delineated except for noting it to be very important. Mostofsky (1978) has proposed four mechanisms by which anxiety may provoke seizure activity: (1) direct physiochemical change; (2) indirect neurophysiological modulation; (3) psychophysiological modulation; and (4) schedule-induced effects.

Anxiety reduction via relaxation training, biofeedback, and systematic desensitization has been reported with adults (cf. Mostofsky & Balaschak, 1977), but little work appears to have been conducted with children. One case study by Ince (1976) did describe the utilization of relaxation training and desensitization in reducing seizures in a 12-year-old epileptic boy. The treatment initially involved the development of several hierarchies of anxiety-arousing situations and focused on the removal of anxiety that the child experienced concerning school. Complete relaxation was achieved within two treatment sessions. Relaxation was followed by 8 weeks of systematic desensitization. Twice during each session, following relaxation, the subject was instructed to slowly say "Relax" to himself 10 times, so as to associate the key word with bodily relaxation. He was also told to say the key word to himself repeatedly whenever he felt the onset of a seizure approaching. During baseline, the child was noted to have up to 10 grand mal and 26 petit mal seizures per week. By the end of the 17th week of treatment, the child experienced a seizure-free week. Both grand mal and petit mal seizures were reduced by the 30th session. These effects were maintained at a 6-month follow-up.

Biofeedback. Biofeedback involves instructing the subject to generate a certain bioelectrical pattern of waveform. Information is then fed back to the subject regarding his or her performance. Research into the use of biofeedback to reduce seizures was largely stimulated by the work of Sterman and his colleagues (Sterman & Friar, 1972; Sterman, 1973; cf. Mostofsky & Iguchi, 1982). These researchers focused their efforts on training animals to sensory motor rhythms (SMR), which consisted of 12–15 Hz activity. They discovered a marked decrease in susceptibility to monomethylhydrazine (MMN)-induced seizures in SMR-trained animals. Attempts to extend the findings to clinical work with humans were successful (Sterman & Friar, 1972; Sterman, McDonald, & Stone, 1974; Sterman, 1973). However, other studies (cf. Mostofsky & Iguchi, 1982; Mostofsky & Balaschak, 1977) produced mixed results and noted increased seizure activity when SMR biofeedback training was stopped.

As with many of the other procedures, relatively little work has been done with children using SMR biofeedback training. One such study, however, is reported by Finley, Smith, & Etherton (1975). The subject was a 13-year-old boy with a history of seizures dating from age 20. The training procedure employed was similar to that utilized by Sterman. The subject was reinforced with money for every 5 sec of uninterrupted SMR activity. The detection of a spike and/or a wave discharge was followed by the appearance of a red light. The subject attempted to turn out the red light and to keep it off as long as possible. The results showed that the boy's SMR activity increased from 10% to 65% as a function of biofeedback training. A concomitant reduction in seizures was noted.

Extinction (Habituation). The term *extinction procedures* in this instance relates to the repeated presentation of a stimulus or a stimulus condition known to evoke a seizure without the seizure's occurring. This usually involves one of two strategies. First, the seizure-provoking stimulus is introduced at subthreshold levels and is then gradually increased. Or second, the presence of the seizure-evoking stimulus is paired or associated with some non-seizure-evoking stimulus and then adjusted in its presence. An example of the second strategy would be the presentation of a non-seizure-evoking auditory stimulus whenever a seizure-evoking photic stimulus appeared. To the extent that the auditory stimulus sustained nonseizure responding, extinction regarding the photic seizure-producing stimulus could then occur. Forster (1969) has been a leader in developing these techniques for treating what have been referred as *reflex epilepsies.*

Attempts to use this procedure with children have been reported (Booker, Forster, & Klove, 1965; Forster, Ptacek, & Peterson, 1965; Forster, Booker, & Ansell, 1966). Auditory, visual, and combined auditory-visual stimuli have been used. Three or four children reported in the above studies showed a significant decrease in seizure frequency. The fourth child refused to wear the apparatus and thus did not complete the treatment. In one case (Forster, *et al.*, 1966), a 7-year-old girl known to have 20 minor seizures per day was exposed to 60 hr of extinction by means of stroboscopic stimulation produced by specially designed hearing-aid eyeglasses. While in treatment, the child averaged approximately one seizure per day, and four seizure-free days occurred in a 3-week period.

Forster *et al.* (1965) suggested that their approach was effective because the auditory clicking device served to elicit a nonseizure response, thus allowing extinction to seizure-producing stimuli. Alternatively, it has been suggested that the non-seizure-producing stimulus may well serve to divert the subject's attention from the seizure-producing stimulus (i.e., inattention). Therefore, any stimulation that leads to a competing response could effectively reduce seizure activity. Studies with adults using this competing-response paradigm seem to support this contention (cf. Mostofsky & Balaschak, 1977). Although most of the studies in this area have relied on exteroceptive stimuli, Forster (cited in Mostofsky & Balaschak, 1977) had indicated that seizures might be more broadly viewed "in a larger context of *communication disorders* in which the cognitive variables constitute a major contribution to both the generation and termination of seizures" (p. 737). This explanation would appear to open the door to the use of such stimuli as self-verbalizations as a means of controlling seizure frequency by diverting the subject's attention from seizure-provoking stimuli.

Childhood Obesity

Introduction

Childhood obesity is rapidly becoming a major health problem in the United States. Estimates of the percentage of children who are overweight varies with the criteria used but have ranged as high as 26% (Weiss, 1977). Perhaps equally surprising is an estimated increase from 12% to 20% in the incidence of obesity over the past 20 years (Mayer, 1973). There are many factors that contribute to or are associated with childhood obesity, including familiality (genetics), metabolic and endocrine factors, adipose hypercellularity, and environment. The predominating factor, if there is one, is likely to vary among children. It does appear that the longer a child stays obese, the more recalcitrant the condition becomes to treatment. Various estimates have noted a 70–80% likelihood that 9- to 12-year-old children who are obese will also be obese as adults (Abraham & Nordsieck, 1960; Lloyd, Wolf, & Whelen, 1961; Stunkard & Burt, 1967). Increased risk of diabetes, coronary artery disease, and hypertension have also been associated with childhood obesity (cf. Janzen, 1980). A separate but equally devastating effect is the trauma experienced by obese children through rejection, jokes, etc. (cf. Drabman, Jarvie, & Cordua y Cruz, 1982). These figures could support the need for a unified interdisciplinary and concentrated effort in the prevention and treatment of childhood obesity.

Treatment

Traditional Medical Approaches. Obese children have traditionally been exposed to one or more of the following treatments: (1) caloric restriction, (2) anorectic drugs, (3) physical exercise, (4) therapeutic starvation, (5) by-pass surgery, or (6) changes in habit patterns (Coates & Thoresen, 1978). Caloric restriction via nutritional counseling is perhaps the most time-honored approach. It usually takes the form of intermittent and few meetings with the child and/or the parent to review the nutritional guidelines and the imposing of a diet. The research data have shown this procedure, when used by itself, to fail repeatedly (cf. Coates & Thoresen, 1978; Drabman et al., 1982; Weiss, 1977). Anorectics, diuretics, and hormones have been used in the treatment of childhood obesity. Amphetamines were supposedly used to suppress appetite but were found to have little value above dietary restriction (Bray, 1972) and created a potential for habituation and abuse (Knittle, 1972; Grollman, 1975). Diuretics offer little but

short-term reductions and may yield metabolic imbalances and nutritional deficiencies. Thyroid hormones may help some by increasing metabolic rate and caloric expenditure. However, the otherwise healthy child is at risk because of the demands placed on the body (Grollman, 1975; Rivlin, 1975).

Exercise has been shown to be effective in weight reduction (Moody, Wilmore, & Girandola, 1972; Keys, 1955). But the maintenance of exercise and the long-term benefits when it is not part of a treatment package have been discouraging. Little needs to be said about the potential problems of therapeutic fasting and the risks involved for disrupting normal growth and development. If conducted in a hospital setting under medical supervision, it *might* be useful in a small minority of cases. But it clearly cannot be said to be a viable option for the majority of overweight children. By-pass surgery, though often thought of as only for adults, is being witnessed with increased regularity in the child and adolescent populations. The results have been less than encouraging whether the surgery is of the gastric or the jejunoileal type, particularly in light of the risk factors (cf. Coates & Thoresen, 1978; Drabman et al., 1982).

Behavioral. Considering the magnitude of the problem and the amount of research on obese adults, there has been surprisingly little systematic research on the use of behavioral procedures in the treatment of childhood obesity. There have been some case studies (Dinoff, Richard, & Colwick, 1972; Foxx, 1972) and work with adolescents (Gross, Wheeler, & Hess, 1976; Weiss, 1977), which will not be detailed here. They have been reviewed elsewhere (Coates & Thoresen, 1978).

One of the earlier studies on children was conducted by Rivinus, Drummand, and Combrinck-Graham (1976). Ten children (8–13 years old), 35% or more overweight, were exposed to a treatment program consisting of self-monitoring, stimulus control, and reinforcement for desirable behaviors. A daily caloric intake was set, but nutritional education was minimal. Weekly sessions included eating dinner in a cafeteria setting where instructions were given regarding food selection and the parents modeled appropriate eating behaviors. Of the 10 subjects, 9 completed the 10-week treatment program and demonstrated an average weight loss of 6.1 lb. Weight decrease continued and reached 9.2 lb at a 20-week follow-up, but it averaged only 6.7 lb at a 120-week follow-up. Considering growth rate and the pretreatment rate of weight gain, as one must in treating children, these data appear very encouraging.

Other studies have also examined the effects of treatment "packages" (Aragona, Cassady, & Drabman, 1975; Epstein, Wing, Steranchak, Michelson, & Dickson, 1979; Kingsley & Shapiro, 1977; Wheeler & Hess, 1976). Aragona et al. (1975) were one of the first groups to employ parent training in the treatment of childhood obesity. The subjects were 15 overweight females 5–10 years of age assigned to either a response-cost-plus-reinforcement, a response-cost-only, or a no-treatment control group. Sessions occurred weekly for 12 weeks. The parents were instructed in exercise management, nutrition, and stimulus control procedures. They recorded their child's food intake, calories, and weight. Portions of refundable deposit were returned to the parents contingent on their attendance, their record keeping, and their child's meeting a specified weight-loss goal. In addition, the parents in the response-cost-plus-reinforcement group received instructions on how to engage their children in behavioral contracts targeting the relevant behaviors. The subjects in the response-cost-plus-reinforcement group lost an average of 11.3 lb (range 9.0–13.3), the response-cost-only group lost an average of 9.5 lb (range 2.3–13.7), and the no-treatment control subjects showed a gain of .9 lb (range −4.5–+4.5). The 31-week follow-up showed a return to baseline weight. The experimenters speculated that unprogrammed reinforcement of weight-loss-relevant behaviors by parents in the response-cost-only group probably accounted for the similarity in outcome of the two groups.

Wheeler and Hess (1976) compared the effects of individualized behavior therapy provided to mother–child (MC) pairs to no treatment for a control group. The treatment focused on instructions and the use of stimulus control, self-monitoring, and reinforcement procedures. Emphasis was placed on tailoring the treatment to fit the lifestyle of the family.

MC pairs were seen in 30-min sessions every other week, with the intersession interval increasing over time. The treatment time averaged 7.3 months. Of the original sample, 46% dropped out within the first four sessions. The treatment completers showed a decrease in percentage overweight of 4.1%, in comparison with a 3% and a 6% increase for dropout and treatment controls, respectively. Though statistically significant, these data can hardly be seen as clinically meaningful, as the subjects were an average of 40.4% overweight to begin with.

The modification of specific food-related behaviors has been demonstrated by Epstein and his colleagues (Epstein, Masek, & Marshall, 1978; Epstein, Parker, McCoy, & McGee, 1976). Epstein et al. (1976) showed that eating rates could be reduced effectively through instructions and positive reinforcement. Collateral behaviors incompatible with eating (i.e., talking, laughing, and moving about in a chair), though not targeted, decreased along with bite rate. Sip rate, however, was not affected throughout the study. Decreased bite rate was associated with a significant decrease in food consumption, but no weight loss was recorded. An analysis of food preference according to intake records kept by observers showed nonobese and obese children to differ only in that the nonobese consumed more bread and the obese showed a preference for more milk products.

In the second study, Epstein, Masek, and Marshall (1978) assessed the effects of increased premealtime activities on the amount consumed and the effects of instruction, praise, and token reinforcement on consumatory behavior in six obese children aged 5–6. Foods were grouped into three categories, red, yellow or green, according to their nutritional value and their caloric density. The colors corresponded to those of a traffic light, indicating that the child should not eat "reds," should eat some "yellows," and could eat all the "greens" he or she wanted. Food consumption was recorded during lunch and breakfast. Activity was increased through a 10-min period of prelunch structured play and exercise. When increased activity was introduced, a slight reduction in the consumption of "reds" and "yellows" was noted as compared with baseline. When prompts, praise, and token reinforcement were introduced for correct consummatory behavior, the intake of "reds" decreased to near zero, and there was a reduction in "yellows" and a significant increase in "greens." The treatment effects were replicated by means of a withdrawal design. The mean percentage overweight was decreased from 43.3% to 37.9% during the 7-month study, but it had increased to 52% at follow-up. The number of calories consumed during breakfast was reduced from 529 to 392, and from 487 to 380 during lunch.

Family Involvement. The importance of family involvement in the treatment of obesity was suggested by the work of Stuart and Davis (1972), Mahoney and Mahoney (1976), and Brownell, Heckerman, Westlake, Hayes, and Monti (1978) with adults. It has also been implicated by Aragona *et al.* (1975), Coates and Thoresen (1982), Wheeler and Hess (1976), and Gross *et al.* (1976). Kingsley and Shapiro (1977) have examined the effects of maternal participation on childhood obesity. Four groups were used: (1) a no-treatment control group (NT); (2) the child alone (C); (3) mother–child pairs (MC); and (4) mother only (M). The treatment consisted of exposure to a program like that of Stuart and Davis (1972), with nutritional education, self-monitoring of intake, caloric counting, and written instructions to parents on how to effectively employ positive reinforcement for their child's compliance. The treatment consisted of eight weekly sessions attended by the child only, the mother and the child, or the mother only. Each of the treatment groups lost more weight (1.6 kg) than the control group (.9 kg), but there were no differences between the treatment groups. However, the mothers in the M group showed a greater weight loss than the other mothers, and it was maintained. A 5-month follow-up of the children showed normal expected weight gains and no differences between the treatment groups. Although it would appear that parental presence does not make a difference, the authors did note resentment on the part of the mothers in the C group, who were excluded from treatment.

A second study examining family involvement was conducted by Epstein *et al.* (1979): 6 of 13 obese children and their mothers were assigned to a behavior modification group, and 7 mother–child pairs were assigned to a nutritional education group. Group therapy sessions occurred weekly for 7 weeks, with follow-up meetings monthly for 3 months. The mothers and their children were seen separately. Both the behavior modification and the nutrition education groups received instructions in diet and nutrition education. Calisthenics and a one- to two-mile walk occurred during each session. Each parent in both treatments participated in a contingency contract specifying the return of a refundable deposit contingent on fulfilling the requirements of this study. In addition, the behavior modification group was exposed to self-monitoring, training in social reinforcement, modeling, a slowed-down eating rate, and regular phone contact. Behavioral contracting for self-monitoring, not eating "red foods," and weight loss was also included for the behavior modification group. The data showed that the behavior modification group lost more weight, 7.2 lb (3.5 kg) versus 3.9 lb (1.8 kg), and showed a greater decrease in percentage overweight, 11.6% versus 5.1%. (Pretreatment percentage overweight was 69% for behavior modification group and 62% for the nutrition education group.) These differences were maintained at 3 months posttreatment. The authors noted a high correlation ($r = +.66$) between mother and child weight loss in the behavior modification group but not in the nutrition education group ($r = -.01$). They interpreted these data as suggesting the utility of changing eating and exercise habits at the family level.

Hyperactivity

Introduction

It is estimated that from 3% to 10% of schoolchildren demonstrate enough problem behaviors to be classified as hyperactive or hyperkinetic, and males are so diagnosed more often than females (Office of Child Development, 1971; Sleator, Von Neuman, & Sprague, 1974). Other labels that have been applied to hyperactive children include *maturational lag, hyperkinetic reaction, immaturity of the nervous system, minimal cerebral dysfunction, minimal brain damage,* and *minimal brain injury.* The later two names are fairly common but are incorrect, as most children with hyperactivity are not brain-damaged. The new DSM III offers yet another classification, as it describes attentional deficits with and without hyperactivity.

At one time, the hyperactive or hyperkinetic child was characterized as demonstrating a short attention span, restlessness, and overactivity. The definition, however, is misleading since there are many disorders of childhood that can encompass these problems. The term *minimal brain dysfunction* (Wender, 1971) has come into prominence. Others have looked at drug responsiveness as a means of defining hyperactivity, which carries with it its own sets of problems. Most recently, K. D. O'Leary (1980) suggested that the most ''reasonable'' approach is to regard hyperactivity as a set of behaviors, such as excessive restlessness and short attention span, that are qualitatively different from those of other children of the same sex and age. These behaviors should be confirmed by the use of measurement scales such as the Teacher's Rating Scale (TRS; Conners, 1969). In addition, O'Leary also suggested that one must be able to rule out chronic medical or neurological disease and severe behavioral disturbances as major contributing factors to the hyperactivity. Finally, it is suggested that it must be shown that hyperactive behaviors persist across time and situations. Safer (1982) described what he called ''developmental hyperactivity.'' The essential features of this disorder are hyperactivity, which is usually associated with inattentiveness; a learning impediment or lag; misconduct; and immaturity.

Hyperactive children generally manifest their behavior throughout the elementary-school years. Their hyperactivity may begin to decrease from ages 13–15 years, but a relatively high level of restlessness frequently persists into young adulthood and adulthood. Even with decreasing symptomatology at puberty, the data suggest that hyperactive children have a lower chance of successful adjustment in adolscence and adulthood than nonhyperactive children (Mendelson, Johnson, & Stewart, 1971; Menkes, Rowe, & Menkes, 1967; Stewart, 1970). Historically, it is interesting to note that very little was written about the hyperactive child before about the last 20 years (K. D. O'Leary, 1980).

Treatment

Medication. Stimulant medication is one of the most common forms of treatment for the hyperactive child. Although first employed in the early 1900s, it has only been since the 1960s that its popularity has become evident. The percentage of children taking stimulant medication has risen steadily throughout the 1970s and was estimated at about 2.1% in 1977 (Safer, 1982). The most commonly prescribed stimulants are Ritalin (methylphenidate), Dexedrine (dextroamphetamine sulfate), and Cylert (pemoline). The popular media and the pharmaceutical advertisements have probably contributed heavily to the increased use of psychostimulants (K. D. O'Leary, 1980), which seems to be ''outrunning'' the rate with which research data are being produced.

In summarizing the use of stimulants, Safer (1982) noted that beneficial effects are achieved in over 70% of hyperactive children as compared to 10%–40% using placebos. In adequate doses, 35%–50% showed dramatic improvement, 30%–40% moderate improvement, and 15%–20% little or no change. Significant amounts of data exist showing that stimulant medications generally lead to increased attention, increased cooperativeness, and decreased disruptiveness in the classroom (cf. Cantwell & Carlson, 1978; Connors & Werry, 1979; Safer & Allen, 1976). The effect of stimulants on social behavior appears beneficial but remains under investigation. Questions have been raised about whether the observed effects are due to increased attention and decreased disruptiveness or are somehow mediated more directly by the medication (K. D. O'Leary, 1980). One study has found that children under stimulant medication initiated less social contact than when they were not medicated (Whalen, Henker, Collins, Finck, & Dotemoto, 1979).

Changes in schooi achievement also remain under scrutiny. Though positive changes have been reported by some (Bradley, 1937) they have not been found in most studies (cf. K. D. O'Leary, 1980). Consolidation of newly learned behavior does not appear to be facilitated (Rie & Rie, 1977), and there is some concern that learning under stimulant medication may be state-dependent, although it does not appear so under therapeutic doses (Aman & Sprague, 1974). One problem regarding this issue of increased academic performance has been the relative lack of long-term studies. Studies that are three to six months in length yield equivocal data with no consistent increases (Gittelman-Klein & Klein, 1976; Hoffman, Engelhardt, Margolis, Polizos, Waizer, & Rosenfeld, 1974). There is a strong likelihood that because of their improved attention and conduct under stimulant medication, the children only "appear" to be learning more.

S. G. O'Leary and Pelham (1978) have summarized the concerns over the use of medications as the sole treatment for hyperactivity. These concerns include the following: (1) there is no documentation of the long-term effect on academic achievement; (2) no long-term effect on disruptive social problems has not been demonstrated; (3) increases in heart rate and blood pressure, along with decreased rate of height and weight gains, although reversible, are present; (4) the medication may have deleterious long-term effects; and (5) because of the anorexic and sedative effects, medication is generally not administered in the late afternoon. For these reasons and because of some of the obvious beneficial effects of medication, greater attention is being given to a more in-depth examination of the interactions between the medications and the environment and the possibility of combining medication with behavioral therapies.

Whalen et al. (1979) focused on "social ecology," its effects on classroom behavior, and its interaction with medication. Though inattentiveness or "distractibility" is a major feature of the hyperactive child, it is clear that little is known about the environmental conditions that correlate with this problem (Doleys, 1976). Whalen et al. compared hyperactive boys on and off Ritalin with hyperactive boys on placebo, as well as comparison nonhyperactive boys in a "quasi-naturalistic setting." External stimulation (quiet versus noisy) and the type of tasks (self-paced versus other-paced) were manipulated. In general, these authors found that hyperactive boys on pla-

cebo tended to be much less attentive, more active, and more disruptive than their peers. Self-paced activities and high noise level both were shown to have detrimental effects on classroom behavior. A medication-by-situation interaction was observed. These data would appear to suggest that environmental conditions may (1) impact upon the child's behavior in a classroom and (2) could act synergistically or antagonistically with medication.

Behavioral Treatments

Positive Reinforcement. Hyperactive behavior has frequently been treated through the use of behavioral therapies (Gardner, 1970). One of the more common techniques has been the use of positive reinforcement with a token economy to strengthen incompatible behavior (Werry & Sprague, 1970). A number of studies carried out in the classroom have demonstrated the effectiveness of the use of these procedures in decreasing hyperactive behavior (Doubros & Daniels, 1966; Edelson & Sprague, 1974; Patterson, Jones, Whittier, & Wright, 1965), and increasing attending behavior (Allen, Henke, Harris, Baer, & Reynolds, 1967; Quay, Sprague, Werry, & McQueen, 1967; Walker & Buckley, 1968). Patterson et al. (1965) described a program in which token reinforcement was used to bring about significant increases in attention. Tokens were given after each 10 sec of uninterrupted attending. Doubros and Daniels (1966) used a token economy with six hyperactive mentally retarded children between the ages of 6 and 13. A checklist of hyperactive behaviors was constructed for each child. The children earned tokens for appropriate play during a 15-min play situation. A significant reduction of hyperactive behaviors was noted as a function of the treatment and continued through a 2-week follow-up. Edelson and Sprague (1974) instituted a token economy in a classroom that focused on the reinforcement of cooperative behavior. A substantial reduction in hyperactive behaviors and destructive acts along with a significant increase in attention level and class cooperation resulted. The removal of the token system was associated with the return of these behaviors to baseline levels.

Allen *et al.* (1967) focused on the time spent on a specific activity. Systematic programming of adult social reinforcement resulted in a decrease in the number of activity changes to 50% of preconditioning levels. Quay *et al.* (1967) examined procedures for modifying visual orientation in a group of five hyperactive children. The children were of normal intelligence and had been placed in a class for behavior problem students. The subjects were seated at desks in a semicircle around the teacher, with a small box containing a light mounted inside the box on the top of each desk. Each subject was observed for five 10-sec segments during each experimental session and was reinforced for attending on a variable ratio schedule. Reinforcement consisted of the light's flashing, followed by candy and/or social praise. Attending increased significantly under the candy-plus-social-reinforcement condition and decreased when the treatment was withdrawn. Similar effects were documented in studies by Krop (1971) and Mitchell and Crowell (1973), who used candy, praise, and contingent attention to increase attending behavior and to decrease "hyperactive" behavior. Such reinforcement procedures have also been effectively applied in groups (Schofield, Hedlund, & Worland, 1974; Pratt & Fischer, 1975).

Parents as Therapists. The importance of working with parents in counseling or guidance relationships has often been pointed out (Wender, 1971; Safer, 1982). Fraizer and Schnieder (1975) described a procedure carried out by parents to eliminate inappropriate hyperactive behavior during and following mealtime by employing a multiple-baseline procedure using contingent attention and time-out. The parents were trained to give positive attention to appropriate behavior and to ignore inappropriate behavior. Time-out was employed for inappropriate behaviors. The rate of inappropriate behavior decreased significantly and remained low for approximately 5 weeks thereafter. Furman and Feighner (1973) reported on the beneficial effects of videotape feedback in teaching parents operant techniques with their hyperactive children. The parents worked on specific target behaviors

and improvements in communication. Wiltz and Gordon (1974) worked with the parents of a 9-year-old hyperactive and aggressive boy. The family spent five consecutive days in an apartment-like setting with observational facilities. The training included instructional materials, prompting, modeling, and feedback. A follow-up by telephone revealed a significant reduction in noncompliance and destructive action.

Self-Regulation. Meichenbaum and Goodman (1971) suggested that impulsive or hyperactive children may be deficient or may have experienced inadequate training in controlling their motor behavior via self-commands. In their original study, these authors showed that children increased their response latency on a discrimination task after self-instructional training. However, the number of errors performed by the children did not decrease. Bornstein and Quevillon (1976) used a self-instructional package with three overactive preschool children 4 years old. The dependent variable was on-task behavior in the classroom. The treatment consisted of one massed self-instructional session that lasted for approximately 2 hr. During the training: (1) the experimenter modeled the task while talking out loud to himself or herself; (2) the subject performed the task while the experimenter instructed out loud; (3) the subject then performed the task, talking out loud to herself or himself while the experimenter whispered softly; (4) the subject performed the task, whispering softly, while the experimenter made lip movements but no sound; (5) the subject performed the task making lip movements without sound while the experimenter self-instructed covertly; and (6) the subject performed the task with covert self-instruction (Meichenbaum & Goodman, 1971; Bornstein & Quevillon, 1976). The content of the verbalizations that were modeled generally fell into one of four categories: (1) questions about the task; (2) answers to questions in the form of cognitive rehearsal ("Oh, that's right, I'm supposed to copy that picture"); (3) self-instructions that directed the task ("First, I draw this line, then I draw that line"); and (4) self-reinforcement ("How about that, I did it right!"). Significant and meaningful increases in the percentage of on-task behavior were noted immediately after self-instructional training. The treatment gains were maintained. The use of a multiple-baseline design across subjects helped to demonstrate that the effect was indeed a response to self-instructional training rather than to other extra-experimental factors.

A second study in this area was performed by Friedling and O'Leary (1979). These authors attempted to replicate the Bornstein and Quevillon (1976) results using older (7- to 8-year-old), nonmedicated hyperactive children. The dependent variable included on-task behavior in the classroom and performance on reading and arithmetic tasks when the difficulty was varied. The experimental group received self-instructional training in a 90-min session. A control group received the same amount of time with the experimenter but without training in providing self-instructions. This initial intervention did not prove effective in producing any significant changes. Therefore, it was replicated by providing the treatment group with two additional 40-min sessions on consecutive days. Again, the percentage of on-task and academic behavior did not change significantly. The authors then instituted a token economy wherein reinforcers were provided for on-task behavior. This manipulation did prove successful in significantly increasing the percentage of on-task behavior for both groups.

Although other researchers (K. D. O'Leary, 1968; Hartig & Kanfer (1973) have shown self-instructions to be effective in increasing the moral behavior of children, there appears to be some question about whether similar effects will be achieved in modifying the behavior of hyperactive children. It may be that there is an interaction between self-instructional treatment and the level of task performance (high versus low) and/or the complexity of the task (Friedling & S. G. O'Leary, 1979). That is, if the behavior already exists in the child's repertoire and can be easily performed by the child, then self-instructional procedures may be more effective than if the desired response is extremely complex and/or is relatively "weak."

Relaxation and Biofeedback. Because of the apparent cognitive and overt hyperactivity noted in children diagnosed as hyperactive, it was only natural that at some point consideration would be given to the use of relaxation techniques to help diminish this overt activity. One such study was conducted by Lupin, Braud, and Duer (1974). They presented relaxation instructions via a tape recorder to small groups of hyperactive children. Several physiological measures and behavioral ratings were taken before and after the treatment sessions. A group of children who were not exposed to the taped relaxation sessions were used as a control. The authors noted reduced forehead muscle tension, emotionality, and aggressiveness following the presentation of the tapes. Although not directly concerned about the reduction of hyperactive behavior in the classroom or at home, Putre, Loffio, Chorost, Marx, and Gilbert (1977) were interested in the relative effectiveness of a relaxation and control tape in producing a reduction in muscle tension. Twenty hyperactive boys ranging in age from 7 to 13 listened either to a relaxation tape utilizing the typical progressive relaxation instructions or to a control tape consisting of a story read from an adventure book. The tapes lasted approximately 15 min and were listened to on a daily basis for 2 weeks. Measurement of forehead muscle tension occurred periodically. The researchers reported no significant difference between the groups, and both showed a significant decrease in muscle tension (mean 34%).

Braud, Lupin, and Braud (1975) extended this work to the use of biofeedback technology. The subject was a 6.5-year-old hyperactive boy exposed to 11 sessions of frontalis electromyographic (EMG) biofeedback. The child was instructed to turn off the tone that signaled the presence of muscle tension. Muscle tension, as measured by the EMG, and overt activity decreased within and across sessions. The authors noted that the child was able to control his hyperactivity during a 7-month follow-up. Improvements were also noted on achievement tests, reports of self-confidence, and behavior at school and at home.

Combination Therapies. Although stimulant medication and behavior therapy have both been shown to be effective in treating various problems of the hyperactive child and some studies have found one to be better than the other, (Gittelman-Klein, Klein, Abikoff, Katz, Gloisten, & Kates, 1976), neither can be said to be the treatment of choice. Perhaps for this reason, increasing attention is being given to combined and more comprehensive therapies.

In one of the earlier studies, Christensen and Sprague (1973) studied two troups of six children. One group received behavior modification and a placebo, the other behavior modification and methylphenidate. Seat activity, as measured by a stabilimetric cushion, and performance on daily quizzes were examined. The behavior modification-plus-methylphenidate group showed lower rates of activity, but there was no different between the two groups in the number of correct answers on daily quizzes. In a study using mentally retarded, institutionalized "hyperactive" children, Christensen (1973) found significant improvement across a variety of academic and activity measures when behavior modification was applied. The effects did not appear to be enhanced by the addition of methylphenidate. Wolraich, Drummond, Salomon, O'Brien, and Sivage (1978) compared a combination (behavior therapy plus stimulant medication) treatment with behavior therapy alone. No difference was found between the two interventions. However, this may not have been an adequate test because of the short treatment duration (2 weeks) and a relatively low dose of methylphenidate (.3 mg/kg). In addition, these results are inconsistent with those of Gittelman-Klein *et al.* (1976), who, although finding medication to be more effective than behavior therapy over an 8-week treatment, did note that stimulant medications of considerably higher dosages enhanced the effects of behavior therapy.

S. G. O'Leary and Pelham (1978) looked at the utility of behavior therapy when applied after a stimulant medication was withdrawn. They found a significant increase in off-task and other maladaptive behavior when hyperactive children were taken off stimulant medication. The rebound was reduced to on-drug levels of behavior during a 4-month, 18-session (on the average) behavioral-intervention program involving parents and teachers. The authors noted that (1) there was individual variability in the subjects' responses to behavior therapy; (2) the treatment tended to be more

effective in changing social behavior than in increasing attention skills; and (3) the changes noted in the classroom were highly correlated with the cooperation and commitment shown by individual teachers and principals. Although the therapy was effective in ameliorating the rebound effects observed following the withdrawal of the stimulant medication, the expense of such treatment in time and dollars, as well as the motivation required of the family, cannot be ignored in its evaluation.

In a recent paper, Pelham, Schnedler, Bologna, and Contreras (1980) used a 3-week medication probe period to evaluate the effects of combining stimulant medication with behavior therapy. The behavior therapy was ongoing and consisted of an average of 12 sessions across 5 months. The treatment included (1) weekly parent training sessions, with individual families focusing on the development and use of contingency management; (2) teacher training in behavioral approaches; and (3) child tutoring in self-instruction techniques. The dependent measures included classroom observations, teacher ratings, clinic observations, and parent ratings. In general, the results showed that behavior therapy was effective in reducing the target behaviors, but not maximally so. Increased on-task behavior and decreased parental punishment with some reinforcement were noted. Both medication and behavior therapy appeared to increase on-task behavior, but only behavior therapy was shown to increase the amount of work completed correctly. Behavior therapy was found to be as effective as low doses of methylphenidate, but not as effective as high doses. Medication seemed to have an incremental effect even after 13 weeks of behavior therapy. Even with the behavioral intervention, the subjects were not "normal" in their interpersonal relationships and social skills. On the basis of these data, the authors emphasized the potential of stimulant medications at therapeutic doses, as an adjunct to behavior therapy. They further emphasized that in both clinical and analogue research, the timing of the ratings should be carefully considered because the medication effects fluctuate during the day. The importance of the use of multiple dependent measures that cover a variety of behavioral domains was also pointed out, as was individual variation in reactions to medication and behavior therapy. In discussing multiple measures, they noted that low doses of psychostimulants appear to have their effect on cognitive abilities as reflected in on-task behavior, whereas higher doses seem to have a beneficial effect on interpersonal behavior and compliance of the type often found through teacher ratings.

References

Abraham, S., & Nordsieck, M. Relationship of excess weight in children and adults. *Public Health Reports,* 1960, *75,* 1516–1521.

Adams, K. M., Klinge, V., & Keiser, T. W. The extinction of a self-injurious behavior in an epileptic child. *Behaviour Research and Therapy,* 1973, *11,* 351–356.

Alexander, A. B. Systematic relaxation and flow rates in asthmatic children: Relationship to emotional participants and anxiety. *Journal of Psychosomatic Research,* 1972, *16,* 405–410.

Alexander, A. B. Behavioral methods in the clinical management of chronic asthma. In R. B. Williams & W. D. Gentry (Eds.), *Behavioral approaches to medical practice.* Cambridge: Ballinger, 1977.

Alexander, A. B., Miklich, D. R., & Hershoff, H. The immediate effects of systematic relaxation training on peak expiratory flow rates in asthmatic children. *Psychosomatic Medicine,* 1972, *38,* 388–394.

Alexander, A. B., Chai, H., Creer, T. L., Miklich, D. R., Reane, C. M., & Cardoso, R. R. deA. The elimination of chronic coughing by response suppression shaping. *Journal of Behavior Therapy and Experimental Psychiatry,* 1973, *4,* 75–80.

Allen, E. K., Henke, L. B., Harris, F. B., Baer, P. M., & Reynolds, N. J. Control of hyperactivity by social reenforcement of attending behaviors. *Journal of Educational Psychology,* 1967, *58,* 231–237.

Aman, M., & Sprague, R. L. The state-dependent effects of methylphenidate and dextroamphetamine. *Journal Nervous and Mental Diseases,* 1974, *158,* 268–279.

Aragona, J., Cassady, J., & Drabman, R. S. Treating overweight children through parental training and contingency contracting. *Journal of Applied Behavior Analysis,* 1975, *8,* 269–278.

Ashkenazi, Z., & Wisdom, S. *Elimination of head rolling in an epileptic retarded child.* Unpublished manuscript, Ministry of Health, Beer Sheba, Israel, 1957.

Balaschak, B. A. Teacher implemented behavior modification in a case of organically based epilepsy. *Journal of Consulting and Clinical Psychology,* 1976, *44,* 218–223.

Blanchard, E. B., & Ahles, T. A. Psychophysical disorders. *Behavior Modification,* 1979, *3,* 535–549.

Booker, H. E., Forster, F. M., & Klove, H. Extinction factor in startle (accusticomotor) seizures. *Neurology,* 1965, *15,* 1095–1103.

Bornstein, R., & Quevillon, R. The effects of a self-instructional package on overactive preschool boys. *Journal of Applied Behavior Analysis,* 1976, *9,* 179–188.

Bradley, C. The behavior of children receiving benzedrine. *American Journal of Psychiatry,* 1937, *94,* 579–585.

Braud, L. W., Lupin, M. N., & Braud, W. G. The use of electromyographic biofeedback in the control of hyperactivity. *Journal of Learning Disabilities,* 1975, *8,* 21–26.

Bray, G. A. Clinical management of the obese patient. *Postgraduate Medicine,* 1972, *51,* 125–130.

Brownell, K. D., Heckerman, C. L., Westlake, R. J., Hays, S. C., & Mont, P. M. The effect of couples training and partner cooperativeness in the behavioral treatment of obesity. *Behaviour Research and Therapy,* 1978, *16,* 323–333.

Cantwell, D. P., & Carlson, G. A. Stimulants. In J. S. Werry (Ed.), *Pediatric psychopharmacology: The use of behavior modifying drugs in children.* New York: Brunner/Mazel, 1978.

Christensen, D. *The combined effects of methylphenidate (Ritalin) and a classroom behavior modification program in reducing the hyperkinetic behavior of institutionalized mental retardes.* Unpublished doctoral dissertation, University of Illinois, 1973.

Christensen, D. E., & Sprague, R. L. Reduction of hyperactive behaviors by conditioning procedures alone and combined with methylphenidate (Ritalin). *Behaviour Research and Therapy,* 1973, *11,* 331–334.

Coates, T. J., & Thoresen, C. E. Treating obesity in children and adolescents: A review. *American Journal of Public Health,* 1978, *68,* 143–151.

Coates, T. J., & Thoresen, C. E. Treating obesity in children and adolescents: Is there any hope? In J. M. Ferguson, & C. B. Taylor (Eds.), *Advances in behavioral medicine.* Englewood Cliffs, N.J.: Spectrum, 1981.

Conners, C. K. A teacher rating scale for use in drug studies with children. *American Journal of Psychiatry,* 1969, *126,* 884–888.

Conners, C. K., & Werry, J. S. Pharmacotherapy of psychopathology in children. In H. C. Quay, & J. S. Werry (Eds.), *Psychopathological disorders of childhood* (2nd Ed.). New York: Wiley, 1979.

Creer, T. L. The use of time-out from positive reinforcement procedure with asthmatic children. *Journal of Psychosomatic Research,* 1970, *14,* 117–120.

Creer, T. L., & Miklich, D. R. The application of a self-modeling procedure to modify inappropriate behavior: a preliminary report. *Behaviour Research and Therapy,* 1970, *8,* 91–92.

Creer, T. L., & Yoches C. The modification of an inappropriate behavioral pattern in asthmatic children. *Journal of Chronic Diseases,* 1971, *24,* 507–513.

Creer, T. L., Weinberg, E., & Moulk, L. Managing a hospital behavior problem: Malingering. *Journal of Behavior Therapy and Experimental Psychiatry,* 1974, *5,* 259–262.

Creer, T. L., Chai, H., & Hoffman, A. A single application of an aversive stimulus to eliminate chronic cough. *Journal of Behavior Therapy and Experimental Psychiatry,* 1977, *8*(1), 107–109.

Danker, P. S., Miklich, D. R., Pratt, C., & Creer, T. L. An unsuccessful attempt to instrumentally condition peak expiratory flow rates in asthmatic children. *Journal of Psychosomatic Research,* 1975, *19,* 209–213.

Davis, M. H., Saunders, D. F., Creer, T. L., & Chai, H.

Relaxation training facilitated by biofeedback apparatus as a supplemental treatment in bronchial asthma. *Journal of Psychosomatic Research,* 1973, *17,* 121–128.

Department of Health, Education, and Welfare. *Vital and Health Statistics, 1973, Prevalence of selected chronic respiratory conditions.* Washington, D.C.: USDHEW, Public Health Service, Series 10-No. 84, HRA-74-1511, September 1973, p. 17.

Dinoff, M., Richard, H. C., & Colwick, J. Weight reduction through succession contracts. *American Journal of Orthopsychiatry,* 1972, *42,* 110–113.

Doleys, D. M. Distractability and distracting stimuli: inconsistent and contradictory results. *Psychological Record,* 1976, *26,* 279–287.

Doubros, S. G., & Daniels, G. J. An experimental approach to the reduction of overactive behavior. *Behaviour Research and Therapy,* 1966, *4,* 251–258.

Drabman, R. S., Jarvie, G. J., & Cordua y Cruz, G. D. Childhood obesity: Assessment, etiology, risks and treatment. In D. M. Doleys & T. B. Vaughn (Eds.), *Assessment and treatment of developmental problems.* Englewood Cliffs, N.J.: Spectrum, 1982.

Edelson, R. I., & Sprague, R. L. Conditioning of activity level in a classroom with institutionalized retarded boys. *American Journal of Mental Deficiency,* 1974, *78,* 384–388.

Eggleston, P. A. Asthma in childhood. In H. F. Conn (Ed.), *Current therapy.* Philadelphia: Saunders, 1976.

Epstein, L. H., Parker, L., McCoy, J. F., & McGee, G. Descriptive analysis of eating regulation in obese and nonobese children. *Journal of Applied Behavior Analysis,* 1976, *9,* 407–415.

Epstein, L. H., Masek, B. J., & Marshall, W. R. A nutritionally basic school program for control of eating in obese children. *Behavior Therapy,* 1978, *9,* 766–778.

Epstein, L. H., Wing, R. R., Steranchuk, L., Michelson, J., & Dickson, B. *Comparison of family basic behavior modification and nutrition education for childhood obesity.* Paper presented at the AABT, San Francisco, December 1979.

Feldman, G. M. The effect of biofeedback training on respiratory resistance in asthmatic children. *Psychosomatic Medicine,* 1976, *38,* 27–34.

Finley, W. W., Smith, H. A., & Etherton, M. D. Reduction of seizures and normalization of the EEG in a severe epileptic following sensorimotor biofeedback training: A preliminary study. *Biological Psychology,* 1975, *2,* 189–203.

Forster, F. M. Conditioned reflexes and sensory-evoked epilepsy: The nature of the therapeutic process. *Conditioned Reflex,* 1969, *4,* 103–114.

Forster, F. M., Ptacek, L. J., & Peterson, W. G. Auditory clicks in extinction of stroboscopic-induced seizures. *Epilepsia,* 1965, *6,* 217–225.

Forster, F. M., Booker, H. E., & Ansell, S. Computer automation of the conditioning therapy of stroboscopic induced seizures. *Transactions of the American Neurological Association,* 1966, *91,* 232–233.

Foxx, R. M. Social reinforcement of weight reduction: A case report on an obese retarded adolescent. *Mental Retardation,* 1972, *10*(4), 21–23.

Fraizer, V. R., & Schneider, H. Parental management of inappropriate hyperactivity in a young retarded child.

Journal of Behavior Therapy and Experimental Psychiatry, 1975, *6,* 246–247.

Freedman, S. S., & Pelletier, G. A. Asthma in childhood: Treatment of 1070 cases. *Annals of Allergy,* 1970, *28,* 133–141.

Friedling, C., & O'Leary, S. G. Teaching self-instruction to hyperactive children: A replication. *Journal of Applied Behavior Analysis,* 1979, *12,* 211–219.

Furman, S., & Feighner, A. Video feedback in treating of hyperkinetic children: A preliminary report. *American Journal of Psychiatry,* 1973, *130,* 792–796.

Gardner, J. E. Behavior therapy treatment approach to a psychogenic seizure case. *Journal of Consulting Psychology,* 1967, *31,* 209–212.

Gardner, J. E. A blending of behavior therapy techniques in an approach to an asthmatic child. *Psychotherapy: Theory, Research and Practice,* 1968, *5,* 46–49.

Gardner, J. M. Behavior modification in mental retardation: A review of research and analysis of trends. In C. M. Franks & R. Rubin (Eds.), *Progress in behavior therapy.* New York: Academic Press, 1970.

Gittelman-Klein, R., & Klein, D. F. Methylphenidate effects in learning disabilities. *Archives of General Psychiatry,* 1976, *33,* 655–664.

Gittelman-Klein, R., Klein, D. F., Abikoff, H., Katz, S., Gloisten, A. C., & Kates, W. Relative efficacy of methylphenidate and behavior modification in hyperactive children: An item report. *Journal of Abnormal Child Psychology,* 1976, *4,* 361–379.

Grollman, A. Drug therapy of obesity in children. In P. J. Collipp (Ed.), *Childhood obesity.* Acton, Mass.: Publishing Science Group, 1975.

Gross, M. A., Wheeler, M., & Hess, K. The treatment of obesity in adolescents using behavioral self-control. *Clinical Pediatrics,* 1976, *15,* 920.

Hartig, M., & Kanfer, F. H. The role of verbal self-instruction in children's resistance to temptation. *Journal of Personality and Social Psychology,* 1973, *25,* 259–267.

Hock, R. A., Rodgers, C. H., Reddi, C., & Kennard, D. W. Medicopsychological interventions in male asthmatic children: An evaluation of physiological change. *Psychosomatic Medicine,* 1978, *40,* 210–215.

Hoffman, S., Engelhardt, D. M., Margolis, R. A., Polizos, P., Waizer, J., & Rosenfeld, T. Response to methylphenidate in low socioeconomic hyperactive children. *Archives of General Psychiatry,* 1974, *30,* 354–359.

Ince, L. P. The use of relaxation training and a conditioned stimulus in the elimination of epileptic seizures in a child: A case study. *Journal of Behavior Therapy and Experimental Psychiatry.* 1976, *7,* 39–42.

Jacobson, E. *Progressive relaxation.* Chicago: University of Chicago Press, 1938.

Janzen, G. S. Parental modeling and re-enforcement in the treatment of childhood obesity. Unpublished dissertation, University of Alabama, 1980.

Keys, A. Body composition and its change with age and diet. In E. S. Eppright, D. Swanson, & C. A. Iverson (Eds.), *Weight control.* Ames: Iowa State University Press, 1975.

Khan, A. V. Effectiveness of biofeedback and counterconditioning in the treatment of bronchial asthma. *Journal of Psychosomatic Research,* 1977, *21,* 97–104.

Khan, A. V., & Olson, D. L. Deconditioning of exercise-induced asthma. *Psychosomatic Medicine*, 1977, *39*, 382–392.

Khan, A., Staerk, M., & Bonk, C. Role of counter-conditioning in the treatment of asthma. *Journal of Psychosomatic Research*, 1974, *18*, 89–92.

Kingsley, R. G., & Shapiro, J. A comparison of three behavioral programs for the control of obesity in children. *Behavior Therapy*, 1977, *8*, 30–36.

Kinsman, R. A., Luparello, T. O., O'Banion, K. O., & Spector, S. L. Multidimensional analysis of the subjective symptomology of asthma. *Psychosomatic Medicine*, 1973, *35*, 250–267.

Kinsman, R. A., O'Banion, K., Resnikoff, P., Laparello, T. J., & Sheldon, S. L. Subjective symptoms of acute asthma within a hetenogenous sample of asthmatics. *Journal of Allergy and Clinical Immunology*, 1973, *52*, 384–396.

Kinsman, R. A., Spector, S. L., Shucard, D. W., & Luparello, T. J. Observations on patterns of subjective symptomatology of acute asthma. *Psychosomatic Medicine*, 1974, *36*, 129–143.

Knapp, T. J., & Wells, L. A. Behavior therapy for asthma: A review. *Behaviour Research and Therapy*, 1978, *16*, 103–115.

Knittle, J. L. Obesity in children: A problem of adipose tissue development. *Journal of Pediatrics*, 1972, *81*, 1048–1059.

Kotses, H., Glaus, K. D., Crawford, P. L., Edwards, J. E., & Scherr, M. S. Operant reduction of frontalis EMG activity in the treatment of asthma in children. *Journal of Psychosomatic Research*, 1976, *20*, 453–459.

Krop, H. Modification of hyperactive behavior of a brain-damaged, emotionally disturbed child. *Training School Bulletin*, 1971, *68*, 49–54.

Lloyd, J. K., Wolf, O. H., & Whelen, W. S. Childhood obesity: A long-term study of height and weight. *British Medical Journal*, 1961, *2*, 145–148.

Lupin, M., Braud, W. G., & Duer, W. F. *Effects of relaxation upon hyperactivity using relaxation tapes for children and parents.* Paper presented at the 11th Annual Convention for Learning Disabilities, Houston, February 1974.

Mahoney, M. J., & Mahoney, K. Treatment of obesity: A clinical explanation. In B. J. Williams, S. Martin, & J. P. Foreyt (Eds.), *Obesity: Behavioral approaches to dietary management.* New York: Brunner/Mazel, 1976.

Mathison, D. A. Asthma. In H. F. Conn (Ed.), *Current therapy.* Philadelphia: Saunders, 1976.

Mayer, J. Fat babies grow into fat people. *Family Health*, 1973, *5*, 24–38.

Meichenbaum, D., & Goodman, J. Training impulsive children to talk to themselves: A means of developing self-control. *Journal of Abnormal Psychology*, 1971, *77*, 115–126.

Mendelson, W., Johnson, N., & Stewart, M. A. Hyperactive children as teenagers: A follow-up study. *Journal of Nervous and Mental Diseases*, 1971, *153*, 273–279.

Menkes, M. M., Rowe, J. S., & Menkes, J. H. A 25-year follow-up on the hyperkinetic child with minimal brain dysfunction. *Pediatrics*, 1967, *39*, 393–399.

Miklich, D. R. Operant conditioning procedures with systematic desensitization in a hyperkinetic asthmatic boy.

Journal of Behavior Therapy and Experimental Psychiatry, 1973, *4*, 177–182.

Mitchell, D. W., & Crowell, P. J. Modifying inappropriate behavior in an elementary art class. *Elementary School Guidance and Counseling*, 1973, *8*, 34–42.

Moody, D. L., Willmore, J. H., & Girandola, R. W. The effects of a jogging program on the body composition of normal and obese high school girls. *Medicine and Science in Sports*, 1972, *4*, 210–213.

Moore, N. Behavior therapy on bronchial asthma: A controlled study. *Journal of Psychosomatic Research*, 1965, *9*, 257–276.

Mostofsky, D. I. Epilepsy: Action for improving socialization and family support. In L. G. Perlman (Ed.), *The role of vocational and rehabilitation in the 1980's.* Washington, D.C.: National Rehabilitation Association, 1978.

Mostofsky, D. I., & Balaschak, B. A. Psychological control of seizures. *Psychological Bulletin*, 1977, *84*, 723–750.

Mostofsky, D. I., & Iguchi, M. Y. Behavior control of seizure disorders. In D. M. Doleys, R. L. Meredith, & A. R. Ciminero (Eds.), *Behavioral medicine: Assessment and treatment strategies.* New York: Plenum Press, 1982.

Neisworth, J. T., & Moore, F. Operant treatment of asthmatic responding with the parent as therapist. *Behavior Therapy*, 1972, *3*, 95–99.

Office of Child Development, Department of Health, Education, and Welfare. Report of the conference on the use of stimulant drugs in the treatment of behaviorally disturbed young school children. Washington, D.C.: U.S. Government Printing Office, 1971.

O'Leary, K. D. The effects of self-instruction on immoral behavior. *Journal of Experimental Child Psychology*, 1968, *6*, 297–301.

O'Leary, K. D. Pills and skills for hyperactive children. *Journal of Applied Behavior Analysis*, 1980, *13*, 191–204.

O'Leary, S. G., & Pelham, W. E. Behavior therapy and withdrawal of stimulant modification in hyperactive children. *Pediatrics*, 1978, *61*, 211–217.

Ounstead, C., Lee, D., & Hunt, S. J. Electroencephalographic and clinical changes in an epileptic child during repeated phobic stimulation. *Electroencephalography and Clinical Neurophysiology*, 1966, *21*, 388–391.

Patterson, G. R., Jones, R., Whittier, J., & Wright, M. A. A behavior modification program for the hyperactive child. *Behaviour Research Therapy*, 1965, *2*, 217–220.

Pelham, W. E., Schnedler, R. W., Bologna, N. C., & Contreras, J. A. Behavioral and stimulant treatment of hyperactive children: A therapy study with methylphenidate probes in a within subject design. *Journal Applied Behavior Analysis*, 1980, *13*, 221–236.

Phillip, R. L., Wilde, G. J. S., & Day, J. H. Suggestion and relaxation in asthmatics. *Journal of Psychosomatic Research*, 1972, *16*, 193–204.

Pratt, S. J., & Fischer, J. Behavior modification: Changing hyperactive behavior in a children's group. *Perspectives in Psychiatric Care*, 1975, *13*, 37–42.

Putre, W., Loffio, K., Chorost, S., Marx, V., & Gilbert, C. An effectiveness study of relaxation training tape with hyperactive children. *Behavior Therapy*, 1977, *8*, 355–359.

Quay, H., Sprague, R., Werry, J., & McQueen, M. Conditioning visual orientation of conduct problem in the classroom. *Journal of Experimental Child Psychology,* 1967, *5,* 512–517.

Renne, C. M., & Creer, T. L. Training children with asthma to use inhalation therapy equipment. *Journal of Applied Behavior Analysis,* 1976, *9,* 1–11.

Rie, E. D., & Rie, H. E. Recall, retention and Ritalin. *Journal of Consulting and Clinical Psychology,* 1977, *45,* 967–972.

Rivinus, T. M., Drummond, J., & Combrinck-Graham, L. A group behavioral treatment program for overweight children: Results of a pilot study. *Pediatric Adolescent Endocrinology,* 1976, *1,* 212.

Rivlin, R. S. The use of hormones in the treatment of obesity. In M. Winick (Ed.), *Childhood obesity.* New York: Wiley, 1975.

Safer, D. J. Hyperactive-attentional disorders. In D. M. Doleys & T. B. Vaughn (Eds.), *Assessment and treatment of developmental problems.* New York: Spectrum, 1982.

Safer, D. J., & Allen, R. P. *Hyperactive children: Diagnosis and management.* Baltimore: University Park Press, 1976.

Schaefer, C. E., Millman, H. L., & Levine, G. F. *Therapies for psychosomatic disorders in children.* San Francisco: Jossey-Bass, 1979.

Scherr, M. S., Crawford, P. L., Sergent, C. B., & Scherr, C. A. Effect of biofeedback techniques on chronic asthma in a summer camp environment. *Annals of Allergy,* 1975, *85,* 289–295.

Schofield, L. J., Hedlund, C., & Worland, J. Operant approaches to group therapy and effects on sociometric status. *Psychological Reports,* 1974, *35,* 83–90.

Schultz, J. H., & Luthe, W. *Autogenic training: A psychophysiologic approach in psychotherapy.* London: Grune & Stratton, 1959.

Sherwood, S. L. Self-induced epilepsy: A collection of self-induced epilepsy cases compared with some other photo-convulsive cases. *Archives of Neurology,* 1962, *6,* 63–77.

Sirota, A. D., & Mahoney, M. J. Relaxation on cue: The self-regulation of asthma. *Journal of Behavior Therapy and Experimental Psychiatry,* 1974, *5,* 65–66.

Sleator, E. K., Von Neuman, A., & Sprague, R. L. Hyperactive children. *Journal of the American Medical Association,* 1974, *229,* 316–317.

Sterman, M. B. Neurophysiologic and clinical studies of sensorimotor EEG biofeedback training: Some effect on epilepsy. *Seminars in Psychiatry,* 1973, *5,* 507–525.

Sterman, M. B., & Friar, L. Suppression of seizures in an epileptic following sensorimotor EEG feedback training. *Electroencephalography and Clinical Neurophysiology,* 1972, *33,* 89–95.

Sterman, M. B., McDonald, L. R., & Stone, R. K. Biofeedback training of the sensorimotor electro-ence-

phalogram rhythm in man: Effects on epilepsy. *Epilepsia,* 1974, *15,* 395–416.

Stewart, M. A. Hyperactive children. *Science American,* 1970, *222,* 94–98.

Stuart, R. B., & Davis, B. *Slim chance in a fat world: Behavioral control of obesity.* Champaign, Ill.: Research Press, 1972.

Stunkard, A. J., & Burt, V. Obesity and body image: II. Age of onset of disturbances in body image. *American Journal of Psychiatry,* 1967, *123,* 1443–1447.

Vachon, L., & Rich, E. S. Visceral learning in asthma. *Psychosomatic Medicine,* 1976, *38,* 122–130.

Walker, H. M., & Buckley, N. K. The use of positive reinforcement in conditioning attending behavior. *Journal of Applied Behavior Analysis,* 1968, *1,* 245–250.

Weiss, A. R. A behavioral approach to the treatment of adolescent obesity. *Behavior Therapy,* 1977, *8,* 720–726.

Wender, P. H. *Minimal brain dysfunction in children.* New York: Wiley-Interscience, 1971.

Wender, P. H. *The hyperactive child: A handbook for parents.* New York: Crown Publishers, 1973.

Werry, J. S., & Sprague, R. L. Hyperactivity. In C. G. Costello (Ed.), *Symptoms of psychopathology.* New York: Wiley, 1970.

Whalen, C. K., Henker, B., Collins, B. F., Finck, D., & Dotemoto, S. A social ecology of hyperactive boy: Medication by situation interactions. *Journal of Applied Behavior Analysis,* 1979, *12,* 65–81.

Wheeler, M. E., & Hess, K. W. Treatment of juvenile obesity by successive approximation control of eating. *Journal of Behavior Therapy and Experimental Psychiatry,* 1976, *7,* 235–241.

Wiltz, N. A., & Gordon, S. B. Parental modification of a child's behavior in an experimental residence. *Journal of Behavior Therapy Experimental Psychiatry,* 1974, *5,* 107–109.

Wolraich, M., Drummond, T., Salomon, M., O'Brien, M., & Sivage, G. Effects of methylphenidate alone and in combination with behavior modification procedures on the behavior and academic performance of hyperactive children. *Journal of Adolescent Child Psychology,* 1978, *6,* 149–161.

Wright, L. Aversive conditioning of self-induced seizures. *Behavior Therapy,* 1973, *4,* 712–713.

Wright, L. Psychology as a health profession. *Clinical Psychologist,* 1976, *29,* 16–19.

Yorkston, N. J., McHugh, R. B., Brady, R., Serber, M., & Sergent, H. G. S. Verbal desensitization in bronchial asthma. *Journal of Psychosomatic Research,* 1974, *18,* 371–376.

Zlutnick, S. I., Mayville, W. J., & Moffat, S. Modification of seizure disorders: The interruption of behavioral chains. *Journal of Applied Behavior Analysis,* 1975, *8,* 1–12.

Author Index

449

Subject Index